Air Transportation

Now in its ninth edition, *Air Transportation: A Global Management Perspective* by John Wensveen is a well-proven, accessible textbook that offers a comprehensive introduction to the theory and practice of air transport management. In addition to explaining the fundamentals, the book transports the reader to the leading edge of the discipline, using past and present trends to forecast future challenges and opportunities the industry may face, encouraging the reader to think deeply about the decisions a manager implements.

The word "Global" has been added to the subtitle for this edition, reflecting an increased emphasis on worldwide operations, including North America, Latin America/Caribbean, Europe, Asia-Pacific, the Middle East, and Africa. The ninth edition focuses on the "Age of Acceleration," addressing trends related to emerging technologies, such as autonomy, artificial intelligence, augmented reality, virtual reality, 3-D printing, data analytics, blockchain, and cybersecurity. New material includes extra information on airport management and operations, air carrier business models, aviation risk, safety and security, and how changing political landscapes impact the aviation industry. Enhanced content is supported by the addition of new chapters and online supplemental resources, including PowerPoint presentations, chapter quizzes, exam questions, and links to online resources.

This wide-ranging textbook is appropriate for nearly all aviation programs that feature business and management. Its student-friendly structure and style make it highly suitable for modular courses and distance-learning programs, or for self-directed study and continuing personal professional development.

John Wensveen is Chief Innovation Officer at Nova Southeastern University and Executive Director of the Alan B. Levan | NSU Broward Center of Innovation, responsible for overseeing a multimillion-dollar public–private partnership to support the growing entrepreneurial ecosystem in South Florida with local, regional, national, and international impact. John is also the official advisor to the Mayor of Broward County on innovation, technology, and entrepreneurship and is an Official Member of the Forbes Technology Council. John is a TEDx speaker and his higher education experience includes faculty and senior leadership positions at Miami Dade College, Purdue University, Dowling College, and Embry-Riddle Aeronautical University. John's entrepreneurship and industry experience includes senior leadership positions at Mango Aviation Partners, Radixx International, Airline Visions, InterVISTAS, Marriott Vacation Club International, MAXjet Airways, and Canada 3000 Airlines. John is a certified IATA instructor and earned Master's and Ph.D. degrees in International Air Transport and Business from Cardiff University (U.K.) and a B.A. in Geography and Transportation Land Use Planning from the University of Victoria (Canada).

Ninth Edition

AIR TRANSPORTATION

A GLOBAL MANAGEMENT PERSPECTIVE

John Wensveen

Routledge
Taylor & Francis Group
LONDON AND NEW YORK

Designed cover image: © Getty Images

Ninth edition published 2023
by Routledge
4 Park Square, Milton Park, Abingdon, Oxon, OX14 4RN

and by Routledge
605 Third Avenue, New York, NY 10158

Routledge is an imprint of the Taylor & Francis Group, an informa business

First edition published by Wadsworth Publishing Co Inc 1984
Eighth edition published by Routledge 2015

British Library Cataloguing-in-Publication Data
A catalogue record for this book is available from the British Library

Library of Congress Cataloging-in-Publication Data
A catalog record has been requested for this book

ISBN: 9780367364489 (hbk)
ISBN: 9780367364472 (pbk)
ISBN: 9780429346156 (ebk)

DOI: 10.4324/9780429346156

Typeset in Palatino
by Apex CoVantage, LLC

Access the Support Material: www.routledge.com/9780367364489

The ninth edition of this book is dedicated to the aviation industry and all the victims, families, and friends impacted by the COVID-19 global pandemic. This dark time in the history of humankind has brought death, economic destruction, and the aviation industry has changed forever. Despite the challenges faced, the aviation industry is resilient, resulting in new opportunities and sustainable strategies that will make this sector stronger and more successful than ever.

CONTENTS

FIGURES

TABLES

ABOUT THE AUTHOR

John Wensveen is Chief Innovation Officer at Nova Southeastern University and Executive Director of the Alan B. Levan, NSU Broward Center of Innovation, responsible for overseeing a multimillion-dollar public–private partnership to support the growing entrepreneurial ecosystem by attracting and retaining industry-leading entrepreneurs, technology, sources of investment capital, and supporting resources to create a premier innovation center and technology hub.

Prior to this role, John served as the Vice Provost of Academic Schools at Miami Dade College providing direct leadership and direction for the College's professional education programs. He was responsible for creating corporate relationships with local, regional, national, and international boards and organizations and with leaders of foreign governments, businesses, and non-governmental organizations.

John has extensive academic leadership experience, including Professor and Head of the School of Aviation & Transportation Technology at Purdue University, Dean of the School of Aviation at Dowling College, and Professor of Airline Management at Embry-Riddle Aeronautical University.

John has held a variety of industry leadership positions, including Partner/EVP at Mango Aviation Partners, Global Head of Airline Advisory Services at Radixx International, President of Airline Visions, Executive Consultant at InterVISTAS, Senior Director at Marriott Vacation Club International, Vice President of International Affairs at MAXjet Airways, Director of Strategy and Communications at Corporate Visions, and Manager of Pacific Rim Flight Operations & Passenger Services at Canada 3000 Airlines.

John is an External Instructor at the International Air Transport Association (IATA), a Certified Instructor at the Turkish Aviation Academy (Turkish Airlines), and a frequent contributor to the media. He also provides expert witness testimony, and is author of two leading industry books including a "best-seller" (*Air Transportation: A Management Perspective* and *Wheels Up: Airline Business Plan Development*).

John earned Master's and Ph.D. degrees in International Air Transport and Business from Cardiff University (U.K.) and a B.A. in Geography and Transportation Land Use Planning from the University of Victoria (Canada). Currently, he is working toward the U.S. Coast Guard, Masters Upgrade (100 Gross ton license) certification.

In his free time, John is an avid boater, scuba diver, recreational pilot, and enjoys hitting the open road in the RV.

FOREWORD

As you start this journey to learn more about the aviation industry, or any other industry for that matter, my advice to you is to "express massive curiosity." That's one of the mantras that has defined my career, and I'll explain.

I started my career in economics and public policy, and then moved to finance at a leasing company where I was intrigued by how businesses find ways to solve problems, finance assets and structure deals. I deeply immersed myself in these transactions and was later recruited to join an airline to manage financial planning with no previous industry experience. I didn't know much about airlines, but I had a mentor who taught me and let me run with anything I could get my hands on. Everyone approaches their career differently, and it's important for me to always learn something new and have someone working with me who is willing to teach.

Now that I'm in aviation, I'm addicted to it and fascinated by the pace and the competitive dynamics. You can delve into a diverse range of functions from engineering, airfield management, airport negotiations, sales strategies, and capacity planning, while still enjoying all the ins and outs of travel. Airlines are a high fixed-cost business with expensive assets, and, generally speaking, your seat on a plane is some of the most valuable real estate in the world. Even the challenges with things like commodity fluctuations, competitive dynamics, weather, and airport operations that arise on a day-to-day basis create interesting puzzles to solve. There are many challenges; however, it's all worth it when we out-perform competitors and empower our guests, to visit family and friends and go places they've never been. The happiness and satisfaction that come from adding flights to underserved markets and helping people experience the world is unmatched. That's the energy that drives me every day.

Our Spirit team is the best in the business. Spirit re-invented the way airlines work in North America with an unbundled, high value business model that's now mainstream in the airlines and beyond. For example, chances are that you've already "cut the cord" on your cable provider and are subscribing only to what you want – similar to the approach many different airlines now take. Much of the talk of "disruptive" companies tends to gravitate toward the tech industry. However, as you read this book, you'll see Spirit's fingerprints all over the industry, from heightened competition to the democratization of air travel.

The most notable change for me in this new edition is the increased focus on emerging technologies and this so-called Age of Acceleration. In 2023, keep your eyes open when you travel because innovation powers your journey. Expect to see more advances in self-service, biometrics, and automation in guest service functions. On the engineering side, significant advances in engine technology, aerodynamics, lighter seats, and more are resulting in substantial increases in fuel efficiency and lowered noise levels, helping the industry become a better steward of the environment.

Our industry is growing exponentially and needs smart people like you. I hope you get a foot in the door, because a very rewarding career awaits you.

Ted Christie
President and CEO, Spirit Airlines

PREFACE

Since the last edition of this book was published, the global aviation industry was hit hard by the COVID-19 global pandemic and, at the time of writing, just when things were starting to turn in a positive direction, the world was introduced to the Omicron variant, sparking travel bans across the world. Air transportation is used to historical trends and challenges but the COVID-19 situation has been the largest barrier faced in the history of aviation. In 2019, the global industry was reaching record levels in terms of market size valued at $818 billion, but in 2020 this figure dropped to $359 billion. Fortunately, in 2021, this figure increased to an estimated $472 billion, showing positive signs, but due to ongoing global pandemic issues, the ability to forecast recovery is more than a challenging exercise. For 2023, the global market size was $841 billion reflecting positive signs of recovery.

As presented in previous editions of this book, aviation is the most high-profile industry sector and continues to be one of the most neglected related to investment supporting infrastructure needed for success. The global pandemic situation is a reminder of the long-term challenges aviation faces, including climate change, slim profit margins, strict regulations, aging infrastructure, the constant need for financial support, and emerging technologies creating new competitive forces. In many ways, the industry is on a life support system, frequently requiring assistance to make sure it keeps breathing. Now is the time to rethink what a resilient industry should be and how all stakeholders can provide input into reinventing this sector that ultimately links the global economy. Unfortunately, this statement is easily said but very difficult to accomplish because the aviation industry is so focused on today rather than tomorrow.

The ninth edition of this book provides a 30,000-foot view of the global air transportation industry and breaks down to regional overviews where applicable. Despite being an international industry, all six regions of the aviation world, as defined by the International Air Transport Association (IATA), have their own sets of trends, challenges, opportunities, and strategies. The goal of this book is to educate the reader on all the different aspects that make up air transportation, securing the knowledge to reason accurately and objectively about the challenges and opportunities impacting the industry.

CHANGES IN THE NINTH EDITION

Writing a book is a challenge for an author when the content relies on current data. Unfortunately, by the time of publication, some of the data is outdated or new information impacts the state of the industry, which may result in revising certain sections. With this said, the chapter outline in the ninth edition has been designed to provide foundational knowledge, no matter what circumstances impact the industry, and the reader should understand that certain facts and figures can be taken at face value while others should not be, given how quickly the industry changes. The ninth edition increases the focus on the international scene, including North America, Latin America/Caribbean, Asia-Pacific, Europe, Middle East, and Africa while addressing emerging technologies that will change the aviation landscape forever. The impact of the COVID-19 global pandemic is discussed in various chapters as this catastrophic event has also irrevocably changed the aviation industry. At the time of writing, the industry was still recovering from this crisis and the true impact is not known. However, it is safe to assume that the aviation industry will become more proactive in order to be more reactive when the time comes. Tables, figures, statistics, key terms, and review questions have been updated.

TEACHING AND LEARNING AIDS

The substantive content of a textbook is only part of what makes it usable in the classroom or learning environment; for the book to be effective, its content must be taught by instructors and industry professionals and learned by students as well as those in the workforce seeking new skills, upskilling, and reskilling. To facilitate the process, this edition continues to pay particular attention to teaching and learning aids, such as the following:

1. *Chapter Outlines.* Each chapter opens with an outline of the major topics to be covered.
2. *Chapter Checklists.* After the outline, each chapter includes a checklist of objectives that students should be able to accomplish on completing the chapter.
3. *Relevancy.* Most of the examples, applications, and extensions of the basic material are drawn from and apply to the air transportation environment of the last two decades.
4. *Staying Power.* The text is designed to have staying power over the years. It emphasizes the underlying principles, practices, and policies that will not change appreciably over time. It is recognized that instructors will supplement the material with current, topical applications and events.
5. *Figures and Tables.* Important points in each chapter are illustrated with strong visual materials.
6. *Logical Organization and Frequent Headings.* Air transportation can easily become overwhelming in its multitude of topics, concepts, practices, and examples. The material covered here has been put in a systematic framework so that students know where they have been, where they are, and where they are going in the text. Frequent headings and subheadings aid organization and readability.
7. *Key Terms.* Each chapter concludes with a list of key terms used in the text.
8. *Review Questions.* Review questions at the end of each chapter address important points.
9. *Appendix.* One chapter includes an appendix that is of practical interest and that reinforces the material covered.

10 *Career Appendix.* This edition, once again, includes an appendix on jobs in the air transportation field and ways to get them.
11 *Glossary of Air Transportation Terms.* All key terms appearing at the end of each chapter, as well as many other terms used in the text and others of significance in air transportation, are included in the glossary.
12 *Complete Index.* The book includes a complete index to help students find needed information.
13 *PowerPoints.* Supplemental content in the form of slides are available for the reader via the publisher.

INTENDED AUDIENCE

Because the aspirations of most students of air transportation (and, for that matter, most career paths) lead to the airline segment of the air transportation industry, the major focus of this text is on the management functions and organization of airlines. However, the significance and contribution of general aviation is not overlooked.

This book is intended for three somewhat different audiences with similar interests: students enrolled in a course such as "Air Transportation" or "Airline Management"; students in transportation and traffic management programs who wish to gain more insight into the air transportation industry because most of their classes concentrate on surface transportation modes; and individuals who work for an airline and want to gain a better understanding of managerial aspects. Too often, an airline employee, as a specialist, sees only a limited part of the overall operation and has little, if any, knowledge of such important subjects as marketing, pricing, scheduling, and fleet planning. Even individuals within marketing—reservations, for example—have little appreciation of their company's growth strategies and market segmentation. These employees are simply too busy fulfilling the functions of the particular job description.

ORGANIZATION OF THE TEXT

The following is an outline of *Air Transportation: A Global Management Perspective*, ninth edition.

Part One *An Introduction to Air Transportation*

Chapter 1 "The Airline Industry: Trends, Challenges, and Strategies." This chapter provides the reader with a solid overview of the different stages of development impacting the airline industry alongside past, present, and future trends. In addition, the main challenges and strategies are presented leading into a discussion on the new breed of airlines.

Chapter 2 "Aviation: An Overview." This chapter introduces the reader to the characteristics, scope, and economic significance of the aerospace industry and its major segments – the government market and the commercial market for air transport and general aviation aircraft. The air transportation industry is clearly defined, and its contribution to the economy is discussed in depth.

Chapter 3 "Historical Perspective." This chapter provides a historical sketch of U.S. airlines and general aviation, including the federal legislation that has affected their growth and development. The Airline Deregulation Act of 1978 and the circumstances leading up to it are thoroughly explored. The postderegulation era from 1978 to the 2020s is discussed, including changes in the structure of the industry and new airlines entering the market (low-cost carriers, virtual carriers, and mega-carriers). The impact of the COVD-19 global pandemic is presented, including the impact on the different regions of the world.

Chapter 4 "Air Transportation: Regulators and Associations." This chapter discusses the roles played by the four primary federal agencies that interface with both segments of the air transportation industry: the Department of Transportation (DOT), the Federal Aviation Administration (FAA), the Transportation Security Administration (TSA), and the National Transportation Safety Board (NTSB). The offices at the Department of Transportation responsible for carrying out the remaining functions of the former Civil Aeronautics Board (CAB) are thoroughly explored. The purpose and major functions of the prominent aviation trade associations are also described.

Chapter 5 "The General Aviation Industry." This chapter concludes Part One by reviewing the general aviation industry, including its statistics and a description of widely diverse segments according to their primary use categories. Other topics include the role of general aviation airports, FAA services to general aviation, and the general aviation support industry, including manufacturers, the fixed-base operators, and the users of general aviation aircraft, and emerging technologies impacting general aviation.

Part Two *Structure and Economics of the Airlines*

Chapter 6 "The Airline Industry." This chapter reviews the current structure of the U.S. airline industry and its composite financial and traffic statistics. A complete discussion of the postderegulation expansion, consolidation, and concentration of the industry is included. The growing role of regional carriers and new types of airlines is thoroughly discussed. This chapter also includes a section on airline certification, including types of and requirements for certification and offices within the DOT responsible for this important function. The current trend of intra-industry agreements, such as code sharing and other cooperative efforts, and the impact of the COVID-19 global pandemic, are described in detail.

Chapter 7 "Economic Characteristics of the Airlines." This chapter deals with the economic characteristics of oligopolies in general and the unique characteristics of airlines in particular. Attention is also given to the economic forces in the postderegulation period that have led to the creation of mega-carriers. The significance of airline passenger load factors is thoroughly explored. This chapter also discusses how the industry has changed since the events of 9/11 and current global events, including the COVD-19 global pandemic.

Part Three *Managerial Aspects of Airlines*

Chapter 8 "Airline Management and Organization." The opening chapter of Part Three introduces the reader to the principles and practices of airline management and organization. The different levels of management within an airline are explored, along with the functions of management planning, organizing, staffing, directing, and controlling. This is followed by a comprehensive review of organization planning and a description of a typical major air carrier's organizational structure, including the purpose and function of various administrations and departments. Departmentalization and the need for new divisions within the organization, such as safety and security and training, are introduced.

Chapter 9 "Forecasting Methods." Forecasting is extremely important in the management of airlines. All planning involving personnel and equipment needs is based on forecasts of future traffic and financial expectations. For this reason, this chapter naturally precedes all of the chapters relating to the other managerial aspects of airlines. The purpose of this chapter is to expose the reader to the primary forecasting methods used by firms engaged in air transportation while also showing the impact of global crises like the COVID-19 pandemic.

Chapter 10 "Airline Passenger Marketing." This chapter begins with a discussion of how the marketing of air transportation has changed over the years. The marketing mix (product, price, promotion, and place) is analyzed in depth, and the consumer-oriented marketing concept of the late 1990s and 2020s is discussed. Various current airline marketing strategies are then explored, including such intensive approaches as gaining deeper market penetration, increasing product development, and developing new target markets. Direct marketing, computerized reservation systems (CRSs), travel agents, frequent flyer programs, business-class service, code sharing, hub-and-spoke service, advertising and sales promotion, and emerging technology platforms are all highlighted.

Chapter 11 "#Mastering the Art of Airline Social Media." This chapter discusses social media and how airlines exercise their presence on social media. The objectives of the airlines' presence on social media as well as the major aspects of social media campaign development are presented. Several examples of airline best practices in crisis management through social media are included, as well as airline best practices in driving customer service and revenue. The chapter concludes with a section on the future of airline social customer care.

Chapter 12 "Airline Pricing, Demand, and Output Determination." This chapter focuses on pricing, certainly one of the most volatile of the "four Ps" of marketing since deregulation. Subjects include the determinants of airline passenger demand and elasticity of demand. The types of airline passenger fares are discussed, followed by in-depth coverage of the pricing process, including pricing strategies and objectives, pricing analysis, and the steps involved in analyzing fare changes. The important role of inventory, or yield, management is addressed as well. This is followed by an in-depth discussion of airline operating costs, profit maximization, and output determination in the short run.

Chapter 13 "Air Cargo." After a brief discussion of the history of air cargo in the United States, the reader is introduced to the importance of air express and air freight today, and to the expectations for future growth in the industry. The market for air freight is then covered, including the types of air freight rates. Special air freight services are discussed, as are factors affecting air freight rates and security.

Chapter 14 "Principles of Airline Scheduling." Unquestionably one of the most critical and yet most difficult tasks facing airline management is scheduling equipment in the most efficient and economical manner. This chapter deals with the many internal and external factors that affect schedule planning. Types of schedules and financial charges are discussed, along with several examples of how a carrier goes about putting a schedule together. The chapter concludes with a discussion of hub-and-spoke scheduling and its importance in the competitive postderegulation environment of the 1980s, 1990s, 2000s, 2010s, and 2020s, in addition to how the use of historical data is changing due to global events.

Chapter 15 "Fleet Planning: The Aircraft Selection Process." The decision to purchase new aircraft is certainly one on which management expends a great deal of time and effort. This crucial decision will entail millions of dollars, and its effects will remain with the carrier for years. The reader is introduced to the aircraft selection process, first from the standpoint of the manufacturer and then from the individual carrier's viewpoint. The trend toward leasing is thoroughly explored. All of the inputs to the process are addressed, as are the criteria by which a carrier evaluates a particular aircraft. The next generation of aircraft technologies are introduced, including supersonic travel. The chapter concludes with an appendix demonstrating the fleet-planning process at American Airlines.

Chapter 16 "Airline Labor Relations." Representing more than one third of a typical carrier's operating expense, labor is certainly one of the most important areas of concern to management. This chapter opens with a thorough discussion and analysis of the Railway Labor Act, followed by a review of the collective bargaining process under the act. A historical sketch of airline union activity in the United States, beginning in the 1930s through the postderegulation period, is also provided. This chapter educates the reader on trends affecting future development of human resources departments. The chapter ends with an overview of the collective bargaining process in recent years, its impact on the carriers, and growing challenges associated with the industry's need to train, recruit, and retain skilled talent.

Chapter 17 "Airline Financing." This chapter takes up the problem of airline capital financing. The major sources of funding are examined, followed by a discussion of the sources and the use of funds over the two decades following the introduction of jets. The final portion of this chapter deals with funding sources in the 2020s and the important subjects of cash management and financial planning, especially given recent events, including how the COVID-19 global pandemic has impacted risk mitigation and sources of funding.

Part Four *The International Scene*

Chapter 18 "International Aviation." The final chapter rounds out the text coverage of air transportation by adding the dimension of international aviation. Air transportation plays a significant role in the movement of passengers and cargo between countries, and this chapter discusses how the various international conferences and conventions have shaped worldwide aviation. The last section of the chapter covers the international aviation market following the passage of the International Air Transportation Competition Act of 1979. The subjects of globalization and international airline and airport alliances are thoroughly explored in addition to regional trends. A new era associated with crowdfunding and cryptocurrency is introduced.

Appendix "Career Planning in Aviation." This appendix provides a structured approach to the all-important subject of career planning. Students are taken through the steps of choosing and getting their first job in aviation, identifying sources of career information, developing résumés, and preparing for interviews. Included are numerous job descriptions from all segments of the aviation industry.

ACKNOWLEDGMENTS

My passion for aviation began at the age of three when I had to evacuate a Boeing 747 with an engine fire. I was dressed in a U.S. Air Force pilot's uniform proudly displaying my wings. Little did I know the events of that day would change the course of my life and fly me down a path to a lifelong career in aviation. As a small child, my dream was to learn to fly and after a few hours playing with the stick and rudder, and a few years of maturity, I realized my real passion was aviation business.

I owe many thanks to the pioneers of aviation and the entrepreneurs of today that continuously amaze me with new developments. There are few industries in existence where one can go to sleep at night and wake up the next morning faced with challenges that did not exist the day prior. The excitement created by the daily stresses of this business keeps me going and striving toward the design of the ultimate airline business model. Is this even possible?

Many thanks are owed to industry sources who provided a great deal of material that was extremely helpful in putting together this textbook. Thank you to: the Department of Transportation, Research and Innovative Technology Administration, Transportation Security Administration, National Transportation Safety Board, Federal Aviation Administration, Airlines for America, Regional Airline Association, National Business Aviation Association, Aircraft Owners and Pilots Association, International Civil Aviation Organization, and the International Air Transport Association. Additional thanks to Airbus Industrie and The Boeing Company.

A very special thank you is owed to two aviation professors for assisting with revisions of the ninth edition of this text. Dr. Benedikt Badanik, Air Transport Department, University of Zilina (Slovakia) co-authored Chapter 11. Dr. Robert O. Walton, College of Business, Worldwide Campus, Embry-Riddle Aeronautical University, co-authored Chapters 2 and 13. I cannot thank you both enough for the tremendous effort and attention to detail. You are both super stars!

A textbook of this nature cannot come together without the assistance of a team. Thank you to Dr. Alexander Wells for believing in me many years ago and passing on the legacy to take *Air Transportation: A Global Management Perspective* to the next level. Thank you to the team at Routledge Publishing, especially Lusana Taylor-Khan for assisting with hours of editing. Thank you to Nova Southeastern University student assistant, Jonathan R. Boulanger, for assisting with hours of research. I am excited to watch your entrepreneurial journey.

My professional career has been an amazing ride and all of these experiences led to my current role as Chief Innovation Officer at Nova Southeastern University and Executive Director of the Alan B. Levan, NSU Broward Center of Innovation. Thank you George L. Hanbury II, Ph.D., President and CEO of Nova Southeastern University. I am so proud to work under your leadership and I appreciate the guidance you provide as I strive toward my ultimate professional career goal. Thank you Alan B. Levan, Chairman, BBX Capital Corporation, Chairman and CEO, Bluegreen Vacations for believing in me to advance the vision of the Alan B. Levan | NSU Broward Center of Innovation initiative, as well as to create the "The World's First Theme Park for Entrepreneurs™".

I also want to thank inspirational leaders in the world of transportation, particularly Lisa Lutoff-Perlo, CEO of Celebrity Cruises, who is a model leader and a constant innovator, overseeing the most innovative cruise line in the world. I have learned many lessons from the cruise line industry which have created opportunities for me to think strategically in the world of aviation.

There are numerous other people throughout the world that I must thank for supporting my career over the years, including my family. Thank you Mom, Dad, and Kristy for your support in my early days. Thank you Clyde and Sherry Berry for welcoming me into the family with open arms. Thank you to my step-daughter, Madison. I cannot wait to see how your entrepreneurial journey advances. Finally, there are no words that can show appreciation for the love and support my wife, Lisa Berry-Wensveen, gives in supporting the long days and nights it takes to have a successful career. I am forever grateful. Thank you to my two special Frenchie dogs, Fiona and Finlay, who make me smile each and every day, and Annabelle my crazy cat!

John "Air Bear" Wensveen

PART ONE

An Introduction to Air Transportation

CHAPTER 1

The Airline Industry
Trends, Challenges, and Strategies

CHAPTER CHECKLIST • YOU SHOULD BE ABLE TO:

- Define the four stages of development impacting the airline industry
- Discuss the main trends impacting the global airline industry, including regional challenges
- Describe and discuss the main critical financial issues and challenges associated with air transportation
- Understand the main strategies for global aviation in order to achieve success
- Discuss the different types of air carriers evolving and the main factors behind success and failure
- Describe how evolving new technology may impact the future of aviation, including space travel and high-speed ground transportation

INTRODUCTION

In previous editions of this book, Chapter 1 provided an overview of the air transportation and aerospace industries. Given the volume of change constantly occurring in the aviation industry, it is important for the reader to have a full understanding of the global airline industry before proceeding with the other chapters in the book. Having knowledge at the macro level will assist the reader in better understanding the other chapters presented.

DOI: 10.4324/9780429346156-2

This chapter provides a background on the current global industry, including a regional analysis, discusses current and future evolvement of the industry in terms of trends, discusses challenges and strategies impacting the industry, discusses the new breed of airlines, and discusses why airlines fail and what can be done to achieve success. Chapter 1 presents an overall framework to supplement the other chapters in the book. As a result, some information presented in this chapter will be repeated in other chapters and discussed in greater detail.

STAGES OF DEVELOPMENT IMPACTING THE AIRLINE INDUSTRY

Historically, the United States aviation industry has been the center of focus for discussions related to history, change, challenges, and strategies. One of the main reasons for this is because the U.S. has traditionally been at the forefront of evolvement in the aviation industry and that is the one major reason why the bulk of reference material on the market is heavily concentrated on the U.S. airline industry. However, as the rest of the world experiences increased change in political environments, different regions of the globe are becoming more important in terms of change, resulting in decreased emphasis on the U.S. industry. Although some experts disagree, there are four stages of development impacting the airline industry in terms of maturity. Some regions of the world have skipped a step or two, resulting in both positive and negative results for the industry. With that said, the logical stages of development include regulation, liberalization, deregulation, and in some cases, re-regulation. The first three stages of development are discussed in greater detail throughout the book.

Stage I: Regulation

At one point in time, the bulk of the global airline industry was heavily regulated, meaning governments had strict control of the industry in terms of air fares, routes, and market entry of new airlines. The main factors resulting from a regulated environment include, but are not limited to, the following: strict ownership control of airlines, limited to no competition on selected routes, limited markets served, limited city-pair frequency, high air fares for passengers, government bail-outs for air carriers in distress, and incentive to achieve airline profitability.

Stage II: Liberalization

In a liberalized environment, there is less government control of the industry compared to a regulated environment. Although liberalization generally brings positive results to the industry, one large barrier to implementation is that the global airline industry cannot implement seamlessly or simultaneously. However, the industry does recognize the need to implement where appropriate and, as of mid-2011, the industry appears to be moving forward in a positive direction with increased bilateral negotiations between countries. As per the International Air Transport Association (IATA), liberalization allows for expansion into new markets, diversification into new products, specialization in niche products, and market exit for air carriers not able to succeed in specific competitive markets.

Stage III: Deregulation

In a fully deregulated environment, government controls like entry and price restrictions for air carriers are removed, allowing airlines to serve any given route and freely compete with other carriers. In many ways, deregulation is the opposite of regulation. Generally speaking, air fares are substantially decreased, safety is improved, and service quality increases (i.e., route frequency, total number of miles flown, on-time performance, frills and amenities). In the case of the United States, selected small- and medium-sized airports have not felt the true benefits of deregulation because of the limited amount of competition in each market.

Stage IV: Re-regulation

In 2007, the United States airline industry entered formal discussions regarding the possibility of re-regulating the industry as a result of merger discussions between American Airlines and Northwest Airlines, and United Airlines and Continental Airlines.

In a re-regulated environment, the government would have a role in pricing and restrict airlines from selling air fares below actual cost. Re-regulation would also result in changes to the **Railway Labor Act**, as discussed in later chapters of the book, where unions would not be permitted to strike, resulting in binding arbitration. Suggested changes also include restricting airlines to utilizing larger aircraft on certain city-pairs resulting in decreased frequency. Also, the air traffic control system would be updated to increase efficiency of the national air transport system and decrease delays at hub airport facilities throughout the country. As the airline industry restructures, it appears there will be increased expansion, increased consolidation, and increased concentration.

By 2014, a number of changes impacted the U.S. airline industry as a result of merger deals between legacy airlines. The industry moved from having eight major players to essentially four. American Airlines and US Airways merged to create a new American Airlines. Delta and Northwest merged to create a new Delta. United and Continental merged to create a new United. Southwest and AirTran merged to create a new Southwest.

Some industry experts argue that the U.S. airline industry is in a re-regulation phase given the Justice Department's decision to allow such mergers to occur. Experts argue that consolidation in the industry reduces competition, ultimately creating monopolies at select key airports across the country. Experts on the other side argue consolidation is a positive thing for the industry as it creates new opportunities for **low-cost carriers** and new start-ups.

As of 2023, the regulatory environment had not changed much since the period of deregulation but there were a number of air carrier mergers and acquisitions that transpired, stimulated by deregulation. In the U.S., all trends indicate a lesser number of air carriers in existence in the future. In 1995, there were a total of 95 air carriers operating compared to 21 in 2021. Interestingly, the number of classified major air carriers increased from 11 in 1995 to 18 in 2021 according to the U.S. Bureau of Transportation. What happens in the next decade in terms of deregulation vs. re-regulation will be dependent on the success of the existing air carrier structure. Unfortunately, it is not possible to forecast the future as the airline industry is unpredictable and volatile.

PAST, PRESENT, AND FUTURE TRENDS

The Global Airline Industry

Since the terrorist attacks on the United States on September 11, 2001, the global airline industry has experienced four phases of evolvement: survive, adapt, recover, and rethink. The rethink phase is an ongoing process, forcing air carriers worldwide to constantly enhance business models to achieve profitability while maintaining a safe and efficient operation. In the new operating environment, airlines are no longer defined as airlines but as businesses where only the fittest survive. If the bottom line is not met, the air carrier disappears and is often replaced by a new competitor, or an existing competitor expands its operation.

Scenarios

In the past decade and a half, the global airline industry has faced a long list of negative scenarios resulting in high barriers for successful operations. Some of these scenarios include: the 2003 outbreak of **Severe Acute Respiratory Syndrome (SARS)**, the Iraq War, the Afghan War, the ongoing Syrian crisis, the 2008–2012 financial crisis, and the COVID-19 global pandemic that commenced in 2019 and was still wreaking havoc in 2022. In the year 2022 onwards, airlines will be forced to prepare for additional scenarios whether they occur or not. The mentality is shifting from something "could" happen to it "will" happen. Preparation includes developing a flexible business plan, allowing the airline to adapt to most any environment. Historically, well-established airlines have not done a great job adapting to fluctuating environments because of their dependency on legacy-based systems. New air carriers, particularly those known as "low-cost" carriers, have been able to withstand changes in the global environment because their business models incorporate flexibility. With that said, not all such airlines have been able to survive. Moving forward, airlines must prepare for globalization, changes in the international political landscape, distribution of natural resources (oil, gas, water), internal conflicts (shifts in power), and unintended consequences from good intention, public and international perception, war, terrorism, continued financial issues, and the impact of emerging technologies.

The Top Frustrations in Aviation

The airline industry is perhaps the most high-profile industry in the world, but it is also considered one of the most neglected in terms of investment. With that said, the airline industry faces a lengthy list of numerous frustrations. For the purpose of discussion, the author highlights what are considered to be the top frustrations impacting aviation today (in random order). These include fuel and oil, pollution control, personnel cutbacks, access to skilled and qualified talent, global economic woes, and recurring safety lapses. Additional areas of debate include costs associated with **Air Navigation Service Providers (ANSP)**, government interference, the environment and efficient infrastructure, and security and taxation. Such topics are discussed in greater detail throughout the book.

The Top Three Costs for Airlines and Typical Airline Operating Expenses

The top three costs for most airlines, in any order, are: fuel, labor, and maintenance. In the United States, fuel was approximately 20–40 percent of airline operating costs in the year 2020 as per IATA. In 2020, for the first time in a number of years, fuel consumption decreased to 10.28 billion gallons compared to 18.27 billion gallons in 2019 due to a reduced number of flight operations brought about by the COVID-19 global pandemic. Actual costs associated with airline operations vary region by region, country by country, and company by company. In the U.S., the Air Transport Association (ATA) produces a Passenger Airline Cost Index on a quarterly basis. The author recommends the reader consult the ATA website to get a better understanding of costs associated with operating an airline. The Index takes into account the following costs: fuel; labor; aircraft rents and ownership; non-aircraft rents and ownership; professional services; food and beverage; landing fees; maintenance material; aircraft insurance; non-aircraft insurance; passenger commissions; communication; advertising and promotion; utilities and office supplies; transport-related; and other operating expenses.

The Aviation and Aerospace Almanac lists typical operating expenses as: ticketing, sales, promotion; general administrative; fuel and oil; station expenses; passenger services; maintenance and overhaul; flight crew; depreciation and amortization; landing and associated airport charges; en route facility charges; and other operating costs. For specific percentage breakdowns of costs, the reader is encouraged to review ICAO Air Transport Reporting Form EF-1.

REGIONAL ANALYSIS

Airlines are important to the global economy because they link regional economies with the rest of the world. When the economy is doing well, airlines tend to profit, but when the economy is not doing well, airlines tend to lose profit, often being the first and hardest hit industry in turbulent times.

In order to better understand the aviation industry, it is important to have a global understanding of how the industry functions as well as a regional understanding. Just because one region is successful, it does not mean another region is following similar patterns. However, the effects of a region do have positive and negative impacts on other regions, causing what is called the domino effect or a chain reaction.

At the end of 2009, the aviation industry suffered from a global economic crisis, the implications of which will never be fully known. According to IATA, airlines worldwide lost a combined US$11 billion in 2009 due to rising fuel costs and reduced earnings on fares and cargo. Despite indications of certain economies returning to positive environments, the positive impact on air carriers worldwide has been slow to grow. As a result, airlines have been shrinking capacity to accommodate reduced bookings for first- and business-class travel. Typically, when the economy suffers, the volume of business travel is reduced or eliminated by many corporations, negatively impacting high-end fares.

By the end of 2012, business confidence had bottomed out and there was the expectancy that business activity would increase dramatically. However, by early 2014, this trend had not occurred. In 2013, GDP growth averaged 2 percent compared to 2.2 percent in 2012 with developed nations doing better than developing nations like India, Brazil, and China. In 2013, oil prices were approximately US$109 per barrel while jet fuel averaged US$126 per barrel. The 2013 fuel bill for the global airline industry was approximately US$213 billion or 31 percent of total costs. In 2013, passenger growth fell to 5 percent from 5.3 percent in 2012. IATA expected worldwide passenger numbers to reach 3.12 billion by end of 2013/early 2014, combined with record load factors of 80.2 percent. Demand for air cargo is declining and in 2013, growth was only 0.9 percent, forcing airlines to focus on passenger traffic. Air cargo revenue reached a peak in 2011 declining to $59 billion in 2013 while passenger revenue increased, reaching $565 billion. In 2020, air cargo revenue reached a record $175 billion and passenger revenue was $189 billion resulting in a 69 percent negative difference over 2019. The COVID-19 global pandemic had a positive impact on air cargo revenue and the complete opposite for passenger revenue. 2020 will be forever known as "the year we would like to forget."

According to IATA, in 2021 the global airline industry's fuel bill was approximately $100 billion resulting in an increase of 28% over 2020. The 2022 estimated fuel bill is $132 billion and industry net losses are expected to be approximately $52 billion following an estimated $138 billion

Table 1.1 Regional Regulatory Trends

Region	Regulation	Liberalization	Deregulation	Privatization
North America	No	No	Yes	Privatization
Latin America	No	No	Yes	Privatization
Europe	No	Yes	No	Privatization
Asia-Pacific	No	Yes	Yes	Privatization
Middle East	No	Yes	No	Limited
Africa	No	Some	No	Cautious

dollar loss in 2020. Interestingly, the price of crude oil ultimately increased from approximately $54 per barrel to $70 per barrel in 2021.

Table 1.1 highlights current regional regulatory trends. Depending on what direction regional and global economies take, such regulatory trends may alter to adapt to the changing environment. It is expected the volume of airline consolidation will increase to compensate for increased operating costs and increased competition in specific markets.

North America

In terms of regulatory trends for North America, Canada has experienced the privatization of airlines, airports, Air Traffic Control (ATC), and the rise of the low-cost airline. The United States has experienced the rise of the low-cost carrier, government control of airports, the development of secondary airports, major airline debt, bankruptcies, mergers, stagnant domestic passenger growth, and increased international growth. U.S. domestic routes have been hit hard in recent years. Mexico has experienced government control of the industry and bankruptcies, in addition to the emergence of the low-cost airline.

Although most U.S. airlines utilize a hub-and-spoke strategy as defined later in this book, some airlines are now implementing **de-hubbing** or de-peaking strategies to spread flights more evenly throughout the day, allowing airlines to use their resources in a more efficient manner. Such a strategy also allows for a reduction in energy which ultimately reduces airport congestion. Aircraft fleets are becoming more simplified as airlines realize the high costs of operating mixed fleets. Automation initiatives are being implemented to improve customer service and enhance productivity. Airlines are changing distribution methods with a huge reliance on the Internet for ticket sales and there is a shift in in-flight services to more economical offerings.

Consolidation seems to be a modern trend as seen with recent mergers among the legacy airlines. Additionally, the subject of regulation has reappeared and there is talk about the possibility of moving from a deregulated environment to a re-regulated environment.

Europe (European Union)

In terms of regulatory trends for Europe, the Third Package was implemented in 1997 creating a fully liberalized environment. Airlines have privatized and the region has experienced the growth of low-cost airlines and the growth of alliances, including airlines and airports. Competition between different modes of transportation and emerging technologies has impacted the airline industry, especially the use of high-speed rail. The theme for the future of the European Union (EU) is "leadership in air transport regulation." National pride continues to be an issue for the industry and many challenges will continue to be faced as the EU expands its geographic boundaries.

In recent years, Europe has experienced slow growth among the six main regions, partly due to economic instability in select regions of the Eurozone. Airlines serving the intra-European markets are not performing as well as airlines serving long-haul markets. Additionally, Europe is facing increased competition by hubs in the Middle East where airline connectivity is more efficient and less costly, and all trends indicate Europe is losing ground in terms of ability to be the gateway for connectivity to other regions of the world.

Asia-Pacific

In terms of regulatory trends for Asia-Pacific, the region has experienced managed liberalization and change has been slow compared to North America and Europe. However, things are changing quickly due to diversified air transport policies consisting of everything from open skies to protectionist policies. The region has felt the positive rewards of strong growth since late 2001, especially in markets such as Australia, China, India, Japan, Republic of Korea, and the **Association of Southeast Asian Nations (ASEAN)**. Interestingly, the busiest route in the world is Jeju International to Seoul Gimpo and it is the only route with more than 1 million seats (1.5 million) according to IATA.

The region is somewhat unique in the sense that there is no regional organization providing many opportunities as well as challenges. Megacarriers and small international carriers co-exist and there are limited interline agreements despite having the largest share of the world economy. There has been increased growth in the development of airline alliances and the region faces increased airport and airspace congestion as well as competition. There is a dire need for airport expansion and construction, and for advanced navigational equipment to improve efficiency and enhance safety measures; all requiring significant investment which is estimated at $6.5 billion per year.

The Asia-Pacific region is quickly emerging in terms of passenger and cargo demand, growing at a rate higher than all other regions of the world, and is officially holding the number one spot for Revenue Passenger Kilometres (RPKs) and Freight Tonne Kilometres (FTKs). For the foreseeable future, the Asia-Pacific region will experience passenger traffic growth at a rate of 5.3 percent and freight traffic at a rate of 3.9 percent according to the International Civil Aviation Organization (ICAO).

Due to the decreased demand for air cargo, Asia-Pacific has been hit fairly hard, resulting in flat performance. Air cargo operators in Asia-Pacific have the largest cargo fleets, forming a direct correlation with demand.

Middle East

In terms of regulatory trends for the Middle East, the region has experienced fairly stagnant growth in recent years due to the great divide between rich and poor. Historically, the passenger market was limited, forcing airlines to bank on repeat travel by passengers. Today, airlines are implementing low-cost strategies and there has been an emergence of low-cost carriers. The Middle East is strategically positioned and the use of efficient hub airports has resulted in a stronger presence in the long-haul markets. Safety and security continue to be issues which require addressing.

Africa

In terms of regulatory trends for Africa, airlines do not really contribute much to the economy due to the low propensity to fly. Standards are low compared to other regions of the world, particularly when looking at safety and the environment. North Africa appears to be growing at a higher rate compared to other parts of the region. North Africa's air transport is estimated at 4–6 percent year over year with the recognition that there are certain years where demand could dip due to unforeseen circumstances. There has been increased stability in the region which will hopefully increase the propensity to fly variable over the next decade. However, in 2022, as a result of the COVID-19 global pandemic, Africa has been hit hard with the closure of four major air carriers and a number of additional companies in financial distress. At the time of writing, Africa is very concerned about a systematic failure that could cripple the aviation industry along with many other sectors.

Africa operates the oldest fleet in the world, mainly due to the low standards issue and lack of capital. According to the **African Airlines Associations (AFRAA)**, more than 17 percent of the world's population resides in Africa and the aircraft fleet accounts for 6 percent of global commercial passenger and cargo aircraft in 2021, meaning the region has the lowest number of aircraft per capita. The average aircraft age in Africa is 17 to 20 years and there continues to be large utilization of what are referred to as Stage I and II aircraft (i.e., Boeing 727). Such aircraft are inefficient to operate, noisy, and damaging to the environment. In 2021, the average age of a South African Airways aircraft was over 15 years. It is estimated more than 1,000 new aircraft will be required over the next 20 years to replace antiquated technology.

Since 1992, the region has experienced airline integration, restructuring, and commercialization. Gradually, flag carriers have become more self-reliant and there has been increased privatization and less government control in the industry. There is a strong need for training, especially at the management levels, to cope with global trends. In addition, there is the need for autonomy in civil aviation authorities and improved and additional infrastructure. Airlines need to learn to work together as partners rather than compete and it is expected that as the industry matures, low-cost carriers will enter certain markets.

Latin America/Caribbean

In terms of regulatory trends for Latin America/Caribbean, there is a shift from regulation toward liberalization. Given the geographic size of the region, there are a number of stakeholders involved, resulting in a number of regional air transport liberalization initiatives, including the **Andean Community (CAN)**, the **Caribbean Community (CARICOM)**, the **Southern Common Market (MERCOSUR)**, and the **Association of Caribbean States (ACS)**. The goal of such efforts is to create a standardized set of policies that will ultimately create a fully liberalized environment.

The region has experienced increased passenger growth and competition as well as increased alliances. Airlines are developing corporate strategy and a competitive strategy to cope with competition. There is a strong need for training at the management levels as well as a need for research and development. Brand culture is very important in the region and there has been an increased focus on safety in recent years.

Throughout the region, airlines are thinking as businesses and not necessarily as airlines in the traditional sense. Cost-saving initiatives are being implemented and governments have learned the economic benefits of successful air carrier operations. There is a strong debate about the regional airport system and whether airport privatization has failed or not.

There has been an increased emphasis on improving environmental performance with investments in new technologies, efficient use of infrastructure, more effective use of aircraft operations, and discussions on emissions trading.

The future outlook for the Latin American/Caribbean region is positive with expected continued economic growth resulting in increased traffic demand and increased competitive forces. The region will continue to face infrastructure challenges and high costs of operation, and changes must be made to the taxation system to be more aligned with other regions of the world.

THE INDUSTRY: CHALLENGES AND STRATEGIES

Forces Impacting the Airline Environment and Infrastructure Issues

There are a number of forces impacting the airline environment, including internal and external. The main forces are physical, economic, political and/or legal, socio/cultural, demographic, and technological. Airline management must be aware of all the factors that arise or could arise as applied to each force. The airline has the ability to control certain aspects of the forces but cannot control other aspects. For example, the airline can prepare strategies to combat competition but cannot fully insulate itself from the threat of competition like new entrant carriers (i.e., deregulated/liberalized environment, freedom of entry/exit, aircraft availability) or new substitutes (i.e., telecommunications, video conferencing). The airline does not have control over the power of the customer or the power of market intermediaries.

It has been said that aviation is the highest-profile industry in existence but also the most neglected in terms of infrastructure investment. There has been an ongoing debate about where such investment is needed, and although there is often a strong consensus addressing specific areas, there is frequently strong resistance. For example, in the U.S., ATC technology is antiquated and most agree it should be updated. However, there is the possibility that other countries will be able to tap into U.S. technology and take advantage of it without paying for it.

Capacity in the sky and on the ground is an important topic in the global aviation industry. If there is no additional investment into capacity infrastructure, and demand is greater than capacity, there will be increased congestion and delays resulting in increased costs and loss of economic benefits. Investment into infrastructure development will result in an efficient air transportation system with economic benefits being realized. The above will be discussed in greater detail throughout the book.

Airlines must plan for the future when it comes to the changing regulatory requirements for pilot training. This is a global challenge and each country of the world will be impacted. For example, in the U.S., pilot training is a current challenge due to the 2013 Federal Aviation Administration (FAA) ruling, known as Public Law 111–216 ("The 1,500 Rule"), that says all commercial pilots must have a minimum of 1,500 flight hours to be hired by an airline (FAR Part 121). Prior to this ruling, the minimum hourly requirement was 250. The rule does not apply to all commercial pilots as there are exceptions for those who have been employed as military pilots and students graduating from select undergraduate programs from accredited colleges and universities. In short, the new rule was passed to increase safety in an airline environment by providing enhanced training and increased experience before holding a first officer position. The 1,500 Rule stems from a Congressional mandate following the 2009 crash of a Colgan Air Bombardier Q400.

Critical Financial Issues and Challenges

As previously stated, the global airline industry will continue to face critical financial issues and challenges. Table 1.2 outlines some of the major factors corporations must address in order to succeed.

Table 1.2 Financial Issues and Challenges Impacting Air Transportation

Cost controls	World economy
Access to capital markets	Irrational pricing and predatory action by major carriers
Insurance	Over-capacity
Foreign currency exposure	Cash flow and ability to self-finance
Fleet replacement and price of new aircraft	Debt/equity ratios
Industry losses and inconsistent profitability	Taxation
Cost of funds and low yield on surplus funds	Ownership issues
Productivity and labor reform	

Table 1.3 Challenges Impacting Global Air Transportation

Bankruptcy and shut downs	"Generic" vs. "Airline" business plan
Flexible strategic plan	Treat as a "business"
Regulation, liberalization, deregulation	Rising costs (fuel, oil, labor, maintenance, security)
New generation airlines vs. legacies	Restructuring and alliances
Excessive capacity	Competition from other modes of transportation and technology
Customer (target, loyalty)	Organizational design
Internal challenges	Overall strategy
Duplication of work structures	Functional and departmental barriers
Staff relations and new types of employees	Legacy system dependencies
Lack of compromise	Air carrier ownership and control
Sustainability of air carriers and safeguards	Physical and environmental constraints
Air transport and the global trade mechanism	Consumer protection and passenger rights
Impact of technology (aircraft, e-commerce, Internet, Computer Reservation Systems, Global Distribution Systems) on liberalization process	Future approaches to regulatory reform Pilot training requirements Access to qualified and skilled talent

Global Aviation Challenges in the 21st Century

The global aviation industry will face a long list of challenges in the 21st century due to the new operating environment resulting from the tragic terrorist attacks on the U.S. in 2001 and changing political environments. Table 1.3 outlines some of the major challenges that are discussed throughout the

Table 1.4 Strategies for Global Aviation

Understand the reality of change and become flexible	Revitalize strategy
Development of new types of air carrier business models	Focus on the customer and ask what they want
Eliminate duplication of work structures	Organizational accountability
Turn staff relations into strengths	Update airline systems
Build partnerships (alliances, interactive marketing)	Act decisively
Diversify the business (core and non-core)	Create new ways to reduce future costs and spending of capital
Increase efficiency	Reduce dependence on local, national, and international economies
Airlines must take control of business issues	Work in partnership with other organizations

book. The reader will gain a better understanding of most topics, plus additional ones, in upcoming chapters.

Global Aviation Strategies in the 21st Century

The global aviation industry is learning to adapt to the multiple changing environments in which it operates. The incorporation of flexible strategies is becoming more important than ever in the development and implementation of new business models with various types of businesses under the umbrella of air transportation. Table 1.4 outlines some of the global aviation strategies the industry must address. The reader will gain a better perspective on some of these topics as they are presented throughout the book.

THE NEW BREED OF AIRLINES

Since the terrorist attacks on the U.S. on September 11, 2001, the global industry has gone through multiple phases of development, including survive, adapt, recover, and rethink. The latter phase is an ongoing phase that will never end, forcing air carriers to constantly rethink business strategies. The main advantage of having to rethink regularly is that it forces management at the leadership level to strengthen the core business for long-term survival and success. As airlines rethink their business models and new entrants emerge based on new business platforms, new breeds of airlines will emerge and succeed as well as emerge and fail. The ultimate business model will probably never be developed because of the impossibility of being able to predict the future of the industry and all the factors that influence its growth. Although a frustrating scenario, excitement is added to the industry with the challenge of becoming the best.

There are different categories of air carriers to be discussed in Chapter 6, ranging from the true legacy airline to the regional/commuter, to the low-cost airline to the specialized airline —including the network specialist, the product specialist, and the price specialist. Before discussing any of the above in greater detail, the reader should know that the term "low-cost airline" has been a major buzz word in the industry over the past decade and there is the belief that low-cost means an efficient operation with "cheap" air fares.

As the airline industry continues to mature, new technologies are creating opportunities for new forms of transportation. Space tourism is now a reality with names like Richard Branson, Elon Musk, and Jeff Bezos breaking barriers. Billionaires are revolutionizing the way in which humans travel and 2020/2021 was perhaps one of the most impactful periods in terms of breaking boundaries. On May 30, 2020, Elon Musk's company, SpaceX, launched the first private spacecraft to the International Space Station. On July 20, 2021, Jeff Bezos and his company, Blue Origin, successfully completed travel to space followed by Richard Branson and his company, Virgin Galactic, on July 11, 2021.

High speed transportation on the ground is going to compete with air travel, and the Virgin Hyperloop technology is positioned to go head-to-head with air carriers. On November 8, 2020, Virgin Hyperloop transported the first passengers on a test run, opening opportunities for expansion. The technology propels passengers or cargo in high-speed pods, essentially in a vacuum tube capable of reaching speeds in excess of 1,000 km/h (three times faster than high-speed rail and ten times faster than traditional rail). Eventually, Virgin Hyperloop will be running operations in the U.S., Europe, Middle East, and India.

Discombobulated Syndrome: What the Heck Does Low-cost Mean?

Low-cost airline is a frequently misused and misinterpreted phrase even by industry experts. For the purpose of debate, there is no such thing as a low-cost airline but the reader can decide if that is true or not by consulting the chapters in the book. It is important to have a basic understanding of the above issue prior to moving forward with the readings so that there are no misconceptions about terminology used in the content. The industry tends to use numerous definitions for low-cost operations, and the author wants to alert the reader of such because often multiple definitions mean the same thing. For example, a low-cost airline might refer to the following: low-cost carrier (LCC), low-cost/no frills carrier (LCC/NF), low-fare/high-value carrier (LFHV), less frills carrier, value carrier, budget carrier, or new generation carrier. The author refers to the above as discombobulated syndrome.

In upcoming chapters, the new breed of air carriers, discussions on the new airline/airport system, and newly developing trends in airline alliances will be introduced to the reader.

FAILING AND ACHIEVING SUCCESS

Historically, airlines have failed and airlines have achieved success in all regions of the world. As already mentioned, no business model is perfect and there is always room for improvement. Many lessons will be learned throughout the chapters in this book and the reader will recognize common traits leading to failure.

Failures in Airline Business Planning

Some of the common failures in airline business planning will now be highlighted and later discussed in upcoming chapters.

Undercapitalization is a common basis for failure. Existing airlines rarely have enough capital to keep up with high operational costs, and start-up airlines rarely have enough capital to either launch the company or remain in business. Access to funding has become increasingly difficult and will most likely become more difficult until the global economy becomes more stable.

Overexpansion is another common trait associated with failure. There is often a common belief that bigger is better, and sometimes leadership feels it is better to have larger access to a market over a competitor rather than operate a successful and efficient operation. In certain cases, when an airline grows to a certain size, often measured by the amount of annual revenue, the airline has no choice but to continue growing due to various factors, including size of infrastructure.

Lack of flexibility is a major negative factor impacting airlines worldwide. The business platforms of legacy carriers are often based on old regulatory environments designed to operate in a specific type of environment that no longer exists. Unfortunately, because the legacy carrier is often too established, it has difficulty adjusting to changing environments. However, newer carriers have a major advantage over legacy carriers because business platforms are developed which incorporate flexible strategic parameters, allowing the airline to adapt to multiple changing environments as necessary.

"Wrong" money and "wrong" leadership are negative contributors when an airline seeks to be successful. Wrong money is invested by parties that do not understand the nature of the operation and, as a result of having an active voice in the decision-making process, ultimately lead to the demise of an organization. Wrong leadership includes having the wrong person in the wrong job and in some cases, having the right person in the wrong job. Airlines, no matter how big or small, should make sure only right money is invested into the organization and the right people should be placed in the right positions.

Unable to obtain sustainable, competitive advantage is a large factor contributing to failures in business planning. This is one of the reasons why some air carriers believe in the "bigger is better" philosophy. Market dominance is often more important than achieving profitability but as access to capital is decreased and government bail-out packages decrease, airlines will be forced to restructure strategies if they wish to remain afloat.

Finally, a failure to demonstrate revenue growth and profitability is a major failure in airline business planning. This is difficult to achieve but it must be done. Failure to identify market need is a common mistake made in the development of the airline business plan. It must be superior to any potential competitors' business plan and should be able to gain the attention of investors.

Achieving Success

The reader will quickly learn of the many failures associated with different types of businesses in the air transportation industry. There is a large focus on air carrier operations as this book concentrates on this, but it also introduces the reader to other aspects of air transportation, including general aviation, air cargo, and aerospace. In terms of discussing how to achieve success in the industry, airlines are the primary focus. The reader should be aware that different success strategies apply to different aspects of air transportation depending on the specific focus. However, as success relates to airlines, success can be achieved by following, but not being limited to, some basic factors, including: development of a solid airline business plan (not a generic business plan); incorporating flexibility; diversifying business structures; recruiting and hiring the right leadership; implementing steady and moderate growth strategies; implementing effective cost-cutting strategies; practising aircraft fleet commonality; seeking reasonable capital requirements; ensuring that available tonne-mile remains congruent with demand (route/network realignment/optimization); shifting capacity to take advantage of routes and markets where depressed currency will significantly increase value-for-money opportunities; improving balance sheets and credit ratings (prudent capital planning); developing strategies to counter continuing pressure on yields; carefully evaluating new partnerships and alliances; responding to consumer needs rather than dictating; creating an environment that enhances labor/management relationships with cooperation; engaging in effective lobbying efforts to influence critical government policies, laws, regulations, and taxes; eliminating inefficiencies; increasing productivity to the greatest extent possible; and having a long-term vision rather than concentrating on "today".

KEY TERMS

Air Navigation Service Providers (ANSP)
African Airlines Associations (AFRAA)
Andean Community (CAN)
Association of Caribbean States (ACS)
Association of Southeast Asian Nations (ASEAN)
Caribbean Community (CARICOM)
COVID-19

deregulation
de-hubbing
liberalization
low-cost carrier (LCC)
Railway Labor Act
regulation
re-regulation
Severe Acute Respiratory Syndrome (SARS)
Southern Common Market (MERCOSUR)

REVIEW QUESTIONS

1 List the four stages of development impacting the airline industry and briefly describe how each has impacted the future direction of the industry.
2 What are the top frustrations in aviation today? Describe each. What are additional areas of debate?
3 What are the top three costs for an airline typically? In addition, list other typical airline operating expenses. What is the name of the index that produces such costs? How often is the index published?
4 What are the six aviation regions of the world? Describe the regulatory trends associated with each region.
5 What are the main forces impacting the airline environment? What are the main infrastructure issues?
6 What are the main failures in airline business planning? Describe each in detail.
7 Other than airline travel as we know it today, what other forms of transportation are being developed? Describe how this emerging technology could impact the future of the airline industry.

CHAPTER 2

Aviation
An Overview

Revised and updated by Dr. Robert O. Walton, College of Business, Embry-Riddle Aeronautical University Worldwide, U.S.A.

CHAPTER CHECKLIST • YOU SHOULD BE ABLE TO:

- Define *aerospace industry* and describe its basic characteristics and economic magnitude
- Discuss some of the problems faced by the government market
- Describe the current economic outlook for the three segments included in the civil aviation market
- Identify and briefly describe the factors affecting commercial transport sales
- Define related aerospace products and services
- Define *air transportation industry* and distinguish between certificated air carriers and general aviation
- Describe the impact of the air transportation industry on the economy
- Describe how air transportation contributes to the efficient conducting of business and affects personal and pleasure travel patterns

INTRODUCTION

In a short span of 120 years, we have gone from making a few test flights to orbiting celestial bodies, from sliding along sand dunes to spanning oceans, from performing feats of isolated daring to depending on aviation in our everyday lives. Speeds have increased a thousandfold, as have altitude and range capability. No longer is the sky the limit. Ahead lie risks and rewards

DOI: 10.4324/9780429346156-3

as vast as space itself. We have the promise of new airliners that fly with greater fuel efficiency, huge air freighters that move the nation's goods, an expanding general aviation fleet, and of the peaceful uses of space for exploration and research.

COVID-19 Pandemic

In early 2020 the novel human coronavirus disease 2019 (COVID-19) spread throughout the world, and countries started closing borders and restricting travel. By March 2020 U.S. airlines started canceling a huge number of flights, and by May 2020 almost all air passenger travel was halted. The air transportation system did not start to return to normal until 2022, and experienced major problems restarting the system since many of the flight/cabin crews, ground crews, and security personnel had been furloughed. This downturn in the industry skews the data that is presented in this book. While data through 2022 may have been available, to paint a more accurate picture of the industry as a whole, data prior to the pandemic may be presented. This is not to say that the data during the pandemic is bad as it is not. However, history and future text will have to consider the true impact of COVID-19 on the industry, just as it does with past economic cycles and armed conflicts.

THE AEROSPACE INDUSTRY

The **aerospace industry** includes those firms engaged in research, development, and manufacture of all of the following: aerospace systems, including manned and unmanned aircraft; missiles, space-launch vehicles, and spacecraft; propulsion, guidance, and control units for all of the foregoing; and a variety of airborne and ground-based equipment essential to the testing, operation, and maintenance of flight vehicles. In the United States, virtually all of the major firms in the aerospace industry are members of the **Aerospace Industries Association (AIA)** or the **General Aviation Manufacturers Association (GAMA)**. Founded in 1919 and based in Washington, D.C., the AIA is a trade association representing the nation's manufacturers of commercial, military, and business aircraft, helicopters, aircraft engines, missiles, spacecraft, and related components and equipment. GAMA, also based in Washington, D.C., is the trade association that represents the interests of manufacturers of light aircraft and component parts. Many other countries have similar aviation industry associations to support their respective industries, for example in Germany, the German Aerospace Industries Association (BDLI) plays an analogous role to the AIA.

The defense industry is more insulated from the economic and global impact of events such as 9/11 and COVID-19. While the civilian aviation market may go through ups and downs due to these external events, the defense market tends to be relatively stable or expands during times of armed conflict, real or perceived. The civilian aircraft market is more volatile and quickly affected by world events (e.g., pandemics, economic cycles, and armed conflicts). Together Airbus and Boeing make up over 90 percent of the commercial aircraft market. In 2018, Boeing generated about $163 billion, but this fell to only $62 billion in 2021 during the height of the COVID-19 pandemic.

These facts underline the unique status of the aerospace industry. Its role as principal developer and producer of defense, space, and other government-required systems in large measure dictates the industry's size, structure, and product line. Because it operates under federal government procurement policies and practices, the industry is subject to controls markedly different from those of the commercial marketplace. But the aerospace industry is also a commercial entity, and it must compete in the civil market for economic and human resources with other industries less fettered by government constraints. Its dual nature as government and commercial supplier makes the aerospace industry particularly important to the national interest. Its technological capabilities influence national security, foreign policy, the space program, and other national goals. Also, the efficacy and safety of the national air transportation system depends to a considerable degree on the quality and performance of equipment produced for the airlines and the airways operators.

Naturally, such an industry is vital to the U.S. economy, especially in the following areas:

1 *Trade balance.* The excellence of U.S. aerospace products has created strong demand abroad, with the result that the industry consistently records a large international trade surplus. In 2021, the U.S. aerospace industry maintained a positive trade balance at a value of $40.6 billion.
2 *Employment.* The aerospace industry is one of the nation's largest manufacturing employers. The industry represents about 1.4 percent of all employment in the United States with average wages about 41 percent above the national average.
3 *Research and Development.* The industry conducts more **research and development (R & D)** than any other industry, and R & D is a major long-term determinant of national economic growth.
4 *Impact on the Economy.* The aerospace industry has a significant impact on the U.S. economy and represents about 1.8 percent of the total U.S. GDP. In 2021, the industry contributed an economic value of $382 billion to the U.S. economy.
5 *Impact on Other Industries.* A great many new aerospace-related products and processes have spun off from the initial aerospace requirement and have provided value to other industries, both in sales and in productive efficiency. In addition, the aerospace industry is a large-scale user of other industries' goods and services: it has been estimated that for every 100 aerospace jobs created, another 73 are created in other industries.

Each of these factors represents a significant contribution to the U.S. economy; collectively, they elevate aerospace to a key position among the nation's major industries.

Characteristics of the Industry

The history of the aerospace industry has been a saga of continuing adjustment to changing national policy and economic conditions. Since 1960, fluctuating government demands and a variety of international events have teamed up to produce a roller-coaster-like sales curve: up to a peak, down to a valley. Over the years, the industry's operations have become increasingly complex, with each increment of complexity heightening the industry's problems in adapting to change. Today, the industry's unique characteristics make the adaptive process extraordinarily difficult. An understanding of the difficulties is best promoted by an explanation of how the industry has been transformed in the past 70 years.

Prior to 1950, the industry was relatively unsophisticated. Its product line was entirely aeronautical—aircraft, engines, propellers, avionic components, and accessories. Long-run production of many airplane types was the order of the day. The labor force, during the post-World War II retrenchment period, was less than one-fifth of the later peak. Three-fourths of the workers were moderately skilled production workers. R & D was an essential prelude to production, but the subsonic aircraft being built then were less demanding of technological advance, and R & D represented a considerably less significant portion of the total workload than it does today.

The transformation began in the early 1950s with the production of the jet-powered supersonic military airplane, which brought about across-the-board changes in the industry—new types of engines, totally different airframes, different on-board equipment, new tooling and facilities, and, most importantly of all, a vastly greater degree of complexity in products and the methods employed in producing them. New airplane performance dictated that far greater emphasis be placed on R & D. The combination of R & D and product complexity required a major shift in the composition of the work force to include ever-increasing numbers of scientists, engineers, and highly skilled technicians. All of these changes resulted in increased emphasis on an ever more sophisticated managerial process.

While the industry was adjusting to these changes, it inherited a new responsibility: development and production of guided missiles, particularly long-range ballistic weapons. Then came another major change: the application of turbine power to commercial airliners, whose resemblance to military jets ended with their propulsion systems. The need to transport large numbers of people at high subsonic speeds and multimile altitudes involved a further modification of the industry's methods. Finally, in the late 1950s, the industry was assigned still another responsibility: fabrication of equipment to meet the nation's goals in space exploration.

Each of these changes compounded the need for change throughout the entire industry—more R & D, greater product complexity, more personnel per unit produced, higher skill levels in the work force, longer program development time, and greater need for new facilities with only single-program utility because of their specialized natures. Such changes contributed to higher costs of end products, and the demand in the 1960s and 1970s for still more advanced aerospace systems further escalated both the rate of change and the costs—for example, the production and operation of the Concorde supersonic passenger jet from 1970 until it ended operation in 2003. The Concorde required advanced technology learned through the production of military aircraft.

The introduction of the Boeing 787 Dreamliner in 2011 was the next big step in new technology for aircraft. Built from lighter carbon fiber, the 787 was the first commercial passenger jet whose airframe was much lighter than the traditional aluminum airframes. In the 2020s, the rise of additive manufacturing (3D printing) and the possibility of autonomic flight operations are on the horizon.

In defense output, cost—together with the greater capability of the individual system—influenced a trend away from volume production and toward tailored manufacture of fewer types of weapons and fewer numbers of each type.

This evolution has left the aerospace industry with a set of characteristics unique in U.S. manufacturing:

1 Performance demands for new systems require continual advancement of the technological frontier, which in turn involves unusual degrees of uncertainty and risk.
2 Because the government is the principal customer, the product line is subject to revisions in program levels occasioned by changing requirements and funding availability.
3 Equipment that challenges the state of the art is necessarily costly, the more so because requirements generally dictate short production runs, negating the economies of large-scale production.
4 Technologically demanding programs require personnel emphasis in the higher skill levels. Hence, labor input per unit of output is substantially larger than in other manufacturing industries.
5 The combination of technological uncertainty and long lead times, often 7–10 years and frequently longer, between program initiation and completion, makes advance estimation of costs particularly difficult.
6 Because there are few customers and relatively few programs, competition for the available business is intense.

Economic Profile of the Industry

The aerospace industry is composed of about 60 major firms operating some 1,000 facilities, backed by thousands of subcontractors, vendors, and suppliers. The principal product line—aircraft, missiles, space systems and related

FIGURE 2.1 Revenue of Top Ten Aerospace Manufacturers in 2021 (in billions of U.S. dollars)

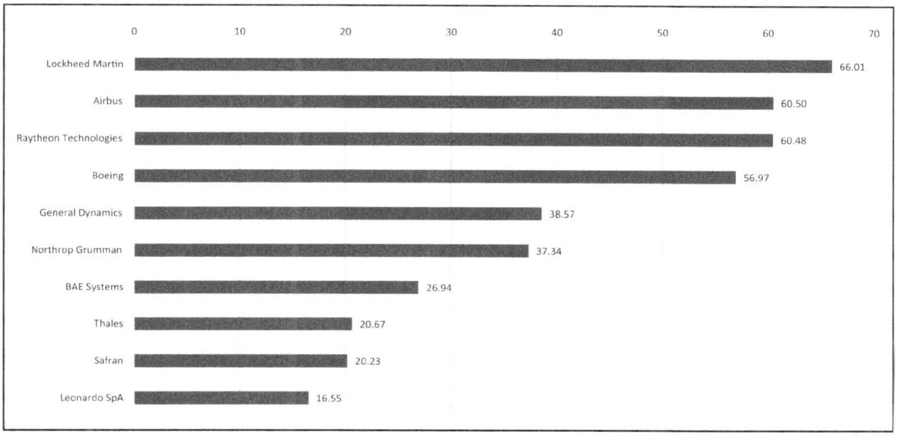

Source: Statista (Financial Times; Thomson Reuters; Various sources)

engines, and parts and equipment—is characterized by high performance and high reliability, and hence high technology and high unit value.

Half of the top ten aerospace manufacturers in the world are U.S. firms, based on revenue. Lockheed Martin was the largest in 2021, followed by Airbus, Raytheon Technologies, and then Boeing. Figure 2.1 provides the list of the complete top ten firms with revenues.

Sales in the U.S. aerospace and defense market in 2020 totaled $874 billion, down 2.8 percent from 2019. Civil aerospace made up about 80 percent of the exports in 2020, with 15 percent in the defense aerospace, and 15 percent in related products and services. Related products and services include all nonaircraft, non-space vehicle, and nonmissile products, and services produced or performed by those companies or establishments whose principal business is the development or production of aircraft, aircraft engines, missile and spacecraft engines, missiles, or spacecraft.

Changes in aerospace product sales are driven by the dynamics of the industry's customer base. During the 1980s, the Cold War environment set the tone for increased U.S. defense spending, and aerospace companies responded accordingly. In 1987, industry sales to the Department of Defense (DOD) accounted for 56 percent of total aerospace business. Yet federal spending priorities have gradually changed. The end of the Cold War and pressures to balance the federal budget led to spending cuts in defense programs. Aerospace sales to the DOD fell substantially between 1987 and 1999. Then there was a slight rise in defense spending in 2000 and 2001, largely as a result of the nation's war on terrorism following the tragedy of September 11, 2001. Higher procurement spending occurred in 2002–2012 as the global war on terrorism continued, and again in the early 2020s with the rise in concerns over China and the invasion of Ukraine by Russia.

The aerospace industry represents one of the nation's largest employers, with approximately 2 million workers on the rolls at the end of 2020. A labor-intensive industry, aerospace employs as many salaried as production workers; the highest such ratio among comparable industries. The emphasis on high-tech R & D in the aerospace industry demands a greater number of scientists, engineers, and technicians than are utilized by most industries. At its peak, the aerospace industry employed almost 30 percent of all U.S. scientists and engineers engaged in R & D.

Testifying to the excellence of U.S. aerospace products is the strong performance of the industry on the international market. The industry has a significant impact on the U.S. balance of trade. Back in 1967, aerospace exports reached the $2-billion-a-year level, and in succeeding years, they rose sharply, mainly because of deliveries abroad of advanced-technology commercial jetliners. In 1973, the industry set an all-time export record of more than $5 billion, and in 1974, that figure increased by almost $2 billion. In 1981, there was another substantial increase to a new record of $17.6 billion, and in 1986, the figure rose to $19.7 billion, which represented 9.6 percent of total U.S. exports. In 2005, exports topped $67 billion, and in 2008, exports exceeded $95 billion. By 2019, exports reached $148 billion, but then settled back to $90 billion in 2021 due to the downturn in the aviation industry brought on by the COVID-19 pandemic. At the same time, aerospace imports have traditionally amounted to only a fraction of the value of goods exported. Thus, aerospace has consistently shown a substantial trade surplus.

Industry Suppliers

Aerospace products perform very sophisticated functions and are complex and costly to manufacture. Because of this, aerospace companies do not attempt to design and assemble finished products entirely in-house. Instead, companies specialize and, where appropriate, contract work out to other companies. A major aircraft manufacturer may use over 15,000 suppliers in its transport manufacturing activities.

The largest amount of economic activity involved in the assembly of aerospace products occurs among aerospace companies themselves. One aerospace firm may be responsible for the design, assembly, systems integration, and final testing of a product, such as an aircraft. That company subcontracts work to other aerospace manufacturers, who supply aircraft wings, tails, and engines. These relationships vary from program to program, with companies exchanging roles as prime contractor and subcontractor. This process also involves subcontractors from around the globe—for example, Boeing sources from over 75 different countries. Major aircraft components are also sourced worldwide. For instance, the Boeing 787 Dreamliner wings are produced in Japan, the central fuselage and horizontal stabilizers are from Italy, and landing gears are produced in France, just to give a few examples.

Much of the aerospace sector's impact on the U.S. economy arises from the industry's position as a major consumer of goods and services supplied by firms outside of aerospace. These services include legal assistance, advertising, accounting, and data-processing activities. Other service industries that are prominent aerospace suppliers include wholesale and retail trade, finance, and insurance.

The importance and value content of electronic components in aerospace end products have grown significantly in recent years. Items such as antennas, electronic connectors, and liquid crystal displays are included within this commodity category. Their growing share of the value of aerospace systems and vehicles is due principally to two factors. First, electronic component costs are being driven upward by Pentagon demands for state-of-the-art technology. This demand, coupled with the short production runs inherent in most military programs, has increased technology unit costs. Second, in an attempt to restrain military spending, the DOD has postponed new product acquisitions and instead has been upgrading some existing weapons systems with improved avionics. The costs of electronic components are clearly rising relative to those of other inputs.

Other important commodities purchased by the aerospace industry include: primary, nonferrous metals (for example, copper, aluminum, lead); radio, TV, and communications equipment; and scientific and controlling instruments.

The Government Market

Despite growing percentages of nongovernment and nonaerospace business, industry activity is still dominated by government contracts with the DOD and the National Aeronautics and Space Administration (NASA); a factor that has important effects on the industry's economic status.

Defense Contractors. The optimism that followed the breakup of the former Soviet Union was replaced by the reality of the Persian Gulf War in 1990/1991 and what it signified: continued regional threats from various corners of the world. Fast on the war's heels came the conflict in the Balkans and an understanding that peace was equally threatened by European regional and ethnic tensions. Then the various Middle East operations that the U.S. conducted in the 2000s and 2010s were followed by the rising concern of Russia's invasion of Ukraine in 2022 and potential hostilities from China.

Leading up to the catastrophic events of 9/11, defense companies experienced decreases in business as a result of dwindling government contracts. Companies cut costs by trimming personnel at all levels. In the United States, aerospace sales to the DOD declined from a high of $61.8 billion in 1987 to $47.6 billion in 2001. Total employment fell from 1.3 million in 1987 to an estimated 794,000 at year-end 2000, largely as a result of defense cutbacks. Military aircraft-related jobs declined from 656,000 in 1986 to 459,000 by 2000. Despite the drops in business, defense companies impacted by fewer contracts overcame the challenge of keeping key technical teams in place to maintain the technology capabilities on which the chances for future contracts rest. In 2006, business picked up as a result of continued terrorism threats and political instability in the Middle East, peaking in 2011. Defense spending in the U.S. has remained high through the early 2020s due to the re-emergence of a pseudo cold war after Russia invaded Ukraine in early 2022 and the rise in hostile rhetoric from China against Taiwan.

Companies are also focusing on improving their design and manufacturing processes and procedures, such as concurrent engineering and inventory control, to enhance productivity and competitiveness. They are restructuring by eliminating less profitable lines of business and adding new capabilities. Many companies are striving for greater balance between defense and commercial work, while others concentrate on the core defense business in which they are strong.

The industry continued its consolidation throughout the 1990s. The merger of Martin Marietta and GE Aerospace made Martin Marietta the largest defense electronics company in the world until the mid-1990s, when Lockheed purchased Martin. Lockheed went on to purchase the tactical aircraft business from General Dynamics, which significantly strengthened that company's position as a leading producer of fighter aircraft. The purchase by Hughes Aircraft of the missile division from General Dynamics enabled Hughes to move into a joint lead with Raytheon in missile production and sales until Raytheon acquired Hughes' missile division. In 1998, Texas Instruments became a part of Raytheon. Later, Boeing acquired the Hughes satellite division. Other major acquisitions were the purchase by Loral of LTV's missile division and by the Carlyle Group and Northrop of LTV's aircraft division. More recently, in 2020, United Technologies and Raytheon merged to create Raytheon Technologies with $74 billion in net sales at the time of the merger.

In addition to consolidation in the defense sector, some companies with existing civil and military product mixes are taking steps to expand their nondefense activities or to move into related areas. Boeing is allocating resources to its new 787 transport program. Raytheon purchased the corporate jet unit of British Aerospace to expand its commercial aircraft business. Textron purchased General Dynamics' Cessna Aircraft Company. But these were only the most sizable and newsworthy of many mergers and acquisitions as aerospace and related business divisions switched hands.

U.S. companies teamed up to perform R & D and to bid on government work. They are setting up joint ventures and other arrangements (sometimes including foreign partners) to apply technology developed for military purposes to commercial aerospace and nonaerospace markets. The anticipated growth of the civil aircraft business invites the application of technology to commercial avionics, air traffic control systems, and aircraft maintenance and upgrades.

Other civil business opportunities being sought include: highway traffic management; the electric car market; hazardous waste and weapons disposal; high-speed data transmission; environmental sensing; space satellite communications; law enforcement (aircraft surveillance, "smart" computer-linked police cars, biosensing of drugs and bomb-making chemicals); large-screen television and home TV satellite service; software conversion; factory automation; light-rail systems; and cellular telephone systems. Although the range of new business is extensive, it will take time to develop markets.

NASA. The days of the Apollo program, when annual real increases in U.S. government space spending were the norm, are long past. The *Challenger* space shuttle disaster of January 28, 1986, and reduced spending on discretionary programs resulted in greater congressional scrutiny of civil space budgets. In addition, space efforts have been tempered by the diminished competition from the Russian space program and the end of the ideological competition between the leading capitalist and the major communist nations. The loss of the Space Shuttle *Columbia* on February 1, 2003, has led to further examination of space spending. As the Shuttle program came to a close, private space firms (e.g., Virgin Galactic, Blue Origin, SpaceX, and Boeing Space Launch System) emerged to fill in the demand for commercial space flight, support of resupply to the International Space Station, and providing launch capacity for satellites.

Many U.S. policymakers recognized the importance of space from a technical, environmental, and commercial standpoint. As defense programs shed skilled workers, a healthy space sector is viewed as a mechanism that can reabsorb some of the talent that becomes available. In addition, the commercial segment of the industry, particularly telecommunications, has been a growth area in an otherwise troubled aerospace market. Environmental problems are receiving greater attention today, and the ability to monitor global warming, ozone depletion, and climatic changes from space is a valuable capability. A variety of space platforms are needed to meet these needs.

The cumulative effect of these opposing forces is a NASA budget that, while not declining, is also not showing any signs of real growth. Since 1990, NASA spending has been flat. In addition, some funds that once were earmarked for space programs were instead shifted into aeronautical projects. Consequently, U.S. government funding for civil space activities is not expected to rise significantly any time soon. Companies remaining in this business will have to be very skillful at selecting which space programs will demonstrate returns within a zero-growth NASA budget. This situation may prompt U.S. companies to seek foreign opportunities with greater vigor.

In 2010, President Barack Obama cancelled NASA's space Constellation program due to ongoing financial woes in the U.S., resulting in a $9 billion budget cut to replace the Space Shuttle program with Orion spacecraft and Ares rockets. Additionally, in late 2013, due to budget cuts, NASA cancelled the Advanced Spacecraft Power Program. This program focused on creating new plutonium power technology to be used in spacecraft that cannot use solar energy to propel through space. While some critics claim the White House is against planetary exploration, the Biden administration has shown support for the Artemis program which intends to re-establish manned moon landings.

The Civil Aviation Market

The United States, traditionally, has been the largest market outside of the former Soviet Union for commercial transports, helicopters, and general aviation aircraft. Close ties between U.S. manufacturers and their domestic customers have provided U.S. aerospace companies with a solid sales base.

Although the domestic market will remain vital to U.S. aircraft programs, the economies of scale necessary for success in today's commercial market compel manufacturers to take an international approach. This is due to the fact that an enormous amount of capital is required to cover the development and tooling costs associated with a new program. For example, the cost of launching a commercial transport program today is approximately $5 billion. Manufacturers must wait about four years before deliveries begin and revenue is generated from their initial investments. Compared to other industries, the customer base for commercial passenger jets is limited and the volume of orders is low. Generally, between 400 and 600 aircraft must be sold before a program reaches the break-even point. And in some cases, this break-even point is much higher. For example, Boeing initially projected the need to sell 1,100 787s before the break-even point was reached. These market characteristics also apply to other civil aircraft manufacturing sectors. Consequently, every sale is important in order to pay back the nonrecurring costs of R & D and production tooling and to make a profit. This is why exports are an integral part of the product and marketing strategies of civil aircraft companies. Since 1990, foreign sales have accounted for between 60 and 70 percent of commercial transport and civil helicopter sales, and about 40 percent of general aviation aircraft sales. Total civil aerospace exports reached more than $64 billion in 2013 and topped $148 billion in 2019. The largest export destinations of U.S. aerospace products in 2020 were to Germany, France, Canada, the United Kingdom, and Japan and accounted for about 40 percent of all U.S. aerospace and defense exports.

Civil aircraft manufacturers have had a global view for some time, as their export figures indicate, but recent changes in market conditions have increased the need for them to remain committed to an international strategy.

Air Transport. The principal civil aviation product is the airline transport. The traditional and obvious difficulty in this area is the fact that sales depend on the financial health of another industry—the world's airlines. The need for new jetliners is evident. The world transport fleet is aging, and the older, less efficient aircraft must be replaced. After reaching a high of 589 units in 1991, the number of shipments declined precipitously during the early 1990s as the economy went into recession and the airlines lost $13 billion during the first four years. The economy rebounded by the mid-1990s,

FIGURE 2.2 Number of U.S. Produced Transport Aircraft Deliveries (2000–2021)

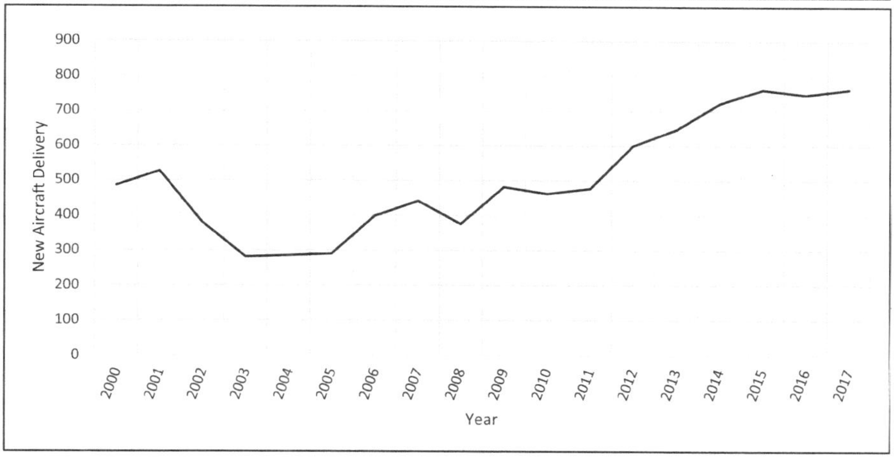

Note: Data was not reported 2018–2022
Source: Bureau of Transportation Statistics, U.S. Sales or Deliveries of New Aircraft, Vehicles, Vessels, and Other Conveyances

and the orders poured in as the airline industry returned to profitability. The number of transport aircraft shipments reached a peak of 620 in 1999, when the industry recorded record profits. Once again, the economy slowed down in 2000 and fell into recession in 2001. The tragedy of September 11, 2001, exacerbated the decline, and the carriers lost $7.7 billion for the year. Transport aircraft shipments followed the decline during the first few years of the 21st century. However, from 2005–2018, the number of aircraft shipped has increased steadily but drastically dropped after 2019 during the COVID-19 pandemic (Figure 2.2).

Before World War II, more than two dozen companies were in the business of designing and building large commercial airliners—large at that time meaning 20 seats or more—almost all for airlines in their home countries. Today, the number of prime manufacturers of large airliners—and that now means 100-plus seats—is down to just a few: Boeing and Airbus being the largest producer by far, but growing in the 100-plus seat market are Embraer, Bombardier, and the relatively new entry of Comac which started operations in 2008.

The winnowing-out in this industry has happened for many reasons, the chief one being the cost of developing new aircraft. As one generation of aircraft has succeeded another, the costs of building the latest aircraft and designing its successor have risen exponentially. Combined with the uncertainties of the marketplace, the spiraling cost of development and early production of new aircraft has made the commercial aircraft business a risky venture.

Since deregulation in the late 1970s, the trend has been toward less and less differentiation within the airline industry as the airlines have competed more and more on the basis of price and schedule, and as some of the oldest and proudest names in the industry have disappeared through merger or bankruptcy. In making their purchasing decisions, the airlines, in turn, have increasingly focused on a single factor: which of the various aircraft available to them in a few distinct categories is the low-cost solution to the task of carrying a certain number of passengers a certain distance? Each of the two major competitors strives to enter new markets ahead of the other by developing new and more cost-efficient aircraft, and each one tries to defend its markets in the absence of any natural barriers on the strength of being the low-cost producer.

Boeing has been able to maintain approximately 60 percent of the market for large jet transports in an increasingly competitive global market. The company's commercial transport products include the 737, 757, 767, and 777 models, with the latest jet in commercial operation, the 787, entering service in 2011. Boeing's most formidable competitor has been and will continue to be Airbus Industrie. Airbus launched its first aircraft, the A300, just 50 years ago, and 55 years after Boeing launched the Boeing Model 2—their first financial success. By 1995, Airbus had captured approximately 30 percent of the worldwide market for commercial jet transports. Airbus's goal is to further increase its market share in the United States and abroad; the company's largest aircraft, the 555-seat A380, made its maiden flight in 2005, and aimed to see that this goal was reached. The A380 made its first commercial flight with Singapore Airlines on October 25, 2007, between Singapore and Sydney. However, the existence of the A380 was short-lived and Airbus stopped production in 2021 after only delivering 251 aircraft. At the

FIGURE 2.3 Aircraft Deliveries by Manufacturers (2000–2020)

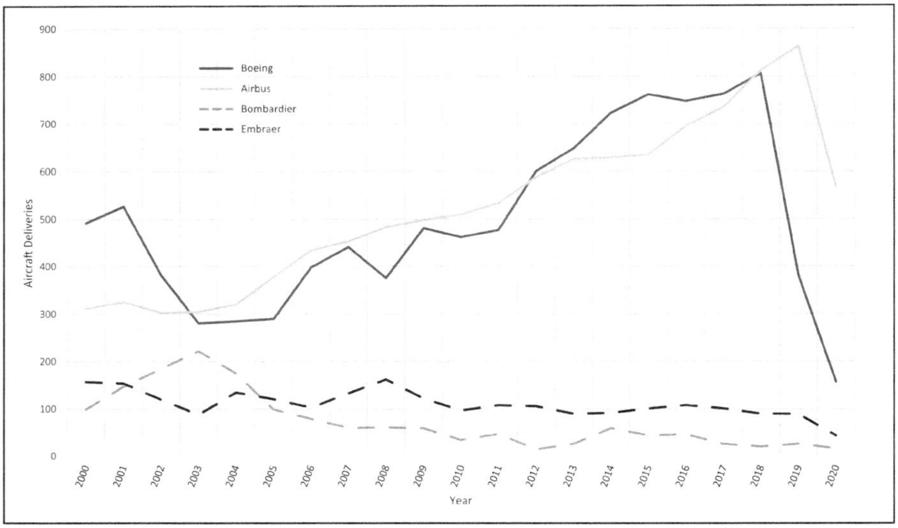

Sources: Airbus, Boeing, Bombardier, Embraer via Statista

start of production, it was estimated that a minimum of 270 aircraft would have to be delivered to attain break-even.

While Airbus got a late start in the commercial aircraft market, finally in 2003 Airbus caught up with Boeing and delivered more aircraft. Since 2003, Airbus and Boeing have been fighting for lead producer, changing places several times (see Figure 2.3).

Extensive levels of government subsidization by France, Germany, the United Kingdom, and Spain have enabled Airbus to develop a full family of aircraft without ever having made a profit, to price these aircraft without full cost recovery, and to offer concessionary financing terms to customers. Boeing and McDonnell-Douglas objected strenuously to this practice, claiming unfair competition. Airbus, in turn, claimed that Boeing and McDonnell-Douglas benefited over the years from the large military contracts that have offset a large part of their R & D expenses. In fact, the United States has long had a defense budget double that of Western Europe, with a large investment in military aircraft R & D and long production lines. Finally, in 2004 the U.S. filed a case with the World Trade Organization (WTO) claiming that Airbus had received illegal government subsidies. The European Union (EU) filed a countersuit, alleging that Boeing had received subsidies from the U.S. Government for its R & D projects. The WTO found that both Airbus and Boeing received unfair government subsidies but in 2019 allowed the U.S. to impose tariffs on the EU, and then in 2020 the WTO allowed the EU to impose tariffs on the U.S. Finally, in 2021, the U.S. and the EU agreed to suspend tariffs and end the dispute.

The cost of developing new airplanes has become staggering. Every time a company like Boeing moves forward with a new program, it is essentially putting its entire net worth on the line. Enormous front-end investments must be made for a return that will not be realized until many years later—if at all. Boeing's program to develop and manufacture the 350-seat 777 airplane provided a good example of the enormity of the challenge. The company spent billions to develop the new airplane, which involves several thousand suppliers and over 800,000 different parts.

Boeing's most recent addition to the aircraft fleet is the 787 Dreamliner, originally scheduled to enter service in May 2008. However, production was delayed numerous times and the maiden flight took place on December 15, 2009. The aircraft entered commercial service in late 2011 with All Nippon Airways (ANA) as the launch customer. The first such aircraft was delivered to ANA in July 2011 for final testing. The Boeing 787 Dreamliner is a mid-sized, wide-body, twin-engine aircraft seating 210 to 330 passengers, and is the most fuel-efficient airliner in the industry due to the use of composite materials in the construction process. Airbus Industries' latest aircraft product is the A350, which entered commercial service in 2015. The A350 is a long-range, mid-sized, wide-body, twin-engine aircraft seating 270 to 412 passengers depending on variant and configuration. This aircraft, constructed primarily of carbon fiber-reinforced plastic, is lightweight and competes against the Boeing 777 and 787 Dreamliner.

As Airbus and Boeing continue to compete, they are forced to develop new products and services that are attractive to an existing and potential customer base. Both manufacturers are going head-to-head on the development of new aircraft technology that will revolutionize the future of air transportation. Airbus launched the A350 in response to Boeing's B787 Dreamliner. Both aircraft are twin-engines capable of flying 250 to 300 passengers on long-distance routes at costs much less than today's modern aircraft. Both aircraft are lighter in weight than previous aircraft, consisting of composite materials amounting to significant decreases in fuel costs.

Even a redesign of existing aircraft can be a major risk for airline manufacturers. Boeing learned this the hard way with the introduction of the 737Max. What should have been a simple upgrade from an existing well-accepted aircraft almost destroyed the entire program after two accidents within the first two years of operations.

Although the cost of developing new airplanes is enormous, the cost of not moving ahead is even greater. A company's ability to maintain its position as a global aerospace manufacturer depends fundamentally on its capitalizing on new market opportunities. In instances in which the market is limited or the barriers to entry are prohibitively high for one company, international collaboration may be the wave of the future.

Although U.S. aerospace companies have dominated the global market for many years, the use of overseas suppliers for components and subassemblies is increasing. There is nothing strange about that, because two-thirds of the world market for large airliners exists outside the United States. Though companies in countries such as Italy and Spain have been major suppliers for many years, the nations of Asia and the Pacific Rim collectively have been distinctly minor suppliers. That is bound to change, for two reasons: those same countries already account for a substantial portion of the world market for commercial airliners (20 percent and growing rapidly), and they plainly have both the desire and the capability to participate in the production of new aircraft.

Unquestionably, international collaboration is a key strategy in the broader effort to remain competitive in the aerospace industry. Joint programs in which the partners share costs offer a means of generating the requisite capital for advanced commercial airplane and engine development in the face of high and rising costs. They also give the U.S. companies involved access to foreign markets that might otherwise be denied to them in view of the trend toward directed procurement. Offsetting these advantages to some extent is the fact that joint U.S.-foreign ventures inevitably strengthen the technological capabilities of foreign industry. In short, sharing American know-how might prove costly in the long run, because it further enhances the competitive posture of foreign companies. But sharing, it should be remembered, is a two-way street.

In addition to the two large aircraft manufacturers, Airbus and Boeing, it is important to note the increased importance of other companies involved in the regional jet manufacturing industry. Airbus and Boeing products focus on medium and long-haul operations, while regional jet products focus on short and medium-haul markets catering to the 60–120 passenger range. The two leading manufacturers in this category are Bombardier (Canada) and Embraer (Brazil). Both manufacturers have invested heavily into the future of emerging markets where the propensity to fly variable is increasing. China is a huge potential market for both companies, with forecasts indicating the country will require close to 1,000 regional jets in the 60–120 seat category between 2011 and 2030. However, more competition in this sector is starting to emerge with the Chinese producer Comac, whose C919 aircraft conducted its maiden flight in 2017.

Factors Affecting Commercial Transport Sales

Continued market leadership of U.S. aircraft manufacturers is closely tied to the existence of healthy, profitable U.S. airlines. The huge size of the U.S. domestic market has been important to U.S. manufacturers by providing them with the broad base of demand necessary to launch new aircraft programs. Traditionally, over 40 percent of commercial jets on order from U.S. manufacturers have been delivered to U.S. airlines. Large order volumes help manufacturers spread costs over a larger production run, which allows them to reduce their unit costs and be more competitive. Now more than ever, as they seek the export sales crucial to market leadership, manufacturers need the foundation of a strong U.S. sales base.

By the end of 1993, the airline industry was in a tailspin. Passenger and freight traffic was stagnant, aircraft by the hundreds had been placed in storage, industry losses and debts were mounting, and aircraft orders were being canceled. The downturn had also spread to the commercial transport sector, and aircraft manufacturers were forced to scale back production and lay off thousands of workers.

By 1997, however, the airline industry was again taking off. Air traffic and profits were back up, and net orders for U.S. transports jumped from 256 in 1995 to 620 in 1999. The pace of this recovery left commercial aircraft producers struggling to keep up.

Civil aviation has a history of cycles, and with the slowdown of the economy in 2000 shipments began to tumble, and again during the economic crises of 2008–2009. Finally, the COVID-19 pandemic almost brought civil aviation to a standstill in 2020–2021, but by 2022 showed signs of a quick recovery. Aircraft companies are implementing programs to reduce these market swings. Also, some economists are suggesting that business cycles in general should be less severe due to factors such as deregulation and global competition. Nevertheless, several factors strongly influence cycles in the air transport industry.

Today, Boeing and Airbus maintain a 99 percent market share of the global commercial aircraft market. However, Boeing holds a larger market share in the U.S. followed by the Asia-Pacific, making up 70 percent of its revenues in 2018. Airbus's largest market is the Asia-Pacific followed by Europe, and this makes up 65 percent of their gross revenue.

Economic Growth. Economic growth has a tremendous impact on the civil aviation market. It is important because it broadly influences the demand for air transportation services, which, in turn, affects aircraft orders and deliveries. During periods of economic growth, companies build and service new outlets, which leads to an increase in business travel. In addition, family incomes generally rise, which results in greater spending on leisure travel. Yet, the reverse is also true: when economic output falls, businesses close facilities, unemployment rises, and air traffic declines.

The correlation between economic growth and air travel has been recognized by analysts for many years. A generally accepted rule of thumb holds that there is a 2.5–3 percent increase in world air traffic for every 1 percent increase in world economic growth.

Inflation. Inflation is important because it influences economic growth. When prices are stable, interest rates tend to be low, and this encourages investment and business expansion. When prices rise quickly, interest rates also climb. Eventually, high interest rates will inhibit economic activity, which can put a damper on air traffic. Because high interest rates raise the cost of borrowing, they can also make aircraft financing prohibitive. In addition, inflation can result in escalating labor and fuel costs. When this happens, airlines are faced with the unpleasant choice of either absorbing those higher costs or raising their fares.

Inflation has grounded the airline industry on more than one occasion. In 1970, 1973, 1978, 1991, 2007–2008, and 2020–2021, air carriers faced rising fuel and labor costs. During those same years, inflation also plunged the major world economies into a recession, causing air traffic and airline profits to decline.

During the recent recessionary periods (1990–1994, 2000–2002, and 2008–2009), and the COVID-19 pandemic, air carriers sustained huge losses. Airlines have attempted to control their costs and have made it clear to aircraft manufacturers that they want the price of planes to come down. Aircraft companies have reduced their prices through implementation of long-term programs aimed at cutting costs and improving efficiencies: efforts that should benefit airlines well into the future.

Fleet Capacity. The passenger load factor is used to measure airline capacity utilization. The indicator is expressed as a percentage, relating the number of passengers flown to available seats. When load factors are low, airlines have more excess lift capacity than when load factors are high. High load factors and rising air traffic place airlines under pressure to buy aircraft. If load factors are rising during a business cycle, this also suggests that airline revenues are improving. This is important if airlines are planning to order aircraft because it enhances their ability to purchase or lease planes.

The passenger load factor for world airlines rose during the latter half of the 1990s, and orders for new aircraft reached record levels. Unfortunately, as was the case in previous economic downturns, air traffic declined in the early 2000s and load factors fell, prompting the air carriers to reduce fleet capacity and cancel orders. By year-end 2006, load factors were at "normal" levels (running about 76 percent) and in some cases higher than ever. By 2014, load factors hit 80 percent and continued to climb to a peak of 82.6 percent just before the COVID-19 pandemic caused load factors to fall below 60 percent. It is expected to take several years for load factors to return to pre-COVID levels, however by 2022 demand quickly returned and the recovery may be quicker than expected.

Replacement Aircraft. Airlines order aircraft to increase their capacity; they also purchase new transports to replace their older, less efficient models. The advancing age of current fleets and continued increase in demand suggests that replacement orders should be on the rise through the mid to late 21st century.

Airline Profitability. Commercial transports are expensive assets: smaller models start at approximately $89 million (e.g., 737–700) and jumbo jets cost over $338 million (e.g., 787). To make these types of purchases, air carriers need to raise capital in the financial markets, and, therefore, they need to demonstrate to potential investors that their operations are profitable. After losing billions of dollars in the early 1990s, the airlines returned to profitable operations in the latter half of the decade. Airline stocks were soaring and optimism prevailed as the carriers entered the new century. The economy slowed down in the spring of 2000 and went into recession in 2001, followed by the tragedy of September 11, 2001. Once again, the carriers experienced record losses in 2001 and 2002. US Airways filed for bankruptcy, and other major carriers were not faring much better. Massive employee furloughs took place during these years. United won $5.8 billion in wage and benefit concessions from its employees to stave off bankruptcy. By the end of 2002, the industry was in shambles. Over 90 percent of the passengers were flying on discount fares and low-cost carriers were eating away at market share from the old-line airlines. The market started to recover during the 2010s but then took on massive losses during the COVID-19 pandemic.

However, the future looks bright, Boeing is projecting a demand of 41,000 new aircraft by 2041. It is believed that more than 50 percent of new aircraft will replace older ones. The remaining aircraft orders will be required for fleet growth. The bulk of new aircraft will be single-aisle, targeting emerging markets and low-cost carrier models.

A Cyclical Industry. The civil aviation market is cyclical. This is important to recognize to fully understand the environment surrounding transport orders and deliveries. Since 1971, orders for U.S. transports have peaked several times. These cycles are set in motion by the underlying forces of economic growth and recession and are further magnified by the nature of aircraft manufacturing.

In the retail industry, items often sit on store shelves for weeks before they are sold, and buyers usually can take their purchases home the day they are bought. But aircraft are too expensive to build and then keep in inventory. Instead, they are manufactured only after an order is placed. This creates a time lag between order and delivery dates that can last several years.

Also, in the retail industry, there are many suppliers. If a customer has to wait for delivery from one supplier, that customer can go to another vendor offering a more immediate response. But again, the aircraft industry is different. Building a commercial transport takes an enormous investment, limiting the number of manufacturers in the business. If the order line for aircraft fills up, customers have little recourse but to wait.

If aircraft demand rises, manufacturers will initiate a new program or increase their production rates. Unfortunately, due to the tooling and supplier links that must be set up and the bottlenecks that can develop among strategically important suppliers, reaching full implementation takes time.

These situations can create an imbalance between demand and supply that causes orders and deliveries to swing abruptly. Yet there is also a behavioral side to these cycles. Airlines and aircraft leasing companies worry that they might miss a market upturn if they are placed near the end of an ordering line. At the first sign of a market turnaround, they frequently scramble en masse to place orders. This creates a surge in orders that can push back delivery dates even further. As a result, air carriers near the end of the line might, in fact, receive their deliveries years later, as air traffic is subsiding. These deliveries then create an overcapacity problem, causing aircraft orders to swing downward. Manufacturers who had just invested in greater production capability now find themselves with excess capacity, and a shutdown reverberates through the industry.

These cycles are disruptive, and aircraft manufacturers are working to minimize them. Companies have launched efforts to shorten the product development phase and reduce the time gap between aircraft order and delivery. This is being accomplished by adapting computer-aided design and manufacturing technologies that obviate the need to build mock-ups. To improve program communication and efficiency, manufacturers are using concurrent engineering, which involves establishing teams of design, development, production, and sales people at the beginning of a program. Prime contractors are strengthening their relationships with their suppliers and increasing the two-way flow of information. Boeing, specifically, is overhauling its production and systems software to simplify the way it tracks and handles millions of parts.

Future Trends in Air Transport. The air transport sector has shown a strong tendency to recover from downturns with renewed vigor. Overall, transport deliveries have been rising for the past 50 years. This suggests that deliveries will continue to climb in the future. In fact, transport manufacturers and analysts alike project that deliveries will almost double over the next two decades. The key assumption here is that the international economy will continue to grow.

General Aviation

After record shipments of 17,817 units in 1978, the U.S. **general aviation** segment of the aerospace industry, which manufactures light aircraft and components, has experienced a downward trend in sales that lasts to this day. After reaching a low of 928 units shipped in 1994, industry shipments increased for the remainder of the decade and through the years until 2007.

FIGURE 2.4 U.S. General Aviation Aircraft Shipments (2000–2020)

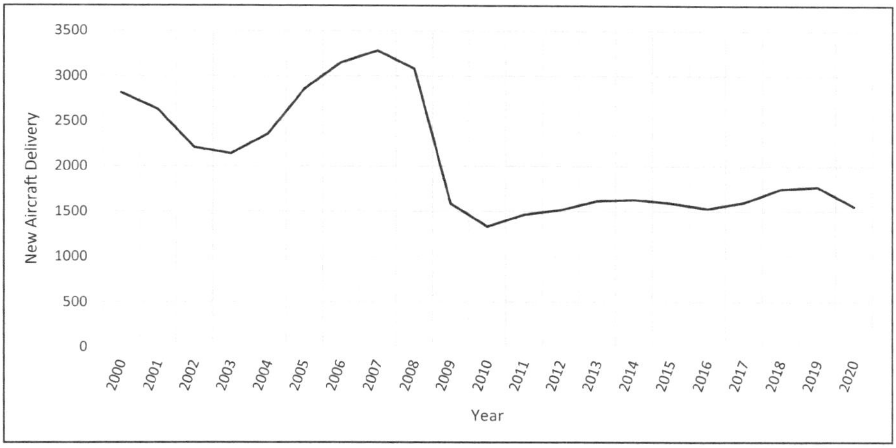

Source: Bureau of Transportation Statistics, U.S. Sales or Deliveries of New Aircraft, Vehicles, Vessels, and Other Conveyances

A large drop in demand (about 50 percent) for general aviation aircraft occurred after the 2008–2009 recession and demand has not yet returned to pre-2008 levels. After 2008, delivery of general aviation aircraft remained steady at about 1,500 aircraft per year (see Figure 2.4). Historically, the economic cycle of the general aviation industry closely paralleled that of the national economy. This relationship changed during the 1980s and early 1990s. High aircraft prices, interest rates, operating expenses, and product liability costs all contributed to the downward cycle. Other analysts cited changing lifestyles, tax laws, and foreign competition as further reasons for the sluggish sales performance in the past.

The general aviation industry has undergone deep and broad structural changes. The major independent manufacturers have been taken over by conglomerates. Textron acquired Cessna from General Dynamics in 2014, and Beech from Raytheon in 2013. Both Cessna and Beech now operate as separate brands under Textron Aviation. Piper emerged from bankruptcy and is now owned by the government of Brunei.

Business use of light aircraft tends to remain strong despite economic downturns for several reasons. Small aircraft are fuel-efficient. In fact, they use less fuel per seat-mile than any other form of air transportation. Even light twin-engine aircraft perform better in terms of fuel usage than the extremely efficient Boeing 777.

Furthermore, airlines require considerable ground support facilities, such as tugs, shuttle buses, baggage trucks, and heated and air-conditioned offices and terminals, most of which use petroleum-based energy. Rarely is a major airline terminal as close to a person's ultimate destination as is a general aviation airport. Private-use aircraft can fly straight to their destinations, whereas airlines frequently use indirect routes with one or more stops along the way. This has been particularly true in recent years with the establishment of hub airports by the major carriers.

The efficient use of time is another reason general aviation will expand. As our energy problems deepen and the airlines seek to make more efficient use of costly fuel, it will be increasingly difficult to reach many locations via scheduled carriers. Only those routes that generate high load factors will continue to be viable, which means that the trend will be toward decreased airline service. Fewer than 5 percent of the nation's airports have airline service now, and the majority of flights serve only 30 major centers. It often is not possible using the airlines to travel in one day between such cities as New York and Lexington, Kentucky; Chicago and Charleston, West Virginia; or San Francisco and Salem, Oregon. In the future, general aviation will be the only time-effective means of travel between many of the places business-people need to go.

Helicopters. Sales of U.S.-manufactured civil helicopters increased from the turn of the century through 2008, starting with the delivery of 493 units in 2000 and growing to a peak of 1,084 in 2008 (see Figure 2.5). As with the trend seen in general aviation, the recession of 2008 caused a drop in demand of almost 50 percent by 2009, and the market has continued to generally decline since then with only 455 units produced in 2018. It should be noted that much of U.S. manufacturer Bell Helicopter's production is based in Canada and thus is not counted as a U.S. export when shipped abroad.

FIGURE 2.5 U.S. Helicopter Shipments (2000–2018)

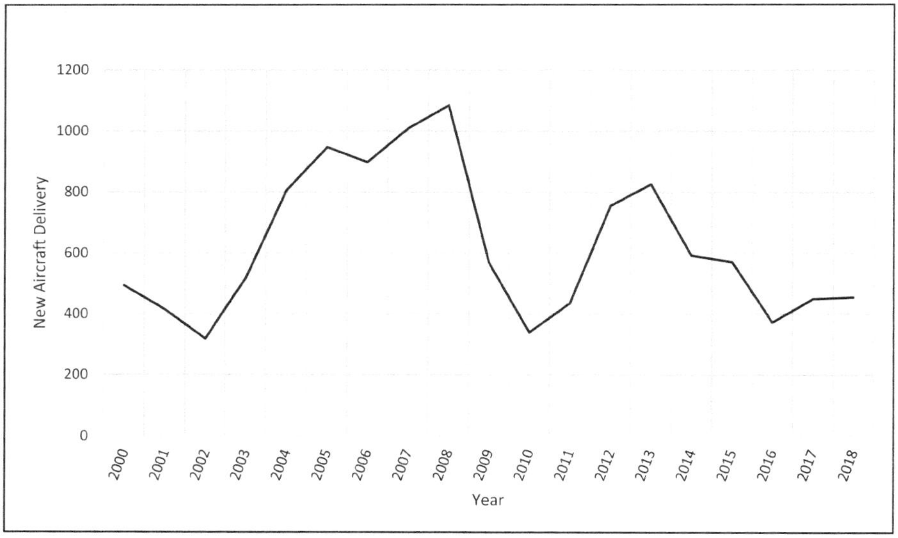

Source: Bureau of Transportation Statistics, U.S. Sales or Deliveries of New Aircraft, Vehicles, Vessels, and Other Conveyances

FIGURE 2.6 Helicopter Manufacturers' Market Share (2020)

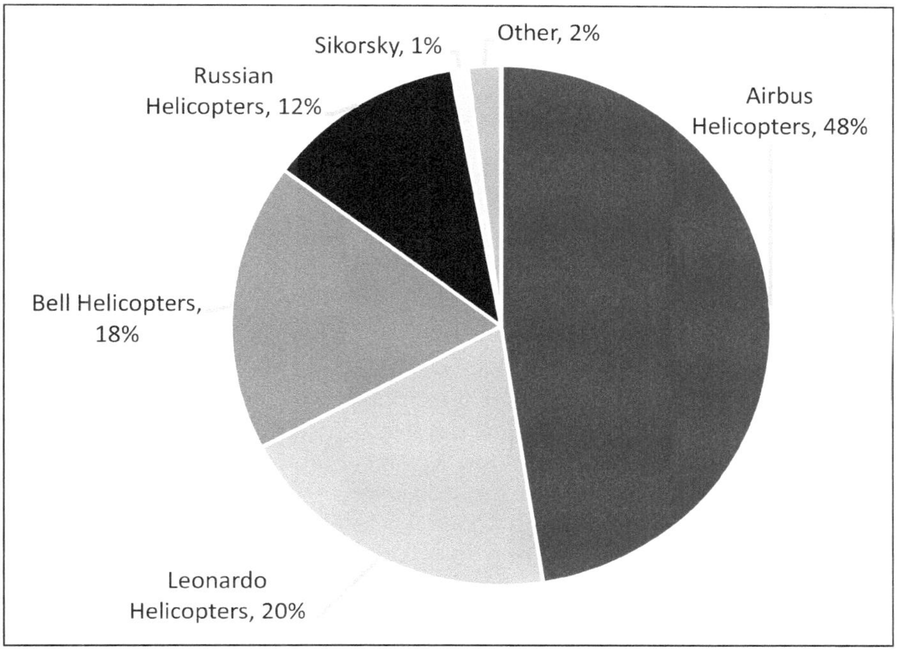

Source: Airbus

Today, lightweight single-engine models dominate U.S. rotorcraft shipments produced mainly by Robinson, while French/German-owned Eurocopter is the largest manufacturer of larger, more expensive models. Overall, foreign manufacturers should continue to increase their share of the total world market into the future. The three major U.S. helicopter manufactures are Bell, Robinson, and Sikorsky. Figure 2.6 provides an overview of the global helicopter manufacturers' market share in 2020.

Related Products and Services

Technology is simply knowledge, and it has a high degree of transferability: the know-how acquired in exploring aerospace frontiers can be put to work to provide new products and services of a nonaerospace nature, with resultant benefits to the economy as a whole.

For many years, the aerospace industry has pursued a program of technology transfer in an effort to make broader use of its wealth of know-how. The transfer process has been hampered by the lack of an aggregated market, such as that provided by the federal government or the airlines in aerospace work. In nonaerospace activity, the industry has operated largely on a single-project, single-location basis, working with individual federal, state, and local government agencies and other customers to transfer technology in such areas as medical instrumentation, hospital management, mass transportation, public safety, environmental protection, and energy.

THE AIR TRANSPORTATION INDUSTRY

The **air transportation industry** includes all civil flying performed by certificated air carriers and general aviation. Because this industry is the major focus of this text, it is important to define exactly what we mean by the terms *certificated air carriers* and *general aviation.*

The Civil Aeronautics Act of 1938 defined and established various classifications within aviation:[1]

> "Air carrier" means any citizen[2] of the United States who undertakes-. . . to engage in air transportation.[3]
>
> "Air transportation" means interstate-. . . transportation.[4]
>
> "Interstate air transportation"-. . . mean[s] the carriage by aircraft of persons or property *as a common carrier for compensation or hire.*[5] [Emphasis added.] No air carrier shall engage in any air transportation unless there is in force a certificate issued by the Civil Aeronautics Board authorizing such air carrier to engage in such transportations.[6]

Reading these sections of the act together, one sees the airline business as defined by Congress. The key words are italicized: *common carrier* and *compensation or hire.* Therefore, the appropriate term for airlines is not *commercial airlines,* but **certificated (common) air carriers**.

Having legally defined air carrier aviation, the act went on to define other types of aviation in a second category in the following way:

> "Air commerce" means interstate . . . commerce or any operation or navigation of aircraft within the limits of any Federal airway or any operation or navigation of aircraft which directly affects, or which may endanger safety in interstate air commerce.[7]
>
> "Interstate air commerce" . . . mean[s] the carriage by aircraft of a person or property *for compensation or hire-*. . . or the operation or navigation of aircraft in the conduct or furtherance of a business or vocation, in commerce-. . . between any State and any other State . . .[8]

The first paragraph, which is all-inclusive and embraces all non-air carrier aviation, defines *general aviation* as we know it: noncommercial or *private* use. That paragraph is modified by the second one quoted, which goes on to define two subparts of general aviation: (1) *business* aviation, where the aircraft is used "in the conduct or furtherance of a business or vocation," and (2) *commercial* aviation, where people are carried for compensation or hire, but not as a common carrier—note that those words are omitted. Today, general aviation is commonly described as "all civil aviation except that which is carried out by the certificated airlines." This segment of the industry will be covered in detail in Chapter 5, "The General Aviation Industry." Chapter 6 provides an in-depth review of the airline industry.

Contribution to the Economy

Over the past 70 years, the air transportation industry has become an increasingly important part of the U.S. economy. Aviation is the nation's dominant intercity mode of transportation for those passengers and goods that must be transported quickly and efficiently. It has become so universal that no one questions aviation's importance as an essential form of transport.

Aviation employs many thousands of people, and thousands more work in aviation's support industries, such as hotels, restaurants, rental cars, real estate, construction, and manufacturing. Individuals in these industries benefit economically from aviation regardless of whether they actually fly.

Aviation's final "products" are passengers and cargo safely and efficiently delivered to their destination. In 2019, U.S. airlines carried 811 million passengers, up 4.3 percent over 2018 and registered 16 billion ton-miles of cargo on approximately 8 million scheduled departures. Although scheduled airlines provide service to about 800 communities, over 5,000 communities of all sizes can access the air transportation system via publicly owned general aviation airports, including nonscheduled, on-demand, and charter flights.

Most people are familiar with the aviation elements that they see and use—airports, airlines, and general aviation aircraft. They also might be familiar with some of the support elements—baggage services, travel agents, and others. However, the aviation industry is much more than that; it includes an intricate set of suppliers of a wide variety of goods and services, all of which benefit economically from aviation. With economic deregulation of airlines in the late 1970s, air cargo networks were able to facilitate just-in-time shipping, providing expanded services at lower costs. Optimization of just-in-time shipping allows short production and development cycle times and eliminates excessive inventory in the logistics chain, regardless of facility location. Without the availability of ubiquitous, reliable, efficient air express service, U.S. businesses would be unable to realize the competitive economies of just-in-time production. Air transportation offers many cost advantages—lower lead times, quicker customer response times, improved flexibility, and reduced inventory. Many high-tech, high-value industries have embraced air transport for its time and cost advantages in manufacturing and distribution, and because it improves delivery reliability by providing time-definite guarantees.

One-stop shopping has become extremely important to businesses in their selection of logistics service providers and air cargo carriers. The ability to use a carrier that will provide door-to-door service with single-vendor control makes the entire logistics chain much less complicated than the traditional method of using several providers with different delivery functions. The major integrated carriers provide seamless trucking, warehousing, and distribution service functions in addition to air cargo. As a consequence, shippers are increasingly substituting blended air and surface transportation services provided by (or through) a single carrier.

Contribution to Efficient Conduct of Business

Air transportation is now as much a part of our way of life as the telephone or the computer. Speed, efficiency, comfort, safety, economy—these are the symbols of both modern society and modern air transportation. If you need to get somewhere in a hurry, and most businesses do, because time means money, then fly—comfortably, safely, and economically.

Air transportation has enabled employees of business and government organizations to reach any point in the world within hours, whether flying by air carrier or a general aviation aircraft. Certain values are associated with this timeliness:

1 Quicker on-the-spot decisions and action
2 Less fatigue associated with travel
3 Greater mobility and usefulness of trained, experienced executives, engineers, technicians, troubleshooters, and sales personnel
4 Decentralized production and distribution
5 The ability to expand market areas through more efficient use of management and sales personnel

To visualize a world without modern air transportation, consider the world of 1940, when surface transportation was still in its prime and air transportation was in its infancy. The 800-mile New York–Chicago trip took 17 hours each way on the fastest rail routing. The same trip today can be made in a couple of hours. Also consider the thousands of smaller communities now served by business representatives flying in and out the same day—it took days and weeks to cover the same territory back in the 1940s.

Impact on Personal and Pleasure Travel Patterns

In 1940, few people had ever flown in a scheduled airliner. By 1960, one-third of U.S. adults had flown; by 1981, two-thirds of the population over 18 years of age had been airline passengers; and by 2006, over 85 percent of the adult population had flown on a commercial flight. The impact of the air age on personal and pleasure travel has been at least as great as it has been on business travel. And airline fares remain a bargain compared to the price increases of other products and services over the past 60 years.

The combination of speed and economy has altered people's ideas about personal travel. In 1940, only a few wealthy individuals traveled to places like Florida or Hawaii, much less to Europe. Today, thousands of college students fly to Europe during the summer. Entire regions have developed into strong tourist-oriented centers because air transportation has made them accessible to vacationers from many areas. The economic development of such areas as Florida, Hawaii, Puerto Rico, Las Vegas, Phoenix, and San Diego can be attributed to the access provided by air transportation.

Emerging Sectors

There are four aerospace sectors that are expected to see major growth in the near future. They are: space applications, advanced air mobility (AAM), small unmanned aerial systems (UAS), and sustainable aviation fuels. After NASA closed the space shuttle program, an opportunity opened for commercial space to develop. Currently, SpaceX and Space Launch Systems provide most of the space lift capacity to NASA, however others are also trying to enter the market. Advanced air mobility vehicles can support previously underserved communities with passenger and cargo movement using advanced new aircraft. The AAM market is expected to grow to $115 billion by 2035. The growth of UAS market is expected to continue with a projected worth of over $52 billion by 2025. As problems are worked out to integrate UAS into the national aerospace system this growth will accelerate. Finally, sustainable aviation fuels might provide a solution to reduce the aviation industry's carbon footprint. While the industry has made steps by using cleaner and more efficient jet engines, there is still a long way to go.

The aviation industry is always evolving to meet the future demand for air transport, whether terrestrial or celestial. A healthy and strong aerospace sector is important to the economy of a country; however, the industry does operate in an international market, both for talent, raw material, subcomponents, and customers so an international view of the industry is required to fully understand the market.

KEY TERMS

aerospace industry
Aerospace Industries Association (AIA)
General Aviation Manufacturers Association (GAMA)
research and development (R & D)
related products and services
general aviation
air transportation industry
certificated (common) air carriers

REVIEW QUESTIONS

1 Define *aerospace industry*, and describe the role of both the AIA and the GAMA. The industry is a vital factor in four particular areas of the U.S. economy. What are they?
2 How has the aerospace industry changed since the 1950s? What are the unique characteristics of the aerospace industry?

3 Describe the aerospace industry in terms of its major products and its sales during the 1990s and 2000s. What are related aerospace products and services?
4 Describe the outlook for the civil aviation market in the early to mid-21st century.
5 What is the primary cause for consolidation in the commercial aircraft manufacturing industry? Why has there been a greater emphasis on international cooperation in building aircraft components and subassemblies?
6 List and briefly describe the major factors affecting commercial transport sales. How does the cyclical nature of civil aviation affect aircraft manufacturing?
7 What are some of the factors that led to the decline in general aviation aircraft sales? Why have the corporate and commuter segments of the general aviation industry done so much better than the personal-use segment? What is the outlook for helicopter sales?
8 Define *air carrier, interstate air transportation,* and *air commerce.* Both air carriers and general aviation fly "for compensation or hire." What distinguishes the two?
9 Discuss the impact of the air transportation industry on the U.S. economy in terms of dollar expenditures and jobs.
10 Describe the contribution of air transportation to the efficient conduct of business and its impact on personal and pleasure travel.
11 What is meant by emerging market opportunities in air transport? Which manufacturers have invested into the future of developing nations?
12 What are the four emerging sectors in aerospace? Explain each.

Notes

1 The language has been rearranged and certain words omitted for the purposes of clarity.
2 A citizen may be an individual or a corporation.
3 Section 101(3).
4 Section 101(10).
5 Section 101(2).
6 Section 401(a) [Certificate of public convenience and necessity]. A common carrier is a person or company in the business of transporting the public or goods for a fee.
7 Section 101(4).
8 Section 101(2).

CHAPTER 3

Historical Perspective

CHAPTER CHECKLIST • YOU SHOULD BE ABLE TO:

- Discuss some of the early attempts to provide air mail service in the United States
- Explain the significance of the Kelly Act and the Air Commerce Act of 1926
- Identify some of the breakthroughs in commercial aircraft development from 1918 to 1958
- Describe the events that led to the development of commercial jet air transportation
- Summarize the major economic developments in air transportation during the four decades from 1938 to 1978
- Discuss the reasons the federal government got into the business of regulating the air carriers
- Understand the significance of the federal legislation leading up to deregulation in the 1970s
- Give a brief summary of the deregulation movement before the Airline Deregulation Act of 1978
- Describe the major provisions of the Deregulation Act of 1978
- Identify some of the changes that took place in the airline industry during the two decades following deregulation
- Discuss early general aviation and how Beech, Cessna, and Piper began

DOI: 10.4324/9780429346156-4

- Explain the reasons for the decline in general aviation aircraft sales starting in the late 1970s
- Understand the impact of the events of September 11, 2001, on the aviation industry
- Understand the impact of the events of the COVID-19 global pandemic on the aviation industry
- Introduce the concept of new aircraft technology for the 21st century, including Small Aircraft Transportation System and Urban Air Mobility

INTRODUCTION

In 1914, most of the world was too preoccupied with World War I to notice that for a fare of $5 (more if the passenger weighed over 200 pounds), a person could buy a ticket for a one-way trip in an open-cockpit Benoist flying boat that flew across Tampa Bay, connecting Tampa and St. Petersburg. The land journey took an entire day; the flight took about 20 minutes. On January 1, 1914, the mayor of St. Petersburg became the first passenger on a regularly scheduled airline using heavier-than-air aircraft in the United States. Financed by P. E. Fansler and flown by Tony Janus, this primitive operation folded after four months when it ran into financial trouble. A humble beginning for the now-giant industry.

Between 1912 and 1916, the Post Office Department made several attempts to obtain federal appropriations for the transportation of mail by air, but no appropriations were granted until 1916. In that year, Congress made funds available for the establishment of proposed air mail routes; several in Alaska and one between New Bedford, Massachusetts, and Pawtucket, Rhode Island. The Post Office Department issued ads inviting bids on the routes, but no bids were forthcoming because of the lack of planes suitable for the services.

The development of large bombing planes during World War I demonstrated that the airplane could be used for fast commercial and mail transportation. In 1918, Congress appropriated $100,000 to the Post Office Department for the development of an experimental air mail service and for the purchase, operation, and maintenance by the Post Office Department of what were referred to as "aeroplanes." Thus was born the air transportation industry.

THE FORMATIVE PERIOD: 1918–1938

After preliminary studies, the first regular air mail route in the United States, 218 miles in length, was established on May 15, 1918, between New York City and Washington, D.C. One round trip was made every day except Sunday, and an intermediate stop in Philadelphia enabled the receipt and discharge of mail and the servicing of the planes. The service was conducted jointly by the United States War Department and the Post Office Department. The War Department furnished the planes and pilots and performed the operation and maintenance, and the Post Office Department attended to the sorting of the mail, its transport to and from the airport, and the loading and discharge of the planes. This joint arrangement continued until August 12, 1918, when the Post Office Department assumed exclusive responsibility for the development of a larger-scale mail service.

The New York–Washington air mail route was discontinued on May 31, 1921, because of the need for economy and the failure of Congress to specifically authorize the route.

The Post Office Department Service

When the Post Office Department took over the entire air mail service in 1918, including personnel and equipment and the complete operation and maintenance of the domestic air mail service, it shouldered a formidable task. This period in the history of the air mail service represented a trial stage during which the Post Office Department experimented with airplane equipment, weather service, night flying, flying and ground service arrangements, routes, postage rates, and other areas in which additional data were required before the service could be placed on a sound basis and operated nationwide over regular routes. Initially, the Post Office Department acquired a number of airplanes from the War and Navy Departments, rebuilding or remodeling the planes to transport mail. Safety and carrying capacity were the principal qualities sought when selecting or remodeling the planes. Later, the Post Office Department acquired planes especially designed for carrying mail. The success of the first experimental route led to the extension of the service through the establishment of a transcontinental route between New York City and San Francisco.

Weather conditions were one of the most serious difficulties faced in establishing the air mail service. The Weather Bureau of the Department of Agriculture was enlisted to provide the pilots with adequate weather information. Improvements were made in the design of planes, in airplane motors, and in airway marking and communication facilities, which made it possible to operate the air mail service in weather that would have prevented flying in the early years of the service.

One of the many contributions of the Post Office Department to the development of aviation during this period of experimentation and development was the demonstration of the practicability of regular night flying over regular routes on fixed schedules. In 1923, using data compiled by the War Department, the Post Office Department studied the feasibility of regular night flying. Army planes had done a considerable amount of night flying during the war. In addition, airplanes had been flown at night occasionally before these experiments, but regularly scheduled route flying had not been attempted.

A lighted airway was established between Cheyenne, Wyoming, and Chicago, and emergency landing fields were located along the airway and equipped with lights. Pilots made experimental night flights over the routes. In August 1923, a regular schedule of night flying was established between Chicago and Cheyenne, and in July 1924, regular night service was established on the transcontinental route.

Other Post Office Department air mail routes were added or discontinued as need for the routes was demonstrated or the lack of need became apparent. One of the most important routes, the overnight service between New York and Chicago, was established on a regular schedule of five nights a week in 1925 and on a nightly basis in 1926.

The Post Office Department experimented with various types of airplanes in actual flight conditions during this period. At first, planes that could be acquired by the government at nominal prices were used in air mail service. Later, the steady increase in volume of mail traffic necessitated the development of a type of plane capable of carrying more than 500 pounds. The government accepted competitive bids, and the Post Office Department began purchasing mail planes that were faster and that had twice the mail-carrying capacity of the earlier types.

By 1925, domestic air mail service in the United States had progressed to the point that the feasibility of regular service had been adequately demonstrated. Facilities for air transportation had been established, and the desirability of continued direct government operation or private operation under contract with the government was widely discussed. The U.S. government traditionally had arranged with railroads, steamship lines, and other carriers for the long-distance transportation of mail, with the Post Office Department providing the services incident to the collection, sorting, local transportation, and delivery of the mail.

Contract Mail Service

The third stage in the development of air mail service was ushered in by the Contract Air Mail Act of 1925, the so-called Kelly Act, named after its sponsor, Clyde Kelly (see the section "Federal Legislation and the Airlines"). The Kelly Act authorized the postmaster general to enter into contracts with private citizens or companies for the transportation of mail by air.

Shortly thereafter, the joint congressional committee on civil aviation, which had been established at the request of the Department of Commerce, decried in its report how much the United States lagged behind Europe in aviation. In response to these findings, President Calvin Coolidge appointed a select board of prominent business leaders, headed by Dwight Morrow, to make recommendations regarding the development of aviation in the United States. The Morrow board essentially confirmed the findings of the joint committee and recommended the separation of civil and military aviation, with the former under the auspices of the Commerce Department. This pleased the secretary of commerce, Herbert Hoover, who was a strong proponent of aviation. Out of all this came the Air Commerce Act of 1926, which, in effect, got the federal government back into the aviation business, this time as a regulator of those budding carriers created by the Kelly Act (see the section on "Federal Legislation and the Airlines").

The Post Office Department first set up short **feeder routes** (designed to feed traffic into the main-line trunk route) between various cities and scheduled the start of a transcontinental **Columbia route** once the short lines were working satisfactorily. Businessmen, lured by the Kelly Act's allowance of 80 percent of the air mail revenue to the contractor who carried it, flooded the Post Office Department with more than 5,000 bids. From these, the department chose the operators of 12 feeder, or **CAM (contract air mail)**, routes linking cities throughout the nation (see Figure 3.1).

On November 15, 1926, the Post Office Department advertised for bids on proposals for service on two sections of the transcontinental air mail route—the New York–Chicago and the Chicago–San Francisco sections. An acceptable proposal at a satisfactory rate of compensation for the Chicago–San Francisco section was submitted by the **Boeing** Airplane Company and Edward Hubbard. This service was later incorporated as the Boeing Air Transport Company. At first, no satisfactory bid was received for the New York–Chicago section, but on March 8, National Air Transport's bid was accepted.

Service on the Chicago–San Francisco route was relinquished to Boeing by the Post Office Department on June 30, 1927. Boeing's entry into commercial aviation had far-reaching effects. To clear the Rocky Mountains, Boeing produced a new airplane, the B-40, powered by the new air-cooled Pratt & Whitney 400-horsepower (hp) Wasp radial engine and equipped to carry two passengers in addition to its mail cargo. Subsequently, Boeing and Pratt & Whitney joined forces to become United Aircraft and Transport Company.

Service on the New York–Chicago route began on September 1, thus placing the air mail service in the same relationship with the Post Office Department as the mail service provided by the railroads, steamship lines, and other mail contractors.

The air mail contracts provided the genesis for several of today's airlines. Colonial Airlines, which won CAM route 1 between New York and Boston, was the predecessor of American Airlines. Western Air Express, operator of CAM 4 from Los Angeles to Salt Lake City, eventually became part of TWA. Northwest Airlines picked up CAM 9 from Chicago to Minneapolis after the original contractor gave it up. United absorbed the operators of two western carriers, Varney Speed Lines, operator of CAM 5, and Pacific Air Transport, operator of CAM 8. After a struggle to gain majority stock interest, United also gained control of the carrier along the eastern segment of the transcontinental route, National Air Transport, which had flown specially designed planes on CAM. In the midwest, the biggest name in automobiles, Henry Ford, emerged as a major force on the aviation scene by winning the contracts for CAM 6 and CAM 7 between Detroit, Chicago, and Cleveland. Ford's venture into aviation gave a skeptical public new confidence in air transport—if the astute auto manufacturer was willing to get into the business, there must be something to it.

FIGURE 3.1 The First Contract Air Mail Routes. Airline feeder routes were contracted to private operators in 1926. The transcontinental express sections were set up in 1927, and commercial air travel across the United States became a reality.

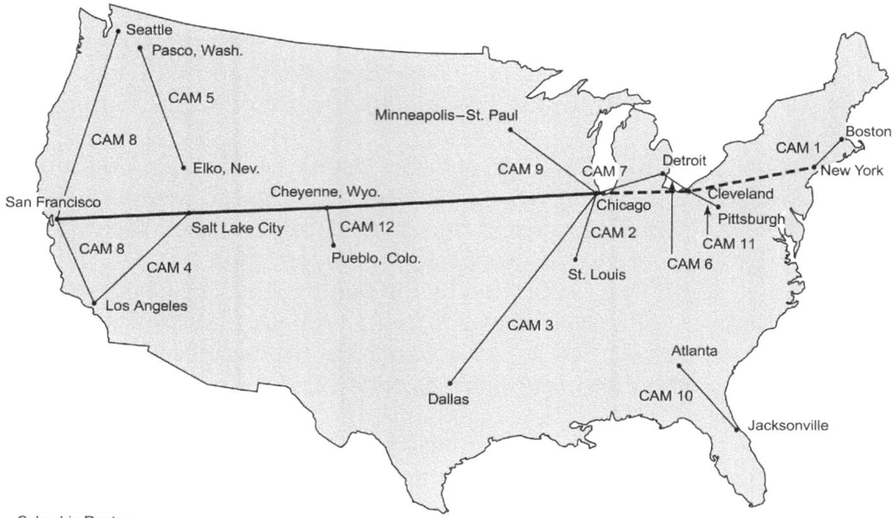

Columbia Routes:
——— Western Express Route – Boeing Air Transport – July 1, 1927
- - - - Eastern Express Route – National Air Transport – September 1, 1927

Feeder Routes:

Route No.	Company	Route	Began Operating
CAM 1	Colonial Airlines	New York – Boston	June 18, 1926
CAM 2	Robertson Aircraft Corp.	Chicago – St. Louis	April 15, 1926
CAM 3	National Air Transport	Chicago – Dallas	May 12, 1926
CAM 4	Western Air Express	Los Angeles – Salt Lake City	April 17, 1926
CAM 5	Varney Speed Lines	Elko, Nev. – Pasco, Wash.	April 6, 1926
CAM 6	Ford Air Transport	Detroit – Cleveland	February 16, 1926
CAM 7	Ford Air Transport	Detroit – Chicago	February 15, 1926
CAM 8	Pacific Air Transport	Los Angeles – Seattle	September 15, 1926
CAM 9	Charles Dickenson	Chicago – Minneapolis	June 7, 1926
CAM 10	Florida Airways Corp.	Atlanta – Jacksonville	September 14, 1926
CAM 11	Clifford Ball	Cleveland – Pittsburgh	April 21, 1927
CAM 12	Western Air Express	Pueblo, Colo. – Cheyenne, Wyo.	December 15, 1926

Ford branched out in 1926 by acquiring the Stout Metal Aircraft Company in Stout City, Michigan, and began construction of the famous "Tin Goose". The Ford Trimotor, as it was officially designated, had three-engine reliability, as well as greater altitude capability and a larger payload capacity than any of its predecessors. From the time of its first flight in 1926 to its retirement from TWA in 1934, the Tin Goose was reliable, relatively slow at 85 knots, very strong, and rather uncomfortable.

In the meantime, passenger service could only improve. In 1927, an airplane called the Lockheed Vega made its first flight, heralding the age of fast, comfortable travel for more than a mail sack and pilot.

In 1928, weather information was transmitted by teletype, and in the decade that followed, that network expanded rapidly to bring pilots the kind of information that was essential to safe, reliable service. By 1929, the Graf Zeppelin had flown around the world, and James H. Doolittle had made the first successful instrument landing. In that same era, Hamilton Standard produced the first hydraulic variable-pitch propeller. The technology was advancing, but would any company running an airline be profitable enough to buy it?

Postmaster General Brown and the Airlines

Walter Folger Brown was postmaster general under President Herbert Hoover in the late 1920s. An attorney from Ohio, Brown combined astute vision with a ruthless will to ensure the success of the Post Office's mission to develop commercial aviation. Both Hoover and Brown disliked reckless competition as much as they did monopolies, and they both sought industry stability, efficiency, and growth—specifically, strong companies with regulated competition. Consequently, Brown spurred the adoption of another amendment to the Kelly Act, the McNary-Watres bill. Known as the Air Mail Act of 1930, it empowered the postmaster general to consolidate air mail routes if he thought that would serve the public interest.

Brown redrew the air map of the United States, forcing small operators out of business and awarding the bulk of the air mail business to a handful of airlines he considered to be well run, financially stable, and efficient. In May 1930, he invited the heads of the larger airlines to Washington for a series of meetings that came to be called the **Spoils Conference**. It was an apt name, for the spoils literally went to those participants who supported Brown's plan to establish three main mail routes—central, northern, and southern—out of the original CAM routes. United (a fusion of mostly west coast CAM companies) would get the northern route; Avco (the Aviation Corporation, a holding company that later became American Airlines) would get the southern route. The central route would go to a merger of Western Air Express and Transcontinental Air Transport (TAT), which had hired Charles Lindbergh to survey routes for a passenger service based on alternating rail and Ford Trimotor flights that would allow for coast-to-coast travel in the unheard-of time of 48 hours. Western had also shown considerable interest in passenger travel, although its route was for only the most rugged of individuals. Western's Harris "Pop" Hanshue was not the type to be forced into anything, and he fought Brown all the way, eventually compromising by accepting stock and a position in the new company. Hanshue agreed to the establishment of a new airline named Transcontinental and Western Air Express, in which TAT and Western held the majority of stock. Brown's plan seemed to succeed until 1934, when a scandal erupted in Washington. Although Brown had been quite candid about the fact that he wanted the air mail business awarded according to proven performance and financial solidity, newspaper reporter Fulton Lewis, Jr., discovered the result of Brown's philosophy. Ludington Airlines, flying the triangular Washington–Philadelphia–New York route, had bid 25 cents a mile on the mail contract between these cities but had lost out to Eastern Air Transport, a much bigger line that had bid 89 cents a mile. When his newspaper would not publish the story, Lewis approached Senator Hugo Black of Alabama, who was chairing a Senate committee investigating maritime mail contracts. When Black heard the story, he quickly added air mail contracts to his investigation.

After some lengthy hearings in which a number of supposed scandals were uncovered, Black had stirred up the public and President Franklin D. Roosevelt to a point that all prior contracts were immediately canceled. Roosevelt ordered the Army to begin flying the mail; a decision that had tragic consequences. Even though Postmaster General James Farley had argued against the cancellation, the public's wrath fell on him more than on the president when one Army plane after another crashed in poor weather that the pilots were completely unequipped to handle.

Although Black's hearings ultimately revealed no illegalities in Brown's arrangements—even the supposed bidding scandal was explained to everyone's satisfaction as a more complex arrangement than it first appeared—Black still came out the winner. He talked Roosevelt into supporting a bill to separate the airframe companies from the airlines, to reopen competitive bidding, and to bar all the attendees of the Spoils Conference from further participation. It was pure punitive politics, but at least the Army was out of the mail business. Not only had a number of pilots lost their lives, but it had cost the Army $2.21 a mile to fly 16,000 miles of routes, compared to 54 cents a mile to cover 27,000 miles for the airlines.

The Air Mail Act of 1934 was signed into law by President Roosevelt after Senator Pat McCarran's effort to legislate an independent regulatory body was defeated. The act authorized new one-year contracts that were subject to review before renewal. The Interstate Commerce Commission was involved as a regulator of rates, and the secretary of commerce was empowered to specify what equipment was suitable for each route. To placate smaller airlines anxious to acquire portions of the big routes, Postmaster General Farley added a provision that barred all prior contract holders from bidding anew. Obviously, this meant the end of the airlines as an industry. The government that had created them under Brown was now preparing to destroy them under Farley. Farley privately advised all the airlines to reorganize, which is how American Airlines, Eastern Airlines, and United Airlines all came to be.

Of greatest consequence was the provision that severed aircraft manufacturers from the airlines themselves. Boeing had to pull out of United; Avco gave up American; North American sold its TWA holdings; and General Motors surrendered its stock in both Eastern and Western. A new era had dawned, one in which the airlines would guide their own destinies.

The Turning Point for the Airlines

Certain aspects of the industry were looking up. Both the Boeing 247 and the DC-1 had made their first flights during 1933, rendering immediately obsolete such antiquated fixtures as the Trimotor and the Curtiss Condor—the last of the biplane transports.

Boeing's all-metal, low-wing, twin-engine monoplane was the first modern airliner. Nevertheless, the 247 was not a success, serving as an illuminating example that in the airliner market, the design that is first to the finish line does not necessarily win the race. The 247 was spectacular: faster than most fighter planes and able to carry ten passengers in unaccustomed luxury. It won the Collier Trophy for speed and endurance in 1933, as well as the favor of William A. Patterson, who became president of United Airlines after the previous president resigned during the Brown scandal.

Patterson bought 60 of the Boeings for $4 million, at the time the largest single purchase of airplanes in history—and a bigger order than Boeing could really handle. The order tied up the company's assembly lines for a year, forcing TWA and American to look elsewhere for planes. Unfortunately for Boeing, their search took them to a small manufacturer headed up by Donald Douglas.

The 247 originally was to have been built with the new Pratt & Whitney air-cooled Hornet engines, but United's pilots vetoed those engines; they trusted only the reliable Pratt & Whitney Wasp engine. The 247 would have carried 14 passengers with Hornets, but the United version could carry only ten with the smaller Wasps, and thereby Boeing won the battle but lost the war.

In 1932, Jack Frye, president of TWA, had gone to Douglas with a proposal for a trimotor airliner. Douglas knew that the Wright Cyclone would eliminate the need for the third engine, offering seats for 14 in a twin-engine airplane. Thus, when Boeing slammed the door on TWA and American, Douglas was able to show them something better—four more passengers than the 247 could carry for the same operating cost. The resulting DC-1, which quickly stretched to the DC-2, was a colossal gamble for Donald Douglas, and the debt he incurred developing it was not paid off even by TWA's eventual order for 25 planes. Boeing sold 75 of the 247s—but that was all. Lufthansa bought two that served as models for some of Germany's World War II bombers, so advanced was the 247's design and performance. United soon switched to the Douglas airplanes as well, in order to remain competitive with American and TWA. But if the 247 had been built with the proper engine, there might never have been a Douglas airplane to consider.

The 247 caused a setback for Boeing, but it did serve as the stimulus for the DC family—a line of airplanes that are generally credited with moving the airlines from their pre-1933 red-ink days to times of solid profit. The DC-3, which was introduced as the Sleeper Transport (the DST) in response to a specification written by American Airlines' C. R. Smith, not only increased the speed and comfort of travel, thereby winning passengers who had not been willing to brave an airliner before, but also operated reliably and profitably. The plane was incredibly strong, an attribute that is largely credited to an engineer named Jack Northrop. Its development also introduced the importance of operating costs to airline managers, who were mostly new to the business and therefore willing to try new ideas. The

DC-3 was the first airplane to instill a feeling of confidence in air travel, as measured by the fact that its safety record encouraged the introduction of the first air travel insurance in 1937.

The Arrival of the Professional Airline Manager

Once the 1934 Air Mail Act had become law, a new group of managers emerged who would prove to be the most dominant personalities thus far in the short history of air travel. The pioneers had been long on courage, but they came up short when it came to business acumen. Curiously, few of the leaders we now associate with their respective companies actually founded their airlines. The major exception is Juan Trippe, the former Navy pilot who launched Pan American World Airways in 1927 with a rented seaplane because the Fokker he ordered didn't show up on time. Another exception was Tom Braniff, whose brother Paul was one of his first pilots. A third founder, though he came along later, was the colorful Bob Peach of Mohawk Airlines (now part of US Airways).

For the most part, however, the men who became the giants of the industry worked their way up from less exalted positions. For example, William A. Patterson, who boldly signed for $4 million worth of Boeings, was only a vice-president at United when the massacre of 1934 moved him up. As late as 1934, after the Air Mail Act had gone into effect, C. E. Woolman was only general manager of Delta, but he would lead the company's development as its president in the decades to follow. The president of Eastern was Ernest R. Breech; Eddie Rickenbacker didn't join until the following year, as general manager. And TWA was about to elect Jack Frye as president, but he was only a vice-president for the ten-month period preceding his election.

The industry needed strong leadership at this point in its development, and these individuals would enjoy some of the longest and most successful tenures in U.S. business history. This group of dynamic individuals seemed to share one outstanding trait—the ability to take risks against great odds and keep going in the face of adversity. And between 1929 and 1933, the adversity was great indeed. The airlines had a fatality rate 1,500 times that of the railroads and 900 times that of buses; in 1932, the carriers had 108 accidents, 16 of them fatal. And not until the 1940s did passenger revenues exceed the income from mail payments. If that wasn't bad enough, the industry learned early on that the years when its fleet needed modernization and expansion usually preceded times of economic stagnation, recession, tight money, and slack air travel.

Just before World War II, some events took place that influenced the future of the airlines and redirected the way they conducted their operations. Considering their awful safety record at the time, it is hard to fault the decisions that led to the changes, but few would ever have guessed at the eventual outcome.

On December 1, 1935, the first airway traffic control center was formed in Newark, New Jersey, to inform by radio all pilots in the vicinity as to the whereabouts of other air traffic during instrument conditions. Significantly, it was the airlines themselves that first staffed the facility. They had seen the need for such a practice and had hastened to take action. In less than a year, the Bureau of Air Commerce was arranging to take over air traffic control, a landmark event that seemed less significant at the time than it does in retrospect. The government was now irretrievably involved in the direct operation of the airlines.

That same year, Senator Bronson Cutting was killed when his Transcontinental and Western flight crashed in Missouri. An immediate investigation was launched into the safety function of the Bureau of Air Commerce. Also in 1935, the British installed a top-secret network of radar transceivers along their coast and equipped their military aircraft with an early transponder known as IFF (for "identification, friend or foe").

By 1936, Socony-Vacuum Oil Company was producing 100-octane aviation gasoline by a method known as catalytic cracking, which efficiently derived large quantities of high-quality fuel from petroleum stock. Shortly thereafter, Captain Carl J. Crane invented a system for totally automatic landings and successfully tested the devices at Wright Field in Ohio. It seems surprising now to realize that so many major technological advances were available so early. That they arrived when they did may well have had a decisive effect on how the government dealt with what it saw as its obligation to ensure the safety of passengers, for this was a time of fierce debate that would culminate in a significant piece of legislation.

THE GROWTH YEARS: 1938–1958

1938–1945

The laws relating to air commerce were a hopeless mess. Three agencies held power in various intertwined areas: the Post Office Department, the Commerce Department, and the Interstate Commerce Commission. In an effort to clean legislative house, President Franklin D. Roosevelt solicited and received recommendations for a new, inclusive body of regulations. The result was the Civil Aeronautics Act of 1938, which established the Civil Aeronautics Authority (see the section "Federal Legislation and the Airlines").

When World War II broke out, Roosevelt made arrangements to nationalize the airlines, and had it not been for the strong opposition of the Air Transport Association (ATA), this arrangement might well have become permanent. Just a few days after the Japanese attack on Pearl Harbor, Roosevelt had signed an executive order that would have allowed him to seize the airlines, but the president of the ATA talked him out of it, pleading that the carriers could do a better job if they were left to run a global wartime transportation system themselves. The order was rescinded.

Still, aviation in all its forms contributed to the war effort. Everything that flew became at least quasi-military: the Civil Air Patrol went out on coastal patrols, and the airlines contracted the bulk of their fleets to the

Army. The military also enlisted most of the pilots who had staffed the airlines, and routes were revised drastically to allocate the remaining resources to the war effort rather than the needs of the traveling public.

Production was converted overnight: the DC-3 became the C-47 and was even more legendary in its accomplishments as a military airplane than as its civilian counterpart. At the beginning of the war, U.S. transports were the most highly evolved aircraft the military had, and certainly the most tried and tested. The war shrank the airlines themselves to insignificance, but the industry had never been more than the sum of the skill and equipment that turned it into an efficient military force as easily as they had made it a profitable business.

The Postwar Years

Out of World War II came the DC-4 and the Constellation, two high-performance, long-range airplanes that later prepared the industry for the jet era. The C-54 (the military designation for the DC-4) had its beginnings back in 1936 as the DC-4E; an abortive design that combined the forward end of a DC-3 with four engines and a triple tail. Meanwhile, George Mead of Pratt & Whitney had undertaken the task of getting that company back into the transport business; its military success had been phenomenal, but Wright Aeronautical had dominated the commercial market with the DC-3. The new Pratt & Whitney R-2000 engine met the specifications for the final version of the DC-4—an entirely new Douglas design that first flew in 1942, just in time to become the Army's C-54 Skymaster.

Simultaneously, Lockheed was building the Constellation, which had Wright engines, a pressurized airframe, and the triple tails that Douglas abandoned; it first flew in 1943. It is significant that air cargo became a worthwhile notion during the war. Freight was first carried in the C-47, the C-54, and the Constellation—the old passenger carriers—and later in airplanes such as the C-82s, which were designed specifically to move freight. Although the airlines could not benefit financially from these new airplanes until after the war, it mattered little. The aircraft existed, and the fact that the military produced them in large numbers simply made them available cheaply as postwar surplus.

The complex operations of war also hastened the improvement of communications techniques, and radar became a high-priority project that would lay the foundation for modern air traffic control. Military air traffic operations in high-density environments became a valid model to be further improved upon and modified to fit the needs of the airlines.

The immediate postwar era was a stagnant time for the airlines. President Harry S. Truman's administration was plagued by heated rivalries and political infighting over routes and revenues. With thousands of aviators available after the war, a large number of airlines sprang up. Trunk routes were already taken by the prewar companies, but many feeder routes were up for grabs. The established carriers viewed with horror the thought of government subsidies for new feeder lines, arguing that they should provide the feeder service. The Civil Aeronautics Board assured the larger carriers that the newly established feeders would be carefully monitored and not allowed to compete with airlines flying the trunk lines. Some of the first feeders established were Allegheny, Mohawk, Piedmont, North Central, Frontier, Bonanza, Ozark, and Pacific.

Overexpansion furnished enough trouble for the airlines, but the nonscheduled airlines that sprang up all over the nation provided more. These airlines, naturally, made runs between major population centers, which cut into the trunk lines' traffic.

The Berlin airlift in 1948–1949 represented an unequaled opportunity to develop experience in high-volume air freight and contributed to the sense of optimism about air freight as a viable business. Independent lines specializing in carrying only freight were formed, and the first experiments in using helicopters to carry the mail to inner-city heliports were conducted. In 1947, Los Angeles Airways succeeded in gaining approval for the first scheduled helicopter service.

Boeing tried to bounce back with its 377 Stratocruiser, modeled after the military B-29 Superfortress. Its success was limited, however, and Boeing turned its attention to military jet aircraft. Meanwhile, Convair and Martin twin-engine planes with pressurized cabins flew short-haul routes to feed the ever-growing giant airlines that crossed the entire country in nonstop leaps. Aviation records fell as new and improved models of Constellations, DC-6s, and DC-7s with reciprocating power plants appeared. The United States had emerged in the postwar years as the aircraft manufacturing leader.

The British aircraft manufacturing industry met with government officials after the war to decide whether to try to challenge the lead of the United States with conventional transports or to take another approach. They decided to leapfrog—to gamble on producing the first jet airliner. The result was the de Havilland Comet jetliner. It made its first flight in July 1949, and it entered service with BOAC in May 1952. In January 1954, a Comet plummeted into the Mediterranean, killing all 35 passengers and crew members; in April 1954, a second Comet ripped apart and plunged into the sea after takeoff from Rome. All Comets were grounded while officials conducted a thorough investigation to ascertain the cause of the crashes. In February 1955, the investigators determined that metal fatigue in the hull had led to explosive decompression.

Technological advances were coming so fast that the old pioneers of the airlines were soon left behind. Airplanes quickly became machines of awesome complexity, requiring systems no one person could ever entirely understand. Increasingly, it was the government that recognized this, and beginning in 1947, the Civil Aeronautics Authority (CAA) began certifying three new classes of flight personnel: flight radio operators, navigators, and engineers—a symbol of the era of the technocrat. Landings became routine at 42 terminal airports used by 12 of the airlines. In 1948, three engineers at the Bell Telephone Laboratories invented the transistor, while distance-measuring equipment (DME) and very high frequency (VHF) omnirange loomed as the answer to a need for improved air navigation aids. By 1951, Pratt & Whitney was testing its 10,000-pound-thrust J57, which would make the development of the Boeing 707 possible.

Very quietly, in 1953, a study was completed showing for the first time that the airplane had become the prime mover of travelers on trips of more than 200 miles. This only confirmed what the young executives in the airline marketing departments already knew. The way to win the public was to sell not "transportation," but "travel," and that took new and ingenious methods.

If U.S. engineers weren't willing to experiment with turbojets, they could at least go halfway with turboprops, and Capital Airlines tried the British-built Vickers Viscount amid press parties that featured demonstrations of how one could balance a quarter on the edge of one's meal tray, so smooth were the new turbine engines. But when Lockheed tried the same approach with its Electra turboprop, the result was one of the most expensive recall campaigns ever. Although the airplane eventually proved to be one of the most efficient ever built, its image suffered when critics questioned its structural integrity. Lockheed eventually redesigned the wings and engine nacelles on 165 of the airplanes.

Boeing had never really prospered in the commercial business since the DCs had stolen the thunder from its 247. The 307 and 377, though praiseworthy for their implementation of revolutionary features, had not really been successful. Fortunately, Boeing had been blessed with an endless succession of contracts for heavy military equipment that kept it afloat.

At great financial risk, Boeing built a jet tanker, the military KC-135, whose purpose was to fuel the Boeing-built B-47 jet bomber. The air force tested the plane and bought it. Boeing then approached the airlines, proposing a jet airliner based on the Boeing jet tanker. The airlines were lukewarm to the proposal and declined to invest any money in research. Once more, Boeing risked its own funds, this time to develop the Boeing 707.

When, in 1955, Pan Am announced its order not only for the 707 but also for the Douglas DC-8, Boeing had spent $185 million on jet transport development. It marked the end of one era, and the beginning of another.

MATURITY – JETS ARRIVE: 1958–1978

The jets were coming, and by 1956 the CAA recognized the inevitable and held a conference to plan for the jet age. The challenges were enormous, not only for the airlines, for whom 30 years of parts and maintenance experience became obsolete overnight, but also for the government, because safe operations were their responsibility. Then, in 1956, an event occurred that defied all the odds: a TWA Super Constellation and a United DC-7 collided over the Grand Canyon, killing 128 people. Suddenly, it was a crowded sky, and the outcry for reform was loud and clear. The answers, of course, were sought in technology.

If a pair of conceptually obsolete piston airliners could have a midair collision, what would happen with jets, which went 50 percent faster?

The seemingly impossible collision between two airplanes in what had once seemed a boundless sky was a pivotal event in the history of airline travel, for it brought the issue of the control of each flight by some central authority to the fore, made air traffic control mandatory, and increased demands for precision. It also paved the way for the next major piece of legislation.

The Grand Canyon mid-air collision was followed by two more bad accidents, and in 1958, there was a virtual stampede to push a law through Congress creating a new Federal Aviation Agency (FAA)—an independent and comprehensive government agency to control all aviation matters, both civil and military. Centralized air traffic control began less than a month after the bills were introduced. President Dwight D. Eisenhower pressed for passage, and the FAA was born.

Just as the turboprops entered service in 1958, the 707 began flying overseas routes. The turboprop aircraft had a relatively short life with the major carriers. It was American Airlines that began 707 service between the coasts a year later. With the advent of the 727, one of the most efficient transport airplanes ever built and one that became as widely flown as the DC-3 and the DC-9, the airlines soon disposed of all their reciprocating propeller equipment. For a while, Eastern used some older airplanes on its shuttle flights between the northeast corridor cities of Boston, New York, and Washington, but they were soon replaced.

On December 30, 1969, Boeing achieved certification of an airplane that revolutionized airline travel forever. Just as the original B-707 brought vibration-free, over-weather jet-engine flying to passengers, the giant 747 was to bring low-cost travel to the masses. Once again, Pan Am led the way by introducing jumbo-jet service across the Atlantic in January 1970. An economic downturn dried up orders for the plane between 1969 and 1972, but after that initial setback, orders began to flow in a steady stream.

The Boeing 747 was unmatched. It was able to carry about 380 passengers in an eight- or even ten-abreast, twin-aisle, mixed-class layout and brought a new term to commercial aviation: "wide-body." The humpback profile of the airplane resulted from an early decision to maximize freight-carrying capability; the tilt-up nose on the 747F (freighter) and 747C (convertible) versions allowed direct insertion of cargo containers. Doing so required a cockpit that was removed from the main deck and a generous afterbody for streamlining, and, at Juan Trippe's insistence, an upper-deck, first-class lounge was added in the area behind the cockpit.

The Boeing 747 has reigned supreme over the world's air routes for more than a quarter of a century. More than a thousand 747s have already been built, and production continues. Wisely, other manufacturers did not try to challenge Boeing head-on. The tri-jet Douglas DC-10 and the Lockheed L-1011, under development at the same time as the 747, were only about three-quarters of its size. Containing about 270 seats, the planes were intended to satisfy the requirements of air routes that did not generate sufficient traffic to justify the deployment of the giant Boeings. The DC-10 entered service on August 5, 1971, and the TriStar on April 26, 1972. Both suffered severe setbacks. A DC-10 suffered a spectacular crash at the world's busiest airport, Chicago's O'Hare, on May 25, 1979. Production of the TriStar was disrupted by the bankruptcy of its engine manufacturer, Rolls-Royce.

A latecomer to the wide-bodied airliner field was the **Airbus**. It was first conceived simultaneously by Hawker-Siddeley, which had taken over de Havilland, in Great Britain and by Bréquet-Sud in France. The basic design of this twin-engined variant on the wide-bodied principle took shape in the late 1960s. The wings for what became the A300 series were built by a European consortium of airframe manufacturers. Air France put the first version of the Airbus, as it quickly became known, into service in May 1974.

Boeing had not been neglecting other projects during the years of the 747 program. The three-engine 727 short-haul airliner began as a 100-seat regional carrier, eventually stretching into lengthened versions that matched the 707's length. Both the 727 and the 737 used the fuselage cross-section of the 707 series, giving short-range customers amenities similar to those found on the longer trips. The twin-engine 737, certificated in July 1967, was designed to compete with Douglas's DC-9.

Since the jets took over, the airline industry has introduced one technological advancement after another: flight recorders, weather radar, terrain-avoidance systems, and so on. During this era, the airlines passed from a period of high risk to a period of virtually no risk at all. With the passage of the Airline Deregulation Act of 1978 (see the section "Federal Legislation and the Airlines"), the airline industry moved into an era of new challenges.

ECONOMIC DEVELOPMENTS PRIOR TO DEREGULATION

The period from 1938 to 1978 witnessed truly phenomenal growth in domestic and international air transportation. Over the years, U.S. airlines received many new route authorizations, both domestic and international. Table 3.1 shows the growth in the number of certificated domestic route miles of the leading carriers during 40 years of regulation. The number of U.S. city pairs connected by scheduled airline service grew in step with expanded route miles. Internationally, limited service was provided in 1938 by a handful of scheduled U.S. airlines (principally Pan American Airways and its related companies) and a half dozen or so significant foreign airlines. By 1978, these numbers had increased to 21 U.S. and 73 foreign airlines.

Air passenger traffic also grew at an astonishing rate. The number of passengers (domestic and international) carried by U.S. airlines increased from a little over 1 million in 1938 to almost 267 million in 1978. In addition, in 1978, foreign airlines carried some 16 million passengers to or from the United States. With increases in average length of journey, there was an even greater growth in U.S. airline passenger miles, from 533 million in 1938 to 219 billion in 1978. The air transport industry thus emerged as one of the nation's major industries. Over the four-decade period, revenues increased from $58 million to $22.8 billion, and total airline assets increased from under $100 million to over $17 billion.

Table 3.1 Growth of Certificated Domestic Routes (miles)

Airline	1938	1978
American	6,826	43,755
Delta	1,091	50,380
Eastern	5,276	43,576
Northwest	2,507	30,927
TWA	5,749	29,127
United	5,321	48,709

Source: CAB Statistical Reports.

The air transport industry also became a major employer. Total direct airline employment increased from about 13,000 to well over 300,000. In addition, hundreds of thousands of people were employed in the manufacture of civil transport aircraft, engines, and accessories; at airports; in travel agencies; and in the vast range of other related service, supply, and support activities.

Technological development was spectacular, not just in aircraft but in the air transport system infrastructure as well. In terms of aircraft, this 40-year period witnessed the evolution from the propeller-driven, 21-passenger DC-3 to the 400-seat, wide-body Boeing 747 jet that, in addition to a full passenger load, has cargo capacity equal to the load-carrying capability of five DC-3s. Aircraft nonstop range, with full payload, grew to over 6,000 miles.

Accompanying these developments were quantum improvements in safety, speed, comfort, and overall convenience for the users of air service. A truly integrated air transport system was developed that enabled the public to buy tickets from virtually any airline (and from many thousands of travel agents) for travel on multiple airlines and to check baggage at the point of origin for delivery at the destination regardless of how many airplane or airline changes were made en route.

At the same time, technological advances combined with economies of scale to produce lower unit costs, helping make it possible to hold the line on prices over this 40-year period. Despite a consumer price inflation rate of almost 400 percent from 1938 to 1978, average fares per passenger mile remained remarkably stable (see Table 3.2). The increase from 1968 to 1978 reflected not only acute inflation but also the sharp fuel cost increases following the 1973 oil embargo.

The air transport industry also met the congressional objective of assisting the national defense. As reported by the CAB in its 1942 Annual Report to Congress: "Pearl Harbor brought real meaning and new force to the national defense standard so wisely written into the Civil Aeronautics Act during peacetime." The airlines, domestic and international, went on wartime footing and contributed significantly to the war effort. Subsequently, they helped break the Berlin blockade, provided important contributions in the Korean and Vietnam wars, and furnished emergency and

Table 3.2 Average Yield per Revenue Passenger Mile (cents)

	All Route Carriers*	Domestic Trunk Lines	International Trunk Operations
1938	5.50¢	5.12¢	8.34¢
1948	6.30	5.73	8.01
1958	5.80	5.58	6.46
1968	5.46	5.45	4.95
1978	8.35	8.14	7.50

Source: CAB Statistical Reports.
*Includes local service carriers, whose yields were higher than those of domestic trunk lines and international trunk operations.

evacuation assistance in dozens of other critical situations around the globe. And by 1978, the formal Civil Reserve Air Fleet, available with crews for military call-up at defined stages of national emergency, contained 298 commercial aircraft, of which 216 were large intercontinental units.

The U.S. air transport system, by far the largest in the world, was also the best in just about every respect. And this contributed, in no small measure, to the worldwide supremacy of the U.S. aerospace industry, exporting as it did many billions of dollars' worth of aircraft, engines, components, and parts.

All of this was accomplished through private enterprise with an early phase out of government subsidies except for limited types of service in the public interest. Exact early figures do not exist, because the CAB did not identify the "compensatory" element in total mail pay until 1951. For fiscal 1951, slightly over $75 million was paid in subsidies, equal to slightly over 7 percent of total industry revenues. In 1951, subsidy recipients, by category, were:

Domestic trunks	$18.9 million
Local service	$17.1 million
International, overseas, and territorial	$39.3 million
Total	$75.3 million

For calendar year 1977, by coincidence, almost the same levels of subsidies ($76.7 million) were distributed, but none went for domestic trunks or international services, which had long functioned without government financial support. The recipient groups in 1977 were:

Local service	$72.2 million
Alaskan carriers	$ 4.5 million
	$76.7 million

Subsidies in 1977 represented only 0.3 percent of total industry revenues.

The 40-year period of air transport regulation saw a steady increase in the number of operators on specific domestic routes. In 1978, few markets with significant traffic existed that were served by only one airline. And in international service, there was a steady and substantial increase in the number of operators (U.S. and foreign) over virtually all commercially important routes.

This 40-year period also saw changes in the structure of the U.S. airline industry. A number of the original "grandfather" trunk-line carriers (5 of the original 16) merged with or were acquired by other airlines; there were no bankruptcies among them. During the same period, new categories of carriers, as well as new carriers, were licensed, including eight local-service and three all-cargo companies, and ten charter airlines. This latter group played a significant role in offering lower-priced transportation and developed a strong presence in certain markets, particularly for transatlantic flights.

Despite problems and inadequacies, few could reasonably deny the brilliant success of the 1938 regulatory scheme. There was a high level of public satisfaction with U.S. airlines. A *U.S. News & World Report* survey revealed that out of 21 defined categories of U.S. industry, the airlines were rated the highest for "giving the customer good value for money."

Table 3.3 U.S. Schedule Airlines Operating Revenues and Profits, Before and After Interest Expense (millions of dollars)

	Operating Revenue ($)	Operating Profit ($)	Interest Expense ($)	Operating Profit (Loss) After Interest Expense ($)
1968	7,753	505	222	283
1969	8,791	387	283	104
1970	9,290	43	318	(275)
1971	10,046	328	331	(3)
1972	11,163	584	307	277
1973	12,419	585	368	217
1974	14,699	726	420	306
1975	15,356	128	402	(274)
1976	17,506	723	372	351
1977	19,917	908	373	535
1978	22,884	1,365	539	826

Source: Air Transport Association (ATA) Annual Reports.

In only one respect did the airlines perform poorly: compared with other broad industry groups, the airline business was not highly profitable. Coincidentally, 1978, the last year of regulation, was by far the most profitable year over the 40-year period.

Any review of airline profitability must also take into account the extremely cyclical nature of the business. It is highly leveraged, because the marginal cost of additional traffic (and the marginal savings from less traffic) at any given level of capacity is very low. As a result, the swings in profitability from recession to good times and back to recession can be very wide. This is well illustrated by how the 1970–1971 and 1974–1975 recessions affected airline financial performance (see Table 3.3). It is interesting to note that ATA computations of rate of return on investment showed, for example, positive returns of 1.2 percent in 1970, when the industry reported a net loss of $201 million, and 2.5 percent in 1975, when it reported a net loss of $84 million. Profit margin provides a meaningful financial yardstick. Based on these computations, airline profit margins from 1967 to 1977 averaged only 1.7 percent, versus 4.8 percent for U.S. manufacturing companies.

FEDERAL LEGISLATION AND THE AIRLINES

The authority of the federal government to regulate interstate and overseas aviation and air transportation derives from the Constitution of the United States, which grants to Congress the right to regulate interstate and foreign commerce, to regulate the postal service, to make treaties with foreign nations, and to provide for the national defense. The rationale for regulation is rooted in the economic and physical characteristics of the air transport industry. The major reasons are listed here:

1 *To Stabilize the Industry.* The air transportation industry is a public utility that is important to the commercial and social welfare of the nation. The need to stabilize modes of transportation so that they could serve the public at reasonable prices spurred the introduction of economic regulation of water transportation, railroads, and, later, highways. In the case of air transportation, the industry was somewhat unstable in its early years of growth, even though safety regulations and federal subsidies through air mail contracts were in place from the beginning. Industry instability was one of the primary reasons for bringing air transportation under a system of regulation.

   Air transportation's early years were characterized by fierce competition among numerous budding carriers, fluctuating prices, unreliable service, and high turnover among carriers. Overcapacity in the industry and the competitive bidding process for air mail contracts were said to have led to absurdly low bids and disastrous price wars. This atmosphere was not conducive to investment by the financial community, and without outside capital funding, the fierce little competitors that made up the industry in its early years could not acquire the equipment they needed. Later, in the early 1930s, the air carriers themselves sought federal regulation, realizing that the history of transportation demonstrated that the absence of such regulation led to evils from which not only the public but also the industry itself would suffer. By 1938, the air transportation industry was experiencing critical financial difficulties: many of the major lines faced the threat of bankruptcy, and much of the original investment in airlines had been dissipated. Financial difficulties were also aggravated by a series of accidents in the winter of 1936–1937 that undermined public confidence. The fact that rail and highway transportation was already regulated set a precedent for regulation that encouraged its enactment in air transportation.

2 *To Improve Air Safety.* The industry was, and still is, largely dependent on government aid to maintain the safe flow of traffic. Federal regulation of air transportation safety was in effect from the early years. It was recognized that safety regulation could not reach its maximum effectiveness if the industry was unstable and if the carriers were financially weak and unable to afford the necessary safety precautions and devices. Therefore, economic regulation was intended, in part, to stabilize air transportation so that the carriers would have the financial capacity to pay for whatever was needed to conform with safety regulations pertaining to the design, operation, and maintenance of aircraft.

3 *To Reduce Cash Subsidies.* Another reason, although minor, for regulating air transportation was the fact that air carriers had been subsidized through the air mail program since the mid-1920s. It was believed that the subsidies needed could be reduced by stabilizing the industry through economic regulation. A financially strong and stable airline industry would need smaller subsidies from the federal government.

Other reasons for regulation included the fact that the industry used the airspace over the entire United States, over other nations, and over international waters. Consequently, it naturally fell under federal rather than state jurisdiction. Another reason was the industry's role in the national defense. This was evidenced as early as World War II, when the airlines, flying under contract for the military, provided the backbone of the Air Transport Command. Under contracts with the military for airlift services, the airlines played a significant role during the Korean and the Vietnam wars. In addition, a joint program between the Department of Defense and the airlines, the Civil Reserve Air Fleet (CRAF), was designed to augment military airlift capability in the event of a national emergency.

Early Federal Legislation

The first steps the federal government took to regulate aviation and air transportation occurred in connection with the development of the air mail service. In May 1918, the air mail service was inaugurated on an experimental basis by the Post Office Department and the Army. In August of the same year, the service was taken over as a Post Office Department operation. On February 2, 1925, Congress enacted the Contract Air Mail Act, usually known as the Kelly Act, and as such gave birth to the airline industry. This law authorized the postmaster general to contract with private individuals or companies engaged in air transportation service for the transportation of air mail. By 1927, all the air mail services of the Post Office Department had been turned over to the air transportation companies, and new routes were established to be operated by air mail contract carriers. The effect on air passenger transportation of the establishment of contractual relationships between the Post Office Department and the air mail carriers can scarcely be overemphasized. The subsidies received by the air mail contractors enabled a number of airlines to establish passenger services. Indeed, it would have been impossible for some companies to exist without the air mail contracts.

The Kelly Act was amended in 1926 to provide higher rates of compensation. Subsequent air mail legislation was important because of the relationship of this type of regulation to the broader legislation dealing with the regulation of air transportation. The pioneer legislation of this type, because it laid the foundation for all future regulation of air transportation, was the Air Commerce Act of 1926, also known as the Bingham Parker Act.

The Air Commerce Act of 1926

The Air Commerce Act of 1926 imposed on the secretary of commerce and the Department of Commerce the duty of promoting and fostering the development of commercial aviation in the United States. The act authorized the Department of Commerce to encourage and develop facilities necessary for air navigation and to regulate and maintain them.

The act did not initially create a new bureau within the Department of Commerce. Rather, the intention was to distribute the duties imposed by the act among the then-existing agencies of the department.

The objective of the Air Commerce Act was to stabilize civil or commercial aviation in such a way as to attract adequate capital to the fledgling industry and to provide it with the assistance and legal basis necessary for its development. The law emphasized the federal government's role in the development of civil air transportation more than it stressed its responsibility for regulating the business aspects of air transportation. The act was designed to encourage the rapid development of commercial aviation, as indicated by the legislative history of the act.

In introducing the bill that became the Air Commerce Act, the Senate Committee on Interstate Commerce stated that "although Americans built the first airplanes capable of flight, and were the first to learn how to fly heavier-than-air machines, and hold more world records than do the citizens of any other nation, commercial aviation has not advanced as rapidly in the United States as had been hoped and expected." This act defined **air**

commerce as transportation, in whole or in part, by aircraft, of persons or property for hire, and the navigation of aircraft in furtherance of or for the conduct of a business. The act made it the duty of the secretary of commerce to encourage air commerce by establishing civil airways and other navigational facilities to aid aerial navigation and air commerce.

The regulation of aviation provided for in the act included the licensing, inspection, and operation of aircraft; the marking of licensed and unlicensed craft; the licensing of pilots and of mechanics engaged in aircraft work; and the regulation of the use of airways. Several different governmental agencies or departments were empowered to perform functions relative to carrying out the provisions of the act:

1 The Department of Commerce was entrusted with the administration and enforcement of major portions of the act. An assistant secretary for aeronautics was appointed in 1927 to administer the duties assigned to the department.
2 The secretary of the treasury was given the duty of providing regulatory rules for entry, clearance, and customs regulations for aircraft engaged in foreign commerce.
3 The secretary of labor was empowered to deal with all immigration problems relative to air transportation.
4 The Weather Bureau of the Department of Agriculture was authorized to supply meteorological information.
5 The secretary of war was authorized to designate military airways.
6 The Bureau of Standards of the Department of Commerce was directed to undertake R & D to improve air navigation facilities.

Through this distribution of functions in connection with aviation and air transportation, Congress sought to utilize as many of the existing governmental agencies as possible, thus avoiding or reducing the need to create additional and duplicating federal agencies, especially for air transportation and aviation. Consequently, no separate bureau was initially set up in the Department of Commerce. However, in July 1927, a director of aeronautics was appointed, who, under the general direction of the assistant secretary for aeronautics, was in charge of the work of the Department of Commerce in the administration of the Air Commerce Act.

In November 1929, because of the increasing volume of work incident to the rapid development of aviation, it was necessary to decentralize the organization. Three assistants and the staffs of the divisions under their respective jurisdictions were assigned to the assistant secretary of commerce for aeronautics. These included a director of air regulation, a chief engineer of airways, and a director of aeronautics development to assist in aeronautical regulation and promotion. The organization was known as the Aeronautics Branch of the Department of Commerce.

The work was further reassigned by executive order of the president in 1933, so as to place the promotion and regulation of aeronautics in a separately constituted bureau of the Department of Commerce. An administrative order of the secretary of commerce provided for the establishment of the Bureau of Air Commerce in 1934. The bureau consisted of two divisions: the Division of Air Navigation and the Division of Air Regulation.

A revised plan of organization for the Bureau of Air Commerce, adopted in April 1937, placed all the activities of the bureau under a director, aided by an assistant director, with supervision over seven principal divisions: airway engineering, airway operation, safety and planning, administration and statistics, certification, inspection, and regulation. A policy board was formed to deal with all matters affecting policy within the bureau, and an advisory board, consisting of civilian and other representatives of all aviation interests, was appointed to advise the bureau.

Additional Air Mail Acts

The Air Mail Act of 1930, known as the McNary-Watres Act, was passed by Congress on April 29, 1930. It provided the postmaster general with unlimited control over the air mail route system. The postmaster general could now extend or consolidate routes if he thought it would serve the public interest. The act also tightened the provisions under which contractors were reimbursed for carrying the mail and provided additional remuneration for contractors flying multi-engine aircraft and using the latest navigational aids.

In February 1934, the postmaster general annulled all domestic air mail contracts, and the transportation of the mail was assigned temporarily to the Air Corps of the U.S. Army. This action was taken because the postmaster general had evidence that there was a conspiracy to defeat competitive bidding.

The arrangement with the Air Corps continued from February 20 to May 16, 1934. Then, after the reorganization of the commercial air transportation companies according to government requirements as a precondition to submitting bids for air mail contracts, the commercial companies submitted bids, and new contracts were awarded.

The Air Mail Act of 1934, passed on June 12 and known as the Black-McKellar Act, provided temporary contracts and gave the Interstate Commerce Commission (ICC) the responsibility of periodically adjusting the rates of compensation to be paid to the air transport companies for the carriage of the mail within the limitations imposed by the act. The ICC was required by law to review annually the rates of air mail pay to ensure that no company was earning unreasonable profits. Each air mail contractor was required to submit for examination and audit by the ICC its books, accounts, contracts, and business records and to file semiannual reports of all free transportation provided. The ICC was also authorized to investigate any alleged unfair practices and competitive services of companies transporting air mail that adversely affected the general transport business or earnings on other air mail routes, and to order the practices or competition to be discontinued if unfair conditions were found to exist. The act also provided that after July 1, 1938, the aggregate cost of air mail transportation to the government could not exceed the anticipated revenue from air mail.

The ICC organized the Bureau of Air Mail to administer the regulation of air mail compensation under its direction.

In addition, the act separated the manufacturing companies from connections with airlines and forbade interlocking directorates, overlapping interests, and mutual stock holdings. By 1938, two general categories of "air carriers" had developed. The first, economically more significant, group was composed of the air mail contractors that flew over established routes and transported persons, property, and mail. The second group, the so-called fixed-base operators, was composed of persons operating airports, flying schools, crop-dusting services, and so forth, who also carried persons and property on an air taxi basis in small, nontransport-type aircraft.

The Civil Aeronautics Act of 1938

On June 23, 1938, the Civil Aeronautics Act was approved by President Roosevelt. This act substituted a single federal statute for the several general and air mail statutes that, up to this time, had provided for the regulation of the aviation and air transportation industry. The act placed all the functions of aid to and regulation of aviation and air transportation within one administrative agency consisting of three partly autonomous bodies—a five-member Civil Aeronautics Authority (CAA), a three-member Air Safety Board, and an administrator—and attempted to demarcate executive, legislative, and judicial functions.

Members of this composite agency or administration were appointed by the president with the advice and consent of the Senate. No term was stated for the administrator, but members of the other two agencies were appointed to office for terms of six years. The act required members of the three agencies to devote full time to their duties and forbade them from having financial interest in any civil aeronautics enterprise.

The five members of the Civil Aeronautics Authority performed quasi-judicial and legislative functions related to economic and safety regulations. The administrator performed purely executive functions related to the development, operation, and administration of air navigation facilities, as well as promotional work in aviation. The Air Safety Board was a quasi-independent body created for the purpose of investigating and analyzing accidents and making recommendations to eliminate the causes of accidents.

The personnel, property, and unexpended balances of appropriations of the Bureau of Air Commerce of the Department of Commerce and of the Bureau of Air Mail of the Interstate Commerce Commission, which had administered air mail payments under the Air Mail Act of 1934, were transferred to the new Civil Aeronautics Authority. The transfer of the responsibilities of the Bureau of Air Commerce to the Civil Aeronautics Authority, effected in August 1938 under provisions of the Civil Aeronautics Act, brought to a close a 12-year period during which the development and regulation of civil aeronautics were under the jurisdiction of the Department of Commerce.

The Civil Aeronautics Authority exercised all quasi-legislative and quasi-judicial powers conferred by the act and all executive powers of appointment with respect to its officers and employees. It took control of the expenditures of the administrator and the Air Safety Board and of all other executive powers of appointment with respect to the exercise of these quasi-legislative and quasi-judicial powers.

The administrator, appointed by the president, exercised executive powers with respect to the development of civil aeronautics and air commerce; the fostering, establishment, and maintenance of air navigation facilities; and the regulation and protection of air traffic.

The Air Safety Board was appointed by the president, by and with the approval of the Senate. It acted independently of the Civil Aeronautics Authority, and in performing its investigations of accidents, it reported on the facts and probable causes and recommended preventive measures to avoid future accidents.

The Civil Aeronautics Authority was directed by Congress, in the declaration of policy of the Civil Aeronautics Act, to regulate air transportation in the public interest by performing six functions:

1 Encouraging and developing an air transportation system adapted to the present and future needs of domestic and foreign commerce, the postal system, and national defense
2 Regulating air transportation so as to preserve its inherent advantages, promoting the highest degree of safety and sound conditions in the industry, improving relations among air transport companies, and coordinating transportation by air carriers
3 Promoting adequate, economical, and efficient transportation service by air carriers at reasonable charges, and prohibiting unjust discrimination, undue preferences or advantages, and unfair or destructive competitive practices
4 Preserving competition in keeping with the sound development of an air transportation system for commerce, the mail service, and national defense
5 Promoting the development of air commerce and safety
6 Encouraging the development of civil aeronautics

The act extended federal regulation to all phases of aeronautics, to all persons engaged in flying, and to all instrumentalities of aviation with the exception of the actual acquisition and operation of airports. This was accomplished by what has been termed a rather unusual use of definitions. *Air commerce* was defined by the act to mean all interstate, overseas, or foreign air commerce, or the transportation of mail by aircraft, or any operation or navigation of aircraft within the limits of any civil airway, or any operation or navigation of aircraft that directly affected or that might endanger safety in interstate, overseas, or foreign air commerce. This last clause provided for a degree of federal control over intrastate aviation, because a private pilot might use an airway in intrastate operation that could endanger the safe conduct of interstate commerce.

Under several reorganization plans in 1940, the Air Safety Board was abolished and its functions transferred to the five-member Civil Aeronautics Authority, which was redesignated the Civil Aeronautics Board (CAB). The administrator of civil aeronautics (whose organization was then known as the Civil Aeronautics Administration, or CAA, and later as the Federal Aviation Agency, or FAA) was placed under the Department of Commerce. The respective duties of the board and the administrator were delineated a broad outline. The CAB, although administered within the Department of Commerce for housekeeping purposes, retained its status as one of the so-called independent regulatory agencies, such as the Interstate Commerce Commission, the Federal Communications Commission, the Federal Power Commission, and the Securities and Exchange Commission.

Under the later 1958 Federal Aviation Act, the board was designated an "independent" agency. The FAA, successor to the CAA, was not assigned to any executive department, but was considered an "executive agency" as opposed to an independent regulatory commission.

Economic Functions of the CAB

The broad language of the Declaration of Policy, with its somewhat conflicting objectives, left the CAB with considerable discretion in its administration of the act. The CAB's decisions were final, subject to court review, but even here the act provided that the "findings of fact by the CAB, if supported by substantial evidence, shall be conclusive." This was a significant obstacle to efforts to overturn CAB decisions, particularly because the "findings" in most route and rate proceedings (which were at the heart of the regulatory scheme) were predictive or judgmental in character.

Whatever the complexities encountered in practice, the licensing system was simple in concept: no one could engage in the business of public air transportation unless authorized to do so by a "certificate of public convenience and necessity" issued by the CAB. To obtain such certificates, applicants were required to convince the CAB that they were "fit, willing, and able" to perform the proposed transportation "properly" and that "such transportation is required by the public convenience and necessity." This, of course, led right back to the extremely general congressional objectives set forth in the Declaration of Policy.

The CAB also had broad authority to attach to any certificate "such reasonable terms, conditions, and limitations as the public interest may require," and it exercised such authority. Certificates were often very detailed. They specified intermediate and junction points and, in some cases, required or prohibited stops or through services. Often, the carriage of traffic between certain pairs of cities named in a certificate, or even the carriage of certain categories of traffic, was prohibited. An important aspect of the regulatory system was that airlines could not lawfully suspend or abandon services without CAB approval.

Regulation of international routes differed from that of domestic routes. Most important, CAB decisions with respect to international route applications of both U.S. and foreign airlines were subject to "the approval of the President." The Supreme Court eventually held the president's decision to be unreviewable. Also, foreign air carrier applications were generally based on preexisting intergovernmental air transport agreements that granted route rights to the airline designated by the foreign government. This alone was almost invariably considered sufficient to meet the statutory standard applicable to the grant of foreign airline route applications (that the proposed transportation "will be in the public interest").

Passenger fares and cargo rates were also subject to strict regulation. Carriers were required to file formal tariffs, establishing prices charged and applicable terms and conditions. These tariffs had to be filed in advance and could be "rejected" (for technical reasons) or "suspended" (for perceived substantive problems). Fares and rates were to be "just and reasonable," and discrimination (with its panoply of related legal terms such as "undue or unreasonable preference or advantage," "unjust discrimination," and "undue or unreasonable prejudice or disadvantage") was prohibited. Once a given tariff became effective, it had to be observed; all forms of rebating were prohibited.

Standards for evaluating the reasonableness of fares and rates were as general as those for awarding routes. Thus, among other factors, the CAB was to consider "the need in the public interest of adequate and efficient transportation of persons and property by air carriers at the lowest cost consistent with the furnishing of such service; and the need of each air carrier for revenue sufficient to enable such air carrier, under honest, economical, and efficient management, to provide adequate and efficient air carrier service." In practice, the CAB applied public utility "rate of return on investment" principles in its rate reviews and rate making, and all carriers generally were required to charge like amounts for like services.

As for international routes, the CAB had to share authority over international rates with foreign governments. The obvious complexities were greatly ameliorated, in practice, by broad worldwide acceptance of the International Air Transport Association (IATA) as a forum for meetings and rate agreements among international airlines, subject to approval by interested governments.

The CAB also established rates to be paid to airlines by the Post Office Department for the carriage of U.S. mail, both domestic and international; this was the mechanism for providing the subsidy that all air carriers initially required. Thus, while the mail rates were to be "fair and reasonable," one of the factors to be considered was

> the need of each – . . . carrier for compensation for the transportation of mail sufficient to insure the performance of such service, and, together with all other revenue of the air carrier, to enable such air carrier under honest, economical, and efficient management, to maintain and continue the development of air transportation to the extent and to the character and quality required for the commerce of the United States, the Postal Service, and the national defense.

When the CAB was establishing commercial rates, subsidy allowances were based on a "rate of return on investment" analyses.

Although route and rate regulation had the most direct and visible impact on public service, the CAB also exercised a broad range of other economic controls over the air transportation industry. Thus, it could (and did) prescribe in detail the accounts and records to be maintained by air carriers and the reports to be submitted. Agreements between air carriers had to be filed with the CAB, whose approval was required for certain specified interlocking relationships and for air transport-related mergers, consolidations, and acquisitions of control. At the same time, however, CAB approval of such agreements granted immunity from the general antitrust laws. The CAB also was authorized to investigate and terminate "unfair or deceptive practices or unfair methods of competition in air transportation."

One further economic provision of the Civil Aeronautics Act warrants mention in light of deregulation legislation and postderegulation developments. It relates to labor relations between the airlines and their employees. In recognition of the "public interest" characteristics of air transportation, air carriers were required to comply with the provisions of the Railway Labor Act, which prescribed an elaborate system for resolving disputes.

The Federal Aviation Act of 1958

In 1958, President Eisenhower, citing midair collisions of aircraft that had caused a number of fatalities, asked Congress for legislation to establish "a system of air traffic management which will prevent within the limits of human ingenuity, a recurrence of such accidents." Congress responded by enacting the Federal Aviation Act of 1958, which was signed into law on August 23, 1958. The new law created the Federal Aviation Agency (FAA), which was given authority over the nation's airspace. The FAA combined the existing functions of the CAA, the aviation functions of the secretary of commerce, the duties of the Airways Modernization Board, and the safety and regulatory functions of the CAB.

Under the new law, however, the CAB retained its jurisdiction over route allocation, accident investigation, and fare applications. The 1958 act expressly empowered the FAA administrator to regulate the use of the navigable airspace by both civilian and military aircraft, to establish air traffic rules, to conduct necessary research, and to develop air navigation facilities. The act also provided that military aircraft be exempt from air traffic rules in the event of urgent military necessity and provided for restricted airspace zones for security identification of aircraft.

The 1958 act left the economic regulatory provisions virtually unchanged but made several revisions to the safety program. Although the CAB retained its duties in the fields of air carrier economic regulation and aircraft accident investigation, the board's power to enact safety rules was transferred to the administrator of the FAA, with the result that the latter official promulgated the regulations and standards. The CAB's role in safety rule-making was limited to participation as an interested party in

FAA proceedings. A second important revision of prior law concerned procedure in cases involving suspension and revocations of safety certificates. Whereas under former law only the CAB could suspend or revoke in the first instance, the new act provided for initial action by the administrator, subject to the certificate holder's privilege of appeal to the board.

Apart from these matters, the FAA administrator wielded essentially all the powers and duties his predecessor had under the 1938 act, plus a clearer authority to allocate the navigable airspace between military and civilian users.

In the spring of 1967, Congress created the Department of Transportation. The FAA as such was in effect abolished, and in its stead was established within the new department a Federal Aviation Administration, headed by an administrator. The FAA's functions were transferred to the Department of Transportation, where, for the most part, they were placed under the Federal Aviation Administration, where they remain today. The Department of Transportation Act also transferred the CAB's accident-investigating and related safety functions to the new department and, in turn, immediately redelegated them to a new independent agency called the National Transportation Safety Board.

The Deregulation Movement

Despite remarkable advances under the regulatory system established in 1938, as well as broad public satisfaction with the airline system, air regulation gradually came under increasing criticism, particularly from academic economists. This criticism gained strong momentum in the mid-1970s, and between 1977 and 1979, a veritable revolution was accomplished in both domestic and international U.S. air transport policy.

The infancy of the air transport industry, and then World War II, produced an initial period free from serious criticism, but the basic economic regulatory policies of the Federal Aviation Act eventually came under attack. The key issue, as might be expected, was the relative desirability of free competition in this industry versus the supposed need for tight government control of entry, exit, pricing, and other issues. As early as 1951, in a study titled *Federal Control of Entry into Air Transportation*, Lucille Keyes questioned both the theoretical and empirical bases for the regulatory system. In 1962, Richard E. Caves, in *Air Transport and Its Regulators*, concluded that "the air transport industry has characteristics of market structure that would bring market performance of reasonable quality without any economic regulation."

Despite increased criticism and occasional congressional studies that led to minor regulatory changes, it was not until 1975 that certain factors began combining for a successful push to **deregulation**. Traditional distrust of government regulation in general became sharply focused on air transportation through a series of economic and regulatory developments. Adversity struck the industry in 1970 when large increases in capacity, resulting from the advent of wide-body jet aircraft, coincided with a serious economic recession. This, in turn, led to widely criticized CAB regulatory policies, including a four-year moratorium on all new-route cases and approval of a series of agreements among airlines to limit capacity over certain major routes. At the same time, CAB pricing policies (which set industry-wide standards based on average industry costs) were increasingly viewed as fostering inefficiency, higher costs, and higher prices. Critics pointed to the experience of several intrastate carriers in California and Texas (not regulated by the CAB) that charged lower per-mile fares for comparable distances than the CAB-regulated airlines and that operated more profitably.

The storm might have passed had it not been for the Arab oil embargo of 1973 and the ensuing massive increase in fuel costs. Airline operating costs soared, while traffic decreased due to the recession. One result was a series of fare increases. However, with cost increases exceeding increases in yields, another period of poor airline earnings followed. This latter factor added to the list of arguments for regulatory reform the contention that the airlines themselves would be better off with some form of deregulation.

It was in this atmosphere that two influential reports were released. One was a special CAB staff study on regulatory reform, dated July 1975. It concluded: "Protective entry control, exit control, and public utility-type price regulation under the Federal Aviation Act are not justified by the underlying cost and demand characteristics of commercial air transportation. The industry is naturally competitive, not monopolistic." The study recommended that protective entry, exit, and public utility-type price controls in domestic air transportation be eliminated within three to five years by statutory amendment.

At about this same time, an influential report was released by the Subcommittee on Administrative Practice and Procedure of the U.S. Senate Judiciary Committee, headed by Senator Edward Kennedy. The report's repeated message was that prices should and would be lower with a more competitive system. The CAB's practices, the subcommittee report concluded, while effective in promoting industry growth, technological improvements, and reasonable industry profits, had not been effective in maintaining low prices. The report further stated that it was economically and technically possible to provide air service at significantly lower prices, bringing air travel within the reach of the average citizen. With the sudden increase in antiregulation sentiment, President Gerald Ford's administration in 1975 sponsored the first deregulation bills. This started the legislative process that culminated in the Airline Deregulation Act of 1978.

Even before the act's passage, however, the CAB had begun its own administrative journey on the road to deregulation. First, Chairman John E. Robson, who took office in 1975, gradually relaxed the moratorium on scheduled service routes of his predecessor. Supplemental (charter) airlines were given greater opportunities through the expansion of the scope of permissible charters. The CAB also permitted greater carrier flexibility to reduce fares. These initial cautious moves gained enormous momentum under Chairman Alfred E. Kahn, appointed by President Jimmy Carter in

1977. Under his vigorous leadership, the CAB soon began processing and approving applications for new operating authority, particularly when the applicants promised lower fares. To enforce compliance with such promises, awards were made for short terms, with renewal dependent on performance. The CAB also was much more receptive to route realignments and elimination of restrictions, as well as to exit from those markets to which entry had been liberalized. During this same period, the Carter administration sought agreements with foreign governments to permit more international competition and was prepared to authorize as much international service by U.S. airlines as foreign governments would accept.

There was also far greater receptivity to fare reductions. Indeed, CAB Chairman Kahn carried it to the point of justifying dismissal of a complaint against illegal rebating by stating: "The law prohibits departure from tariffs, but departures from tariffs are good for competition. Rebating as we see it is a consequence of noncompetitive rate levels, and the best theoretical remedy is to reduce fares."

The Carter administration's support for deregulation was an important factor, but the movement was also aided by improved industry profitability. Some observers attributed the industry's profitability to the CAB's new procompetition policies. Actually, however, from 1976 to 1978, the industry was merely experiencing its traditional cyclical upturn after the sharp downturn in 1975.

There was, of course, substantial opposition to any significant relaxation of regulation from most airlines, from airline labor unions, and from financial institutions with investments in the industry. Their arguments covered a broad range of concerns, including these:

1 Possible worsening of the industry's excellent safety record
2 Probable concentration of service on dense traffic routes, with a consequent deterioration of service on others, especially those serving small communities
3 Impairment of the air transportation "system," with its conveniences of through-baggage handling, interline ticketing, and so on
4 Destructive and predatory price competition, resulting in earnings deterioration and, ultimately, increased industry concentration
5 Reduced ability to re-equip and to finance other available technological advances
6 Adverse impact on airline employees

But these arguments failed to halt the drive for deregulation. Indeed, although what finally emerged as the Airline Deregulation Act of 1978 was working its way through congressional hearings and reports, and although the bills themselves were undergoing various revisions, a mini-deregulation bill was passed by Congress with little fanfare or public notice. This was the deregulation of domestic all-cargo service, which became law in November 1977. Actually, it entered the statute books buried in a package of changes attached to a bill dealing with war risk insurance.

The technique for all-cargo deregulation was simple and effective. Any airline that, under the authority of a certificate or exemption, had provided any scheduled domestic all-cargo service during 1977 could, within 45 days after passage of the law, apply for authority for any and all other domestic all-cargo service, and the CAB was directed to grant the application promptly. At any time within one year after passage, anyone could apply for a domestic all-cargo certificate, which was to be granted within 180 days of application, unless the CAB found that the applicant was not "fit, willing and able." In addition, the CAB's authority to regulate domestic cargo rates, whether carried on combination or all-cargo aircraft, was limited to those cases in which the board found, after a hearing, that the rates were discriminatory, preferential, prejudicial, or predatory. The preexisting test of "unjust or unreasonable" was eliminated, and the CAB was specifically precluded from suspending proposed cargo rates pending a hearing.

In March 1978, another deregulation law dealing with cargo was passed. It gave charter airlines the same immediate opportunity to obtain certificates for scheduled all-cargo service that was made available to scheduled carriers by the 1977 law.

The Airline Deregulation Act of 1978

The Airline Deregulation Act of 1978 dealt primarily with domestic air transportation. There was still substantial practical recognition of the fact that no one government could by itself deregulate international service. As a result, Congress established a new Declaration of Policy applicable only to domestic air transportation; the preexisting policy statement continued to apply to international air transportation.

The overriding theme of the act was competition. There was to be maximum reliance on competition to attain the objectives of efficiency, innovation, low prices, and price and service options while still providing the needed air transportation system. "Competitive market forces" and "actual and potential competition" were "to encourage efficient and well-managed" carriers "to earn adequate profits and to attract capital." At the same time, however, Congress was responsive to small-community needs and pressures, and so the act called for "maintenance of a comprehensive and convenient system of continuous scheduled interstate and overseas airline services for small communities and for isolated areas in the United States, with direct federal assistance where appropriate."

Restrictions on entry into domestic service were to be gradually eliminated over the next several years, with complete elimination by the end of 1981 (subject to CAB determination that particular applicants were "fit, willing and able"). The standard for granting route applications was immediately changed from the preexisting requirement, that the proposed transportation "is required by the public convenience and necessity," to a finding that it "is consistent with" the public convenience and necessity. Further, the burden was now on opponents to prove lack of such consistency.

Several special provisions were made for the three-year interim. First, any certificated airline (scheduled or charter) had the right of entry to one new route in each of the three years before complete open entry. Second, subject to certain limitations, carriers could lay claim to unused authority of other carriers. And third, the CAB was authorized to issue experimental certificates for temporary periods.

The new law contained other entry-related provisions that liberalized the preexisting regime, including the following:

1 *Domestic Fill-up Rights on International Flights.* For example, an international carrier flying from Los Angeles to Rome via New York could be given authority, even though not previously possessed, to carry domestic traffic between Los Angeles and New York on at least one round-trip flight a day.
2 *Removal of Restrictions.* All "closed-door" restrictions contained in domestic certificates were eliminated. Thus, if an airline was authorized to fly from City A to City B to City C but prohibited from carrying traffic from B to C, that restriction was eliminated. Congress also ordered simplified and expedited procedures for reviewing applications to remove other types of certificate restrictions, domestic or international.
3 *Suspension and Reduction of Service.* Provisions were adopted that greatly simplified the ability of carriers to reduce or eliminate service.

The CAB was also directed to establish simplified procedures for disposing of certificate applications and requests for amendment or suspension of certificates, and the board was given relatively short deadlines for reaching decisions.

The ultimate liberalization of entry occurred, as scheduled, on December 31, 1981, when the sole barrier to unrestricted domestic entry was the requirement that the applicant be "fit, willing and able"—a finding that had already been made for all existing certificated airlines. For practical purposes, all airlines (and virtually all would-be airlines) are now free to serve, or to cease serving, any and all domestic routes and cities.

Congress did recognize the need to ensure continued service to communities that might otherwise have been abandoned or provided an unacceptable service level under deregulation. The traditional subsidy program for local-service carriers, which was directed more toward sustaining the carriers than to maintaining specific service to small communities, was to be phased out by the end of 1985, and a new program of subsidies to guarantee essential air transportation to specific communities was established. All cities named in any certificate were automatically eligible, and unless the city is served by at least two airlines, the CAB (or, now, the Department of Transportation, to which this responsibility was transferred) was required to determine what and how much service is "essential." **Essential air service** for any given city is defined as scheduled service, at specific minimum frequency and at fair rates, to one or more other cities with which it has a community of interest. Whenever it is found that a city will not receive essential air transportation without subsidy inducement, applications to perform subsidized service must be sought and an award made at an established rate of compensation. Under the Airline Deregulation Act, this program was to be continued until 1988; it was subsequently renewed for another ten years.

The act specified a number of other changes affecting CAB authority over operating rights, including these:

1 *Expanded Authority to Grant Exemptions from Economic Regulatory Provisions.* The standard for granting exemptions was considerably eased, and, for the first time, exemptions could be granted to foreign airlines.
2 *Specific Validation for Certain Liberalized Charter Rules That Were Under Court Challenge.*
3 *Limitation of the President's Authority to Overrule the CAB in International Route Cases.* Formerly, there were no statutory standards for presidential review and no deadlines for any action. Now, the president could only disapprove such decisions for foreign policy or national defense reasons.

The act also dealt with domestic fares. Pending almost complete deregulation at the end of 1982, the general criteria for CAB consideration in exercising its rate regulation functions were amended to give more weight to the desirability of low fares and increased pricing and service options. The act also created a zone of reasonableness for domestic passenger fares geared to "standard industry fare levels," which, in turn, were based on July 1, 1977 fares, adjusted periodically for changes in average operating costs. Within this zone, the CAB could not suspend as unreasonable any fare as much as 50 percent lower or 5 percent higher than the "standard" fare.

There were major changes in the antitrust area as well. Certain types of interairline agreements, transactions, and relationships were removed from CAB jurisdiction and thus left subject to federal antitrust laws. For those transactions still requiring CAB approval (such as mergers), the standard for approval more closely conformed to general antitrust principles. In addition, the previous automatic immunity from antitrust laws for any transaction or agreement approved by the CAB was repealed. The CAB was given discretionary power to grant immunity when specifically requested.

Strong labor opposition to the act led to the inclusion of an employee protection program. This program was intended to provide for preferential hiring and financial assistance to eligible airline employees who lost their jobs or suffered pay cuts because of bankruptcy or major downsizing of a carrier due to the change in regulatory structure caused by the act. Although the program was to be administered by the secretary of labor, the CAB was to determine the circumstances under which the protective provisions become operative. (The CAB never did find that any employees were entitled to protection under that statutory test.)

The most dramatic of the Deregulation Act's provisions was the CAB's demise ("sunset"). On January 1, 1985, the CAB ceased to exist altogether, and its authority over subsidies and foreign air transportation was transferred to the U.S. Department of Transportation (DOT). First, however, late in 1984, Congress made some changes to the 1978 act, primarily to ensure continued consumer protection and to transfer authority over mergers and agreements to the DOT rather than to the Department of Justice.

POSTDEREGULATION EVOLUTION

With market entry opened up by deregulation, a series of major changes occurred in the industry's structure. Because the routes of greatest traffic volume and financial appeal were those originally within the trunk system, this is naturally where most exploitation of the free-entry opportunity occurred. Trunk carriers themselves moved into one another's territories, entering markets they had previously desired but been unable to obtain. For the trunk carriers as a group, the substantial movement into one another's markets essentially represented a standoff in the sense that, while all of these carriers gained new opportunities, they also lost markets as other carriers moved into their own previous territory.

Merger Mania

In July 1979, Southern Air Lines and North Central Airlines merged to create Republic Airlines. Not content with what was basically still a regional route system, Republic purchased Hughes Airwest in November 1980 and expanded its route system to the west coast. With this merger of three local-service carriers into one major carrier, the industry consolidation phase began.

Pan American merged with National Airlines in 1980, theoretically to obtain a domestic route system. However, the real significance of this merger was not that Pan American eventually won the rights to take over National, but rather that Texas International Airlines lost. With the profits from the sale of its National Airlines stock, Texas International started New York Air in January 1981. In January 1982, the Texas Air Corporation was set up to operate New York Air. In October 1982, the Texas Air Corporation purchased Continental Airlines and combined it with Texas International. Continental continued to operate as a separate entity, but Texas International went out of existence.

On a single day in December 1978, Braniff Airways was the most aggressive former trunk carrier in picking up dormant route authorities, inaugurated service to 16 new cities and 32 new city-pair markets. Unfortunately, it became the first victim of deregulation, forced to cease operations in May 1982. Many factors contributed to Braniff's demise, including a high debt structure, a recession-weakened demand for transportation, and dramatically higher fuel prices. Eastern Airlines subsequently acquired Braniff's prized Latin American routes. In 1991, American Airlines would acquire these routes after the demise of Eastern.

Merger activity remained fairly dormant for the next couple of years, reappearing again in March 1985, when Southwest Airlines purchased

Muse Air (later to be renamed TransStar Airlines), one of its major competitors in Texas markets. However, merger actions began in earnest again in fiscal 1986.

People Express acquired Frontier Airlines during the fourth quarter of 1985 and continued its acquisitions in 1986 by purchasing Provincetown-Boston Airlines in January and Britt Airways in February. In September 1986, People Express was acquired by Texas Air Corporation. In April 1986, Texas Air had added Rocky Mountain Airways to its empire, and by September, Eastern Airlines was under its corporate umbrella.

In May 1986, Delta acquired two commuter airlines: Atlantic Southeast and Comair. By the end of the year, Delta completed the purchase of Western Airlines. In September of that same year, Trans World acquired Ozark Air Lines, while Northwest Airlines, which had acquired Mesaba Airlines in 1984, acquired Republic Airlines. Meanwhile, United acquired Pan American's Pacific routes during the year, and American acquired Air California in November 1986.

Allegheny Airlines, a former local-service carrier ambitious to become a major carrier in the deregulated environment, changed its name to USAir in October 1979. By 1985, it had acquired Pennsylvania Airlines, and in April 1986, it added Suburban Airlines, followed by Pacific Southwest Airlines in December of that same year. Then, in December 1986, USAir acquired another former local-service carrier: Piedmont Airlines. Piedmont had acquired Henson Airlines in 1983, followed by Empire Airlines in 1985 and Jetstream International in July 1986.

The consolidation movement that began in 1979 has had a profound impact on the structure of the commercial airlines industry, and its effects are still being felt. Continental Airline Holdings (the former Texas Air), which in the 1980s had been taken into and out of bankruptcy by its former owner, Frank Lorenzo, wound up in bankruptcy once again in 1990, when its overleveraged balance sheet proved too heavy a burden in a time of high fuel costs and a recessionary economy.

Fifty-three years of aviation history came to an end in January 1991 when Eastern Airlines, to the surprise of few in the industry, finally ceased operations after a lengthy struggle for survival. Incorporated in 1938, Eastern was one of the nation's original four trunk airlines. Plagued by labor problems and operating under Chapter 11 bankruptcy since March 1989, Eastern was pushed over the brink by the outbreak of the Persian Gulf War, which resulted in rising fuel costs and decline in travel during the recessionary early 1990s.

In April 1991, American Airlines acquired Eastern's routes to 20 destinations in 15 Central and South American countries, and in December of that year, it struck deals for Continental's Seattle–Tokyo route authority and for TWA's remaining U.S.–London routes. American had already purchased TWA's Chicago–London route in 1989.

By the end of 1991, another aviation pioneer went out of business: Pan American, whose history traced back to 1927, when it began flying the mail between the Florida Keys and Havana. Later, it pioneered transpacific service with its flying boats, and it was the first carrier to fly both the Boeing 707 and 747. Its financial problems began in earnest with the acquisition of National Airlines shortly after deregulation.

In 1991, Delta solidified its position in the ranks of the "big three" carriers by acquiring first the Pan American Shuttle and later the bulk of Pan American's transatlantic and European systems. The Delta Shuttle began operating between Boston, New York, and Washington, D.C., in September 1991. Competition on the shuttle route stepped up a notch when USAir took over operation of the Trump (formerly Eastern) Shuttle.

Meanwhile, in the early 1990s, United Airlines acquired first Pan American's Latin American routes and then Pan American's London routes. In 1991, United also completed the purchase of its primary United Express partner, Air Wisconsin, rescuing that carrier from potential bankruptcy.

In January 1992, TWA went into Chapter 11 bankruptcy. In its filing, TWA listed assets of $2.7 billion and liabilities of $3.5 billion. Subsequently, it sold its London routes from Philadelphia and Baltimore to USAir. Earlier, it had sold the bulk of its London routes to American. The Persian Gulf War and a recessionary economy contributed to the addition of America West in 1991 to the list of bankrupt U.S. carriers. Another new-entrant carrier since deregulation, America West became a major airline in 1990 after rising from regional to national status. The fifth largest carrier, Northwest, was also in financial difficulty by early 1992 due to its leveraged buyout in 1989. Northwest's problems affected another new-entrant carrier born in the deregulation era: Midway Airlines. One of the few remaining new entrants during the deregulation era and the purchaser of Air Florida, Midway went out of business in November 1991 when Northwest backed out of an agreement to acquire the carrier. Founded in 1979, Midway grew into a national carrier by 1990. Two true success stories during the deregulation period have been Federal Express and Southwest Airlines. Both carriers were founded in the early 1970s and have been consistently profitable over the years.

In the late 1990s and early 2000s, new types of air carriers emerged as a result of cost-cutting strategies by the major airlines, expansion of niche markets, and competitive forces. Recent trends indicate that four types of air carriers are growing: new-entrant/low-cost, regional/feeder, megacarrier, and virtual carrier. New-entrant carriers include airlines such as Spirit and JetBlue. Regional/feeder carriers continue to expand as major airlines realize the benefit of feeder traffic to the main hub airports. Megacarriers are forming as major airlines partner up with other major airlines in order to reduce costs and increase market share. Because of the high costs of launching a new airline, more virtual carriers exist than ever before. Such carriers subcontract most of their services out to other companies, therefore reducing investment risk.

Regional/Commuter Airlines

Spurred on by deregulation, many regional/commuter airlines entered the market in the early 1980s. Simultaneously, the major carriers sought to extend their high-density markets by increasingly dominating their hub airports and sloughing off less profitable routes. The hub system, which has proliferated since deregulation, establishes a number of routes connected to a central hub airport where passengers are collected from feeder flights, transferred to other flights on the same line, and are then carried to their ultimate destination. This trend encouraged regional airlines to offer service linking small cities and providing connections to hub airports. Flying primarily turboprop aircraft and requiring less ground-based infrastructure, the regional airlines could operate such routes more profitably than the major carriers and provide a needed service.

In 1985, there was a dramatic growth in the number of code-sharing agreements between regional airlines and the major carriers. These code-sharing agreements varied from partial or outright ownership to pure marketing alliances devoid of any ownership by the major carriers. A somewhat predictable outgrowth of these agreements has been the identification of commuter partners with the business name of the major airline partner. Just as in the contract experiments with local airlines in the late 1960s, many independent commuter airlines conduct operations under a "service mark" similar to that of their major carrier partners. Thus, commuter airliners bearing such names as Continental Express, United Express, American Eagle, and Northwest Airlink are flying the skies. The evolution of the relationships with the large air carriers has led to further route rationalization policies on the part of the larger partners in the form of transferring an increasing number of short-haul jet routes to their regional partners. The result has been a process of industry consolidation, increasing concentration, integration, and transition to jet equipment.

From a high of 246 carriers in 1981, the number of regional/commuter operators declined to 124 in 1995. By 2004, there were 74 such operators in business carrying a total of 134.7 million passengers. Although the number of carriers in this market showed a steady decrease, the number of passengers carried shows a steady increase. Interestingly, the number of hours flown on an annual basis is gradually increased indicating that regional/commuter operators, although decreased in number, became larger in size resulting in increased market share, longer flights, and better utilization of aircraft. Because of the increased integration of operations with the large air carriers (through code-sharing agreements and partial or total acquisition of the regionals) the success of many regional airlines is closely tied to the success of their larger partners.

Although the number of carriers has declined overall, the size of the dominant carriers has risen dramatically. This has resulted in increased industry concentration, with the top 50 carriers accounting for approximately 98 percent of the total passenger enplanements and revenue passenger miles (Table 3.4).

As of the end of 2021, there were 61 certificated operators in the U.S. compared to 71 when the last edition of this book was published. Interestingly, from 1995 to 2021, there has been a steady decrease in the number of certificated operators in existence with the bulk of decline focused on small air carriers.

More sophisticated, modern aircraft are added to the regional airline fleet each year. The average trip length for the regional airline passenger has increased, as has the transition from piston to turboprop and jet equipment. In 2021, the number of regional air carriers operating at U.S. airports was extensive.

Table 3.4 Top U.S. Airports for Regional Flights Year 2021 (ranked by number of regional airline departures)

Rank	Airport Name	Airport Code	Regional Departures	Total Departures	Regional Share
1	Dallas	DFW	136,523	289,202	47.21%
2	Chicago	ORD	173,942	279,645	62.20%
3	Atlanta	ATL	61,260	273,289	22.42%
4	Denver	DEN	71,915	219,912	32.70%
5	Charlotte	CLT	109,727	194,734	56.35%
6	Los Angeles	LAX	36,830	161,677	22.78%
7	Seattle	SEA	62,690	155,114	40.42%
8	Phoenix	PHX	34,151	142,883	23.90%
9	Boston	BOS	40,386	129,364	31.22%
10	Houston	IAH	69,074	126,278	54.70%
11	Las Vegas	LAS	5,383	122,964	4.38%
12	Detroit	DTW	63,471	117,745	53.91%
13	Minneapolis/ St Paul	MSP	54,317	114,477	47.45%
14	Orlando	MCO	4,286	107,102	4.00%
15	San Francisco	SFO	33,336	105,486	31.60%
16	Philadelphia	PHL	49,050	95,167	51.54%
17	Salt Lake City	SLC	40,445	95,108	42.53%
18	Newark	EWR	31,247	94,380	33.11%
19	John F. Kennedy Int'l	JFK	12,227	91,893	13.31%
20	Fort Lauderdale	FLL	8,256	85,954	9.61%
21	Miami	MIA	17,016	84,611	20.11%
22	Baltimore	BWI	7,529	78,850	9.55%
23	New York LaGuardia	LGA	34,162	74,831	45.65%
24	Washington	DCA	32,830	71,033	46.22%
25	Nashville	BNA	16,876	66,457	25.39%
26	Washington	IAD	38,610	64,603	59.77%

Rank	Airport Name	Airport Code	Regional Departures	Total Departures	Regional Share
27	Honolulu	HNL	11,087	62,426	17.76%
28	St Louis	STL	23,513	62,314	37.73%
29	Tampa	TPA	6,723	61,175	10.99%
30	Chicago	MDW	895	61,037	1.47%
31	San Diego	SAN	8,968	60,091	14.92%
32	Portland	PDX	27,046	56,682	47.72%
33	Dallas	DAL	1,720	53,201	3.23%
34	Houston	HOU	2,571	45,176	5.69%
35	Austin	AUS	3,178	40,733	7.80%
36	San Jose	SJC	8,318	39,156	21.24%
37	Sacramento	SMF	7,789	38,257	20.36%
38	Pittsburgh	PIT	19,613	37,795	51.89%
39	Raleigh/ Durham	RDU	13,272	37,003	35.87%
40	Kansas City	MCI	11,856	35,191	33.69%
41	Oakland	OAK	2,064	35,069	5.89%
42	New Orleans	MSY	4,060	34,741	11.69%
43	Indianapolis	IND	15,009	33,141	45.29%
44	Fort Myers	RSW	1,540	32,644	4.72%
45	Kahului	OGG	11,733	31,775	36.93%
46	Cincinnati	CVG	18,399	31,481	58.44%
47	Cleveland	CLE	12,910	31,033	41.60%
48	Columbus	CMH	15,772	29,975	52.62%
49	Santa Ana	SNA	6,093	29,895	20.38%
50	Anchorage	ANC	12,026	29,557	40.69%

Source: Regional Airline Association.

New-Generation Airliners

In the early 1980s, after years of flying the once-revolutionary Boeing 727, 737, and 747 and the McDonnell-Douglas DC-8, DC-9, and DC-10, the airlines were ready for newer, more efficient designs, not simply retooled versions of the old ones. If the two dominant U.S. airframe manufacturers would not supply them, foreign sources, notably the Airbus Industrie consortium from Europe, would oblige. After all, the U.S. commuter airliner industry had been dormant during the 1970s, losing market share to firms such as British Aerospace, Embraer of Brazil, Dornier of Germany, and ATR of Italy.

To hold its market share, Boeing introduced two new airliners, the 757 and the 767, certificated in October 1984 after a development process that may have cost as much as $3 billion. Both were giant twin-engine airplanes with underwing powerplants supplied by GE/Snecma, Pratt & Whitney, or Rolls-Royce. Flown by two-person crews, they could carry 190 persons in the narrow-body 757 version or 230 in the wide-body 767. The new planes filled the niche between the 115–145-seat 737 and the smallest 420-seat 747. The 757 quickly supplanted the aging 727 with its greater efficiency, and the roomy 767 proved to be economical on the transatlantic routes.

With the increasing reliability of modern jet engines, the FAA had approved extended twin-engine operations (ETOPS) over routes that did not meet the FAR 121.161(a) requirement for continuous availability of a landing site within one hour of single-engine cruising. Historically the province of three-engine DC-10s and L-1011s as well as four-engine Boeing and Douglas airliners, the new 120-minute ETOPS exemption allowed the 767 to fly to Europe without deviating over an uneconomic northern route to stay near land.

First approved in February 1985 for TWA's Boeing 767-200, the basic criteria for ETOPS was a documented in-flight engine shutdown rate of less than 0.05 per 1,000 hours of operation, or less than 1 shutdown per 20,000 hours. Given that mature turbine power plants were experiencing shutdown rates as low as 0.02 per 1,000 hours, the risk assumed by flying over routes that would require two or even three hours of single-engine cruising to reach a diversionary airport was quite small. Within eight years, ETOPS had become so commonplace that 400-seat twin-engine airliners, such as the Airbus A330 and Boeing 777, were being developed for the North Atlantic run.

Meanwhile, the 737 became the most-built jetliner in 1987, surpassing the 727's previous record of 1,832. More than 3,000 of the 737s have been sold to date, and the 300-series, introduced in 1981, began a new cycle for this phenomenally successful aircraft. The 737-300, -400, and -500 are all equipped with new-technology GE/Snecma CFM-56 turbofans and "glass cockpits" with electronic flight instrumentation (EFIS) replacing the old mechanical flight directors and engine gauges. EFIS had been introduced previously on the 757 and 767.

The 747-400 appeared in 1988 with an extended upper deck, bringing the total seating up to 660 in the all-tourist configuration (550 on the main deck and 110 on the upper deck, 65 more than the 200B). Featuring Pratt & Whitney PW 4000, General Electric CF6-80C2, or Rolls-Royce RB 211-524D4D engines, the 747-400 is capable of flying 7,200 miles—1,000 more than the 747-300.

McDonnell-Douglas was able to remain a presence in the airliner business during the 1980s and 1990s, but with stiff competition from Boeing and Airbus, it saw its market share drop to 10 percent by the mid-1990s. The stretched DC-9-80 became known as the MD-80, subsequently growing into the MD-81, MD-82, MD-83, MD-87, and MD-88, with each model differing chiefly in gross weight and wing size. An MD-90 version with further updating was rolled out in February 1993. Glass cockpits became the norm, along with flight management systems that choreographed flights for maximum efficiency. The last DC-10 came off the production line in 1989, and in January 1990, the MD-11 made its maiden flight. Powered by new engines, the new airliner grosses over 600,000 pounds at takeoff and can carry over 400 passengers. The panel features six 8-inch cathode-ray tube displays, replacing all the mechanical gauges of the DC-10, and with the aid of flight management computers, the plane is simpler to fly, even with two pilots. The MD-11 offers the option of manual cable controls when the autopilot is not engaged, rather than the full fly-by-wire systems popularized by the Airbus A320.

By the early 1990s, more and more airliners were being built in component form, with only the final assembly taking place at the parent company's plant. In the case of the MD-11, the wings were built in Canada, the winglets were produced by Italy's Aeritalia, the tailcone came from Mitsubishi, and the control surfaces were manufactured by companies such as Embraer and CASA.

Boeing, seeking to close the gap between the 767 and 747, developed the 777—an even larger twin-engine airliner capable of carrying 305–440 passengers. Powered by huge General Electric, Pratt & Whitney, or Rolls-Royce fan-jet engines in the 74,000- to 92,000-pound-thrust class, with fan diameters approaching 10 feet, the 777 offers efficiency, size, and long-range capability. One of the 777's unique options is its folding wing tips, which reduce the 200-foot wingspan to less than 160 feet for simplified docking at crowded gates.

It should be noted that in 1997, Boeing and McDonnell-Douglas merged to become one company, leaving Airbus Industrie as the primary competitor. The merger was a strategic move to expand Boeing's presence in the increasingly competitive aircraft manufacturing market. The merger was anticipated to bring an estimated $48 billion in revenues per year. After the merger, Boeing moved its corporate headquarters from Seattle to Chicago.

By 2011, Boeing and Airbus continued to remain the largest aircraft manufacturers in the world, constantly competing to outperform the other in terms of sales. New aircraft technology resulted in increased sales and for the first time since 2000, Boeing was once again the number one aircraft manufacturer, leaving Airbus in the number two position. Boeing's production of the B787 Dreamliner captured the industry by storm as airlines strived toward operating fuel-efficient twin-engine aircraft on long-haul flights.

By year end 2013, Airbus achieved record sales and deliveries beating out Boeing. Airbus received a total of 1,619 aircraft orders worth a value exceeding $240 billion and a total of 626 planes delivered. Airbus launched the A350 in 2015 with Qatar Airways followed by Singapore Airlines and did so with great success in order to compete against the Boeing 787 Dreamliner. Fortunately for Airbus, they did not experience technical issues similar to those of the Boeing Dreamliner, which negatively impacted Boeing both financially and from a branding perspective. Although Airbus was somewhat late to the game in terms of launching the A350, the delay was well received by the industry, giving Airbus time to make sure the new technology was mature before going to market.

In 2021, Airbus accepted 771 gross orders and received 264 cancellations due to the COVID-19 global pandemic resulting in 507 net new orders, while Boeing accepted 909 gross orders and received 430 cancellations for a total of 479 net new orders. It seems the title of "king" changes regularly and the neck-and-neck race will continue for many years to come.

September 11, 2001—A New Era in Aviation

On September 11, 2001, the world was shocked to hear about the biggest disaster in the history of aviation. Four commercial airline flights were hijacked simultaneously (United Airlines Flight 93, Newark to San Francisco; American Airlines Flight 77, Washington Dulles to Los Angeles; United Airlines Flight 11, Boston to Los Angeles; and American Airlines Flight 175, Boston to Los Angeles). Flight 93 missed its intended target, believed to be the White House, and crashed into a field in Somerset, Pennsylvania, killing all 45 persons on board. Flight 77 was flown directly into the Pentagon, the citadel of world strategic military planning, killing 189 persons. Flight 11 was flown directly into the north tower of the World Trade Center in New York City, killing all 92 persons on board the aircraft. Flight 175 was flown directly into the south tower of the World Trade Center, killing all 65 persons on board. In the end, more than 3,000 people lost their lives on 9/11 as a result of the acts of fanatic terrorists.

Because of the events of 9/11, security at airports, as well as security at high-risk events outside aviation, was stepped up significantly. The global aviation business was hit hard financially and recovery is still ongoing. It was estimated in October 2002 that airlines in the United States would lose a total of $8 billion by the end of the fourth quarter for the same year. Some analysts said that these estimated losses were optimistic and that $10 billion would be a more likely figure.

Since the events of 9/11, a number of airlines around the world have declared bankruptcy with some closing their doors forever. In this new era of air transportation, air carriers have been forced to implement cost-cutting strategies in order to survive. Such strategies are discussed in later chapters.

COVID-19 Global Pandemic

In late 2019, the COVID-19 global pandemic shocked the world and, at the time of writing, the air transport sector is still suffering as the pandemic continues. Forced travel restrictions impacted all six regions of the world, including Africa, Asia-Pacific, Europe, Latin America/Caribbean, Middle East, and North America.

According to the International Civil Aviation Organization (ICAO), the impact of COVID-19 has resulted in unprecedented passenger traffic declines. There was a 60 percent decline in 2020 compared to 2019, 49 percent decline in 2021 compared to 2019, and 29 percent in 2022 compared to 2019. To put this in perspective, in 2020, airlines reduced seat capacity by

50 percent, equating to a reduction of 2,703,000 passengers and a $372 billion loss in gross passenger operating revenues. In 2021, airlines reduced seat capacity by 40 percent, equating to a reduction of 2,201,000 passengers and a $324 billion loss in gross passenger operating revenues. By 2022, U.S. domestic air travel demand faced moderate recovery but international demand remained flat. Interestingly, in terms of regional recovery, Latin American/Caribbean, North America, and Europe were recovering faster in terms of total seat capacity compared to the other regions of the world by mid-2022. In 2021, Europe supported more than 50 percent of global international traffic. The future is impossible to forecast but many leading industry experts agree that 2022–2025 will be the recovery years for the global air transport industry and the length of time to fully recover will most certainly impact data related to economic growth, employment, trade, and tourism. Despite the impact of COVID-19, long-term forecasts predict the aviation sector will support close to 100 million jobs and generate close to $6 trillion in GDP.

GENERAL AVIATION

World War I ended in November 1918, and several thousand Curtis Jennies, which cost the U.S. government close to $17,000 apiece, became surplus and sold for as much as $750 for a new plane with an OX-5 engine, and as little as $50 for a used one. Although most World War I pilots returned to other professions, a group of them with flying in their blood became **barnstormers**. Living from hand to mouth and acting as their own mechanics, the members of this happy-go-lucky group put on air shows and took the local townsfolk for rides, usually for about five minutes, and charged whatever the traffic would bear.

With the passage of the Air Commerce Act in 1926 and its requirements for the licensing of pilots, maintenance requirements, and other regulations, the barnstormer era came to an end. A number of these colorful individuals settled down and became known as **fixed-base operators**, providing everything from flight instruction, to sale of aircraft and fuel, to maintenance work. General aviation had been born.

The Home of General Aviation

Wichita, Kansas, was a boom town in the 1920s. Since its founding in 1870, the city had ridden the boom-to-bust roller coaster in cattle and oil. Aviation, however, was the boom that would last. Wichita had the right terrain—flat (the city was called the world's largest natural airport). It had the right weather—clear. It also seemed to attract the right people. Matty Laird and Jake Moellendick began work in April 1920 on the first Laird Swallow aircraft. They soon hired three other aviation enthusiasts, who in time developed their own companies: Buck Weaver, who started Weaver Aircraft Company (WACO), Lloyd Stearman, and Walter Beech. The last two, along with another barnstormer by the name of Clyde Cessna, pooled their talents in 1925 to form the Travel Air Manufacturing Company.

The first Travel Air plane, built of welded metal tubing, as opposed to wood framing, won the 1925 Ford Reliability Tour with Walter Beech at the controls. In the 1926 Reliability Tour, Beech flew a Travel Air 4000 monoplane equipped with instruments that permitted blind flying; the first time such a feat had ever been attempted. By 1929, when the company was bought by Curtiss-Wright Corporation, Travel Air was producing 25 percent of all commercial aircraft in the United States. Beech, who worked for Curtiss-Wright until 1932, then embarked on what proved to be his greatest challenge: the start of Beech Aircraft Corporation. He soon announced plans to build a four-place cabin biplane that would fly 200 miles per hour. Impossible—or so the critics thought. Two months after Beech Aircraft introduced its first airplane, the stagger-wing Model 17, the sleek biplane flew off with first place in the prestigious Texaco Trophy Race in Miami. A string of triumphs followed as Beechcrafts won five major races in 1936 alone, including the Denver Mile-High Air Race and the Bendix Transcontinental Speed Dash. Beechcrafts continued to pick up trophies into the next decade. In 1937, the Model 18 Twin Beech was born. Employment peaked during the World War II years, and in 1946, Beech introduced the V-tail Bonanza, which has had the longest production record of any general aviation aircraft.

By 1934, economic conditions had improved sufficiently to allow Clyde Cessna to open his own small factory in Wichita and to install his nephew, Dwane Wallace, a recent aeronautical engineering graduate, as plant manager. Wallace was not paid a salary, but he did have the opportunity to design, build, test, fly, sell, and race the company's products. Wallace set about designing the C-34, a high-wing, four-place cabin monoplane with a 145-hp Warner Super-Scarab engine. After months of anxious flight tests and tedious refinements, the C-34 was entered in the 1935 Detroit News Trophy Race, part of the prestigious National Air Races. The C-34 won the day, and the attendant publicity vastly enhanced Cessna's reputation as a builder of fast, efficient aircraft.

Wallace's next project was a light, inexpensive trainer-utility airplane that was easy to fly and not too sophisticated to build. By 1939, the T-50 was flying, and by 1940, it was in production and ready for buyers. Among the first was the Canadian government, followed by the U.S. Army Air Corps. By 1945, some 5,000 of these trainers had been produced. After the war, Cessna introduced the 120/140 series, which was followed by the 190/195 series. These strong but simple single-engine aircraft helped Cessna survive the postwar shakeout of many small manufacturers of general aviation aircraft and also helped propel the company into the 1950s.

Wichita is the home of another man whose name is famous in corporate aviation: William Lear, gambler, inventor, discoverer, promoter, and industrialist, who developed the highly successful corporate Lear jet.

Mr. Piper and His Cubs

At 48 years of age, William T. Piper was a successful Pennsylvania oilman when he invested in the Taylor Aircraft Company in 1931. He was a superb salesman with a clear idea of what would make a light aircraft successful. His formula was simple: build easy-to-fly machines and price them low enough to attract buyers. After an abortive attempt to design a glider, Taylor Aircraft developed the E-2 Cub—an excellent example of Piper's vision of the simple airplane.

The name of the company was changed to Piper Aircraft Corporation in 1936, and the subsequent models were called J-2 and J-3. The PA-11 came next in the Cub line, and then the PA-18 Super Cub, which had essentially the same structural and aerodynamic configuration as the 1932 E-2. To this day, more than one-third of the over 120,000 aircraft produced by Piper since 1937 have been Cubs, and 80 percent of U.S. pilots in World War II received their initial training in that two-place tandem design. Piper Aircraft Corporation boomed and then nearly busted during the difficult days after World War II.

The Post-World War II Years

The Aircraft Owners and Pilots Association (AOPA) had 22,000 members by the mid-1940s (384,915 members as of 2002), and their motivations were the same then as now: to protect private flying from the depredations of the airlines and the assaults of bureaucrats who want to build empires around the commercial airlines and legislate the private flier out of the skies. The AOPA is the largest, most influential aviation association in the world. The term *general aviation* was coined to remove the imagined onus of the term "private flying" from the industry. General aviation denotes aviation used for vital, useful, general purposes, much like those for which the private automobile is used.

The light-aircraft manufacturers, with few exceptions, envisioned their products becoming as popular as the automobile in the years to come. After a banner year in 1946, the manufacturers realized that the general public had perhaps been oversold on light-plane flying and that they could not hope to have a mass-production industry comparable to the auto industry.

In 1947, a year before Cessna introduced its 170, which eventually developed into the 172, the world's most successful light plane, the industry was beginning to flounder.

With manufacturing companies turning belly up all over the place, delivery ramps were clogged with unsold airplanes. At the end of 1947, sales were down 44 percent from 1946, and the downward trend continued well into 1949. But this period also represented a major turning point for the light-aircraft manufacturers, as executives began to look at the future from a different angle. The future lay in developing a fleet of airplanes that would provide solid, comfortable, reliable business transportation—aircraft that could operate in instrument conditions with high enough speed and long enough range. A certain number of training airplanes would have to be built to get new people started flying, but a utility airplane that business-people could afford and on which the manufacturer could make a fair profit was the target design for the future.

Production in 1951 was only 2,477 units. General aviation continued to limp along, although the ranks of the manufacturers were decimated. Beech, Bellanca, Cessna, Piper, and Ryan were still trickling airplanes off the production lines, but not all of these companies were sure that they could hang on much longer.

Things were not all bad in the early 1950s: more ground-based navigation stations were built, improved static-free radios were installed, and factory options on more and more airplanes became available. Bill Lear produced the first light-plane three-axis autopilot in 1951 and made cross-country flying easier and more relaxing. Toward the end of the year, about the time that Ryan was dropping the production of the Navion, a new company, Aero Design and Engineering, offered its five-place Aero Commander to the business community; and Mooney unveiled its single-place $1,000 Mooney Mite. That same year, Piper put a nosewheel on its little Pacer and renamed it the Tri-Pacer, which sparked a new surge of interest in light planes for fun as well as for business.

By 1953, things were starting to turn around for the industry. Engineers in Wichita and Lock Haven made careful note of the growing acceptance of light twins for business. Cessna discontinued the 195 model in 1953 and produced the four-place 180, a more powerful successor to the successful 170. Piper stayed with the Tri-Pacer and the Super Cub, and Beech was backlogged with orders for the Bonanza, the Twin-Bonanza, and the Super-18. The National Business Aircraft Association held its first meeting, in St. Louis, which was attended by 9 manufacturers and suppliers along with 50 voting members and 16 associates (the annual NBAA meeting today attracts over 10,000).

In 1954, Cessna and Piper introduced their four-place light twins, the 310 and the Apache, both of which represented the beginning of a long line of descendants. Many companies had entered the avionics business, including ARC, Bendix, Collins, Lear, Mitchell, and Wilcox, to name a few. Month after month, new autopilots were coming out for light planes.

The Maturing of General Aviation

As the 1950s turned into the 1960s, general aviation was developing an unmistakable stability and purpose. Though pleasure flying was far from extinct, the general aviation airplane clearly was developing into a viable means of business transportation. In ten years, the general aviation fleet had more than doubled to 60,000 aircraft—over half of which were equipped for instrument flying. General aviation had become a major part of the nation's transportation system, with an inventory of light aircraft that were fully capable of flying people in comfort 1,500 miles in one day to thousands of places not served by the commercial air carriers.

Beech brought out the Travel Air, to be followed by the Baron, the Queen Air, and the King Air. Cessna put tricycle landing gear on its 170s and 180s in developing the 172 and 182 series, which became the best-selling airplanes in history. Piper discontinued the Tri-Pacer and entered the Cherokee, Comanche, and Twin Comanche into the market. Many of the old names, such as Bellanca, Mooney, Navion, and North American, would also enjoy a comeback.

By 1965, the general aviation aircraft fleet had grown to 95,000 airplanes, and production that year totaled 11,852 new aircraft. The following year, a record 15,768 units were produced. General aviation growth during the late 1960s paralleled growth in the economy and all segments of aviation at that time.

Nothing added more to the growing importance of general aviation than the advent of turbine power. The business jet and turboprop were introduced to corporate users. At first, there were just a few Lockheed JetStars, North American Sabreliners, Beechcraft King Airs, and Grumman Gulfstreams. It wasn't long before Bill Lear arrived in Wichita with the idea of turning a small Swiss fighter aircraft into a business jet. Both the Sabreliner and the JetStar were designed as military utility aircraft. Lear would go on to sell hundreds of Learjets and, like Piper and his Cubs, his name would become synonymous with a certain kind of transportation.

In 1970, the manufacturers of light aircraft established a strong and effective lobbying and public relations organization in Washington: the General Aviation Manufacturers Association (GAMA). The National Business Aircraft Association (NBAA) blossomed into a highly professional Washington-based service organization for business users. The Aircraft Owners and Pilots Association (AOPA) and other special-aircraft-use organizations developed into effective lobbying groups. The Federal Aviation Administration (FAA), under administrator Jack Shaffer, appointed a deputy administrator for general aviation.

Despite an economic recession during the first two years of the 1970s and an oil embargo in 1973, general aviation continued to grow, reaching a high point in 1978, with 17,811 units produced. By the late 1970s, both manufacturers and users began to feel a confidence in general aviation that they had seldom enjoyed before. Perhaps for the first time, the general aviation community perceived that potential problems related to government controls, charges, fees, and taxes, as well as restrictive legislation, were manageable. However, fundamental changes were taking place in the industry. Fuel prices rose dramatically during the 1970s, and manufacturers looked to more fuel-efficient aircraft for the future. Airspace congestion was another problem that the industry had been studying since the mid-1960s. As a result, the Airport and Airway Development Act of 1970 was passed to provide the revenue needed to expand and improve the airport and airway system over a ten-year period. Finally, the industry was faced with ever-increasing federal regulation during the 1970s. Terminal control areas (TCAs) were introduced around the country's busiest airports, which required two-way communication with air traffic control (ATC), VHF omnidirectional range (VOR) navigation capability, and altitude-reporting transponders. Increasing regulations particularly affected the personal-pleasure pilot.

It was also during the 1970s that the attention of the general aviation industry started focusing on product liability. As the number of lawsuits and the size of awards increased, insurance premiums shot up, from $51 per new airplane in 1962 to $2,111 in 1972. This trend was a sign of things to come for aircraft manufacturers and, no doubt, one of the major causes of the precipitous decline in the production of general aviation aircraft during the 1980s.

Unfortunately, the 1980s brought on a new round of challenges for the industry. Soaring interest rates and a depressed economy during the early 1980s had an effect on sales. Aircraft shipments dropped from 11,877 in 1980 to 9,457 in 1981 and to 4,266 in 1982. By 1994, the number had reached a record low of 928 units. Once again, the ranks of the manufacturers were being thinned. Raytheon Company acquired Beech in 1980, and in 1984, Lear-Siegler took over Piper as part of a buyout of Bangor Punta, its former parent. Piper changed ownership several more times before the end of the decade. General Dynamics took over Cessna, the last independent of the "big three" manufacturers of general aviation aircraft. By 1986, Cessna decided to drop its piston-aircraft production.

Low unit sales of general aviation aircraft during the 1980s and early 1990s have been attributed to the ever-increasing cost of new aircraft with relatively few design changes since the 1970s, higher fuel and other operating expenses, including maintenance and hangar charges, and the availability of used aircraft. Other analysts cite product liability costs and changing tastes and preferences among the traditional business and pleasure aircraft users. Interests in sports cars and boats, the operation of which requires less training, seemed to peak during the 1980s. Another financial pressure working against aircraft ownership involved the passage of the Tax Reform Act of 1986, which eliminated the 10 percent investment tax credit (ITC). Finally, foreign aircraft manufacturers entered the traditionally U.S.-dominated market in a much bigger way during the 1980s.

Although the U.S. economy experienced impressive growth and interest rates declined during the latter part of the 1980s, general aviation failed to recover. By 1992, the number of general aviation aircraft manufactured in the United States had dropped below 1,000 for the first time since the end of World War II. Between 1978 and 1994, flying hours declined by about 45 percent, and the active general aviation fleet, after reaching a peak of 220,943 aircraft in 1984, fell to 170,660 by 1994. More importantly for the future growth of the industry, the number of student and private pilot certificates issued dropped by almost 50 percent between 1978 and 1994.

General Dynamics apparently found the field of general aviation to be too far removed from its core military business, which was in decline during the post-Cold War period, so Cessna was sold to Textron in 1992. This caused much speculation in general aviation circles about a return to light-plane production, because Textron also owned the manufacturer of Lycoming engines, which had been used in Cessna's 152, 172, 172 RG, T182, and 182 RG models, and it would be logical to create a market for them. However, Textron also owned Bell Helicopter, and there was about as much chance of Cessna switching over to helicopter production as to start building Lycoming-powered light planes again. Cessna was satisfied building Caravan single-engine turboprops, operated primarily under contract to Federal Express over small-parcel freight routes. Cessna was also content with its line of six business jets, ranging from the 10,400-pound Citation Jet, powered by FJ44 fan jets from Williams Research, to the speedy 31,000-pound Citation X with its two huge Allison GMA 3007C engines. More than 2,000 Citations have been sold since September 1972, when the first one was delivered; plane number 2,000, a Citation VII, was rolled out on March 30, 1993.

Piper limped along through the downturn of the 1980s but still celebrated its fiftieth anniversary in 1987. However, a series of ownership changes had left it ill-equipped to make the tough managerial decisions needed in hard times. In 1970, control passed from the Piper family to Bangor Punta Corporation, itself acquired by Lear-Siegler in 1984. In turn, Lear-Siegler was taken over by investment bankers Forstmann Little in the mid-1980s. Then, with shutdown imminent, private entrepreneur M. Stuart Millar bought Piper in May 1987 with the idea of returning it to owner-management. Piper dropped its product liability insurance in an attempt to discourage lawsuits, prices were cut, and enthusiasm ran high. Unfortunately, the company slipped into Chapter 11 bankruptcy in 1991, unable to build airplanes cheaply enough to fill the large backlog of orders taken at bargain prices. It was purchased in April 1992 by another entrepreneur, A. Stone Douglas. A trickle of airplanes continued to flow from the production lines under the protection of the court. Finally, in July 1995, the New Piper Aircraft Corporation was formed from the assets sale of Piper Aircraft Corporation.

Beech survived by concentrating on its traditional role as a supplier of business airplanes. With over 90 percent of the executive turboprop market firmly in the hands of the various King Airs, ranging from the seven-passenger King Air C-90B to a ten-passenger Super King Air 350, only limited plant space was devoted to piston-aircraft production. However, Beech still offered its four-place Bonanza F-33A, a six-seat Bonanza A-36 or turbo-charged B36TC, and a twin-engine Baron 58. These finely crafted, piston-powered planes served to introduce future King Air buyers to Beech quality.

Beech acquired the rights to Mitsubishi's Diamond business jet in 1986, giving it a fast entry into the business jet field, just above the largest King Air. This was actually Beech's third attempt at jets. The company had entered into marketing agreements for the French-made Morane-Saulnier MS-760 in 1955 and the British-made Hawker BH-125 in the 1970s, but neither venture had been overly profitable. This time, however, Beech was in a position to take over the production of its jets, which it redesigned and built as the Beech Jet-400A.

The rest of the U.S. general aviation industry held on through the 1990s by staying small, merging, or diversifying. Mooney had been owned by the French firm Euralair since 1984 and was still building single-engine aircraft in the Kerrville, Texas plant it occupied in 1953. Learjet was sold to the Canadian firm Bombardier, but it remained based in Wichita. The stretched Model 55 grew into the Model 60, certificated in late 1992.

Specialty aircraft builders hung on by exploiting their particular niche, such as manufacturers of fabric-covered tail-wheel airplanes (Husky, Maule, Taylorcraft, American Champion), amphibian flying boats (Lake), custom-made and steel-tube classic aircraft (Bellanca, Waco Classic), and other personal airplanes (Commander's 114 B and the American General Tiger—a rebirth of the Grumman AA-58).

Signs of optimism appeared in 1994 with the passage of the General Aviation Revitalization Act, which limited products liability suits, and with Cessna's announcement that it would resume production of single-engine aircraft in 1996. The New Piper Aircraft Corporation was formed, and in 1995, general aviation aircraft shipments finally increased after an 18-year decline. Unquestionably, the 1990s brought new challenges to the industry. But as the history of general aviation shows, this is hardly a novel situation.

Today, the manufacturing of **light-sport aircraft (LSA)**, has become a popular trend. They are easy to fly, economical to operate, and relatively cheap to purchase compared to conventional aircraft. The LSA market continues to grow with a diverse range of domestic and international suppliers offering sale prices from $45,000 to $200,000. Popular aircraft include Cessna's 162 Skycatcher, Cirrus' SR Sport (Cirrus SRS), and the innovative Tecnam line. This relatively new form of technology has provided more affordable options for pilot training, general aviation use, corporate transport, and surveillance as examples.

Business Aviation

Although business or corporate flying had its foundations in the 1930s, when petroleum companies, newspaper publishers, and manufacturers owned and operated their own aircraft, it wasn't until the late 1950s that business flying really took off. The turbine engine was one of the major factors.

Since the end of World War II, corporate operators had relied heavily on former military aircraft that were converted to civilian use. The Lockheed Lodestar and Ventura were examples. Pacific Airmotive Corporation's Lodestar conversion, the Learstar, was one of the most sought after of its kind. It offered 280-mph speed and 3,800-mile range. The DC-3 and its military version, the C-47, fit well into the corporate fleets. Many corporate flight departments operating today got started with Beech D-18s or E-18s, each powered by 450-hp Pratt & Whitney R985 radial engines.

But the end was signaled for the large radial-engine business aircraft with Grumman Aircraft Corporation's announcement in 1957 that it intended to build the first made-for-business-aviation, turbine-powered airplane. It would be called the Gulfstream, and it would cost a half-million dollars.

Lockheed was first on the turbojet scene with its JetStar, but the big winner in the jet competition was North American Aviation's T-39 Sabreliner.

The DH-125 twin-jet airplane by de Havilland followed, and a short time later, Dassault of France was ready with its Model-20 Falcon.

By the mid-1960s, turboprops abounded. The Turbo Commander and King Air could be seen on many ramps, and there was talk of the coming of the Mitsubishi MU-2. But perhaps the favored aircraft among Fortune 500 companies was the Beechjet.

Deregulation has had a twofold effect on general aviation. First, corporations and businesses with widely scattered plants, mines, mills, construction sites, and so on have found it essential to establish flight departments equipped with high-performance aircraft to minimize executive trip time, increase employee productivity, and maintain a high level of cohesion and control of far-flung operations. Second, the proliferation of hub-and-spoke operations for commercial traffic has expanded scheduled regional and commuter airline systems, which feed about 70 percent of their passengers from widely scattered, low-density airports into large, high-density terminals, where they can continue their trips on the major carriers. The regional/commuter airlines serve many communities in the continental United States, providing air links to communities that might otherwise be cut off from fast, efficient air transportation.

However, the proliferation and expansion of the new regional carriers does not mean that all business and corporate requirements for efficient, nonscheduled air transportation have been met. The current hub-and-spoke pattern may be economically more efficient than the elaborate multipoint network it replaced, but some passengers must pay for this in time-consuming layovers and other inconveniences during their trips. For business and executive travelers, time is of great importance—a commodity companies have shown themselves willing to pay for through the purchase of business aircraft.

Will New Technology Affect the Future of Corporate Aviation?

It was not too long ago that the main function of corporate aircraft was to transport executives between destinations regardless of the financial cost factors. Often, the aircraft was not flown enough in a year to make it a viable mode of transport for the organization, because its use was limited to a small number of key people.

Today, organizations must reduce costs wherever possible in order to remain competitive in the global marketplace. For the most part, the days of the "royal barge" have disappeared as corporate aircraft operators have learned about the high costs of operating such aircraft. More and more, corporate aircraft are used not just by key executives but by employees of all levels within an organization. Some organizations continue to underutilize aircraft but there might be advantages to doing this, depending on what kind of business is transacted on board the aircraft or at a destination. Other organizations fully utilize corporate aircraft and use this technology as a shuttle between destinations while maximizing the load factor.

Aircraft technology has "shrunk" the world, and it is becoming more important to be able to visit more destinations within a short period of time. As the need for travel increases, expenses increase. Locations that were previously not accessible by commercial and corporate aircraft need to be accessed.

New technology is being developed by government, industry, and academic partners for a type of aircraft that can safely and affordably move people and goods among underutilized airports in urban, suburban, and rural locations throughout the United States. This new technology has been commonly known as the **Small Aircraft Transportation System (SATS)**. The project reached its conclusion with a proof-of-concept demonstration in June 2005 at Danville, VA. Demonstrations are intended to show policy-makers and the public that this new technology can work.

Under SATS, each aircraft will hold four to ten people, including the pilot(s). Each aircraft will be outfitted with digital avionics suites with satellite-based navigation systems, on-board computers that permit coordinated control and display of aircraft system operation and status, and synthetic vision that allows operations in low-visibility environments. A computer display will show a three-dimensional view of the flight path, terrain, obstacles, traffic, and weather, with superimposed guides for the pilot to fly any flight plan selected. These aircraft will have simpler controls than any aircraft currently flying, making the aircraft easier to operate. The conventional throttle and mixture controls will be replaced by a single lever power control. The yoke and pedals will be replaced by a simple joystick control.

Because of the simplicity of this technology, the amount of flight training required will be reduced, and techniques used will be simplified. It is expected that a person will receive private pilot certification with instrument rating in an economical and accelerated single course. SATS aircraft will have access to the Internet and the Public Switched Telephone Network (PSTN) for airborne communications. Each aircraft will also have access to weather graphics, traffic information, and ground facility information, allowing operators to schedule reservations for meetings, accommodations, car rentals, and restaurants while en route.

SATS aircraft will not be dependent on current air traffic control (ATC) systems because of the use of satellite-based navigation information. Each aircraft will know its exact location from takeoff to landing, reducing the number of delays currently imposed by ATC systems. For corporate operators, this will mean a more efficient environment to conduct business. Each SATS aircraft will "beam" its location and intent to other SATS aircraft in the vicinity and to local ATC facilities, reducing routing and scheduling constraints. Once SATS matures, it will integrate with the National Airspace System.

It has been determined that approximately 5,000 existing SATS Portal Airports throughout the nation will be utilized. For the most part, these are airports equipped with fixed-base operators (FBOs), offering a comfortable environment with accessible parking and check-in, baggage handling, food service, office support, ground transportation, access to accommodation, and aircraft service and maintenance. Some 10 percent of Florida's airports were used for SATS demonstrations using primarily professional pilots. Avionics will be what is commercially available. SATS will have "multi-modal" connectivity, and it is expected that these airports will all remain in operation as SATS airports.

For corporate operators, SATS will reduce travel time and eliminate the need to fly in and out of congested airports. No more airport lines and no more connecting flights! Departures and arrivals will take place within a 30-minute radius of one's home or office, permitting more reasonable travel times and increased travel range. It should be noted that although SATS technology will continue to evolve, the SATS name will most likely change.

In 2005, new aircraft technology flew for the first time with a number of new companies starting operations in 2006 and 2007. Such aircraft are based on technology design guidelines, system standards, and certification standards developed by the Advanced General Aviation Transport Experiments (AGATE) Alliance. The AGATE Alliance was a public–private partnership that existed from 1994 to 2001.

Although the SATS program is technically over, the concept still exists and is now referred to as **Urban Air Mobility (UAM)** which concentrates on creating a safe and efficient transportation system incorporating automated aircraft for the movement of people and cargo. The concept is to operate a system within urban and suburban zones at low altitude that can use existing helipads and air traffic control (ATC) services without the need to build the necessary infrastructure from the ground up. In the United States, the FAA is including UAM in the strategic planning process, and in Europe, the European Union Aviation Safety Agency (EASA) is collaborating with industry expecting to launch UAM around 2025. According to EASA, the first operations will transport people and cargo, and although the technology will be autonomous in nature, a pilot will be onboard for safety measures.

KEY TERMS

air commerce
Airbus
barnstormers
Boeing
Columbia route
contract air mail (CAM)
deregulation
essential air service
feeder route
fixed-base operator
light-sport aircraft (LSA)
Small Aircraft Transportation System (SATS)
Spoils Conference
Urban Air Mobility (UAM)

REVIEW QUESTIONS

1 When was the first regular domestic air mail service provided? Who flew the mail in the years before 1925? What was the major significance of the Kelly Act? Of the Air Commerce Act? Who was the successful bidder on the Columbia route? What was the name of the aircraft specifically designed to carry mail on the Columbia route? Who were six of the first 12 carriers on the newly established CAM routes?

2 What role did Walter Folger Brown play in developing the early CAM routes? What was the Spoils Conference? Which three carriers picked up the northern, central, and southern cross-country routes? What event prompted Senator Black to investigate air mail bidding practices? What was the significance of the Air Mail Act of 1934?

3 What was the first modern airliner? How did Douglas Aircraft get started? Describe several technical developments that took place in the 1930s. Why did the federal government tighten its grip over the industry toward the later 1930s?

4 Who were the leading commercial aircraft manufacturers in the post-World War II period? What was Boeing doing at the time? What position did the CAB take when the major carriers wanted to establish feeder routes after the war? What major decision did the British make? Why? Briefly describe some of the technical advances that took place in the early 1950s.

5 How did Boeing arrive at the design for the 707? What were some of the events leading up to the establishment of the Federal Aviation Agency? List and briefly explain several major economic developments in air transportation during the four decades from 1938 to 1978.

6 Describe some of the reasons government is rooted in the economic and physical characteristics of the air transport industry. What was the major object of the Air Commerce Act of 1926? How did the act define "air commerce"? Which governmental agencies or departments were empowered to perform functions relative to carrying out the provisions of the act? Why did Congress choose to spread the workload over so many units of government?

7 What was the primary purpose of the Civil Aeronautics Act of 1938? What does the following statement mean: "The five members of the CAA exercised quasi-judicial and quasi-legislative functions"? Describe four of the six functions of the CAA. What was the significance of the reorganization plans of 1940? Briefly describe five economic functions performed by the CAB. Describe some of the features of the Federal Aviation Act of 1958.

8 What were some of the events leading up to the passage of the Airline Deregulation Act of 1978? Describe the position of the CAB regarding deregulation under the chairmanship of Alfred E. Kahn. List some of the arguments against deregulation. What is the overriding theme of the act? What are the major changes under the act?

9 Explain how the certificated airline industry has changed since deregulation in terms of expansion, consolidation, and concentration. Describe the role of commuter/regional carriers and the reasons they have experienced significant growth despite their shrinking numbers during the 1980s. Identify some of the new-generation aircraft that have arrived in the postderegulation period.

10 How was the term fixed-base operator coined? Who were some of the early general aviation aircraft manufacturers? What was the prevailing thinking of the light-aircraft manufacturers after World War II? What did they decide to do that subsequently turned the industry around? When did things start to look up? Describe the growth of general aviation during the 1960s and 1970s. What were some of the causes for the slowdown in unit sales during the 1980s and early 1990s? When did the large corporate aircraft arrive on the scene? What effect has airline deregulation had on general aviation and corporate aviation?

11 How will the development of concepts like SATS and UAM impact the future of aviation? How will this impact aircraft manufacturers, general aviation, commercial airline operations, public services, and private vehicles in the future?

CHAPTER 4

Air Transportation
Regulators and Associations

CHAPTER CHECKLIST • YOU SHOULD BE ABLE TO:

- Discuss the primary role of the DOT and its administrations
- Describe the major functions of the FAA, including some new developments in air traffic control and engineering
- Identify the steps involved in a major-accident investigation by the NTSB
- Compare and contrast the following airline associations: Airlines Clearing House, Airline Tariff Publishing Company, and Air Cargo, Inc.
- Describe the primary purpose of the Airlines for America and the Regional Airline Association
- Distinguish between the International Civil Aviation Organization and the International Air Transport Association

INTRODUCTION

In 1961 and 1962, seven major studies of transportation and its regulation were released by various federal agencies and study groups.[1] Although the recommendations of these studies varied, they generally supported relaxation of federal regulations and greater reliance on market forces.

In response to the continuing problems of the U.S. transportation system, President John F. Kennedy delivered a special transportation message

DOI: 10.4324/9780429346156-5

to Congress on April 5, 1962. In that address, Kennedy criticized the existing regulatory structure as inconsistent and outdated and recommended a number of federal regulatory and promotional changes. He proposed more flexible carrier rate making and suggested that minimum rate regulation should be eliminated on bulk and agricultural shipments involving common carriers. He also recommended extension of the agricultural and fishery exemptions to all carriers. His message stressed what he perceived to be inconsistencies in taxation policies and user charges in transportation. To remedy this situation, he urged repeal of the 10 percent tax on railroad and bus transportation and simultaneously called for an increase in user charges in air transportation. He also suggested implementation of a waterway usercharge program to recover federal outlays in that area. Additionally, Kennedy sought to promote more even-handed treatment of intercity transportation modes by reducing CAB subsidies to local-service carriers and abolishing such subsidies to trunk lines.

Obviously, President Kennedy believed that the future viability of the national transportation system required major regulatory and promotional changes. His suggestions were subsequently incorporated into legislation and submitted to Congress. In the hearings that followed, many of his recommendations met with resistance strong enough to kill the legislation in committee. Nevertheless, several of Kennedy's recommendations, particularly those related to expansion of the user-charge concept (that those who use the airways and airlines should bear the costs for the service received) were reflected in subsequent statutes.

In 1966, President Lyndon B. Johnson also chose to deliver a special transportation message to Congress. Departing from Kennedy's economic regulatory theme, Johnson focused instead on the need for coordination of the national transportation system, reorganization of transportation planning activities, and active promotion of safety.

In his address, President Johnson contended that the U.S. transportation system lacked true coordination and that this resulted in inefficiency. He advocated creation of a federal Department of Transportation (DOT) to promote coordination of existing federal programs and to act as a focal point for future research and development efforts in transportation. The new agency would also become actively involved in transportation policy review and critique, although the economic regulatory functions of the Interstate Commerce Commission (ICC), Civil Aeronautics Board (CAB), and Federal Maritime Commission were to be unaffected. This was not a new proposal. In fact, a cabinet-level transportation agency had first been proposed in 1870. Another major focus of President Johnson's remarks was transportation safety. He suggested creation of a National Transportation Safety Board to investigate major accidents and to make relevant recommendations to the appropriate federal bodies. The board was to be placed under the auspices of the secretary of transportation yet remain independent of DOT operating units. In another safety matter, Johnson called for establishment of a new highway safety program to be administered by the DOT.

Other recommendations contained in the Johnson message dealt with a broad range of topics, including development of supersonic aircraft, control of aircraft noise, and research and development involving high-speed ground transportation.

THE DEPARTMENT OF TRANSPORTATION

Congressional hearings were held on several bills involving most of President Johnson's recommendations. Although some opposition was expressed to specific proposals, there was general support for creation of the Department of Transportation. The legislation creating the agency was approved in October 1966. The DOT commenced operations on April 1, 1967, and Alan S. Boyd was appointed the first secretary of transportation.

The objectives that Congress set for the organization were stated in the act that created the DOT:

> To assure the coordinated, effective administration of the transportation programs of the Federal government; to facilitate the development and improvement of coordinated transportation service, to be provided by private enterprise to the maximum extent feasible; to encourage cooperation of Federal, State, and local governments, carriers, labor, and other interested parties toward the achievement of national transportation objectives; to stimulate technological advances in transportation; to provide general leadership; to develop and recommend to the President and Congress for approval national transportation policies and programs to accomplish these objectives with full and appropriate consideration of the needs of the public, users, carriers, industry, labor, and the national defense.

The secretary of transportation is a cabinet member appointed by the president with the advice and consent of the Senate. The secretary reports directly to Congress.

Figure 4.1 illustrates the organization of the DOT, including its main components. The department has more than 60,000 full-time, permanent employees and maintains more than 3,000 field offices in the United States and foreign countries. The secretary of transportation oversees and coordinates the activities of ten administrations within the department.

The Federal Aviation Administration

Chief among the day-to-day operations of the Federal Aviation Administration (FAA) is promotion of aviation safety while ensuring efficient use of the nation's navigable airspace. (See the more detailed description of FAA activities later in this chapter.)

FIGURE 4.1 Organization of the U.S. Department of Transportation (USDOT)

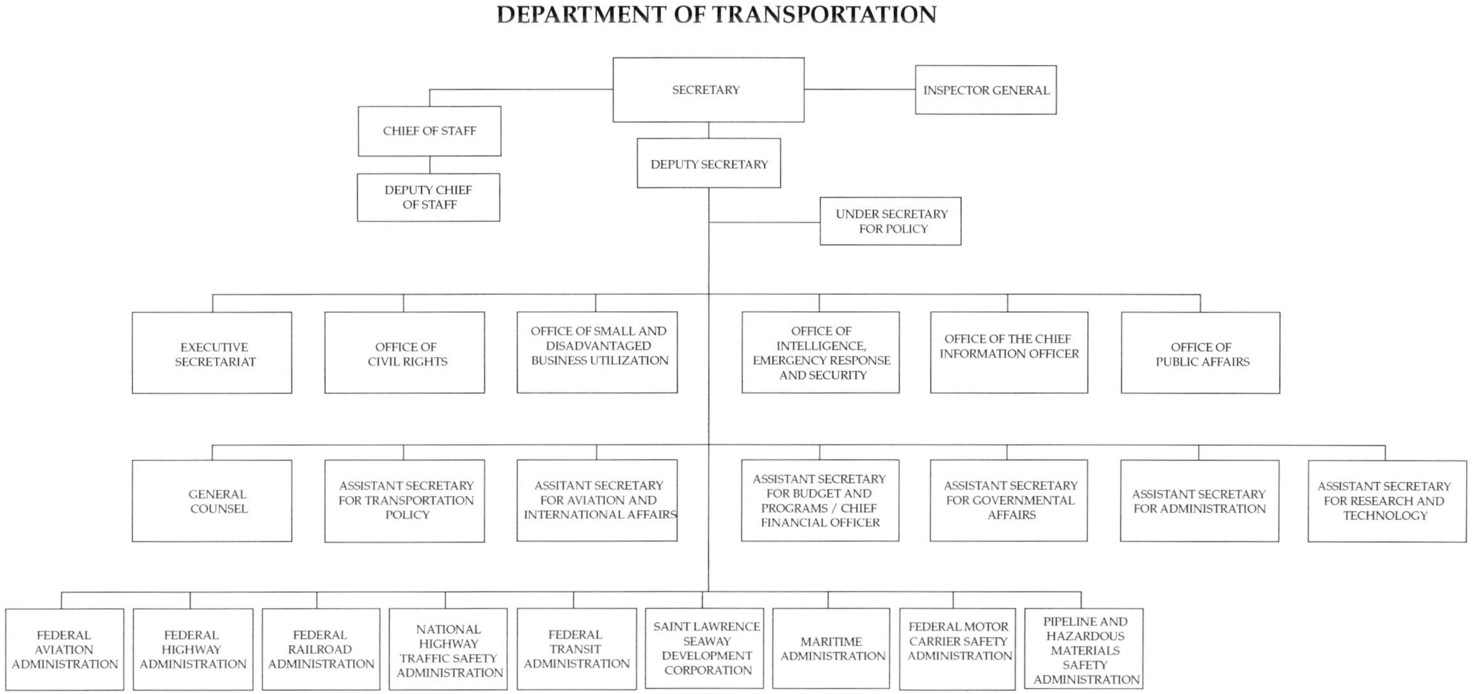

Source: U.S. Department of Transportation (USDOT)

Note: In 2003, the Transportation Security Administration (TSA) and the U.S. Coast Guard (USCG), and related Office of Inspector General (OIG) responsibilities, were transferred from the Department of Transportation to the Department of Homeland Security (DHS).

The FAA carries out its responsibilities in aviation safety by doing the following:

1 Issuing and enforcing safety rules and regulations
2 Certificating "aviators," aircraft, aircraft components, air agencies, and airports
3 Conducting aviation safety-related research and development
4 Managing and operating the national airspace system

There are over 700,000 active FAA-licensed pilots, including more than 250,000 student pilots; in addition, the FAA issues licenses for approximately 60,000 other pilots annually. In order to handle the more than 5,000 aircraft in the sky at any given time, the FAA employs more than 14,000 air traffic controllers across approximately 700 facilities.

The FAA operates and maintains 22 air route traffic control centers, 684 airport traffic control towers, 135 flight service stations, three international flight service stations, 1,041 VHF Omnidirectional Range (VOR), 1,344 non-directional beacons, 310 airport surveillance radars, and 1,231 instrument landing systems. It also has a technical center in Atlantic City, New Jersey, where new aeronautical equipment is tested, and a training academy in Oklahoma City.

Of the 19,200 airports in the United States, about 5,000 are publicly owned. Of these, 850 serve both airline and general aviation activity. The remainder primarily serve general aviation.

The FAA also reviews blueprints and specifications of all new aircraft designs and certifies their fitness to fly after extensive ground and air tests.

The Federal Highway Administration

Approximately one out of two people in the United States old enough to drive owns an automobile today, and approximately four out of five have driver's licenses. When they drive, they use the finest, most extensive system of streets and highways in the world.

Most of these roads, including the limited-access interstate system, were built with assistance from the Federal Highway Administration (FHA). Federal-aid highways make up a network of some 900,000 miles and carry about two-thirds of the nation's motor vehicle traffic. Today, the FHA is responsible for more than 615,000 bridges nationwide and the highway system carries approximately 11.9 billion tons in freight.

The FHA is responsible for administering the federal-aid program with the states and for working with them in planning, developing, and coordinating federal-aid construction of primary, secondary, urban, and interstate roads. It also regulates and enforces federal requirements for the safety of trucks and buses engaged in interstate or foreign commerce and governs the safe movement over the nation's highways of such hazardous cargoes as explosives, flammable materials, and toxic substances.

The agency also works with the U.S. Forest Service, the National Park Service, and other federal agencies in designing and building principal roads in national forests, parks, and Native American reservations and assists foreign governments in the various phases of highway engineering and administration.

The organization of the FHA extends from its headquarters in Washington, D.C., to encompass a broad regional and field structure. The field organization consists of nine regions, each of whose regional headquarter offices oversee a geographic group of states. In addition, an operating division office is located in each state (usually in the state capital), the District of Columbia, and Puerto Rico.

The Maritime Administration

The Maritime Administration (MARAD) became an operating unit of the DOT on August 6, 1981. Like its predecessor agencies, dating back to the creation of the U.S. Shipping Board in 1916, the MARAD is responsible for developing and maintaining a merchant marine capable of meeting U.S. requirements for both commercial trade and national defense. This dual government role supports the principle that a well-balanced merchant marine and maritime industry is vital to U.S. seapower and contributes to the nation's economic strength and security.

To accomplish its objectives, the MARAD performs these functions:

1 Administers financial aid programs to assist U.S. shipbuilders and ship operators
2 Sponsors research and development programs to enhance the maritime industry's productivity and competitiveness
3 Develops promotional and marketing programs to generate shipper support for U.S.-flag vessels engaged in foreign trade
4 Promotes the domestic shipping industry and U.S. port development
5 Trains ships' officers at the U.S. Merchant Marine Academy at Kings Point, New York, and provides support to state maritime schools
6 Negotiates bilateral maritime agreements and participates in international maritime forums
7 Maintains the National Defense Reserve Fleet for timely deployment in national emergencies

The St. Lawrence Seaway Development Corporation

With the Atlantic Ocean at one end and the Great Lakes at the other, the St. Lawrence Seaway provides a 2,300-mile staircase, carrying ships from sea level to an elevation of 600 feet through an intricate series of locks and dams. The seaway is operated jointly by the U.S. St. Lawrence Seaway Development Corporation and the Canadian St. Lawrence Seaway Authority.

The St. Lawrence Seaway Development Corporation was created by legislation in 1954 to construct the U.S. facilities of the St. Lawrence Seaway navigation project. Since 1959, when the seaway was opened to deep-draft navigation, the Seaway Corporation has been charged with the operation and maintenance of that part of the seaway between Montreal and Lake Erie within U.S. territorial limits and with development of the full seaway system from the western tip of Lake Superior to the Atlantic Ocean—a distance of 2,300 miles.

All operations, maintenance, and capital improvement costs are paid from revenues obtained from tolls charged to vessels that pass through the Montreal–Lake Ontario section of the seaway. The U.S. share of these tolls is 29 percent. Seaway Corporation offices are located in Washington, D.C. and Massena, New York. The two U.S. seaway locks, which are named after President Dwight D. Eisenhower and Congressman Bertrand H. Snell, are located on the St. Lawrence River near Massena.

Bulk cargoes represent the largest percentage of the seaway's traffic volume, and among these, grains and iron ore predominate. Export coal from the United States, however, is a rapidly growing bulk cargo. Iron and steel compose most of the seaway's general cargo traffic. In recent years, the number of commercial vessels moving through the Seaway Corporation's locks have averaged 4,500 annually, and they carry over 50 million tons of cargo. A large number of recreational boats also travel through the seaway each year. The normal shipping season runs from early April through mid-December, when the seaway freezes over. The Seaway Corporation has approximately 170 employees, most of whom work in Massena.

The Federal Transit Administration

Mass transportation is more than just buses and subways. It includes streetcars, ferries, carpools, and commuter trains. And it is vital to millions of people who use this means of travel to get to work, shop, or obtain essential services.

The Federal Transit Administration (FTA) encourages planning and establishment of areawide urban transportation systems and provides assistance to state and local governments in financing such systems. It helps develop improved mass transportation facilities and provides financial assistance for equipment. A large part of its work is in developing new techniques and methods to be used in the mass transportation field.

Urban transportation investments by the federal government began on a modest level in 1961. All major elements of the mass transportation programs were transferred to the DOT and the Urban Mass Transportation Administration (UMTA) in 1968.

Since 1970, urban mass transportation assistance has been significantly expanded. New legislation passed in Congress in 1978 established a $16.4 billion grant-and-loan program for public transit capital and operating assistance and small urban and rural programs through 1982. A discretionary capital grant program was authorized through 1990. The Intermodal Surface Transportation Efficiency Act of 1991 renamed the Urban Mass Transportation Administration as the Federal Transit Administration.

Since the capital assistance programs began, more than 5,400 new rail cars, 43,000 new buses, and 18 ferry boats have been purchased by hundreds of local transit authorities and systems. Many other capital investments have also been made in renovated facilities and equipment. All of these programs have helped improve the mobility of citizens, conserve energy, reduce traffic congestion, and improve the nation's environment.

The United States Coast Guard

The United States Coast Guard (USCG) was part of the DOT until 2003. In this year, both the USCG and Transportation Security Administration (TSA) were transferred to the Department of Homeland Security (DHS).

Created by Alexander Hamilton in 1790 to apprehend smugglers, the United States Coast Guard over the years has seen its role and mission expand tremendously. Coast Guard personnel go out on more than 70,000 search-and-rescue missions each year and save hundreds of lives, and they have become world famous for their life-saving skills.

But the Coast Guard's assignments are many. It patrols for oil spills, inspects ships for safety defects, enforces fishing laws, operates the nation's only fleet of icebreakers, and plays a vital role in law enforcement by intercepting drug smugglers attempting to enter the country by sea. It also plays a continuing role in intercepting illegal immigrants who try to reach the U.S. by ship. In addition, the Coast Guard operates a worldwide marine navigation system and guards the nation's ports against sabotage, subversive acts, accidents, and other threats.

An important task for the Coast Guard is boating safety, which benefits the hundreds of thousands of recreational boaters in this country. It operates a national boating safety program that encompasses research and development of safer boating practices and equipment, enforces boating safety standards, and conducts a vast educational program on safety practices for the boating public.

The Coast Guard Auxiliary, a volunteer organization of civilians, assists in the boating safety program.

The National Highway Traffic Safety Administration

The National Highway Traffic Safety Administration (NHTSA) is the agency within the DOT responsible for reducing highway accidents and the deaths and injuries that result from them. The agency carries out its congressional mandate by working to improve the safety characteristics of motor vehicles and conducting a national safety program in cooperation with state and local governments, industry, and private safety organizations.

The agency, created by Congress in 1966, is authorized to issue motor vehicle safety standards based on specified levels of performance and to investigate possible safety defects in vehicles and to direct their recall and repair without cost to consumers.

In its highway safety activities, the agency has identified six types of state and local safety programs that are most effective in reducing accidents, alcohol countermeasures, police traffic services, occupant protection, traffic records, emergency medical services, and safety construction on and improvements to existing roads. The alcohol countermeasures program, which seeks to get drunk drivers off the roads, and a nationwide effort to induce motorists to wear their safety belts are currently the two top-priority programs of the agency.

The Federal Railroad Administration

The Federal Railroad Administration (FRA) ensures that the nation has a safe, efficient, and progressive railroad network. The FRA issues standards and regulations to enhance railroad safety and conducts safety research and development. It also fosters growth of an efficient and economically viable system for movement of freight throughout the country.

Since its beginning in 1967, the agency also has provided major policy guidance for the DOT on legislative matters affecting rail transportation. The FRA helped guide through Congress legislation establishing the quasi-public corporation Amtrak to manage and operate intercity rail passenger service. Under provisions of the Northeast Rail Service Act of 1981, Amtrak is now engaged in carrying commuter rail passengers.

Under the Railroad Revitalization and Regulatory Reform Act of 1976, the FRA assists railroads that are unable to obtain necessary funds for track and equipment rehabilitation in the private capital market. The FRA also has the authority to provide assistance to states to enable them to maintain local rail freight service. Currently, the FRA is reducing the size of these two programs to reflect the railroad industry's lessened need for federal assistance.

Research and Innovative Technology Administration

The Research and Innovative Technology Administration (RITA) was created in 2005 to advance transportation science, technology, and analysis, and to improve the co-ordination of transportation research. RITA replaced the Research and Special Programs Administration (RSPA) that was established in 1977. The RSPA was responsible for a number of programs involving safety regulation, emergency preparedness, and research and development. Emphasis was given to hazardous material transportation and pipeline safety, transportation emergency preparedness, safety training, and multimodal transportation research and development activities, including programs with the university community.

Surface Transportation Board

The Surface Transportation Board (STB), created as a result of the ICC Termination Act of 1995, is an economic regulatory agency. The main role of the STB is to resolve railroad rate and service disputes as well as review railroad mergers. The STB acts as an adjudicatory and regulatory body.

Federal Motor Carrier Safety Administration

The Federal Motor Carrier Safety Administration (FMCSA) was created in 2000 as a result of the Motor Carrier Safety Improvement Act of 1999. The main role of the FMCSA is to prevent commercial motor-vehicle related fatalities and injuries by ensuring safety in motor carrier operations. The FMCSA interacts with federal, state, and local enforcement agencies, the motor carrier industry, and a diverse range of types of groups.

Pipeline and Hazardous Materials Safety Administration

The Pipeline and Hazardous Materials Safety Administration (PHMSA) was created in 2004 as a result of the Norman Y. Mineta Research and Special Programs Improvement Act of 2004. The main role of the PHMSA is to develop and enforce regulations for the safe, reliable, and environmentally sound operation of the 2.6-million-mile pipeline transportation system and approximately 1 million daily shipments of hazardous materials by land, sea, and air.

THE FEDERAL AVIATION ADMINISTRATION

Now an operating arm of the Department of Transportation, the Federal Aviation Administration traces its ancestry back to the Air Commerce Act of 1926, which led to the establishment of the Aeronautics Branch (later reorganized as the Bureau of Air Commerce) in the Department of Commerce, with authority to certificate pilots and aircraft, develop air navigation facilities, promote flying safety, and issue flight information (see Chapter 2). The government acted just in time. In May 1927, Charles Lindbergh bridged the North Atlantic in 33 hours, generating new interest and enthusiasm for aviation in both Europe and the United States.

Aviation continued to grow and expand at a very rapid rate in the decade after Lindbergh's historic flight, creating a need for new machinery to regulate civil flying. The result was the Civil Aeronautics Act of 1938, which established the independent Civil Aeronautics Authority with responsibilities in both the safety and economic areas. In 1940, the machinery was readjusted, and the powers previously vested in the Civil Aeronautics Authority were assigned to a new Civil Aeronautics Administration (CAA), which was placed under an assistant secretary in the Department of Commerce, and to the semi-independent Civil Aeronautics Board (CAB), which had administrative ties with the Department of Commerce but reported directly to Congress.

The CAA performed a useful service during World War II but proved unequal to the task of managing the airways in the postwar years because of the tremendous surge in civil air traffic and the introduction of new high-performance aircraft. In 1958, the same year jets entered commercial service, Congress passed the Federal Aviation Act, which created the independent

FIGURE 4.2 Organization of the Federal Aviation Administration

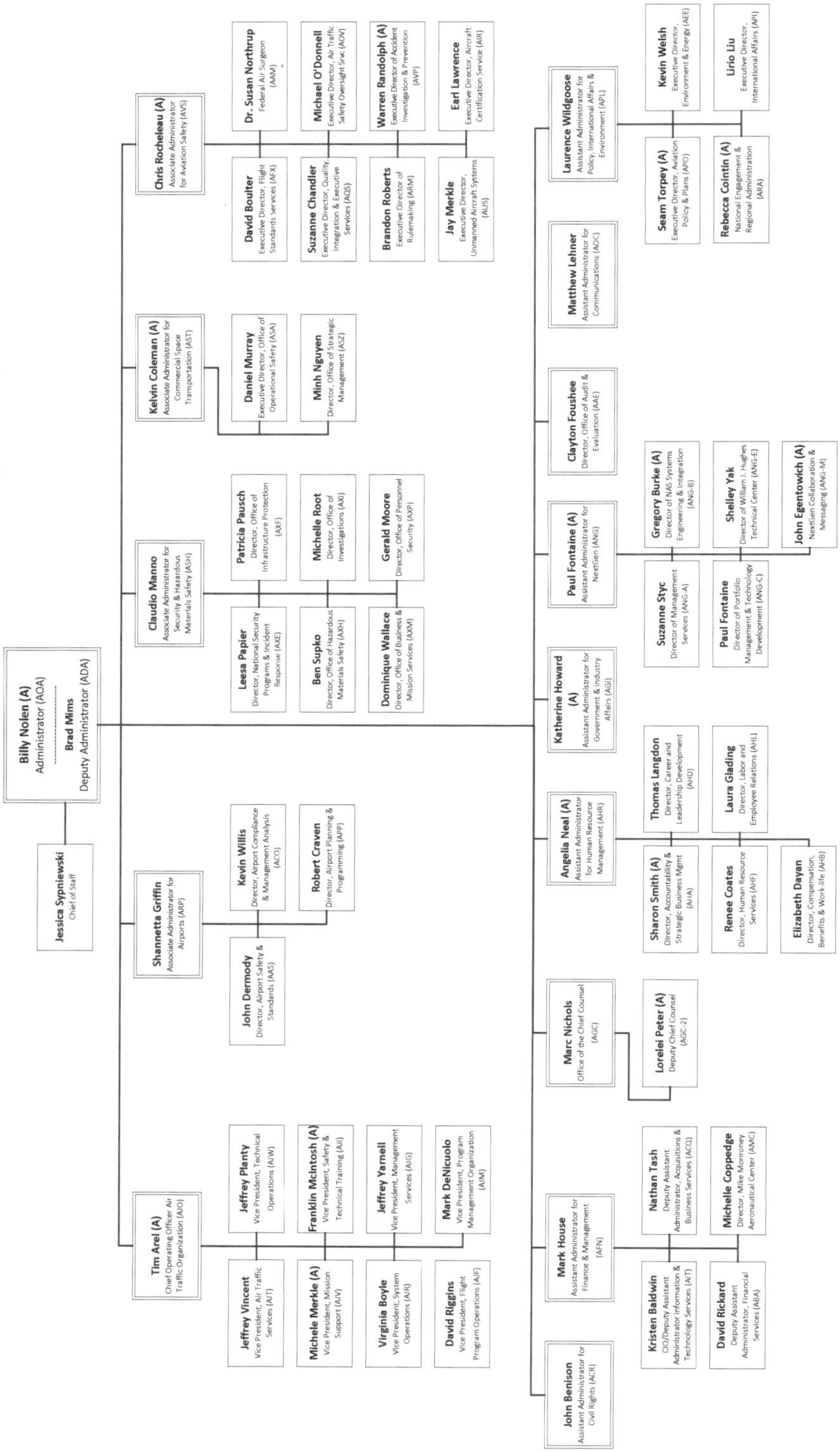

Source: Federal Aviation Administration (FAA)

Federal Aviation Agency with broad new authority to regulate civil aviation and provide for the safe and efficient utilization of the nation's airspace.

In April 1967, the Federal Aviation Agency became the Federal Aviation Administration and was incorporated into the new DOT, which had been established to give unity and direction to a coordinated national transportation system. The FAA's basic responsibilities remain unchanged, however. While working with other administrations in the DOT in long-range transportation planning, the FAA continues to concern itself primarily with the promotion and regulation of civil aviation to ensure safe and orderly growth. Figure 4.2 shows the organizational chart for the Federal Aviation Administration.

Major Responsibilities

Air Traffic Control. One of the FAA's principal responsibilities is the operation and maintenance of the world's largest and most advanced air traffic control and air navigation system. Almost half the agency's work force of more than 52,000 people are engaged in some phase of air traffic control. They staff 400 airport control towers, 22 air route traffic control centers, and 91 flight service stations. The FAA also employs 12,000 technicians and engineers to install and maintain the various components of this system, such as radar, communications sites, and ground navigation aids. The FAA operates its own fleet of specially equipped aircraft to check the accuracy of this equipment from the air.

Almost all airline flights and many general aviation flights operate under **instrument flight rules (IFR)** regardless of weather conditions. This means that they are followed from takeoff to touchdown by air traffic control to ensure that each flies in its own reserved block of airspace, safely separated from all other air traffic in the system.

A typical transcontinental flight from Los Angeles to New York, for example, involves almost a dozen air traffic control facilities. From the air traffic control tower at Los Angeles International Airport, the flight is transferred, or "handed off," first to the terminal radar control room and then to the air route traffic control center at Palmdale, California. The Salt Lake City center takes control next, and depending on the route, it may be followed by the Denver, Kansas City, Chicago, Cleveland, and New York centers. Approximately 30 miles from John F. Kennedy International Airport, the flight is handed off to the radar approach control facility serving all New York airports and, finally, to the JFK air traffic control tower, which issues final landing instructions. Only when the aircraft is safely on the ground and has taxied clear of other traffic does the FAA's responsibility for the safety of the passengers and crew on that particular flight end.

When weather conditions permit, many general aviation pilots follow **visual flight rules (VFR)**, which means they maintain separation from other aircraft on a "see and avoid" basis. Although VFR flights essentially are outside the air traffic control system except in busy terminal areas, they must follow well-established rules designed to maximize the safety of such operations. VFR flight also is banned from certain heavy-use airspace, such as along the jet routes above 18,000 feet.

VFR pilots rely heavily on the FAA's network of 91 flight service stations to obtain preflight and in-flight briefings, weather information, suggested routes, altitudes, and other information important to flight safety. The flight service station also is a friend in need to VFR pilots who are lost or otherwise in trouble. In addition, these facilities will initiate search-and-rescue operations when a VFR aircraft is overdue at its reporting station or destination airport.

To keep pace with the rapid growth of aviation, the FAA has implemented a computer-based, semi-automated air traffic control system at all of the 20 en route centers that service the contiguous United States and at all major terminal facilities. The system tracks controlled flights automatically and tags each aircraft with a small block of information written electronically on the radar scopes used by controllers. Included in this data block are aircraft identity and altitude—information that previously had to be acquired by voice communications, thereby imposing a burden on both pilots and controllers, contributing to radio frequency congestion, and providing the possibility of human error.

Similar automated radar systems, tailored to the varied traffic demands of terminal locations, already have been installed and are operational at more than 60 large- and medium-hub airports. Another 80 systems have been installed at airports in the small-hub category.

FAA plans call for the en route and terminal systems to be tied together nationwide in a common network for the exchange of data. The capabilities of the automated system also are being upgraded to include additional air traffic management functions, such as automatic prediction and resolution of air traffic conflicts, metering and spacing of en route aircraft, and flow control of aircraft in the terminal area.

Aircraft and Aviator Certification. No air traffic control system, no matter how automated, can function safely and efficiently unless the people and machines using the system measure up to certain prescribed standards. The FAA therefore has been charged with responsibility for establishing and enforcing standards relevant to the training and testing of aviators and the manufacture and continued airworthiness of aircraft.

There are approximately 180,000 civil aircraft in the United States, and the FAA requires that each be certificated, or licensed, as airworthy by the agency. Both the original design and each subsequent aircraft constructed from that design must be approved by FAA inspectors. Even home-built aircraft require FAA certification.

In the case of new transport airplanes, such as the new breed of fuel-efficient jets (Boeing 777 and 787, Airbus A380 and A350), the certification process may take years. The FAA's involvement begins when the aircraft is still in the blueprint stage. FAA aeronautical engineers work side by side with factory engineers throughout the entire building process, checking on the progress of the numerous components, such as the fuselage, wings, landing gear, and tail surfaces, to ensure quality of workmanship and conformity to an approved design. The same watchfulness is exercised over the design and manufacture of aircraft engines, propellers, and instruments.

When the new aircraft prototype is finished, it must pass an extensive series of ground and flight tests. If all goes well, the airplane receives a **type certificate** to show that it meets FAA standards of construction and performance. This is followed by the issuance of a **production certificate** to the manufacturer when its capability of duplicating the type design has been established. Finally, each airplane off the line receives an **airworthiness certificate** attesting to the fact that it conforms to the type certificate and is safe to fly.

Small aircraft get the same close attention during design, construction, testing, and production as do big ones. Some factories do a sufficient volume of business to require FAA inspectors on the job full-time; others may not, but the inspection procedures are identical, and FAA inspectors personally make final checks.

Once an aircraft starts flying, the FAA is concerned that it remains airworthy. Therefore, the FAA approves airline maintenance programs, setting the times for periodic inspections and overhauls of various aircraft components such as engines, propellers, instruments, and communications and flight systems. The FAA also certifies repair stations that perform the required maintenance checks and the needed repairs and alterations on general aviation aircraft—those flown by businesspersons, commercial and industrial operators, air taxi operators, and private individuals. All of these facilities are checked at regular intervals by FAA inspectors.

The end result of all these efforts is reflected in statistics that show that mechanical or structural defects account for only a relatively small percentage of aviation accidents. The key element in the safety equation is still the human one. For this reason, the FAA requires that everyone directly involved in the operation, maintenance, and direction of airplanes have a valid certificate from the agency with appropriate ratings. Included are pilots, flight engineers, navigators, aviation mechanics, air traffic controllers, aircraft dispatchers, and parachute riggers. In addition, the FAA certifies both pilot and mechanic schools and the instructors who teach in these institutions.

Airport Aid and Certification. One of the FAA's most significant efforts is aimed at expanding and modernizing the nation's airport facilities to meet projected traffic demands. The agency was given broad power to pursue this objective by the Airport and Airway Development Act of 1970, which replaced the Federal Airport Act of 1946 and established both the Airport Development Aid Program (ADAP) and the Planning Grant Program (PGP). The act expired at the end of fiscal 1980, and appropriations have been made on an annual basis since then.

Although the present airport system in the United States includes some 19,200 facilities, only one-third of these are publicly owned. The rest are in private hands, and the majority are closed to the public.

Under the ADAP, the FAA was authorized to allocate funds for airport improvement and construction projects. During this ten-year program, the agency allocated more development money than it did during the entire 26-year history of the previous Federal Aid Airport Program. Funds were allocated on a cost-sharing basis for such projects as acquisition of land; construction of runways, taxiways, and aprons; purchase of fire and crash-rescue equipment; and installation of lighting and navigation and landing aids.

The purpose of the PGP was to promote the orderly and timely development of the nation's airport system by assisting state and local authorities in identifying present and future air transportation requirements. Grants were made for two types of planning projects: (1) preparation of master plans at individual airports and (2) development of statewide or regional airport system plans. The FAA paid three-fourths of the cost of a planning project, with the local agency contributing the remainder.

The Airport and Airway Development Act of 1970 also authorized the FAA to issue operating certificates to airports receiving service to ensure their safe operation. In keeping with this directive, the agency subsequently adopted new regulations that set safety standards in 18 areas, including the availability of firefighting and rescue equipment, reduction of bird hazards, marking and lighting of runways and taxiways, handling and storage of dangerous materials, and marking and lighting of obstructions.

The first phase of the certification program was limited to the approximately 500 airports that receive regularly scheduled service by certificated air carriers using large aircraft and account for 96 percent of all airline passenger enplanements in the United States. The FAA completed certification of these airports in May 1973. The second phase involved those airports serving certificated air carriers that conduct operations on an irregular or unscheduled basis or operations with small aircraft. FAA operating certificates had been issued to more than 700 airports by the end of 1980. The FAA also assists airport owners in designing, constructing, and maintaining airports in keeping with aviation requirements, national safety standards, and state-of-the-art design and engineering technology. This is accomplished by the issuance of standards, published in the form of advisory circulars, that are mandatory for grant recipients and have worldwide acceptance as technical advisory documents. Advisory circulars cover such areas as airport paving, drainage, and lighting, and runway, taxiway, and apron design.

Environmental Protection. In addition to safety, the FAA also has important responsibilities to make airplanes compatible with the environment by controlling noise and engine emissions. The agency considers these efforts of critical importance in ensuring the future growth and development of civil aviation in the United States.

Significant progress has already been made since the introduction of wide-body jets, such as the Boeing 747, the DC-10, and the Lockheed 1011 in the early 1970s. Although the engines that power these aircraft generate 2.5 times the thrust of any engine previously used in commercial service, they are only about half as loud as their predecessors. In addition, they are virtually smoke-free.

The FAA also has initiated regulatory action designed to quiet older jets presently in service by requiring that they either be modified with noise suppression devices or phased out of service. In addition, engine noise standards have been developed for the new generation of aircraft and the supersonic transports.

Civil Aviation Security Program. Another major FAA responsibility is the Civil Aviation Security Program. Efforts in this area are aimed at preventing or deterring such criminal acts as air piracy, sabotage, extortion, and other crimes that could adversely affect aviation safety. Key elements of the program include required screening of all enplaning airline passengers and a search of their carry-on baggage. A law enforcement officer also must be present at each screening station during the boarding process. In addition, airport operators are required to establish a security system that will keep unauthorized persons from gaining access to air operations areas.

Implementation of these regulations in early 1973 and negotiation of an agreement with the Cuban government on the disposition of hijackers at about the same time produced a dramatic turnaround in the hijacking situation. After averaging almost 30 per year from 1968 to 1972, the number of hijacking attempts dropped to five in 1977 and has remained at around that number ever since.

Civil aviation security was strengthened further in August 1974 when Congress passed the Anti-Hijacking Act of 1974, which gave statutory force to the FAA's security regulations. And in July 1978, the industrialized nations of the world agreed at a summit meeting in Bonn, Germany, to act together to cut off all air service to and from countries that refuse to extradite or prosecute aircraft hijackers. In addition, the secretary of transportation is authorized to act against foreign carriers operating in the United States that do not meet minimum security standards.

Engineering and Development. The FAA supports all of its safety, security, and environmental programs with extensive engineering and development (E & D) projects, conducted in part through contracts with industry, other government agencies, and universities. Much of the E & D work, however, is done in-house at the FAA Technical Center in Atlantic City, New Jersey, and the transportation systems center in Cambridge, Massachusetts. Aeromedical research is done at the FAA's Civil Aeromedical Institute in Oklahoma City.

A continuing priority of the agency's E & D work is further automation of the air traffic control system to help controllers keep aircraft safely separated as air traffic increases. Warning systems, for instance, have been added to the automated systems at the busiest air traffic facilities to alert controllers when aircraft under their control are dangerously close to the ground or to one another. Work is under way to develop other computer systems that will assist controllers in handling higher traffic loads with increased efficiency and safety.

The FAA has also developed **collision avoidance systems** that operate independently of the air traffic control system but are compatible with it. These electronic devices warn pilots directly of potential conflicts with other aircraft and show how to avoid them. The first of these systems, designed for use in en route airspace and at airports with light to moderate traffic, were in operation by 1981. The FAA continues to develop and test more sophisticated collision avoidance systems for effective operation in congested airspace.

An important element in an effective collision avoidance system for high-use airspace is the discrete address beacon system (DABS), which is being developed by the FAA to upgrade the present air traffic control radar beacon surveillance system. Essentially, DABS is an improved transponder, but it will provide a data link for use with a ground-based anticollision system. It will also be the basis for other system improvements, such as automatic metering and spacing to improve the flow of traffic and automatic weather reporting.

Supplying pilots with accurate and timely weather information, particularly in hazardous weather, is another major E & D program goal. Among the efforts under way to achieve this safety goal are the development and demonstration of automated weather observation systems for airports without control towers, testing of a wake vortex advisory system that warns pilots of potentially dangerous air turbulence in approach and departure paths, and low-level wind shear alert systems to help pilots cope with wind shear during the critical stages of approach and landing. In addition to enhancing safety, these weather systems will help reduce delays and conserve fuel and will enable more efficient use of airport capacity.

The FAA also has an extensive aeromedical research program to explore the human factors that affect the safety and advancement of civil aviation. Current research efforts include studies of crash impact and survival, the toxic hazards of burning cabin materials after a crash, and the effect of aging and stress on pilots' performance.

In addition, the FAA conducts a comprehensive health program for more than 24,000 air traffic control specialists. The program provides a complete annual physical examination and certain laboratory procedures to determine whether controllers are fit to perform their demanding duties and to preserve their usefulness by early detection of correctable diseases.

Other FAA Activities

Because the United States is the recognized world leader in aviation, the FAA has a vital role to play in international aviation matters. For example, in cooperation with the State Department's Agency for International Development, it sends civil aviation assistance groups abroad to provide technical aid to other nations. The FAA also trains hundreds of foreign nationals every year at the Mike Monroney Aeronautical Center in Oklahoma City.

The FAA also works with the International Civil Aviation Organization (ICAO) in establishing worldwide safety and security standards and procedures, provides technical advice on the export and import of aviation products, and handles certification of foreign-made aircraft engines and parts under the terms of bilateral airworthiness agreements.

The FAA also participates with the National Transportation Safety Board (NTSB) in the investigation of major aircraft accidents to determine if any immediate action is needed to correct deficiencies and prevent a recurrence. In addition, the agency investigates most nonfatal and many fatal general aviation accidents on behalf of the NTSB, although the responsibility for determining probable cause remains with the board. The FAA also operates a public-use airport at its Technical Center outside Atlantic City, New Jersey.

THE TRANSPORTATION SECURITY ADMINISTRATION

On November 19, 2001, President George W. Bush signed into law the Aviation and Transportation Security Act, which, among other things, established a new Transportation Security Administration (TSA) within the Department of Transportation headed by the undersecretary of transportation for security. In March 2003, the TSA was moved to the Department of Homeland Security. This act was implemented to achieve a secure air travel system and was formed as a result of the tragic events of September 11, 2001. For the first time in U.S. aviation history, airport security became a direct federal responsibility. The TSA protects the nation's transportation systems to ensure freedom of movement for people and commerce by setting the standard for excellence in transportation security through its people, processes, and technologies.

The TSA is responsible for federal security screening operations for passenger air transportation and intelligence information related to transportation security; managing and carrying out program and regulatory activities; discovering, preventing, and dealing with threats to transportation security; research and development activities related to enhancing transportation security; coordinating intermodal transportation security, including aviation, rail, other surface transportation, and maritime transportation; and overseeing most transportation-related responsibilities of the federal government during a national emergency.

The TSA issues and administers Transportation Security Regulations (TSR), which were formerly rules of the FAA. These rules were transferred to the TSA when the TSA assumed control of the FAA's civil aviation security function on February 17, 2002. The general contents of the TSR cover the responsibilities of the undersecretary of transportation for security, investigative and enforcement procedures, passenger civil aviation security service fees, aviation security infrastructure fees, protection of sensitive security information, civil aviation security, airport security, aircraft operator security (air carriers and commercial operators), foreign air carrier security, indirect air carrier security, and aircraft security under general operating and flight rules.

In 2003, the TSA, along with the U.S. Coast Guard, were transferred from the DOT to the Department of Homeland Security (DHS).

THE NATIONAL TRANSPORTATION SAFETY BOARD

Created by the Department of Transportation Act of 1966, the NTSB officially came into being by executive order on April 1, 1967. Actually, it was on May 2 that the first five-member board, appointed by the president with the advice and consent of the Senate, was sworn into office.

The board was to be independent in its operations, but for housekeeping purposes, it was made a part of the new Department of Transportation. Nearly eight years later, the Transportation Safety Act of 1974 established the board as an entirely independent agency and broadened the board's statutory mandate for investigation of certain surface transportation accidents. The new act also strengthened the NTSB's position in pressing for action by the DOT on board safety recommendations. The secretary of transportation was required to respond, in writing, within 90 days of each recommendation to the DOT and to give detailed reasons whenever the DOT rejected a recommendation. The NTSB, in turn,

FIGURE 4.3 Organization of the National Transportation Safety Board

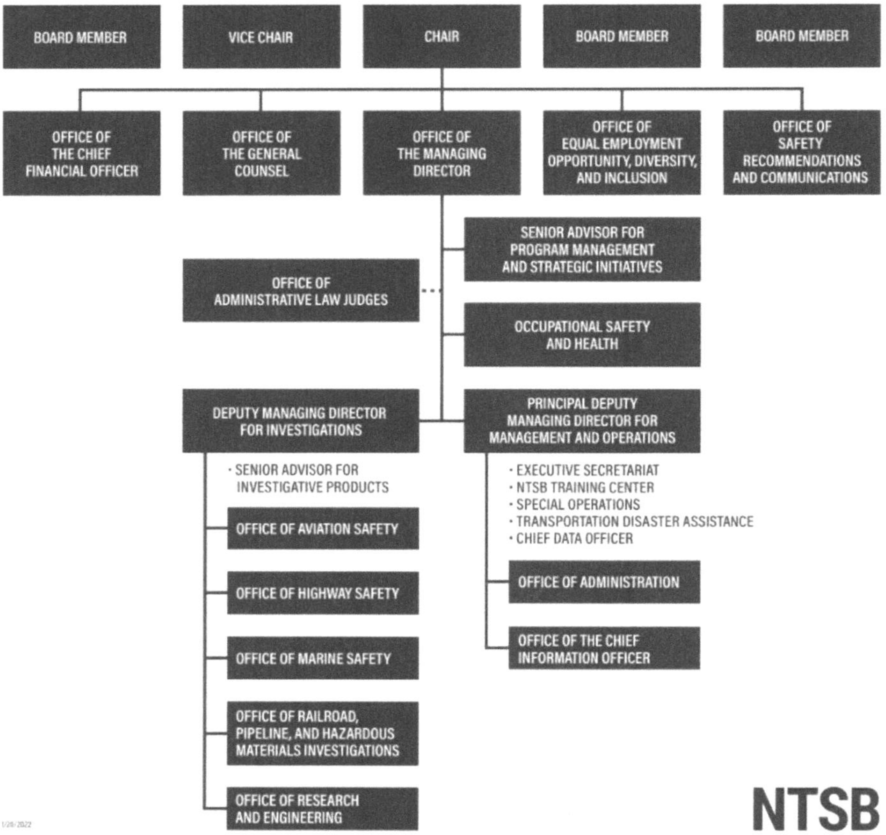

Source: National Transportation Safety Board (NTSB); www.ntsb.gov/about/organization/Pages/default.aspx

instituted a formal procedure for monitoring responses to recommendations and for evaluating them.

In 1982, the 1974 legislation was amended to give the NTSB "priority over all other investigations—. . . by other Federal agencies" in surface transportation cases. Provision was made for participation of other agencies in board investigations, and the board's rights to examine physical evidence were extended specifically to "any vehicle, rolling stock, track, or pipeline component" involved in an accident. Figure 4.3 shows the organizational chart for the NTSB.

The board is composed of five members appointed by the president and confirmed by the Senate, two of whom are designated by the president for two-year terms to serve as chair and vice-chair. The full term of a member is five years. The board's headquarters are in Washington, D.C., and field offices are located in Anchorage, Atlanta, Chicago, Denver, Fort Worth, Los Angeles, Miami, Kansas City, New York City, and Seattle.

Scope and Responsibilities

The NTSB is required to determine the probable cause of the following:

1 Civil aviation accidents
2 Highway accidents selected in cooperation with the states
3 All passenger train accidents, any fatal railroad accident, and any railroad accident involving substantial damage
4 Major marine accidents and any marine accident involving a public and a nonpublic vessel
5 Pipeline accidents involving a fatality or substantial property damage

Under the Transportation Safety Act of 1974, the board is required to take these actions:

1 Conduct special studies on safety problems
2 Evaluate the effectiveness of government agencies involved in transportation safety
3 Evaluate the safeguards used in the transportation of hazardous materials
4 Review appeals from aviators and merchant sailors whose certificates have been revoked or suspended

Safety Board Publications. The board's Public Inquiries Section maintains a public docket at its headquarters in Washington, D.C. The docket contains the records of all board investigations, all safety recommendations, and all safety enforcement proceedings. These records are available to the public and may be copied, reviewed, or duplicated for public use. The board makes public all of its actions and decisions in the form of accident reports, special studies, safety effectiveness evaluations, statistical reviews, safety recommendations, and press releases.

Aviation Safety. Aviation is the largest of the NTSB's divisions. The board investigates hundreds of accidents annually, including all air carrier accidents, all in-flight collisions, fatal general aviation accidents, and all air taxi commuter accidents. The major share of the board's air safety recommendations are directed to the FAA. The recommendations have resulted in a wide range of safety improvements in areas such as pilot training, aircraft maintenance and design, air traffic control procedures, and survival equipment requirements. The board also is empowered to conduct special studies of transportation safety problems, widening the focus on a single accident investigation to examine a safety problem from a broader perspective. In the past, for example, the board has conducted special studies in the areas of weather, crash worthiness, in-flight collisions, and commuter airlines.

In 1967, the NTSB inherited the entire Bureau of Safety of the Civil Aeronautics Board, a professional staff with a history of more than 50 years of pioneering work in civil aviation accident investigation. Its go-team organization and its emphasis on specialized study of all facets of an accident had been recognized for its excellence and emulated throughout the world.

In the NTSB's 40-year history, airline safety has improved steadily. In 1967, the airline fatal accident rate was 0.006 per million aircraft miles flown. By 1980, it was down to 0.001 per million miles, a reduction of 83 percent. And on January 1, 1982, U.S. airlines completed 26 months without a catastrophic crash of a pure-jet transport; never before had there been two calendar years without such an accident. The airlines flew more than a half-billion passengers on over 10 million flights in that 26-month period—more than a half-trillion passenger miles. The aerial transportation involved would have taken every man, woman, and child in the country on a flight of more than 2,000 miles.

In 1985, there were four fatal accidents, including two by the major carriers, ending the downward trend in accident rates. The fatal accident rate declined during the late 1980s, reaching another low of 0.023 per 100,000 departures by year-end 2005. By 2014, the rate remained around the same. The chance of a passenger on a major carrier being involved in a fatal accident is still about 1 in 3 million.

Steps Involved in a Major Accident Investigation

In the event of a major accident, the NTSB follows clearly delineated procedures, as outlined here.

1 *The go-team.* One of the more publicly visible aspects of a major NTSB accident investigation is the board's use of the **go-team** concept. The go-team, which is on 24-hour alert, is a group of board personnel whose members possess a wide range of accident investigation skills. In aviation, for example, a go-team roster could include one of the five members of the safety board, an air traffic control specialist, and experts trained in witness interrogation, aircraft operations, and aircraft maintenance records. In the case of a railroad accident, the go-team is similar, but the specialties vary, typically consisting of track engineers, locomotive and signal experts, and operations specialists. Some go-team members are intermodal in that their area of expertise

is applicable to each transportation mode. Human-factors experts fall into this category, as do the board's metallurgists, meteorologists, and hazardous materials experts.

2 *At the site.* The length of time a go-team remains on the accident site varies with need, but generally a team completes its work in 7–10 days. However, accident investigations often can require off-site engineering studies or laboratory tests that may extend the fact-finding stage.

3 *In the laboratory.* The NTSB operates its own technical laboratory to support investigators in the field with unbiased analysis. For example, the laboratory has the capability to read out aircraft cockpit voice recorders (CVRs) and decipher flight data recorders (FDRs). These so-called black boxes provide investigators with a profile of an aircraft during the often-crucial last minutes of flight. But the board's read out capability is not confined to aviation. Similar techniques are applied to marine course recorders taken from ships involved in accidents. Metallurgy is another of the laboratory's skills. Board metallurgists perform postaccident analyses of wreckage parts ranging from aircraft components to railroad tracks. The laboratory is capable of determining whether failures resulted from inadequate design strength, excessive loading, or deterioration in static strength due to metal fatigue or corrosion.

4 *The safety recommendation.* The **safety recommendation** is the NTSB's end product. Nothing takes a higher priority; nothing is more carefully evaluated. The recommendation is vital to the board's basic role of accident prevention, because it is the lever used to bring changes in procedures and improvements in safety to the nation's transportation system. With human lives involved, timeliness is also an essential part of the recommendation process. As a result, the board issues a safety recommendation as soon as a problem is identified, without necessarily waiting until an investigation is completed and the probable cause of an accident determined. In its mandate to the board, Congress clearly emphasized the importance of the safety recommendation, stating that the board shall "advocate meaningful responses to reduce the likelihood of recurrence of transportation accidents." Each recommendation issued by the board designates the person or the party expected to take action, describes the action the board expects, and clearly states the safety need to be satisfied. To emphasize the importance of the safety recommendation, Congress has required the DOT to respond to each board recommendation within 90 days.

5 *The public hearing.* After an accident, the NTSB may decide to hold a public hearing to collect additional information and to air at a public forum the issues involved in an accident. The hearing is presided over by a member of the board, and witnesses testify under oath. Every effort is made to hold the hearing promptly and close to the accident site.

6 *The final report.* With the completion of the fact-finding phase, the accident investigation enters its final stage—analysis of the factual findings. The analysis is conducted at the NTSB's Washington headquarters, and the result is a statement of what the board terms "the probable cause of the accident." The **final report** on the accident is then presented to the full five-member board for discussion and approval at a public meeting in Washington. The entire process, from accident investigation to final report, normally takes several months. Accidents investigated by the board's field investigators are reported in brief format.

MAJOR AVIATION ASSOCIATIONS

Airline-Related Associations

Airlines for America
1275 Pennsylvania Avenue NW, Suite 1300
Washington, DC 20004
www.airlines.org

Founded in 1936, the **Air Transport Association of America (ATA),** now known as **Airlines for America (A4A)**, is the trade, service, and lobbying organization representing major airlines in the United States. Through the A4A, member airlines pool their technical and operational knowledge to form a single integrated airline system serving thousands of communities throughout the nation.

Of all A4A activities, safety and security, sustainability, modernization, and strategic policy is foremost. Other objectives include the improvement of passenger and cargo traffic procedures, economic and technical research, and action on legislation affecting the industry.

The interests and goals of the airlines as an industry are achieved through a system of councils and related committees made up of airline and A4A staff members working together. The committee structure also includes the Air Traffic Conference, whose function is to develop industry standards through intercarrier agreements. These agreements make it possible for a member of the public to walk into the office of virtually any airline or travel agent in any city and buy a ticket that will take him or her to any point served by that airline or any other scheduled airline throughout the world. The same service is available to a person making a shipment by air freight.

Regional Airline Association
1201 15th Street NW, Suite 430
Washington, DC 20005
www.raa.org

The **Regional Airline Association (RAA)**, renamed in 1981 (formerly the Commuter Airline Association of America), represents those airlines engaged in the scheduled air transportation of passengers and cargo, primarily in local, feeder, and short-haul markets, throughout the United

States and its territories. The RAA is chartered to promote a healthy business climate for the growth of regional and commuter services by working with government, other organizations, and the public on issues affecting the industry. Through cooperation and education, the RAA seeks to foster the development of the industry.

Other Airline Associations

Airlines Clearing House
1275 Pennsylvania Avenue NW, Suite 1300
Washington, DC 20004

The **Airlines Clearing House (ACH)** is a corporation, wholly owned by the larger certificated airlines, through which the interline accounts of airlines, certificated and regional, are settled on a net basis each month. Regional airlines, by participating as associate members, are able to realize all the billing and clearance benefits without the necessity of purchasing stock in the corporation.

Each member air carrier submits a recap sheet on the fifteenth of each month to the Airline Clearing House bank showing accounts due from every other member, covering both passenger and freight. The bank nets these accounts and notifies each airline on the twentieth of the month of their net debit or credit position in the Clearing House. Settlement is made on the twenty-eighth, with penalties levied for failure to pay. Flight coupons and air bills are sent to the appropriate airline for a follow-up audit, with an opportunity for subsequent Clearing House adjustments.

Each participating carrier is requested to maintain an account at the Airlines Clearing House bank. The Airlines Clearing House performs the clearing functions without charge. The cost of such items as printing, postage, bulletin correspondence, and maintenance of the manual of procedures is nominal. Reimbursement for such costs is billed to all members and associate members on an annual basis. When making application as an associate member, commuter airlines are required to have interline agreements with at least one member or associate member of the Clearing House.

Airline Tariff Publishing Company
Washington Dulles International Airport
45005 Aviation Drive
Dulles, VA 20166
http://atpco.net

The **Airline Tariff Publishing Company (ATPCO)**, wholly owned by Air Canada, Air France, All Nippon Airways, American Airlines, British Airways, Delta Air Lines, Hawaiian Airlines, KLM Royal Dutch Airlines, LATAM Airlines, Lufthansa German Airlines, and United Airlines is employed by the airlines to publish and distribute fares and cargo rates to the travel industry. ATPCO publications list joint fares tariffs, commuter local fares tariffs, commuter airline cargo local rules and rates, small-package rates, and air cargo memorandum tariffs. ATPCO distributes these tariffs to travel agents, airline rate desks, and other companies in the business.

Air Cargo, Inc.
1819 Bay Ridge Avenue
Annapolis, MD 21403
www.aircargocommunities.com

Air Cargo, Inc. is a service organization owned by the scheduled airlines of the United States. Air Cargo, Inc.'s complete system of airline and air freight services involves three distinct areas: local air freight pickup and delivery, air and truck and container pickup and delivery, and loading and unloading. Regional airlines may contract for the services of Air Cargo, Inc. as associate members.

Aircraft-Manufacturing Associations

Aerospace Industries Association
1000 Wilson Boulevard, Suite 1700
Arlington, VA 22209
www.aia-aerospace.org

The **Aerospace Industries Association (AIA)** is the national trade association that represents U.S. companies engaged in research, development, and manufacture of such aerospace systems as aircraft, missiles, spacecraft, and space-launch vehicles; propulsion, guidance, and control systems for the flight vehicles; and a variety of airborne and ground-based equipment essential to the operation of the flight vehicles. A secondary area of industry effort, grouped under the heading "nonaerospace products," consists of a broad range of systems and equipment generally derived from the industry's aerospace technological expertise but intended for applications other than flight.

The AIA functions on national and international levels, representing its membership in a wide range of technological and other relationships with government agencies and the public. To facilitate its work at the national level, the AIA is a member of the Council of Defense and Space Industry Associations (CODSIA), a coordination medium for six industry associations with mutual interests related to federal government procurement policies. In international activities, the AIA cooperates, whenever it is practical, with trade associations in other countries, both individually and through the International Coordinating Council of Aerospace Industry Associations (ICCAIA), an informal body of the world's national aerospace associations. The AIA also serves as secretariat for TC 20, the aircraft/space group of the International Organization for Standardization (ISO).

General Aviation Manufacturers Association
1400 K Street NW, Suite 801
Washington, DC 20005
www.generalaviation.org

The **General Aviation Manufacturers Association (GAMA)** is an independent trade organization representing 52 U.S. companies that produce over 95 percent of the nation's general aviation aircraft and equipment. The GAMA represents the joint interests of the general aviation sector in Washington and provides insight into the industry's role in the U.S. transportation system.

Aviation Distributors and Manufacturers Association
PO Box 3948
Parker, CO 80134
www.adma.org

The **Aviation Distributors and Manufacturers Association (ADMA)** represents distributors and manufacturers of aviation parts, supplies, and equipment in all matters of national importance. The ADMA cooperates with various government agencies, including the FAA, and represents this segment of the industry in all issues relating to federal legislation, regulations, orders, and other government activities. Like the GAMA, it provides a focal point for all other elements in the industry to determine what can be done through industry efforts to make prospective purchasers and the public at large aware of the advantages and usefulness of given aviation products. The ADMA conducts research in connection with operations of members to promote efficiency and economy in the distribution of aviation parts, supplies, and equipment.

General Aviation Associations

National Business Aviation Association
1200 G Street NW, Suite 1100
Washington, DC 20005
www.nbaa.org

The **National Business Aviation Association (NBAA)** represents more than 4,000 businesses and corporations that generate more than one-third of the gross national product of the United States. Members fly more than 5,500 aircraft in the conduct of business, from single-engine planes and helicopters to intercontinental jets of airliner size. More than half the members own and operate one or more aircraft.

At the national level, the NBAA is concerned with fuel allocation and availability, discrimination in the use of airports and airspace, aircraft noise and the environment, flight service station requirements, weather reporting services, federal taxes for the use of airports and air traffic control systems, customs services, and any federal regulation that has a bearing on business aircraft use.

There is no other spokesperson for business aviation before Congress, the DOT, the FAA, the Department of Energy, the IRS, the U.S. Customs Service, or any other federal agency. Staff members interpret business aviation's requirements, accomplishments, and activities; analyze government proposals, rules, and regulations for the effect on members; generate public information programs; and coordinate, when appropriate, with other national aviation associations. As needed, staff members turn to the entire membership for assistance.

Aircraft Owners and Pilots Association
421 Aviation Way
Frederick, MD 21701
www.aopa.org

The **Aircraft Owners and Pilots Association (AOPA)** represents more than 384,915 members who own or fly general aviation aircraft and fly for personal and business purposes.

The AOPA works closely with the FAA, the DOT, the NTSB, Congress, and other aviation organizations, both local and national, to ensure that the interests of its members and the entire general aviation community are well represented.

Safety in flying has always been of prime concern to the AOPA. By 1950, that area of activity had expanded to the degree that a separate organization, the AOPA Foundation, Inc., was developed to concentrate on aviation safety and educational programs. In 1967, the foundation was redesigned and named the AOPA Air Safety Foundation.

During the 1960s, AOPA's success in effectively representing the general aviation population gained worldwide recognition. Spearheaded by the AOPA, the International Council of Aircraft Owner and Pilot Associations (IAOPA) was formed. The goal was to bring to other nations around the globe the same flying freedom and professional representation that the AOPA obtained in the United States.

Although service to its members remains its primary consideration, the AOPA aggressively pursues the total public acceptance of general aviation.

National Association of State Aviation Officials
1390 Chain Bridge Road, #A106
McLean, VA 22101
www.nasao.org

The **National Association of State Aviation Officials (NASAO)** represents 47 state aviation agencies, as well as Puerto Rico's Aviation Department. Its members are the aeronautics commissions and departments created under the laws of the various states to foster, develop, and regulate aviation at the local and state levels.

The primary purpose of the NASAO as an association is to foster and encourage cooperation and mutual aid among the states, as well as federal and local governments, in developing both state and national air transportation systems that will be responsive to the needs of all users of aviation. By working to coordinate various state laws, regulations, and programs with those of the federal government, the NASAO seeks to develop operational uniformity among the states and to minimize conflict between and duplication of state and federal efforts in the development of an integrated national air transportation system.

International Aviation Associations

International Civil Aviation Organization
Place de L'Aviation Internationale
PO Box 400
Montreal, P.Q., Canada H3A2R2
www.icao.org

The principal aim of the **International Civil Aviation Organization (ICAO)** is to develop the principles and techniques of international air navigation and to foster the planning and development of international air transportation. The specific goals of the ICAO include the following:

1 Ensure the safe and orderly growth of international civil aviation throughout the world
2 Encourage the arts of aircraft design and operation for peaceful purposes
3 Encourage the development of airways, airports, and air navigation facilities for international civil aviation
4 Meet the needs of the peoples of the world for safe, regular, efficient, and economical air transport
5 Prevent economic waste caused by unreasonable competition
6 Ensure that the rights of contracting states are fully respected and that every contracting state has a fair opportunity to operate international airlines
7 Avoid discrimination between contracting states
8 Promote safety of flight in international air navigation
9 Promote generally the development of all aspects of international civil aeronautics

The ICAO has a sovereign body, the Assembly, composed of 191 signatory states. The Assembly meets at least once every three years and is convened by a Council. Each contracting state is entitled to one vote, and decisions of the Assembly are made by a majority of the votes cast except where otherwise stipulated in the convention. At this session, the complete work of the organization in the technological, economic, legal, and technical-assistance fields is reviewed in detail, and guidance is given to the other bodies of the ICAO for their future work.

The Council is a permanent body responsible to the Assembly. Contracting states are elected by the Assembly for three-year terms. In the election, adequate representation is given to states of chief importance in air transport. States not otherwise included that make the largest contribution to the provision of facilities for civil air navigation, or whose designation will ensure that all the major geographic areas of the world are included, also are represented on the Council.

The Council, the Air Navigation Commission, the Air Transport Committee, the Committee on Joint Support of Air Navigation Services, and the Finance Committee provide the continuing direction of the work of the organization. One of the major duties of the Council is to adopt international standards and recommended practices and to incorporate these as annexes to the Convention on International Civil Aviation. The Council may act as an arbiter between member states on matters concerning aviation and implementation of the convention, and it may investigate any situation that presents avoidable obstacles to the development of international air navigation. In general, it may take whatever steps are necessary to maintain the safety and regularity of operation of international air transportation.

International Air Transport Association
800 Place Victoria
PO Box 113
Montreal, P.Q., Canada H421M1
www.iata.org

Whereas the ICAO's major focus is on setting standards for the safe and orderly flow of air transportation throughout the world, the **International Air Transport Association (IATA)** is primarily concerned with tariff coordination, including the coordination of fares, rates, and charges, and rates and levels of travel agent commissions. It provides a forum for member states to discuss these matters collectively and to enable them, if they wish, to develop and adopt agreements on fares, rates, and commissions that are submitted to their respective governments for approval.

The IATA's work begins only after governments have promulgated a formal exchange of traffic and other rights (bilateral air transport agreements) and have licensed the airlines selected to perform the service. But from that point on, the activity of the IATA spreads through virtually every phase of air transport operations.

The basic source of authority in the IATA is the annual general meeting, in which all active member states have an equal vote. Year-round policy direction is provided by an elected executive committee (of airline chief executives), and its creative work is largely carried out by its traffic, technical, financial, and legal committees. Coordination of fares and rate agreements is entrusted to the IATA tariff coordination conferences, with separate meetings addressing passenger and cargo issues and establishing agreements valid for periods of up to two years.

Members of IATA committees are nominated by individual airlines, and, subject to the regulation and review of the executive committee, they serve as experts on behalf of the entire industry. In the traffic conferences, however, delegates act as representatives of their individual companies. Although the executive committee fixes the terms of reference of these conferences, their decisions are subject only to the review of governments and cannot be altered by any other part of the association. The day-to-day administration of the IATA is carried out by a nine-member executive management board, headed by a director general.

KEY TERMS

Aerospace Industries Association (AIA)
Air Cargo, Inc.
Air Transport Association (ATA)
Aircraft Owners and Pilots Association (AOPA)
Airline Clearing House
Airline Tariff Publishing Company
airworthiness certificate
Aviation Distributors and Manufacturers Association (ADMA)
collision avoidance system
final report
General Aviation Manufacturers Association (GAMA)
go-team
International Air Transport Association (IATA)
International Civil Aviation Organization (ICAO)
instrument flight rules (IFR)
National Association of State Aviation Officials (NASAO)
National Business Aviation Association (NBAA)
production certificate
Regional Airline Association (RAA)
safety recommendation
type certificate
visual flight rules (VFR)

REVIEW QUESTIONS

1 Describe some of the events that led to the creation of the Department of Transportation. What are the primary objectives of this department? Briefly describe the major role of each of the 11 administrations under the DOT.
2 The FAA has its roots in which early piece of legislation? When was the FAA created as an agency? Describe some FAA functions with regard to air traffic control, aircraft and aviator certification, airport aid and certification, environmental protection, civil aviation security programs, and engineering and development. How does the FAA interface with the ICAO and the NTSB?
3 Briefly describe the genesis of the NTSB. What is the board's primary function? What are some of its other functions? Give the steps involved in a major accident investigation. What is included in a safety recommendation? A final report?
4 What is the primary function of the following associations: the A4A, RAA, AIA, GAMA, ADMA, NBAA, and AOPA? Describe the

functions performed by the following airline associations: Airlines Clearing House; Airline Tariff Publishing Company; Air Cargo, Inc.?

5 What is the primary purpose of the NASAO?

6 Compare the roles of the ICAO and the IATA. How are they similar? Different?

Note

1 See Roy J. Sampson and Martin T. Farris, *Domestic Transportation: Practice, Theory, and Policy*, 3rd edition. (Boston, MA: Houghton Mifflin, 1975), p. 486.

CHAPTER 5

The General Aviation Industry

CHAPTER CHECKLIST • YOU SHOULD BE ABLE TO:

- Define *general aviation* and describe its segments in terms of primary use
- Give a statistical summary of general aviation in terms of total aircraft, number of aircraft produced annually, type of aircraft, number of pilots, and number of airports
- Discuss the major factors affecting the general aviation industry in the postderegulation period
- Distinguish between business and executive uses and between various types of commercial and non-commercial uses of general aviation aircraft
- Distinguish between the various types of general aviation airports
- Explain several of the services provided by the FAA to general aviation pilots
- Describe the relationship between manufacturers, the service industry, and users
- List the major functions of a medium to large FBO
- Discuss the factors causing businesses to seek the benefits of their own transportation
- Explain how emerging technologies are impacting the future of general aviation

DOI: 10.4324/9780429346156-6

INTRODUCTION

Ask people today what commercial aviation is, and they will undoubtedly tell you that it is the airlines. The public is aware of the existence and operation of what are commonly called the "commercial airlines" because of both representations of them in television and motion pictures and recurrent coverage in magazines and newspapers, including a vast advertising campaign by the air carrier industry. The millions of air travelers who pass through the major transportation centers of New York, Chicago, Atlanta, Miami, Los Angeles, and other cities have had personal experience with airlines.

As a result of these direct and vicarious exposures to air transportation, the huge role played by the airlines in the nation's transportation system is almost universally recognized. Unfortunately, most people regard the airlines as the only form of air transportation.

General aviation is the largest segment of aviation based on number of aircraft, number of pilots, and number of airports and communities served. It is a multi-billion-dollar industry that generates over $247 billion annually in economic activity and employs more than 1.3 million total jobs. Because of its efficiency and productivity, general aviation has become an important business tool. The majority of hours flown by general aviation aircraft are for business and commercial purposes. It is truly an integral part of the national transportation system and the U.S. economy. But there is no legal definition of general aviation, and it is commonly described in relatively negative terms as "all civil aviation except that carried out by the commercial airlines."

The term was invented in the early 1950s by the then **Utility Airplane Council** (forerunner of GAMA) of the Aerospace Industries Association (AIA) to describe the operations of the "utility" aircraft produced by the light-plane manufacturers and to distinguish them from the airplanes made by the large-airplane manufacturers, the members of the AIA, who produce aircraft (missiles and space) equipment for the airlines and the military. With the passage of time, the term general aviation came to be applied to a heterogeneous group of close to 220,000 aircraft of vastly diverse usage, performance characteristics, and cost.

General aviation is the aerial application plane that treats one out of every five tillable acres of land, which facilitates greater food production and keeps the cost of food low. It is the land developer making survey flights and the police officer observing traffic. It is the family on a vacation trip and the air ambulance flying a mercy mission. It is the relaxation of a brief flight on a Sunday afternoon.

It is the air taxi bringing passengers to the airline or picking them up at the terminal to whisk them to a distant off-airline point. It is the business traveler who travels to and from many cities making deals and decisions affecting the welfare of thousands of employees. It is the spare part flown in to keep an assembly line running. It is the bush pilot in Alaska, ferrying people, mail, and supplies from towns to wilderness areas.

Unquestionably, general aviation is the dominant force in the sky, including as it does over 90 percent of the civil air fleet, 75 percent of civil

Table 5.1 GAMA General Aviation Airplane Shipments and Billings (in $ Millions) by Airplane Type Manufactured Worldwide (1994–2020)

	Piston Airplanes				Turboprop		Business Jet				
Year	Single-Engine	Multi-Engine	Total Units	Billings	Units	Billings	Units	Billings	Total Turbine Units	Grand Total Units	Grand Total Billings
1994	544	77	621	$ 111	233	$ 714	278	$ 2,924	511	1,132	$ 3,749
1995	605	61	666	$ 169	285	$ 774	300	$ 3,351	585	1,251	$ 4,294
1996	731	70	801	$ 191	320	$ 864	316	$ 3,881	636	1,437	$ 4,936
1997	1,043	80	1,123	$ 238	279	$ 913	438	$ 6,019	717	1,840	$ 7,170
1998	1,508	98	1,606	$ 377	336	$ 1,011	515	$ 7,216	851	2,457	$ 8,604
1999	1,689	112	1,801	$ 440	340	$ 930	667	$ 10,190	1,007	2,808	$ 11,560
2000	1,877	103	1,980	$ 512	415	$ 1,323	752	$ 11,661	1,167	3,147	$ 13,496
2001	1,645	147	1,792	$ 541	422	$ 1,210	784	$ 12,117	1,206	2,998	$ 13,868
2002	1,591	130	1,721	$ 483	280	$ 868	676	$ 10,427	956	2,677	$ 11,778
2003	1,825	71	1,896	$ 545	272	$ 837	518	$ 8,616	790	2,686	$ 9,998
2004	1,999	52	2,051	$ 692	319	$ 997	592	$ 10,405	911	2,962	$ 12,093
2005	2,326	139	2,465	$ 805	375	$ 1,189	750	$ 13,161	1,125	3,590	$ 15,156
2006	2,513	242	2,755	$ 857	412	$ 1,389	887	$ 16,555	1,299	4,054	$ 18,815
2007	2,417	258	2,675	$ 897	465	$ 1,593	1,137	$ 19,347	1,602	4,277	$ 21,837

(Continued)

Table 5.1 (Continued)

	Piston Airplanes				Turboprop		Business Jet				
Year	Single-Engine	Multi-Engine	Total Units	Billings	Units	Billings	Units	Billings	Total Turbine Units	Grand Total Units	Grand Total Billings
2008	1,943	176	**2,119**	**$ 945**	538	**$ 1,953**	1,317	**$ 21,948**	**1,855**	**3,974**	**$ 24,846**
2009	893	70	**963**	**$ 442**	446	**$ 1,589**	874	**$ 17,443**	**1,320**	**2,283**	**$ 19,474**
2010	781	108	**889**	**$ 415**	368	**$ 1,300**	767	**$ 18,000**	**1,135**	**2,024**	**$ 19,715**
2011	761	137	**898**	**$ 441**	526	**$ 1,365**	696	**$ 17,235**	**1,222**	**2,120**	**$ 19,042**
2012	817	91	**908**	**$ 428**	584	**$ 1,359**	672	**$ 17,108**	**1,256**	**2,164**	**$ 18,895**
2013	908	122	**1,030**	**$ 571**	645	**$ 1,821**	678	**$ 21,058**	**1,323**	**2,353**	**$ 23,450**
2014	986	143	**1,129**	**$ 635**	603	**$ 1,849**	722	**$ 22,015**	**1,325**	**2,454**	**$ 24,499**
2015	946	110	**1,056**	**$ 601**	557	**$ 1,651**	718	**$ 21,877**	**1,275**	**2,331**	**$ 24,129**
2016	890	129	**1,019**	**$ 631**	582	**$ 1,949**	666	**$ 18,480**	**1,248**	**2,267**	**$ 21,059**
2017	936	149	**1,085**	**$ 595**	563	**$ 1,720**	677	**$ 17,885**	**1,240**	**2,325**	**$ 20,201**
2018	952	185	**1,137**	**$ 642**	601	**$ 1,869**	703	**$ 18,054**	**1,304**	**2,441**	**$ 20,564**
2019	1,111	213	**1,324**	**$ 772**	525	**$ 1,664**	809	**$ 21,077**	**1,334**	**2,658**	**$ 23,515**
2020	1,155	157	**1,312**	**$ 717**	443	**$ 1,370**	644	**$ 17,942**	**1,087**	**2,399**	**$ 20,029**

Source: GAMA

operations at FAA-towered and untowered airports, and 80 percent of the total certificated pilots in the United States.

General aviation is impactful worldwide and the International Council of Aircraft Owner and Pilot Association (IAOPA), a non-profit federation of 82 autonomous, nongovernmental, national general aviation organizations, includes the following in its definition: corporate aviation fractional ownership programs, business aviation, personal and private travel, air tourism, recreational flying, and air sports. Aerial application includes agricultural flights, banner towing, firefighting, medical evacuations, pilot training, search and rescue, sightseeing, skydiving, and medical transportation.

GENERAL AVIATION STATISTICS

General aviation has no reporting requirements comparable to those of the certificated air carrier industry. As is the case with operators of private automobiles, general aviation operators do not have to report to anyone on the specifics of their flights. The only statistics gathered by the government (the FAA) are based on an annual survey requesting every aircraft owner to report the number of flight hours for the previous year by **primary use category**: corporate, business, personal, instructional, aerial application, aerial observation, sightseeing, external load, air tour, air taxi, medical, and other. Table 5.1 outlines general aviation shipments and billings by airplane type manufactured worldwide (1994–2020). At the time of publication, data for 2021–2022 was not reported.

Factors Affecting General Aviation

Fundamental changes have taken place in the general aviation industry. Before 1978, changes in the industry mirrored changes in the economy. If the economy was strong and growing, so was general aviation; if a slowdown occurred, general aviation lagged as well. However, since the long and precipitous decline of aircraft shipments began in the late 1970s, this expected relationship has not held.

General aviation took off in the 1960s as the economy grew at a rapid pace, fueled by the Vietnam War and President Lyndon B. Johnson's "Great Society" social programs. General aviation manufacturers enjoyed a heyday, introducing new models and producing an average of more than 9,000 airplanes per year. Four airplanes in particular that were introduced in the 1960s—the Cessna 172, the Piper Cherokee, the Beechcraft King Air 90, and the Lear 23—proved to be bellwether designs for years to come. The general aviation fleet almost doubled during the 1960s, and new-aircraft shipments reached a high of 15,768 units in 1966.

The expansion of all segments of aviation continued into the 1970s, with more airplanes sold in this decade than before or since. The general aviation aircraft fleet increased from 131,743 to 211,045 aircraft, and production hit a high of 17,811 aircraft in 1978. New aircraft were introduced in record numbers, particularly trainers such as the Piper Cherokee and

Tomahawk models, the Cessna 150 and 152, and the Beech Sierra and Sundowner, to name a few.

However, some clouds loomed on the horizon. As fuel prices soared during the 1970s, manufacturers began to focus on more fuel-efficient aircraft. Airspace congestion was another problem that the industry had been studying since the mid-1960s. As a result, the Airport and Airway Development Act was passed in 1970 to provide the funding to expand and improve the airport and airway system over a ten-year period. And terminal control areas (TCAs) were introduced to the country's busiest airports; these required two-way communications with air traffic control (ATC), VOR navigation capability, and altitude-reporting transponders. Increasing regulations affected the personal-pleasure pilot in particular.

During the 1970s, the general aviation industry also began focusing on the issue of product liability. The number of lawsuits and the size of awards were rising, and not surprisingly, so were insurance premiums—from $51 per new airplane in 1962 to $2,111 in 1972. This was a sign of things to come for the aircraft manufacturers and, no doubt, a key reason for the steep drop in the production of general aviation aircraft during the 1980s. Product liability insurance costs for the general aviation airframe builders totaled about $135 million in 1985, and based on unit shipments of 2,029 aircraft that year, the costs exceeded $70,000 per airplane. This was more than the selling price of many basic two- and four-place aircraft.

These phenomenal cost increases during the first five years of the 1980s came at a time when the industry's safety record continued to improve. Improved safety notwithstanding, the number of product liability suits continued to increase. Even more significant was the exponential growth in settlements, judgments, and legal costs. By 1986, Cessna Aircraft Company decided to drop its piston-aircraft production and self-insure up to $100 million. Piper decided to operate without the benefit of product liability coverage, and Beech insured the first $50 million annual aggregate exposure with its own insurance company.

Other factors were also working against the private business and pleasure flier. Airline deregulation in 1978 at first caused a decrease in the use of business aircraft, as the air carriers, including many new ones, served new markets and competed for customers by lowering fares. But as the airlines concentrated their flights at hub cities and merger mania struck the industry in the early 1980s, service to many smaller communities was dropped or severely cut back as competition decreased. The use of corporate aircraft started to rebound, and the major manufacturers focused more attention on turboprops and jets. By this time, these manufacturers had been purchased by larger conglomerates. In 1980, Beech Aircraft was acquired by Raytheon Company. Cessna was acquired by General Dynamics in 1985 and then sold to Textron in 1991. France's Euralair, an air charter, executive jet, and cargo operator, bought Mooney in 1984. Piper's owner, Bangor Punta Corporation, was bought by Lear-Siegler, which, in turn, was bought by investment banker Forstmann Little and then in 1987 by entrepreneur M. Stuart Millar.

Unfortunately, the recession of the early 1990s and costly liability claims forced the company into Chapter 11 bankruptcy by 1992.

In the early 1980s, general aviation followed the rest of the economy into a recession. Interest rates were at an all-time high when President Ronald Reagan took office in 1980. Everything from housing starts to durable goods sales, including autos and general aviation aircraft sales, plummeted. The economy began to recover in 1983, but general aviation did not, for a number of reasons. No doubt the high interest rates of the late 1970s and early 1980s had an effect at the beginning of the slide. Acquisition costs, including those for avionics equipment, rose sharply during the early to mid-1980s, despite very little change in the design or features of the typical single-engine aircraft. Used aircraft were readily available, and prospective buyers were reluctant to purchase new equipment at considerably higher prices. Total operating expenses—including fuel, maintenance, hangar charges, and insurance—all steadily increased during the 1980s, making it more expensive for the occasional flier.

Another major factor, discussed previously, was the sharp rise in product liability claims, which caused the light-aircraft manufacturers to concentrate on their higher-priced line of turbine equipment. The growth in number and availability of regional and commuter airline service to many smaller communities also likely reduced the desirability of using private general aviation aircraft when planning business or pleasure trips. And changing tastes and preferences among the traditional business and pleasure aircraft users may have contributed to the decline in the 1980s, even as interest in sports cars and boats seemed to peak. The level of professionalism required to fly even a light aircraft in today's air traffic environment has grounded many private pleasure fliers. Some of these individuals chose to fly much less expensive ultralights and kit planes in uncontrolled airspace.

Another financial pressure working against aircraft ownership resulted from passage of the Tax Reform Act of 1986, which eliminated the 10 percent investment tax credit. This was followed by a luxury tax on boats and planes, which only exacerbated the problem of declining new aircraft sales. Finally, foreign aircraft manufacturers entered the traditionally U.S.-dominated market in a much bigger way during the 1980s. In the 1970s, U.S. general aviation aircraft manufacturers held a dominant position worldwide. But since 1981, imports of general aviation airplanes have exceeded U.S. exports in dollar value. Many foreign governments supported their fledgling aviation industries through subsidization of research, development, production, and financing, and foreign manufacturers continued to gain an ever-increasing foothold in the U.S. market. Aircraft made abroad accounted for more than 50 percent of all aircraft delivered to U.S. customers. Even in the high-end market, sales of foreign-manufactured business jets accounted for almost 40 percent of all business jets sold here in the early 1990s.

Meanwhile, shipments of new U.S.-manufactured general aviation aircraft continued to fall, reaching a low of 928 units in 1994. As a result of the industry's devastating decline, due largely to product liability lawsuits, Congress passed the General Aviation Revitalization Act (GARA) in 1994. The GARA ushered in a new wave of optimism in the general aviation industry.

With some exceptions, the GARA imposed an 18-year statute of repose, limiting product liability suits for aircraft having fewer than 20 passenger seats not engaged in scheduled passenger-carrying operations. Cessna immediately announced that it would resume production of single-engine aircraft in 1996. The New Piper Aircraft Corporation was formed, and in 1995, general aviation aircraft shipments finally increased after a 17-year decline.

In 1997, the optimism so prevalent in the industry since the passage of the GARA was evidenced by the release of new products and services, expansion of production facilities, increased student starts, increased aircraft shipments, and record-setting gains in aircraft billings. These conditions suggested continued improvement in the general aviation industry in 1998 and beyond. According to a poll of Aircraft Owners and Pilots Association (AOPA) members conducted in March 1992, only 41 percent said that they were optimistic about the future of general aviation. In response to a similar poll in January 1997, 51 percent responded optimistically, and by April 1998, the poll of certificated pilots reported that 74.5 percent of its members thought the state of aviation was the same or better than it had been. This renewed optimism among the pilot community, aircraft manufacturers, and the industry as a whole could be directly attributed to the strong economy and the passage of the GARA in 1994.

In January 1997, Cessna delivered its first new single-engine piston aircraft since 1986. In addition, Lancair International, Diamond Aircraft, and Mooney also produced new piston models. Galaxy Aerospace rolled out its new business jet in the fall of 1996. Aerospatiale and Renault joined forces to produce light-aircraft piston engines for certification in 1999. Piper announced plans to manufacture the Meridian, a single-engine turboprop which first flew in 1999.

New manufacturing facilities opened to support expanded production. Cirrus Design broke ground on two facilities to support production of the SR 20. Also, Sabreliner started a large expansion program at their Missouri facility.

In 1999, Cessna announced plans and orders for the new Citation models—the CJ1, CJ2, Sovereign, and Ultra Encore. Raytheon announced that it would begin deliveries of its Premier I, an entry-level jet that featured a composite fuselage with metal wings, in 2000. Mooney delivered its first Eagle in 1999.

Boeing Business Jets announced its plan to build a larger version of its long-range corporate jet, the BBJ-2. Boeing Business Jets, a joint enterprise of Boeing and General Electric, entered the market in 1998 with the long-range BBJ, which was based on a hybrid of the 737-700/800 aircraft. Twenty-eight aircraft were delivered in 1999. Airbus and Fairchild were also marketing business jets that are based on aircraft originally designed for commercial operations.

During the 1990s, fractional ownership programs offered by Executive Jets' NetJets, Bombardier's Flexjet, Raytheon's Travel Air, Flight Options, and TAG Aviation grew at a rapid pace. From 1993 through the end of 1999, these five major fractional ownership providers increased their fleet size and shareholders at average annual rates above 65 percent. Despite this record growth, only a small percentage of this market has been developed.

Fractional ownership programs are filling the niche for corporations, celebrities, and businesspeople who do not fly enough to warrant having their own flight department. Fractional ownership providers offer the customer a more efficient use of time by providing a faster point-to-point travel time and the ability to conduct business while flying. In addition, shareholders of fractional ownership find the minimum start-up concerns and easier exiting options of great benefit.

The 1990s truly represented a revitalization of the industry. Total billings in 1999 soared 35.1 percent over 1998, reaching $7.9 billion, and units shipped increased from 2,200 to 2,504, or 12.6 percent. Put into perspective, general aviation sales in 1999 were quadruple those of 1991. The last year of the decade also marked the first time in the GAMA's history that both billings and shipments increased for five consecutive years. It marked the first full year of deliveries of the Cessna 206H Stationair and T206H Turbo Stationair. Deliveries of the composite-construction Cirrus Design SR 20 began, and Mooney Aircraft Corporation began production of the Ovation 2—a faster and more fuel-efficient version of the firm's best-selling model, the Ovation.

The biggest jump in 1999 sales revenue, similar to 1998, was in the turbofan aircraft segment. Sales rose 23.9 percent, in large part because of strong incremental growth and fractional ownership programs. The decade closed with across-the-board growth in general aviation activity, corporate flight departments, fractional programs, and charter flights.

The new millennium started out with a continuation of the 1990s. New manufacturing facilities were being built and old facilities expanded. Sales of general aviation aircraft continued to set new records for value of aircraft shipped. Much of this record sales value was for aircraft at the higher priced end of the general aviation fleet—turbine-powered aircraft—and is likely due in part to the increase in fractional ownership. More than 900 turbine aircraft were delivered in 2000 (see Table 5.2) as production capacity soared to keep up with record backlogs in manufacturers' order books. Cessna, for example, doubled the number of Excels it delivered and increased Bravo production by 50 percent. Dassault Falcon Jet deliveries reached 73, five more than in 1999, and its backlog of orders increased. Learjet 45 deliveries were up from 43 in 1999 to 71 in 2000. Even deliveries of the venerable Raytheon Hawker 800 XP increased by 22 percent. Total turbine production decreased in the early 2000s but hit a record 1,850 in 2008. Production levels for 2011 decreased due to the global economic slowdown but numbers were up to 1,323 by 2013.

Piston-aircraft shipments grew by almost 11 percent, buoyed by an infusion of new technology from Lancair and Cirrus Design and by increased piston deliveries from Cessna's Independence, Kansas plant. The year 2000 saw the first deliveries of Lancair's Columbia 3000. Cirrus delivered 95 new four-seat SR 20 models. Cessna piston deliveries increased to 912 units.

However, clouds were on the horizon, and by 2001 the economy slipped into a recession. While sales reached another high, largely the result of strong turboprop and jet sales, the total number of shipments fell for the first time in six years. Unexpected events, such as the tragedy on September 11, 2001, the economic slowdown during the first three years of the new millennium, and the increase in costs related to fuel and liability, vividly demonstrate that the future, as in the past, will bring new challenges to the general aviation industry.

From the early 2000s to 2020, general aviation aircraft sales remained stable, and in some years, there were small increases in terms of shipments. By the end of 2021, GAMA reported increased shipments for turboprop, business jet, and helicopter deliveries over the prior year but there was a decrease in the number of shipments for piston aircraft. Despite the COVID-19 global pandemic that started in 2019, the general aviation sector proved to be resilient despite workforce and supply-chain challenges.

During the global pandemic, the commercial aviation sector was hit hard but the general aviation sector showed positive gains as there was a shift in customer demographics due to changing business and personal needs. Before the global pandemic, urban centers were the primary business centers and as a result of new work options, primarily focused on remote workers utilizing virtual offices, suburban zones benefited with increased populations. In many cases, primary residences in urban areas became second homes while suburban or remote homes became the new primary residence. This, combined with customers seeking to increase safety awareness, resulted in increased demand for general aviation transport. Historical data and emerging trends indicate that fractional aircraft programs are growing, having a negative impact on the commercial aircraft sector serving business centers.

Uses of Aircraft

The size and diversity of general aviation makes it difficult to categorize for statistical purposes. Aircraft flown for business during the week may be used for personal transportation on weekends, the same way a family car is used. Instructional aircraft may be used for charter (air taxi) service or rented to customers for business or personal use. An air taxi airplane may be used for advanced flight instruction or for rental to business- or personal-use customers, and so on. Nevertheless, the FAA has broken down the numbers of general aviation aircraft by type and primary use, from which a further analysis can be made on the basis of solicited reports from the users (see Table 5.2).

Business Aviation. The **National Business Aviation Association (NBAA)** defines business aviation as falling into two categories: **business aircraft use** and **corporate aircraft use**.

1 *Business aircraft use.* Any use of an aircraft not for compensation or hire by an individual for the purpose of transportation required by a business in which he or she is engaged (in other words, personally flown)
2 *Corporate aircraft use.* Any use of an aircraft by a corporation, a company, or another organization for the purpose of transporting its employees and/or property not for compensation or hire and employing professional pilots for the operation of their aircraft

Business aircraft complement airline services in satisfying the nation's business transportation requirements. Although airlines offer transportation to the largest cities and business centers, business aviation specializes in many areas where major airlines cannot satisfy demand. More than 440,000 general aviation and air taxi aircraft are flown throughout the world, providing quick, safe, and reliable transportation whenever and wherever business needs require them. Of the 440,000 aircraft, approximately 211,000, or 48 percent, are flown in the U.S. alone.

Business aviation operators use all types of aircraft, from single- and twin-engine piston-powered airplanes, helicopters, and turboprops to the fastest jets, to ensure maximum business effectiveness. Over two-thirds of the Fortune 500 companies operate business aircraft, and virtually all of these aircraft operators are members of the **National Business Aviation Association (NBAA)**. The NBAA is the principal representative of business aviation before Congress and the regulatory agencies, such as the FAA. It represents more than 11,500 members operating over 10,000 aircraft. NBAA member companies earn annual revenues amounting to approximately $5 trillion, employing more than 19 million people worldwide. Turbojets are the most widely used type of aircraft. Over one-half of NBAA members have turbojets, approximately 20 percent have turboprops, and about 10 percent use multi-engine piston-powered aircraft. Although most of these aircraft are operated domestically, an increasing number are utilized to expand markets overseas.

Numerous examples of typical traveling schedules purport to demonstrate the advantages of business aircraft over the commercial airlines. Because of the proliferation of airline hub-and-spoke systems since deregulation, flying business aircraft directly between airports has become a big advantage. The monetary-equivalent savings in terms of executives' time that would otherwise be spent in traveling to and from air carrier airports and in waiting for scheduled air carrier flights, plus hotel expenses, meals, and rental car expenses, loom large on the benefit side of such calculations. Normally unquantified are the advantages of flexibility and prestige (which may or may not bring about pecuniary benefits) and the fact that private meetings can be held in privately owned aircraft.

The same is also generally true of smaller businesses, which have discovered the benefits of maintaining their own aircraft. It is not unusual for general aviation aircraft operators to hold business meetings in several cities hundreds of miles apart—on the same day.

Table 5.2 General Aviation and Part 135 Number of Active Aircraft by Primary Use 2008–2019 (Aircraft in Thousands)

General Aviation Use	2019	2018	2017	2016	2015	2014	2013	2012	2011*	2010	2009	2008
Personal	141.8	143.2	139.7	142.1	139.7	135.7	133.9	141.3		150.9	152.3	154.4
Business Without Paid Flight Crew1	15	15.5	17.3	16.2	15.9	15.8	15.9	17.5		21.7	22.4	22.4
Business with Paid Flight Crew2	11.1	11	11.1	9.8	11.3	11.9	10.7	9.4		10.4	10.5	11.7
Instructional	18	17	16.1	15.8	15.7	13.2	13.4	12.8		15.4	14.1	15
Aerial Application Agriculture	3.1	3.3	4.1	3.2	3.3	3.1	3.6	3.6		3.3	3.2	3.1
Aerial Observation	4.1	4.8	4.4	6.1	5.5	6	4.8	5.3		5.9	5.3	5.3
Aerial Application Other	1.1	1	1.4	0.8	0.9	0.9	1	0.8		0.7	0.8	1
External Load	0.3	0.2	0.3	0.3	0.3	0.3	0.3	0.4		0.2	0.2	0.4
Other Work	1	1	1.7	1.3	1.3	1.2	1	0.9		0.8	1.2	0.9
Sightseeing	1	1	1.3	1.1	1.2	1.7	1.1	1.1		1.5	0.8	0.7
Air Medical	0.3	0.3	0.4	0.4	0.5	0.6	0.4	0.3		0.2	0.5	0.4
Other	5	4.8	4.5	6.1	5.7	4.9	4.5	6.2		4.3	4	4.8
General Aviation Use Total	**201.9**	**203**	**202.3**	**203.3**	**201.1**	**195.2**	**190.5**	**199.7**		**215.3**	**215.3**	**220.2**
On-Demand FAR Part 135 Use												
Air Taxi	6.6	6.3	6.5	5.8	6.5	6.9	7.3	7.1		6.5	7	6.9
Air Tours	0.7	0.6	0.5	0.6	0.5	0.4	0.5	0.5		0.5	0.4	0.4
Air Medical	1.8	1.8	2.5	2.1	1.9	1.8	1.6	1.8		1.1	1.2	1.2
On-Demand FAR Part 135 Use Total	**9.1**	**8.8**	**9.5**	**8.5**	**8.9**	**9.2**	**9.4**	**9.4**		**8.1**	**8.6**	**8.5**
Total General Aviation and On-Demand FAR Part 135 Use	**211**	**211.7**	**211.8**	**211.8**	**210**	**204.4**	**199.9**	**209**		**223.4**	**223.9**	**228.7**

*2011 data not reported.
Source: www.faa.gov

Fractional ownership has also become an important option today. Companies or individuals own a fraction of an aircraft and receive management and pilot services associated with the aircraft's operation. Fractional ownership allows companies that have never before used business aircraft to experience many of the advantages of business aviation quickly and without typical start-up considerations associated with traditional flight departments. It also allows existing flight departments to supplement their current aircraft when needed.

Today's business aircraft are quieter, more efficient, and safer than ever before. Much like computers, business aircraft are powerful business tools that can make a company more profitable by enabling it to make better use of its most valuable assets—time and personnel.

Personal Flying. All flying that is not common carrier for hire, business flying, or commercial flying, as defined to this point, is **personal flying**. Personal transportation by air is not economically regulated; a personal plane is like a personal car. When the owner (or renter) uses a car or plane for a business trip, it becomes a business automobile or a business aircraft. But there is no way to tell whether a car or an airplane is being used for business or for pleasure simply by looking at it. A multimillionaire may own a large airplane as a purely private conveyance, with no business use. However, because the majority of privately owned (as distinguished from company-owned or corporate-owned) aircraft are of the light single- or light twin-engine variety, it is appropriate to discuss this important segment of the general aviation industry at this time.

Although the range and endurance of light airplanes is well documented (for example, with Lindbergh's *Spirit of St. Louis*, a high-wing monoplane similar in size to a Cessna 180, and his Lockheed Sirius, in which he flew over the North Pole to the Orient; and with Wiley Post's Lockheed Vega), the public impression is that the planes are good only for short hops in a limited area. In the early 1950s, Bill Odom flew a single-engine Bonanza from Hawaii to Seattle nonstop, then went back to the Islands and flew the same airplane nonstop to Teterboro, New Jersey. Max Conrad flew a 125-hp Piper Pacer across the North Atlantic and back to visit his family in Europe. He also flew a Piper Comanche from Casablanca to Los Angeles nonstop. In 1959, a Cessna 172 was flown for 65 days without landing, which is equivalent to circling the world six times nonstop.

Just as automobiles and boats are used for personal transportation and recreation, personal flying is a legitimate use of the sky. An aircraft is an efficient and effective business tool, but it is also a pleasant recreational vehicle. Thousands of private pilots use their aircraft to visit friends and relatives, attend special events, and reach remote vacation spots.

These aircraft are also flown by doctors, lawyers, accountants, engineers, farmers, and small-business owners in the course of their business. Typically, such persons use their aircraft partly for business and partly for pleasure. They differ primarily from the purely business flier with respect to the type of aircraft flown. A much higher proportion of the 100,000 aircraft they fly are single-engine piston aircraft.

A number of organizations represent the interests of the business and pleasure flier; by far the most important is the **Aircraft Owners and Pilots Association (AOPA)**. This organization, headquartered in the Washington, D.C. area, includes approximately 384,915 members, who own about 70 percent of the active general aviation aircraft in the United States. In addition to its function as congressional liaison, the AOPA provides a variety of services for its members, many of which are designed to enhance air safety.

Instructional Flying. Instructional flying accounted for roughly 12,800 aircraft in 2012. This category includes any use of an aircraft for purposes of formal instruction, either with the instructor aboard or when the student is flying solo but is carrying out maneuvers according to the instructor's specifications. Close to 90 percent of the aircraft used for instruction are of the single-engine type.

Obtaining a private pilot's license for business or personal reasons is the primary goal for many students. Others use it as a stepping stone to an airline or military aviation career. Most people learn to fly through a local **fixed-base operator (FBO)**. FBOs provide fuel and service, and they also rent and sell airplanes. They usually have a professional flight instructor on staff who provides ground and flight instruction. Many individuals also learn to fly through a local flying club that offers flight training. Such clubs are made up of groups of individuals who own aircraft and rent them to members. They usually offer flight instruction and other flying-related activities to their members. In addition, many vocational and technical schools, colleges, and universities offer aviation programs that include flight training.

Commercial and Industrial Aviation. The remaining aircraft use categories are broken down as follows:

1 *Aerial Application*. Any use of an aircraft for work purposes related to the production of foods and fibers for health control measures, in which the aircraft is replacing farm implements or ground vehicles for the particular task accomplished. This includes fire-fighting operations and the distribution of chemicals or seeds in agriculture, reforestation, and insect control. Approximately 3,600 aircraft are used for **aerial application**. The majority are single-engine piston aircraft.

2 The use of aircraft in agriculture is a major factor in the production of food and fiber all over the world. The Japanese, Russians, and Chinese are spending huge amounts of money to apply fertilizers, to spread seeds in inaccessible locations, to control pests, and to harvest crops using aircraft. Although the public image of crop dusters is that they are flying daredevils who operate flimsy crates and pollute the environment, the fact is that aviation is a major factor in the production of cotton, vegetables, and beef (by seeding and fertilizing grazing lands) and in the eradication of pests, such as the fire ant, the screw worm, and the gypsy moth. But it is also an expensive business. These specially designed aircraft, such as the Cessna Ag Truck and Ag Husky, cost in excess of $150,000 each. Needless

to say, the operators, many of whom have fleets of as many as 50 aircraft, are involved in big business, requiring bank loans for equipment renewal, which, in turn, requires insurance coverage. But if the business was as hazardous as many think it is, no banker or insurance company would deal with it.

3 The air-dropping of chemicals and fire-retardant slurry by aircraft is a major weapon in the control of forest and brush fires from the pine woods of New Jersey to the Florida Everglades, and from the forests of the Big Sky country to the hills of southern California. This aviation specialty is seldom seen by most members of the public.

4 Resort operators have found that the spraying of light oils and suspensions by aircraft (as distinguished from agricultural use of similar aircraft) has enhanced their business by eliminating the irritations of small flying insects. In addition to eliminating a nuisance, aerial application of pesticides has been highly effective in controlling, and in many cases eliminating, diseases transmitted by insects, such as malaria.

5 *Aerial observation.* Any use of an aircraft for aerial mapping or photography, survey, patrol, fish spotting, search and rescue, hunting, or highway traffic advisory not included under FAR Part 135. Over 5,300 aircraft are included under this category.

6 Land use planners, real estate developers, beach erosion engineers, businesspeople seeking new industrial sites, and public officials and highway designers all use photographs taken from aircraft in their deliberations.

7 Commercial fishing fleets have found that their operations are more productive and profitable when they can be directed to concentrations of fish schooling far from the shore. Therefore, the use of light aircraft for that purpose has evolved to become an integral part of the fishing industry.

8 Major metropolitan police departments have found that road patrols by aircraft are a highly effective means of monitoring the flow of traffic during morning and evening rush hours and apprehending lawbreakers. Most police air patrols are performed in aircraft leased from general aviation operators.

9 Another specialized service usually performed on a contract basis is flying at very low levels along public utility rights of way to inspect the integrity of energy lines and to check for transformer failures, broken insulators, short circuits, or line breaks. Inspection by air is frequently the only economical means of performing such service.

10 *Aerial other.* Approximately 800 aircraft fall into other aerial pursuits such as aerial advertising, weather modification, and wildlife conservation.

11 On the basis of "cost per thousand," key words in the advertising business, a towed banner or a message written in smoke over a city will draw a larger audience for the cost than any other form of advertising. A banner towed over a sports stadium or along a hundred miles of crowded beach is seen by more people than a similar message

carried for the same price in any other communication medium. A sky message written over Manhattan on a clear day can be seen by 10 million people at one time. Aerial advertising is a highly specialized—but very lucrative—part of commercial aviation.

12 Weather modification and wildlife conservation functions of commercial aviation are usually performed on a contract basis and require special expertise. The creation of both rainfall in arid regions and snow in ski resort areas has been accomplished recently. The Fish and Wildlife Service retains commercial operators to survey herd and flock movements and to count the size of herds, as well as to air-drop food when natural forage is unavailable.

It is impossible to assign a specific value to these commercial aviation operations. However, without them, we would pay far more for clothing, fibers, and food products. Similarly, the protection of natural resources, land planning, and disease and pest control are important, but their value is difficult to compute in dollars.

Sightseeing, Air Tours, and Air Taxi. Aircraft flown for the purpose of *sightseeing and air tours* totalled over 1,700 in 2019. Sight-seeing includes flying conducted under FAR Part 91, whereas air tours are conducted under FAR Part 135 (see Table 5.2). More than one-half of the sightseeing flights are made in lighter-than-air aircraft. The majority of air tours are conducted in rotorcraft and lighter-than-air aircraft. *Air tours* flown over widely diverse areas such as the Florida Keys or the Grand Canyon have become very popular with tourists.

Air taxi or charter firms serve as on-demand passenger and all-cargo operators. This category covers all types of aircraft, including single- and multi-engine piston and turbine aircraft and rotorcraft operating under FAR Part 135. The great advantage of the on-call air taxi or charter operator is its flexibility.

Chartering an airplane is similar to hiring a taxi for a single trip. The charterer or air taxi operator provides the aircraft, flight crew, fuel, and all other services for each trip. The charteree pays a fee, usually based on mileage or time, plus extras such as waiting time and crew expenses. Using an air taxi is particularly attractive for a firm that requires an airplane only infrequently or seldom needs a supplement to its own aircraft. Firms will also charter when they need a special-purpose aircraft, such as a helicopter.

As commercial operators, air taxi firms must conform to more stringent operating and maintenance requirements. In addition, each air taxi or charter operator, regardless of the type of airplanes used, must have an air taxi certificate on file with the FAA. This certificate is issued by the FAA after proper application procedures have been followed, the plane has been inspected, and certain minimum insurance coverages and limits have been obtained.

External Load and Medical. External load includes aircraft under FAR Part 133. The majority of aircraft under this category are rotorcraft used for external load operations, such as hoisting heavy loads and hauling logs from remote locations. If it were not for general aviation aircraft, primary helicopters that transport heavy, expensive drilling equipment, as well as people, day and night, good weather and bad, America's dependence on foreign oil would be far greater and would surely impact negatively on the American consumer.

The *medical* category is also dominated by helicopters, which represent more than 50 percent of the aircraft flown to carry people or donor organs for transplant. There are times when the American Red Cross needs to transport emergency supplies to disaster victims or blood of rare types or in large quantities. The entire medical emergency evacuation process was changed when state and local governments began establishing "MEDEVAC" units to respond to critically injured persons such as those involved in auto accidents. The survival rate in life-threatening injuries is greatly enhanced when a person can be transported quickly to nearby hospitals. There are over 1,100 aircraft used in the external load and medical categories.

Other Flying. The final category of general aviation craft includes a wide variety of over 6,200 single-engine and multi-engine aircraft used for purposes not included under the other categories. Examples include aircraft used for research and development, testing, demonstration, and government purposes.

Close to one-third of the aircraft in this category are government aircraft. These aircraft, most of which were designed for civilian use, log millions of hours a year on government business. Agencies and departments such as Agriculture, Commerce, Energy, the EPA, Health and Human Services, Interior, Justice, State, Transportation, Treasury, NASA, and TVA use aircraft to perform a wide variety of tasks, including:

Aerial photography
Agricultural application
Drug interdiction
Fire fighting
Flight inspection
Law enforcement
Pollution control
Powerline and pipeline patrol
Scientific research and development
Search and rescue
Surveying
Transportation of government personnel

Airports

Actually, the term *general aviation airport* is a common misnomer. All airports are general aviation airports, including those used by the certificated air carriers, which are sometimes referred to as "air carrier airports."

In addition, many airports that are not certificated for air carrier service may be used by air carrier charter flights if the facilities are adequate. Or, to put it another way, air carriers may use so-called general aviation airports as well.

The FAA issues an annual report on landing facilities in the United States and its possessions. As of 2022, the gross number of aircraft landing facilities was given as 19,542 (see Table 5.3). However, this figure is not restricted to airports but includes other forms of landing facilities not used by conventional aircraft, such as heliports, STOLports (short-takeoff-and-landing airports), and seaplane bases. It also includes airports located on American Samoa, Guam, and U.S. Trust Territories.

Private-Use Airports. **Private-use airports** are those that are not open to the general public but are restricted to use by their owners and the invited guests of the owners on an exclusive-use basis. Such airports are comparable to private roads or driveways.

Public-Use Publicly Owned Airports. There are 5,211 **publicly owned airports** in the United States, ranging in size from the enormous Dallas–Fort Worth and JFK layouts to the small grass fields owned by local communities. All of these airports may be used by light general aviation aircraft. Fliers intending to use any airport can consult government or industry publications to ascertain its capacity and equipment.

An airport owned by a government body can usually be regarded as permanent and stable, particularly if federal funding has been obtained for improving the facilities.

Public-Use Privately Owned Airports. It is estimated that close to 40 percent of the **public-use privately owned airports** in the United States are not permanent; they disappear from the roster of available landing places because of economic, political, or personal reasons. The disappearance of public-use privately owned airports is a matter of deep concern to the entire general aviation industry, because once an airport is lost, it can never be

Table 5.3 Number of U.S. Airports

Number of U.S. Airports	2021
TOTAL Airports	20,061
Public Use, total	5,211
Private Use, total	14,850
Military Owned	313
Certificated, total	519
General Aviation, total	19,542

Top 10 U.S. GA Airports Ranked by Itinerant Operations, 2021

Rank	Airport	State
1	Van Nuys (VNY)	CA
2	Phoenix Deer Valley (DVT)	AZ
3	Centennial (APA)	CO
4	Ernest A. Love Field (PRC)	AZ
5	Long Beach Daugherty Field (LGB)	CA
6	Portland-Hillsboro (HIO)	OR
7	Phoenix-Mesa Gateway (IWA)	AZ
8	Falcon Field (FFZ)	AZ
9	Grand Forks International (GFK)	ND
10	Gillespie Field (SEE)	CA

Top 20 U.S. Airports Ranked by Passenger Operations, 2021

Rank	Airport	State
1	Hartsfield-Jackson Atlanta International (ATL)	GA
2	Los Angeles International (LAX)	CA
3	Chicago O'Hare International (ORD)	IL
4	Dallas-Fort Worth International (DFW)	TX
5	Denver International (DEN)	CO
6	John F. Kennedy International (JFK)	NY
7	San Francisco International (SFO)	CA
8	McCarran International Airport (LAS)	NV
9	Seattle-Tacoma International (SEA)	WA
10	Charlotte Douglas International (CLT)	NC
11	Orlando International (MCO)	FL
12	Miami International (MIA)	FL
13	Phoenix Sky Harbor International (PHX)	AZ
14	Newark Liberty International (EWR)	NJ
15	George Bush International (IAH)	TX
16	St. Paul International (MSP)	MN
17	Boston Logan International (BOS)	MA
18	Detroit Metropolitan Wayne County (DTW)	MI
19	Fort Lauderdale-Hollywood International (FLL)	FL
20	Orlando Executive Airport (ORL)	FL

Sources: NBAA, www.faa.gov

replaced. Without ready access by air to a community, the transportation utility of aircraft is seriously eroded.

FAA Services

The most widely used service provided by the FAA to general aviation pilots is the **flight service station (FSS)** network of 75 facilities for collecting and disseminating weather information, filing flight plans, and providing in-flight assistance and aviation advisory services. This figure includes automated flight service stations. Air carriers have their own meteorological service, and their instrument flight plans are prefiled by computer. (These are called "canned" flight plans.) General aviation flight plans are filed individually via FSS facilities.

Flight service stations are the sole means of general aviation's filing of flight plans, which are required under actual instrument conditions but are optional in good weather. They are the sole source from which to obtain legal weather information, either in person (face-to-face briefings) or by telephone or, when airborne, by air/ground radio communications.

The FSS system is vital to general aviation operations, and it is used by pilots at every level, from student pilots to air transport-rated pilots of large business jets. Flight service stations are indispensable to all general aviation flight operations.

Whenever there is an active control tower in an airport, all traffic is required to comply with its direction of aircraft in flight and on the ground. However, not all airports (to be accurate, not all air carrier-served airports) have control towers. There are 680 airports in the United States with traffic control towers. With the exception of the major hubs that serve large metropolitan areas, general aviation is the primary user of the tower-controlled airports.

The busier tower-controlled airports have an additional facility to ensure the safe and expeditious movement of air traffic: radar. Many civil airports have terminal radar approach control (TRACON), and military airport radar facilities are also available to general aviation pilots who operate in the areas of their coverage. When using airports with such equipment, the majority of general aviation pilots use radar assistance because it is available, and in some cases, required.

Another service available to all fliers is the en route air traffic control complex, which consists of 24 air route traffic control centers (ARTCCs). These centers provide radar air traffic separation service to aircraft operating on instrument flight plans within controlled airspace. No aircraft may operate when the visibility or ceiling falls below prescribed limits unless an instrument flight plan has been filed under instrument flight rules (IFR). Air carrier aircraft, particularly those operated by certificated air carriers, operate under instrument flight rules all the time, no matter how good the actual weather may be, as a matter of course. General aviation pilots who are instrument qualified, or instrument "rated," tend to file instrument flight plans only when they must fly in adverse weather.

THE GENERAL AVIATION SUPPORT INDUSTRY

The economies of all businesses require interrelated and carefully balanced relationships among three players: the manufacturers, the service industry, and the users. The small size of general aviation makes this "triangle" exceptionally vulnerable because, in comparison with, say, the automobile industry, the market is so limited in terms of the number of units. Only a relatively small reduction in the flow of goods and money can wreak havoc throughout the industry.

The Manufacturers

Approximately 15 U.S. airframe manufacturers are involved in designing and constructing light (or small) and large aircraft for the various segments of general aviation. The number of aircraft these manufacturers produce varies greatly, from 17,811 units in 1978 to as few as 2,646 in 2020 (see Table 5.1). The export market also experienced a long recessionary period. Exports typically represent about one-third of total aircraft shipments.

Beginning in 1979, general aviation aircraft shipments steadily declined. The decline in aircraft sales has been accompanied by a decrease in the number of student and private pilots. Between 1979 and 2005, the number of individuals holding a student pilot certificate declined from 210,180 to 87,213 and the number of private pilots declined from 343,276 to 228,619. By 2021, the number of private pilots decreased to 161,459 resulting in a pilot shortage challenge for the U.S. aviation industry. As of 2021, there were a total of 720,605 active airmen certificates held including student, recreational, sport, private, commercial, airline transport, rotorcraft, and glider pilots compared to 610,576 in 2012.

The failure of the industry to respond to the economic recovery of the mid-1980s, which was one of the most robust in the past 50 years, was puzzling. Historically, the economic cycle of the general aviation industry has clearly paralleled that of the national economy. Possible reasons for the industry's slump were discussed in the section "Factors Affecting General Aviation," earlier in this chapter.

In any case, a number of steps were taken to reverse the downward trend in sales. One of the most significant was the passage of the General Aviation Revitalization Act, which would curtail product liability suits. Also, there has been an industrywide effort to promote the use of general aviation aircraft for business purposes and to increase the number of student starts. "No Plane, No Gain" is a joint NBAA/GAMA advocacy program to actively promote business aviation. This innovative program taps all segments of the media to identify, document, and disseminate the benefits of business aviation. In 1996, AOPA and GAMA invited all general aviation businesses, associations, and organizations to join in a new industry alliance to attract new pilots, called "GA Team 2000." Unlike previous efforts, this program targeted new pilots based on research completed by GAMA's Piston-Engine Aircraft Revitalization Committee (PEARC) in 1995 and strategic planning by AOPA earlier that same year. Renewing the pipeline of new pilots is the keystone on which all other industry revitalization needs will build. Many analysts believe that increasing the industry's current number of student starts from about 50,000 a year in the late 1990s to at least 100,000 is needed to re-establish a healthy pilot base and, at the same time, to create demand for a new fleet of piston-powered airplanes.

Following passage of the General Aviation Revitalization Act of 1994, manufacturers resumed production of existing popular designs, incorporating upgraded airframe, engine, and avionics technology. The result is overall improvement of the perceived value of new aircraft, offsetting higher purchase prices in the eyes of prospective buyers. Today's piston-engine aircraft fleet has an average airframe age of 28 years, and one-fourth of the fleet is over 35 years old.

Renewed research and development and improved certification regulations aimed at replacing this outdated technology base has already brought advanced systems like electronic ignitions to market. Also, the NASA-sponsored Advanced General Aviation Transportation Experiment (AGATE) is well under way. The wide-ranging AGATE program involves a joint research consortium with broad manufacturer participation and cost sharing. Its primary goals are to improve small piston-engine aircraft cockpit displays and integration, icing prevention and avoidance systems, engine controls, manufacturing methods, and pilot training methods.

Although there is some diversification in the industry (such as military contracts and military/industrial subcontracts with major military/air carrier manufacturers), the financial health of the manufacturers requires a sales volume equal to the manufacturing volume over the long run, or else surplus inventories build up and production must be curtailed in accordance with good business practice. Of course, there are other segments of the general aviation industry besides the airframe manufacturers, such as manufacturers of engines, avionics (aviation communications and navigation radio equipment), flight instruments, and autopilots, all of which are used only in aviation and are directly affected by any diminution in the sales rate of aircraft. However, this subject is not within the scope of this book.

Tables 5.4, 5.5, and 5.6 show the general aviation aircraft in production and usually available in the United States. The economy slowed by the end of 2000 and went into a recession in 2001. Shipments declined in 2001 as a result of the recessionary economy and the tragic events surrounding September 11, 2001. By 2006, aircraft orders picked up over 2001 with many industry experts claiming the industry was getting "back on track." Despite positive growth in the early 2000s, the industry faced a steep decline in aircraft production in 2007, 2008, 2009, and 2010, but the industry picked up from 2011–2014. Between 2014 and 2021, general aviation aircraft production remained fairly stagnant in the piston, turboprop, and jet-engine markets.

Table 5.4 Worldwide Piston-Engine Airplane Shipments by Manufacturer, 2004–2021

	2004	2005	2006	2007	2008	2009	2010	2011	2012	2013	2014	2015	2016	2017	2018	2019	2020	2021
Adam Aircraft	**0**	**2**	**4**	**3**	**0**	**0**	**0**	**0**	**0**	**0**	**0**	**0**	**0**	**0**	**0**	**0**	**0**	**0**
A500	-	2	4	3	-	-	-	-	-	-	-	-	-	-	-	-	-	-
Air Tractor	**n/a**	**n/a**	**n/a**	**n/a**	**n/a**	**n/a**	**n/a**	**n/a**	**1**	**0**	**1**	**1**	**0**	**1**	**0**	**0**	**0**	**0**
AT-401B	n/a	n/a	n/a	n/a	n/a	n/a	n/a	n/a	1	0	1	1	0	1	0	0	0	0
Alpha Aviation	**0**	**0**	**5**	**13**	**1**	**0**	**0**	**0**	**0**	**0**	**0**	**0**	**0**	**0**	**0**	**0**	**0**	**0**
120T	-	-	-	2	-	-	-	-	-	-	-	-	-	-	-	-	-	-
160A	-	-	5	9	1	-	-	-	-	-	-	-	-	-	-	-	-	-
160Ai	-	-	-	2	0	-	-	-	-	-	-	-	-	-	-	-	-	-
American Champion	**94**	**89**	**60**	**70**	**54**	**26**	**37**	**29**	**18**	**26**	**30**	**19**	**19**	**15**	**13**	**10**	**14**	**20**
7EC Champ	-	-	1	21	7	1	0	3	0	3	1	1	2	-	-	-	-	-
7ECA Citabria Aurora	2	3	2	4	3	2	2	1	0	0	2	1	0	0	2	0	0	0
7GCAA Citabria Adventurer	12	12	6	6	2	1	2	0	0	0	0	0	0	0	2	0	0	0
7GCBC Citabria Explorer	24	26	16	8	8	4	4	6	3	1	3	0	1	2	1	1	2	4
8GCBC Scout	18	9	14	8	10	8	15	13	7	6	7	6	10	8	5	6	8	11
8KCAB Super Decathlon	38	39	21	23	24	10	14	6	8	10	14	6	6	5	3	3	4	5
8KCAB Xtreme Decathlon	-	-	-	-	-	-	-	-	-	6	3	5	0	0	0	0	0	0

(Continued)

Table 5.4 (Continued)

	2004	2005	2006	2007	2008	2009	2010	2011	2012	2013	2014	2015	2016	2017	2018	2019	2020	2021
Aviat Aircraft	**42**	**47**	**0**	**0**	**0**	**0**	**0**	**0**	**0**	**0**	**0**	**0**	**0**	**0**	**0**	**0**	**0**	**0**
A-1B Husky	30	41	n/a	n/a	n/a	n/a	n/a	n/a	n/a	n/a	n/a	n/a	n/a	n/a	n/a	n/a	n/a	n/a
Husky Pup	3	1	n/a	n/a	n/a	n/a	n/a	n/a	n/a	n/a	n/a	n/a	n/a	n/a	n/a	n/a	n/a	n/a
S-2C Pitts	9	5	n/a	n/a	n/a	n/a	n/a	n/a	n/a	n/a	n/a	n/a	n/a	n/a	n/a	n/a	n/a	n/a
AVIC General	**0**	**0**	**0**	**0**	**0**	**0**	**0**	**0**	**0**	**0**	**0**	**0**	**26**	**22**	**14**	**12**	**14**	**13**
Y5B	n/a	n/a	n/a	n/a	n/a	n/a	n/a	n/a	n/a	n/a	n/a	n/a	4	5	4	2	7	10
LE500	n/a	n/a	n/a	n/a	n/a	n/a	n/a	n/a	n/a	n/a	n/a	n/a	11	5	0	0	6	3
A2C	n/a	n/a	n/a	n/a	n/a	n/a	n/a	n/a	n/a	n/a	n/a	n/a	11	12	10	10	1	0
Columbia Aircraft (prev. Lancair)	**78**	**114**	**185**	**152**	**0**	**0**	**0**	**0**	**0**	**0**	**0**	**0**	**0**	**0**	**0**	**0**	**0**	**0**
Columbia 300	-	-	-	-	-	-	-	-	-	-	-	-	-	-	-	-	-	-
Columbia 350	28	25	39	34	-	-	-	-	-	-	-	-	-	-	-	-	-	-
Columbia 400	50	89	146	118	-	-	-	-	-	-	-	-	-	-	-	-	-	-
Cirrus Aircraft	**553**	**600**	**721**	**710**	**549**	**266**	**264**	**255**	**253**	**276**	**308**	**301**	**317**	**355**	**380**	**384**	**347**	**442**
Cirrus SR20	91	116	150	112	115	28	42	48	84	32	31	31	35	46	65	53	56	81
Cirrus SR22	459	475	565	588	427	238	165	105	81	112	117	128	133	135	135	131	107	131
Cirrus SR22T	-	-	-	-	-	-	57	102	88	132	160	142	149	174	180	200	184	230
Cirrus SRV	3	9	6	10	7	-	-	-	-	-	-	-	-	-	-	-	-	0

CubCrafters	**n/a**	**n/a**	**n/a**	**n/a**	**n/a**	**n/a**	**n/a**	**47**	**58**	**63**	**60**	**52**	**34**	**27**	**19**	**16**	**9**	**50**
CC11-100 Sport Cub S2	n/a	n/a	n/a	n/a	n/a	n/a	n/a	2	0	2	0	0	0	1	-	-	-	-
CC11-160 Carbon Cub SS	n/a	n/a	n/a	n/a	n/a	n/a	n/a	38	57	52	53	47	24	6	3	3	5	-
CC18-180 Top Cub	n/a	n/a	n/a	n/a	n/a	n/a	n/a	7	1	9	7	5	2	6	7	5	2	-
CC19-180 XCub	-	-	-	-	-	-	-	-	-	-	-	-	8	14	9	8	2	-
Carbon Cub LSA & E-AB	-	-	-	-	-	-	-	-	-	-	-	-	-	-	-	-	-	23
Xcub/NX Cub E-AB	-	-	-	-	-	-	-	-	-	-	-	-	-	-	-	-	-	17
CC19 XCub/ NXCub	-	-	-	-	-	-	-	-	-	-	-	-	-	-	-	-	-	10
Daher (prev. SOCATA EADS)	**5**	**9**	**0**	**0**	**0**	**0**	**0**	**0**	**0**	**0**	**0**	**0**	**0**	**0**	**0**	**0**	**0**	**0**
TB-9 Tampico	0	1	-	-	-	-	-	-	-	-	-	-	-	-	-	-	-	-
TB-10	3	4	-	-	-	-	-	-	-	-	-	-	-	-	-	-	-	-
TB-20	0	1	-	-	-	-	-	-	-	-	-	-	-	-	-	-	-	-
TB-21	2	3	-	-	-	-	-	-	-	-	-	-	-	-	-	-	-	-
TB-200	0	0	-	-	-	-	-	-	-	-	-	-	-	-	-	-	-	-

(Continued)

Table 5.4 (Continued)

	2004	2005	2006	2007	2008	2009	2010	2011	2012	2013	2014	2015	2016	2017	2018	2019	2020	2021
Diamond Aircraft	**261**	**329**	**438**	**471**	**308**	**163**	**130**	**185**	**156**	**139**	**202**	**144**	**132**	**137**	**134**	**233**	**239**	**240**
HK-36	-	-	-	-	-	13	10	3	3	1	0	1	-	-	-	-	-	-
DA-20	58	54	55	58	69	14	31	40	32	14	16	22	20	8	3	0	8	23
DA-40	203	207	220	232	154	98	57	72	93	102	136	75	48	60	45	126	143	122
DA-42	-	68	163	181	85	38	32	70	28	22	50	44	34	36	50	77	62	55
DA-50	-	-	-	-	-	-	-	-	-	-	-	-	-	-	-	-	-	7
DA-62	-	-	-	-	-	-	-	-	-	-	-	2	30	33	36	30	26	33
Discovery Aviation (prev. Liberty)	**0**	**2**	**29**	**38**	**33**	**13**	**14**	**3**	**0**	**0**	**0**	**0**	**0**	**0**	**0**	**0**	**0**	**0**
XL2	-	2	29	38	33	13	14	3	0	-	-	-	-	-	-	-	-	-
Extra Aircraft	**n/a**	**n/a**	**n/a**	**n/a**	**n/a**	**n/a**	**n/a**	**n/a**	**27**	**29**	**31**	**27**	**27**	**25**	**24**	**25**	**22**	**22**
EA300	n/a	n/a	n/a	n/a	n/a	n/a	n/a	n/a	27	29	31	27	27	25	24	25	22	22
Flight Design GmbH	**n/a**	**n/a**	**n/a**	**n/a**	**n/a**	**n/a**	**n/a**	**89**	**76**	**89**	**88**	**59**	**23**	**32**	**43**	**63**	**38**	**41**
F2	-	-	-	-	-	-	-	-	-	-	-	-	-	-	-	-	2	6
ASTM CT Series	n/a	n/a	n/a	n/a	n/a	n/a	n/a	89	76	89	88	59	23	32	43	63	36	35
ICON Aircraft	**0**	**0**	**0**	**0**	**0**	**0**	**0**	**0**	**0**	**0**	**0**	**0**	**5**	**10**	**44**	**41**	**22**	**18**
A5	-	-	-	-	-	-	-	-	-	-	-	-	5	10	44	41	22	18
Mahindra Aerospace (prev. GippsAero)	**20**	**22**	**20**	**17**	**19**	**11**	**14**	**10**	**14**	**12**	**17**	**14**	**9**	**9**	**7**	**12**	**2**	**0**
Airvan 8	20	22	20	17	19	11	14	10	14	12	17	14	9	9	7	12	2	0

Maule Air Incorporated	**25**	**27**	**38**	**36**	**27**	**7**	**4**	**4**	**9**	**6**	**2**	**13**	**3**	**0**	**0**	**0**	**0**	**0**
M-4-180A, V	-	1	7	5	-	-	-	-	-	-	1	-	-	-	-	-	-	-
M-7-235, A, B, C	8	11	8	6	7	1	3	-	1	-	1	-	1	n/a	n/a	n/a	n/a	n/a
M-7-260, C	3	4	2	4	4	4	-	1	3	4	-	-	1	n/a	n/a	n/a	n/a	n/a
MT-7-235	1	2	9	2	6	2	-	-	1	-	-	-	-	-	-	-	-	-
MT-7-260	0	2	4	-	-	-	-	-	-	-	-	-	-	-	-	-	-	-
MX-7-180, A, B, C, AC	5	3	4	6	4	-	1	1	1	1	-	12	1	n/a	n/a	n/a	n/a	n/a
MXT-7-160	-	-	-	-	-	-	-	-	-	-	-	-	-	-	-	-	-	-
MXT-7-180, A, AC	8	4	4	12	6	-	-	2	3	-	-	-	-	-	-	-	-	-
M-8-235	-	-	-	1	-	-	-	-	-	-	-	-	-	-	-	-	-	-
M-9-235	-	-	-	-	-	-	-	-	-	1	-	1	-	n/a	n/a	n/a	n/a	n/a
Mooney International Corporation	**37**	**85**	**75**	**79**	**65**	**19**	**2**	**0**	**0**	**0**	**1**	**11**	**7**	**7**	**14**	**9**	**0**	**0**
M20M Bravo	9	20	5	1	-	-	-	-	-	-	-	-	-	-	-	-	-	-
M20R Ovation	-	-	-	-	-	-	-	-	-	-	-	-	-	-	-	-	-	-
M20R Ovation 2	28	65	63	20	21	4	0	0	0	0	0	3	1	2	-	-	-	-
M20U Ovation Ultra	-	-	-	-	-	-	-	-	-	-	-	-	-	1	7	2	0	0
M20S Eagle 2	-	-	-	-	-	-	-	-	-	-	-	-	-	-	-	-	-	-

(Continued)

Table 5.4 (Continued)

	2004	2005	2006	2007	2008	2009	2010	2011	2012	2013	2014	2015	2016	2017	2018	2019	2020	2021
M20TN Acclaim	-	-	7	58	44	15	2	0	0	0	1	8	6	1	-	-	-	-
M20V Acclaim Ultra	-	-	-	-	-	-	-	-	-	-	-	-	-	3	7	7	0	0
Pacific Aerospace Corporation	**0**	**0**	**0**	**0**	**0**	**0**	**0**	**0**	**0**	**0**	**0**	**0**	**0**	**0**	**0**	**1**	**1**	
CT/4E Airtrainer	6	-	-	-	-	-	-	-	-	-	-	-	-	-	-	-	-	-
E-350 Explorer	-	-	-	-	-	-	-	-	-	-	-	-	-	-	-	-	1	1
Piper Aircraft, Inc.	**163**	**193**	**189**	**168**	**216**	**61**	**135**	**104**	**126**	**154**	**136**	**111**	**93**	**108**	**173**	**246**	**201**	**161**
PA-28-161 Warrior III	18	37	19	27	23	8	23	15	20	2	3	20	5	0	0	0	-	-
PA-28-181 Pilot 100i	-	-	-	-	-	-	-	-	-	-	-	-	-	-	-	-	11	38
PA-28-181 Archer III	19	16	29	16	7	1	21	2	4	48	45	25	42	72	107	182	149	89
PA-28R-201 Arrow IV	12	9	5	8	1	0	4	0	2	1	8	5	7	9	7	0	3	0
PA-32-301FT Piper 6X	24	18	10	12	0	-	-	-	-	-	-	-	-	-	-	-	-	-
PA-32-301XTC Piper 6XT	14	16	11	-	-	-	-	-	-	-	-	-	-	-	-	-	-	-
PA-32R-301 Saratoga II HP	9	8	10	-	-	-	-	-	-	-	-	-	-	-	-	-	-	-
PA-32-301T Saratoga II TC	31	37	37	39	12	-	-	-	-	-	-	-	-	-	-	-	-	-
PA-34-220T Seneca V	10	12	26	22	27	7	22	21	17	22	10	8	3	1	2	3	1	0

PA-44-180 Seminole	11	29	11	14	24	5	16	16	22	23	22	17	10	17	37	40	22	15
PA-46-350P Malibu Mirage/ M350	15	11	31	30	21	7	26	33	49	42	37	34	26	9	20	21	15	19
PA-46R-350T Matrix	-	-	-	-	101	33	23	17	12	16	11	2	-	-	-	-	-	-
Pipistrel	**0**	**0**	**0**	**0**	**0**	**0**	**0**	**0**	**0**	**0**	**0**	**0**	**0**	**19**	**22**	**24**	**30**	**74**
SW 121 Virus	-	-	-	-	-	-	-	-	-	-	-	-	-	19	22	24	17	26
SW 128 Velis Electro	-	-	-	-	-	-	-	-	-	-	-	-	-	-	-	-	13	48
Quartz Mountain Aerospace	**0**	**0**	**0**	**0**	**11**	**0**	**0**	**0**	**0**	**0**	**0**	**0**	**0**	**0**	**0**	**0**	**0**	**0**
QMA 11E	-	-	-	-	11	-	-	-	-	-	-	-	-	-	-	-	-	-
SONACA Aircraft	**0**	**0**	**0**	**0**	**0**	**0**	**0**	**0**	**0**	**0**	**0**	**0**	**0**	**0**	**2**	**8**	**19**	**19**
Sonaca 200	-	-	-	-	-	-	-	-	-	-	-	-	-	-	2	8	19	19
Symphony Aircraft (prev. OMF)	**1**	**10**	**5**	**0**	**0**	**0**	**0**	**0**	**0**	**0**	**0**	**0**	**0**	**0**	**0**	**0**	**0**	**0**
Symphony 160	1	10	5	-	-	-	-	-	-	-	-	-	-	-	-	-	-	-
TECNAM Aircraft	**n/a**	**n/a**	**n/a**	**n/a**	**n/a**	**n/a**	**n/a**	**n/a**	**n/a**	**197**	**190**	**191**	**191**	**171**	**180**	**205**	**154**	**203**
ASTM - LSA	n/a	n/a	n/a	n/a	n/a	n/a	n/a	n/a	n/a	108	108	102	73	72	63	60	46	75
P2002JF	n/a	n/a	n/a	n/a	n/a	n/a	n/a	n/a	n/a	33	18	20	33	20	18	21	8	6
P92JS	n/a	n/a	n/a	n/a	n/a	n/a	n/a	n/a	n/a	15	7	4	7	3	3	3	0	0

(Continued)

Table 5.4 (Continued)

	2004	2005	2006	2007	2008	2009	2010	2011	2012	2013	2014	2015	2016	2017	2018	2019	2020	2021
P2002JR	n/a	n/a	n/a	n/a	n/a	n/a	n/a	n/a	n/a	2	-	-	-	-	-	-	-	-
P2008JC	n/a	n/a	n/a	n/a	n/a	n/a	n/a	n/a	n/a	19	36	24	24	19	35	39	40	41
P2006T	n/a	n/a	n/a	n/a	n/a	n/a	n/a	n/a	n/a	20	21	21	32	39	41	40	22	28
P2010P Twenty Ten	-	-	-	-	-	-	-	-	-	-	-	20	22	18	20	34	22	36
P2012 Traveller	-	-	-	-	-	-	-	-	-	-	-	-	-	-	-	8	16	17
Textron Aviation (Beechcraft)	**93**	**99**	**118**	**111**	**103**	**56**	**51**	**54**	**36**	**70**	**72**	**41**	**45**	**36**	**34**	**22**	**20**	**0**
Beechcraft Bonanza A/G36	62	71	80	73	63	36	22	24	12	35	32	23	25	13	15	7	12	0
Beechcraft Baron B/G58	31	28	38	38	40	20	29	30	24	35	40	18	20	23	19	15	8	0
Textron Aviation (Cessna Aircraft)	**654**	**822**	**865**	**807**	**733**	**355**	**261**	**413**	**283**	**206**	**220**	**271**	**217**	**238**	**193**	**196**	**294**	**254**
CE-162 SkyCatcher	-	-	-	-	-	1	22	168	19	-	-	-	-	-	-	-	-	-
CE-172R Skyhawk	32	37	87	133	55	16	8	26	27	-	-	-	-	-	-	-	-	-
CE-172S Skyhawk SP	204	314	322	240	228	110	77	77	113	106	155	143	100	129	129	126	241	166
CE-182T Skylane	196	241	140	161	109	58	64	40	48	13	0	33	50	46	31	33	27	38
CE-T182T Turbo Skylane	133	118	187	140	105	75	36	37	19	26	-	-	-	-	-	-	-	-

CE-206H Stationair	22	29	25	20	17	3	4	11	16	3	-	-	-	-	-	-	-	-
CE-T206H Turbo Stationair	67	83	104	111	95	46	42	53	40	37	43	51	36	40	32	37	26	50
CE-350 Corvalis	-	-	-	1	14	5	1	0	1	-	-	-	-	-	-	-	-	-
CE-240 TTx (prev. CE-400 Corvalis TTx)	-	-	-	1	110	41	7	1	0	21	22	44	31	23	1	-	-	-
Tiger Aircraft	**19**	**15**	**3**	**0**	**0**	**0**	**0**	**0**	**0**	**0**	**0**	**0**	**0**	**0**	**0**	**0**	**0**	**0**
AG-5B Tiger	19	15	3	-	-	-	-	-	-	-	-	-	-	-	-	-	-	-
WACO Classic Aircraft	**n/a**	**n/a**	**n/a**	**n/a**	**n/a**	**n/a**	**n/a**	**5**	**6**	**7**	**11**	**10**	**7**	**6**	**6**	**3**	**5**	**3**
2T-1A-2	-	-	-	-	-	-	-	-	-	1	6	6	3	1	1	1	2	1
YMF-5D	n/a	n/a	n/a	n/a	n/a	n/a	n/a	5	6	6	5	4	4	5	5	2	3	2
XtremeAir GmbH	**n/a**	**n/a**	**n/a**	**n/a**	**n/a**	**n/a**	**n/a**	**9**	**9**	**8**	**9**	**0**	**0**	**0**	**0**	**0**	**0**	**0**
XA41	n/a	n/a	n/a	n/a	n/a	n/a	n/a	4	2	2	0	n/a	n/a	n/a	n/a	n/a	n/a	n/a
XA42	n/a	n/a	n/a	n/a	n/a	n/a	n/a	5	7	6	9	n/a	n/a	n/a	n/a	n/a	n/a	n/a
Total Number of Airplanes	**2,051**	**2,465**	**2,755**	**2,675**	**2,119**	**977**	**912**	**1,207**	**1,072**	**1,282**	**1,378**	**1,265**	**1,155**	**1,218**	**1,302**	**1,509**	**1,431**	**1,561**
% Change	8.0%	20.2%	11.8%	-2.9%	-20.8%	-53.9%	-6.7%	n/a	-11.2%	n/a	7.5%	-8.2%	-8.7%	5.5%	6.9%	15.9%	-5.2%	9.1%
Total Billings for Airplanes ($M)	**692**	**805**	**857**	**897**	**945**	**442**	**415**	**441**	**428**	**571**	**635**	**601**	**631**	**596**	**642**	**772**	**735**	**837**
% Change	27.0%	4.7%	4.7%	4.7%	5.3%	-53.1%	-7.7%	n/a	-3.0%	n/a	11.1%	-5.3%	5.0%	-5.6%	7.7%	20.3%	-4.8%	13.7%

Source: GAMA

Table 5.5 Worldwide Turboprop Shipments by Manufacturer, 2006–2021

	2006	2007	2008	2009	2010	2011	2012	2013	2014	2015	2016	2017	2018	2019	2020	2021
Air Tractor	**n/a**	**n/a**	**n/a**	**n/a**	**n/a**	**130**	**168**	**174**	**145**	**113**	**112**	**133**	**141**	**119**	**123**	**163**
AT-402A	n/a	n/a	n/a	n/a	n/a	0	1	0	0	0	4	5	8	4	5	0
AT-402B	n/a	n/a	n/a	n/a	n/a	9	21	33	20	11	10	15	25	16	17	18
AT-502A	n/a	n/a	n/a	n/a	n/a	3	1	2	1	0	8	17	25	22	19	31
AT-502B	n/a	n/a	n/a	n/a	n/a	57	81	70	61	36	22	32	29	27	21	29
AT-504	n/a	n/a	n/a	n/a	n/a	4	6	2	3	3	1	5	1	1	3	7
AT-602	n/a	n/a	n/a	n/a	n/a	10	10	18	14	14	16	7	8	10	6	12
AT-802	n/a	n/a	n/a	n/a	n/a	26	18	9	10	8	5	6	3	3	6	3
AT-802A	n/a	n/a	n/a	n/a	n/a	21	30	40	36	29	40	39	34	30	41	45
AT-802AF	-	-	-	-	-	-	-	-	-	10	3	6	5	5	1	11
AT-802F	-	-	-	-	-	-	-	-	-	2	3	1	3	1	4	7
AVIC General	**0**	**0**	**0**	**0**	**0**	**0**	**0**	**0**	**0**	**0**	**6**	**2**	**0**	**0**	**0**	**0**
Y12 Series	n/a	n/a	n/a	n/a	n/a	n/a	n/a	n/a	n/a	n/a	6	2	0	0	0	0
Daher	**42**	**46**	**60**	**36**	**38**	**38**	**38**	**40**	**51**	**55**	**54**	**57**	**50**	**68**	**53**	**68**
Kodiak 100	-	-	-	-	-	-	-	-	-	-	-	-	-	20	11	17
TBM 700	-	-	-	-	-	-	-	-	-	-	-	-	-	-	-	-
TBM 850	42	46	60	36	38	38	38	40	-	-	-	-	-	-	-	-
TBM 900	-	-	-	-	-	-	-	-	51	55	8	-	-	-	-	-
TBM 910	-	-	-	-	-	-	-	-	-	-	-	29	29	11	1	2

TBM 930	-	-	-	-	-	-	-	-	-	-	46	28	21	2	-	-
TBM 940	-	-	-	-	-	-	-	-	-	-	-	-	-	35	41	49
Epic Aircraft, LLC	**0**	**0**	**0**	**0**	**0**	**0**	**0**	**0**	**0**	**0**	**0**	**0**	**0**	**0**	**7**	**10**
E1000	-	-	-	-	-	-	-	-	-	-	-	-	-	-	7	1
E1000 *GX*	-	-	-	-	-	-	-	-	-	-	-	-	-	-	-	9
Extra Aircraft	**0**	**0**	**0**	**0**	**0**	**0**	**2**	**1**	**2**	**0**	**0**	**0**	**0**	**0**	**0**	**0**
EA500	-	-	-	-	-	-	2	1	2	-	-	-	-	-	-	-
Maule Air Incorporated	**0**	**0**	**1**	**0**	**0**	**0**	**0**	**0**	**0**	**0**	**0**	**0**	**0**	**0**	**0**	**0**
M-7-420AC	0	0	1	0	0	0	0	0	0	0	0	0	0	0	0	0
Pacific Aerospace Corporation	**5**	**10**	**15**	**12**	**11**	**10**	**10**	**6**	**4**	**5**	**8**	**7**	**11**	**6**	**1**	**0**
PAC 750XL	5	10	15	12	11	10	10	6	4	5	8	7	11	6	1	0
Piaggio Aerospace	**19**	**21**	**30**	**24**	**11**	**14**	**5**	**2**	**2**	**3**	**3**	**2**	**4**	**3**	**0**	**1**
P.180 Avanti	-	-	-	-	-	-	-	-	-	-	-	-	-	-	-	-
P.180 Avanti II	19	21	30	24	11	14	5	2	2	-	-	-	-	-	-	-
P.180 Avanti Evo	-	-	-	-	-	-	-	-	-	3	3	2	4	3	0	1
Pilatus	**90**	**98**	**100**	**105**	**84**	**69**	**67**	**69**	**76**	**74**	**100**	**86**	**83**	**83**	**82**	**90**
PC-6 Porter	n/a	6	3	5	5	6	5	4	10	4	9	1	3	0	0	2
PC-12	90	92	97	100	79	63	62	65	66	70	91	85	80	83	82	88

(Continued)

Table 5.5 (Continued)

	2006	2007	2008	2009	2010	2011	2012	2013	2014	2015	2016	2017	2018	2019	2020	2021
Piper Aircraft, Inc.	**49**	**53**	**52**	**29**	**25**	**32**	**32**	**34**	**36**	**27**	**34**	**47**	**56**	**44**	**43**	**46**
PA-46-500TP Meridian/ M500	49	53	52	29	25	32	32	34	36	27	12	12	18	20	7	7
PA-46-600TP M600	-	-	-	-	-	-	-	-	-	-	22	35	38	24	36	39
Quest Aircraft Company	**0**	**1**	**7**	**24**	**14**	**13**	**15**	**28**	**30**	**32**	**36**	**31**	**23**	**0**	**0**	**0**
Kodiak 100	-	1	7	24	14	13	15	28	30	32	36	31	23	-	-	-
Textron Aviation (Beechcraft)	**140**	**157**	**172**	**119**	**90**	**92**	**89**	**135**	**127**	**117**	**106**	**86**	**94**	**93**	**62**	**71**
King Air C90 / GTx	52	46	66	44	28	29	27	27	21	15	11	13	12	13	8	-
King Air B200 / B250 / B260	42	58	54	37	24	25	22	36	35	28	32	28	30	31	20	22
King Air 350/i/ER/B360	46	53	52	38	38	38	40	72	71	74	63	45	52	49	34	49
Textron Aviation (Cessna Aircraft)	**67**	**79**	**101**	**97**	**95**	**93**	**107**	**105**	**94**	**102**	**84**	**69**	**92**	**83**	**51**	**54**
CE-208 Caravan 675	8	11	12	12	8	10	11	11	13	9	13	10	13	12	8	12
CE-208B Grand Caravan	59	68	89	85	87	83	96	94	81	93	71	59	79	71	43	42
Thrush Aircraft, Inc.	**n/a**	**n/a**	**n/a**	**n/a**	**n/a**	**35**	**51**	**51**	**36**	**29**	**39**	**43**	**38**	**26**	**20**	**24**
S2R-T34	n/a	n/a	n/a	n/a	n/a	30	39	20	10	8	10	15	16	16	8	14
S2RHG-T65	n/a	n/a	n/a	n/a	n/a	1	0	1	0	0	2	1	1	0	0	0
S2R-T660	n/a	n/a	n/a	n/a	n/a	1	0	1	1	7	17	6	6	4	7	9

S2R-G10	n/a	n/a	n/a	n/a	n/a	3	3	2	1	0	0	0	0	0	0	0
S2R-H80	n/a	n/a	n/a	n/a	n/a	0	9	27	24	14	10	21	15	6	5	1
Viking Air Ltd.	**0**	**0**	**0**	**0**	**0**	**n/a**	**n/a**	**n/a**	**n/a**	**n/a**	**n/a**	**n/a**	**9**	**n/a**	**n/a**	**n/a**
DHC-6 Series 400 Twin Otter	-	-	-	-	-	n/a	n/a	n/a	n/a	n/a	n/a	n/a	9	n/a	n/a	n/a
Total Number of Airplanes	**412**	**465**	**538**	**446**	**368**	**526**	**584**	**645**	**603**	**557**	**582**	**563**	**601**	**525**	**442**	**527**
% Change	24.5%	12.9%	15.7%	-17.1%	-17.5%	n/a	11.0%	10.4%	-6.5%	-7.6%	4.5%	-3.3%	n/a	n/a	-15.8%	19.2%
Total Billings for Airplanes ($M)	**1,389**	**1,593**	**1,953**	**1,589**	**1,300**	**1,365**	**1,359**	**1,821**	**1,849**	**1,651**	**1,949**	**1,720**	**1,869**	**1,664**	**1,370**	**1,806**
% Change	16.9%	14.6%	22.7%	-18.7%	-18.2%	n/a	-0.4%	33.9%	1.5%	-10.7%	18.0%	-11.7%	n/a	n/a	-17.7%	31.8%

Source: GAMA

Table 5.6 Worldwide Business Jet Shipments by Manufacturer, 2005–2021

	2005	2006	2007	2008	2009	2010	2011	2012	2013	2014	2015	2016	2017	2018	2019	2020	2021
Airbus	**9**	**11**	**13**	**11**	**13**	**15**	**10**	**9**	**6**	**5**	**4**	**1**	**0**	**1**	**6**	**5**	**11**
Airbus Corporate Jet (all models)	9	10	12	9	11	-	-	-	-	-	-	-	-	-	-	-	-
ACJ318	-	-	-	-	-	2	2	2	1	0	1	0	0	0	0	0	0
ACJ319	-	-	-	-	-	8	6	6	4	1	1	0	0	0	0	-	-
ACJ319neo	-	-	-	-	-	-	-	-	-	-	-	-	-	-	2	0	2
ACJ320ceo	-	-	-	-	-	3	1	0	0	4	1	0	0	1	0	1	0
ACJ320neo	-	-	-	-	-	-	-	-	-	-	-	-	-	-	4	2	2
ACJ321	-	-	-	-	-	-	-	-	1	0	0	0	0	0	0	0	0
ACJ321neo	-	-	-	-	-	-	-	-	-	-	-	-	-	-	-	-	2
ACJ330	-	-	1	1	1	1	1	1	0	0	1	1	0	0	0	0	3
ACJ340	-	1	0	1	1	1	0	0	0	0	0	0	0	0	0	0	0
ACJ350	-	-	-	-	-	-	-	-	-	-	-	-	-	-	-	2	2
Avcraft (prev. Fairchild)	**1**	**0**	**0**	**0**	**0**	**0**	**0**	**0**	**0**	**0**	**0**	**0**	**0**	**0**	**0**	**0**	**0**
Envoy 3	1	-	-	-	-	-	-	-	-	-	-	-	-	-	-	-	-
Boeing Business Jets	**4**	**13**	**7**	**6**	**6**	**12**	**8**	**12**	**7**	**10**	**11**	**4**	**10**	**6**	**2**	**1**	**2**
Boeing Business Jet	3	12	7	3	3	4	8	2	5	3	4	1	0	2	0	0	0
Boeing Business Jet 2	1	1	0	1	0	2	0	2	1	2	1	0	0	0	0	0	0
Boeing Business Jet 3	-	-	-	2	1	4	0	0	0	0	1	0	0	0	0	0	0
Boeing Business Jet Max 7	-	-	-	-	-	-	-	-	-	-	-	-	-	0	0	0	0

Boeing Business Jet Max 8	-	-	-	-	-	-	-	-	-	-	-	-	-	2	0	1	2
Boeing Business Jet Max 9	-	-	-	-	-	-	-	-	-	-	-	-	-	0	0	0	0
Boeing 737-800	-	-	-	-	-	-	-	-	-	-	-	2	1	0	0	0	0
Boeing Business Jet 747	-	-	-	-	-	-	-	8	0	0	0	0	3	0	0	0	0
Boeing Business Jet 767	-	-	-	-	1	0	0	0	0	0	0	0	0	0	0	0	0
Boeing Business Jet 777	-	-	-	-	1	2	0	0	0	1	1	1	3	2	0	0	0
Boeing Business Jet 787	-	-	-	-	-	-	-	-	1	4	4	0	3	0	2	0	0
Bombardier	**188**	**213**	**224**	**247**	**173**	**150**	**182**	**179**	**180**	**204**	**199**	**162**	**138**	**137**	**142**	**114**	**120**
Learjet 31A	-	-	-	-	-	-	-	-	-	-	-	-	-	-	-	-	-
Learjet 40/XR	21	26	57	48	33	16	24	24	1	-	-	-	-	-	-	-	-
Learjet 45/XR	28	30								-	-	-	-	-	-	-	-
Learjet 60/XR	18	15	23	26	13	12	19	15	10	1	-	-	-	-	-	-	-
Learjet 70 / 75 / 75 Liberty	-	-	-	-	-	-	-	-	18	33	32	24	14	12	12	11	10
Challenger 300/350	50	55	51	60	33	29	37	48	55	54	68	62	56	60	76	44	44
Challenger 601	-	-	-	-	-	-	-	-	-	-	-	-	-	-	-		
Challenger 604 / 605 / 650	36	29	35	44	36	38	43	34	32	36	25	25	21	23			
Global 5000 / 5500	17	18	46	52	51	49	53	54	62	80	73	51	45	41	54	59	27
Global 6000 / 6500 / Express	13	22															

(Continued)

Table 5.6 (Continued)

	2005	2006	2007	2008	2009	2010	2011	2012	2013	2014	2015	2016	2017	2018	2019	2020	2021
Global 7500	-	-	-	-	-	-	-	-	-	-	-	-	-	1	-	-	39
CL 850/870/890	5	18	12	17	7	6	6	4	2	0	1	0	2	0	-	-	-
Cirrus Aircraft	**0**	**0**	**0**	**0**	**0**	**0**	**0**	**0**	**0**	**0**	**0**	**3**	**22**	**63**	**81**	**73**	**86**
SF50	-	-	-	-	-	-	-	-	-	-	-	3	22	63	81	73	86
Dassault Aviation	**51**	**61**	**70**	**72**	**77**	**95**	**63**	**66**	**77**	**66**	**55**	**49**	**49**	**41**	**40**	**34**	**30**
Falcon 50	-	-	-	-	-	-	-	-	-	-	-	-	-	-	-	-	-
Falcon 50EX	5	5	2	1	-	-	-	-	-	-	-	-	-	-	-	-	-
Falcon 900B	-	-	-	-	-	-	-	-	-	-	-	-	-	-	-	-	-
Falcon 900C	1	-	-	-	-	-	-	-	-	-	-	-	-	-	-	-	-
Falcon 900DX	2	4	10	4	1	3	-	-	-	-	-	-	-	-	-	-	-
Falcon 900EX	-	-	-	-	-	-	-	-	-	-	-	-	-	-	-	-	-
Falcon 900EX EASy	16	16	18	19	17	17	1	-	-	-	-	-	-	-	-	-	-
Falcon 900LX	-	-	-	-	-	4	11	7	11	8	-	-	-	-	-	-	-
Falcon 2000	6	6	1	-	-	-	-	-	-	-	-	-	-	-	-	-	-
Falcon 2000DX	-	-	-	3	1	-	-	-	-	-	-	-	-	-	-	-	-
Falcon 2000EX	-	-	-	-	-	-	-	-	-	-	-	-	-	-	-	-	-
Falcon 2000EX EASy	21	30	33	24	3	-	-	-	-	-	-	-	-	-	-	-	-
Falcon 2000LX	-	-	-	-	23	30	20	22	8	-	-	-	-	-	-	-	-
Falcon 2000LXS	-	-	-	-	-	-	-	-	3	18	-	-	-	-	-	-	-
Falcon 2000S	-	-	-	-	-	-	-	-	12	13	-	-	-	-	-	-	-

Falcon 7X	-	-	6	21	32	41	31	37	43	27	-	-	-	-	-	-	-
Falcon 2000S / 2000LXS / 900LX / 7X / 8X	-	-	-	-	-	-	-	-	-	-	55	49	49	41	40	34	30
Embraer	**20**	**27**	**36**	**38**	**122**	**145**	**99**	**99**	**119**	**116**	**120**	**117**	**109**	**91**	**109**	**86**	**93**
Phenom 100/EV	-	-	-	2	97	100	41	29	30	19	12	10	18	11	11	6	6
Phenom 300	-	-	-	-	1	26	42	48	60	73	70	63	54	53	51	10	9
Phenom 300E	-	-	-	-	-	-	-	-	-	-	-	-	-	-	-	40	47
Legacy 450	-	-	-	-	-	-	-	-	-	-	3	12	14	14	15	0	-
Legacy 500	-	-	-	-	-	-	-	-	-	3	20	21	15	9	11	1	-
Praetor 500	-	-	-	-	-	-	-	-	-	-	-	-	-	-	3	10	14
Praetor 600	-	-	-	-	-	-	-	-	-	-	-	-	-	-	13	18	17
Legacy 600/650E	20	27	36	36	18	11	13	17	21	18	12	9	7	4	5	1	-
Lineage 1000/E190 Head of State	-	-	-	-	5	5	3	2	4	3	3	2	1	0	0	0	-
Shuttles (ERJs and E-Jets)	-	-	-	-	1	3	0	3	4	0	0	0	0	0	0	0	-
Emivest (prev. Sino Swearingen)	**0**	**1**	**1**	**0**	**2**	**0**	**0**	**0**	**0**	**0**	**0**	**0**	**0**	**0**	**0**	**0**	**0**
SJ30-2	-	1	1	0	2	-	-	-	-	-	-	-	-	-	-	-	-
Gulfstream Aerospace Corporation	**89**	**113**	**138**	**156**	**94**	**99**	**99**	**94**	**144**	**150**	**154**	**121**	**120**	**121**	**147**	**127**	**119**
G100/G150 (pre. IAI Astra)	26	42	59	68	19	24	21	11	23	33	34	27	30	29	-	-	-
G200 (prev. IAI Galaxy)																	

(Continued)

Table 5.6 (Continued)

	2005	2006	2007	2008	2009	2010	2011	2012	2013	2014	2015	2016	2017	2018	2019	2020	2021
G280	-	-	-	-	-										33	22	16
G300/350/400/450 (prev. GIV/GIVSP)	63	71	79	88	75	75	78	83	121	117	120	94	90	92	-	-	-
G500/G550 (prev. GV/GVSP)																	
G500/G550 (prev. GV/GVSP), G650, G650ER																	
G500/G600/G550/G650/G650ER	-	-	-	-	-	-	-	-	-	-	-	-	-	-	114	105	103
Honda Aircraft Company	**0**	**0**	**0**	**0**	**0**	**0**	**0**	**0**	**0**	**0**	**2**	**23**	**43**	**37**	**36**	**31**	**37**
HA-420 HondaJet	-	-	-	-	-	-	-	-	-	-	2	23	43	37	36	31	37
ONE Aviation Corp. (prev. Eclipse Aero)	**0**	**1**	**98**	**161**	**0**	**0**	**0**	**0**	**0**	**12**	**7**	**8**	**6**	**0**	**0**	**0**	**0**
Eclipse 500	-	1	98	161	-	-	-	-	-	-	-	-	-	-	-	-	-
Eclipse 550	-	-	-	-	-	-	-	-	-	12	7	8	6	0	0	-	-
Pilatus	**0**	**0**	**0**	**0**	**0**	**0**	**0**	**0**	**0**	**0**	**0**	**0**	**0**	**18**	**40**	**41**	**45**
PC-24	-	-	-	-	-	-	-	-	-	-	-	-	-	18	40	41	45
Textron Aviation (Beechcraft)	**141**	**140**	**162**	**160**	**98**	**73**	**52**	**32**	**6**	**0**	**0**	**0**	**0**	**0**	**0**	**0**	**0**
Premier I/A	30	23	54	31	16	11	11	3	-	-	-	-	-	-	-	-	-
Hawker 400XP	53	53	41	35	11	12	1	-	-	-	-	-	-	-	-	-	-
Hawker 750	-	-	-	23	13	5	7	-	-	-	-	-	-	-	-	-	-
Hawker 800XP	58	8	-	-	-	-	1	-	-	-	-	-	-	-	-	-	-

Hawker 850XP	-	56	35	15	3	1	0	-	-	-	-	-	-	-	-	-	-
Hawker 900XP	-	-	32	50	35	28	22	17	-	-	-	-	-	-	-	-	-
Hakwer 1000	-	-	-	-	-	-	-	-	-	-	-	-	-	-	-	-	-
Hawker 4000	-	-	-	6	20	16	10	12	6	-	-	-	-	-	-	-	-
Textron Aviation (Cessna Aircraft)	**247**	**307**	**388**	**466**	**289**	**178**	**183**	**181**	**139**	**159**	**166**	**178**	**180**	**188**	**206**	**132**	**167**
CE-510 Citation Mustang	-	1	45	101	125	73	43	38	20	8	8	10	7	-	-	-	-
CE-525 Citation CJ1	14	-	-	-	-	-	-	-	-	-	-	-	-	-	-	-	-
CE-525 Citation CJ1+	4	25	34	20	14	3	2	-	-	-	-	-	-	-	-	-	-
CE-525 Citation M2	-	-	-	-	-	-	-	-	12	46	41	38	39	34	34	24	34
CE-525A Citation CJ2	23	1	-	-	-	-	-	-	-	-	-	-	-	-	-	-	-
CE-525A Citation CJ2+	-	36	44	56	21	17	15	19	15	2	-	-	-	-	-	-	-
CE-525B Citation CJ3	48	72	78	88	40	20	22	21	15	6	-	-	-	-	-	-	-
CE-525B Citation CJ3+	-	-	-	-	-	-	-	-	-	10	23	25	26	37	37	21	26
CE-525C Citation CJ4 Gen2	-	-	-	-	-	19	48	44	33	28	33	29	23	29	33	23	27
CE-550 Citation Bravo	21	18	-	-	-	-	-	-	-	-	-	-	-	-	-	-	-
CE-560 Citation Ultra	-	-	-	-	-	-	-	-	-	-	-	-	-	-	-	-	-
CE-560 Citation Encore	13	12	-	-	-	-	-	-	-	-	-	-	-	-	-	-	-
CE-560 Citation Encore+	-	-	23	28	5	5	4	-	-	-	-	-	-	-	-	-	-
CE-560 Citation Excel	-	-	-	-	-	-	-	-	-	-	-	-	-	-	-	-	-

(Continued)

Table 5.6 (Continued)

	2005	2006	2007	2008	2009	2010	2011	2012	2013	2014	2015	2016	2017	2018	2019	2020	2021
CE-560 Citation XLS	64	73	82	72	7	-	-	-	-	-	-	-	-	-	-	-	-
CE-560 Citation XLS+	-	-	-	8	37	22	27	31	31	22	21	19	18	21	22	13	19
CE-650 Citation VII	-	-	-	-	-	-	-	-	-	-	-	-	-	-	-	-	-
CE-680 Citation Sovereign	46	57	65	77	33	16	19	22	5	-	-	-	-	-	-	-	-
CE-680 Citation Sovereign+	-	-	-	-	-	-	-	-	8	28	18	11	9	6	8	6	3
CE-680A Citation Latitude	-	-	-	-	-	-	-	-	-	-	16	42	54	57	58	26	34
CE-700 Citation Longitude	-	-	-	-	-	-	-	-	-	-	-	-	-	-	13	18	24
CE-750 Citation X	14	12	17	16	7	3	3	6	-	-	-	-	-	-	-	-	-
CE-750 Citation X+	-	-	-	-	-	-	-	-	-	9	6	4	4	4	1	1	-
Total Number of Airplanes	**750**	**887**	**1,137**	**1,317**	**874**	**767**	**696**	**672**	**678**	**722**	**718**	**666**	**677**	**703**	**809**	**644**	**710**
% Change	0.0%	18.3%	28.2%	15.8%	-33.6%	-12.2%	-9.3%	-3.4%	0.9%	6.5%	-0.6%	-7.2%	1.7%	3.8%	15.1%	-20.4%	10.2%
Total Billings for Airplanes ($M)	**13,161**	**16,555**	**19,347**	**21,948**	**17,443**	**18,000**	**17,235**	**17,108**	**21,058**	**22,015**	**21,877**	**18,480**	**17,885**	**18,054**	**21,077**	**17,942**	**18,951**
% Change	0.0%	25.8%	16.9%	13.4%	-20.5%	3.2%	-4.2%	-0.7%	23.1%	4.5%	-0.6%	-15.5%	-3.2%	0.9%	16.7%	-14.9%	5.6%

Source: GAMA

Significance of Pilots to Aircraft Manufacturing

The significance of pilots to the growth in airframe manufacturing cannot be overstated. Traditionally, the industry has looked at pilots in two ways. First of all, as people who would learn to fly and, in some form or fashion, then buy an airplane, pilots might buy a new or used aircraft or join a flying club or rent from an FBO. In essence, however, they were purchasing the aircraft, either in total or by the hour. The manufacturers also looked at pilots as those who would fly their products for a living with the air carriers or with military, corporate, utility, agricultural, air ambulance, state, local, or federal government, or other operations.

The overwhelming majority of business aircraft sales are by companies that already own and operate an aircraft and are acquiring more capable, new equipment. The awareness of aviation—the influences that go into creating the potential for a company to use aircraft as a business tool—comes significantly from pilots. Over the years, manufacturers have recognized that one of the key indicators of aircraft usage or acquisition by a company is the presence of a pilot, even a noncurrent pilot, in the senior management ranks of a company. These advocates inside the company are often much more influential in the sales process than the manufacturers' sales and marketing staffs.

The Aviation Service Industry

All civil aircraft are directly affected by the safety regulations of the FAA, which require that repairs, maintenance, and installation of parts be done by FAA-licensed personnel. In addition, all aircraft must go through a cyclical reinspection on at least an annual basis—a function that can be carried out only by FAA-licensed mechanics and must be approved by authorized inspectors designated by the FAA.

Major air carriers have their own maintenance facilities for periodic and progressive maintenance of airframes, engines, and avionics equipment, but many local-service carriers, most commuter airlines, and all but a few major general aviation business aircraft operators rely on the services of specialized support business operations.

The Functions of FBOs. General aviation sales, service, and support operations are carried out by free-enterprise businesses that are known in the industry as fixed-base operators, or FBOs. By the very nature of the aviation business, any of these operations must be concentrated at or close to an airport, usually at one or two spots at an airport, and often while sharing the airport with air carrier and military operations. The FBOs provide the ground services and support required by general aviation and, at some locations, the major airlines and military units. They are comparable to the collocation of all automobile support services (gas station, garage, body shop, parts, sales, driver training, and so on) at one site. The following outline summarizes the operations of a typical general aviation FBO:

1 Administration of the business
2 Line services
   a Fueling
   b Sale of lubricants
3 Aircraft storage
   a Bulk hangarage
   b T-hangarage
   c Outdoor tiedowns
4 Aircraft maintenance
   a Major repairs and reconstruction
   b Minor repairs
   c Annual inspections and relicensing
5 Engine maintenance
   a Minor
   b Major
   c Remanufacture
6 Avionics
   a Sales
   b Service
      i Maintenance
      ii Recertification
7 Aircraft sales and rentals
   a New aircraft
   b Used aircraft
8 Flight instruction
   a Primary
   b Advanced
      i Instrument
      ii Multi-engine
   c Recurrent
9 Parts sales and service
   a Tires, brakes, and bearings
   b Batteries
10 Specialized commercial functions
   a Aerial application
      i Aerial advertising
      ii Utility-line surveillance
      iii Pest control

Not all FBOs perform all of these functions; indeed, some may specialize in only one or two categories. However, an FBO normally performs at least six of the functions listed, either as part of the business or by leasing space out to specialists who perform the functions on the owned (or leased) premises. An FBO, then, is like a shopping mall manager who is charged with making a profit on each of the many, widely diverse individual business operations within the orbit of the overall operation.

The Size and Scope of FBOs. As previously mentioned, over 5,000 airports are open to public use in the United States, of which approximately 800 are served by air carriers and by general aviation. Of the 4,200 airports that might be called purely general aviation airports, not all are attended (which entails at least a fueling function), and not all of those that are attended have service all the time; many are seasonally attended (summer resorts, for example), and many are attended only during daylight hours. At the same time, many of these airports offer service 24 hours a day, and many large airports have several FBOs competing for aviation business.

The best guess is that there are about 3,500 FBOs of different sizes at public-use airports in the United States. They fall into four categories.

1 *Major FBOs.* These FBOs are located at major airports and are fully equipped to handle the servicing and maintenance of all types of aircraft, from the large air carriers used by major service carriers and business corporations to single-engine aircraft. Many of the major FBOs have multi-plex operations, as do some of the medium-size FBOs, but most major FBOs have a single operations base. Some FBOs are affiliated with a franchise and operate nationally and internationally, whereas others are independently owned and operated but have a network affiliation with other independents. Some of the largest FBOs are part of a larger corporation whose interests extend beyond the FBO industry. Gross revenue exceeds $50 million, and investments in FBOs run into the hundreds of millions of dollars, including leaseholds and equipment.
2 *Medium-size FBOs.* The difference between the major and the medium-size FBOs is chiefly the size of the investment, for most medium-size operators are also located at air carrier-served airports. They must be able (by contract with the lessor) to remove and repair any aircraft that might use their facility in the event that such aircraft becomes disabled on the ramps or runways. The investment in a medium-size FBO may run as high as $50 million, and sales volumes are generally in the range of $5 million to $25 million.
3 *Small FBOs.* Of the 3,500 FBOs, approximately 2,000 fall into this category. Many of them are known in the business world as "mom-and-pop shops," doing business on a shoestring using the cash drawer system: at the beginning of the year, there is so much money in the till; during the year, some goes out and some comes in; and at the end of the year, whatever is left is profit. The vulnerability of such operations in the modern business environment should be evident.

   The vast majority of the small operators have no business training. Small FBOs are started by someone who loves aviation: an aeronautical specialist, a pilot, a mechanic, or a technician, such as an engine rebuilder or a radio expert or a sheet metal fabricator. Then the business grows to meet the increasing demands of the aviation public.

Beginning as a flight instruction or repair facility, the small FBO develops a clientele, and as the flying public learns of the operation, functions are added: fueling, hangarage, tiedowns. In a short time, the specialist becomes a generalist and blossoms out into a classic multiservice FBO, with numerous employees and increasing investments—an aviation shopping mall that the operator may not be educationally equipped to operate in a businesslike way. Because FBOs, in general, are the major contact between the manufacturers and the general public for the sale of new aircraft and for flight instruction, the small FBOs reflect a fragility in the industry that must be corrected if general aviation is to be of value to the nation.

4 *Special FBOs.* Some extremely specialized aviation operations found at public airports do not qualify as true FBOs but are nevertheless necessary to aviation. These include engine manufacturers and remanufacturers, avionics and propeller specialists, and certain flight training specialists who do nothing but recurrent flight training for professional or semiprofessional pilots of high-performance aircraft. These operations are separate from and do not compete with the true FBOs, but they fall within the category simply because they are located at the same airport.

FBOs and the Bottom Line—Profitability. As noted previously, fixed-base operators vary widely in size, scope of services offered, type of facility, size of investment, and management expertise. They may range from the small grass-field mom-and-pop shops that offer minimum services to huge complexes that service the large general aviation business jets and are located at hub airports. No matter how large or how small, they share a challenge: they must operate at a profit in a narrowly defined business, or they will go belly-up.

There can be no general aviation air transportation without a nationwide system of FBOs to support it. Not only are FBOs the interface between the manufacturers and the public, and thus the principal outlet for aircraft sales, but they also provide fueling, routine (and major) maintenance, inspection and relicensing facilities, storage, and general aviation terminal buildings. No one can plan a trip by general aviation aircraft unless such support facilities are available at both ends of the trip (at least fueling capability). FBOs are the backbone of general aviation transportation. However, many are running so close to the line of unprofitability that any reduction of their business, especially in the realm of new-and used-aircraft sales and fuel sales (the two staple sources of income for FBOs), will put them in a loss position. The same possibility exists for the large multiplex operations, despite their huge size. The problems are the same; only the numbers are larger. The advantage that the large operators have over the small ones is that they practice modern business techniques and can absorb some losses over a period of time by maintaining cash reserves, which the small operators frequently do not have.

An aspect of economic vulnerability that is seldom recognized is that of financing. Except for the very smallest FBOs, the operation of the business depends on credit and loan arrangements from commercial banks. Aircraft floor plans, equipment loans, mortgages, and construction loans run into substantial figures and substantial overhead payments. If for any reason an operator is unable to repay loans or to keep current in the obligations to the trade, to fueling suppliers, and to others, so that loans are called or turned over to creditors, the operation can disappear overnight.

There is a serious corollary to this: once a bank has been exposed to such a loss, it is justifiably leery of making subsequent loans to successor operators. A general aviation business failure affects the entire industry far more than a comparable failure of a small business in other industries, which usually are more widely distributed and require far less financing in their normal operations. Because the FBO is the economic gateway for general aviation to thousands of communities and the sole threshold for general aviation transportation, the economic impact can be enormous in the event of its business failure.

In the post-World War II era and continuing through the 1950s, 1960s, and 1970s, the number of FBOs increased dramatically. Much of the expansion of the industry after World War II can be directly related to the G.I. Bill, which provided funding for the majority of flight training that occurred throughout this period. Flight training was clearly a catalyst for growth in the industry, as newly licensed pilots created additional demand for aircraft, which increased manufacturing- and sales-related activities and, ultimately, increased demand for aircraft fueling, maintenance, and other services.

In the late 1970s and early 1980s, many nonaviation investors were overwhelmed by the attractiveness of the FBO industry. Many of these individuals lacked the operational and managerial expertise, which is typically acquired only after years of actual hands-on operating experience, required to properly meet the needs of aviation consumers. By 1980, it was estimated that more than 10,000 FBOs were operating throughout the United States. At the same time, the economy was plagued by an undesirable combination of double-digit inflation and interest rates. Additionally, during this period, the funds required to acquire and/or develop FBOs were readily available from a multitude of sources, including savings and loans, commercial banks, finance companies, and private investors. Combine this with the decline in aircraft sales beginning in 1979, and the result was a situation in which the number of FBOs far exceeded the demand. The dramatic consolidation which occurred throughout the 1980s was the result of a market desperately trying to reach a rational balance between the number of FBOs (supply) and the services and needs (demand) of aviation consumers.

With approximately 3,500 FBOs in business by 2021, the supply is approaching equilibrium with the level of demand that now exists for FBO products and services. As a result, the industry is now apparently in a position to develop and sustain rational growth and profitability.

THE AVAILABLE MARKET – THE USERS

The critical issue of aircraft and equipment sales on a constant-flow and increasing-flow basis through the dealer-distributor network eventually depends on the absorption of the product by the end users—the people who spend money to purchase such equipment. In the highly competitive new- and used-aircraft sales market (and used aircraft are relicensed annually and upgraded by equipment replacement), the fortunes of the manufacturers are largely dependent on the quality of service provided by their dealers and distributors and on the general state of the national economy.

There are two classifications of aircraft use: (1) transportation, in which the user travels from one point to another, whether for business or for pleasure, and (2) local flight, mostly for the sheer fun of flying. Flight training and certain special uses discussed earlier in the chapter really do not belong in the transportation category, nor does local flying, although the aircraft involved obviously have a transportation capability. The transportation market is our point of focus.

The Business Market

The general aviation manufacturers made the business judgment in the early 1950s to concentrate on the business market, where there is a continuing and growing need for swift, reliable transportation. Business aviation, one of the most important segments of general aviation, is made up of companies and individuals who use aircraft as tools in the conduct of their business.

Business aircraft are utilized by all types of people and companies, from individuals who often fly rented single-engine piston-powered airplanes, to sales or management teams from multinational corporations, many of which own fleets of multi-engine turbine-powered aircraft and employ their own flight crews, maintenance technicians, and other aviation support personnel.

Many large companies use business aircraft to transport priority personnel and cargo to a variety of far-flung company or customer locations, including sites overseas. Often, business aircraft are used to bring customers to company facilities for factory tours and product demonstrations. Companies and individuals, such as salespeople and doctors, use business aircraft to cover regional territories within several hundred miles of their home bases. Although the overwhelming majority of business aircraft missions are conducted on demand, some companies maintain scheduled operations, known as corporate shuttles, which are essentially in-house airlines.

Most corporations that operate business aircraft use modern multi-engine turbine-powered jets, turboprops, or turbine helicopters that are certified to the highest applicable transport category standards. Aircraft built specifically for business use vary from four-seat short-range piston-powered airplanes to two- or three-engine corporate jets that can carry up to 20 passengers nearly 7,000 miles nonstop. Some companies even use airline-type jets, such as 737s and 757s, and helicopters for business transportation.

Business aircraft operated by larger companies usually are flown by two-person professionally trained crews whose primary, if not exclusive, responsibility is to fly company aircraft. Some smaller operators of business aircraft, especially businesspeople who pilot their own aircraft, typically use one pilot to fly piston-powered machines.

Although the majority of business aircraft are owned by individuals or companies, businesses also utilize business aviation through arrangements such as chartering, leasing, fractional ownership, time-sharing, interchange agreements, partnerships, and aircraft management contracts.

Business aircraft generally are not flown for hire. Thus, the majority of U.S.-registered business aircraft are governed by Part 91 of the Federal Aviation Regulations (FARs). U.S.-registered business aircraft that can be flown for compensation are regulated by FAR Part 135, which covers on-demand commercial operations. Regardless of how business aircraft are utilized, they are chosen because they provide safe, efficient, flexible, and reliable transportation.

Of all the benefits of business aircraft, flexibility is probably the most important. Companies that fly general aviation aircraft for business purposes can control virtually all aspects of their travel plans. Itineraries can be changed instantly, and business aircraft can be flown to thousands more destinations than are served by the airlines.

Business aircraft are productivity multipliers that allow passengers to conduct business en route in complete privacy while reducing the stresses associated with traveling on commercial carriers. Passengers who fly by business aircraft never have to worry about missed connections, lost baggage, overbooking, air carrier maintenance standards, or airline security. And in recent years, business aircraft have compiled a safety record that is comparable, and sometimes superior, to that of the airlines. As the preceding discussion suggests, businesses increasingly are seeking their own transportation for a variety of reasons.

Concentration of Air Carrier Service. The United States has the finest scheduled air transportation in the world. The service points, equipment, personnel, and schedules are as excellent and as much in the public interest as it is humanly, mechanically, and economically possible to make them. But this does not alter the fact that there still exist vast voids in airline service, infrequent schedules in the majority of places served, and the necessity of using roundabout routes, with time-consuming layovers and frequent changes, unless one is traveling between the major metropolitan areas.

Increased concentration of certificated air carrier service gave rise to the commuter carriers in the early 1970s. It is simply not economically viable to service many hundreds of smaller communities with large jet equipment. In 2021, scheduled air service was provided to approximately 680 airports, with approximately 70 percent of these communities depending exclusively on regional service.

In addition, the scheduled service provided to many of the 680-odd airports is sparse and generally offered only at the most popular times of day. With a shift toward long-haul flights between primary hubs, many medium-size cities are experiencing a decrease in frequency of flights and a curtailment of nonstop service between middle hubs and major hubs. These conditions are frequently the basis for the purchase, charter, or lease of a business aircraft.

Decentralization of the Industry. The demographics of our nation are changing. Firms are decentralizing by moving or establishing facilities in parts of the country far removed from the central headquarters in order to follow the shifting sources of labor resulting from the mobility of the labor force. We are experiencing a large-scale migration of people of all ages to the Sunbelt states. The population of some metropolitan areas in southwestern states grew more than 200 percent between the last two census counts. Cities ranked in the top 20 based on population saw a radical rearrangement of rank during the ten-year period, with cities in the Sunbelt moving up on the list. This shift in population has created a need to shift marketing emphasis. All this again adds up to a need for more business travel and better communications.

Flexibility. Flexibility is the key word in business aircraft: flexibility to go when and where necessary. The key to flexibility is airport facilities. The shorter the time spent between the office and the aircraft, the greater the benefits of the business airplane. This flexibility of destinations not only serves in direct point-to-point travel but also is one factor that is making business aviation one of the biggest feeders of passengers to the airlines. More and more airline passengers are going all the way—making the whole trip—by air. Business and private airplanes feed passengers into major terminals; charter and air taxi services let long-distance jetliner passengers swiftly complete their journeys to cities hundreds of miles distant from airline stops.

Shortage of Management Personnel. The most valuable asset a company has is its human resources. In basic terms, a business's success is based on the degree to which it applies this asset to its problems and opportunities.

In a working year, each executive has only about 2,000 hours of regular working time in which to be in the right places at the right times with the right decisions. A 40-year career thus offers only 80,000 working hours. For both company benefit and personal advancement, each hour takes on precious significance.

This need to make productive use of time is a concern of all executives—seeing that they themselves, and all employees in their areas of responsibility, use their time most efficiently. Investments are made in time and motion studies to produce operating practices that achieve the most results in the least time. New equipment is obtained either to reduce the number of hours required for a certain operation or to achieve greater production in the same number of hours. Telephones and faxes are used instead of messengers and mail; calculators and computers are acquired. The business aircraft is a time machine that compresses distances into minutes and hours. It does for travel what computers, telephones, and programmed milling machines do for other areas of a company's operations.

Reliability and Capability of Today's Business Aircraft. The wide variety of business aircraft available, from single-engine piston aircraft to corporate jet, can meet almost any need a business might have: a single-engine Cirrus for a sales representative covering a tristate area, a light twin for a regional manufacturer, and a Cessna Citation for a national firm with widespread operations.

Federally regulated specifications control design engineering, method of manufacture, mechanical functions, flight operating limits, airworthiness, and maintenance standards. All systems and accessories are subject to regulation, and minimum safety standards are set for structural strength and stress. One single-engine aircraft can require over 15,000 individual inspections during manufacture. The industry's concern with building safe aircraft can best be seen in the fact that virtually all models are structurally stronger than the FAA requires. In fact, each company exceeds the FAA minimums in almost all respects. The industry has both a moral obligation and an economic self-interest in building safe aircraft—a manufacturer with a poor safety record cannot continue to exist.

The general aviation accident rates over the past 15 years attest to the reliability and capability of today's business aircraft. The accident rate per 100,000 aircraft hours flown has steadily decreased since 1972.

In short, business aviation will continue to grow because companies recognize the benefits of speed, economy, and convenience. Specific benefits of using business aircraft can be summarized as follows:

1 *Time savings.* Business aircraft not only reduce flight time by providing point-to-point service but also decrease total travel time by utilizing smaller airports closer to final destinations. Also, the office environment of a business aircraft allows travel time to become productive time.
2 *Flexibility.* People who travel by business aircraft do not have to alter their schedules to conform to those of commercial carriers. Consequently, they have the freedom to change course en route and to leave and arrive according to their own schedules.
3 *Reliability.* Business aircraft are engineered and built to the highest standards, and companies that maintain their own aircraft have complete control over the readiness of their fleets.
4 *Safety.* In recent years, business aircraft have compiled an outstanding safety record that is comparable to or better than that of the airlines.
5 *Improved marketing efficiency.* Business aircraft not only extend the reach of a sales force but also quickly and easily bring customers to the point of sale.
6 *Facilities control.* Business aircraft help management extend its control by facilitating personal visits to remote company sites.

7 *Personnel and industrial development.* The mobility that business aircraft provide company employees can accelerate training, orientation, and teamwork.
8 *Privacy and comfort.* Conversations on business aircraft are confidential, and cabins can be configured to accommodate virtually any special needs of passengers.
9 *Efficiency.* Business aviation enables a company to maximize its two most important assets: people and time.
10 *Security.* A company that uses business aviation controls all aspects of its air travel, including the visibility of its employees on sensitive missions.

Some of the intangible benefits of business aviation—enhanced management productivity and better customer relations—may be difficult to quantify, but they are no less important to a company than direct financial returns on investments.

A community with no aviation gateway for economic development is obviously at a competitive disadvantage compared to one that has one. Many studies on the economic impact of general aviation airports on communities conclude that a small town without an airport is in the same position as a community that was bypassed by a canal or railroad 100 years ago. Close proximity to an airport is always near the top of the list of prime factors a business considers when planning a major move to a particular area.

The Personal Market

As of 2021, the FAA reported 720,605 active pilots in the United States, including 161,459 private pilots, many of whom own, rent, borrow, and lease small aircraft for business and pleasure purposes (see Table 5.7).

It is easy to become caught up in the business and economic aspects of general aviation and the contribution it makes to a locality's economy and to overlook another important part of general aviation's contribution—personal flying. There is a widely held attitude that commercial airlines are a business and so are important but that personal flying is simply a frivolity. However, one must keep in mind that the certificated airlines carry almost as many people for personal and recreational reasons as they do for business purposes. On special charters, virtually all the passengers are on pleasure trips on every flight.

The flexibility of transportation offered by general aviation is not restricted to business use. By light plane it is possible for a citizen of the mid-Atlantic states or the midwest to visit the warm climate of Florida for the weekend or to fly from Montgomery, Alabama to the Canadian lakes in a few hours.

Air transportation for vacationing is unabashedly advertised by the air carriers. It should not be overlooked as an important aspect of general aviation.

Thousands of single-engine aircraft are flown within 100 miles of home on nice days—comparable to jaunts in small sailboats or on a pair of skis.

Table 5.7 Estimated Active Airmen Certificates Held as of December 31, 2021

CATEGORY	2021	2020	2019	2018	2017	2016	2015	2014	2013	2012
Pilot Total	**720,605**	**691,691**	**664,565**	**633,317**	**609,306**	**584,362**	**590,039**	**593,499**	**599,086**	**610,576**
Student 1/	250,197	222,629	197,665	167,804	149,121	128,501	122,729	120,546	120,285	119,946
Recreational (only)	85	105	127	144	153	175	190	220	238	218
Sport (only)	6,801	6,643	6,467	6,246	6,097	5,889	5,482	5,157	4,824	4,493
Airplane 2/										
Private	161,459	160,860	161,105	163,695	162,455	162,313	170,718	174,883	180,214	188,001
Commercial	104,610	103,879	100,863	99,880	98,161	96,081	101,164	104,322	108,206	116,400
Airline Transport	163,934	164,193	164,947	162,145	159,825	157,894	154,730	152,933	149,824	145,590
Rotorcraft (only) 3/	13,191	13,629	14,248	15,033	15,355	15,518	15,566	15,511	15,114	15,126
Glider (only) 4,5/	20,328	19,753	19,143	18,370	18,139	17,991	19,460	19,927	20,381	20,802
Pilot Total w/o Student Category 1/	**470,408**	**469,062**	**466,900**	**465,513**	**460,185**	**455,861**	**467,310**	**472,953**	**478,801**	**490,630**
Flight Instructor Certificates 6/	**121,270**	**117,558**	**113,445**	**108,564**	**106,692**	**104,382**	**102,628**	**100,993**	**98,842**	**98,328**
Instrument Ratings 6,7/	**317,169**	**316,651**	**314,168**	**311,017**	**306,652**	**302,572**	**304,329**	**306,066**	**307,120**	**311,952**
Remote Pilots 9/	**254,587**	**206,322**	**160,302**	**106,321**	**69,166**	**20,362**	**N/Ap**	**N/Ap**	**N/Ap**	**N/Ap**

(Continued)

Table 5.7 (Continued)

CATEGORY	2021	2020	2019	2018	2017	2016	2015	2014	2013	2012
Non Pilot—Total 8/	**733,127**	**724,307**	**714,201**	**688,002**	**671,222**	**652,943**	**728,329**	**717,399**	**707,155**	**701,291**
Mechanic 8/	313,093	306,301	301,087	292,002	286,268	279,435	342,528	341,409	338,844	337,775
Repairmen 8/	37,261	36,741	36,294	35,382	35,040	34,411	39,363	39,566	39,952	40,444
Parachute Rigger 8/	7,230	7,014	6,800	6,430	6,192	5,851	8,846	8,702	8,491	8,474
Ground Instructor 8/	74,105	71,991	69,991	67,784	66,423	65,053	70,957	71,755	72,493	73,599
Dispatcher 8/	23,835	23,286	22,598	21,465	20,664	19,758	23,754	23,113	22,401	21,862
Flight Navigator	30	36	40	58	64	67	102	115	126	141
Flight Attendant	249,043	248,742	245,699	231,355	222,037	212,607	200,319	188,936	179,531	172,357
Flight Engineer	28,530	30,196	31,692	33,526	34,534	35,761	42,460	43,803	45,317	46,639

Note: The term airmen includes men and women certified as pilots, mechanics, or other aviation technicians.

1/ In July 2010, the FAA issued a rule that increased the duration of validity for student pilot certificates for pilots under the age of 40 from 36 to 60 months.
This resulted in the increase in active student pilots to 119,119 from 72,280 at the end of 2009.
Starting with April 2016, there is no expiration date on the new student pilot certificates, which generates a cumulative increase in the numbers.

2/ Includes pilots with an airplane only certificate. Also includes those with an airplane and a helicopter and/or glider certificate. Prior to 1995, these pilots were categorized as private, commercial, or airline transport, based on their airplane certificate. In 1995 and after, they are categorized based on their highest certificate. For example, if a pilots holds a private airplane certificate and a commercial helicopter certificate, prior 1995, the pilot would be categorized as private; 1995 and after as commercial.

3/ See table 7 for the total number of pilots with a helicopter certificate.

4/ See table 8 for the total number of pilots with a glider certificate.

5/ Glider pilots are not required to have a medical examination. Beginning in 2002, glider pilots with another rating but no current medical are counted as "Glider (only)."

6/ Not included in total.

7/ Special ratings shown on pilot certificates do not indicate additional certificates.

8/ Historically, numbers represented all certificates on record. No medical examination required. In 2016, Federal Regulation required that airmen without a plastic certificate no longer be considered active. Therefore, starting with 2016, those airmen with a paper certificate only were excluded.
Data for 1996 and 1997 are limited to certificates held by those under 70 years of age.

9/ Remote pilot certification started in August 2016. These numbers are not included in the pilot totals.

N/Ap Not applicable.

Source: FAA, AOPA, GAMA

They are flown for the sheer fun of flying, not for transportation. Many pilots who start off as weekend pilots tend to upgrade into high-performance equipment, to obtain higher ratings and pilot privileges, and eventually to become business as well as pleasure air travelers in light aircraft.

EMERGING TECHNOLOGIES IMPACTING GENERAL AVIATION

Today, humans live in an age of acceleration and disruption and in many ways, the future is already here. The big question should be, "What are we going to do about it?" Emerging technologies have always been part of aviation's DNA, propelling the industry to move forward resulting in faster aircraft as one example. As we look toward the future, emerging technologies that we know of, and those that haven't been invented yet, will have significant impact in terms of experience, economics, and mindset. Examples of emerging tech include artificial intelligence (AI) and machine learning, augmented reality (AR), virtual reality (VR), big data, analytics, IT automation, Fintech, software development, connected technologies, cloud technologies, cybersecurity, quantum computing, spatial computing, block chain, cryptocurrency, and non-fungible tokens (NFTs). There is so much happening in the world of technology that it requires a separate book.

Aviation has always been a leader in the development and implementation of new technology with the military sector leading, followed by general aviation and commercial aviation. The need to transport people and goods more quickly is an area of focus including short, medium, and long-haul distances. Now, we can add space travel as the next frontier for personal and commercial transportation purposes.

Advanced Air Mobility (AAM) is a major opportunity for future transport and it is gaining attention as evidenced by the establishment of the Advanced Air Mobility Coordination and Leadership Act that authorizes the U.S. Secretary of Transportation to establish an interagency working group to plan for the advancement of operating advanced air mobility aircraft. The easiest way to explain AAM is that new types of aircraft will utilize new technologies in a diverse range of operating environments. For example, electric vertical takeoff and landing (eVTOL aircraft) are expected in city centers utilizing traditional heliports and next generation vertiports.

Next Generation Air Transportation System (NextGen) is the FAA's initiative consisting of interlinked programs, portfolios, systems, policies, and procedures to enhance flight operations within the **National Airspace System (NAS)**. NextGen incorporates radar-based surveillance and satellite monitoring of aircraft resulting in straight-line routing with decreased dependence on ground-based navigational aids. Ultimately, successful implementation of NextGen will reduce flight times meaning less fuel burn and improving environmental emissions.

The Concorde was famed for supersonic travel and, unfortunately, it ultimately failed due to high fuel consumption resulting in high costs for the aircraft operators (British Airways, Air France). Technology has come a long way since the Concorde last flew and supersonic transport aircraft are now being developed with the ability to fly higher and longer distances and at faster speeds. The challenge with supersonic technology is making it financially feasible and environmentally friendly when it comes to noise. To be classified as supersonic, the aircraft must fly faster than the speed of sound (Mach 1). **Supersonic business jets (SSBJ)** are a potential new class of small supersonic aircraft that will bring a new set of trends, challenges, opportunities, and strategies. At the time of writing, there were approximately ten manufacturing companies developing supersonic technology ranging from small to large aircraft with Boom Overture taking the lead. Boom's invention has a passenger capacity of 65 to 88, a cruising altitude of 60,000 feet, a speed of Mach 1.7, and a range of 4,250 nautical miles or 4,888 miles. Imagine flying Tokyo to Seattle in 4.30 hours instead of 8.30 hours, Paris to Montreal in 3.45 hours instead of 7.15 hours, or Los Angeles to Sydney in 8.30 hours instead of 14.30 hours. Interestingly, although the aircraft will be marketed to the business aviation and commercial aviation sectors, the first company to sign an aircraft purchase agreement was United Airlines.

Unmanned aircraft systems (UAS), often referred to as drones, are another great example of how technology will change aviation. Today, drones are widely used by military, utility companies, agriculture, construction, and search and rescue as examples. Drones are attractive because there is no need for a human pilot in the air and the technology can be controlled from the ground and, in most cases, by an individual. As UAS technology further develops, additional challenges will arrive in terms of how such aircraft technology operates within airspace as they start to transport passengers and cargo.

KEY TERMS

Advanced Air Mobility (AAM)
aerial application
Aircraft Owners and Pilots Association (AOPA)
business aircraft use
corporate aircraft use
electronic vertical takeoff and landing (eVTOL)
fixed-base operator (FBO)
flight service station (FSS)
International Council of Aircraft Owner and Pilot Associations (IAOPA)
National Airspace System (NAS)
National Business Aviation Association (NBAA)
Next Generation Air Transportation System (NextGen)
personal flying
primary-use categories
private-use airport
publicly owned airport
public-use privately owned airport

supersonic business jet (SSBJ)
unmanned aircraft systems (UAS)
Utility Airplane Council

REVIEW QUESTIONS

1 Why do the airlines seem to receive all of the attention when general aviation is actually the largest segment of aviation? Why do you think the general aviation aircraft manufacturers broke away from the A4A (formerly AIA) to form GAMA?

2 List the primary-use categories. Distinguish between business and corporate use. What is the primary role of NBAA? AOPA? Define aerial application, aerial observation, and aerial other. What is the significance of these segments of aviation to our economy? Give some examples. What type of aircraft use falls into the "other flying" category?

3 Discuss some of the factors that led to the decline in general aviation aircraft sales in the postderegulation period. What was the primary reason for the light-aircraft manufacturers discontinuing the production of single-engine piston aircraft?

4 Discuss the significance of the General Aviation Revitalization Act. How have the manufacturers responded in recent years?

5 Approximately how many airports are there in the United States? How many public-use airports? Approximately how many airports in the United States are served by the certificated and noncertificated carriers?

6 What are the primary services provided by the FAA to general aviation pilots?

7 Describe some of the steps that have been taken by the general aviation community to reverse the downward trend in aircraft sales.

8 Why is the general aviation support industry like a three-legged milk stool? Discuss the important interrelationship among manufacturers, the service industry, and users. Name six general aviation aircraft manufacturers. Why are the FBOs considered the backbone of general aviation? Describe six or seven services provided by a typical medium-size FBO. Distinguish between a large or medium-size FBO and a small mom-and-pop operator. What are some of the special FBOs at a typical public-use airport? What is the primary reason for the tremendous decline in the number of FBOs during the 1980s and early 1990s? What is happening with FBO growth in the 2000s?

9 Why did the general aviation aircraft manufacturers concentrate on developing aircraft to meet the needs of the business market as early as the 1950s? What are some of the factors that have caused businesses to seek the benefits of their own transportation? List the benefits of using business aircraft.

10 Why did the Concorde ultimately fail and what are some of the challenges expected with the modernization of supersonic transport?

From your perspective, do you think this technology will be positive or negative for the National Airspace System? Explain your answer using examples.

11 Explain what emerging technologies are and how they are changing the general aviation sector. Identify the three main emerging technologies presented in this chapter and explain how each will impact general/business aviation and commercial aviation.

PART TWO

Structure and Economics of the Airlines

CHAPTER 6

The Airline Industry

CHAPTER CHECKLIST • YOU SHOULD BE ABLE TO:

- Define *trunk*, *supplemental*, and *local-service carriers*, and describe their role in the prederegulation era
- Describe some of the problems faced by the CAB and the air carriers prior to deregulation
- Compare and contrast the major and national carriers at the time of deregulation and during the subsequent years, in terms of expansion, consolidation, and concentration
- Discuss some of the innovations pioneered by the major air carriers in the early 1980s that had a profound effect on the structure of the industry
- Explain the role of the regional carriers in the air transport system
- Describe the airline certification process and DOT reporting requirements
- Highlight the significant traffic and financial statistics during the period 1960–2021, and demonstrate the cyclical nature of the airline industry

INTRODUCTION

In Chapter 2, the airlines were referred to as a segment within the air transportation industry. This chapter deals with the airlines as a separate

DOI: 10.4324/9780429346156-8

industry. In order to avoid confusion about the term *industry*, it is best to define it at the outset.

An *industry* can be defined as a number of firms that produce similar goods and services and therefore are in competition with one another. In this sense, the airline industry is a segment or part of the broader air transportation industry. Several hundred U.S. companies engage in the carriage of persons or goods by air. Broadly defined, the airline industry consists of a vast network of routes that connect cities throughout the country, and indeed, the world. Over this network, a large number of airlines carry passengers and cargo on scheduled service. According to the U.S. Bureau of Transportation Statistics T-100 Market data, for the year 2021, air carriers transported 605,927,200 domestic passengers, 94,244,352 international passengers, for a total of 700,171,552 passengers. The reported data was significantly less than previous years due to the COVID-19 global pandemic and fortunately, at the time of writing, there was an increase in passenger demand as the airline industry showed a positive sign toward recovery. In comparison, for the year 2019, air carriers transported 811,545,260 domestic passengers, 241,435,921 international passengers, for a total of 1,052,981,181 passengers.

STRUCTURE OF THE AIRLINE INDUSTRY

Growth and Regulation

To clarify the structure of the industry at the outset, it is useful to define the industry. When the Civil Aeronautics Act was passed in 1938, only a handful of air carriers operated regular schedules over prescribed routes, and when they received government certification, they became known as *certificated route, scheduled air carriers*, a term that is used to this day. The act empowered the Civil Aeronautics Board (CAB) to structure the interstate airline industry through regulation of passenger fares, air mail rates, route entry and exit, mergers and acquisitions, and intercarrier agreements. The CAB immediately "grandfathered" the routes of 23 existing airlines, which later became known as **trunk carriers** (a term borrowed from the trunk railroads of the day). By definition, trunk carriers were airlines certified to operate on medium- and long-haul interstate routes. These carriers came under Section 401 of the board's regulations and thus were sometimes referred to as **401 carriers.** To be exempt from 401 certification, a carrier could not exceed a takeoff weight of 12,500 pounds (roughly the weight of a DC-3), which effectively limited aircraft to 19 passengers. Typically, two or three carriers provided service in a given market, although in some instances routes were covered by only one carrier. The CAB set standard fare levels to ensure cross-subsidization between profitable and unprofitable routes. Carriers were required to charge equal fares for equal distances. Cost increases were passed along to customers, and the CAB allowed the airlines to earn a reasonable rate of return.[1]

Originally, there were two general classes of common-carrier air transportation: (1) the trunk airlines, which provided scheduled service on fixed routes, and (2) small nontransport carriers, principally operating from a fixed base, which furnished service on request, without schedules. For the nonscheduled carriers, transportation services were incidental to the principal business activities of sale and service of aircraft and flight instruction.

After World War II, a number of enterprising aviation entrepreneurs purchased war surplus DC-3s (C-47s) and DC-4s (C-54s) and began to transport people and cargo for compensation or hire with no fixed routes or schedules, much in the manner of tramp steamers. These operations, usually cutthroat in the worst sense of the term, became known as nonscheduled, or "nonsked," air carriers to the public and as "large irregular air carriers" to the CAB, which was powerless to regulate them until the Civil Aeronautics Act was amended by Congress. The act was amended after World War II to create *supplemental air carriers* and *supplemental air transportation*[2] so that such operations also required certificates of public convenience and necessity. Originally designed to supplement the capacity provided by the trunk carriers, by the 1960s the **supplemental air carriers** had truly become competitive carriers, and by the 1970s the name supplemental had lost all meaning. Some carriers provided scheduled passenger and cargo services, whereas others concentrated on cargo only.

In the postwar period, there were also many feeder routes to be granted. The trunk lines claimed that they had grandfather rights (original certification) to provide such service feeding into the trunk routes, but their pleas were to no avail; the CAB chose instead to certificate a whole new level of service. The CAB assured the trunks that the feeders would be carefully watched and not permitted to provide service between the major metropolitan areas. The CAB awarded each local-service carrier a regionally centered route system that fed the trunks with additional passengers. These **local-service carriers**, which provided intrastate service to small communities, were exempt from CAB economic regulation, and many were eligible for government subsidies to cover operating losses. The charter services charged lower fares, did not operate published schedules, and were also exempt from CAB regulations.

Nineteen local-service airlines were certificated by the board between 1945 and 1951. Some of the first feeder lines, as they became known, were Allegheny (US Airways and now American); Mohawk and Lake Central (US Airways and now American); Frontier (Continental and now United); Bonanza, Southwest, and West Coast (later Hughes Airwest, later part of Republic, later part of Northwest and now Delta); North Central and Southern (later part of Republic, later part of Northwest and now Delta); Piedmont (US Airways and now American); and Ozark (which became part of TWA, which is now part of American Airlines).

During the 1950s and 1960s, subsidization of most local-service and many trunk routes continued. Local subsidy costs, exacerbated by fares deliberately set below marginal costs in accordance with the CAB formula, escalated rapidly as the local-service carriers added routes and replaced their original DC-3 aircraft with larger equipment. In an effort to reduce subsidy costs, the CAB at first shifted some low-density trunk routes to the local service carriers. When this approach failed, longer and potentially more profitable routes, often in direct competition with the trunk routes, were awarded. Despite this overlap of local-service and trunk carrier routes, the CAB largely maintained its vision of a bilevel industry. Trunk airlines served long-distance routes between major cities, while local-service carriers provided connecting service from smaller cities to trunk destinations. Consequently, many itineraries required a change of airlines. Because of poorly coordinated flight schedules, significant delays awaiting a connecting flight were common. Faced with suppressed routing and pricing options, the airlines competed on services such as meals, movies, and seating comfort.

Despite these problems, the industry grew rapidly, enjoying more than a tenfold growth in passengers between 1950 and 1970. Technological advances embodied first in the long-range DC-6 and Constellation aircraft and then in the first-generation commercial jet transports provided steady improvements in productivity. Jet transportation greatly increased the trunks' capacity levels and allowed them to schedule more frequent flights. Airlines that added capacity gained a disproportionate share of market traffic because customers were most likely to call the airline with the widest range of travel options. The purchase of new aircraft left both the trunk and the local-service carriers with weakened earnings and balance sheets, while competition intensified in the high-density markets, where business travelers sought maximum convenience. In the meantime, subsidies to the local-service carriers continued to increase. Air fares, though high, remained nominally stable but declined in real terms throughout the period. High fares, however, limited air travel to business and affluent passengers.

The industry's problems worsened during the Arab oil embargo of the 1970s. Between 1969 and 1978, fuel costs rose 222 percent (to 20 percent of operating expenses); inflation boosted labor costs (to 45 percent of operating expenses); and the stagnation of the gross national product curtailed demand growth (from 18 percent to 4 percent per annum).

Calls for regulatory reform first appeared in the early 1970s. Prohibited from competing on fares and routes, carriers responded by increasing flight frequency, lowering seating density, and adding ever more extravagant in-flight service. Anticipating continued rapid traffic growth that accompanied the introduction of jet aircraft, the major carriers placed new wide-body aircraft in service, exacerbating existing overcapacity. Load factors fell from 70 percent in 1950 to 50 percent by 1970. With the transition to jet aircraft complete, productivity gains that had cushioned the economic consequences of falling load factors slowed. The industry's financial health weakened.

The CAB responded to the deteriorating financial conditions by increasing its regulatory interventions. In addition to the ongoing denial of new carrier applications, it imposed a route moratorium on existing carriers, approved a 20 percent fare increase, and sanctioned capacity limitation agreements among the trunk carriers. These actions raised alarm outside the CAB, resulting in a consensus in government and academia that regulatory distortions imposed unacceptable burdens on the economy and society and did little to address the industry's underlying structural problems.

Sensing a winning issue, Senator Edward Kennedy held congressional hearings in 1975 sharply critical of CAB policies. Studies comparing intrastate airlines operating outside CAB control with the trunk carriers projected fares 50 to 70 percent lower if the industry was deregulated.

Deregulation

In response to the criticism, the CAB reversed its policies, beginning with the approval of new route applications. In 1977, it consented to American Airlines' request for "super saver" discounts some 45 percent below existing coach fares. When American Airlines' traffic grew as much as 60 percent in response, the solution to overcapacity seemed at hand. Other carriers quickly filed and received CAB approval for similar discounts. De facto deregulation was under way.

In 1978, now with the active encouragement of new CAB Chairman Alfred Kahn, Congress passed the Airline Deregulation Act. The act mandated that the CAB phase out its route approval authority over three years and its regulation of fares over five years, and that it pass its remaining functions to the Department of Transportation. The CAB ceased operation at the end of 1984.

MAJOR AND NATIONAL CARRIERS

That deregulation was a landmark event in the history of the U.S. airline industry is illustrated by the fact that five of the top 12 airlines of 1978, as measured by revenue passenger miles (RPMs), no longer exist (see Tables 6.1 and 6.2). Eastern (no. 4) and Braniff (no. 8) went bankrupt; Western (no. 7) was absorbed by Delta; National (no. 10) was absorbed by Pan Am; Pan Am (no. 6) broke itself up into parts, with most going to Delta and United; the remnant of Pan Am then dissolved in bankruptcy. Deregulation fueled a trend toward concentration of business with a new cluster of "megacarriers," with a number of small and midsize airlines being absorbed in the process.

The immediate consequence of deregulation was that the established carriers faced competition on many fronts. First, they competed vigorously among themselves, motivated in part by the belief that market share would determine the ultimate survivors in a restructured industry. This meant new routes and lower prices, which led to more available seat-miles but lower load factors, as capacity outstripped new passenger traffic, and to lower passenger revenue yields because of the reduced fares.

The competition within the established industry was intensified by three innovations pioneered by the major carriers in the early 1980s that collectively represent a radical change from the regulated era. Although each of the measures offered initial competitive advantage to the first movers, in the aggregate these innovations appear to have contributed to the very high volatility of industry revenues. First, airlines established "hub-and-spoke" route structures, designed to funnel traffic from outlying regions for further transit, at very high load factors, to major destinations. But hubs are very expensive to establish and maintain because of the high infrastructure costs; the high fixed costs hinder easy adjustment of route structures in response to changing patterns of demand, and the overall route structure produces more connections on long-distance routes, which is disfavored by full-fare business travelers. The hub-and-spoke structure also left the airlines vulnerable in the 1990s to low-fare carriers that fly point to point between destination city-pairs. Among other factors, the point-to-point carriers gain the advantage of higher aircraft utilization than do the hub-and-spoke carriers, which have to provide time in their schedules of long-distance routes for the arrival of feeder flights.

Second, the airlines adopted frequent-flier programs designed to enhance brand loyalty among business travelers and to exploit the differences between regional and national (or international) airlines in terms of more desirable destinations. The frequent-flier programs proved to be expensive to administer, and the potential liability of accruing free travel credits was an unwelcome overhang on an airline's financial statement. Moreover, the frequent-flier programs came to play a somewhat perverse role in the design of route structures, in which destinations were added or retained to avoid the potential loss of frequent fliers.

Third, the airlines developed sophisticated reservations systems that they used for at least two purposes: (1) to skew in their favor the display

Table 6.1 U.S. Airline Passenger Traffic for the Top 12 Air Carriers, 1978

Airline (ranked by RPMs)	Revenue Passenger Miles (millions)	Percentage of Total
United	39,399	18.46
American	28,987	13.78
Trans World	26,967	12.7
Eastern	25,183	11.86
Delta	23,332	10.99
Pan American	21,054	9.91
Western	10,188	4.8
Braniff	9,604	4.5
Continental	8,626	4.1
National	7,892	3.7
Northwest	7,018	3.3
Allegheny	4,083	1.9
Total	212,333	100.0%

Source: Air Transport Association Annual Report, June 1979

Table 6.2 Top U.S. Airlines by Market Share, 2021

2021 Rank	Carrier	2021 Market Share (percentage)
1	American	19.5%
2	Southwest	17.4%
3	Delta	16.3%
4	United	12.9%
5	Alaska	5.4%
6	JetBlue	5.3%
7	Spirit	4.9%
8	SkyWest	3.4%
9	Frontier	3.3%
10	Hawaiian	1.7%
Other	Other	9.9%
Total		100.0%

Source: www.statista.com

of scheduling information on the screens that were used in travel agents' offices, and (2) to establish yield management programs. In accumulating data about traffic patterns and demand for particular flights, airlines could engage in sophisticated price discrimination in the effort to maximize revenues. For example, based on historical information and current demand, an airline could decide seat allocations for cut-rate, advance-planning leisure travelers versus full-fare, last-minute business travelers. However, the combination of hub-and-spoke route structures and such efforts at fine-tuning led to complicated rate structures that facilitated price competition (because disciplining defectors from a particular benchmark fare was harder) and thus lowered passenger revenue yields.

The established carriers also faced competition from new entrants with significantly lower cost structures. Prominent examples in the early 1980s were People Express and New York Air, which brought an extremely low fare structure into lucrative markets in the northeast, and Southwest and Texas Air, which operated on a similar basis in the southwest. Interestingly, in 2013 a group of aviation enthusiasts and investors attempted to recreate People Express with the primary base of operations being Newport News/Williamsburg International Airport. As of mid-2014, the proposed airline start-up had not taken flight. These new entrants were not part of the industry's collective bargaining structure; they paid their employees well below the industry average, often 50 percent below industry scale, and, because of the absence of work rules, employed far fewer employees per available seat-mile.

The consequence of the dramatically changed competitive environment was financial distress for many carriers. For example, in an effort to operate on a national (and international) scale, Braniff expanded very rapidly but failed to fill seats. It went into Chapter 11 in 1982 and was liquidated shortly thereafter. An ailing Continental was taken over in a 1982 hostile tender offer by Texas Air, run by Frank Lorenzo. A year later, Lorenzo pushed Continental into Chapter 11 and, in a controversial move, voided the union contracts. Immediately thereafter, half the work force was fired and wages were cut by nearly 50 percent. Continental survived the machinists' strike that preceded the bankruptcy and the pilots' strike that followed by dramatically reducing fares. Continental was a major carrier with a well-developed route structure, and so its cut-rate fares put further pressure on industry profitability.

Thus, the airlines are an example of an industry sector subject to exogenous shocks that have undermined many of its previous ways of doing business. Not only did deregulation expose the airlines to powerful competitive forces that undermined profitability, but it also eliminated the implicit protection under government regulation against collapse and bankruptcy. As a result, the industry made a transition to a new structure in 2013 creating different classifications to define air carriers. Group III included air carriers with annual gross revenues over $1 billion. Group II included air carriers with annual gross revenue over $100 million to $1 billion. Group I included air carriers $100 million and under. Subgroups were broken down to $20 million to $100 million, and under $20 million. Today, air carrier group definitions are outlined in Figure 6.1.

FIGURE 6.1 The Structure of the Airline Industry by Carrier Group Definitions

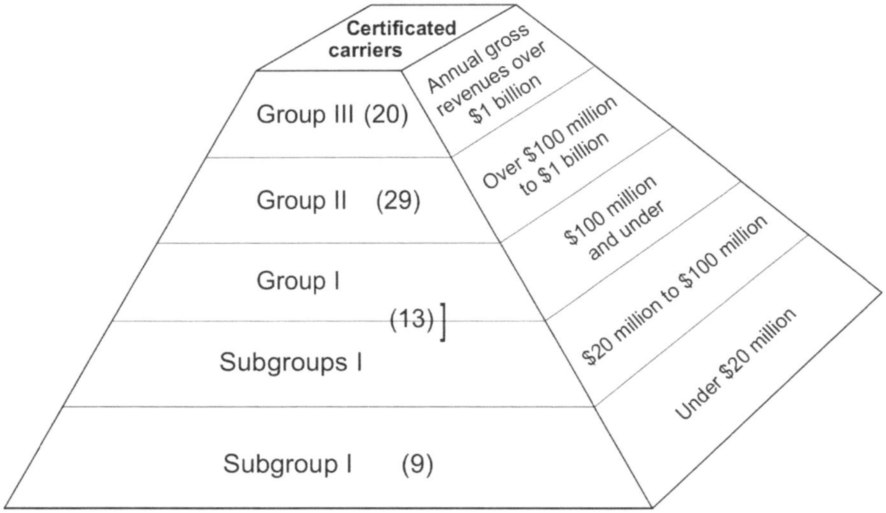

Majors: Air carriers with annual operating revenues exceeding $1,000,000,000
Nationals: Air carriers with annual operating revenues between $100,000 and $1,000,000
Large Regionals: Air carriers with operating revenues between $20,000,000 and $99,000,000
Medium Regionals: Carriers with annual operating revenues less than $19,999,999 or operating aircraft with 60 or fewer seats (18,000 pounds maximum payload)
Source: U.S. Department of Transportation

REGIONAL CARRIERS

Early Growth

Out of several thousand air taxi operators in January 1964, only 12 offered scheduled services, all to noncertificated points. By the end of 1968, there were over 200 scheduled air taxi operators. This explosive early growth in what became the regional/commuter airline industry resulted in part from the economic opportunity created by the service gap left by the withdrawing local-service carriers. Another important factor was the availability of new aircraft that were small enough to be exempt from CAB economic regulation yet large enough to carry profitable loads in scheduled short-haul operations.

Regulatory and economic changes in the 1960s improved the climate for the growth of scheduled air taxis. In 1964, the FAA promulgated Federal Aviation Regulation (FAR) Part 135, which defined the operational and safety rules of the industry. In 1965, the CAB amended its regulations to allow these carriers to transport mail and to provide service between certificated points, often as replacements for trunk or local-service airlines. In 1964, American Airlines contracted with Apache Airlines to replace it in serving Douglas, Arizona; this was the first "air taxi replacement agreement." In 1968, Allegheny Airlines (now US Airways) greatly expanded this concept by contracting its unprofitable routes to 12 independent commuters operating under the name "Allegheny Commuter"; this network continues today. The CAB officially recognized the commuter industry in 1969, defining a commuter air carrier as an air taxi operator that either (1) performs at least five round-trips per week between two or more points and publishes flight schedules that specify the times, days of the week, and origins and destinations of such flights, or (2) transports mail by air under contract with the U.S. Postal Service. By August 1978, 26 commuter airlines were providing replacement service for certificated carriers at 59 points, mostly without direct financial assistance.

During the 1970s, passenger enplanements on commuter carriers grew at an annual rate of slightly over 13 percent, compared with a 7 percent growth rate for the combined trunk and local-service airlines and a 3 percent annual growth rate in real gross national product.

As part of airline deregulation in 1979, the trunk and local-service carriers began their second stage of withdrawal from smaller communities. The commuters saw yet another opportunity to serve the traveling public and eagerly moved to provide service. Under congressional mandate, communities that stood to lose service as part of deregulation were placed under the Essential Air Service (EAS) program. As of 2014, more than 163 communities were served by the program in the continental United States, Alaska, Hawaii, and Puerto Rico.

The future of the EAS program has been the focal point of a great debate for a number of years due to the cost of government subsidization. In order for a rural community to be eligible for the EAS program, the United States Department of Transportation outlines the following (www.dot.gov/policy/aviation-policy/small-community-rural-air-service/essential-air-service):

> On August 5, 2011, the President signed the "Airport and Airway Extension Act, Part IV" (Public Law No: 112–27). That law contained a provision which prohibits the Department from providing EAS to communities whose annual passenger subsidies are greater than $1,000 per passenger, regardless of their distance from the nearest hub airport. Subsequently, the "Consolidated and Further Continuing Appropriations Act, 2012" (Public Law No: 112–55, November 18, 2011) waived the requirement that communities receive EAS on 15-seat or larger aircraft.
>
> On February 14, 2012, the President signed the "Federal Aviation Administration (FAA) Modernization and Reform Act of 2012" (Public Law No. 112–95), which contained several additional reforms. First, the law capped the communities in the 48 states plus Puerto Rico that are eligible to participate in the program. (There were no changes in Alaska or Hawaii.) The law states that only those communities that were receiving subsidized EAS at any time between September 30, 2010, and September 30, 2011, or that received a 90-day notice from their incumbent carrier and the Department of Transport would remain eligible for the program. Therefore, no new communities can enter the program should they lose their unsubsidized service. Secondly, the law requires that in order to remain in the EAS program, beginning with fiscal year 2013, subsidized communities must maintain an average of ten passenger enplanements per service day. The law provides exceptions for communities in Alaska and Hawaii, and for those that are more than 175 driving miles from the nearest large or medium hub airport.

Role of the Regional Air Carrier

Today, the regional/commuter airline segment is an integral part of the nation's air transportation system. Regional carriers provide regularly scheduled passenger or cargo service on aircraft predominantly seating fewer than 60 passengers or holding cargo with an 18,000-pound or less payload. Regionals fly pursuant to schedules published in widely used airline schedule guides.

A typical regional flight operates over a trip distance of 100 to 400 miles and at lower altitudes than flights of the long-haul carriers. Regionals operate well-timed frequent flights from outlying communities to the associated hub airports to "interline," or connect, passengers and cargo with other scheduled flights. Seventy percent of all regional passengers make such connections.

Although the growth period of regionals has been relatively short and not without problems, continuing efforts by the industry principals are playing a significant role in helping to forge an integrated and complete air transportation system. Today, nine out of every ten airports in the United States receiving scheduled air transportation are served by a regional air carrier. By year-end 2021, regionals provided frequent and timely air service to more than 600 airports. By contrast, the major airlines served more than 30 percent of the total. Interestingly, between 2006 and 2021, there was an evident decline in the number of departures by U.S. regional airline carriers, indicating mainline carriers have an increased presence and/or other modes of transportation are competing with air travel. For example, in 2020–2022, due to the COVID-19 global pandemic, technology associated with video conferencing competed heavily with air travel.

The certificated regional air carriers provide short-haul air service to small and medium-size communities across the country, typically linking those communities to the nation's larger airports in a hub-and-spoke network. This network of regional air services interconnects each city with others in the system, and the regional airline segment increasingly has become more integrated into the system.

Code Sharing

Approximately 90 percent of regional/commuter airline passengers connect to or from major airlines, saving passengers both time and money, as a result of tight marketing partnerships between regionals and majors known as *code sharing*. Today, close to 80 percent of U.S. regional/commuter carriers offer their service as part of a major airline network and, in the process, have created an integrated service, making regional/commuter airlines a vital link between small communities and the national air transportation system.

Begun as simple marketing arrangements between the majors and their regional/commuter airline partners in 1984, code sharing has developed into sophisticated liaisons that may or may not include some ownership by the major airline. Most code-sharing regional/commuter airlines adopt the paint schemes of their major counterparts. Although the majority of the code-sharing regional/commuter airlines are independently owned and operated, together with their major partners they provide improved service to the small-community passenger. These interline agreements have been attractive to the small carriers, because they offer them access to more passenger traffic, less limited airport facilities, financial support, and marketing intelligence. These marketing partnerships enable regional/commuter airline passengers to check in at their local airport, thereby avoiding long driving times and expensive parking fees. In addition, passengers can obtain boarding passes not only for their initial outbound flight but for their entire trip.

The overwhelming success of these partnerships has afforded the opportunity for regional/commuter partners to upgrade their fleets with new-generation aircraft, complete with the same avionics used by the major carriers. With this new equipment has come new industry service standards that mirror the standards passengers have come to expect from major carriers. The integration of regional/commuter and major airline schedules has also meant well-timed flights, providing fast hub-airport connections. Even for those whose destination is the hub city, regional/commuter airline service offers the out-and-back-in-one-day business trip.

These partnerships have also meant tremendous cost savings to regional/commuter airlines as their major partners assume the reservations functions, which, at the same time, increased passenger and travel agent convenience by offering one-stop shopping. In addition, code sharing means lower air fares, with many regional/commuter segments covered by a small "add-on" fare, sometimes as little as $25. Frequent fliers are also offered mileage credits as much as triple that of the 250-mile average stage length of a regional/commuter airline flight.

In addition, these marketing partnerships mean that small communities, which might otherwise not be served by major jet aircraft, become part of the major airline network. In providing that vital link, regional/commuter airline partners offer savings in both fares and overall transportation costs, frequent departures, convenient connections, and shorter business trips for those not connecting. In short, they have become an integral part of the national air transportation system.

Flight Equipment

The majority of today's regional/commuter airline fleet are prop-jet-powered. New-generation equipment affords the same or more advanced avionics and cockpit instrumentation as even the largest commercial carriers have. In 2013, 25.7 percent of the fleet were turboprop planes, and 94.3 percent were regional jets. The regional carriers continue to rely on jet aircraft for a significant portion of their service. All trends indicate regional/commuter airlines will continue to expand in size, moving from small turbo-prop aircraft to an increased focus on jet aircraft capable of flying a larger number of passengers over greater distances. However, regional/commuter airlines will continue to operate a mixed aircraft fleet as it affords the flexibility to tailor aircraft size to market and frequency needs.

Network expansion will be a key ingredient in the future success of regional/commuter airline growth. As the regional network evolves, competition between regional/commuter carriers and major carriers will increase. In some cases, regional/commuter carriers are already stepping on the toes of the majors causing great concern for both sides. There comes a point with successful regional/commuter carriers when they must decide to grow from being a big fish in a small pond to becoming a small fish in a big pond.

In 2022, according to the Regional Airline Association (RAA), the U.S. regional aircraft fleet includes 1,777 total RAA member operated aircraft—1,571 RAA member aircraft comprised of jets (88.4%), and 206 RAA member aircraft comprised of non-jets (11.6%). The average seating capacity aboard regional aircraft is 65 compared to 2011 when the average was 56, which indicates regional aircraft are increasing in size resulting in a 16 percent increase in seating capacity. The bulk of the regional aircraft fleet includes a diversified range of manufacturers including ATR (ATR-42, ATR-72), Bombardier (CRJ200, CRJ700, CRJ900, Dash 8, Dash 8 Q400), Britten-Norman (Islander), Cessna (402, Caravan, Skywagon), Embraer (E170, E175, ERJ145), Piper (Cherokee, Navajo), and Tecnam (P2012 Traveller). As of 2022, the composition of the regional airline fleet as was follows: ERJ 170/175 (40 percent), CRJ900 (17 percent), CRJ100/200 (16 percent), CRJ700 (14 percent), ERJ135/145 (13 percent).

AIRLINE STATISTICS

To fully understand the structure of the airline industry, it is important to review traffic and financial statistics, including performance measurements. Several excellent, readily available sources can provide this information in a more appropriate and timely manner than can be presented in a textbook. These include the annual reports from the Air Transport Association of America and the Regional Airline Association. Two annual FAA publications that are particularly good are the *FAA Statistical Handbook of Aviation* and *FAA Aviation Forecasts*. Another source for annual statistics and in-depth analysis of all segments of the airline industry is the June edition of *Air Transport World*. Finally, the *World Aviation Directory*, published quarterly, provides a comprehensive industry review and analysis along with statistics.

AIRLINE CERTIFICATION

Certification is the point at which regulatory authorities become involved with the business procedures of establishing a new airline. The purpose of certification is to ensure that any and all functions of an airline's operational methods and procedures are certified as safe, as defined by the regulations set forth by government agencies such as the U.S. Federal Aviation Administration (FAA) and the U.K. Civil Aviation Authority (CAA). Each country has an aviation regulation body, and each controls and regulates the safety concerns and, in some cases, economic concerns, of airlines based within its respective country.

The development of the European Union Aviation Safety Agency (EASA), headquartered in Cologne, Germany, has meant that where once countries had independent aviation regulation agencies, most European countries now fall under the certification and control of the EASA, through the authority of each individual country's regulation board. This has, in some cases, enabled common certification among most European countries.

This chapter introduces the reader to the certification process. The U.S. example will be discussed in detail, walking the reader step-by-step through the five phases of certification including: pre-application, formal application, document compliance, demonstration and inspection, and certification.

The Purpose of Certification

Aviation certification exists primarily, regardless of country, to ensure that commercial airlines, and all other operators of aircraft, meet minimum safety standards before beginning operations. Once operating, air carriers maintain their certified status under the close eye of the certificating agency.

In order to meet the requirements for certification, most countries require that minimum financial, safety-related, and ownership rules be adhered to, and requirements met. For example, the European Union (E.U.) currently caps foreign ownership on airlines to a maximum of only 49 percent of total airline equity. The same can be said of many nations. At the time of writing, the United States also imposes foreign ownership restrictions on airlines. A minimum of 75 percent of the company must be owned and controlled by U.S. citizens according to the U.S. Department of Transportation (DOT). A maximum of 25 percent of the stock (voting) of any airline based in the U.S. may be owned by companies based outside the United States. However, this may change, pending the results of ongoing negotiations between the U.S., the European Union, and other nations.

Within the European Union specifically, there are also ownership and operating laws pertaining to ownership between E.U. member countries. No more than 49 percent of an airline may be owned by a company based outside of the country in which the airline is based. Such rules apply to airlines wishing to be granted route licenses to operate services outside of the European Economic Area (EEA), plus Switzerland and the North. Airlines that are owned fully, or in the majority, by companies from outside of the specific E.U. country are restricted to operations only within the EEA and are not permitted to have route licenses for routes outside of that area.

Financial requirements exist to ensure that the carrier in question has enough financing in place to support operations for up to two years, depending on nation. In some cases, this minimum requirement may include a higher time limit. Some countries do not impose financial constraints on those airlines operating aircraft of a certain size, and some countries do not distinguish between airline sizes or types of operation.

Minimum insurance requirements exist to obtain certification. These requirements cover minimum financial values for hull and liability insurance, business insurance where applicable, and third-party damage insurance. As with financial requirements, these can differ depending on the type of certification required.

Certification enables the company to operate under an air operator's certificate (AOC) that governs safety, and an air carrier operator's license, governing all other minimum requirements. These licenses permit the carrier to fly aircraft of a certain size (or of unrestricted size, depending on the license granted) on a certain collection of routes, where applicable, or within a specified geographical area. Often, however, an operator's license cannot be acquired until an AOC has already been granted.

Types of Certification

In the United States and in much of the European Union, once an airline is certified, it is permitted to fly on any route within a given area, with any combination of route frequency and aircraft type. However, what exactly constitutes "any aircraft type" and "route frequency" can vary depending on the country and type of certification.

In the United States, for example, there are essentially two types of operational certificates under which an airline may operate – Type 14 Commercial Flight Regulation (CFR) Federal Aviation Regulations (FAR) Part 135 Commuter/non-scheduled [Charter] operations, and FAR Part 121 Scheduled operations. While both parts of the FARs enable passenger operations, some of the minimums and insurance issues vary between the two types of certificates. Air carrier certification in the U.S. is currently overseen by the **Certification Standardization and Evaluation Team (CSET)**, which standardizes the approach taken.

Per the FAA, the certification process is one of "goalposts"—where you must meet certain criteria before continuing to the next stage of certification. For example, it is necessary to obtain a "Certificate of Public Convenience and Necessity" in order to become an approved air carrier and this must be done prior to filing the formal application with the FAA.

FAR Part 121 operations are those under which most major airlines operate. These regulations require that three months (90 days) before flight departure, a legally binding schedule be published, by which the airline is legally required to abide.

In addition, FAR Part 121 certification requires the presence and declaration of five specific member positions within the team to start the airline. These positions include a director of safety, responsible for interactions with the certification board concerning safety, a director of operations, a director of maintenance dealing with all maintenance issues, a chief pilot, and a chief inspector. With proper authorization, however, it is possible to waive the requirements for such positions if the FAA deems it to be appropriate. Such waivers are, however, dependent on the size and complexity of the company structure, and such requests are filed usually at the time of formal application.

FAR Part 135 operations are those under which some commuter and non-scheduled airlines operate. These regulations were designed largely for air taxi services and charter operations and do not require the airline to operate on a previously published flight schedule. The result is that, while the operational requirements are less strict with FAR Part 135, some of those requirements – such as the maintenance issues – are actually being brought up to par with Part 121 operations. However, some benefits do exist with Part 135 operations, such as the ability, should it be necessary, to cancel flights without penalty, and remove them from operating schedules, should they exist.

As with FAR Part 121 operations, certification under FAR Part 135 requires certain people within the airline to be declared and specified on the application with certain titles. However, where FAR Part 121 certification requires five members, Part 135 requires a mandatory three, including the director of operations, director of maintenance, and chief pilot. For business purposes, however, it is likely advantageous to include other directors, along with financial experts. It is also possible, as with Part 121 operations, to obtain waivers for such necessary positions from the FAA, depending on the complexity of the operation.

In the U.K., meanwhile, under the CAA, the distinction for an air carrier operator's license is based upon the maximum aircraft size that the carrier may operate. Due to Brexit, previous bilateral aviation safety agreements between the E.U. and third country partners seized to exist effective December 31, 2020.

The Timing of Certification

Certification should be initiated once the business plan has been completed, and once financing has been secured for the venture. The reason that this should not be initiated at an earlier time is that all certification is irrelevant if financing is not available, and it is often the case that certification is not available without specific financing information already existing.

The projected time between initial application and receiving certification is between 12 and 18 months. Certification takes this long because it is necessary for all application information to be thoroughly processed. Also, the certifying body has many demands placed upon itself because it is responsible for certifying more than one airline at once.

The Certification Process

In the United States, certification is done, as a general rule, by the Flight Standards District Office (FSDO) nearest to the intended operating base of the airline at the time of its certification application. In other countries, it may be conducted by the parent aviation authority. However, the step-by-step process below concentrates on the certification process for an FAR Part 121 (Scheduled) operator within the United States.

STEP-BY-STEP U.S. CERTIFICATION BREAKDOWN

The certification process in the United States is divided into five essential parts. The first stage of this is the pre-application stage, followed by formal application, document compliance, demonstration and inspection, and, finally, certification.

Pre-application

During the pre-application phase, it is necessary to discuss with the FAA and declare exactly what types of aircraft, routes, and facilities intend to be used for operations. In addition, a meeting will take place between regulatory representatives and company officials so as to ensure that the company is fully aware of the process they must go through in order to achieve certification. It is necessary at this stage to understand completely what is involved with the formal application, so that it may be done correctly. The initial stage of application encompasses a scheduled visit to the local FSDO where potential applicants meet as a group to learn more about the certification process. The first meeting is treated very informally.

Formal Application

The formal application stage is where, once an understanding has been reached, the company officially outlines its plans. It is necessary to get all this right the first time, and responsibility for such accuracy falls solely on the shoulders of the applicant company. The paperwork required at this stage includes a formal application letter stating aims and objectives, and submission of all company manuals by which the company intends to operate. This includes standard operating procedure (SOP) manuals. The intention here is to ensure that the company meets all operating procedure minimums as set forth by the FAA. All manuals must contain specific information in order to be approved by the FAA. There are a number of consultants within the airline industry that can provide such documentation. In many cases, a consultant will take existing manuals from an FAA approved company and simply tailor the manuals to the likes of the new airline. That being said, the reader should be cautious when it comes to manual production. The management team might have someone on staff that has the ability to produce manuals in-house saving the company substantial money. If the manuals are produced externally, be sure to consult a manual expert with a good reputation and valid references. Such experts often unofficially attend pre-application meetings to introduce themselves to potential applicants.

In the United States, the **Air Transportation Oversight System (ATOS)** implements FAA policy by providing safety controls of business organizations and individuals that fall under FAA regulations. Three major functions define the oversight system including: design assessment (ensures an air carrier's operating systems comply with regulations and safety standards), performance assessment (confirms that an air carrier's operating systems produce intended results including mitigation or control of hazards and associated risks), and risk management (used to manage FAA resources according to risk-based priorities).

Document Compliance

Essentially, this is the part of the certification process where the regulatory authority will review and analyze the documents submitted as part of the formal application phase, and will assess the level to which the company follows all legal minimums, as applicable. These minimums will vary, depending on what type of carrier the company intends to operate.

Demonstration and Inspection

Some parts of this phase may overlap with parts of the previous phase. In order to ensure compliance with the minimums set forth by the FAA, it may be necessary for the company to either demonstrate some of its procedures—such as those associated with emergency evacuation techniques or cabin crew training—in order to ensure safety. During this phase of certification, the FAA has the right to show up on site unannounced and demand the air carrier perform flight operations and simulate different types of scenarios. The purpose of such action is to ensure that the company knows how to handle situations when they arise.

Formal Certification

Provided that no notably negative issues have arisen from the certification process thus far, or that all issues that have arisen have been rectified, the FAA will at this point issue a certificate that allows the company to operate. The certification provided lays down strict operating rules, depending on the type of carrier, and will ensure that the carrier can meet those requirements.

DATA COLLECTION BY THE DOT

Data collection and dissemination are the responsibility of the Bureau of Transportation Statistics (BTS), acting in cooperation with the Office of the Assistant Secretary for Aviation and International Affairs.

Air Carrier Accounting and Guidance

Carriers receiving Section 401 certificates and operating aircraft designed for a maximum passenger capacity of more than 60 seats, or a maximum payload capacity of more than 18,000 pounds, or providing service to a point outside the 50 United States, the District of Columbia, Puerto Rico, or the U.S. Virgin Islands are required to comply with the "Uniform System of Accounts and Reports for Large Certificated Air Carriers." The BTS's Office of Airline Information is responsible for accounting and related systems design and modification, as well as for interpretation of the regulations.

The BTS provides technical accounting expertise and guidance to air carriers and to other government agencies, including the Securities and Exchange Commission. The Regulations Division of the BTS also assists small air carriers participating in the Essential Air Service Program, such as air taxi operators, who may elect to implement the "Voluntary Accounting System for Small Air Carriers," and new or growing certified carriers, who may need assistance in familiarizing themselves with the required accounting systems and related rules in the Uniform System of Accounts.

The BTS continually evaluates the airline industry accounting systems and related rules and coordinates with the Office of Inspector General on the need for audit assistance.

Financial and Statistical Reporting

Air carrier reporting requirements, originally established by the CAB, continue to be in effect until changed by the DOT. Authority to maintain these rules and manage the aviation information program is delegated to the Research and Innovative Technology Administration's (RITA) Bureau of Transportation Statistics.

INDUSTRY AGREEMENTS

Regional airlines have become full partners in the air transportation system. The use of common ticket stock, shared airport facilities, commingled reservation schedules, joint fares, and interline agreements for the handling of baggage, cargo, and other express freight allows regional airlines to play an important role in an integrated system of air transportation.

Approximately half of the top 25 regionals are completely or partially owned by national or major airlines. This trend is expected to continue. Agreements between the larger carriers and regionals can be beneficial to both parties when the aim is to control a bigger share of the traffic. Few regionals have been able to develop enough of their own origination and destination (O & D) traffic to survive in today's competitive market without a partner feeding them traffic. However, as regional airlines grow, this trend is expected to change. Similarly, the larger partner benefits from having a regional carrier feeding traffic into its major hub. In a study titled "The U.S. Regional Airlines Industry to 1996—Markets, Competition and the Demand for Aircraft," the Economist Intelligence Unit of Economist Publications in New York states that the larger carriers now control, through marketing partnerships and acquisitions, three-quarters of the traffic flown by regionals.

Identification Codes and Airline Designators

Every airline that operates scheduled passenger or cargo services with other airlines requires an identification code. The code is printed as the first three digits of the airline's passenger traffic documents and cargo air waybills, and identifies that airline for interline accounting purposes.

Airlines with headquarters in the United States or its territories and possessions request a form code from the Air Transport Association. Airlines with headquarters outside the United States or its territories and possessions request the form code from the International Air Transport Association.

Each airline that operates scheduled passenger or cargo services and publishes its schedules in industry schedule guides, or that participates in the airline communications networks, such as ARINC or SITA, needs an airline designator. The two-letter airline designators are assigned and administered by IATA on behalf of the airline industry.

Publishing Schedules

The flight schedules of passenger-carrying airlines are published in the *Official Airline Guide (OAG)*, the *ABC World Airways Guide*, and the *American Express Sky Guide*; schedules of cargo-carrying airlines are published in the *OAG Air Cargo Guide*, the *ABC Air Cargo Guide*, and *Hereford's Cargo Guide*. There is no charge for publication of direct-flight schedules and fares of commuter air carriers.

Table 6.3 Selected Traffic and Financial Statistics for the Certificated Air Carriers, 1965–2021

	Traffic				Financial		
Year	**Revenue passengers (m)**	**Revenue passenger miles (bn)**	**Available seat-miles (bn)**	**Cargo ton-miles (bn)**	**Operating revenue (bn)**	**Operating expenses (bn)**	**Net profit (or loss) (m)**
1965	102.9	68.7	124.3	2.3	4.9	4.3	367.1
1966	118.1	79.9	137.8	2.9	5.7	4.9	427.6
1967	142.5	98.7	174.8	3.4	6.9	6.2	415.4
1968	162.1	113.9	216.4	4.2	7.8	7.2	209.9
1969	171.9	125.4	250.8	4.7	8.8	8.4	52.8
1970	169.9	131.7	265.1	4.9	9.3	9.2	(200.5)
1971	173.7	135.7	279.8	5.1	10.0	9.7	28.0
1972	191.3	152.4	287.4	5.5	11.2	10.6	214.8
1973	202.2	161.9	310.6	6.0	12.4	11.8	226.7
1974	207.5	162.9	297.0	6.1	14.7	13.9	321.6
1975	205.1	162.8	303.0	5.9	15.4	15.2	(84.2)
1976	223.3	178.9	322.8	6.2	17.5	16.8	563.4
1977	240.3	193.2	345.6	6.6	19.9	19.0	752.5
1978	274.7	226.8	368.7	7.0	22.9	21.5	1,196.5
1979	316.9	262.0	416.1	7.2	27.2	27.0	346.8
1980	296.9	255.2	432.5	7.1	33.7	33.9	17.4
1981	285.9	248.9	424.9	7.1	36.6	37.1	(300.8)
1982	294.1	259.6	440.1	6.8	36.4	37.1	(915.8)
1983	318.6	281.8	464.5	7.6	38.9	38.6	(188.1)
1984	344.7	305.1	515.3	8.1	43.8	41.7	824.7
1985	382.0	336.4	547.8	7.7	46.7	45.2	862.7
1986	418.9	366.5	606.4	9.0	50.5	49.2	(234.9)

	Traffic				Financial		
Year	Revenue passengers (m)	Revenue passenger miles (bn)	Available seat-miles (bn)	Cargo ton-miles (bn)	Operating revenue (bn)	Operating expenses (bn)	Net profit (or loss) (m)
1987	447.7	404.5	648.7	10.0	56.9	54.5	593.4
1988	454.6	423.3	676.8	11.5	63.7	60.3	1,685.6
1989	453.7	432.7	684.4	12.2	69.3	67.5	127.9
1990	465.6	457.9	733.4	12.5	76.1	78.1	(3,921.0)
1991	452.2	447.9	715.7	12.1	75.2	76.9	(1,940.2)
1992	475.1	478.6	752.8	13.2	78.1	80.6	(4,791.3)
1993	488-5	489.7	771.6	14.1	84.6	83.1	(2,135.6)
1994	528.8	519.4	784.3	15.9	88.3	85.6	(344.1)
1995	547.8	540.7	807.1	16.9	94.6	88.7	2,313.6
1996	581.2	578.4	834.7	17.7	101.9	95.7	2,824.3
1997	599.1	605.5	860.8	20.5	109.5	100.9	5,170.6
1998	614.2	619.4	874.1	20.4	113.3	104.0	4,894.0
1999	635.4	651.5	917.8	21.6	118.2	110.3	7,903.0
2000	666.2	692.7	956.9	23.8	130.8	123.8	2,486.0
2001	622.1	651.7	930.5	22.0	115.5	125.8	8,275.0
2002	612.9	641.1	892.5	24.6	107.0	115.5	11,312.0
2003	646.3	656.9	893.8	26.7	118.0	120.0	3,658.0
2004	697.8	731.9	968.0	28.0	131.5	132.9	9,071.0
2005	738.6	779.0	1,003.3	28.0	151.5	151.0	(27,220.0)
2006	744.7	797.4	1,006.3	29.3	165.5	157.8	18,186.0
2007	769.6	829.4	1,037.6	29.5	174.6	165.3	7,691.0
2008	743.3	812.3	1,021.3	28.3	186.1	189.4	(23,747.0)
2009	703.9	769.4	957.1	25.0	154.7	152.3	(2,528.0)
2010	720.5	798.0	972.6	27.9	174.7	164.2	3,665.0
2011	804.5	1,105.9	1,356.0	12	153.2	148.0	5,246
2012	815.3	1,132.5	1,372.7	12.3	156.4	150.4	6,003
2013	826.0	1,169.2	1,412.5	12.4	199.7	139.2	12,000.7
2014	848.1	1,207.7	1,459.9	12.7	169.3	154.6	14,000.6
2015	896.6	1,289.0	1,559.5	13.1	168.9	140.8	24,000.8
2016	932.0	1,374.3	1,667.1	13.4	169.1	143.7	14,000.0
2017	965.4	1,438.8	1,741.1	14.6	175.3	153.9	15,000.3
2018	1,013.6	1,511.7	1,822.0	15.76	187.5	169.8	11,000.8
2019	1,052.8	1,570.3	1,873.8	16.2	196.2	175.4	14,000.8
2020	369	377.8	1,898.9	17.77	77.3	123.8	(3,500.0)
2021	674	699.0	4,891.1	18.49	130.0	147.3	(2,800.0)

Source: U.S. Bureau of Transportation Statistics

Members of the ATA's Passenger Council have established the Interline Traffic Agreement. All scheduled airlines may become parties to the agreement. The agreement becomes binding between parties upon execution of a concurrence.

The agreement gives each airline party the right to sell transportation at the appropriate fares over the lines of other parties with which it has a concurrence and to issue interline tickets providing for such transportation. Parties are required to honor interline tickets issued by another party with which it has concurred. Where interline tickets have been issued under the agreement, the originating airline agrees to check the passenger's baggage to the final destination at the first stopover point, and the down-line airline agrees to accept and transport such baggage.

Interline Agreements

Interlining of air freight within the industry is an effective means of expanding air freight services to customers. The ATA has two specific air cargo agreements available to major, national, and regional carriers: the Air Freight Procedures Agreement and the Small Package Shipment Agreement. Each is a multilateral agreement that prescribes uniform documents and labeling and handling procedures for regular air freight and small-package services.

Airlines may also participate in the International Air Transport Association's multilateral interline traffic agreements as member or nonmember carriers.

Universal Air Travel Plan. Begun in 1936, the Universal Air Travel Plan (UATP) card is one of the world's oldest credit cards. During the early years, the UATP card covered only U.S. domestic airlines. It gained worldwide applicability on October 1, 1948, when international routes were brought into the plan. Today, the UATP card is good for transportation on practically all the world's scheduled airlines flying domestic and global routes. As of 2014, participating airlines now number more than 220. UATP is owned by 30 airline shareholders issued by 18 major airlines, and accepted by more than 250 merchants around the world.

Those carriers desiring to subscribe to this airline credit service can contract through an individual airline by meeting the individual carrier's requirements. Thirty-two airlines ("contracting airlines") are authorized to issue UATP cards, and the cards are honored by all participating carriers. The contracting airline bills the subscriber on a monthly basis for all air transportation used, regardless of the number of airlines involved.

Travel Agencies. As the travel agency industry grew and as travel agents began to generate a larger proportion of airline tickets, a need arose for an efficient system of reporting and accounting for ticket sales. What emerged was the Standard Agent's Ticket and Area Settlement Plan. The plan's most important innovations were a standard ticket stock and a single source to which travel agents reported and accounted for airline ticket sales. Travel agents were issued supplies of standard ticket stock with no carrier identification. In issuing a ticket, the agent fills in the name of the airline on which the seat is being sold. Every week, the travel agent forwards reports of tickets sold to a designated area bank. The agent receives a computerized sales report from the bank for each reporting period. The sales report provides important data on each ticket issued, as well as statistical summaries for the entire reporting period.

The commission paid to travel agents was deregulated in June 1980, allowing airlines to set the commission. With the Interline Settlement of Agent-Issued Documents Agreement, the ATA's Passenger Council has set up a procedure for settling interline service charges at a periodically determined commission rate.

TRAFFIC AND FINANCIAL HIGHLIGHTS: 1960–2021

The history of aviation in the second half of the 20th century is replete with cycles—an experience that is hardly unique to aviation. The aviation cycles we have observed are nothing more than exaggerated reflections of world economic activity. What distinguishes aviation from other forms of economic endeavor is the extent to which it is cyclical: the magnitude of its volatility and the curiously recurring patterns of its various cycles. That is to say, they are big, they are wide, and they tend to repeat themselves each time in a disconcertingly familiar way.

After losing close to $38 million in 1961, the industry climbed steadily upward, reaching a record profit of $427 million by 1966. The downslide reached bottom in 1970, when the industry lost $200 million. The climb back up culminated in new record profits of $1.2 billion in 1978, which were soon followed by record losses of $916 million in 1982. With the exception of 1986, which reflected severe losses by Eastern, Pan American, and TWA, profits rose during the 1980s, reaching yet another all-time high of $1.7 billion in 1988.

After a relatively profitable decade during the 1980s, the airline industry once again sustained heavy losses beginning in 1990. A recessionary economy, high fuel costs resulting from the Gulf War, and the subsequent bankruptcy of several major carriers caused losses of $13 billion for the first half of the decade. The magnitude of this unprecedented loss during the last cycle eradicated nearly a half-century's retained earnings. It placed tremendous stress on the industry's financial statements, on global capital markets, and especially on investors' portfolios. By the mid-1990s, the economy strengthened, the stock market soared, many of the weaker carriers had disappeared, and the industry reported record profits starting in 1995. In 2001, the airline industry ran into great financial trouble leading up to the events of the 9/11 terrorist attacks. These catastrophic events pushed the industry over the edge resulting in record financial losses in late 2001 and 2002. By 2006, the industry was still trying to get back to "normal" operations as a result of numerous challenges from increased cost structures. Table 6.3 highlights traffic and financial performance during this period.

By 2014, the airline industry was stabilized with many airlines reporting profits. The industry was continuing on a positive upswing due to consolidation and major restructuring plans. From 2015 to 2019, the industry experienced record levels in terms of revenue passengers flown and for the most part, air carriers were profitable resulting in aircraft fleet and route network expansion. However, toward the end of 2019, the world faced a global challenge causing the industry to essentially come to a stop and pivot in a new direction. The COVID-19 global pandemic slammed the global aviation industry, forcing air carriers into a negative spiral resulting in massive financial losses in 2020, 2021, and 2022. The actual financial damage caused will never be known and fortunately, at the time of writing, the industry was bouncing back. Cargo volumes were increasing to equivalent levels precrisis, U.S. domestic travel was essentially back to "normal" but international travel continued to take a hit worldwide. The aviation industry is resilient and experts agree that the global pandemic has forced industry and government to think differently and, despite the negative influences experienced, the industry is stronger than before and hopefully better prepared for the next global event. It is not a case of "if" but "when."

Early 1960s

Available seat-miles (ASMs) increased by 45 percent between 1960 and 1963 as more jet equipment was integrated into the airline fleets. **Revenue passenger miles (RPMs)** increased 30 percent during the same period, causing load factors to drop from a high of 63.7 in 1955 to 53.2 in 1963. By 1962, the certificated carriers reached a level of profitability, utilizing jet equipment, that was comparable to profits recorded in 1958 and 1959 principally from nonjet operations. The year 1963 was the first period of solid profitable operations in the jet age.

Late 1960s

Starting in late 1964 and continuing through the first half of 1969, the industry experienced tremendous growth. The economies of jet aircraft reduced unit costs, which enabled carriers to keep fares at about the same level during this period.

In 1965, the industry reached record-level profits and earned a comfortable 12 percent return on investments. The next year would have been just as good were it not for a strike called by the International Association of Machinists (IAM) that shut down five trunk carriers for 43 days.

ASMs increased 136 percent between 1964 and 1969, reflecting the increased capacity provided by the jet equipment. Average seats per mile doubled from 55.0 seats in 1955 to 104.4 seats in 1965. RPMs increased by 114 percent during the period from 1964 to 1969.

Air transportation came of age as more businesses and personal travelers recognized the advantages of speed, economy, and safety it provided. In 1955, first-class travel constituted 59.9 percent of airline travel, but in

1960 it fell to 45.3 percent, and in 1965 to only 21.8 percent. Forecasting that this level of growth would continue into the 1970s, the carriers placed orders of close to $10 billion for larger wide-body equipment between 1966 and 1970.

Signs of an economic downturn appeared in 1969, resulting from an overexpanded economy, which had tried to give us a "Great Society"[3] on the home front at the same time as we were fighting an ever-escalating war in Vietnam.

Early 1970s

The national economic recession that began in 1969 continued throughout 1970, which caused air traffic growth to level off. Total passenger enplanements declined for the first time in the industry's history. Inflation began to plague the airline industry at a rate of about 9 percent in 1970, almost double the national rate. The major portion of this inflationary pressure came from labor settlements, which increased airline wages by some 15 percent in 1970. The CAB kept a tight lid on fares until April 1971, when it finally granted an across-the-board increase of 6 percent, followed by another 3 percent increase later in the year.

Many carriers began cutting flight schedules to eliminate unprofitable flights and reduce uneconomic competition. This began in the second half of 1970 on a unilateral basis, and by May 1971, there were 5.2 percent fewer domestic flights.

Excess capacity, resulting from the use of wide-body jets, prompted the carriers to cancel or stretch out orders for new flight equipment, causing massive layoffs by the aircraft manufacturers. Extensive layoffs of airline employees also took place during the first two years of the 1970s, with some 12,000 people laid off in 1970 and another 10,000 in 1971.

The belt tightening continued into 1972, with carriers eliminating many extras to which the flying public had become accustomed. Gone on many flights were such amenities as free cocktails, snacks, meals at off-mealtime hours, and movies on morning flights. However, overall, things were looking up. Passenger traffic, as measured in RPMs, grew by 12.3 percent in 1972 over 1971, and cargo tonnage carried also increased over the previous year.

During 1973, the airline industry set new records. More than 200 million passengers were enplaned, total operating revenues topped $12.4 billion, and freight revenues reached the $1 billion mark for the first time. In addition, the carriers flew some 16 billion pieces of mail.

For many years, jet fuel prices had remained stable and low. Between 1967 and 1972, fuel prices rose at an annual rate of only 2.6 percent. However, prices rose 8.5 percent between 1972 and 1973, to a 1973 average of 12.8 cents a gallon, and the 1973 Arab oil embargo marked the beginning of the real fuel problem. Between 1973 and 1974, the average price rose from 12.8 cents to 24.2 cents per gallon—an increase of nearly 90 percent in a single year. By late 1974, the economy was sliding into a recession as a result of escalating fuel prices. Airline traffic fell off as businesses and individuals cut back their travel plans. The carriers implemented severe cost-cutting measures, but because of their substantial overhead capacity in facilities and equipment, they lost $84 million in 1975.

Late 1970s

Spurred by an upturn in the nation's economy in the bicentennial year of 1976, airline passenger traffic reached a new high of 223 million passengers, accounting for some 179 billion passenger miles and 6 billion ton-miles of air cargo.

An important factor in bringing air travel to millions of people was the growing role of the travel agent, which became a major part of the airline industry's marketing and sales effort. In 1976, the number of approved travel agencies in the United States and Canada rose to 13,661, up from 12,500 in 1975. U.S. travel agents sold nearly $7 billion worth of domestic and international air transportation in 1976. Airlines paid travel agents $700 million in commissions in 1976—a record 29 percent increase over 1975.

While scheduled air service remained the predominant mode of intercity passenger travel, charter activity really took off. More than 5 million passengers flew civilian and military charter flights of scheduled airlines in 1976—an increase of 25 percent over the previous year.

Again in 1977, the airlines set all-time records in service to air passengers and shippers in domestic and international operations. RPMs increased 8 percent over 1976, and the industry's load factor was 55.9, compared to 55.6 for the previous year. On the gloomy side, fuel prices averaged 36.2 cents per gallon in 1977, compared to 10.4 cents in 1967—a 248 percent increase.

The year 1978 was a major one for the carriers, with operating revenues reaching $22.9 billion and profits reaching $1.2 billion. The Airline Deregulation Act was passed by Congress in October, ushering in a new era of competition in air transportation.

The economy began to slow down in 1979, but the fierce competition for air travelers was just beginning. Revenues increased 19 percent in 1979, primarily as a result of promotional fares, which increased passenger enplanements by 15 percent. Unfortunately, expenses—most notably fuel and labor—increased by 26 percent during the latter 1970s.

Early 1980s

During 1980, ATA member airlines recorded their safest year in history. There was not a single fatality among passengers or flight crews in more than 5 million flights in the United States and throughout the world. In other respects, however, 1980 was a difficult and disappointing year for the industry. Inflation, soaring fuel prices (up more than $3 billion from 1979), and a generally sour economy resulted in a 6 percent decline in passenger enplanements—the sharpest drop in more than 50 years of scheduled air transportation.

In 1981, the trend continued in terms of safety and earnings. Carrying 286 million passengers and logging 7 billion cargo ton-miles on more than 5 million flights, the airlines completed a second consecutive year of jet service without a single passenger fatality. But financial losses mounted in 1981, caused by the recessionary economy, inflation, high interest rates, and the impact of the air traffic controllers' strike during the busy summer months. Severe price competition also contributed significantly to a record-breaking net loss.

In 1982, the industry experienced the worst financial year in its history, recording a net loss of $916 million. This net loss occurred despite a growth in passengers carried and in RPMs and approximately the same level of operating expenses as the previous year. Operating revenues declined for the first time in the history of the U.S. airline industry.

The principal reasons for the industry's poor performance in 1982 were the deep discount fares being offered by the carriers in an intensely competitive environment and the increasing proportion of passengers taking advantage of those fares. The percentage of full-fare-paying passengers fell from 52 percent in 1978 to only 15 percent in 1982.

After three years of severe financial losses totaling $1.4 billion, the industry improved significantly in 1984 with a net profit of $825 million. The economy had rebounded, and the airline industry followed the upswing with a 9 percent increase in passenger enplanements.

Late 1980s

As 1985 began, the Civil Aeronautics Board ended its notable service to the growth and maturity of air transportation. Meanwhile, the industry broke new traffic and revenue records, with net profits of $863 million being recorded.

Stimulated by the greatest ever decline in air fares, a record 419 million passenger enplanements were recorded in 1986, which compares with a 1936 total of 1 million. However, fierce price competition resulted in a net loss of $235 million for the industry and increased the pace of mergers, which reached a peak during 1986.

Optimism returned in 1987 as RPMs increased by over 10 percent and net profits reached $593 million. Net profits of $1.7 billion in 1988 were the highest in the history of the airline industry. That year marked the tenth anniversary of the airlines operating under deregulation, as well as the final year in one of the safest ten-year periods in history in terms of accidents and fatalities. Fares, while rising in 1988, had actually declined in real terms in seven of the previous ten years and had risen only half as fast as the Consumer Price Index since 1978. The hub-and-spoke system, which proliferated after deregulation, was becoming the target for many complaints about increased congestion and reduced competition, despite the fact that more communities were providing more service than ever before.

Airline employment went over 500,000 employees in 1989, and hiring continued at a rapid pace despite some dark clouds on the horizon. There was a long, crippling strike against Eastern Airlines, and fuel prices were rising. Both of these factors had a depressing effect on domestic air travel. The result was that, although several airlines had a good year financially, the industry's overall net profit dropped to $128 million. Though higher fuel prices and a recessionary economy continued to hurt airline earnings in 1990, air travel nonetheless increased significantly in the first half of the year, and there was reason for continued optimism.

Early 1990s

Despite setting new records in passenger enplanements and cargo ton-miles in 1990, the airline industry lost close to $4 billion, virtually all in the fourth quarter, as the result of the Iraqi invasion of Kuwait. Kerosene purchased by U.S. carriers rose from 60 cents a gallon in July, just before the invasion, to a peak of $1.40 per gallon in October. Each 1-cent increase cost the airlines $160 million if carried through the year, and according to estimates, the added fuel costs alone set U.S. carriers back nearly $3 billion. Recession and fear of terrorism caused traffic to fall off so much during the fourth quarter of 1990 and the first quarter of 1991 that some carriers were reluctant to impose fuel-cost-induced fare hikes for fear of driving even more traffic away.

The huge losses forced a number of carriers to cut back severely; to sell off major assets, including international routes, aircraft, and airport gates; and to postpone aircraft orders. Thousands of airline workers were laid off in 1991, including 18,000 Eastern workers, when that pioneer airline closed down in January, followed by Midway in November and Pan Am in December. Three other major carriers—America West, Continental, and TWA—operated under Chapter 11 bankruptcy during 1991 and 1992.

The recession deepened during 1991, and the airlines experienced their second-worst year ever, with net losses of $1.9 billion. All categories of traffic were down in 1991 compared to the previous year. The industry downturn continued in 1992 with an unprecedented loss of $4.8 billion. The year 1993 was characterized by intense public, media, and government interest in the financial condition of the U.S. airline industry. The formation and work of President Bill Clinton's National Commission to Ensure a Strong Competitive Airline Industry was the backdrop for most of the year's activities. The commission held numerous public hearings to examine the many problems and issues facing U.S. airlines, and its August report outlined recommendations and changes in public policy that would improve the financial future of the industry.

Unfortunately, because of competing interests and budgetary constraints, few of the commission's suggestions were implemented. Thus, while the National Airline Commission helped frame the problems of the industry on the national economic agenda, 1993 saw the industry experience its fourth consecutive year of financial losses. By year's end, U.S. airlines had collectively lost $2.1 billion.

Losses shrank in 1994, in large part because of lower fuel prices. Capacity, in terms of available seat-miles, increased only slightly as carriers postponed or canceled purchases of new aircraft. Load factors, measuring the percentage of seats filled, reached record levels, and jet service to smaller markets was replaced with regional/commuter service. Operating revenues increased slowly while prices for both passenger and cargo services declined. Because revenue growth was limited by competition, airlines placed increasing emphasis on reducing or containing costs as the path to profitability.

Mid-1990s to the 21st Century

In June 1995, the U.S. airline industry carried its ten-billionth passenger in scheduled commercial service. The industry also had one of the safest years in its history and, perhaps even more importantly, finally turned the corner financially. The national economy was on the upswing, and net profits reached $2.3 billion. However, the carriers accumulated a lot of new debt in the early 1990s, and the industry's capital requirements in the years to come were enormous as the industry replaced its oldest, noisiest jet equipment.

In 1996, the airlines earned record profits of $2.8 billion, as well as hitting record numbers of passengers and amounts of cargo carried. Passenger traffic increased by 7 percent to 578.4 billion RPMs, and cargo traffic increased by 4.6 percent to 17.7 billion revenue ton-miles. The U.S. economy continued to expand, growing by 2.4 percent and fueling rising incomes for both individuals and businesses. This increase in income, in turn, stimulated additional demand for air travel and shipping. Air traffic was also affected favorably by the expiration and eight-month absence of the 10 percent federal excise tax on airline passenger tickets, the 6.25 percent cargo waybill tax, and the $6-per-passenger international departure tax. In the case of the ticket tax, both airlines and passengers benefited from its absence.

International traffic also experienced strong growth in 1996. The number of international passenger enplanements rose to 50.5 million, with the largest growth rates occurring in the Caribbean and Latin American markets, followed by the Pacific. The Atlantic markets grew more slowly as some U.S. airlines continued to restructure their service.

The two-year period of 1997–1998 was bright for the industry. RPMs rose steadily, passing the 600 billion mark, and net profits remained relatively stable at around $5 billion per year. Load factor was better than 70 percent in both years. Cargo ton-miles shot past 20 billion in 1997, and operating profit margin hit 8.2 percent in 1998.

As the economy began to show signs of slowing in 1999 and 2000, the airlines suffered. There were almost 1 trillion seat-miles available on U.S. airliners in 2000—a record number—and passengers were filling about

72 percent of all available seat-miles on any given flight, but the real bottom line was suffering. Despite solid RPM figures (692.8 billion), net profit, after a brief peak above $5 billion in 1999, nose-dived to $2.5 billion in 2000. Net profit margin had shrunk to a razor-thin 1.9 percent.

It goes without saying that, although the figures for 2001 are obviously and powerfully skewed by the events of September 11, they remain unique in two ways: first, they represent financial shockwaves that were felt by every airline in the industry; second, they were, in and of themselves, the worst ever seen by the U.S. airline industry. Negative numbers appear everywhere in the financial summaries: operating profit margin (-8.7 percent), net profit margin (-6.7 percent), and rate of return on investment (-6.9 percent). Net losses of almost $8 billion were experienced; never before had the airlines experienced so much red ink. Load factors, RPMs, and ASMs were all down from the previous year.

What's more, the aftermath of the terrorist attacks took on a much more human side than these figures show. As schedules began to be cut by large margins in the weeks after the attacks, tens of thousands of airline employees around the country were laid off, furloughed, or forced into early retirement. Over a thousand airplanes were parked, with some airlines choosing to eliminate certain types from their fleets (such as United and its 727 operations). Entire companies were eliminated from the scene (for example, Midway Airlines), while the plights of others became so great that congressional action became inevitable. In late September, the Air Transportation Safety and System Stabilization Act was signed into law, providing some $15 billion of much needed financial assistance to the industry. By year's end, an industry that had been predicted to experience climbing performance indexes in the fourth quarter was instead flatlining.

As of 2010, the airline industry still suffered from the direct and indirect impact of 9/11 and continuously increasing costs (i.e., fuel, labor, maintenance, liability). Airline bankruptcies continued proving any airline, small or large, is vulnerable. US Airways entered bankruptcy on August 11, 2002, and reemerged in 2005 with a restructuring plan that included a merger with America West. The airline was acquired by America West and its partners with the new airline retaining the US Airways name. In December 2002, United Airlines filed for bankruptcy protection, blaming the events of 9/11 for their downfall. However, the rise of low-cost carriers, labor disputes, and problems within the management structure of the company also contributed to financial losses. On February 1, 2006, United came out of bankruptcy. On September 14, 2005, Delta Air Lines filed for bankruptcy for the first time in its 76-year history with a debt load of $20.5 billion. On the same day of Delta's filing, Northwest Airlines also entered into bankruptcy protection for the first time in its 79-year history. Delta merged with Northwest Airlines in February 2009 and entered a consolidation process that ended in February 2010 eliminating the Northwest name. Delta and Northwest now operate under a single operating certificate as granted by the FAA. The transaction was worth an estimated $2.8 billion.

The U.S. Department of Transportation does not maintain an official database recording airline merger and acquisition activity. However, Airlines for America maintains an unofficial database showing related activity from 1930 to 2022 (Table 6.4).

Table 6.4 U.S. Airline Mergers and Acquisitions

Title	Announced	Closed	Resulting Entity
Western Air Express/Standard Airlines	1/22/1930	5/1/1930	Western Air Express
Western Air Express/ Transcontinental Air Transport	11/15/1929	7/16/1930	Transcontinental & Western Air
Delta Air Lines/Chicago and Southern (C&S) Air Lines	4/26/1952	5/1/1953	Delta Air Lines
United Airlines/Capital Airlines	7/28/1960	6/1/1961	United Airlines
Western Airlines/Pacific Northern Airlines	10/28/1966	7/1/1967	Western Airlines
Frontier Airlines/Central Airlines	5/5/1967	10/1/1967	Frontier Airlines
Alaska Airlines/Cordova Airlines	Early 1967	2/1/1968	Alaska Airlines
Allegheny Airlines/Lake Central Airlines	10/19/1967	3/14/1968	Allegheny Airlines (later renamed US Airways)
Alaska Airlines/Alaska Coastal Airlines	3/17/1967	4/1/1968	Alaska Airlines
Pacific Airlines/Bonanza Airlines/West Coast Airlines	6/22/1967	7/1/1968	Air West
American Airlines/Trans Caribbean Airways	1/18/1970	3/3/1971	American Airlines
Allegheny Airlines/Mohawk Airlines	4/14/1971	4/12/1972	Allegheny Airlines (later renamed US Airways)
Delta Air Lines/Northeast Airlines	4/23/1971	8/1/1972	Delta Air Lines
North Central Airlines/Southern Airways/Hughes Airwest	7/14/1978	7/1/1979	Republic Airlines
Pan Am/National Airlines	8/23/1978	1/7/1980	Pan Am
Republic Airlines/Hughes Airwest	3/12/1980	10/1/1980	Republic Airlines
Continental Airlines/Texas Air Corporation	2/9/1981	10/31/1982	Continental Airlines
Southwest Airlines/Muse Airlines	6/25/1985	12/12/1985	Southwest Airlines
Northwest Airlines/Republic Airlines	1/23/1986	10/1/1986	Northwest Airlines
TWA/Ozark Air Lines	3/1/1986	10/27/1986	TWA
Delta Air Lines/Western Airlines	9/9/1986	12/16/1986	Delta Air Lines
Alaska Airlines/Horizon Air	11/19/1986	12/31/1986	Alaska Airlines/ Horizon Air

(Continued)

Table 6.4 ***Continued***

Title	Announced	Closed	Resulting Entity
Continental Airlines/People Express/New York Air/Frontier Airlines	1/12/1987	2/1/1987	Continental Airlines
American Airlines/AirCal	11/18/1986	4/30/1987	American Airlines
US Air/Pacific Southwest Airlines	11/18/1986	5/29/1987	US Air
Alaska Airlines/Jet America	7/23/1987	10/1/1987	Alaska Airlines
US Air/Piedmont Airlines	3/19/1987	8/4/1989	US Air
American Airlines/Eastern Air Lines: Latin Routes	12/19/1989	7/1/1990	American Airlines
American Airlines/TWA: Heathrow Routes	12/16/1990	5/2/1991	American Airlines
Delta Air Lines/Pan Am Airlines (Shuttle and Atlantic Routes)	7/27/1991	11/1/1991	Delta Shuttle
United Airlines/Pan Am: Latin & Caribbean Routes	12/9/1991	5/16/1992	United Airlines
Southwest Airlines/Morris Airlines	12/13/1993	12/31/1993	Southwest Airlines
AirTran Airways/Valujet	7/11/1997	11/17/1997	AirTran Airways
American Airlines/Reno Air	11/19/1998	2/1/1999	American Airlines
Delta Air Lines/Atlantic Southeast Airlines	2/16/1999	3/22/1999	Delta Air Lines
Delta Air Lines/Comair	10/18/1999	10/22/1999	Delta Air Lines
American Airlines/TWA	1/10/2001	4/9/2001	American Airlines
Republic Airways/Shuttle America	4/22/2005	5/9/2005	Republic Airways
SkyWest/Atlantic Southeast Airlines	8/15/2005	9/8/2005	SkyWest/ASA
US Airways/America West Airlines	5/19/2005	9/27/2005	US Airways
Pinnacle Airlines/Colgan Air	1/18/2007	1/18/2007	Pinnacle Airlines/Colgan Air
Southwest Airlines/ATA Airlines	11/19/2008	12/2/2008	Southwest Airlines
Republic Airways/Midwest Airlines	6/23/2009	7/31/2009	Republic Airways
Republic Airways/Frontier Airlines	8/14/2009	10/1/2009	Republic Airways
Delta Air Lines/Northwest Airlines	4/14/2008	12/31/2009	Delta Air Lines
Pinnacle Airlines/Mesaba Airlines	7/1/2010	7/1/2010	Pinnacle Airlines/Mesaba Airlines
United Airlines/Continental Airlines	5/3/2010	10/1/2010	United Airlines
SkyWest/Atlantic Southeast Airlines/ExpressJet Airlines	8/4/2010	11/15/2010	SkyWest/SureJet

Title	Announced	Closed	Resulting Entity
Southwest Airlines/AirTran Airways	9/27/2010	5/2/2011	Southwest Airlines
US Airways/American Airlines	2/14/2013	12/9/2013	American Airlines
Atlas Air/Southern Air	1/19/2016	4/7/2016	Atlas Air Worldwide
FedEx/TNT Express	4/27/2015	5/25/2016	FedEx
Alaska Airlines/Virgin America	4/4/2016	12/14/2016	Alaska Airlines
United Airlines (via ManaAir)/ ExpressJet Airlines	12/18/2018	1/3/2019	United/ExpressJet
Southern Airways/Mokulele Airlines	2/12/2019	3/11/2019	Southern/Mokulele
Mokulele Airlines/Makani Kai Air	6/3/2020	Dec-20	Mokulele
Frontier Airlines/Spirit Airlines	2/7/2022	Pending	TBD
Southern Airways/Air Choice One (Multi-Aero)	3/28/2022	Pending	Southern

Source: Airlines for America

FIGURE 6.2 Oil Prices

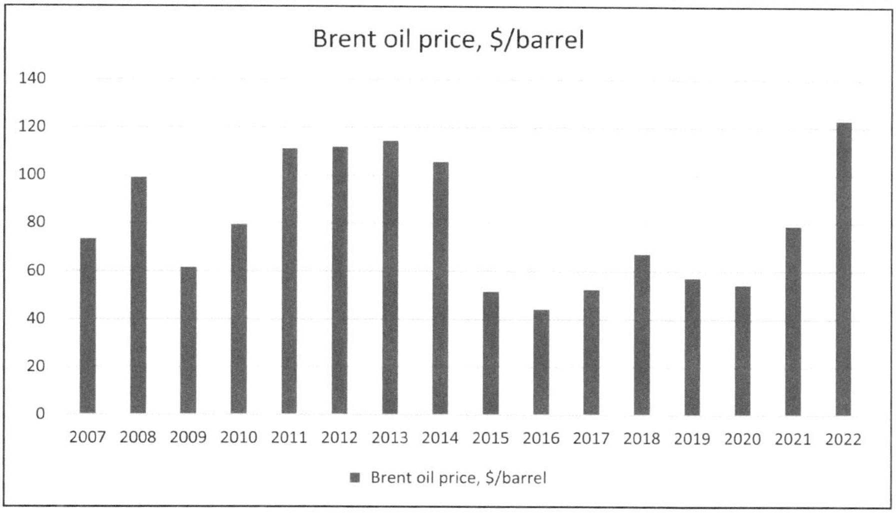

Source: S&P Global Commodity Insights

Aside from the above, one major merger took place in 2010 between United Airlines and Continental Airlines with the resulting entity being United Airlines. This airline became the world's biggest airline in terms of revenue passenger miles and second in aircraft fleet size. The merger was estimated at approximately $3 billion.

One of the biggest surprises in terms of mergers took place in 2011. Southwest Airlines had been successful in terms of growth by acquiring other airlines, including Muse Air in 1985, Morris Air in 1993, and ATA in 2008. In September 2010, Southwest announced it would acquire AirTran Airways in a deal worth $1.4 billion. The merger expanded Southwest's revenue base as well as route network with the addition of Mexico and the Caribbean. From a strategic perspective, the merger provided a major asset for the operators including AirTran's former hub, Atlanta.

From 2012–2013, the U.S. airline industry faced many challenges and changes as did other regions of the world. The world's biggest airline was formed as a result of the December 9, 2013, merger between American Airlines, AMR, and US Airways. The merger was part of American's bankruptcy strategy, essentially creating one large airline under the American brand resulting in 6,700 daily flights to more than 330 destinations, in more than 50 countries. The total employee base was estimated at over 100,000 people. The value of the merger was estimated at $11 billion.

In 2012, the world's airlines showed weak profits with an aggregate profit of $7.6 billion on revenues of $638 billion (1.2 percent net profit margin). Oil hit a record high of $111.80 per barrel while GDP growth was 2.1 percent (Figure 6.2). To compare to 2003, when airlines were in the red, oil was priced at $30 per barrel while GDP was 2.8 percent. In 2013, oil prices increased, hitting a new record high of $114.38 per barrel while world GDP growth was 2.7 percent. Oil prices remained steady from 2014 to 2020 reaching a low of $44.21 per barrel in 2016. However, oil prices took a large increase in 2020 and 2021 due to the COVID-19 global pandemic, causing extra heartache for operators and consequently passengers. At the time of writing, the average price per barrel reached a high of $123 due to an increase in demand and a decrease in supply due to the global pandemic.

As of 2022, many airlines, worldwide, are in the process of developing and implementing transformation programs to reshape business, re-engage employees, and revitalize customer service, focusing on a survive, adapt, recover, rethink mindset. Changes include new partnerships and new investments. Airlines in the emerging markets (Asia, Latin America, Middle East) tend to have more opportunities in terms of growth and potential to profit.

On a global scale, the airline industry is still plagued by extremely high costs and thin margins. Despite the large economic impact the global airline industry has on the economy, it continues to be threatened by inefficient infrastructure and poor regulation. If aviation is to create jobs for the future and drive economic productivity, the industry must learn to collaborate rather than compete. Failure to do so will most likely result in severe consequences both regionally and globally.

KEY TERMS

401 carrier
Air Transportation Oversight System (ATOS)

available seat-miles (ASMs)
CSET
fitness
local-service carrier
major air carrier
national air carrier
regional air carrier
revenue passenger miles (RPMs)
supplemental air carrier
trunk carrier

REVIEW QUESTIONS

1 How did the trunk and local-service carriers evolve? What was the role of the supplemental carriers? Discuss some of the problems faced by the industry in the three decades preceding deregulation. How did the deregulation movement get started?
2 Explain how the certificated airline industry has changed since deregulation in terms of expansion, consolidation, and concentration. Describe several innovations pioneered by the major air carriers in the early 1980s that radically changed the structure of the industry.
3 Describe the role of the major and national carriers. Identify some of the carriers in each category. How did the regional carriers get started? Describe a typical regional carrier in terms of its role in the air transportation system, type of aircraft flown, and route structure. What is meant by *hub-and-spoke network*? Why has the number of regional carriers declined since deregulation? Describe some of the changes that have taken place in this segment of the industry. What is *code sharing*?
4 What is the main purpose of certification? In the United States, what are the different types of certification? Explain the different phases. What is CSET? What is ATOS?
5 Who is responsible for financial and traffic data collection within the Department of Transportation? Describe the role of this government bureau. What is the Interline Traffic Agreement—Passenger? What is the purpose of the Air Freight Procedures Agreement and the Small Package Shipment Agreement? Describe the Universal Air Travel Plan.
6 Highlight the industry's performance, in terms of traffic and finances, during the 1960s, 1970s, and 1990s. Describe the cyclical nature of the airline industry in terms of profitability. What was the reason for the tremendous losses incurred during the early 2000s leading up to 2022? What is the industry forecast for the future?
7 Do you think airlines in the United States will continue to merge? If so, how will the industry respond? If not, what do you think will happen to the industry?

8 The COVID-19 global pandemic impacted the global aviation industry providing numerous unexpected challenges. What are examples of such challenges? How has the industry changed since the global pandemic?

Notes

1 According to the CAB's Domestic Passenger Fare Investigation (DPFI), fares were set according to the following formula: average costs (assuming planes flew 55 percent full) = reasonable return on investment (12 percent) + revenue requirement.

2 Civil Aeronautics Act, Sections 101(35) and 101(36), respectively.

3 Refers to the numerous social programs launched during President Lyndon B. Johnson's administration.

CHAPTER 7

Economic Characteristics of the Airlines

CHAPTER CHECKLIST • YOU SHOULD BE ABLE TO:

- Describe the general characteristics of oligopolies
- Explain how the number of carriers, and their market share, has changed since deregulation
- Identify several of the barriers to entry into the airline industry
- Define *economies of scale*, *scope*, and *density* and discuss how they relate to the airline industry
- Describe the effects of mergers on the airline industry
- Discuss the concept of mutual dependence as it relates to the air carriers
- Explain how the industry is moving toward oligopolistic pricing
- Describe the economic characteristics unique to the airlines
- Explain the significance of load factors in relation to costs and services offered

INTRODUCTION

Economists usually describe the certificated airline industry as closely approximating an oligopolistic market structure. An **oligopoly** (from the Greek *oli*, meaning "few") is an industry composed of a few firms producing either similar or differentiated products. A "few" can be five or ten or 100 firms. A large percentage of our nation's output of goods and services

DOI: 10.4324/9780429346156-9

are produced by oligopolistic industries: steel, automobiles, oil, and aluminum, to mention a few. Oligopolistic industries typically are characterized by high **barriers to entry**. These usually take the form of substantial capital requirements, the need for the technical and technological know-how, control of patent rights, and so forth.

In addition to few sellers, a similar product, and high obstacles to entry, oligopolistic industries tend to share several other characteristics.

1 *Substantial economies of scale.* By **economy of scale**, economists mean decreases in a firm's long-term average costs as the size of its operations increases. Firms in oligopolistic industries typically require large-scale production to obtain low unit costs. Large-scale production is afforded by intensive labor and management specialization of job responsibilities, utilization of the most efficient technology available, and effective use of by-products. If total market demand for the product or service is sufficient to support only a few large firms of optimum size, competition generally ensures that only a few such firms will survive.
2 *Growth through merger.* Many of the oligopolies that exist today have resulted from mergers of competing firms—in mergers that may date back to the late 19th or early 20th century. In 1901, for example, the U.S. Steel Corporation was formed from a merger of 11 independent steel producers. Or think of the number of U.S. automobile manufacturers back in the 1930s, 1940s, and 1950s. Well-known companies like LaSalle, Hudson, Packard, and Studebaker have long since gone. The purpose of most mergers is to gain a substantial increase in market share, greater economies of scale, more buying power in the purchase of resources, and various other advantages that smaller firms do not possess to the same extent.
3 *Mutual dependence.* When there are only a few firms in a market, it matters very much to each firm what its rivals do. Economists call this situation **mutual dependence**. The small number of sellers in an oligopolistic industry makes it necessary for each seller to consider the reactions of competitors when setting prices. In this sense, the behavior of oligopolists in the marketplace may be somewhat similar to the behavior of players in such games of skill as chess, checkers, or bridge. In these games, the participants try to win by formulating strategies that anticipate the possible counterreactions of their opponents.
4 *Price rigidity and nonprice competition.* In an oligopolistic industry, firms find it more comfortable to maintain constant prices and to engage in various forms of nonprice competition, such as advertising and customer service, to hold, if not increase, their market shares. As all firms in an oligopolistic market are price makers (and none price takers), price reductions, when they occur, are sporadic and usually come about only under severe pressures resulting from weakened demand or excessive capacity.

THE AIRLINES AS OLIGOPOLISTS

With the general characteristics of oligopolies as a background, let's see how the airline industry compares and then take a look at several unique characteristics.

Number of Carriers and Market Share

With the easing of CAB regulations and passage of the Airline Deregulation Act, the industry entered an era of intense competition. Major airlines and the former local-service carriers began competing with one another; charter carriers moved into scheduled service; former intrastate carriers, such as Air Florida, Pacific Southwest Airlines, and Southwest, moved into interstate markets; and many new firms began offering service. As a result of this new entry, discount fares proliferated, fare wars began, and total traffic increased dramatically as passengers took advantage of previously unheard-of coast-to-coast fares. The number of RPMs increased dramatically. The established major airlines, with the exception of those that were failing, shared in the traffic growth, but the new entrants made substantial inroads into market share. Between 1978 and 1986, the share of total traffic of the incumbent trunk airlines declined from 94 percent to 77 percent.

In this period, there were 198 certificated (Section 401) carriers providing interstate passenger service in the United States. If we were to add the 36 carriers operating before deregulation, this would give 234 carriers operating at the start of 1987. Unfortunately, instead of the industry expanding, as many proponents of deregulation visualized, 160 of those carriers either were merged, liquidated, decertified, or were not operating or never did operate under a certificate. Therefore, at the start of 1987, only 74 certificated carriers remained. The total number has increased in recent years with the addition of smaller certificated carriers and the demise of some of the larger airlines, including Eastern and Pan Am. The shrinking number of larger carriers has improved the market share of the remaining major carriers, such that the largest carriers now have a somewhat greater market share than before deregulation (although they are not all the same carriers).

Commuter air travel followed a similar pattern, with the number of service providers reaching 246 in 1981 and declining to 109 by the end of 1996. Despite this consolidation, RPMs increased almost sevenfold, from 2.1 billion to 14.2 billion. At the end of 1996, 35 of the top 50 commuter airlines had code-sharing agreements with one or more major or national carriers. Those 50 airlines controlled 99 percent of the total commuter market share.

By 2014, a number of changes occurred in terms of code-sharing agreements, and these changes affected air carriers of all sizes around the world. Because of a large number of bankruptcies (or in the U.S. airlines filing Chapter 11 (with American/AMR in 2011 as the last of the U.S.

legacy carriers to file Chapter 11 and to undergo that restructuring process, which has greatly improved airline labor productivity)), airlines going out of business, and changing partnerships, alliance members were negatively impacted in many cases. Some alliances lost partners, resulting in decreased market share and increased expenses.

By 2022, numerous changes occurred at the global level as a result of an unstable airline industry due to the COVID-19 global pandemic (2019–2022). For the U.S. market, given that we have seen substantial consolidation with a number of mergers, the industry appears to be relatively stable with the remaining four large players (American, Delta Air Lines, United Airlines, Southwest Airlines) all exercising a substantial degree of capacity discipline. On the international scene, the strongest airlines in terms of profit from 2012–2019 were Ryanair (Ireland), British Airways (U.K.), Japan Airlines (Japan), easyJet (U.K.), and Air Canada (Canada). The COVID-19 global pandemic certainly had a negative impact on the global airline industry and virtually all air carriers had to pivot during this time and enter a period of survive, adapt, recover, and rethink. According to McKinsey & Company (2022), air cargo experienced increased demand and high freight rates but passenger airlines were the worst performing area of the aviation industry. In total, the global aviation industry lost $230 billion in 2020 and freight forwarders were the only part of the industry to profit, resulting in a $3.5 billion gain (Table 7.1).

Unquestionably, the airline industry, with its small number of companies and concentration of market share, meets the first characteristic of oligopolist firms. Most analysts expect that the consolidation that began in the early 1980s will continue, with only a handful of major carriers remaining in the future. These carriers will be supplemented by 100 or so smaller airlines providing regional/commuter service. As of 2022, global consolidation continues along with the emergence of small air carriers in different regions of the world. It is impossible to predict the future but factual data indicates the airline industry will be increasingly challenging and competitive.

High Barriers to Entry

One expectation of deregulation was that carriers would have relatively free access to markets because of the mobility of the airlines' chief assets—aircraft. Carriers dominating individual markets would not charge monopolistic fares, according to this theory, because of the ease with which a competitor could enter the market and compete with the incumbent carrier by charging reduced fares. Thus, the mere threat of entry was expected to discipline pricing. Substantial new entry did occur during the early phase of deregulation, but since the mid-1980s, the pace has slowed and the industry has become more concentrated.

Access to many markets has become extremely difficult in recent years because of the difficulty of obtaining terminal space as well as landing and

Table 7.1 Net Income (in Thousands of Dollars $000) All U.S. Carriers, All Regions

Year	Quarter	DOMESTIC	LATIN AMERICA	ATLANTIC	PACIFIC	INTERNATIONAL	TOTAL
2000	1	139,162	58,927	-68,918	-106,308	839	23,702
2000	2	1,570,500	-86,040	250,371	154,724	9,541	1,899,096
2000	3	548,903	33,056	226,224	83,675	45,470	937,327
2000	4	-267,068	6,639	-95,916	5,533	23,388	-327,425
2000	TOTAL	**1,991,496**	**12,581**	**311,761**	**137,623**	**79,238**	**2,532,700**
2001	1	-822,384	76,822	-59,644	-101,160	-3,410	-909,776
2001	2	-774,977	3,683	116,147	-205,108	-62,860	-923,115
2001	3	-2,232,653	-6,375	-44,209	-272,018	-4,848	-2,560,103
2001	4	-3,404,841	-63,631	-194,802	-190,370	-19,871	-3,873,515
2001	TOTAL	**-7,234,855**	**10,499**	**-182,509**	**-768,656**	**-90,989**	**-8,266,509**
2002	1	-2,621,918	-176,148	-372,012	-89,470	9,187	-3,250,361
2002	2	-1,298,581	-44,110	-43,360	-49,899	-33,900	-1,469,850
2002	3	-2,351,704	-67,435	-38,578	-64,051	27,239	-2,494,531
2002	4	-3,056,898	-149,090	-575,563	-288,296	-80,895	-4,150,742
2002	TOTAL	**-9,329,102**	**-436,783**	**-1,029,513**	**-491,717**	**-78,369**	**-11,365,484**
2003	1	-1,085,012	-51,869	-452,157	-330,213	-1,673	-1,920,924
2003	2	606,461	100,285	168,328	-227,315	-340	647,420
2003	3	-642,496	129,566	290,670	-51,195	7,554	-265,900
2003	4	-348,536	107,826	109,623	-42,980	-1,997	-176,064
2003	TOTAL	**-1,469,581**	**285,808**	**116,463**	**-651,702**	**3,543**	**-1,715,469**

(Continued)

Table 7.1 (Continued)

Year	Quarter	DOMESTIC	LATIN AMERICA	ATLANTIC	PACIFIC	INTERNATIONAL	TOTAL
2004	1	-1,622,122	201,821	31,510	-73,884	6,499	-1,456,177
2004	2	-2,018,851	42,467	115,648	-61,035	6,648	-1,915,125
2004	3	-1,702,368	38,782	331,619	94,637	113,802	-1,123,527
2004	4	-4,562,813	30,756	-71,246	-31,241	24,949	-4,609,595
2004	**TOTAL**	**-9,906,154**	**313,825**	**407,530**	**-71,523**	**151,897**	**-9,104,424**
2005	1	-2,956,735	95,583	-202,866	-179,050	35,932	-3,207,135
2005	2	-1,511,275	30,014	207,515	-249,681	36,266	-1,487,161
2005	3	-2,231,293	-43,150	164,743	-293,751	70,285	-2,333,166
2005	4	-13,048,233	-802,628	-2,278,672	-4,111,334	48,434	-20,192,434
2005	**TOTAL**	**-19,747,536**	**-720,181**	**-2,109,279**	**-4,833,816**	**190,916**	**-27,219,896**
2006	1	12,049,285	1,110,214	2,966,133	4,705,502	31,349	20,862,482
2006	2	-642,693	42,078	83,950	-186,742	9,296	-694,110
2006	3	-592,826	190,769	310,776	-109,207	38,787	-161,700
2006	4	-1,770,107	121,001	-172,714	-57,349	58,610	-1,820,559
2006	**TOTAL**	**9,043,659**	**1,464,063**	**3,188,145**	**4,352,204**	**138,042**	**18,186,112**
2007	1	-488,478	303,476	112,807	-39,093	44,269	-67,019
2007	2	3,403,274	368,016	1,224,053	922,144	62,075	5,979,562
2007	3	626,687	242,447	591,292	302,755	37,068	1,800,249
2007	4	-545,608	221,388	120,177	135,670	46,986	-21,387
2007	**TOTAL**	**2,995,875**	**1,135,327**	**2,048,328**	**1,321,476**	**190,398**	**7,691,404**

2008	1	-9,777,777	-335,226	-1,326,883	-151,807	-8,011	-11,599,703
2008	2	-2,254,820	-221,837	-849,465	-953,640	3,106	-4,276,656
2008	3	-2,633,833	171,764	-213,390	-58,070	14,972	-2,718,557
2008	4	-3,507,540	-29,950	-886,774	-499,005	-231,649	-5,154,919
2008	**TOTAL**	**-18,173,970**	**-415,249**	**-3,276,511**	**-1,662,522**	**-221,582**	**-23,749,834**
2009	1	-1,516,128	136,650	-446,958	-63,964	45,643	-1,844,758
2009	2	-344,471	-11,264	-164,482	-114,056	5,612	-628,662
2009	3	-144,230	86,376	-3,069	-58,753	17,452	-102,224
2009	4	-247,244	192,905	-20,067	23,138	100,634	49,366
2009	**TOTAL**	**-2,252,074**	**404,667**	**-634,577**	**-213,634**	**169,340**	**-2,526,277**
2010	1	-704,121	40,958	-146,182	107,467	86,152	-615,726
2010	2	657,279	95,963	396,501	359,678	86,089	1,595,509
2010	3	1,178,343	262,817	397,620	461,467	69,066	2,369,313
2010	4	44,633	235,472	-200,267	174,245	62,815	316,898
2010	**TOTAL**	**1,176,134**	**635,210**	**447,673**	**1,102,857**	**304,122**	**3,665,995**
2011	1	-455,423	177,773	-612,217	37,456	4,263	-848,148
2011	2	1,152,067	151,816	-285,411	-24,198	9,125	1,003,401
2011	3	761,688	420,131	94,273	199,367	6,956	1,482,415
2011	4	-17,775	162,680	-363,956	9,876	-36,306	-245,480
2011	**TOTAL**	**1,440,558**	**912,402**	**-1,167,311**	**222,501**	**-15,962**	**1,392,188**

(Continued)

Table 7.1 (Continued)

ear	Quarter	DOMESTIC	LATIN AMERICA	ATLANTIC	PACIFIC	INTERNATIONAL	TOTAL
2012	1	-213,497	-357,006	-876,974	-196,898	-47,476	-1,691,852
2012	2	1,513,613	-104,616	-293,620	-310,960	-33,105	771,313
2012	3	564,041	187,415	309,960	327,948	-19,657	1,369,708
2012	4	348,019	169,237	-269,382	-240,082	-93,230	-85,437
2012	**TOTAL**	**2,212,176**	**-104,970**	**-1,130,016**	**-419,991**	**-193,468**	**363,732**
2013	1	227,114	290,326	-372,745	-335,847	145,522	-45,631
2013	2	2,147,207	-59,773	299,871	-198,500	-42,398	2,146,407
2013	3	2,384,395	125,408	620,320	83,532	9,086	3,222,741
2013	4	5,763,127	156,472	899,296	610,054	-41,253	7,387,696
2013	**TOTAL**	**10,521,844**	**512,433**	**1,446,741**	**159,239**	**70,956**	**12,711,213**
2014	1	926,580	22,305	-269,343	-145,495	15,751	549,797
2014	2	3,467,788	-54,932	521,443	-120,602	35,687	3,849,384
2014	3	2,828,108	-75,577	633,410	96,429	40,277	3,522,647
2014	4	1,422,907	-131,575	-342,098	-468,313	37,883	518,805
2014	**TOTAL**	**8,645,383**	**-239,780**	**543,413**	**-637,981**	**129,598**	**8,440,634**
2015	1	3,055,504	213,705	152,544	79,301	43,486	3,544,541
2015	2	4,678,728	158,598	655,387	201,055	38,855	5,732,622
2015	3	6,494,263	604,630	1,683,382	888,611	-15,769	9,655,117
2015	4	6,983,407	25,921	407,138	-7,333	38,520	7,447,652
2015	**TOTAL**	**21,211,902**	**1,002,854**	**2,898,451**	**1,161,633**	**105,091**	**26,379,931**

2016	1	2,856,167	362,407	43,896	226,726	5,922	3,495,119
2016	2	4,229,096	279,168	326,080	257,402	2,399	5,094,145
2016	3	3,407,438	266,508	351,436	163,709	6,472	4,195,563
2016	4	2,861,738	141,921	-91,411	-168,870	81,537	2,824,916
2016	**TOTAL**	**13,354,439**	**1,050,005**	**630,002**	**478,968**	**96,330**	**15,609,744**
2017	1	2,647,152	61,452	-134,888	-240,086	-15,375	2,318,254
2017	2	5,046,701	152,157	115,185	-259,166	-59,347	4,995,529
2017	3	3,575,301	380,782	19,548	-87,092	13,447	3,901,986
2017	4	5,752,299	156,080	-227,641	-255,386	163,358	5,588,711
2017	**TOTAL**	**17,021,453**	**750,471**	**-227,796**	**-841,730**	**102,083**	**16,804,481**
2018	1	3,150,849	341,526	319,232	-399,452	20,232	3,432,387
2018	2	3,746,860	150,583	396,013	-215,682	32,741	4,110,516
2018	3	3,473,163	336,129	391,801	-119,818	40,944	4,122,218
2018	4	3,738,630	205,160	11,404	-272,172	80,929	3,763,951
2018	**TOTAL**	**14,109,503**	**1,033,398**	**1,118,450**	**-1,007,124**	**174,844**	**15,429,071**
2019	1	2,732,085	269,912	-146,614	-143,659	-25,952	2,685,771
2019	2	4,891,390	337,052	278,518	-275,831	17,323	5,248,453
2019	3	4,344,519	477,840	323,253	-191,276	-50,583	4,903,753
2019	4	3,737,977	465,079	-76,833	-340,004	-191,673	3,594,546
2019	**TOTAL**	**15,705,970**	**1,549,883**	**378,323**	**-950,769**	**-250,885**	**16,432,523**

(Continued)

Table 7.1 (Continued)

ear	Quarter	DOMESTIC	LATIN AMERICA	ATLANTIC	PACIFIC	INTERNATIONAL	TOTAL
2020	1	-3,227,325	-251,044	-924,766	-553,586	11,288	-4,945,432
2020	2	-8,067,065	-432,403	-1,134,773	-720,025	376,696	-9,977,570
2020	3	-8,799,633	-609,596	-763,418	-386,205	203,505	-10,355,346
2020	4	-4,506,732	-601,501	-715,711	-96,464	295,770	-5,624,637
2020	**TOTAL**	**-24,600,755**	**-1,894,543**	**-3,538,667**	**-1,756,279**	**887,260**	**-30,902,984**
2021	1	-1,350,151	-1,441,636	-411,565	-351,969	197,289	-3,358,032
2021	2	2,810,476	-251,740	-706,843	-64,730	212,698	1,999,860
2021	3	3,638,366	160,776	-424,432	99,150	137,989	3,611,849
2021	4	-461,666	-347,174	-654,875	132,601	236,486	-1,094,628
2021	**TOTAL**	**4,637,025**	**-1,879,774**	**-2,197,715**	**-184,949**	**784,462**	**1,159,049**
2022	1	-2,331,375	-774,464	-1,252,818	42,428	132,284	-4,183,945
2022	2	3,783,643	-151,397	-912,245	89,044	138,084	2,947,130
2022	**TOTAL**	**1,452,268**	**-925,861**	**-2,165,064**	**131,472**	**270,368**	**-1,236,815**

Source: Bureau of Transportation Statistics
Note: All numbers are for scheduled services

take-off rights (slots) at many hub airports and the risk associated with competing with an airline at one of its hubs. A competitor that wishes to challenge another carrier at its hub faces considerable financial outlays. The cost of providing a competitive level of service at a hub is substantial: expenditures for advertising, personnel, and aircraft operations are crucial during start-up, when the competitor attempts to win business away from the major carrier. The risk of being unable to recover these outlays is the largest single deterrent to entry at hub airports. This effect is often referred to as exit barriers or high sunk cost.

It is difficult to compete with a major carrier during start-up because the major carrier has inherent advantages; some result from the scope of its operations, others from marketing. The larger network of the major carrier allows it to increase service at a lower additional cost. In addition, by having an extensive network, the major carrier is more likely to attract passengers, who then form impressions about the quality of service on other routes. Marketing builds on these advantages. Frequent-flier programs make it difficult to lure business travelers away from an incumbent carrier with which they may have already accrued a substantial account balance. And if the incumbent has already established preferred-provider relationships with most of the travel agents around the hub, the new entrant faces an additional competitive disadvantage. Thus, during the months in which a competitor first takes on a major carrier at its hub, the competitor must offer substantial levels of service, which at a minimum include dozens of flights a day. It must also lure frequent fliers away from an incumbent that offers them more opportunities to earn mileage and somehow win over travel agents who have preferred-carrier relationships with the incumbent.

One alternative that the newer carriers, particularly low-cost carriers, have attempted is to focus on another airport serving the same city—for example, serving Chicago's in-town airport (Midway) instead of O'Hare. These airports have considerably lower traffic volumes than the major airports that serve those communities, but they have allowed new entrants to develop niche markets.

Airport terminal capacity can also be a barrier to entry for new and existing carriers seeking to enter new markets. Entering a market requires the ability to lease or develop gates, baggage handling and airport maintenance facilities, and ticketing and passenger waiting areas. Little underused gate capacity and related terminal space is available at major airports in the short term. Over the longer term, it is possible for carriers to enter many markets, but the experience of recent years indicates that such entry is neither easy nor inexpensive.

Airport operators believe that existing capacity limits are exacerbated at many airports because the incumbent airlines, holding long-term leases with majority-in-interest (MII) clauses or exclusive-use agreements, are able to block airport expansions that would provide more capacity for new entrants. In addition, many airport-airline leases contain clauses that prohibit the airport from charging "additional rates, fees, and charges" and from changing its method of calculating landing fees. The airlines can block expansions with these provisions, but only those that would increase their costs without their consent.

Another barrier to entry has become the dominated hubs. As carriers build the connection banks required to make a hub work, their presence in the local market can become so pervasive as to approach being a monopoly. Airlines use hubs to shield some of their output from competition. As more flights are connected to a hub, the number of passengers available to support additional flights grows. Making the connecting banks work for these flights requires many gates because of the desire to minimize the delay between connections. Also, higher-yield originating passengers help provide the numbers needed to support frequent hub service. Because few airports have excess capacity in the short run (and few have enough local traffic to support more than one extensive network of nonstop service), hubs tend to become dominated by one or two major carriers who use up the existing capacity.

Finally, during the 1980s, many new entrants were able to begin operations with used or leased aircraft. Many of the older, noisier Stage 2 aircraft that were in operation had to meet higher Stage 3 noise criteria by 1999. The restrictions reduced the supply of aircraft and required carriers to retrofit or re-engine existing Stage 2 aircraft. Hushkits and re-engine programs were developed for some aircraft. The cost and availability of conversion programs for some of the major aircraft of the fleet were high. In any event, the phaseout of Stage 2 aircraft ultimately increased the cost of entry to the airline industry by reducing the supply of used aircraft and increasing the cost of operating used aircraft.

Economies of Scale

Like all oligopolists, airlines must achieve a large volume of output in order to lower the cost per unit of output (which equals either a seat departure or a seat mile flown as sector length matters too in the concept of economies of scale). To achieve economies of scale in production, the carriers, like other oligopolists, utilize the principle of labor specialization. Because of the number of workers, jobs can be divided and subdivided. Instead of performing five or six distinct operations in the production process, each worker may have only one task to perform. Workers can be used full-time on the particular operations for which they have special skills. Union rules about what specific workers can and cannot do also reinforce this principle. Thus, a skilled machinist with a major carrier might spend an entire career in a particular shop working on one component of the aircraft.

In a small firm, skilled machinists may spend half their time performing unskilled tasks. This makes for higher production costs. Furthermore, the division of work operations that large-scale operations permit gives workers the opportunity to become very proficient at the specific tasks assigned them. The jack-of-all-trades who is burdened with five or six jobs likely will not become very efficient at any of them. When allowed to concentrate on one task, the same worker may become highly efficient. Finally, greater specialization tends to eliminate the loss of time that accompanies the shifting of workers from one job to another.

Large-scale output also permits better utilization of and greater specialization in management. A supervisor who is capable of handling 15 or 20 employees will be underutilized in a small firm with only eight or ten workers. The number of volume-related workers, such as pilots, flight attendants, mechanics, and reservations personnel, can be doubled with little or no increase in administrative costs. In addition, small firms cannot use management specialists to the best advantage. In small firms, sales specialists may be forced to divide their time between several executive functions—for example, market research, sales planning, budgeting, and personnel administration. A larger scale of operations, which can also be a result of larger aircraft rather than just a larger work force, means that the marketing expert can work full-time supervising sales while appropriate specialists are added as needed to perform other managerial functions. Greater efficiency and lower unit costs are the net result. This effect can also be seen in airline fleets. The larger the fleet, the higher the chance of being able to spread some of the fixed cost across more units. As shown by Merkert and Hensher,[1] fleet commonality plays an important role in this as a standardized, one-type-of-aircraft fleet (such as the B737 fleet of Southwest) multiplies that scale effect.

If the volume of output must be reduced because of a decline in traffic, something has to give, or else the firm will experience what economists refer to as **diseconomy of scale**, in which cost per unit begins to rise. In such a case, airlines are forced to furlough volume-related workers as well as administrative personnel. The remaining administrative workers must broaden their responsibilities by taking on new job assignments. Airlines have also attempted to get their volume (mostly unionized) personnel to take on greater responsibilities, but this has been more difficult. The unions question what will happen when increased traffic volumes return and whether workers will still be required to handle work outside their bargained job description. Recent research has also shown that diseconomies of scale exist in airline market where volumes don't fall. By applying econometric models to 66 international passenger airlines, Merkert and Morrell[2] have shown that the optimal airline size is somewhere between 21 and 35 billion available seat-miles capacity and that airlines with more than 125 billion ASMs are definitely too large to operate efficiently.

On the positive, the established carriers can utilize the latest technology available, which also brings about economies of scale. Small firms often are unable to utilize the most efficient and productive equipment. In many cases, the most efficient equipment is available only in very large and extremely expensive units. Furthermore, effective utilization of this equipment demands a high volume of output. This means that only larger carriers can afford and operate the best available equipment efficiently. Global distribution and computerized reservation systems (CRSs) that display airline schedules and prices for travel agents and reservation clerks are an example. CRSs are potent marketing tools, because approximately 70 percent of all reservations made by U.S. travel agents are made through these systems. Most CRSs are owned and operated by the world's major airlines. CRSs have been expanded to make other types of reservations, such as hotel and rental cars. Fees from sales made via the systems are sources of substantial revenue and profits for their owners.

CRSs display considerable economies of scale because of the sheer scale of investment required to compete and the advantage that an airline that owns a CRS has over a nonairline investor interested in developing a CRS. The carriers that developed CRSs have spent hundreds of millions of dollars over many years to bring their systems to their current advanced state (the substantial profits being earned suggest that these investments have been recouped). The incremental revenues CRSs earn are apparently sufficient to allow the carriers to lease such systems to travel agents below cost. Therefore, a potential competitor that is not also an airline would have to develop a system more efficient than those already in use in order to attract travel agents and would have to be able to support the system without generating incremental airline revenues. Given the high cost of system development, the efficiency and economies of scale of the largest systems, and the contribution made by incremental airline revenues, such new competition appears unlikely.

Historically, most airline passengers made trip reservations through travel agents, resulting in fairly high commissions being paid to the travel agent by the airline. Over time, commissions paid have been lowered as airlines realize the high costs of using a middle person in the transaction. Since the late 1990s and early 2000s, airlines have focused on direct selling methods and have decreased the need for the travel agent. Direct selling includes use of the Internet and direct telephone lines to the airline. Direct telephone lines are still costly to use because of high labor and infrastructure costs. However, this is preferred over the travel agent because no commissions are paid. In terms of Internet sales, airlines often advertise on their own website for direct bookings, or tickets can be purchased through other online sources—for example, expedia.com, travelocity.com, hotwire.com, or kayak.com. Some sites offer detailed itineraries, including price, before making a purchase, whereas other sites act as auction houses and no prices are advertised. The customer simply bids a particular price and if accepted by the online system, a credit card is charged and the ticket is issued. Direct selling is the preferred method of sale by the airline because costs are reduced for the organization and savings are passed on to the passenger. Interestingly, Southwest Airlines was the first U.S. airline to reach $1 billion in annual online sales.

The major carriers are also in a better position to utilize by-products of their industry than the small firms are. Selling pre-packaged frozen foods prepared in the company's flight kitchens to a restaurant chain and selling computer services to smaller firms are examples of by-products that lower unit costs. Other examples include contract maintenance and the use of flight simulator time during off-peak periods for greater utilization of equipment and labor, which, in turn, lowers cost per unit.

It is worth noting at this point that those lower unit costs can also be achieved by economies of scope and density, for which airlines provide excellent examples. Economies of scope achieve lower unit costs by producing multiple products, services, or projects at the same time (with combined resources). As airlines typically transport passengers in the upper decks and cargo in the belly hold of their aircraft, the concept of economies of scope clearly applies. Similarly, economies of density are achieved when airlines concentrate their services at hubs in the already discussed strategy of hub-and-spoke-systems.

Growth Through Merger

Another clear characteristic of oligopolists in general, and airlines in particular, is growth through merger. It is a major factor in explaining the small number of firms. The motivations for mergers are diverse. Of immediate relevance is the fact that combining two or more formerly competing firms by merger can increase their market share substantially and enable the new and larger company to achieve greater economies of scale. Another significant motive underlying the urge to merge is the market power that may accompany a merger. A firm that is larger, both absolutely and relative to the market, may have greater ability to control the market for and the price of its service than a smaller, more competitive producer does. Furthermore, the larger firm may gain leverage as a big purchaser by being able to demand and obtain lower prices (costs) in buying goods and services.

Before deregulation, mergers permitted air carriers to purchase wholesale the entire route structure of another carrier instead of applying for one route at a time through lengthy CAB proceedings. Other reasons for merger include eliminating the possibility of bankruptcy in the case of one of the carriers and eliminating competition on certain route segments. Finally, mergers permit carriers to reduce seasonality problems where one carrier's routes complement the others.

In 1950, the certificated trunk airlines of the United States were as follows:

American Airlines
Continental Airlines
Braniff International
Delta Air Lines
Capital Airlines
Eastern Airlines
Chicago and Southern Air Lines
Inland Airlines
Colonial Airlines

Mid-Continent Airlines
National Airlines
Trans World Airlines
Northeast Airlines
United Airlines
Northwest Airlines
Western Airlines
Pan American
World Airways

By 1960, Mid-Continent had been absorbed by Braniff, which filed for bankruptcy in 1982 after overexpanding in the immediate postderegulation period. Chicago and Southern became a part of Delta; Colonial was absorbed into Eastern; and Inland became a part of Western. In 1962, Capital was taken over by United, and by 1972, Northeast was part of Delta. In 1980, National was acquired by Pan Am after a fierce stock battle with Eastern and Texas International. Using its profits from the sale of National stock, Texas International began buying blocks of stock in Continental in 1979 and eventually won control of that airline in 1981. In 1985, People Express acquired Frontier Airlines for $300 million, and a year later People was absorbed by the newly formed Texas Air for the same price. In 1986, Texas Air acquired New York Air, another newcomer since deregulation, and then pulled off its biggest coup: the acquisition of Eastern.

United purchased Pan Am's Pacific division in 1985, and American acquired Air Cal. Merger activity intensified in 1986 when Northwest acquired Republic for $884 million. Republic, a carrier that became a major after deregulation, was the result of a merger of three successful former local-service carriers: Hughes Airwest, North Central Airlines, and Southern Airways. Hughes Airwest had been the result of a merger of four former carriers in the 1960s—Bonanza Airlines, Southwest Airways, Pacific Airlines, and West Coast Airlines. Also in 1986, Trans World acquired Ozark for $250 million, and the merger of Delta and Western combined the nation's sixth- and ninth-largest airlines into one of the remaining megacarriers. USAir (formerly Allegheny) acquired Pacific Southwest early in 1987 and finally won approval from the DOT for the acquisition of Piedmont in October 1987.

In 1991, Eastern finally folded its wings after operating under bankruptcy for close to two years. Midway ceased operations in early 1992. And after struggling for many years, Pan Am finally went out of business that same year. In 1991, it had sold its transatlantic routes to London and beyond to United for $400 million, and finally, in 1992, it sold its Latin American routes to United. In 2002, American Airlines acquired TWA. In late 2005, America West and US Airways merged but continue to operate under separate names. As of mid-2022, the top U.S. airlines were as shown in Table 7.2.

What followed was a wave of mergers and acquisitions, including the so far largest U.S. airline mergers of Northwest Airlines merging with Delta in 2008, United Airlines merging with Continental Airlines in 2012, U.S. Airways merging with American/AMR in 2013 to form the largest airline in the world (when measured in offered capacity), and Alaska Airlines and Virgin America in 2016 (Table 6.4 and Table 7.3). As of September 2022, JetBlue Airways and Spirit Airlines were in formal negotiations to merge but the deal was still pending.

The consolidation in the U.S. market has resulted in a situation where all of the four largest international passenger airlines are based in the U.S. And even in the low-cost sector there was merger activity with Southwest Airlines acquiring AirTran in 2010, which helped Southwest become the fourth largest airline in the world (if measured in offered seats).

The Airline Deregulation Act of 1978 required the CAB to treat airline mergers and acquisitions in a manner more consistent with the antitrust standards applied to almost all other industries. According to the provisions of the act, application of the Sherman Antitrust Act test would be used to prohibit mergers that would result in a monopoly in any region of the country. Application of the Clayton Antitrust Act test would be used to prohibit transactions that would have the effect of substantially lessening competition or that would tend to create a monopoly. The Airline Deregulation Act, however, did give the CAB (and later the DOT) somewhat more latitude in weighing the benefits of mergers (transportation convenience and needs) than is applied in antitrust cases in other industries.

Table 7.2 Top 20 System (Domestic and International) Seats Flown, 2021

Rank	Airline	IATA	ICAO	Total	Percentage Market Share
1	American Airlines	AA	AAL	3,601,274	5.9
2	Delta Air Lines	DL	DAL	3,295,935	5.4
3	Southwest Airlines	WN	SWA	3,176,741	5.2
4	China Southern Airlines	CZ	CSN	2,674,470	4.4
5	China Eastern Airlines	MU	CES	2,501,798	4.1
6	United Airlines	UA	UAL	2,251,170	3.7
7	Air China	CA	CCA	1,768,637	2.9
8	IndiGo	6E	IGO	1,381,818	2.3
9	Turkish Airlines	TK	THY	1,016,020	1.7
10	Alaska Airlines	AS	ASA	863,583	1.4
11	Hainan Airlines	HU	CHH	851,255	1.4
12	Shenzhen Airlines	ZH	CSZ	847,011	1.4

(Continued)

Table 7.2 (Continued)

Rank	Airline	IATA	ICAO	Total	Percentage Market Share
13	Xiamen Airlines	MF	CXA	827,700	1.4
14	Sichuan Airlines	3U	CSC	762,346	1.2
15	Spirit Airlines	NK	NKS	741,118	1.2
16	Shandong Airlines	SC	CDG	695,032	1.1
17	JetBlue Airways	B6	JBU	679,271	1.1
18	LATAM Airlines	LA	LAN	630,727	1.0
19	Aeroflot	SU	AFL	601,307	1.0
20	All Nippon Airways	NH	ANA	599,151	1.0

Source: CAPA – Centre for Aviation; OAG

Table 7.3 U.S. Airline Mergers and Acquisitions

Title	Announced	Closed	Resulting Entity
Western Air Express/Standard Airlines	1/22/1930	5/1/1930	Western Air Express
Western Air Express/Transcontinental Air Transport	11/15/1929	7/16/1930	Transcontinental & Western Air
Delta Air Lines/Chicago and Southern (C&S) Air Lines	4/26/1952	5/1/1953	Delta Air Lines
United Airlines/Capital Airlines	7/28/1960	6/1/1961	United Airlines
Western Airlines/Pacific Northern Airlines	10/28/1966	7/1/1967	Western Airlines
Frontier Airlines/Central Airlines	5/5/1967	10/1/1967	Frontier Airlines
Alaska Airlines/Cordova Airlines	Early 1967	2/1/1968	Alaska Airlines
Allegheny Airlines/Lake Central Airlines	10/19/1967	3/14/1968	Allegheny Airlines (later renamed US Airways)
Alaska Airlines/Alaska Coastal Airlines	3/17/1967	4/1/1968	Alaska Airlines
Pacific Airlines/Bonanza Airlines/West Coast Airlines	6/22/1967	7/1/1968	Air West
American Airlines/Trans Caribbean Airways	1/18/1970	3/3/1971	American Airlines
Allegheny Airlines/Mohawk Airlines	4/14/1971	4/12/1972	Allegheny Airlines (later renamed US Airways)
Delta Air Lines/Northeast Airlines	4/23/1971	8/1/1972	Delta Air Lines
North Central Airlines/Southern Airways/Hughes Airwest	7/14/1978	7/1/1979	Republic Airlines
Pan Am/National Airlines	8/23/1978	1/7/1980	Pan Am

Title	Announced	Closed	Resulting Entity
Republic Airlines/Hughes Airwest	3/12/1980	10/1/1980	Republic Airlines
Continental Airlines/Texas Air Corporation	2/9/1981	10/31/1982	Continental Airlines
Southwest Airlines/Muse Airlines	6/25/1985	12/12/1985	Southwest Airlines
Northwest Airlines/Republic Airlines	1/23/1986	10/1/1986	Northwest Airlines
TWA/Ozark Air Lines	3/1/1986	10/27/1986	TWA
Delta Air Lines/Western Airlines	9/9/1986	12/16/1986	Delta Air Lines
Alaska Airlines/Horizon Air	11/19/1986	12/31/1986	Alaska Airlines/ Horizon Air
Continental Airlines/People Express/New York Air/Frontier Airlines	1/12/1987	2/1/1987	Continental Airlines
American Airlines/AirCal	11/18/1986	4/30/1987	American Airlines
US Air/Pacific Southwest Airlines	11/18/1986	5/29/1987	US Air
Alaska Airlines/Jet America	7/23/1987	10/1/1987	Alaska Airlines
US Air/Piedmont Airlines	3/19/1987	8/4/1989	US Air
American Airlines/Eastern Air Lines: Latin Routes	12/19/1989	7/1/1990	American Airlines
American Airlines/TWA: Heathrow Routes	12/16/1990	5/2/1991	American Airlines
Delta Air Lines/Pan Am Airlines (Shuttle and Atlantic Routes)	7/27/1991	11/1/1991	Delta Shuttle
United Airlines/Pan Am: Latin & Caribbean Routes	12/9/1991	5/16/1992	United Airlines
Southwest Airlines/Morris Airlines	12/13/1993	12/31/1993	Southwest Airlines
AirTran Airways/Valujet	7/11/1997	11/17/1997	AirTran Airways
American Airlines/Reno Air	11/19/1998	2/1/1999	American Airlines
Delta Air Lines/Atlantic Southeast Airlines	2/16/1999	3/22/1999	Delta Air Lines
Delta Air Lines/Comair	10/18/1999	10/22/1999	Delta Air Lines
American Airlines/TWA	1/10/2001	4/9/2001	American Airlines
Republic Airways/Shuttle America	4/22/2005	5/9/2005	Republic Airways
SkyWest/Atlantic Southeast Airlines	8/15/2005	9/8/2005	SkyWest/ASA
US Airways/America West Airlines	5/19/2005	9/27/2005	US Airways
Pinnacle Airlines/Colgan Air	1/18/2007	1/18/2007	Pinnacle Airlines/ Colgan Air

(Continued)

Table 7.3 (Continued)

Title	Announced	Closed	Resulting Entity
Southwest Airlines/ATA Airlines	11/19/2008	12/2/2008	Southwest Airlines
Republic Airways/Midwest Airlines	6/23/2009	7/31/2009	Republic Airways
Republic Airways/Frontier Airlines	8/14/2009	10/1/2009	Republic Airways
Delta Air Lines/Northwest Airlines	4/14/2008	12/31/2009	Delta Air Lines
Pinnacle Airlines/Mesaba Airlines	7/1/2010	7/1/2010	Pinnacle Airlines/ Mesaba Airlines
United Airlines/Continental Airlines	5/3/2010	10/1/2010	United Airlines
SkyWest/Atlantic Southeast Airlines/ExpressJet Airlines	8/4/2010	11/15/2010	SkyWest/SureJet
Southwest Airlines/AirTran Airways	9/27/2010	5/2/2011	Southwest Airlines
US Airways/American Airlines	2/14/2013	12/9/2013	American Airlines
Atlas Air/Southern Air	1/19/2016	4/7/2016	Atlas Air Worldwide
FedEx/TNT Express	4/27/2015	5/25/2016	FedEx
Alaska Airlines/Virgin America	4/4/2016	12/14/2016	Alaska Airlines
United Airlines (via ManaAir)/ ExpressJet Airlines	12/18/2018	1/3/2019	United/ExpressJet
Southern Airways/Mokulele Airlines	2/12/2019	3/11/2019	Southern/Mokulele
Mokulele Airlines/Makani Kai Air	6/3/2020	Dec-20	Mokulele
Frontier Airlines/Spirit Airlines	2/7/2022	7/27/2022	Terminated
Southern Airways/Air Choice One (Multi-Aero)	3/28/2022	Pending	Southern
JetBlue Airways/Spirit Airlines	7/28/2022	Pending	TBD

Source: Airlines.org

In the first few years after passage of the Airline Deregulation Act, before the CAB was dissolved and its antitrust authority shifted to the DOT, several mergers were permitted that were "end-to-end" in character. These mergers involved carriers that did not serve overlapping markets, and some of the mergers actually enhanced service by reducing transaction costs, apparently without reducing competition. For example, Pan American was allowed to merge with National. Several proposed mergers were disapproved because the carriers' routes were "parallel mergers"; that is, the carriers served too many overlapping routes (Eastern–National). Several others were disapproved because of concern about hub dominance and barriers to entry (Continental–Western).

When the DOT was given authority over mergers in 1985, the number of mergers and acquisitions increased from eight between 1980 and 1984 to 18 in 1985 and to 25 in 1986. Most of these mergers did not raise significant competitive issues; many of the small carriers involved in them were in financial difficulty and would have gone bankrupt had they not merged. Some end-to-end mergers may even have facilitated competition, because the combination of two carriers serving different markets helped build a broader, more competitive network.

Because of the complexity of airline networks and competition, it is difficult to specify in advance the conditions under which mergers or acquisitions will be anticompetitive. Some mergers, for example, may facilitate competition between hub networks but simultaneously create opportunities for hub dominance. An overriding question concerns the total number of major carriers that are required to maintain an adequate level of competition. Although the number of firms required to ensure adequate competition necessarily involves some speculation, the main criterion for the adequacy of competition nationwide is the level of competition for passenger flows between competing hub systems. Consumers receive the largest benefits when three or more competitors are operating in the same market, especially if one of the competitors is a new-entrant airline with a low-price marketing strategy.

Having only three carriers nationwide would probably not be adequate to ensure this level of competition. Sufficient barriers to entry exist to prevent three major carriers from being able to compete with one another for hub traffic from every major spoke city. Five or six major airlines, however, would probably constitute a sufficient number of hub systems to ensure the presence of three or more competitors in most major spoke markets, especially when several additional healthy regional and national carriers are offering consumers alternatives in specific regional or niche markets. Five or six nationwide firms that compete with one another at all the large commercial airports may provide much stronger competitive pressure to hold down costs and fares than would ten or 15 carriers competing in less extensive networks. The fewer the number of firms, however, the easier it is for them to form and enforce a tight oligopoly in which industry output is lower and fares are higher than would be the case in a competitive market. For fewer than five or six carriers, the results would depend on the circumstances of the carriers, their markets, and the vigor of the competition among them in the future. But as already indicated, three or four major nationwide carriers are likely to be too few to ensure adequate competition. The positive aspect of this effect is, despite the loss in consumer welfare, that the involved airlines are now, due to coordinated capacity reductions, able to generate profits and more sustainable operations in the future.

Mutual Dependence

Regardless of the means by which an oligopoly evolves, rivalry among a small number of firms clearly interjects a new and complicating characteristic: mutual dependence. Imagine that three carriers—A, B, and C—serve the same route and that each has about one-third of the market. If A cuts its price, its share of the market will increase, but B and C will be directly, immediately, and adversely affected by A's price-cutting. Thus, we can expect some reaction on the part of B and C to A's behavior: B and C may match A's price cut or even undercut A, thereby starting a price war. This response suggests that no firm in an oligopolistic industry will dare to alter its price policies without attempting to calculate the most likely reaction of its rivals. This is consistent with economic theory and characteristic of pricing at concentrated gate- and slot-constrained airports where two or three competitors hold the majority market share. However, not enough oligopoly pricing exists to cover the industry's fixed costs and offset steep discounting in competitive markets. Today, the airline industry sets prices in a highly irrational way. We see evidence of oligopoly and destructive competition side by side. Since deregulation, the full unrestricted Y fare—or basic or standard fare—has almost doubled. With the full fare rising so sharply, relatively few passengers would pay it. Consequently, today, over 90 percent of passengers pay an average of only about 30 percent of the full fare. Only those individuals who absolutely must fly on short notice have to pay full fare.

Discounted fares are targeted at discretionary (vacation) travelers. To dissuade business travelers from using them, they ordinarily come saddled with restrictions—non-refundability, advance purchase requirements, and Saturday night stay-over obligations. However, large corporations and units of the federal government can negotiate a contract rate with airlines that includes the discounted fares but is largely devoid of restrictions.

The intense price competition that characterizes many routes is complicated by the fact that different carriers often attach varying importance to the same route. In many circumstances, a particular route represents an important part of a carrier's network, produces fully allocated profits, and is regarded as part of that carrier's core business. For a second carrier not currently serving that route, on the other hand, it represents an incremental opportunity.

Needing only to recover the marginal costs of adding service with equipment it already has, but adding a service that may be surplus to its needs, the second carrier may choose to facilitate its entry to the route by pricing its services at or just above marginal cost. In this situation, the second carrier will benefit from filling lots of empty seats and contributing, in at least a small way, to covering its fixed costs.

The first carrier, compelled to match the newcomer's price, will suffer significant yield erosion and will be unable to meet its objective of full cost recovery. The new carrier will benefit, but overall, the industry (Carrier A + Carrier B) will move from profit to loss.

The pricing decisions of individual carriers usually make economic sense from the carrier's perspective. But for the industry as a whole, these decisions contribute to the continual price erosion that has restricted the ability of all carriers to increase revenues to keep up with rising costs.

Price Rigidity and Nonprice Competition

Firms in oligopolistic industries are much more comfortable maintaining constant prices than rocking the boat, so to speak, because of mutual dependence and fear of a price war. The tendency has been to fight it out in the nonprice arena, using advertising and increased customer services as the major weapons. This situation prevailed in the airline industry before 1978. At that time, however, the door was opened to new competition, and the airline price wars began.

Under the old regulatory framework, the price of an airline seat was directly related to the cost of producing it. Prices were simply based on costs, allowing for a given rate of return. Carriers were expected to use the resulting profits to cross-subsidize required service on shorter-haul, lower-density routes (on which fares were often held below prevailing costs). Everyone knew the rules and was comfortable with them. The impact of economic recession was blunted by the CAB, which rescued the occasional casualty with repeated doses of fare increases. After the Airline Deregulation Act of 1978, however, things changed, and airline pricing became more complicated.

In theory, the removal of route restrictions after deregulation was supposed to stimulate the entry of new firms into the airline industry and cause existing airlines to expand or shift their operations into other, more profitable markets, thereby forcing fares down and expanding service options in markets in which carriers had previously enjoyed little competition. Indeed, as predicted by theory, most established carriers greatly expanded their networks shortly after deregulation, and many new firms entered the marketplace, creating a competitive environment that produced much lower fares during the mid-1980s. Since 1987, however, virtually all these new entrants have either failed or merged with larger incumbent carriers, while passenger fares have risen.

During the early 1990s, American Airlines tried on several occasions to introduce some sensibility into the fare structure by proposing a simple, four-tiered "value pricing" system that tied fares to distance flown and that more adequately related fares to costs. United and Delta were prepared to emulate the system, but others—like Continental, TWA, and America West, which were going through bankruptcy and facing huge losses—were more interested in cutting fares to generate cash flow.

Given the recessionary economy in the early 1990s and slow industry growth through the late 1990s and early 2000s, prices had not stabilized for several years. As the result of the waves of consolidation and capacity reduction, there appears to be both an oligopolistic market structure and oligopolistic behavior. As a result, prices have not only stabilized but have increased over the last decade with the expected positive results on U.S. airline profitability.

OTHER UNIQUE ECONOMIC CHARACTERISTICS

Government Financial Assistance

Unlike other oligopolistic industries, various government units have played major roles in financing the growth and development of the U.S. airport-airways system. The federal government has played the predominant role in this regard. Until 1970, when the Airport and Airway Development Act was passed by Congress, the national airways system was maintained by the federal government at minimal cost to users of the system. However, the act created a system of user charges that have been levied on airline passengers, shippers, general aviation, and the airlines so that the airways might be self-supporting. The 1970 act and its successor, the Airport and Airway Improvement Act of 1982, provided for continued federal funding of both airway operation and airport development. In many instances, the fees charged for landing aircraft, maintaining office and operational space, and providing maintenance and administrative quarters do not repay the operating costs of the airport. Even when the fees repay operating costs, they typically do not cover capital costs involved in airport expansion. Consequently, the airline industry has historically benefited from the financing of the major cost element of the industry—the airport-airways system—by various governmental units, which until recently levied quite limited charges on system users.

High Technological Turnover

As of 2022, the U.S. scheduled airlines had total assets exceeding $100 billion, of which more than $60 billion was flight equipment. No other oligopolistic industry has such highly mobile assets that represent close to 60 percent of its total assets. Furthermore, technological advances in flight equipment over the short span of approximately 40 years have come at an extremely rapid pace.

Before World War II, the capital requirements of most commercial airlines were modest and were met largely through internal sources—notably profits. The scale of the industry increased, however, and by the mid-1950s, the industry had turned its attention to planning for jet aircraft. The carriers committed almost $2 billion for flight equipment and the associated ground equipment. The first jet aircraft arrived in the late 1950s, and by the mid-1960s, the stretched-version Boeing 727s and 720s were arriving on the scene to accommodate the increased traffic, which required a whole new refinancing cycle. By the mid to late 1960s, plans were being made to purchase larger, wide-body equipment. Between 1966 and 1971, the industry placed orders amounting to $10 billion. The 1970s witnessed dramatic rises in fuel prices, and all attention was focused on developing fuel-efficient aircraft for the 1980s and 1990s. By 1986, industry capital requirements from external sources reached $7 billion. According to a 2022 FlightGlobal report, the growth projected for the global passenger aircraft fleet is estimated to hit $120 billion annually just to fund aircraft.

Airlines have led all other industries in the rate of increase in capital spending over the past three decades. Technological advances and competition have forced the carriers to undertake a re-equipment cycle on an average of every eight years. Besides calling for huge amounts of capital spending, these cycles mean heavy expenses in hiring and training personnel and in modifying facilities to accommodate the new aircraft and associated equipment.

High Labor and Fuel Expenses

Because an airline's costs define the limit of how low it can profitably price its service, and because most airline customers value low prices above all other carrier selection factors, the carrier with the lowest costs has a powerful competitive advantage. The fact that most carriers have a difficult time differentiating their products from those of their competition makes this especially true. Thus, cutting costs to the lowest possible level has become a key strategic necessity in today's airline industry.

Unfortunately, reducing costs is easier said than done. In addition to a carrier's high fixed costs, many of the so-called variable costs, if not completely out of the airline's control, are very difficult to manage. Two of the biggest are labor and fuel expenses.

Airline employees are men and women with highly developed skills and with correspondingly high incomes. In 2008, the industry employed 556,920 people, and the average wage exceeded $56,754 ($75,532 total compensation), which far outpaces all other industries in the United States. In 2020, the U.S. domestic airlines employed 598,760 people at an average salary of $58,246, and by 2022, U.S. domestic airlines employed 413,372 people with the decline attributed to the negative impact of the COVID-19 global pandemic. While airline consolidation has helped the airlines to reduce staff numbers, the data remains clear with fuel and labor the highest cost categories for U.S. airlines. In the U.S., passenger airlines operating costs are broken down as follows: 32.3 percent labor, 17.7 percent fuel, 7.1 percent aircraft rents and ownership, 4.5 percent non-aircraft rents and ownership, 8.6 percent professional services, 1.7 percent food and beverage, 1.9 percent landing fees, 1.4 percent maintenance material, 13.1 percent transport related, and 11.7 percent other.

The high level of unionization in the airline industry, particularly among the more established carriers, also reduces the extent to which labor costs can truly be considered variable. Labor typically represents the largest cost advantage start-up airlines have over more established carriers. Moreover, despite its reliance on high technology, the business is very labor intensive. New entrants often outsource many functions to service providers that pay their employees minimum market rates and provide few, if any, benefits. Because these providers draw from a large pool of experienced workers trained by carriers that have failed, new entrants often offer service that is qualitatively indistinguishable from that offered by long-established carriers.

In contrast, the older carriers operate under the terms of union contracts that prevent them from making changes to match the costs of new entrants. These contracts typically include extraordinarily complex work rules that sharply reduce the carriers' ability to improve labor productivity. Moreover, the work force of the traditional carrier typically is much older than that of a start-up airline, creating an even greater disparity in wage rates, as a ten- or 20-year airline veteran will invariably have achieved a far higher wage than his or her counterpart at a start-up carrier.

No other industry has been subjected to the severe increases in fuel prices that the air carriers have experienced over the past 15 years. Between 1978 and 1981, the price of jet fuel increased by over 153 percent, rising to a peak in May 1981 of $1.052 per gallon in domestic markets and $1.168 in international markets. The trend in jet fuel prices was generally downward for the remainder of the decade. However, in 1990, starting with the heating oil crisis that raised the price of jet fuel by a third, prices soared. Stimulated by the Iraqi invasion of Kuwait, jet fuel, which had sold for as low as 60 cents per gallon, moved very quickly to more than $1.10 per gallon. Although there was no shortage in fuel, prices were driven up in a speculative panic. By 2014, the airlines were hit with increased costs, with fuel being a major contributor. Industry cost expenses increased 14.7 percent in 2008 over the year prior to $165.4 billion. Crude oil prices (per barrel) increased from an average of $26 in 2002 to over $100 in 2008. In July 2008, crude oil hit a record high of $145.21 per barrel and jet fuel hit a high of $4.26 per gallon due to inflation. Fuel prices are heavily influenced by a variety of local and global factors correlated with the price of crude oil. Influencing factors include the global economy, increasing supply tightness, geopolitical insecurity (i.e., the Russian–Ukrainian war), unique production and demand factors, and acts of God. It is estimated that every 1-cent-per-gallon increase costs the industry approximately $160 million. By late 2022, according to IATA, the average global jet fuel price reached $139.50 per barrel with noticeable fluctuations across the globe as follows: Asia and Oceania ($129.54), Europe and CIS ($142.35), Middle East and Africa ($131.32), North America ($143.40), Latin and Central America ($145.32).

Although an airline can maximize its efficiency by purchasing aircraft that burn less fuel than others, fuel-efficient airplanes often have much higher capital costs than less fuel-efficient aircraft do. Moreover, the actual price of fuel is contingent on factors far outside any airline's span of control. Thus, fuel costs are only marginally manageable.

Labor and fuel costs typically represent around 50–60 percent of a carrier's operating expenses.

The Competitive Advantage of Schedule Frequency

The effect of a slight change in departure time on passenger buying behavior creates a powerful incentive for carriers to increase flight frequency, even when there are plenty of seats available on existing flights.

Moreover, when one carrier enjoys a schedule frequency advantage over another on a particular route, the competitive value of that advantage is more than proportional. For example, if Carrier A has six daily flights between two points and Carrier B has only three, the relative strength of Carrier A versus Carrier B is greater than two to one. The reason for this is that Carrier A's customers—in addition to having two times as many chances to match a flight to their needs—will perceive the more frequent service as offering them more flexibility to change their plans at the last minute.

Because airline hub-and-spoke systems provide the most convenient service between the greatest number of cities, most U.S. carriers operate domestic route networks focused around one or more hubs. The fact that customers see the airlines' product, a seat on an airplane, as a relatively undifferentiated product notwithstanding, each time a network-based airline offers a new flight, it commits an additional city to all the others served by the hub, and thus introduces a number of new products. Additionally, by widening the reach of its network, it strengthens its entire existing product line.

When origin-departure city-pairs, time of departure, airport used, and type of service (nonstop versus connecting) combinations are considered, an airline can schedule its resources to offer an enormous range of "products," each with different revenue-generating potential and different costs. Furthermore, once airplanes and facilities are in place, the economics of offering additional capacity are often evaluated on the basis of marginal cost, which is very low as a percentage of total cost.

In most industries, increased production, by itself, does not enhance an individual competitor's sales potential or competitive position. However, in the airline industry, the fact that more capacity represents more schedule frequency, and thus a more desirable product, gives every airline an incentive to use every airplane as intensively as possible. Although this strategy makes sense for each individual carrier, it results in a tendency toward perpetual overcapacity.

Excess Capacity and Low Marginal Costs

The airline industry historically has tended both to produce excess capacity and to price its product below fully allocated costs, although recent data suggests that as a result of consolidation this trend has been reverted in the U.S. (but not elsewhere in the world). The demand of consumers for schedule frequency produces tremendous excess capacity with no shelf life, pushing costs up. The demand of consumers for low prices and the perception that air transportation is virtually an undifferentiated commodity drive prices down to levels that, too often, fail to cover fully allocated costs.

Airlines inevitably produce excessive capacity. Whether regulated or deregulated, from the mid-1950s to the present, U.S. airlines have almost never achieved an average annual load factor exceeding 67 percent (and in most years, load factors were substantially worse than that). In effect, this means that at least one-third of available inventory remains unsold. However, as a result of consolidation and capacity reductions, load factors on average have improved. In 2012, load factors averaged 82.8 percent reaching an all-time high of 83.1% in 2013. Load factors continued to increase with some slight deviations leading up to an industry high of 85 percent in 2019. By 2020, the average load factor decreased to a low of 58.7 percent as a result of the slowdown caused by the COVID-19 global pandemic. By late 2022, the average load factor increased to 74.2 percent with signs of positive growth on the horizon as the world recovered from the pandemic.

On this point, economist Melvin Brenner notes:

> The industry has always had excess capacity, even during boom times. Over-capacity results from: (a) the competitive importance of schedule frequency. Since schedule convenience is one of the most important differentiating characteristics of the airline product, all airlines strive for high scheduled frequency on every important route, and (b) the fact that airlines have very high fixed costs and are therefore incentivized to fly their aircraft as much as possible, even if incremental flying does not produce enough revenue to cover fully allocated costs. Whenever a flight covers variable costs and contributes to overhead, the individual carrier is better off flying rather than not flying. However, the cumulation of the many marginally-justified schedules creates over-capacity for the industry as a whole.[3]

Moreover, that capacity has no shelf life. Once a scheduled flight pulls away from the gate, any empty seats are lost forever. Seeking to sell as much of that perishable inventory as possible, carriers offer the same fares as the lowest-price provider in an effort to grasp an ascending and, too often, elusive break-even load factor and preserve market share.

Excess capacity coupled with perishable inventory leads to marginal cost pricing. The marginal cost of serving one additional customer on a given flight is very low, consisting only of the cost of food, sales commission, incremental fuel burn, and other minor expenses. In general, the marginal cost of an additional passenger is less than one-fourth of the fully allocated costs. But industry costs are disproportionately fixed, with fixed costs accounting for between 80 and 90 percent of total costs. In the high-fixed-cost, price-sensitive airline business, excess capacity has a devastating effect because it motivates carriers to fill aircraft by cutting prices. Other carriers are forced to match, and fare wars erupt. Although a ticket sold below fully allocated costs is unprofitable, any ticket sold at a price above variable cost will make a contribution, albeit often a small one, toward covering the carrier's fixed costs. An empty seat, naturally, makes no such contribution.

Airlines also suffer from the problem that most of their costs are joint costs, spread over an array of functions related to moving passengers and freight throughout their networks. Thus, actual costs are obscured and difficult to ascribe to particular passengers.

In the long run, carriers must recover their fixed costs or face bankruptcy (as scores of airlines have learned). But collectively irrational behavior, such as was exhibited by airlines before regulation in 1938 and after deregulation in 1978, causes costs and prices to fail to achieve equilibrium at a level that covers fully allocated costs and allows an adequate profit. In that sense it is encouraging to see that airline load factors seem to have gone up slightly in recent years.

Sensitivity to Economic Fluctuations

The susceptibility of air transportation demand to the business cycle was underlined by the recession of the early 1990s. Revenue passenger miles and cargo ton-miles declined, and losses soared to record levels.

Although the impact of a recession is not unique to the airline industry, what is different is the fact that as a service industry (unlike durable goods such as automobiles), it is much slower to recover because spending on air travel is discretionary. People have to be working again and the economy has to be well on the way to recovery before spending on air travel starts to pick up momentum. This can take anywhere from 12 to 18 months after the recovery is well under way.

The effects of a recession on air travel are obvious. Both pleasure and business travel is curtailed during periods of sharp and sustained downturn in the general economy. In a recession, people tend to postpone long-distance travel to save not only on airfares but also on the expenses associated with the trip. Companies tend to cut back on business trips or on the number of people sent on a given trip. Travel is one of the expenses a business can cut immediately during tough economic times. Fewer people travel first class, so that the dollar yields realized are reduced.

The impact of a recession on the airlines is intensified by the high rate of traffic growth they experience during periods of prosperity. When the economy moves into a recessionary period, the carriers find themselves with substantial excess capacity. Unlike manufacturing industries, they cannot inventory goods or cut back production until the economy improves. Interest payments to creditors on outstanding debts (primarily flight equipment) must be paid, and facilities that were geared to handle a prerecession volume cannot be closed. Although airlines can furlough certain volume-related employees, they must carefully consider this move because of the extensive retraining costs involved when personnel are brought back as volumes increase.

Close Government Regulation

The close relationship between the airlines and the various units of the federal government was discussed in Chapter 4. Unlike other oligopolistic industries, but like other transportation modes, the airlines have a long history of both support and regulation by government. The FAA regulates most aspects of airline operations that relate to safety and navigation, as well as to environmental conditions. The National Transportation Safety Board investigates all air carrier accidents and makes recommendations to the FAA. Other federal agencies, including the Department of Transportation, Department of Commerce, U.S. Postal Service, U.S. Customs and Border Protection, U.S. Citizenship and Immigration Services, and Department of Justice, regulate less obvious aspects of airline operations and have extensive interaction with the industry. State aviation agencies, local airport authorities, and other branches of local government regulate airline operations in terms of their effect on local airports and airport environs.

THE SIGNIFICANCE OF AIRLINE PASSENGER LOAD FACTORS

One of the most vital statistics in the airline business is load factor. Given the multimillion-dollar investment represented by the modern jetliner, airlines are naturally concerned with equipment utilization. One measure of utilization is the revenue passenger **load factor**. This figure expresses the relationship between available seat-miles and revenue passenger miles realized.

Load factor has a critical impact on the cost and quality of air transportation services offered. Approximately 65 percent of an airline's costs are directly related to the operation of aircraft and are independent of the number of passengers on the aircraft. Therefore, a high load factor will allow the allocation of these costs over a large number of passengers, resulting in lower costs per passenger, which allows for lower fares.

Traffic Peaks and Valleys

All transportation modes must operate during traffic peaks and valleys in order to meet the public need. Buses and commuter trains in every major city are full in one direction during rush hours and virtually empty on the return trip. At midday, in the early morning and late evening, and on weekends, passenger loads are also light. That's the nature of public transportation, whether buses, trains, or planes.

Airline load factors during any one year vary from month to month depending on the season. Daily and hourly load factors fluctuate even more. Averages for the peak day of the peak month might be 75 percent, and for the peak hour 80 percent; many flights in these hours are at or near 100 percent capacity. Furthermore, a nationwide transportation network requires that some flights with light patronage be operated to position aircraft for other flights with higher loads. Flights to Florida in November and December are booked solid, while load factors on flights north are much lower. Flights from Los Angeles to Las Vegas on Friday nights are full and flights back to Los Angeles on Sunday nights are full, but the planes cannot sit idle over the weekend in Las Vegas. They must be used for other service and thus must fly from Las Vegas with little or no traffic and return for the

FIGURE 7.1 Partial Boeing 757 Routing Pattern (two days), Summer 20XX

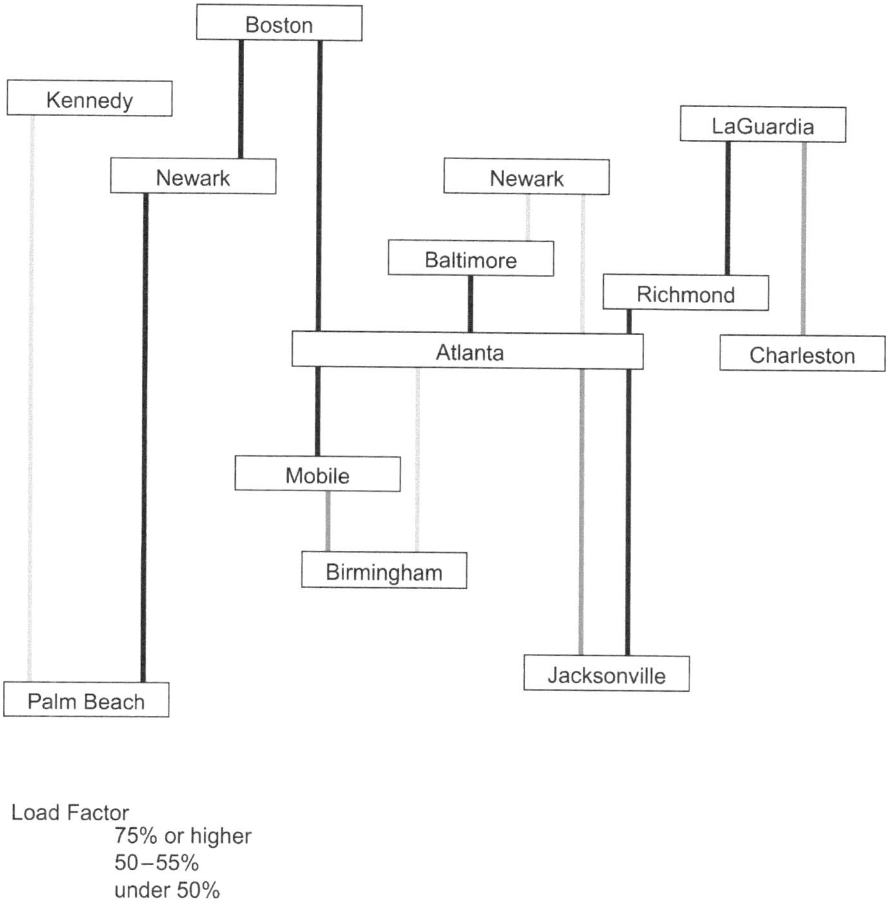

next high-load flight back to Los Angeles on Sunday night. And so it goes for other city-pairs throughout the nation.

Sometimes, aircraft must be flown virtually empty from one city to another late at night or early in the morning to have the plane ready to meet rush-hour demand. These **positioning flights** certainly affect the average load factor figure used to describe air transportation productivity.

Figure 7.1 shows an example of two days out of a summer's Boeing 757 routing pattern. Based on these two days, the carrier had an average load factor of 60 percent. Eight of the 15 flight segments had a load factor of 75 percent or more, and the carrier was forced to turn some passengers away. Three segments averaged about 50 percent, and the remaining four had load factors ranging between 15 and 45 percent.

Capacity versus Demand

Demand for air transport services has always been highly cyclical, with greater or lesser demand depending on time of day, day of the week, and season, as well as on broader market fluctuations from year to year. We know, for example, that discretionary leisure traffic picks up in the summer, thereby allowing the industry to enjoy higher load factors for the third quarter.

On a macro level, when the economy is growing and consumer confidence is strong, demand grows, improving airline load factors and allowing carriers to raise yields and profitability. When the economy falters, however, unemployment rises, consumer confidence declines, and individuals postpone discretionary travel; as a result, airline load factors, yields, and profits suffer.

The realities of public transportation, whether bus, train, or plane, result in an imbalance between the number of seats, or capacity, available and the current demand for travel by the public. The two simply do not mesh at precisely the same time, the same place, and the same rate.

Airlines cannot fine-tune capacity to match demand, because capacity can only be added or taken away in total planeloads. The aircraft unit itself is obviously inflexible; if a given carrier's 757 is equipped with 160 seats, that seat supply on a particular schedule cannot be shrunk or expanded between Thursday and Friday and then changed again for Saturday.

Within limits, the total number of flight frequencies on a given day can be varied, and this is done where feasible. On business routes, for example, it is common to reduce frequencies on Saturdays. However, a number of factors limit the ability to adjust daily seats to daily traffic.

First, many routes have too little flight frequency maintained by each carrier to permit much leeway for canceling trips on a particular day without damaging the overall pattern. Second, the day-of-week pattern of demand does not vary in a precise, predictable, or fully consistent manner. Finally, the schedule pattern on any one route is too interrelated with those of other routes (and with operational constraints of various kinds) to permit an erratically scheduled operation from day to day. As a result of these various factors, the supply of seats is necessarily much more uniform than the demand for them is.

Figure 7.2 shows the number of seats offered each day and the passengers actually carried for a schedule on an intermediate-length segment (Miami–New York). For the month as a whole, the average load on this route was 70 passengers, which produced an average monthly load factor of 68 percent. On the other hand, the average number of empty seats per trip was 32. But as can be seen, at one extreme there were four days when there were more than 60 empty seats, and at the other extreme there were seven days when there were fewer than 15 empty seats.

In the example in Figure 7.2, although space was relatively tighter on some days than on others, on no days was this particular flight completely full. The question may arise as to why there should ever have been any need to turn any passenger away from this scheduled flight. Yet the probability

FIGURE 7.2 Daily Seats and Passengers, One Miami–New York Schedule (hypothetical scenario)

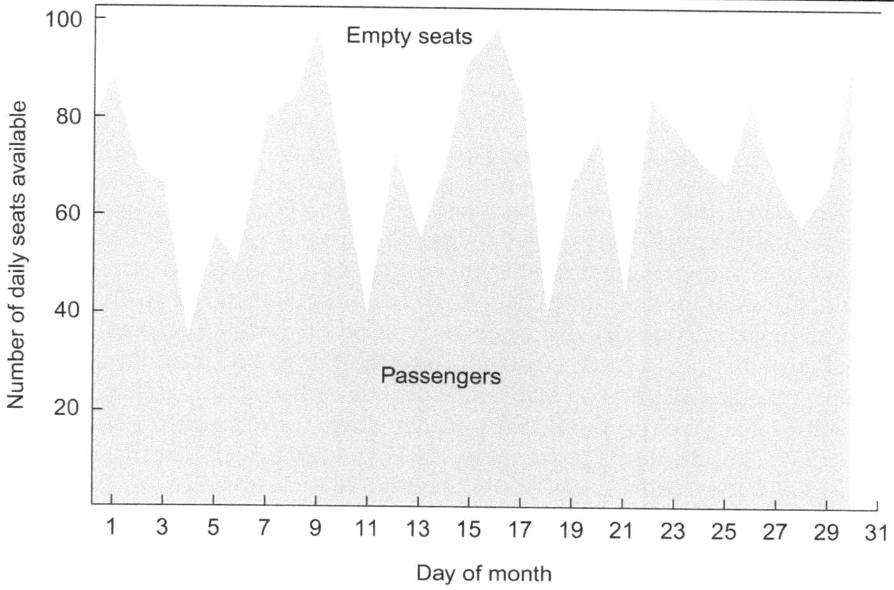

is very high that passengers were indeed turned away on a number of days, even though there were some empty seats at departure time.

The explanation for this lies in the nature of the reservations process and the fact that a flight can be fully booked days or even weeks in advance and then have some of those bookings dissipate by departure time. Passengers originally holding reservations may have to change their plans at the last minute and either cancel their space too late for it to be rebooked or simply become **no-shows**. Thus, the existence of some empty seats at departure time does not eliminate the possibility that prospective passengers were turned away at some time during the booking process. The importance of this factor is indicated by the no-show rate, which at times has run as high as 20 percent.

No-shows are partly offset by **overbooking**, which reflects an attempt by airlines to factor in the mathematical probabilities of no-shows and to adjust seat inventories accordingly. A carrier cannot completely correct for this factor, however, because some allowance must be made for unexpected changes in booking patterns. Therefore, there is still the prospect of unaccommodated demand for any flight that departs with only a few seats empty.

Based on the carrier's no-show rate for a particular flight, it appears likely that flights departing with load factors of 80 percent or more have turned away some passengers. Although the cost benefit of high load factors is easily understood, we now see that there is another side to the coin—the relationship between load factor and service convenience. The higher the load factor, the greater the prospect that a passenger will find his or her desired flight already fully booked when seeking a reservation. There is, in other words, a tradeoff involved in high load factors—the benefit of lower cost per passenger versus the disadvantage of lower service convenience.

Pricing in Relation to Load Factor

One approach that carriers have used quite extensively over the years to improve load factors is **off-peak pricing**. This involves the introduction of a promotional fare designed to attract passengers during an otherwise slack period. Off-peak pricing dates back to the earliest days of the airline industry. The first coach service, for example, was an off-peak night coach.

It has always been recognized that both the public and the industry benefit if the empty seats on low-traffic days are filled with passengers who are willing to travel on those less popular days in exchange for some fare reduction. The additional passengers add very little to costs (primarily meal service), but they add a great deal to the flight's total revenue.

Off-peak pricing has not been without its problems. One problem is the fact that the timing of the peak has varied from route to route and even from one direction to the other on the same route. For example, Dallas–New Orleans might experience its peak traffic on Friday, and Chicago–Los Angeles on Sunday. As another example, the peak hour of the day westbound from New York to Los Angeles is from 5:00 to 6:00 p.m. Yet traveling eastbound on the very same route, the peak departure time is 9:00 a.m., because of the effect of time zones.

Off-peak pricing, by its nature, injects complications into the pricing structure. In contrast, some pricing developments in recent years have aimed for the simplicity of overall fare reductions, applied across the board, without restrictions. Although such overall fare reductions have the welcome effect of reducing the complexity of the fare structure, they do require higher load factors to remain viable, and they cannot themselves channel traffic to off-peak times and days to achieve optimal load factors. Therefore, this particular pricing trend brings into play the full force of high load factors on space restrictions without softening the impact of such restrictions on the normal peak times.

At this point, it is impossible to predict which pricing strategies will prove dominant in the long run. For reasons already indicated, the outcome will have an important bearing on the service-convenience aspect of future load factors.

KEY TERMS

barriers to entry
diseconomy of scale
economy of scale

load factor
mutual dependence
no-show
off-peak pricing
oligopoly
overbooking
positioning flight

REVIEW QUESTIONS

1 Why is the airline industry considered oligopolistic? What are some of the barriers to becoming a certificated carrier today? Compare the barriers today with those before deregulation. How has the number of carriers, and their market share, changed since deregulation?
2 Define *economies of scale*, *scope*, and *density*. How do they apply to the major carriers? When can economies of scale turn into diseconomies of scale? Give several examples of economies of scale in the airline industry today.
3 Why has there been a tendency toward mergers in oligopolistic industries over the years? What are some of the reasons air carriers have merged? What do you think the structure of the airline industry will be like ten years into the future?
4 Why are the carriers so mutually dependent? How have pricing practices changed since the prederegulation days? What was the major form of competition in the prederegulation era? Discuss some of the causes of the price wars in the 1980s. Do you foresee prices stabilizing in the next several years? Why is there a tendency in oligopolistic industries toward price rigidity and nonprice competition?
5 Give some examples of how government (particularly the federal government) has assisted the industry financially over the years. Why is there such a high technological turnover in the industry? When one carrier acquires new flight equipment, why do the other competing lines have to do the same?
6 What are the three major operating expenses of airlines? Why are they so high? How have they changed over the years? Why are labor costs such a competitive advantage for start-up airlines over more established carriers?
7 What is the competitive advantage of schedule frequency? How does it lead to excess capacity? Describe the effect of excess capacity on pricing.
8 Many industries are sensitive to fluctuations in the economy. How does the airline industry differ? How is it different to furlough employees in the airline industry versus the automobile or soft-drink industry?
9 Why has the airline industry been subject to greater government regulation than other oligopolistic industries?

10 Define *load factor*. What is the relationship between load factor and costs per unit? Explain. Why have load factors increased in recent years? Why are all public transportation modes subject to traffic peaks and valleys? How do positioning flights affect load factors?

11 Why can't airlines fine-tune capacity to match demand? Define *no-shows*. When load factors approach 80 percent or higher, we can expect some passengers to be turned away. Why? What is *overbooking*? *Off-peak pricing*?

Notes

1 Rico Merkert and David Hensher, Transportation Research Part A: Policy and Practice, 2011, vol. 45, issue 7, 686–695.

2 www.sciencedirect.com/science/journal/07398859.

3 Melvin Brenner, *Program for Improving Airline Outlook* (unpublished monograph), 1993.

PART THREE

Managerial Aspects of Airlines

CHAPTER 8

Airline Management and Organization

Introduction
Management
The New Corporate Structure
Functions of Management
Organization
The Organizational Chart
Staff Departments
Line Departments

CHAPTER CHECKLIST • YOU SHOULD BE ABLE TO:

- Define *management* and *organization*
- Discuss the different levels of management, and explain each level's role
- Describe the basic functions of management
- Describe the principles of organization planning that are of particular significance to the air carriers
- Explain what is meant by a *line-and-staff organization*
- Identify the typical staff administrations in a major carrier, and describe their primary responsibilities
- List several major departments under each administration, and discuss their individual roles
- Identify the three line administrations found in a typical air carrier, and describe their primary responsibilities
- List several major departments under each of the line administrations, and discuss their individual roles
- Identify the "new" corporate structure used at new-entrant and low-cost carriers.

DOI: 10.4324/9780429346156-11

Table 8.1 BTS Employment at Major Airlines and Select Other Carriers for April 2022

Carrier Group	Carrier Name	Full Time	Part Time	Total
Major	Alaska	16,436	1,715	18,151
	Allegiant Air	4,520	566	5,086
	American	89,379	12,766	102,145
	Atlas Air	4,060	68	4,128
	Delta	85,359	1,795	87,154
	Envoy Air	11,204	4,591	15,795
	Federal Express	199,828	58,334	258,162
	Frontier	5,590	39	5,629
	Hawaiian	5,705	997	6,702
	JetBlue	17,936	4,331	22,267
	Kalitta Air	2,388	11	2,399
	Polar Air Cargo	263	1	264
	Republic Airline	5,949	254	6,203
	SkyWest	12,836	1,556	14,392
	Southwest	59,705	1,212	60,917
	Spirit	10,321	337	10,658
	United	69,124	14,203	83,327
	United Parcel Service	6,760	125	6,885
	TOTAL	**607,363**	**102,901**	**710,264**
National	ABX Air Inc	537	5	542
	Air Transport International	1,084	0	1,084
	Air Wisconsin	1,141	39	1,180
	Aloha Air Cargo	382	70	452
	Amerijet International	963	0	963
	Commutair Aka Champlain Enterprises	1,227	5	1,232
	Endeavor Air	4,902	95	4,997
	GoJet Airlines	1,054	0	1,054
	Horizon Air	2,921	620	3,541
	Lynden Air Cargo	202	1	203
	Mesa	2,737	11	2,748
	National Air Cargo Group Inc dba National	313	0	313
	Northern Air Cargo	438	5	443
	Omni Air International	1,041	3	1,044
	PSA	4,256	0	4,256
	Piedmont	5,188	3,667	8,855
	Sky Lease Cargo	234	42	276

Carrier Group	Carrier Name	Full Time	Part Time	Total
	Sun Country Airlines	1,736	526	2,262
	Swift Air	773	15	788
	USA Jet	495	0	495
	Western Global	391	0	391
	TOTAL	**32,015**	**5,104**	**37,119**
Large Regional	Asia Pacific	79	1	80
	Breeze Aviation Group dba Breeze	650	74	724
	Eastern	274	0	274
	Gulf And Caribbean Cargo	135	0	135
	Jet Aviation Flight Services	687	0	687
	Kalitta Charters II	152	0	152
	Rhoades Aviation dba Transair	114	51	165
	Scott Aviation	108	0	108
	Silver	568	71	639
	Tatonduk Outfitters Limited	346	40	386
	TOTAL	**3,113**	**237**	**3,350**
Medium Regional	21 Air	106	0	106
	ExpressJet Airlines	128	1	129
	Hillwood	86	1	87
	KaiserAir	39	29	68
	Polaris Aviation Solutions	27	15	42
	TOTAL	**386**	**46**	**432**
	GRAND TOTAL	**642,877**	**108,288**	**751,165**

Note: Airlines that operate at least one plane and can carry 18,000 pounds, including fuel, must report monthly employment statistics to the federal government.

Source: U.S. Government, Bureau of Transportation Statistics.

INTRODUCTION

Every organization has goals, whether they be profits, market share, growth, quality of products or services, community image, or any combination of these. **Management** is the process of achieving an organization's goals through the coordinated performance of five specific functions: planning, organizing, staffing, directing, and controlling.

Years ago, when the major carriers were in their formative period, the management process was much simpler. The few employees truly felt that they were part of a team, and they could clearly see how their efforts contributed to meeting the company's goals. Everyone knew what the objectives of the firm were and how each particular job related to them. The lines of communication and span of control were very short. There was an esprit de corps among the employees, from president to the most unskilled worker. In fact, the president probably knew each employee personally.

Today, the major carriers employ as many as 751,165 people (Table 8.1). No longer does the president know the men and women on the line, and many workers on the line have as much allegiance to the union they belong to as they do to the company they work for. It is difficult for individual employees to see exactly how their particular jobs contribute to the corporate goals. The lines of communication are long, and the decision-making process is complex. The airline tends to assume a remoteness from the individual and to become a "thing" that exists, survives, and grows not because of the people who compose it, but in spite of them.

According to Chris Argyris, a noted management theorist, "organizations emerge when the goals they seek to achieve are too complex for any one man. The actions necessary to achieve the goals are divided into units manageable by individuals—the more complex the goals, other things being equal, the more people are required to meet them."[1]

An **organization** is the framework within which the management process can be carried out. It is a structure that enables a large company to attain the same efficiency as or greater efficiency than a small firm run effectively by a few employees. In the highly competitive airline business, an effective organizational structure may prove to be the necessary advantage one firm has over another.

MANAGEMENT

Levels of Management

Terms such as *top management*, *middle management*, and *operating management* are commonly used in business to distinguish the levels of management within an organization. Unfortunately, there is no clear definition of each level, and meanings attached to the terms sometimes differ from one company to another. However, a firm's *top management* is generally considered to be the policy-making group responsible for the overall direction of the company; *middle management* is responsible for the execution and interpretation of policies throughout the organization; and *operating management* is directly responsible for the final execution of policies by employees under its supervision.

Figure 8.1 shows a typical airline pyramid of authority including all three levels of management. The nature of activity carried out at each level is illustrated, with examples showing the organizational breakdown of two administrations and the typical titles of individuals heading up each unit. The term **administration** is generally used to describe a major unit within the company, such as flight operations, marketing, or personnel. **Departments** are the next major breakdown within administrations; **divisions** within departments, and so forth.

The Board of Directors. The chief governing body of a corporation is the board of directors, which is elected by the stockholders. This board ranges

FIGURE 8.1 Typical Airline Pyramid of Authority. The darker shading indicates "doing" kinds of work, such as gathering statistics, making reservations, and maintaining aircraft. The lighter shading indicates activities such as planning, conferring, and formulating policy

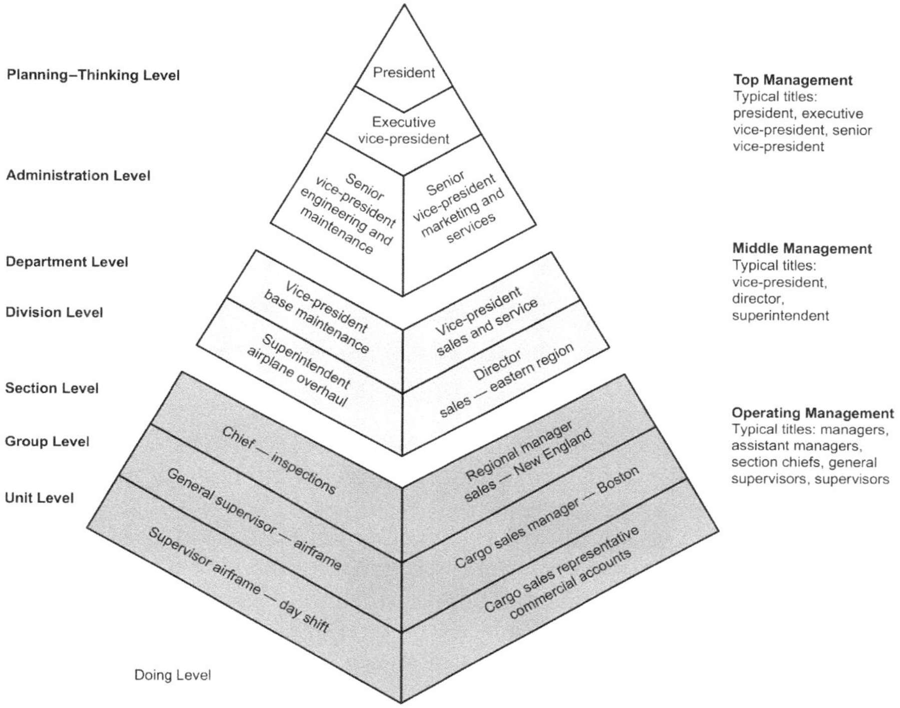

in size from three to 20 or more members and represents a cross-section of prominent individuals from various fields, including banking, insurance, law, and accounting. Airline boards typically include individuals from the hotel and food-processing industries, as well as former political and military leaders. The board of directors is the chief policy-making body of the corporation and the forum to whom the president reports. This body decides the answers to such broad questions as: Should the company be expanded? and Should the company diversify into other fields? The board also has the sole responsibility for the declaration of dividends. The basic decision about a dividend involves other decisions, such as what percentage of the year's earnings should be retained for company use and whether the dividend should be paid in cash or in stock.

The directors of the corporation are responsible for the appointment of a president, secretary, treasurer, and other executive officers who handle the actual details of management. Often, the board elects some of its own members to fill these important posts.

Top Management. Top management is the highest level of management in the organization. The job of top management is to determine the broad objectives and procedures necessary to meet the goals established by the board of directors. Top management will also make recommendations to the board regarding the goals of the company. What distinguishes top management from middle management is not always clear in a given organization, but the individuals in this group usually have many years of experience in all phases of management. Often called key executives, senior executives, or major executives, they usually bear the title of president, executive vice-president, or senior vice-president.

President. This individual is the chief executive officer of the corporation and is responsible for the proper functioning of the business. In the case of airlines, this individual often is a prominent business or political leader with very little airline experience, because the president's primary role is to deal with the financial community, various segments of government, community groups, and so forth.

Executive Vice-President and General Manager. This individual generally has years of airline experience and is responsible for the day-to-day operation of the company. Generally, the senior vice-presidents report to this individual.

Senior Vice-President. This title generally is reserved for those individuals who head up a major administration, such as flight operations, marketing, or engineering and maintenance.

Middle Management. Middle management is the second level of management in the organization and is responsible for developing operational plans and procedures to implement the broader ones conceived by top management. Middle management may be given much leeway in the development of plans, so long as the end result is in keeping with top management's requirements. Decisions on which advertising media to use, how many reservations agents are needed, and what new equipment to purchase are examples of those made by middle management.

Middle management includes individuals who head up departments or divisions within a major administration, such as the advertising department under marketing or the flight procedures and training department under flight operations. Or it might include the simulator division head, who reports to the flight procedures and training department head.

Typical airline titles for individuals in charge of departments and divisions are vice-presidents, directors, and, in the case of maintenance facilities, superintendents.

Operating Management. Operating management is the lowest level in management. It includes managers, assistant managers, section chiefs, general supervisors, and supervisors who head up sections, groups, or units that report to division or department heads. Examples might include the manager of display advertising or the general supervisor of the sheet metal shop. Members of the operating management group are primarily concerned with putting into action operational plans devised by middle management; generally, they do not initiate plans of their own.

Although the direction an airline takes is established by top management, the operating management level is extremely important. Top management makes policies, and middle management makes plans to carry out the policies, but operating management sees that the work the plans call for is actually done. Top management is secure as long as the profit picture is favorable. When a carrier is in serious trouble financially, the board of directors may make changes in the top echelon. Sometimes, a new president and executive vice-president are employed. When this is done, changes at other management levels are not always made by the new top management, because middle management can still make plans to carry out policy, and operating management can still implement plans.

Decision Making

Possibly the foremost responsibility of management at all levels, but especially top management, is the making of decisions. It permeates all functions of management. In accord with the broad operational policies set forth by the board of directors, top managers are confronted daily with the need to decide on courses of action that will enable them to achieve the goals to which their companies are dedicated. In many, if not most, instances, the decisions involve choosing between two or more courses of action. And at the top echelon of management, from which the basic procedural orders for the company's operations emanate, correct decisions may be vital to the continued success of the firm, or even to its survival. Farther down the managerial ladder, the number and importance of decisions made usually decreases, but the decisions made at these levels are nevertheless essential to the well-being of the company.

The ability to make correct decisions in business has long been recognized as a prime attribute of successful management, but until comparatively recently, there has been little apparent need for inquiry into the decision-making process. However, the large carriers now wield vast resources in the areas of finance, capacity, and personnel, and they also face increased competition. Thus, the possible consequences of unwise decisions, both for the companies involved and for the economy, have served to focus the attention of students of business on the methods by which decisions are made, insofar as these can be discovered.

The steps involved in **decision making** include: (1) recognition of the problem involved, (2) definition of the problem and breakdown into its essential parts, (3) the attempt to establish two or more alternative solutions and to evaluate them comparatively, (4) selection of the solution believed to be the most favorable, and (5) adoption of this solution and implementation of it through the issuing of the necessary orders. These steps might be taken in a few moments by a single executive, or they might require a much longer time, depending on the complexity and importance of the problem at hand.[2]

In recent years, a number of changes have brought the decision-making process into sharper focus. From the purely mechanical side, the rapid and extensive development of high-speed computers and data-processing procedures has added immeasurably to the quantity of information available to executives, thereby enabling them to base their decisions on far greater amounts of relevant data than previously.

Second, and what many analysts believe is the most important aspect of airline deregulation, the quality of managers and their decisions has come into question.

Managing air carriers during the regulated era required a different set of skills than those most in demand since deregulation, because of the control that the Civil Aeronautics Board (CAB) exercised over routes, prices, and equipment. By the 1970s, the CAB had effectively stopped granting new routes to the largest trunk carriers, so they were restricted to serving their existing routes. Also, for any carrier, awards of additional routes required a lengthy and expensive regulatory procedure, with no guarantee of success. Trunk or local-service airlines could compete on price to win market share, but only within a fairly limited sphere. The CAB also exercised considerable influence over decisions about the acquisition of aircraft. In this environment, managers needed to be experienced at operating within the confines of CAB regulations, if not adept at lobbying to change them. Many airline managers were indeed quite effective, but skills in marketing and cost control were less important than those in law and politics.

Deregulation gave managers the ability to deploy assets and to price services according to market demand—a freedom exercised daily by managers throughout the rest of the economy. Most top airline executives, however, many of whom had staunchly resisted deregulation, were not prepared for the freedom given to them, nor were they particularly adept at exercising it. Some of the early postderegulation strategic moves by carriers such as Pan American and Eastern, for example, were ineffective and failed to make them cost-competitive or to offer a sharply differentiated product. Because the CAB had protected carriers from failing, managers were also unaccustomed to taking risks that could result in the failure of the firm. Braniff, for example, expanded far too aggressively and was pushed into bankruptcy (for the first time in 1982) by the first major downturn in the economy.

Throughout deregulation, top and middle managers who remained from the regulated era have been either trained on the job or replaced by managers and owners more prepared for marketplace competition. Not all new managers, or new entrant entrepreneurs for that matter, have been successful. Pan American and Eastern were weak before deregulation and have since failed. Other carriers, like American, Delta, and United, have become stronger. Some management innovations developed or expanded during deregulation have been successful at increasing productivity and controlling costs.

THE NEW CORPORATE STRUCTURE

Management Team

New-entrant and low-cost carriers have an advantage over legacy and established carriers when it comes to keeping costs down, efficiency up, and communication flowing. One way of doing this is through the establishment of a lean organizational structure where the "right" people are hired to do the "right" job.

Good management is a key to success and each participant must be able to contribute something to the business. Each position should fit with the experience and skills of the individual and each participant should be able to answer the question, "What do you offer this business venture?" As a rule of thumb, there should be at least one very experienced person on the management team. Often, such an individual is referred to as a "gray hair." To improve success of the company, the ideal person should have a proven business background, preferably as CEO with a middle to large size company. The type of industry does not really matter but an airline background is a definite advantage.

Without offending the reader, there is another rule of thumb that should be considered when discussing the management team. Be cautious of the number of line pilots that make up the management team. Generally speaking, pilots do not make the most effective managers. Pilots are very educated when it comes to aircraft operations but often lack the business skills required to run a successful operation. That being said, more pilots are combining flight hours with academics and during the course of the next decade, it is expected that pilots will be more educated than in the past. In the airline industry, it is often said that there is a surplus of pilots on the market but a lack of qualified pilots in terms of flight experience, combined with academic experience.

The number of people required to make up an efficient management team depends entirely on the type of operation, size of operation, and skills of the individuals. Existing airlines already have a corporate structure in place as mentioned earlier in this chapter. In most cases, the management team is too large and somewhat ineffective due to duplication of work and lack of communication between departments. New airlines starting out have the advantage of being able to establish an effective management team from the start. It is wise to have a small management team initially and grow it as the airline expands. For starters, it is recommended that the management team consist of one lead person acting as president/ CEO. Ideally, this is the optimal position for the "gray hair" mentioned earlier. This individual is the chief executive officer of the corporation, is responsible for the proper functioning of the business, and often involved with the financial community, government and members of the public. Not only should this individual have extraordinary business skills, but they should have good interpersonal skills as communication is an important aspect of this position.

It is also recommended that a second lead person be a part of the management team. This person might be given the title of executive vice-president or senior vice-president. Once the airline is established and growing, it will most likely be necessary to appoint two individuals to fill each title. However, for a new airline starting out, this is not necessary unless massive rapid growth is anticipated over a short period of time. Ideally, the second lead person should have a Vice-President/General Manager title. This person should have a number of years of airline experience at the management level because they are responsible for the day-to-day operation of the airline.

Aside from the two positions previously mentioned, a new airline starting out might consider the following information when forming a management team. Again, keeping the initial team small is important. In the United States, for an air carrier to obtain certification, the management team must have a minimum number of positions. For FAR 121 certification, mandatory positions include: director of safety, director of operations, chief pilot, director of maintenance, and chief inspector. For FAR 135 certification, the mandatory positions include: director of operations, chief Pilot, and director of Maintenance. Depending on the complexity of the operation, it is possible to obtain a deviation from the required basic management positions and qualifications if requested in writing to the FAA. Such a request is normally made when the air carrier submits the formal application letter for certification. However, the air carrier must be able to show the FAA that it can perform the operation with the highest degree of safety under the direction of fewer or different categories of management personnel. Information concerning the required background for each of the positions mentioned can be obtained from the FAA's Advisory Circular (AC) 120-49 entitled "Certification of Air Carriers."

Developing the right management team is a difficult process and in the case of many new airlines planning to commence operations, opportunities often pass by because of the length of time needed to put people in place. In order to speed up the raising of capital and move forward with the certification process, some business plans utilize the reputation of an outside party to act as the "interim" management team. There are a number of consulting companies and expert individuals in the market who will permit use of their name and talents on paper for a fee or some form of compensation. Some firms will put together an entire management team to help get a new airline off the ground. Many existing airlines have found this to be a worthwhile option, but it should be noted that such an option can be expensive and somewhat risky. Be sure to obtain references for all potential members of the management team and do background searches, if necessary. The aviation industry is full of "experts" so be cautious and do not rush into any type of contract until a thorough investigation has been completed. Also, depending on who the primary investors are, they will often have a say on who should be a part of the management team. In many cases, the investor is not the best person to decide who should manage the airline.

Organizational Structure

Most airlines, old and new, tend to operate using the classic pyramid or top-down structure consisting of top management, middle management, and operating management. There is no clear definition of each level, and meanings attached to the terms sometimes differ from one company to another. However, top management is generally considered to be the policy-making group responsible for the overall direction of the company; middle management is responsible for the execution and interpretation of policies throughout the organization; and operating management is directly responsible for the final execution of policies by employees under its supervision. The pyramid is divided into administrations each headed by an individual. For example, major units might include flight operations, marketing, or personnel. Departments are the next major breakdown within administrations; divisions within departments, and so forth.

Although this structure has been used for many years, there are different options to consider. The top three costs for an airline are, in any order: fuel, labor, and maintenance. Increased pressure has been put on the airlines in recent years to implement cost-cutting strategies and one area hit has been labor. Middle management is usually the first to be eliminated during bad times as witnessed in the mid-1980s when the United States faced a major recession. Many airlines have realized that middle level management is not always necessary to run a successful operation and new airlines often eliminate this section of the corporate structure therefore reducing costs and often improving efficiency. When middle management is cut from the picture, work ordinarily done at the department and division levels shifts upward increasing the roles and responsibilities with top management. In other cases, more authority is delegated to the lower or operating level of management.

In today's environment, it is important for an airline to avoid duplication of work structures and improve internal communications where possible. It is also important to create a flexible corporate structure that can expand when necessary and contract if needed without serious harm being done to the business. New start-up carriers have the advantage over existing airlines of being able to tailor a corporate structure that best fits the organization. New corporate structures should provide more authority to individuals at different levels. As authority is delegated, responsibility should be increased with specific positions, therefore changing the nature of the typical top-down or silo system to more of a flat organization. Figure 8.2 visualizes a possible corporate structure suitable for the current aviation environment. Figure 8.3 shows the organizational structure for Spirit Airlines, a successful U.S.-based, low-cost carrier.

The structure previously discussed will also allow the airline to become more diverse when needed. Diversification is one key to success in the airline business but most airlines are not able to diversify despite having all the resources to do so. The typical pyramid structure is designed so that virtually all decisions for the organization are made among a handful of people. As a result, the talents and skills of others are often not utilized and decisions made are sometimes not in the best interest of the airline but in the best interest of upper management or the board of directors. A less formal organizational structure allows diversification to happen because more skills and talents can be tapped into. Access to such resources will permit the airline to initiate new departments when needed and increase the ability of the company to become involved in businesses outside of the core business.

Given the impact of the COVID-19 global pandemic, there is some speculation that select airlines might revise current structures particularly focused on revenue management and pricing departments that ultimately form the core of the business model. During the pandemic, most airlines were forced to furlough personnel and/or eliminate positions and had to be strategic with operations with fewer resources. In many cases, new opportunities were discovered and implemented successfully that could be long-term solutions for success. Such reductions in force ultimately create structural changes and there is an increased need for personnel to be multiskilled and knowledgeable in different areas. As the aviation industry continues to evolve, there is an expectation that organizations will increase their focus on skilled talent and the need to create opportunities for new skills, upskilling, and reskilling.

FIGURE 8.2 Typical New Organizational Structure for New-entrant and Low-cost Carriers

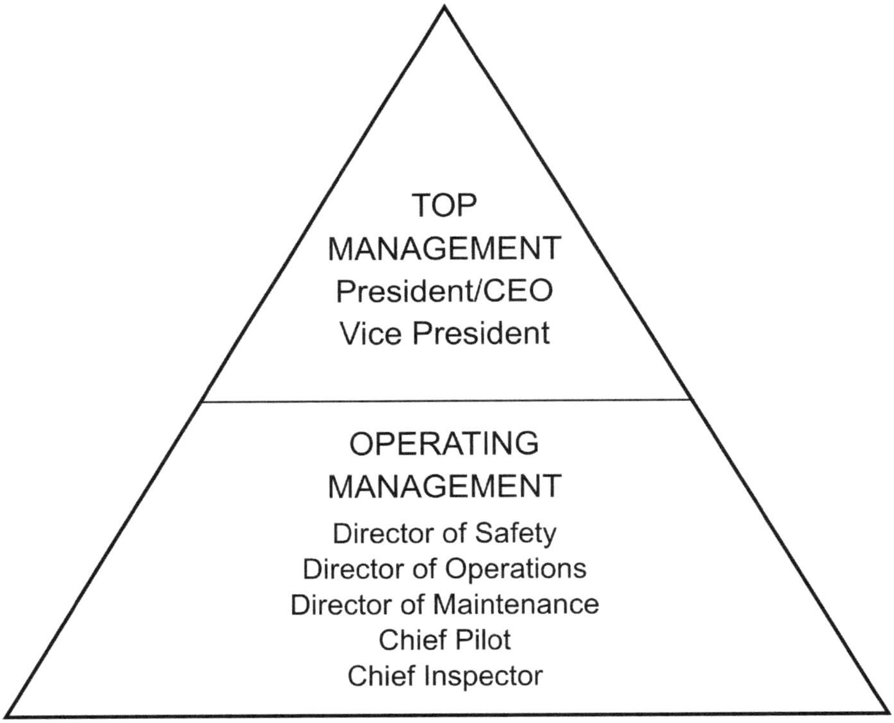

FIGURE 8.3 Organizational Structure for Spirit Airlines

SPIRIT AIRLINES | GENERAL OPERATIONS MANUAL | 2.1.1 Date: 02/28/07 Revision: 40

OPERATIONS ORGANIZATION CHART

FUNCTIONS OF MANAGEMENT

The main **functions of management** are planning, organizing, staffing, directing, and controlling. The key tools of management are supervisory skills, which must be learned and practiced.

Planning

An airline is dependent for its very existence on the ability of its top planners. Failure to forecast the demand for air travel and to plan how to meet a rising or shrinking demand spells the difference between success and failure. The management process begins with **planning**, which sets the stage for what the organization will do, both globally and specifically.

Goals should be established for the company as a whole and for each administration and department, as well as for individual activities. A goal is anything that an organization or group is seeking to do. Some goals are large, such as buying a hotel chain or building a new flight kitchen to serve a growing hub airport. Other goals are small, such as getting a report completed by Friday or handling more reservations calls per hour than last month.

Companywide Goals. These are the general goals an organization wants to achieve. Some examples might be "earn an annual return of 12 percent on our investment," "capture 25 percent of the New Orleans–Memphis market," and "develop a new promotional fare to compete with Airline X."

Administration or Departmental Goals. These goals should be related to—and should lead directly to—the achievement of companywide goals. Some examples might be "improve on-time performance by 10 percent systemwide during the next quarter," "develop and implement a new training program for apprentice-level mechanics in the sheet metal shop," and "hold flight attendant absenteeism to 7 percent."

Individual Goals. These are the goals that specific persons will have to achieve if departmental, division, group, or unit goals are to be met. Some examples might be "increase my cargo sales volume by 10 percent over last year" and "process 10 percent more insurance claims per week."

Management by Objectives. Many carriers operate by a system popularly referred to as **management by objectives (MBO)**, in which employees at all levels are given tangible goals and are held accountable for achieving them (see Figure 8.4). Strategies must be formulated to achieve the goals and objectives of an organization. Consider the company-wide goal just mentioned: "capture 25 percent of the New Orleans–Memphis market." A strategy might include increasing the number of daily flights, including those serving full meals. In a well-designed MBO program, overall goals and strategies of the company and of individual employees are established through discussions between managers and their subordinates. Feedback is provided through follow-up discussions during the period of time set for achieving the goals. Feedback may be in the form of data on quantitative results (such as dollar sales, new accounts, unit costs, aircraft turnaround

FIGURE 8.4 Management by Objectives

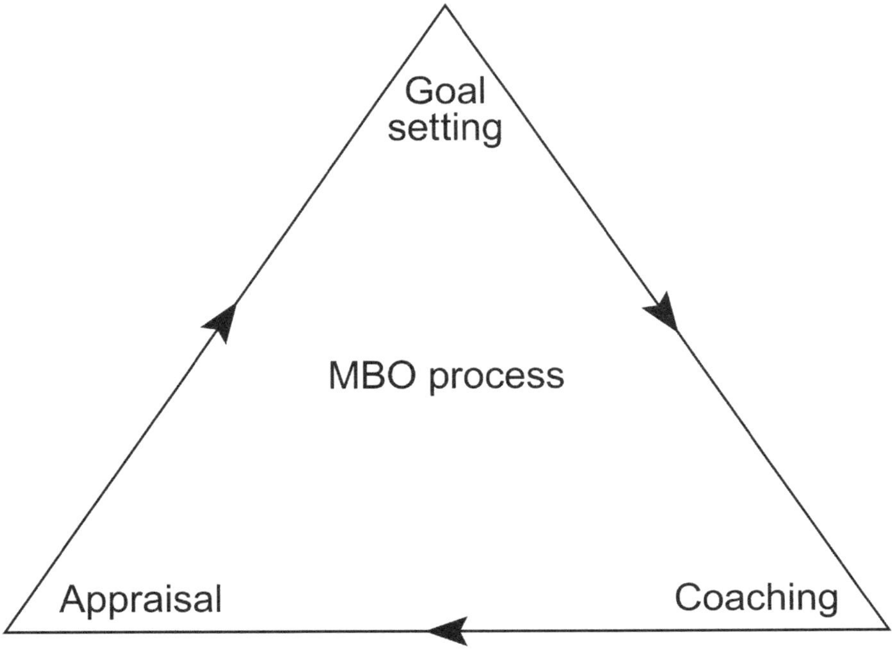

time, or mechanical delays) or data on qualitative results (such as customer complaints, reductions in errors, improvement in image, or development of subordinates). Person-to-person communication, through day-to-day coaching, is particularly important.

With MBO, because employees receive timely, accurate, and fairly complete information on their performance results, they are in a position to take corrective action when necessary. The whole MBO approach assumes that employees will accept responsibility for the achievement of company goals and that they will become committed when the goals are meaningful, attainable, and established through mutual planning.

The final stage of the MBO process is the appraisal of results. At the end of the performance period, the manager and the employee check the employee's progress in achieving the goals. This serves as a time for recognition of good performance and for renewed goal setting.

MBO is a continuous cycle of goal setting, coaching and feedback, and appraisal of results. It is a natural behavioral process that most individuals follow on a daily basis.

Policy and Procedures as Part of Planning. Every airline has a **policy and procedures manual**, usually prepared by the personnel department and containing major sections pertaining to each of the administrations. A policy is a broadly stated course of action that employees should follow in making decisions. A policy is a guide; employees do have some discretion in its implementation. For example, an employment policy for all staff positions above a certain level might be that "preference in employment will be given to college graduates with a management background." Hundreds of policies are in effect at any major carrier, and those of a broad nature are established by top management. Power to make specific policies for the guidance of each department usually is delegated to administration or department heads.

A *procedure* is somewhat like a policy, but it specifies in more detail the kind of action required to handle a specific situation. There are procedures for ordering supplies, training new employees, fueling aircraft, handling customer complaints, and hundreds of other processes within the various administrations, departments, divisions, and so forth.

Rules or *regulations* indicate in very precise terms whether, in a specific situation, something is to be done or not done. An example of a rule is, "Company-authorized headgear and glasses must be worn at all times by all persons who work within 40 feet of the welding operation in Building 7." Rules are important for essentially the same reason as procedures: they save time, because people do not have to think through and ponder each new situation, and they give employees a clear sense of what they can and cannot do.

Organizing

Once plans have been made and policies determined, the job of carrying them out becomes one of organization and operation. Organizing involves the division of work among employees and the determination of how much authority each person will have. More specifically, **organizing** may be defined as the process of logically grouping activities, delineating authority and responsibility, and establishing working relationships that enable the employees, and thus the entire unit, to work with maximum efficiency and effectiveness.

The chief purpose of organization is to establish efficient lines of responsibility and authority designed to (1) provide supervision of all work with a maximum utilization of knowledge and experience to best advantage, (2) efficiently assign and schedule all work with the proper priority observed in projects to be accomplished, (3) provide a means whereby management can be kept informed of the efficiency and dispatch with which each particular unit is fulfilling its function, and (4) establish a sequence of importance in job classifications so that all employees can adequately judge the possibilities for advancement.

Staffing

Staffing involves stationing people to work in the positions provided for by the organizational structure. It includes defining work force requirements for the job to be done, as well as inventorying, appraising, and selecting candidates for positions; compensating employees; and training or otherwise developing both job candidates and current employees to accomplish their tasks effectively.

Directing

Directing includes assigning tasks and instructing subordinates on what to do and perhaps how to do it. Because the supervisor's job is to get things done through other people, effectiveness is closely tied to communicating directives clearly and in a way that will bring about the desired action. It is essential that subordinates understand the orders, or they will not be able to carry them out. In directing people, it is important to know how much information and what kind of information to give them. Orders should be fitted to the receiver; the new employee needs to be instructed in detail, but the experienced worker may need to know only the objectives and then be capable of choosing the means to attain them.

Controlling

Controlling is the measuring and correcting of activities of subordinates to ensure that events conform to plans. Thus, it involves measuring performance against goals and plans, showing where deviations occur and, by putting in motion actions to correct deviations, ensuring accomplishment of plans. Basically, control involves three steps: (1) setting performance standards for the work, (2) comparing actual performance with the standard, and (3) taking corrective action to bring performance in line with the standard.

Standards of both quantity and quality should be determined as precisely as possible. Until they are determined and established, a job will be judged by three different standards: (1) workers' ideas of what constitutes a fair day's work and of what they think might be expected of them, (2) supervisors' ideas of what they would like to have done and of what they think can be done, and (3) top management's criteria and expectations. Whether quantity and quality standards are recognized, they exist, and each level in the organization—workers, operating management, middle management, and top management—may be judging jobs by different standards.

ORGANIZATION

Previously, *organization* was defined as the framework within which the management process can be carried out. More formally, organization is a plan for bringing together the resources of a firm (capital and labor) to the position of greatest effectiveness or productivity. The plan consists of the grouping of operations (labor and equipment) to achieve the advantages of specialization and a chain of command.

Principles of Organization Planning

An internal organizational structure must be designed to enable management at all levels to exercise control of those activities designed to meet the goals and objectives of the firm. To aid management, there are a number of principles of organization. These principles have been developed and practiced by successful firms in various industries and are universally applicable whenever people work together.

Unity of Objectives. The principle of **unity of objectives** states that each administration, department, division, section, group, and unit of the company must contribute to the accomplishment of the overall goals of the firm. For example, the regional sales and services department must be concerned not only with sales but also with how its activities are integrated with all other activities in the company, such as personnel, finance and property, flight operations, and so forth. Each department must accomplish its own goals while at the same time working cooperatively with all other departments. Thus, regional sales and services cannot be planning a major promotional fare campaign offering easier credit terms at the same time as the finance department is embarking on a policy of restricting credit.

Span of Control. The principle of **span of control** states that there is a limit to the number of subordinates a manager can effectively supervise. It is impossible to specify the exact number of subordinates that a manager can supervise for each situation, for that depends on such variables as: (1) the type and complexity of work being performed, (2) the manager's ability, (3) the training of subordinates, (4) the effectiveness of communications, and (5) the importance of time. A customer services agent at an airport might effectively supervise 20 ticket-counter agents, whereas a senior analyst in the revenue accounting department might supervise only three junior analysts due to the analytical nature of the work involved.

Departmentalization. **Departmentalization** is the practice of subdividing both people and functions into groups within an organization to gain the advantages of specialization. Many terms are used for such groups, including administrations, departments, divisions, regional offices, sections, and units. The extent to which an airline is departmentalized depends on the size of the carrier, the complexity of its operations, and its route structure. In other words, in preparing an organizational plan, it is necessary to decide the extent to which tasks are to be subdivided. In a small commuter carrier, the marketing department might consist of 25 people who are involved in everything from schedule planning to soliciting new cargo accounts. In a carrier the size of United Airlines, with 25,000 employees engaged in the marketing function, there is considerable division of labor through departmentalization.

Airlines of the 21st century are expected to focus much of their energy on departmentalization, as such companies diversify their operations. Airlines of tomorrow will need specialized departments. The time to start building is now. New departments might include safety and security, training, and corporate innovation (a think tank where the airline learns to diversify its operation into other types of businesses). As a result of the events of September 11, 2001, and the COVID-19 global pandemic that started in 2019, airlines have focused much attention on enhancing safety and security at all levels.

Focusing energies on training will be important as the industry learns to manage a new generation of employees known as "Millennials." The new generation is outspoken, expectation driven, and motivated. Airlines must create conditions that attract the best people from a large and diversely skilled talent pool. The training department must be able to train these employees quickly to increase employees' value to the company. Such training will include an emphasis on career-effectiveness skills and teaching the manager to manage. The airline's environment will become a resource center for personal growth and development. People are the airline's biggest asset and efficient training programs could mean the difference between success and failure. Southwest Airlines is often considered the most "successful" model in the world and is frequently studied at business schools as a case study. Southwest Airlines established People University providing results-oriented training programs.

Delegation of Authority. Although it is true that the final authority for all decisions rests with the president and board of directors, it is not possible or practical to allow every decision to reach that level. **Delegation of authority** implies that the authority to make decisions should be pushed down to the lowest competent level of supervision. This allows minor decisions to be made at the lower levels of management, and major decisions at the higher levels. However, delegation of authority does not relieve the delegator of the responsibility for the actions of subordinates. A supervisor is always ultimately responsible for the actions of subordinates.

This principle is quite useful for comparing the management styles of various carriers or, for that matter, the same carrier during different periods in its history. Some carriers are very stingy in the delegation of authority to units down the chain of command, whereas others, notably Delta, have always been known for their confidence in their employees to make decisions at the lowest level possible. Southwest Airlines encourages employees to present ideas, often resulting in the employee being empowered to implement the idea.

Levels of Management. This principle holds that the number of **levels of management** in the company should be kept to a minimum. As the number of organizational levels increase, problems in communication increase, inasmuch as each communication must pass through more people as it travels from its point of origin to its final destination.

A carrier must achieve a proper balance between span of control and the number of levels of management if it is to function effectively. If a carrier has too narrow a span of control, many levels of management will be required. With a wide span of control, fewer levels of management will be needed.

During the past 25–30 years, many carriers have gone through periods of rapid growth in numbers of personnel followed several years later by periods of massive furloughs. Without careful analysis of their organizational plans, they have found themselves in recessionary times with whole layers of management that were needed when the traffic volume supported them but that in slack periods represented overstaffing.

Clearly Defined Duties. Every job classification should be clearly defined so that it differs from and does not overlap with other job classifications. All of the major carriers have organizational manuals (usually developed and maintained by the personnel department, except in the case of several of the largest carriers, which have separate organizational planning departments). These manuals include all job descriptions within the company, from president on down. The prerequisites for the job (in terms of education and experience) are included, as is the salary range. Normally, each nonmanagement job description is reviewed by the personnel department every two years in terms of the scope of the job, the functions performed, the number of persons supervised, and the salary range. Management jobs are usually reviewed annually.

Flexibility. A carrier must be flexible so that it can adapt to changing conditions, both internal and external. In today's competitive environment, it behooves management to assess the organizational plan continuously to be sure that it is responsive to the changing marketplace.

Communication. The term communication here means an uninterrupted flow of orders, instructions, questions, responses, explanations, ideas, and suggestions between top management and the rest of the organization. This flow should be two-way—that is, both from management to employees and from employees to management. Aside from the customary orders and instructions concerning normal operations, management frequently wishes to explain some of its policy decisions or to give information regarding a major route expansion, plans for an acquisition or merger, finances, or personnel changes in order to bring about a better understanding among its workers of the salient facts concerning the company. For their part, employees often have ideas for saving time, labor, and materials or have grievances of one kind or another that should reach the ears of management. In planning the details of an organization, provision must be made for the creation and maintenance of a good two-way communications system.

Line and Staff Responsibilities

As a company grows from a simple to a complex organization, it becomes impossible for a small number of executives to assume direct, personal responsibility for functions such as employment, purchasing, market research, labor relations, and public relations. Therefore, as the company grows in size and complexity, assistants to executives are appointed. Specific advisory responsibilities are delegated to these assistants, who frequently carry such titles as "staff assistant accounting" or "assistant to the vice-president of operations for personnel." As the activities of these assistants increase, other personnel are added to assist them. Eventually, the work centering around a special assistant is organized into a department, which is known as a staff department and which supplements the line functions of the organization.

All large carriers are organized using the line-and-staff concept. **Line personnel** are those whose orders and authority flow in a straight line from the chief executive down to lower levels in the organization. Line people are usually involved directly in producing or selling air transportation. Often referred to as volume-related personnel, because they are involved in a particular volume, such as flying hours or number of departures, line personnel have a direct responsibility for accomplishing the objectives of the firm. Examples of line personnel include pilots, flight attendants, mechanics, reservations clerks, and sales personnel.

Staff personnel are those whose orders and authority do not flow in a straight line down from the top of the organization. Although staff people do report to a specific person in the company hierarchy, they may at times perform work for people at levels above or below them. Staff executives are usually technically trained and are employed to advise and inform line and other staff executives on specialized areas, including finance, personnel, legal affairs, medical concerns, and data processing. In short, staff people help line people to work more effectively in accomplishing the primary objectives of the firm. Examples of staff personnel include accountants, budget analysts, employment representatives, market research analysts, industrial engineers, programmers, and company medical staff.

THE ORGANIZATIONAL CHART

Often referred to as the blueprint of the company, the **organizational chart** depicts the formal authority relationships between superiors and subordinates at the various hierarchical levels, as well as the formal channels of communication within the company. The organizational chart helps managers implement organization principles, such as span of control and unity of objectives. The chart can serve as an aid in identifying such organizational deficiencies as one individual reporting to more than one boss or a manager with too wide a span of control.

A major reason advanced for organization charting is that it boosts morale among managers and workers. The chart helps organization members to perceive more clearly where they stand in the company in relation to others and how and where managers and workers fit into the overall organizational structure.

The organizational chart is a static model of the company, because it depicts how the company is organized at a given point in time. This is a major limitation of the chart, because carriers operate in a dynamic environment and thus must continually adapt to changing conditions. Some old positions may no longer be required, or new positions may have to be created to achieve new objectives. Therefore, the chart must be revised and

FIGURE 8.5 The Administrations in a Major Air Carrier's Organization

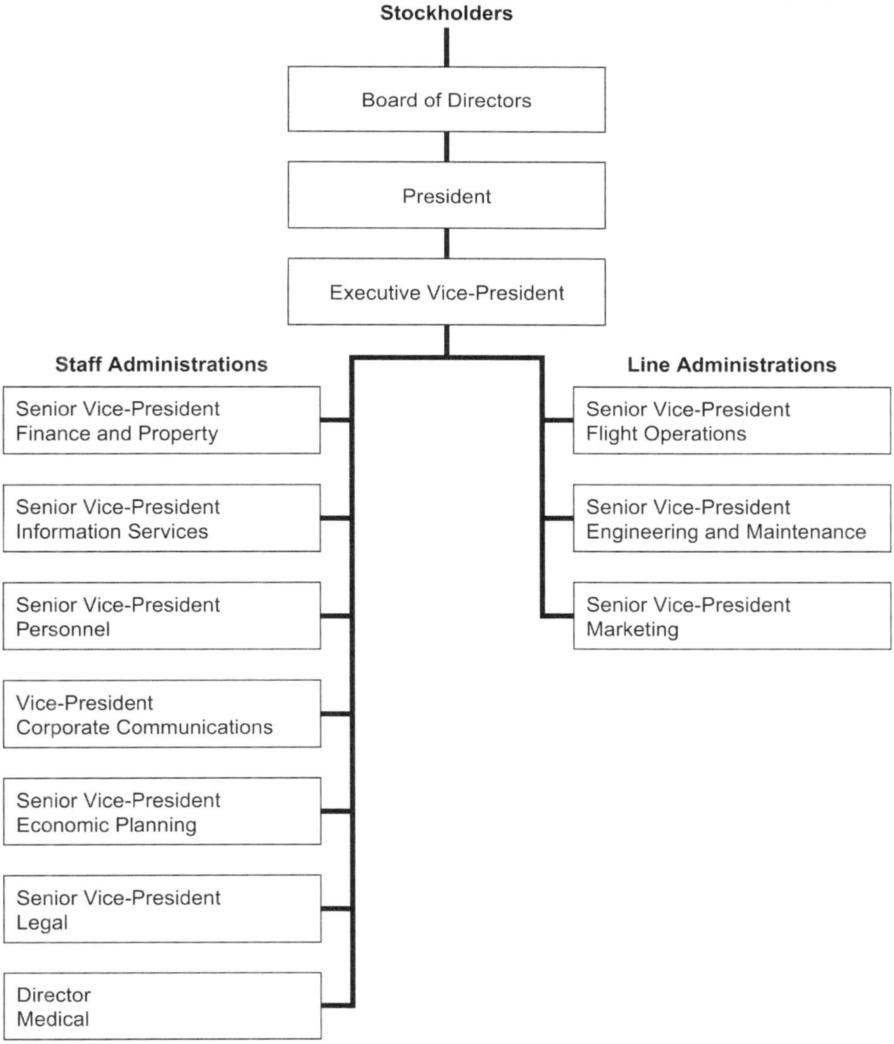

updated periodically to reflect these changing conditions. Like the organization manual, organizational charts generally are maintained by the personnel department or, as in the case of several large carriers, by a separate organization planning department.

Airlines have grown so rapidly in the past 35 years that it is difficult to say that any organizational chart is typical or that the chart of one company at any particular time is the one still in effect even a few months later. However, all airlines do have certain organizational traits in common, such as the administrations, departments, divisions, and so forth into which airline activities are divided. Understandably, the larger the carrier, the greater the specialization of tasks and the greater the departmentalization.

Figure 8.5 shows the administrations normally found in a major air carrier. The following sections describe the major line and staff administrations shown. Figure 8.6 shows a real-life example outlining the organizational structure of Turkish Airlines.

STAFF DEPARTMENTS

Staff departments include those areas that provide a service to the line departments. They are primarily located at the carrier's executive headquarters or at major regional offices.

Finance and Property

The finance and property administration formulates policies for the financing of all activities in the airline and is charged with the receipt and safeguarding of the company's revenues and the accounting of all receipts and disbursements. In carrying out these functions, it administers the activities of: (1) the treasurer's department; (2) facilities and property, which involves the administration of all owned and leased property and equipment; and (3) purchasing and stores, which is a multimillion-dollar business by itself. Airlines purchase everything from uniforms, supplies, parts, and equipment to food, fuel, and hundreds of other items on a daily basis. Other major departments include auditing, accounting, and insurance (see Figure 8.7).

Information Services

Information services is responsible for designing and maintaining the data communications network within the airline. Included in this administration are database administrators, who coordinate the data collection and storage needs of user departments, and systems analysts, who are responsible for analyzing how computer data processing can be applied to specific user problems and for designing effective data-processing solutions. Programmers, who are responsible for developing programs of instructions for computers, work very closely with the user administrations (see Figure 8.8).

FIGURE 8.6 Organizational Structure of Turkish Airlines

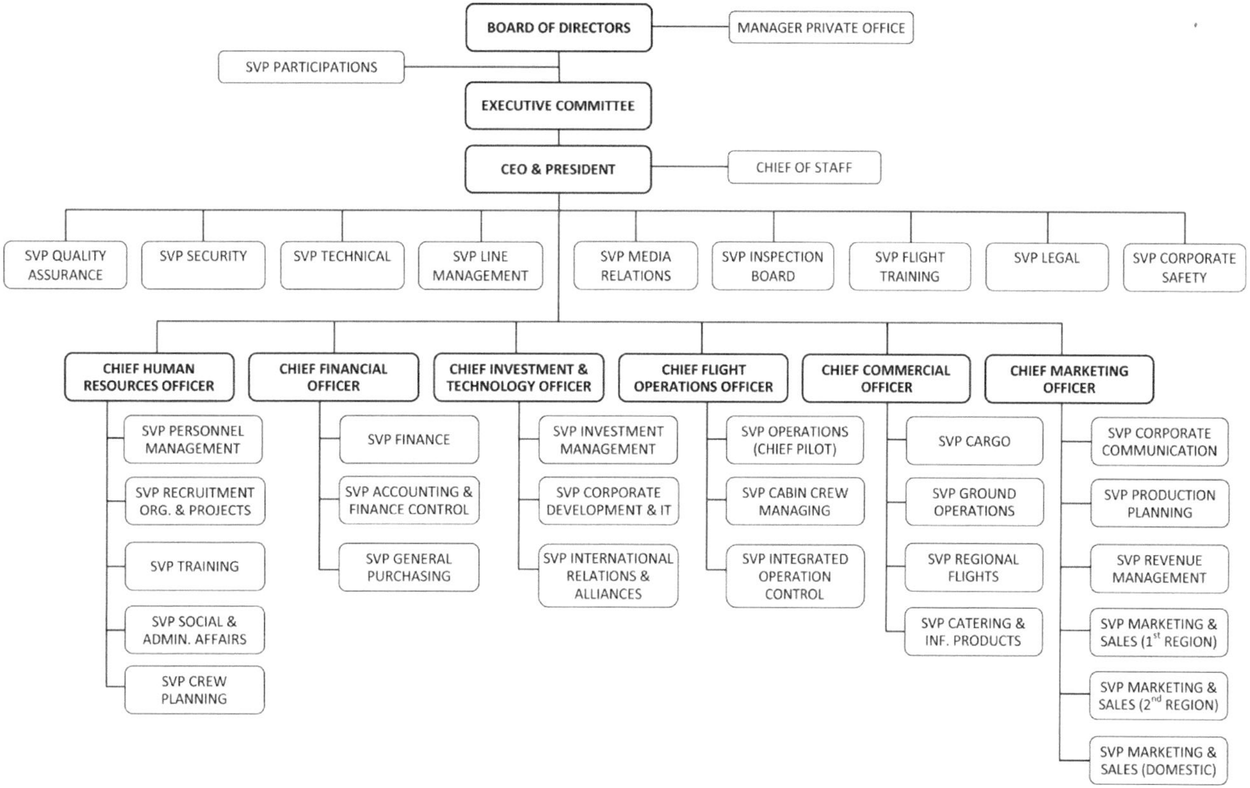

Source: Turkish Airlines (www.turkishairlines.com).

FIGURE 8.7 A Typical Major Air Carrier's Finance and Property Administration (employs approximately 10 percent of the carrier's work force)

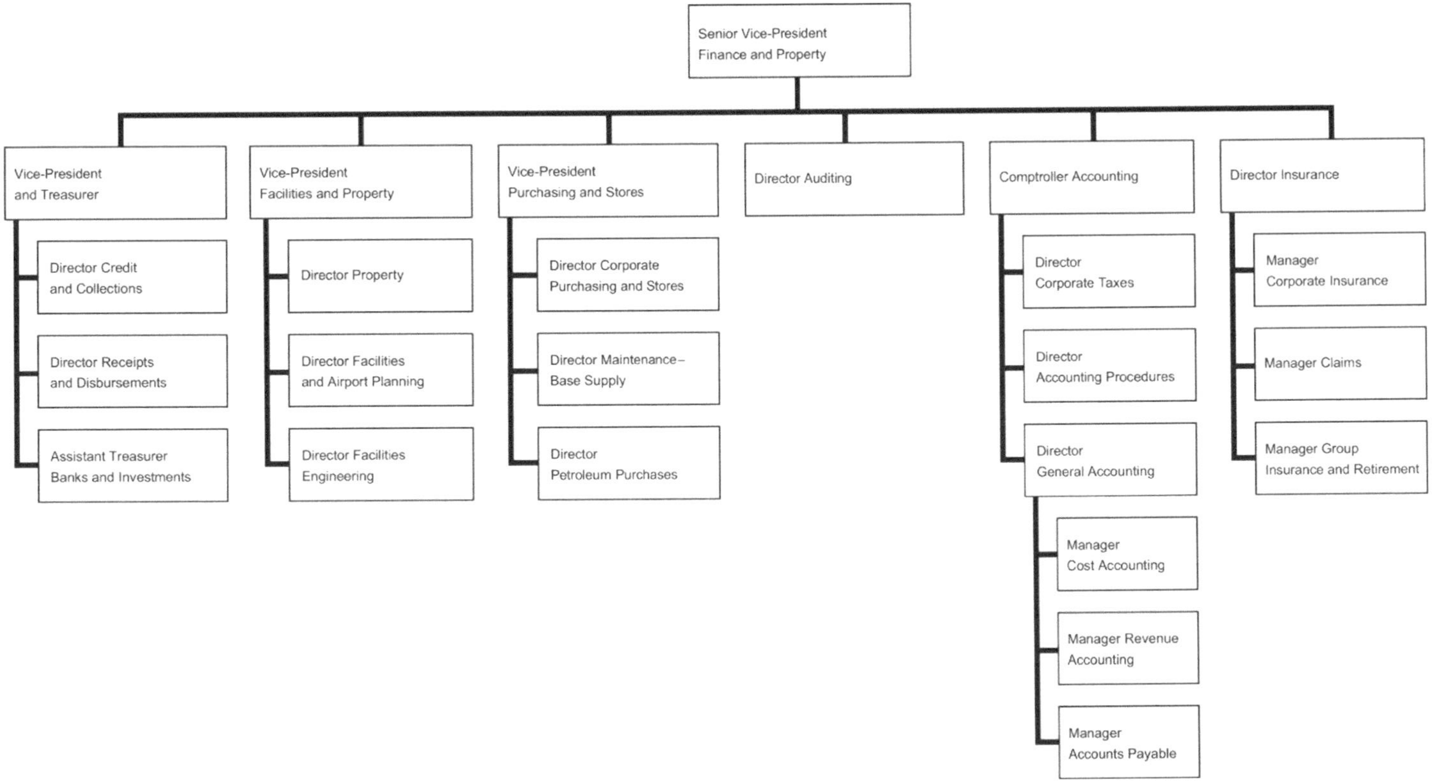

Personnel

The primary goal of the personnel administration is to maintain a mutually satisfactory relationship between management and employees. It is responsible for providing fair and adequate personnel policies. Major departments under personnel include employee development, employee relations, and personnel field services, which encompasses the employment function (see Figure 8.9).

Medical

The medical department provides health services to all employees through physical exams and emergency treatment and establishes health criteria for hiring new employees. In recent years, some major carriers have virtually eliminated their medical personnel, choosing instead to have private physicians and clinics provide medical examinations and other specialized services. Medical service at the major base or at regional facilities is thus limited to emergency treatment (see Figure 8.10).

Legal

Every airline has a legal department under a vice-president or general counsel. This administration is responsible for handling all legal matters, including claims against the company for loss of or damage to the property of others and for injuries to persons. This administration also works closely with government agencies regarding regulatory matters (see Figure 8.10).

FIGURE 8.8 A Typical Major Air Carrier's Information Services Administration (employs approximately 2 percent of the carrier's work force)

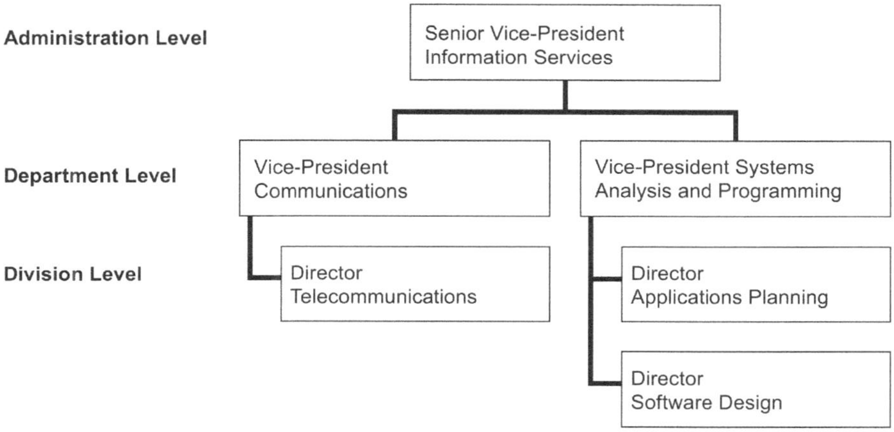

FIGURE 8.9 A Typical Major Air Carrier's Personnel Administration (employs approximately 1 percent of the carrier's work force)

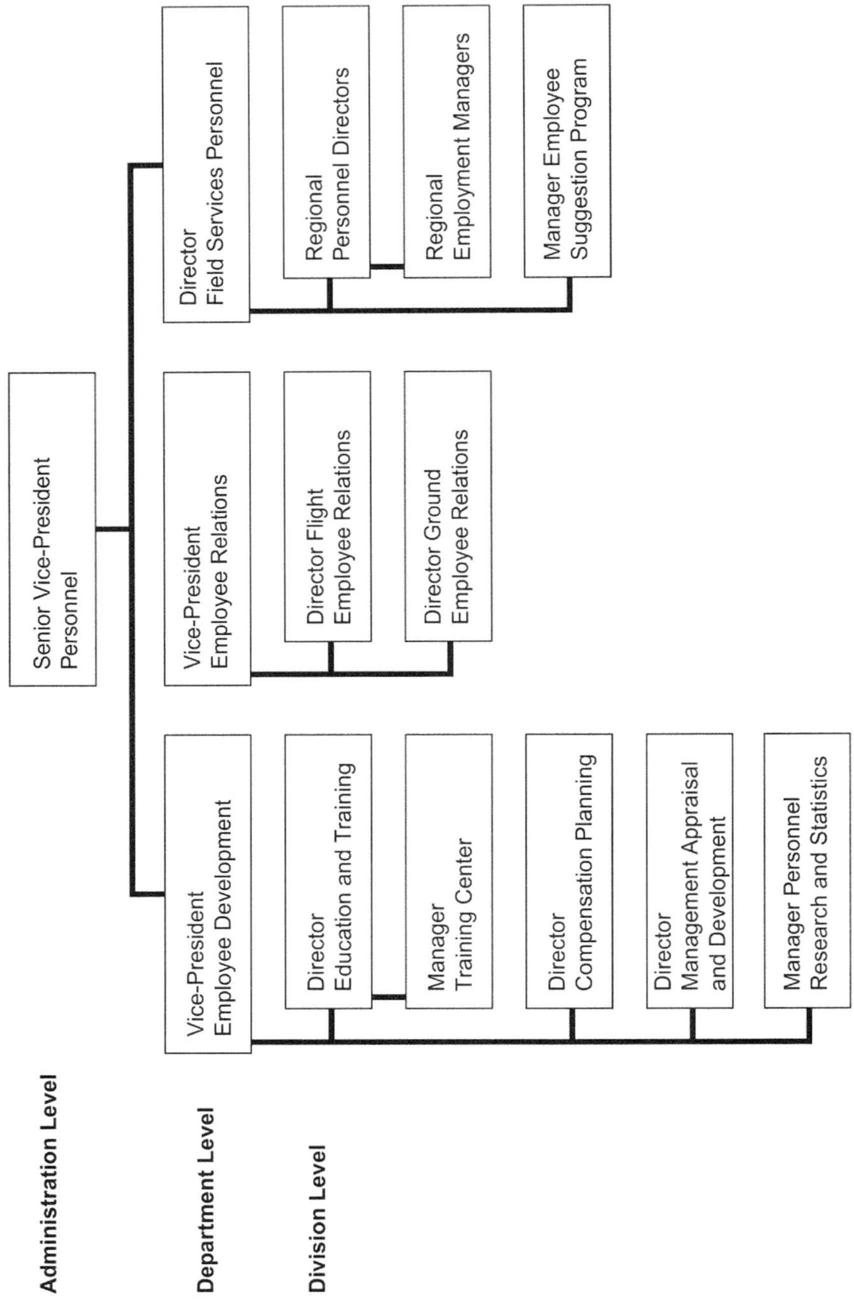

FIGURE 8.10 A Typical Major Air Carrier's Medical and Legal Administrations (employ less than 1 percent of the carrier's work force)

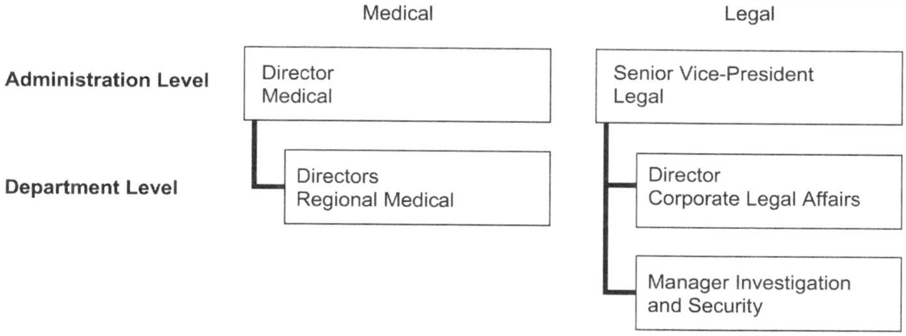

FIGURE 8.11 A Typical Major Air Carrier's Corporate Communications Administration (employs less than 1 percent of the carrier's work force)

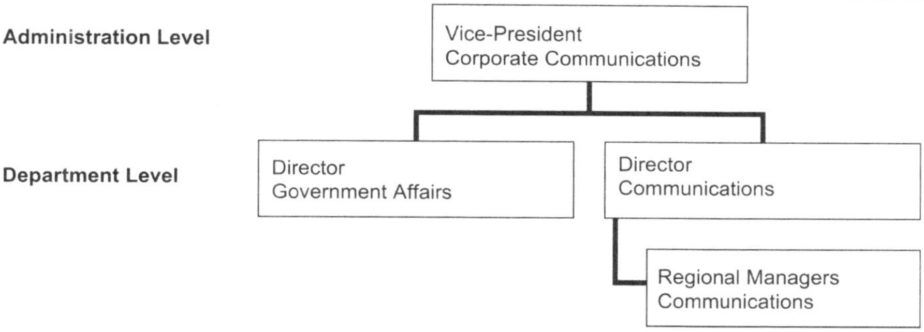

FIGURE 8.12 A Typical Major Air Carrier's Economic Planning Administration (employs approximately than 1 percent of the carrier's work force)

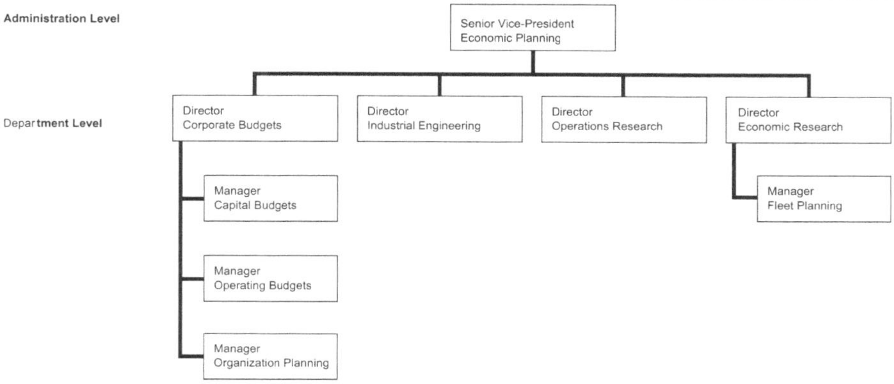

Corporate Communications

This department can be seen as the mouthpiece for the carrier. Most announcements regarding company activities, whether it be an impending strike, weather-caused flight cancellations, or the latest traffic or financial statistics, are made by a representative of this department. This department also has representatives, or lobbyists, in Washington, D.C. and a number of state capitals who are important to the carrier from a legislative standpoint. Legislation regarding increased fuel taxes would be of concern to such individuals (see Figure 8.11).

Economic Planning

The basic function of the economic planning administration is to plan and control the factors that affect the company's economic well-being. This administration develops all long-range forecasts and projects the company's financial returns, including revenues and profit-and-loss statistics, and it develops all cost control and capital expenditure programs. In this capacity, the administration works very closely with top-level management, as well as with all other administrations, in implementing corporate goals (see Figure 8.12).

LINE DEPARTMENTS

Line departments are those administrations that are directly involved in producing and selling air transportation. They include flight operations, engineering and maintenance, and marketing and services.

Flight Operations

The office of the senior vice-president of flight operations is responsible for developing flight-operations policies, procedures, and techniques to promote the safe, efficient, and progressive operation of aircraft. Flight operations must maintain the airline operating certificate in compliance with FAA regulations. In addition, the administration is responsible for developing schedule patterns and procedures for the economic utilization of flight equipment and personnel. It also directs an operations analysis and planning service that effectively plans and exercises continuous control over flight-operations activities throughout the system (see Figure 8.13).

Departmental Level. The vice-president of air traffic and safety develops and recommends ways to promote the safe, economic, and expeditious flow of air traffic from departure to arrival. This executive develops programs for aircraft interior cabin safety and is responsible for safe aircraft operations, navigation aids, and ground communications (teletype and telephone). The vice-president also maintains current information on all airports and airways that may affect operating policies and procedures.

The vice-president of flight procedures and training develops and recommends operating policies, procedures, and techniques for the entire fleet.

FIGURE 8.13 A Typical Major Air Carrier's Flight-operations Administration (employs approximately 10 percent of the carrier's work force)

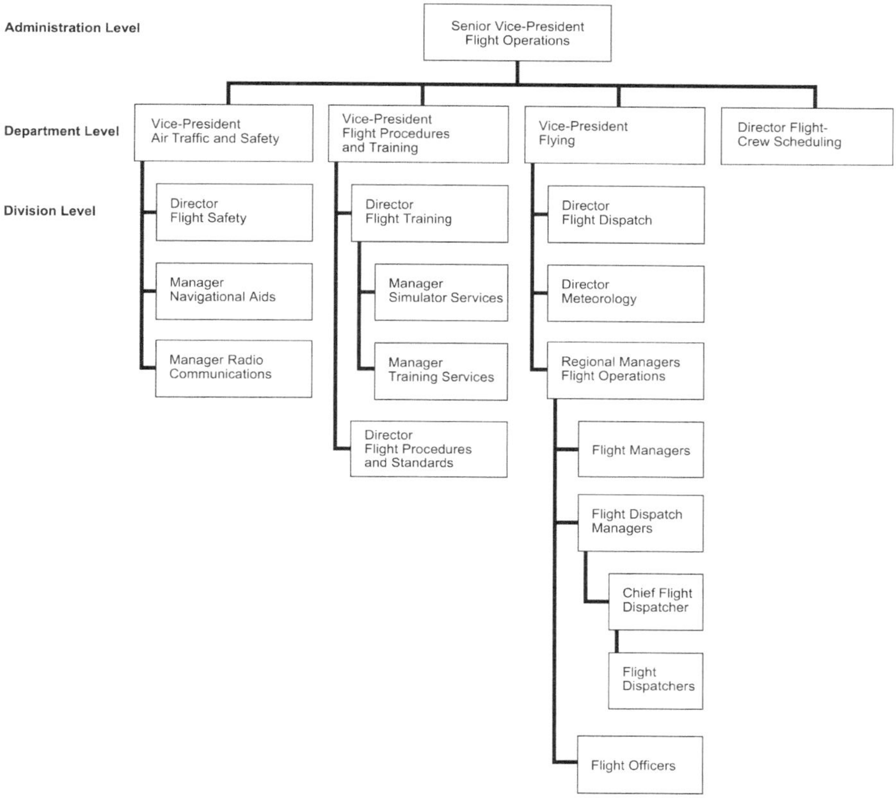

This executive makes recommendations with regard to equipment, such as instruments, controls, power plants, and radios, in addition to directing the flight-operations training department and the flight standards department. The vice-president of flying develops and directs pilot-training programs to enable pilots to meet and maintain proficiency standards required by the airline and the FAA. This executive analyzes the need for pilots within the system to meet schedule requirements and arranges for assignment of new co-pilots, necessary pilot transfers, and furloughs over the entire airline system.

The *director of flight-crew scheduling* is responsible for developing crew schedules for all flight personnel to obtain maximum utilization and availability for each flight.

Division Level. In dispatching aircraft, airlines generally maintain a central control agency, sometimes referred to as **system operations control (SOC)**, that coordinates flight operations, including airplane movements system wide. This agency is headed up by a *director of flight dispatch*. A typical carrier operates 24 hours a day, 365 days a year. *Regional flight dispatch managers* are responsible during their shifts for the overall planning of the flight operations over the entire system. They must consider the technical phases of the operation and coordinate plans with flight dispatchers at adjacent dispatch centers. The goal is to effect safe, efficient, and smooth flow of aircraft operations under existing conditions.

Flight dispatch managers coordinate the activities of their offices in the scheduling of personnel coverage around the clock and are responsible to the regional managers of flight operations. The flight dispatchers are responsible to the chief flight dispatcher for all local activities. They work with flight officers in clearance preparation, covering all details of the proposed flight, including all factors related to the safety of the operation. These factors include: (1) the nature and duration of the flight; (2) weather conditions at various flight altitudes; (3) airway routing; (4) fuel requirements; (5) an alternate flight plan, including airport, if necessary; and (6) the signing of necessary clearance papers after full concurrence with the captain on the proposed plan.

Reporting to the vice-president of flying are usually several *regional managers of flight operations*. Their duties include monitoring all flight-operations policies, methods, and procedures by personal observation and close liaison with flight managers and investigating all irregularities and deviations from established regulations. Regional managers must establish, within their areas and within the limits of airline and FAA guidelines, flight policies and regulations deemed necessary in the interest of safety based on local terrain, weather, and navigational and traffic conditions. Regional managers also hold individual conferences and group meetings with flight managers and flight officers to keep them informed on current company policies, management plans, equipment problems, work planned or in progress for the improvement of equipment, working conditions, personnel problems, grievances, and so forth.

Flight managers are responsible to the regional managers of flight operations for all activities involving flight operations in their area. They monitor the proficiency of pilots by doing en route checks, check flight preparation and execution under various flight conditions, and help and counsel personnel through individual and group meetings.

All pilots report to the flight manager at their domicile. The *captain* is in command of the airplane and, as established by FAA regulations, may take any action deemed necessary to preserve and maintain the safety of the flight. The captain's command commences when the flight is cleared from the loading position. The captain is responsible for determining, before takeoff, that the airplane is loaded within established weight and balance limits and that the required fuel is aboard.

The *first officer* is responsible to the captain for conduct and attention to duty during the flight. The first officer's authority is potential only, capable of being exercised when specifically designated or if the captain becomes incapacitated. The *flight engineer* is also responsible to the captain for conduct and attention to duty during the flight. As new aircraft technology evolves, the flight engineer is being replaced by a computer resulting in two-pilot crews, even for the largest aircraft flying.

Pilots generally are required to arrive one hour before their scheduled flights. In the case of a two-person crew, one pilot reviews the flight plan prepared by SOC, which has been loaded onto the aircraft's computer, while the other inspects the aircraft. The captain will also hold a crew briefing with the flight attendants working the flight.

There are several checklists of tasks that must be completed and items that must be checked before the plane can take off. The checklists used by the major carriers are mechanical rather than paper-and-pencil, requiring the pilot to flip a switch when each necessary task is accomplished; this reduces the likelihood that any check will be left undone. Cockpit procedures are completely standardized, which allows crew members who have never worked together before to operate as an efficient team.

During a given flight, the roles of the cockpit crew members are well defined. There is always one pilot who is flying the aircraft, including takeoffs and landings, and one who is in a support role (checking weight and balance calculations, communicating with SOC, coordinating with air traffic control, monitoring weather data, and so on). Because crews typically work together for at least one month, the captain and co-pilot alternate in these roles. An exception to this is that the captain always taxis the plane, because the tiller that is used in taxiing is on the left side of the cockpit, where the captain sits.

While the aircraft is on the ground, the crew is in contact with the ground controllers, part of the FAA's air traffic control (ATC) system. Ground control directs taxiing aircraft, while tower control handles takeoffs and landings. Once the flight has taken off, it is handed over to departure control, which monitors the flight's first 50–100 miles. Beyond that, the flight is the responsibility of an en route air traffic control center, which handles a large region of the country. During long flights, aircraft pass from center to center until they approach their destination.

Once a flight departs its origin city, keeping track of it and facilitating its on-time completion is the task of SOC. The nerve center of the airline, SOC coordinates and manages the airline's day-to-day and minute-to-minute operations from its facility near the company headquarters. Life at SOC is never routine. Every time something unexpected happens—whether it is a traffic backup, a weather delay, a mechanical problem, a computer outage, an earthquake or a volcanic eruption, a water-main break, a security incident, or any of the other unexpected occurrences that can happen at an airline—SOC experts spring into action.

SOC dispatchers provide the cockpit crew with assistance if a problem occurs en route. For example, if an on-board system fails, a dispatcher arranges for the captain to speak directly with maintenance technicians on the ground to determine if the problem can be rectified in flight. The dispatcher also helps obtain medical advice in the event that a passenger becomes ill during a flight. The dispatcher provides a communications link between the airline's medical department and the captain to discuss the situation, and helps decide whether and where to divert the plane to obtain the appropriate medical treatment.

When the plane gets within 50–100 miles of its destination, the ATC process just described is repeated in reverse. Approach control takes the flight until it is ready to land, at which point it is handed to tower control.

Once the aircraft is on the ground, ground control is in charge of getting it to its designated gate.

Because the captain must do the taxiing, the co-pilot maintains contact with Ground Control and checks to make sure the arrival gate is ready for the aircraft. Once they have successfully guided the plane to the gate, the crew completes a checklist of shutdown duties and makes entries in the aircraft's log. If any maintenance problems arise during the flight, the crew calls them in ahead of time, so that maintenance personnel are ready to address them as soon as the plane arrives.

The basic function of the *director of meteorology* is the administration of the centralized weather service. Meteorologists in this department construct and analyze weather maps and charts to determine what weather phenomena are occurring over various geographic areas at a specific time.

After World War II, the airlines saw the need for a specialized weather service. The forecasting section of the U.S. Weather Bureau could not devote the necessary time to give the airlines the weather information they needed to conduct the safe, smooth, and efficient operation they were striving for. The current airline weather service does not replace but only supplements that of the U.S. Weather Bureau. Whereas the Weather Bureau must consider forecasts to cover all types of aircraft operation nationwide, the airlines focus only on operations over prescribed routes and into prescribed cities.

Weather has a major impact on an airline's ability to meet its objective of safe, comfortable, on-time service. Under federal law, an airline cannot dispatch an aircraft if the forecasted weather is such that the aircraft cannot safely reach its final destination. Aviation forecasts are very detailed and include cloud height, horizontal visibility, and wind speed and direction, because a forecast error of even 30 minutes as to when a storm will arrive at a particular airport can wreak havoc on an airline's operation. Experienced meteorologists use information from governments, satellites, radar, and more than 1,000 airports, as well as constant reports from pilots, to produce hourly forecasts of expected conditions throughout the airline system.

Wind speed and temperature influence how much fuel a flight requires and thus affect how many passengers and how much cargo can be on board. In extreme heat, airplanes taking off from certain runways or anticipating strong head winds need extra fuel and cannot carry as much other weight as planned, which causes some flights to be unexpectedly weight-restricted. In very cold weather, the airplane's wings and fuselage are de-iced to remove any accumulation of ice or snow and prevent further buildup.

Wind conditions dictate the direction toward which an airplane takes off, as well as its allowable take-off weight. Winds also affect travel time, because pilots always try to choose the route and altitude with the least turbulence to give passengers the smoothest possible ride. All of the available weather information goes into the flight plan; and if weather conditions change during midflight, the captain works with SOC to adjust the flight plan accordingly.

The *director of flight training* reports to the vice-president of flight procedures and training and is responsible for the training of flight crews on the airline, including initial training, transition, refresher, requalification, and familiarization training. The training department is divided into three divisions: (1) the ground school, which makes use of audiovisual aids and mockups; (2) flight simulators; and (3) aircraft used for flight training. The *director of flight procedures and standards*, who also reports to the vice-president of flight procedures and training, is responsible for conducting proficiency checks on all flight officers. This includes rating flights for upgrading of first officers, rating flights for transitioning captains, and monitoring flight and simulator training programs conducted by the flight training department.

Engineering and Maintenance

The chief executive officer of engineering and maintenance (E & M) is the senior vice-president, whose responsibilities are as broad as the mission of this administration: to keep the company's equipment in the condition to provide safe and salable air transportation. "Safe," in this sense, implies full compliance with the carrier's own operating specifications and also with all applicable directives and regulations of the FAA. "Salable" means fast and dependable service in up-to-date equipment with comfortable furnishings and decor, without which the company would be unable to compete successfully.

A major carrier's E & M objectives have resulted through the years in the development of an elaborate technical support operation that involves many levels of activity performed at numerous facilities of widely varying capability in accordance with planning and procedures disseminated via a number of media (see Figure 8.14). E & M requires about 25 percent of a carrier's entire work force, and it consumes roughly a fifth of every revenue dollar.

Classes of Stations. From the standpoint of the maintenance function, a major carrier normally divides its many stations served into different **classes of stations**. For example, in descending order of capability, they include: (1) the maintenance base, (2) major stations, (3) service stations, and (4) other stations.

The *maintenance base* is generally conceded to be the largest, most versatile, and best-equipped facility in the system. It is the overhaul and modification center for the carrier's entire fleet, and it has the capability of repairing nearly all aircraft components. Few components must be returned to the manufacturer or sent to outside agencies for reconditioning.

Major stations include the carrier's large hub cities. These stations have relatively large numbers of maintenance people and extensive facilities. They also maintain a substantial inventory of spare parts, mainly supplied by the maintenance base. In general, these stations are capable of providing complete line maintenance of specific types of equipment.

Service stations are large stations served by the carrier but not located at major hub cities with large banks of connecting flights. These stations are well equipped and well staffed with line maintenance personnel, but less so than the major stations.

FIGURE 8.14 A Typical Major Air Carrier's Engineering and Maintenance Administration (employs approximately 25 percent of the carrier's work force)

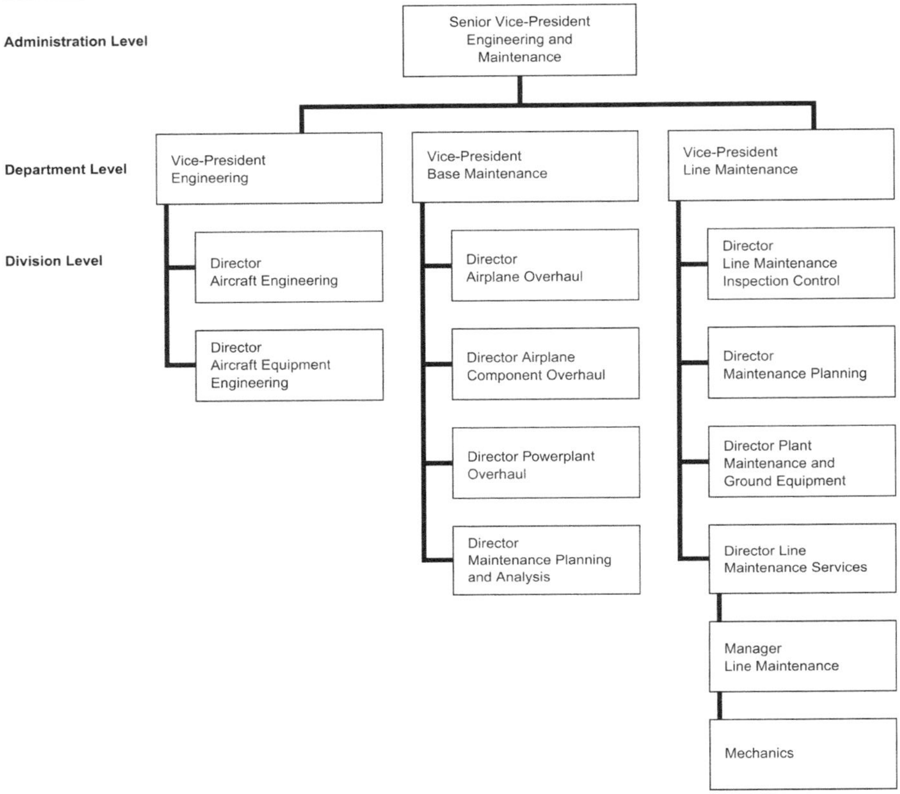

Other stations throughout the system might be designated Class 1, Class 2, and Class 3. Class 1 stations might have only sufficient numbers of licensed people to assure maintenance coverage for each flight before departure. These stations would have minimal facilities and spare parts for performing the assigned work. Class 2 stations might have just enough mechanics and facilities to do routine servicing, such as engine heating, de-icing, aircraft moving, and light maintenance on specific equipment. Ordinarily, the maintenance workload at these stations is so low that the mechanics perform additional tasks. Class 3 stations might exist in smaller cities where there are no licensed maintenance people. They are, therefore, never scheduled to perform maintenance work, and their aircraft servicing is limited to work that has no effect on airworthiness, mainly cargo and passenger handling. Ordinarily, they deal only with through-trips or turnaround flights.

Types of Maintenance. All aircraft must follow an FAA-approved maintenance program that keeps the aircraft in an airworthy condition. Each airline develops its own program, based on the manufacturer's planning documents, but includes adjustments for the airline's own operation. The programs are even different for various operators of the same aircraft type. Although maintained under different programs, aircraft of the same type, utilization, and age will generate approximately the same number of routine maintenance hours during the program cycle. The program cycle is the time elapsed from one overhaul until the next. It generally runs between six and eight years and approximately 20,000 flight hours.

A modern jet aircraft is an assemblage of thousands of parts. For example, a Boeing 787 Dreamliner is made up of 2.3 million parts. These parts constitute many specialized subsystems based on a wide range of technologies. The enterprise of maintaining this highly complex machine usually is classified by both product type (airframe, engine, and components) and the timing and purpose of the work. The latter yields four groupings: (1) **routine scheduled maintenance** (such as airframe and engine checks), (2) **nonroutine maintenance** (structural fatigue repair and corrosion control), (3) **refurbishments** (cabin upgrades and exterior painting), and (4) **modifications** (passenger-to-freight conversions and hushkit installations if applicable). Routine and nonroutine maintenance account for over 95 percent of maintenance activity and spending for most major carriers.

Routine Airframe Maintenance. The most elementary form of routine maintenance is a visual inspection of the aircraft before flight (sometimes called a "walk-around") by pilots and mechanics to ensure that there are no obvious problems such as leaks, missing rivets, or cracks. A "check," the form most routine maintenance takes, comes in several grades, referred to as "letter checks"—A through D—all performed at regular intervals. However, much of "routine" maintenance is unplanned. Up to half of the 400,000 or so tasks involved in a C-check are contingent on the condition of the aircraft.

The following list outlines what each check involves and gives a time frame for its occurrence based on a relatively new narrow-body aircraft. The times and even some of the terminology will differ between airlines.

Overnight Maintenance. At the end of the working day, workers conduct a 1–1½-hour inspection to ensure that the plane is operating in accord with the original equipment manufacturer's (OEMs) minimum equipment list (MEL). This also represents an opportunity to remedy passenger and crew complaints and to implement marketing-driven modifications (such as the installation of telephones), as well as to attend to aspects of FAA Airworthiness Directives (ADs) and Manufacturers' Service Bulletins. This is a chance to do whatever work can be completed in the time allotted so as not to disrupt the aircraft's flight schedule.

A-Check. Roughly every 125 flight hours (two to three weeks), an amplified preflight visual inspection of the fuselage exterior, power plant, and certain readily accessible subsystems, including avionics (aviation electronics) and accessories, is conducted to ascertain the general condition of the aircraft.

B-Check. Approximately every 750 flight hours (three to four months), workers conduct an open inspection of panels and cowlings, during which some preventive maintenance (exterior wash, engine oil spectroscopic analysis, and so on) is performed, oil filters are removed and checked, parts are lubricated as required, and the airframe is carefully examined. The B-check incorporates an A-check.

C-Check. This fundamental airworthiness inspection, which is carried out approximately every 3,000 flight hours or every 15 months, incorporates both A- and B-checks. In addition, components are repaired, flight controls are calibrated, and major internal mechanisms are tested. Other tasks include heavy lubrication, attendance to Service Bulletin requirements, minor structural inspections, flight control rigging tests, engine baroscope inspections, compressor washes, aircraft appearance maintenance, and, usually, some corrosion prevention. The C-check also includes a postcheck flight test.

D-Check. This is the most intensive form of routine maintenance, typically occurring every six to eight years or approximately every 20,000 flight hours. Cabin interiors (including seats, galleys, lavatories, cockpit, furnishings, headliners, and sidewalls) are removed to enable careful structural inspections. Flight controls are examined, and the fuel system is probed for leaks and cracks. The aircraft essentially is stripped to its shell and rebuilt with the intention of returning it to original ("zero-timed") condition as much as possible.

A- and B-checks and overnight maintenance are examples of "line" maintenance: work that can be managed at an airport (sometimes even on the ramp) and that is usually performed overnight so as not to encroach on flight plans. C- and D-checks, however, constitute "heavy" maintenance, demanding special facilities and extensive downtime.

Some airlines employ intermediate layover (IL) checks, a form of so-called progressive (or phased, equalized, or continuous) maintenance that does without a standard D-check by incorporating portions of it across several more frequently scheduled inspections, usually C-checks. In another variation, parts of a C-check are merged with several successive A-checks. The goal in either case is to minimize the time the aircraft is out of service while also balancing workloads.

The maintenance of different components varies considerably. For example, a *consumable* (such as a gasket) is a single-use item that is scrapped whenever it is first removed. An *expendable* (such as a fastener or a cable) is used until it becomes unserviceable. A *repairable* (for example, a turbine or a compressor blade) can be repaired and returned to service a limited number of times. Whereas a repairable tends to be an item, a *rotable* (such as a pump, a fuel control, or a constant-speed drive) is an assembly, usually high-cost and capitalized, and almost never scrapped. It is zero-timed when repaired and thus can be reworked indefinitely. A *life-limited part* (such as a disk, a shaft, a hub, or other major rotating engine unit) must be removed from service after its OEM- or government-imposed life limit, typically 15,000–20,000 cycles. Although a life-limited part (or LLP) can be repaired, in accord with the OEM's manual, its life is not thereby extended.

Since the 1970s, there has been a shift from hard-time removals to "on condition" monitoring. This means that engine and component repairs generally do not occur at fixed time periods or intervals; rather, the timing of routine maintenance is based on the state of the equipment. Thus, instead of detaching an item for inspection and repair after a set number of hours or cycles of operation, technicians consult actual operating data, sometimes collected by sensors or built-in test equipment (BITE), to determine when it requires repair. Engines remain on-wing for the longest possible time to minimize operating cost per flight hour. Safety is enhanced because circumstances that might lead to an in-flight shutdown can be foreseen and prevented. Maintenance planning is improved because removals can be made in concert with other repairs.

In addition, many engines have been designed in modular form, permitting entire sections to be removed and replaced or repaired as needed, rather than having the whole powerplant serviced. Typically, an overhaul shop will view an incoming engine as a group of modules, each of which gets different treatment. Similarly, component repair generally consists of the removal of a component or subcomponent that is later tested and repaired or replaced.

Nonroutine Maintenance. Nonroutine maintenance is either the product of an unforeseen event, such as an accident or random occurrence, or a response to an AD. An example of the first is engine damage due to bird ingestion or an airframe dented by a catering truck. An example of the second, aging aircraft, is worth dwelling on.

Because of concerns about the growing number of older aircraft still flying, the FAA instituted tougher rules several years ago to counter: (1) the repeated cabin pressurization and depressurization that stresses an airframe's structure and skin, resulting, if untreated, in metal fatigue and cracking; and (2) the corrosion caused by long-term exposure to moisture. (Engines are not as vulnerable to aging because periodic maintenance may leave few, if any, original parts.)

Although the average age of the U.S. airline fleet has remained the same during the late-1990s and early 2020s (around 14 years) because of the continued influx of new planes, there remains a cohort of older planes getting older. Close to one-quarter of the fleet has reached 20 years of service, and close to 500 planes are over 25 years old and nearing or exceeding their original design life. Airlines strapped for capital—both start-ups and older carriers—are finding it cheaper to extend the life of an old airplane than to buy a new one.

The problem with this practice is that maintenance costs, special aging regulations aside, grow as an airframe ages. One reason for this is that many parts reach the point at which they can no longer be repaired and must be replaced, which is a costlier proposition. The main reason, though, is the mounting number of nonscheduled procedures that arise. Eventually, the cost of repair approaches a significant fraction of the aircraft's value, and a decision must be made as to whether continued maintenance is cost-efficient. Many aircraft are retired just before a D-check to avoid the over

$1 million expense. But any retirement analysis must also factor in replacement costs, operational costs, and resale value. It is almost certain that operational costs for these aging aircraft (including maintenance) will climb. Interestingly, there are some trends occurring impacting the global aircraft fleet. By 2025, Africa will operate the oldest aircraft fleet followed by the U.S. while India and China will operate the youngest fleet (Statista.com).

Overhaul of Airframes. The real reason for routing an airplane into a maintenance base and opening it up is to give it a thorough structural going over—to inspect and repair. Other reasons are mainly those of convenience. It's easier and probably more economical to change time-controlled units at this time, as well as to do modifications. But these are not essential to an airframe overhaul, and this is not the way most carriers maintain their fleets these days.

It used to be that airplanes were overhauled according to a plan that required a series of seven minor overhauls and a major one. The major overhaul was designed to rework the airplane to a like-new condition—to fit the bits and pieces back together to the exactness of current manufacturing tolerances. The carriers departed from this practice about the end of World War II by developing what was then called a *progressive overhaul* or *progressive maintenance* but should have been described as a *progressive major overhaul.* What this practice did was merely take portions of the work of a major overhaul and incorporate them into the minor overhauls so that all were about equal in workload.

This approach had its advantages, but it didn't go far enough. It did not provide for early sampling of multiple-run items (those not requiring attention at every overhaul), and it resulted in bunching of multiple-run repair-and-return components in the shops. For these reasons, the plan adopted for DC-7s in the 1950s and early 1960s staggered the entry of the airplanes into overhaul. The first eight DC-7s in to the base got eight different treatments, and then the ninth started the cycle over again. Every airplane, on successive visits, received a different one of the eight treatments until it had them all. On each visit, some additional multiple-run items were picked up. The same things weren't necessarily looked into or pulled off of all airplanes just because they were in for the first, second, or third time. Still, after eight visits, each DC-7 had the equivalent of a major overhaul—mostly imposed piecemeal on what had been the seven minor overhauls.

It is considerably different with the jets, although the plan in use is a natural extension of the former progressive one. No longer, though, is the eight-visit cycle in evidence, and no longer is it valid to say that a jet has had the equivalent of a major overhaul after any particular number of visits.

The basic document used in formulating the airframe overhaul plan of a major carrier's jet fleet is the work report prepared by the engineering department for maintaining the structural integrity of the particular aircraft. When this document is approved by the FAA, it becomes a part of the operations specifications, which detail the requirements for continuous airworthiness. Compliance with this document's specifications is mandatory.

A separate work report covers the entire structure, the landing gear, and all control surfaces of each jet airplane type by zones. It spells out the kind of inspection each item is to receive and designates the frequency or interval of inspections. And it further specifies that an approximately equal number of each of the zone inspections are to be made and evenly spaced within each fleet overhaul period. The latter is the provision that largely determines the shape of the overhaul plan for that fleet. A carrier's structural-integrity program thus provides the framework upon which each airframe overhaul is constructed. Other jobs, some related and others not, constitute the body of the overhaul.

Conceivably, an airframe overhaul might be limited in content to a thorough inspection plus the repairs, replacements, and operational checks triggered by it. If this were done, though, a large amount of work would have to be scheduled at other times. This would then necessitate adding to the time and workload of the periodic checks described earlier, or it would lead to special routing of airplanes to a station or base where the work could be done at a time other than check or overhaul.

Generally, however, airlines have preferred to exchange time-controlled units (nonstructural) and do the major modifications at the time of overhaul. But these impose certain penalties on the essential work of the overhaul. In particular, they tend to cause congestion and interference among jobs, and they sometimes upset sequencing of operations and result in delays. All this has prompted some reappraisal of the practice.

In recent years, the lengthening of times between airframe overhauls has led to a shift toward line accomplishment of modification projects, but few time-controlled units are currently scheduled for replacement other than at overhaul. Engines are a notable exception. Jet engine overhauls have never been in phase with airframe overhauls; engines are not ordinarily scheduled for change at the time of an airframe overhaul.

The documents that govern the operational checking of aircraft systems and the removal and replacement of time-controlled units are the engineering and maintenance control (EMAC) cards. The EMAC system, which came into use with the jets, is designed to assemble, disseminate, and control all the information essential to proper maintenance of components and systems, both airframe and engine. It blends with the work reports and the modification project schedules to determine what is involved in overhauls.

Generally, carriers seek to utilize components to their full allowable time. Thus, one-run units are removed and replaced at each overhaul, two-run units at the second overhaul and every second one thereafter, three-run units at the third overhaul and every third one thereafter, and so on. There are some exceptions, however, particularly when sampling or other circumstances indicate benefits of early initial removal and staggering of removals thereafter.

Currently, a big-jet airframe overhaul consumes over 20,000 work hours, including inspector and lead mechanic hours. Of this total, less than 10 percent is involved with inspection, including that called for in the work reports. Over 40 percent involves component changes and systems checkout, about 20 percent modifications, and about 30 percent nonroutine work generated by the inspection. The job takes approximately 15 days in the overhaul dock and two days on the ramp for flight preparation and testing.

Overhaul of Engines and Other Components. In general, overhauls of engines, their accessories, and other components are handled in much the same manner. Components are brought in when either operating time or condition requires it, and the overhaul returns them to specifications laid down by engineering and the manufacturer. A large part of engine overhaul is made up of repair and reconditioning operations, as it is usually beneficial, both economically and from the standpoint of reliability, to reuse seasoned components when they can be reworked to approved specifications.

Scheduled engine changes are planned so as to minimize shipping costs and transit times and to avoid special routing of aircraft. All scheduled big-jet engine changes are handled at the carrier's major base, and all others at compromise locations where routing is convenient and labor is available. When practical, engine changes are made during maintenance checks or airframe overhauls.

Contract Maintenance. There are many reasons an airline contracts with an independent facility to perform maintenance. An airline may not have the personnel or equipment to complete a special project or a large modification to its fleet. An air carrier might also recognize that an independent facility has the expertise in a given area, such as turbine-engine maintenance or heavy-airframe modification, to do the job better and more efficiently than the airline. A newer airline may not have the capital to set up a complete maintenance operation, and an independent facility may be able to perform the same service at a lower cost than an airline because of lower labor costs.

Several other factors have led to the airlines' using outside maintenance service more than in the past. When a carrier expands its fleet, its maintenance capabilities are often stretched to the limit simply providing routine services. Thus, many carriers have found it necessary to go outside to meet their needs. In the past, when airlines had larger maintenance facilities, they were able to handle a big job like standardizing a number of aircraft acquired from another carrier. But deregulation, recessions, lower fares, and higher costs have forced the carriers to keep their maintenance capabilities on the lean side.

Carriers often contract with an independent facility when serving a distant airport at which they have no maintenance support. In addition to providing minor maintenance services, some contracts extend to other functions, such as cleaning and fueling aircraft.

Marketing and Services

The senior vice-president of marketing is a member of a company's top management group and in this capacity brings a marketing focus to its deliberations. As chief executive officer of the largest administration (typically over 50 percent of a carrier's work force), this executive's responsibilities include making decisions about marketing policy, as well as the daily administration of the organization. In the latter capacity, the senior vice-president's office administers the organization's cost control efforts and coordinates and implements personnel policies, including staff training programs. Major departments, generally headed up by vice-presidents, that report to the senior vice-president include advertising, marketing services, services planning, sales planning, sales and services, and food service (see Figure 8.15).

Advertising. Advertising is an extremely important marketing department, particularly in today's competitive environment. The advertising department, working closely with the company's advertising agency, provides expertise on promotional messages, copy, media, and timing. This department may influence, but generally does not determine, the amount of company funds spent on advertising and promotion.

Marketing Services. Marketing services is another extremely important marketing department, as it literally designs the carrier's products and determines the firm's market opportunities. Included are such major divisions as market research and forecasting, pricing, and schedule planning. (For a complete discussion of these important areas, see Chapters 9, 11, and 13.)

Market research and forecasting is charged with the responsibility of systematically gathering, recording, and analyzing data relating to the marketing of air transportation. Operationally, this means forecasting market opportunities and finding out about the market for air transportation—the numbers and types of consumers, the product itself, channels of distribution, and consumer motivation and behavior. With the so-called consumer-oriented marketing concept in use in recent years, whose objective is to furnish consumer satisfaction, market research and forecasting has been recognized by most major carriers as co-equal in status with sales, advertising, new product and services development, pricing, and scheduling (see Chapter 9).

Of all the marketing variables that influence the potential sales of the airline product, *pricing* has certainly received the most attention since deregulation. The pricing division of a major carrier has become one of the most visible areas within the company (see Chapter 11).

Defining what the *schedule planning* division does is simple: all that is necessary is to take the company's marketing goals for a particular period and turn them into a salable schedule that creates volumes of new traffic; beats the competition; makes the most efficient use of personnel, facilities, and aircraft; serves the cities on the system; and earns ever-increasing profits. Scheduling may be the most difficult job in any airline (see Chapter 13).

FIGURE 8.15 A Typical Major Air Carrier's Marketing and Services Administration (employs approximately 50 percent of the carrier's work force)

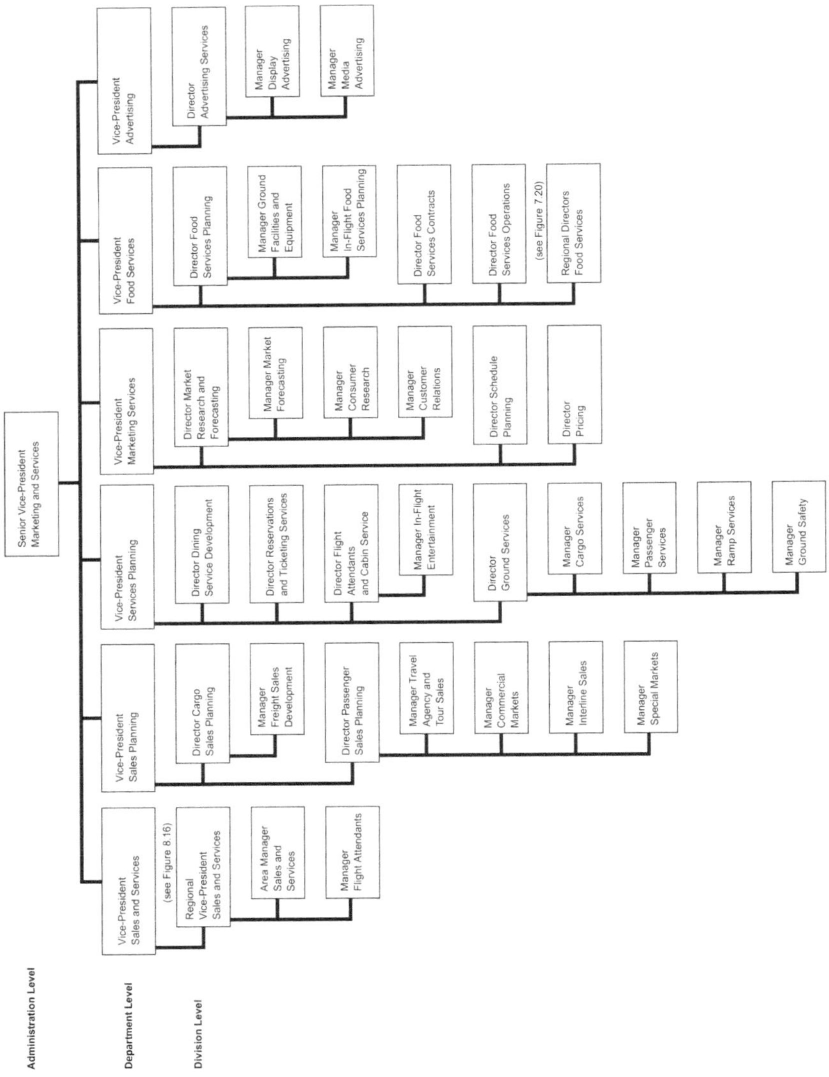

Services Planning. The services planning department is responsible for the development of the in-flight and ground services for the various markets identified by market research and forecasting. These include everything from reservations and ticketing services to in-flight entertainment and dining services. The latter includes such details as the type of meal service aboard various flights, the number of courses, and the various menus.

Sales Planning. Sales planning is concerned with the means by which a carrier's products and services are delivered to consumers. Given the markets developed by market research and forecasting, the prices and schedules, and the services planned for the various markets, it is up to sales planning to develop an approach to reach these target groups. This department works closely with regional sales and services personnel in implementing their plans.

Traditional organizational planning holds that when the number of reporting functions becomes too numerous, a useful solution is to regroup them into several clusters and appoint a manager to each cluster. Accordingly, most of the major carriers have separated the marketing functions into operations and planning. In a sense, the three aforementioned departments—marketing services, services planning, and sales planning—have become staff departments to sales and services.

Sales and Services. Sales and services is concerned with the implementation of the plans formulated by the planning staff (see Figure 8.16). Airline sales management is as old as the carriers themselves, but there have been significant changes since World War II. The social sciences, and especially psychology, have given sales personnel new insights into old problems. Newer organizational methods have increased sales efficiency. To implement the selling function, personnel in this department must have complete knowledge of who consumers are, what makes them purchase the product, and how they can be reached. The planning departments have helped in meeting these selling challenges.

A rationale for the separation of the planning and selling functions is that it is difficult for any individual to give equal time to two tasks and to be equally good at both. Each member of the operating sales force—whether a cargo sales representative, a reservations agent, or a ticket-counter agent—is involved in daily crises, problems, and workloads that detract from long-range thinking and planning. Thus, the planning work gets done better when left to those who specialize in it and who have time to do it. A major criticism is that the planners may do a poor job because they do not understand operating conditions.

It is interesting to note that flight attendants generally report to the regional sales and services personnel. Although their primary purpose aboard aircraft is to serve passengers' needs in the event of an emergency, and although their specific number aboard a flight is determined by federal aviation regulations, they have truly become a part of the marketing game plan.

Food Service. Before 2000, food service was a major business for the large airlines. Many airlines had flight kitchens throughout the system

FIGURE 8.16 A Typical Major Air Carrier's Regional Sales and Services Department

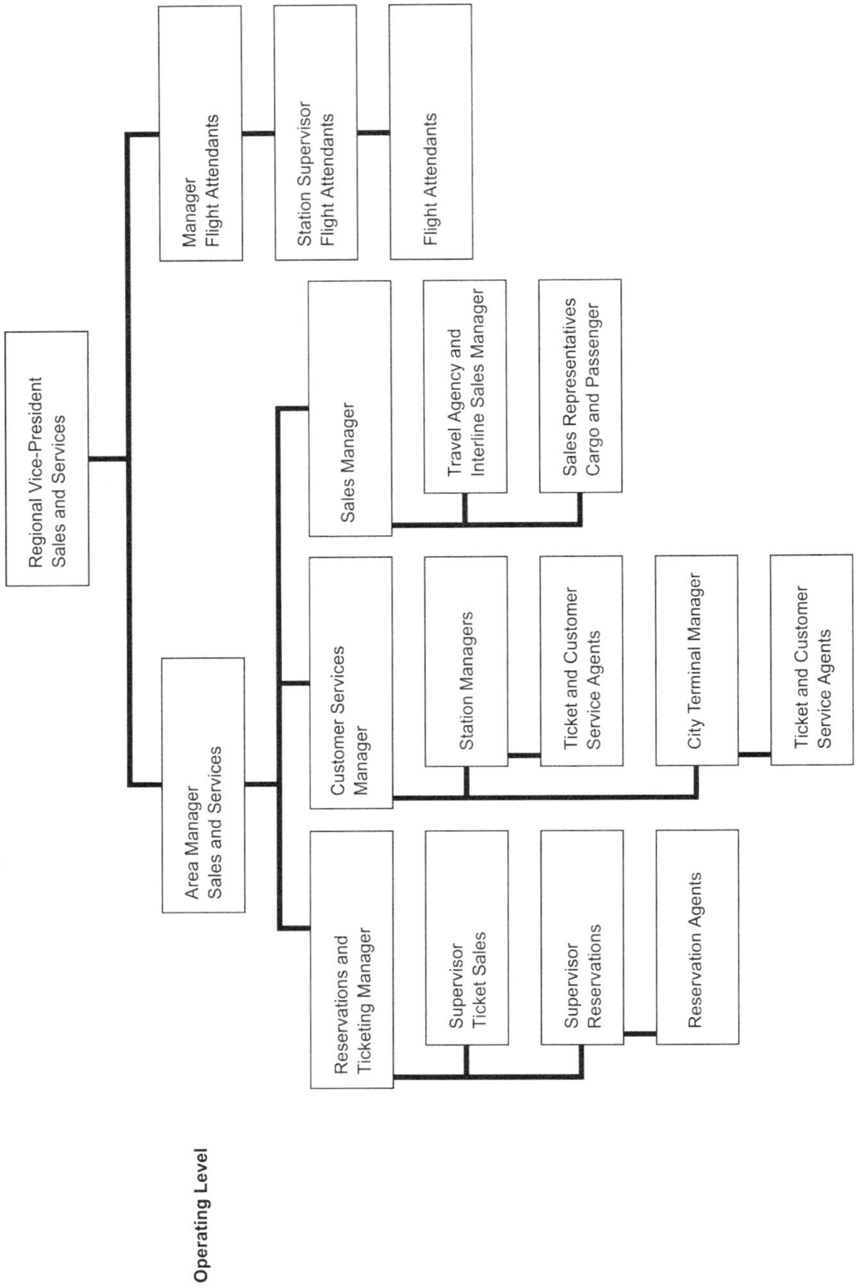

located at major hub airports. These kitchens served thousands of meals per day not only to the carrier's flights but also to those carriers that contracted with the major carrier. The costs of operating a flight kitchen are extremely high, and airlines have realized that costs can be substantially reduced if this service is subcontracted. For those airlines that still operate flight kitchens, Figure 8.17 shows a typical organizational structure.

The Flight – Serving Passengers

The end product of marketing and services is serving customers' needs. The typical airline customer spends more time with the flight attendants than with any other employee group. Thus, the flight attendants have much to do with how an airline's customers feel about the carrier and whether they will fly that airline again in the future. In the eyes of the flying public, the flight attendants *are* the airline, so it is up to the flight attendants to turn every customer into a repeat customer. Although their primary function is ensuring in-flight safety, flight attendants have become an extension of the marketing effort. Flight attendants receive training in aircraft familiarization, customer service, galley equipment, and food and beverage presentation. Through classroom lectures, hands-on demonstrations, and simulations, they become professionals ready to deal with any emergency situation and dedicated to making every passenger's trip comfortable and safe.

Flight attendants are required to sign in at the airport one hour before their flight's scheduled departure time. Flight attendant schedules—like those of the pilots—are based on each flight attendant's preferences, weighted by seniority.

Once they have signed in, flight attendants are required to be at their flight's departure gate 40–50 minutes before departure. At the gate, an agent provides them with the passenger load, a list of the flight's frequent customers, and any special-handling requests (such as passengers who will need a little extra help). Once on board the aircraft, the flight attendants check the emergency equipment and the catering and generally make sure the

FIGURE 8.17 An Air Carrier's Food Service Department

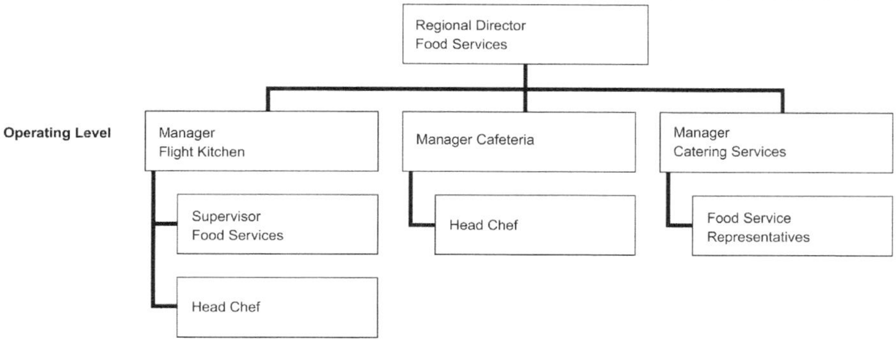

cabin is ready for passengers. On wide-body domestic flights and all international flights, there is a designated first flight attendant, or purser, who has received special training and who supervises and coordinates the activities of the other flight attendants.

When passengers begin to board, one flight attendant will check passenger tickets either at the jet-bridge entrance or at the door of the aircraft. For safety reasons, one flight attendant stays at the back of the plane while the rest assist passengers in finding their seats and stowing their carry-on luggage and, in the first-class cabin, serve a pre-departure beverage. Before the plane can leave the gate, the flight attendants need to make sure that all of the overhead bins are closed and that the passengers are seated and buckled in. Only then can the aircraft leave the gate.

Before take-off, the plane's doors need to be "armed," which means a flight attendant activates an inflatable slide that opens automatically if the doors are opened in an emergency situation. The slides must be deactivated once the plane has landed safely at its destination.

While the captain taxis the plane to its designated runway, the flight attendants make safety announcements and demonstrate the proper use of oxygen masks, seat belts, and—when the plane is to pass over water—life vests and rafts. Before sitting down for take-off, the flight attendants make sure that all passenger seats are upright, that tray tables are up and locked, and that any first-class beverage service items have been collected and put away.

Once the flight is in the air and has reached cruising altitude, the flight attendants can begin their food and beverage service. In the first-class cabin, flight attendants ask passengers for their drink and, when a meal is being served, entree preferences. In the main cabin, the flight attendants prepare the drink cart, with the objective of beginning drink service within 15–20 minutes after take-off. If there is a meal on the flight, beverages are always served first.

It should be noted, due to cost-cutting measures and increased revenue generation, many airlines, domestic and international, now charge passengers for beverages, food, entertainment, and certain services. In some cases, passengers are even charged for carrying "normal" baggage in addition to the seat purchase. It will not be long before an airline creates a unique marketing campaign where they charge passengers based on the comfort and location of a coach class seat. For example, a middle seat might be charged less money than an aisle or window seat.

Before landing, the flight attendants pick up any remaining food and beverage service items and make sure all passenger seat belts are fastened and all tray tables are up and locked. One flight attendant will announce connecting gate information for those passengers who need to catch other flights.

After the plane lands, the flight attendants must remain seated while the captain taxis to the arrival gate. Ramp personnel guide the aircraft to its parking position and, after it comes to a stop, put chocks under its wheels. As soon as that has been done, other workers hook up ground-based power and air-conditioning.

On the airplane, the flight attendants open the door, and as passengers begin deplaning, a mechanic squeezes past them to get a debriefing from the cockpit crew and to see if any maintenance work must be done. Once all the deplaning passengers are off, the cabin cleaners begin cleaning out seat-back pockets, tidying up the cabin, cleaning the lavatories, doing a light vacuuming, and repositioning safety belts for each seat's next occupant. A more thorough cleaning is done each night.

Meanwhile, out on the ramp, airline personnel are unloading baggage, freight, and mail from the airplane's belly compartments and are beginning the process of sorting by various categories and destinations. The bags and cargo must be delivered promptly to passengers and shippers or transferred to other flights if they have not reached their final destination.

If a meal has been served or is planned for the outbound flight, catering trucks pull up to service the first-class and main-cabin galleys. Another truck services the lavatory holding tanks, and in the midst of all this, mechanics deal with any problems reported by the crew and do their own walk-around inspections.

Once all of these processes are complete, customers begin to board the aircraft for its next flight, and everything happens in reverse. Ground workers start loading baggage in the forward belly and freight and mail in the rear. Fuel trucks pull up to refuel most flights. The airplanes also must be "watered." Fresh water is pumped aboard from either a water truck or servicing equipment built into the gate itself. During cold-weather months, de-icing trucks spray fluid on the airplane's wings and fuselage. Ramp crew chiefs are responsible for orchestrating all of the ground-operations activities. Performing all of the required jobs quickly enough for the plane to meet its next departure time requires a great deal of teamwork and cooperation. Although efficiency and customer service are important, the underlying theme of safety pervades all operations.

KEY TERMS

administration
classes of stations
controlling
decision making
delegation of authority
department
departmentalization
directing
division
functions of management
levels of management
line department
line personnel
management
management by objectives (MBO)
modifications

nonroutine maintenance
organization
organizational chart
organizing
planning
policy and procedures manual
refurbishment
routine scheduled maintenance
span of control
staff department
staff personnel
staffing
system operations control (SOC)
unity of objectives

REVIEW QUESTIONS

1 Define *management*. What is meant by the different levels of management? How are they distinguishable? Which titles do we normally find at each level of management?
2 How does decision making differ at the various levels of management? "Sometimes no decision is a decision." Discuss. It has been said that management decision making was easier before deregulation. Do you agree? Why?
3 Why is planning such an important management function within an airline? Who plans? Define *management by objectives*. What is a policy and procedures manual? How does a procedure differ from a rule? Describe the other functions of management.
4 What is an organization plan? Describe the eight principles of organization discussed in this chapter. Why are they so important to the management of airlines?
5 Distinguish between line and staff responsibilities. Why are line workers referred to as volume-related? How did staff organizations get started?
6 What is an organizational chart? What is its purpose? The organizational charts shown in this chapter are fairly comprehensive and reflect the organizational plan for a major carrier. Suppose that you were charged with the responsibility of developing an organizational chart for a medium-size commuter carrier. Develop a chart, including appropriate line and staff departments. (Remember, you are dealing with only a couple hundred employees.)
7 How does the organizational chart of a new-entrant or low-cost carrier compare to a legacy or established airline? What are the main advantages and disadvantages to this type of organization?
8 Which major administration would the following staff departments fall under: telecommunications, corporate insurance, accounts payable, facilities and airport planning, investigation and security,

employee suggestion program, management appraisal and development, publicity, industrial engineering, and fleet planning?

9 Describe the four major departments under flight operations. What is the role of flight dispatch? Briefly describe the flight-crew functions from the time they report to the airport until they arrive at their destination. Why do the major carriers have their own meteorologists?

10 What is the primary role of the E & M administration? Most carriers divide their stations into various classes of maintenance service. Describe the classes. Distinguish between routine scheduled maintenance and nonroutine maintenance. What is the difference between checks A through D? Discuss some of the maintenance problems associated with aging aircraft.

11 What is an overhaul work report? How have major carriers' jet overhauls changed since the early 1960s? Give several reasons air carriers have increased contract maintenance in recent years.

12 Describe the relationship between the following marketing departments: marketing services, services planning, sales planning, and sales and services. Which department would the pricing and schedule planning divisions fall under? Why are they, along with market research and forecasting, so important? Describe the dual role of flight attendants as marketing representatives and safety coordinators. Discuss the importance of teamwork and coordination on the ramp area once an aircraft has been parked.

13 How did the COVID-19 global pandemic impact the need to restructure organizations? What will be the focus of organizations in the future as it relates to personnel otherwise known as talent?

Notes

1 Chris Argyris, *Integrating the Individual and the Organization* (New York: Wiley, 1964), p. 26.

2 Carl Heyel (ed.), *The Encyclopedia of Management*, 2nd edition (New York: Van Nostrand Reinhold, 1963), p. 977.

CHAPTER 9

Forecasting Methods

CHAPTER CHECKLIST • YOU SHOULD BE ABLE TO:

- Discuss the importance of forecasting in relation to analysis, planning, and control
- Compare three basic methods of forecasting
- Describe why causal models are considered the most sophisticated type of forecasting method used today
- Explain what is meant by *trends, cyclical variations, seasonal changes,* and *irregular fluctuations*
- Describe what is meant by *smoothing the variations*
- Explain why judgmental forecasts are often used in conjunction with the other methods of forecasting

INTRODUCTION

Every day, at all levels of management within all segments of the air transportation industry, decisions are made about what is likely to happen in the future. It has been said that business action taken today must be based on yesterday's plan and tomorrow's expectations. Call them expectations, predictions, projections—it all boils down to one thing: forecasting. **Forecasting** is the attempt to quantify demand in a future time period. Quantification can be in terms of either dollars, such as revenue, or some physical volume, such as revenue passenger miles (RPMs) or passenger enplanements. Plans for the future cannot be made without forecasting demand. Planning also plays an important role in any aviation enterprise, but it should not be confused with forecasting. Forecasting is predicting, projecting, or estimating some future volume or financial situation—matters mostly outside of management's control. Planning, on the other hand, is concerned with setting objectives and goals and with developing alternative courses of action to reach them—matters generally within management's control.

DOI: 10.4324/9780429346156-12

A forecast of revenues is not a plan. There must be goals, strategies for attaining them, alternative courses of action, and a realistic fit with other market conditions. Thus, although forecasting is not planning, it is an indispensable part of planning—a management tool for deciding now what the company must do to realize its profit and other goals for the future.

Not only is forecasting done for a given type of demand independently, but forecasts of one type of demand may also be based on other forecasts. Thus, the projection of flying hours for next year is an element in the forecast of future demand for flight personnel, fuel consumption, facilities, and a host of other considerations.

Forecasts are based on historical demand, and for decades the aviation industry has used such data for short, medium, and long-term planning purposes. For the first time in aviation history, the events of 9/11 in 2001 put into question the reliability of data, and just when the industry got back on track, another major global event negatively impacted all stakeholders, catching the world by storm. The COVID-19 global pandemic started at the end of 2019 when clusters of patients began to show symptoms that originated in Wuhan, China. Very quickly, the symptoms spread throughout the world and in March 2020, the **World Health Organization (WHO)** declared the COVID-19 outbreak a pandemic. Immediately, the air transport sector was hit by the law of supply and demand as air carriers throughout the world were forced to stop and revise operations, including cancelation of flights and a decrease in route frequency which also resulted in massive financial losses. For the second time in history, the aviation industry was forced to survive, adapt, recover, and rethink business models because historical data was once again skewed. Interestingly, air carriers learned to advance scenario-based simulation applications whereby different external and internal factors could be tested for outcomes. It is only a matter of time before another global challenge impacts the aviation industry and it is believed that scenario-based simulation exercises will become one of the standards used in forecasting.

THE PURPOSE OF FORECASTING

Each type of forecast serves a particular purpose. Thus, an airline might make a *short-term forecast* of total passenger enplanements between a particular pair of cities to provide a basis for determining station personnel and ground equipment needed, gate availability, and expenses related to these items. Short-term forecasts normally span a period of one month to one year and cover such day-to-day operations as staffing stations, evaluating current competitive situations in the market, and projecting short-term equipment needs.

Medium-term forecasts generally span a period of one to five years and involve such things as route-planning decisions. A *long-term forecast* spans a period of five to ten years and might involve fleet planning decisions and long-term financial commitments. For example, a light-aircraft manufacturer might make a long-term forecast of demand for an aircraft specifically designed to serve the commuter air carrier market and then plan to meet the projected demand. The various forecasts are used by companies to carry out three important management functions—analysis, planning, and control.

A word of caution should be noted when forecasting. When obtaining statistical data, it is important to realize different sources have different reporting methods for the same outcome, meaning actual data might not be accurate. It is very important to use data from reputable sources and have a thorough understanding of how the data was collected, especially when benchmarking against other sources.

Analysis

Every company must make choices among the many markets or submarkets open to it, in addition to deciding on the level of service to offer, the type of aircraft to fly on particular routes, and the type of aircraft to purchase. The choice is greatly facilitated by quantitative estimates of demand. The following situations demonstrate the role of forecasting in the analysis function:

> A major air carrier is trying to decide whether to purchase the Boeing 787 or the A-350. An estimate of operating costs will be a guiding factor.
>
> A regional carrier is trying to decide whether to introduce shuttle service between two cities. The company will be guided by its market research department's estimate of long-term passenger enplanements.
>
> A light-aircraft manufacturer is trying to decide whether to develop a new commuter aircraft. The company will be guided by an estimate of potential sales in this market.

Planning

Every firm must make short-term decisions about the allocation and scheduling of its limited resources over many competing uses; it must make long-term decisions about rates of expansion of capital equipment and funds. Both short-term and long-term decisions require quantitative estimates of demand, as the following situations illustrate:

> A line maintenance supervisor for a national carrier in Dallas wants to identify how many workers will be employed for the next calendar year and needs an estimate of the number of departures at his station by month.
>
> The advertising director for a major carrier wants to promote a new low fare to selected cities and needs a short-term forecast of enplanements as a basis for assigning funds.
>
> The board of directors of a medium-size regional carrier needs a long-term forecast of population growth and business expansion in a particular city to use as a basis for planning future expansion.

Control

A company's actual performance (physical volume or revenues) in the market takes on meaning when it is compared to forecasts. The use of these demand measurements for control purposes is illustrated in these examples:

> A commercial aircraft manufacturer is disappointed with sales to national carriers. The market research department is asked to develop a new forecast of company sales potential in this market.
>
> A regional sales manager of a light-aircraft manufacturer wants to subdivide a sales territory in which sales are unusually high. The salesperson for that territory objects, arguing that the territory has only average sales potential but that she has penetrated the market to a greater degree than her counterparts have. The sales manager asks the research staff to come up with a sales forecast for the territory.
>
> The vice-president of flying for a major carrier asks the administrative staff to reestimate the number of pilots who need to be trained on the B-737 over the next three years because the former number appears to be too large in view of delays in delivery schedule since the original forecast.

FORECASTING METHODS

The choice of forecasting methods should be based on several factors, including availability of data, accuracy of available data, management sophistication, intended forecast use, and availability of electronic data processing. Sophistication in forecasting methods can easily run ahead of data quality and management ability to use the results. Forecasting passenger enplanements for a one-year period on well-established routes, for example, possesses a fundamentally different forecasting problem than estimating enplanements on a new route, and forecasting methods must be chosen accordingly.[1] Annual forecasts are provided by various organizations, such as the FAA, IATA, ICAO, aircraft manufacturers, and so on. The following review of forecasting methods is far from exhaustive, but it suggests the range of methods available.

Causal Methods

Causal (model) forecasts are based on a statistical relationship between the forecasted (dependent) variable and one or more explanatory (independent) variables. There need not be a cause-and-effect relationship between the dependent and the independent variables. A statistical correlation alone is sufficient basis for prediction or forecasting. **Correlation** is a pattern or relationship between the two or more variables. The closer the relationship, the greater the degree of correlation.

In general, a causal model is constructed by finding variables that explain, statistically, the changes in the variable to be forecast. Such variables must have the following characteristics: (1) they must be related statistically to the dependent variable, (2) data on them must be available, and (3) there must be some way of forecasting them, or their relationship to the dependent variable must be lagged (must follow the dependent variable by several months).

Most forecasting methods are based on the assumption that existing patterns and historical relationships will continue in the future. Because this assumption usually holds only for the short term, however, most forecasting methods can provide reasonably accurate forecasts for periods of only one or two years. In the case of aviation, the events of 9/11 led the industry into a very unpredictable era. Historical data once used for forecasting no longer has the same credibility because, essentially, the industry has started over.

The statistical relationship is estimated and verified using statistical analysis. The selection of variables depends on the imagination and resources of the researcher. With the aid of a computer, dozens of candidates can be tested, easily and quickly, once the structure—that is, the mathematical form—of the model has been decided. This, too, may be selected by trial and error.

The availability of data on the variables—or, more specifically, their specific values—is largely determined by the time and resources the researcher has available. Data are the key to specifying the model. Prominent independent variables used in forecasting various segments of the air transportation industry include gross national product (GNP), disposable personal income (DI), and consumer spending on services. Dependent (forecasted) variables might include such things as revenue passengers enplaned, RPMs, and passenger revenues. In the general aviation sector, the level of corporate profits in the economy as a whole correlates well with total business aircraft purchases. Some very sophisticated mathematical models might use 20 or 30 independent variables to forecast a particular set of dependent variables.

For example, let's say we developed the following hypothetical formula, using statistical analysis and based on data covering a 15-year period, that shows the relationship between GNP and the number of active general aviation aircraft in the United States:

$$Y = 8.14 + 0.152X$$

The value of the GNP (X in the equation) is expressed in billions of current dollars, and the resulting estimate of the fleet (Y in the equation), is in thousands of active aircraft. Figure 9.1 demonstrates the closeness of the fit between the forecast model and the observed historical data over a 15-year period.

Once the formula has been established and a high correlation demonstrated, the equation can be used for forecasting purposes. The next step is to obtain current forecasts of the independent variable (GNP in this case). The FAA aviation forecast uses economic forecasts from Chase Econometrics; Data Resources, Inc.; Evans Economics, Inc.; and Wharton Econometric

Associates.[2] These are all highly reputable sources for forecasting major economic aggregates. The forecasted active general aviation aircraft fleet is then determined by plugging in the values for the forecasted GNP over the time period being forecast.

Given unlimited amounts of data, causal models can be constructed that explain almost any market phenomenon. Unfortunately, unlimited amounts of data are rarely available. Shortages of time, money, and personnel; limits on the accessibility of data; deficiencies in measurement techniques—all impose serious constraints on data availability. Often, researchers must be content with secondary data, substitute variables, outdated observations, and inaccurate information. The result is usually an imperfect model, although not necessarily a useless one.

Forecastability, or a lagged relationship with the dependent variable, is essential, because it does little good to construct a forecasting model if the future values of the explanatory variables are as difficult to estimate as those of the dependent variable. The only alternative is to use independent variables whose present values determine the dependent variable's future values.

Causal models are unquestionably the most sophisticated type of forecasting method used today, as well as the most frequently used. However, as mentioned previously, companies use these forecasted data in developing forecasts of their share of the industry (forecasts used for other forecasts). Although causal models are used quite extensively by the FAA, ATA, GAMA, NBAA, and other industry sources, it is important to recognize their limitations:

1 It is sometimes difficult to quantify all of the variables, even though the researcher is aware that these variables have influenced the dependent variable in the past and might continue to do so in the future.
2 It is often assumed that it is easier and more accurate to forecast the explanatory variables (GNP, DI) than the dependent variable (passenger enplanements, cargo/ton-mile). This is important because the forecasted variable is no better than the forecast of the independent variable.
3 It is often assumed that a functional relationship that existed in the past (and upon which the model was built) will exist during the forecasted period.

No one during the mid-1960s boom period in aviation foresaw the magnitude of the recession that occurred in late 1969 and extended through 1972. All indicators pointed to continued expansion throughout the 1970s. Jumbo jets were ordered based on the mid-1960s' forecasts; a major airport expansion program was undertaken, and manufacturers in both commercial and general aviation geared up for a major expansion. And then the bottom fell out. Despite its inadequacies, the science of model building for forecasting purposes has grown increasingly more sophisticated over the past 25 years as a result of the use of computers. Nevertheless, unusual weather conditions, international tensions, labor–management troubles, and a host of other unforeseen factors can disturb an established relationship between variables.

FIGURE 9.1 Hypothetical Correlation Between GNP (independent variable) and Number of Active General Aviation Aircraft (dependent variable)

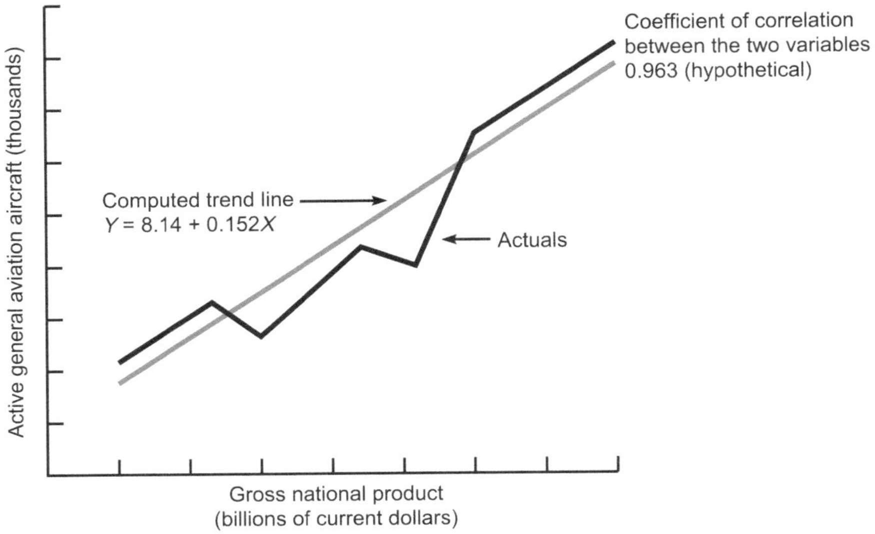

Time-Series or Trend Analysis Methods

Another reasonably sophisticated statistical method of forecasting is **time-series analysis**—the oldest, and in many cases still the most widely used, method of forecasting air transportation demand. In some situations, this method is referred to as **trend extension**. It differs from causal model forecasting in that less causation is embodied in the time series.

Time-series models show the dependent variable as a function of a single independent variable: time. This method is used quite frequently when both time and data are limited, such as in forecasting a single variable (for example, cargo tonnage) for which historical data are obtained. Like the causal models, time-series models are based on a statistical correlation that does not necessarily reflect a real cause-and-effect relationship between the dependent and the independent variable.

Aviation is certainly not static: new-aircraft sales, prices, revenue passenger miles, cargo tonnage, profits, flying hours, on-time performance, and number of departures all fluctuate over time. Time-series or trend analysis is simply a sequence of values expressed at regular recurring periods of time. It is possible from these time-series studies to detect regular movements that are likely to recur and thus can be used as a means of predicting future events.

Forecasting by time-series or trend extension actually consists of interpreting the historical sequence and applying the interpretation to the immediate future. It assumes that the past rate of growth or change will continue. Historical data are plotted on a graph, and a trend line is established.

Frequently, a straight line, following the trend line, is drawn for the future. However, if certain known factors indicate that the rate will increase in the future, the line may be curved upward. As a general rule, there may be several future projections, depending on the length of the historical period studied. Airlines keep numerous records of data of particular concern to them (departures, enplanements, flying hours, and so forth), and when a forecast is needed, a trend line is established and then projected out to some future time. The accuracy of forecasting by historical sequence in time-series or trend analysis depends on predictions of changing factors that may keep history from repeating itself.

The values for the forecasted (dependent) variable are determined by four time-related factors: (1) long-term trends, such as market growth caused by increases in population; (2) cyclical variations, such as those caused by the business cycle; (3) seasonal phenomena, such as weather or holidays; and (4) irregular or unique phenomena, such as strikes, wars, and natural disasters. These four factors induce the following types of behavior in the dependent variable: (1) trends, (2) cyclical variations, (3) seasonal changes, and (4) irregular fluctuations. These types of variations are found throughout the literature of market and economic forecasting. An example of each is given in Figure 9.2, along with a composite they might produce.

Trends. A trend is a long-term tendency to change with time. A variable's trend is a reflection of its statistical relationship with time, exclusive of cyclical, seasonal, and irregular disturbances. Trend functions are described by growth curves, which express, both graphically and mathematically, the underlying pattern of time-related changes. This pattern is usually brought about by such factors as population, GNP, industrialization, changes in technology, and long-term shifts in tastes or preferences. A trend can be inherently positive, such as total air carrier passenger revenues. It can be negative, such as the phasing out of fuel-inefficient aircraft from the airline fleet. Or it can be erratic, as in the case of airline pricing in recent years.

The time period specified for a particular trend varies considerably. Economists frequently define it as any period in excess of that required for a complete business cycle (approximately five years). Airline marketers tend to specify a trend period as equivalent to the approximate lifetime of the service. This can vary from a few months (in the case of some in-flight promotional services, such as two-for-one drinks or special meal service) to a couple of years (for such items as an advertising theme) to an indefinite period (for an essential, such as fuel).

Cyclical Variations. Cyclical variation is the variation of the forecast variable due to the business cycle. The business cycle is the wavelike fluctuation in the level of economic activity that has been associated with the economies of the developed nations since the early years of the Industrial Revolution. The business cycle has never been fully explained by economists, adequately controlled by governments, or satisfactorily predicted by businesses. However, the phenomenon is apparent if any of the common

FIGURE 9.2 Time-related Changes in a Dependent Variable (revenue)

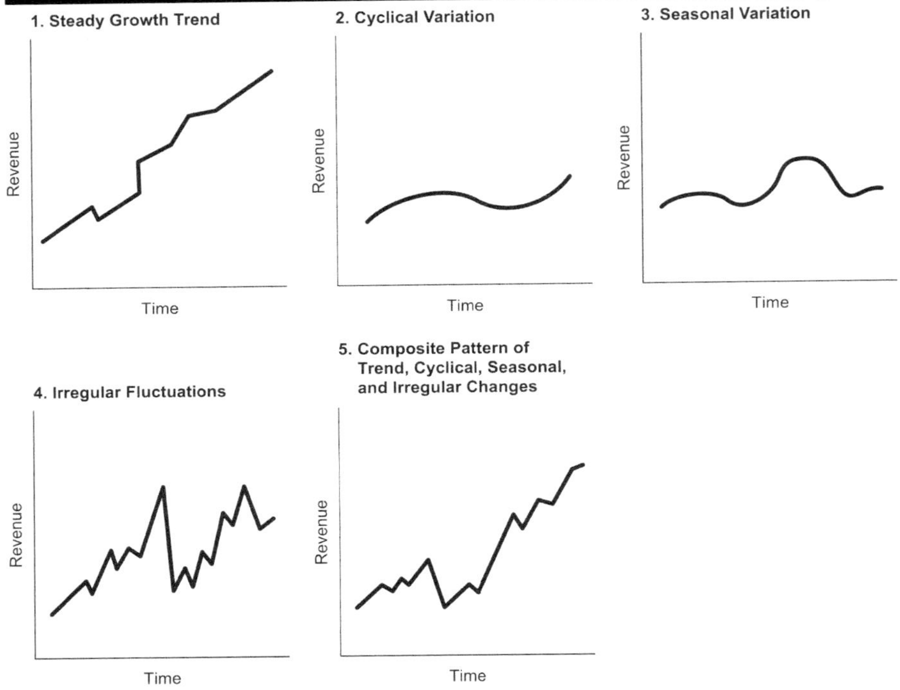

economic indicators (such as GNP, employment levels, stock prices, corporate profits, or capital investment) are plotted over time. The length of individual cycles varies, although they usually last well beyond a couple of years measured from peak to peak or valley to valley. In the United States, cycles range from one to ten years, with four or five years the norm. The magnitude of the fluctuations, measured vertically from peak to valley (or vice versa), varies tremendously and thus far has defied precise forecasting, to the chagrin of most aviation industry analysts.

The business cycle has a significant effect on all segments of the air transportation industry. The level of air travel for business or pleasure purposes is affected by upturns and downturns in the economy. Economists refer to the air transportation industry as being *income elastic*; that is, airplane sales, RPMs, and so forth are very responsive to changes in economic aggregates such as disposable income, personal income, and national income.

Seasonal Variations. Seasonal variation is the variation of the forecast variable associated with the time of year. It is appropriately named, for it is a function of both the weather and the social customs associated with the four seasons (for example, in Florida, the heavy tourist season from Thanksgiving through January 1 or college spring break from March through April). Seasonal fluctuations in the demand for such things as motel rooms, rental cars, and airline travel are quite pronounced.

Irregular Variations. Irregular variations are erratic, nonrecurrent events such as strikes (for example, the air traffic controllers' strike in 1981), blizzards, riots, fires, wars or war scares, price wars, bankruptcies, and other real-world disturbances. Although the disturbance factor is easily identified and the magnitude of its effect can normally be estimated, it seldom can be forecast.

Smoothing the Variations

Cyclical Variations. Cyclical variations can be removed by the forecaster by performing a couple of tasks. The first, and most difficult, task is to estimate the relationship between the forecast variable and the business cycle. The forecaster selects an appropriate index, such as GNP or the Dow Jones stock average, to represent the business cycle. Then, either subjectively or through various mathematical approaches, the forecaster estimates the elasticity (responsiveness) of the forecast variable with respect to the business cycle index. The objective is to determine how much of the fluctuation in the variable was induced by the business cycle. For example, if the index drops 10 percent, how much will the forecast variable change? Once this is determined, the observations of the forecast variable—the values (volumes or financial data) that make up the composite curve—can be adjusted. The forecaster then simply subtracts the cyclical variation, computed for each point in time, from each observation. What remains is a time series or trend line free of cyclical variation. An alternative is to leave the cyclical variation in the data. However, the result is a forecast that reflects the cycle. Depending on the purpose of the forecast, this might, in fact, be the more realistic approach, in that it reflects the uncertainty induced by the business cycle.

Seasonal Variations. The primary reason for removing seasonal variations is to reflect the actual situation more accurately. For example, if Easter week falls in late March one year and in early April the next, increased passenger enplanements, RPMs, revenues, and so forth will appear in the first-quarter statistics one year and in the second-quarter statistics the next year. Unless this is taken into consideration in the forecast, planning for the two quarters will be inaccurate.

Seasonal variation is eliminated by a process called *smoothing*. The most common instruments for this purpose are freehand lines, semi-averages, and moving averages. *Freehand lines* are a convenient way of smoothing out fluctuations in data, but they are obviously imprecise. Using *semi-averages* to smooth out a curve is only slightly more rigorous than using freehand lines. The forecaster simply divides the time series into two equal parts—its first and second halves—and then computes the arithmetic mean (average) of each part. The two means are plotted and a straight line is drawn through the two points to represent the smoothed curve. This line can be expressed mathematically, but the function cannot be evaluated by statistical testing.

The *moving average* is computed by finding the mean of the adjoining observations. This average then replaces the observations used in its calculation. A 12-month moving average would drop the observed data for the first month in the time series when data become available for a new month in the series. The correct number of periods used for a moving average depends on the length of the seasonal cycle and the frequency of the observations. Most seasonal variations have a one-year cycle. If monthly observations are recorded, then a 12-month period moving average will remove seasonal variation.

Irregular Variations. Irregular variations are introduced by a major event such as severe weather conditions or a strike and can usually be identified and measured, or at least estimated, with reasonable accuracy. Either an adjustment can be made in the observed values or the observations taken during the event can be deleted. For example, an evaluation of the long-term trend in passenger enplanements, load factors, and the like would take into consideration the air traffic controllers' strike during the summer of 1981, when service was cut drastically for a period of time.

When forecasters make adjustments or deletions, they should note the fact. Management should be made aware of the effect of these events and the probability of their recurrence. When the effects are severe, such as abnormally harsh weather over several years, and there is a possibility that they will recur, management can sometimes make provisions for them.

The usual order of removing unwanted variation is to remove first fluctuations caused by irregular events, then cyclical variation, and finally seasonal variation. The residual is a true trend. These data can then be plotted and an appropriate curve drawn through, or fitted to, the actual points (scatter points) in what is referred to as a *line of best fit*. Figure 9.3 demonstrates a composite time-series curve after smoothing has been accomplished.

FIGURE 9.3 Composite Time-series Trend Line Used for Forecasting Purposes, After Smoothing Has Been Accomplished

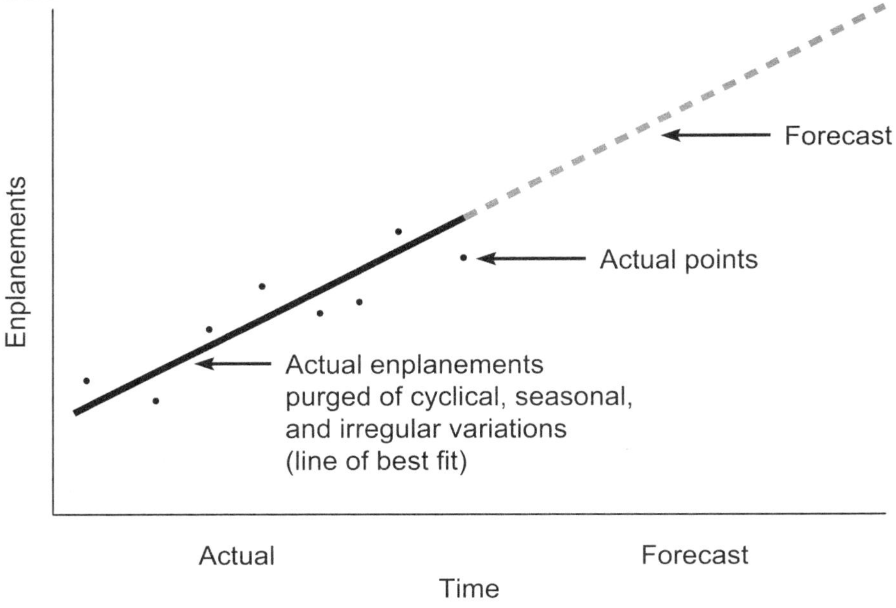

Accuracy of the Causal Models and Time-Series Forecasts

Short-term forecasts are generally more accurate than long-term forecasts because the underlying determinants and the relationships between variables tend to change less in the short run than in the long run. However, short-term forecasts are vulnerable to seasonal variations that, if unaccounted for, can make them unrealistic.

A long-term model is really a trend model, affected only by irregular variations. Developing a trend model is generally the primary objective of the forecaster, because management is interested primarily in the growth or contraction of a particular service.

Forecasts for the economy as a whole usually are more accurate than those for a particular industry within the economy. Consequently, forecasted revenue for the airline industry typically is not as accurate as forecasted GNP. Likewise, an individual company's forecasted share of the industry total usually is less accurate than that of the industry as a whole. And, going one step further, a general aviation aircraft manufacturer's forecast of revenue for a particular model of aircraft generally is less accurate than a forecast for a category of aircraft, such as turboprop aircraft. The reasons for this are basically twofold: (1) the numbers become smaller and less statistically reliable as the forecast becomes more finite, and (2) the number of variables increases as the forecast becomes more finite.

Judgmental Methods

Judgmental forecasts are educated guesses based on intuition and subjective evaluations. Although they are the least rigorous types of forecasts, they are frequently a powerful factor in decision making. Intuition often is the only tool the researcher has, and it can be very accurate. Judgmental methods can be used when either no information or very little historical data exist. They can also be used to adjust forecasts developed by causal models or through time-series analysis. For example, the preface to *FAA Aviation Forecasts, 2020–2040*, states that "FAA aviation forecasts employ projections of key economic variables . . .—These projections are combined with projections of aviation variables and professional judgment."[3]

Acceptance or rejection of a judgmental forecast depends mostly on the reputation of the forecaster, because there are no statistical ways to evaluate it. Very often, a strong leader can push through recommendations based on such forecasts. For example, a vice-president at Cessna felt strongly that there was a significant unexploited demand for a twin-engine airplane with its engines mounted in tandem instead of laterally, as in conventional designs. (This would prevent asymmetric, or out-of-balance, thrust, thereby reducing the hazards of flying with one engine out.) Although his judgment conflicted with forecasts made by more rigorous methods, the company committed itself to the idea. When the product was introduced, sales fell far short of the level the vice-president projected. Instead of backing down, however, the executive insisted that his analysis of demand, and hence of potential sales, was correct and that the fault lay in the design of the aircraft.

He won his point, and the model was not dropped. An alteration in the design (the incorporation of retractable landing gear) made the product acceptable to the market, and sales rose to the level he forecast. The model became, for a time, the most successful product in the firm's line.

As was the case with the Cessna example, judgmental forecasts usually require the backing of a leader because, in the absence of supporting data and objective analysis, they seldom can stand on their own. They are based on experience and partial (usually qualitative) knowledge; their analytical tools are intuition and common sense. They are frequently poorly received, especially when they suggest a future that is substantially different from the present or involve a radically different product or promotional scheme. Aviation is filled with examples—Bill Lear when he first proposed a business jet, or whoever first suggested serving liquor aboard commercial airliners (the president of United Airlines at the time was quoted as saying something to the effect of, "No way, we're not going to become flying taverns").

Judgmental forecasts can be obtained from a number of sources, including expert opinion, sales force opinion, and polls.

Expert Opinion. Expert opinion can come from within or outside the company. Forecasts may be developed by simply drawing on managerial experience within the company. For example, a prediction of next year's cargo tonnage may be obtained from the vice-president of cargo sales. Companies can also tap outside experts for assessments of future market conditions. Various public and private agencies issue or sell periodic forecasts of short- or long-term business conditions for different industries. Leading spokespersons, sometimes referred to as "visionaries," from banking or investment houses report on the status of and outlook for the industry.

An interesting variant of the expert opinion method is used by Lockheed. As a manufacturer of airframes and missiles, the company deals with a relatively small number of customers, each of which accounts for a relatively large percentage of sales. Therefore, Lockheed's forecasting problem is to predict what each particular customer will order during the forecast period. The market research group works up a preliminary forecast on the basis of surveys and causal models. Independently, various Lockheed executives pose as major customers and, in a hardheaded way, evaluate Lockheed's offering in relation to its competitors' offerings. A decision on what and where to buy is made for each customer. The purchases from Lockheed are totaled and reconciled with the statistical forecast to form Lockheed's sales forecast.

The use of expert opinion has several advantages and disadvantages. The primary advantages are that: (1) the forecasts can be made relatively quickly and cheaply, (2) different points of view can be brought out and balanced in the process, and (3) there may be no alternative if historical data are sparse or unavailable, as in the case of new products or services. The primary disadvantages are that: (1) opinions are generally less satisfactory than facts, (2) responsibility for the forecast is dispersed if various managers' opinions are used and if good and bad estimates are given equal weight, and (3) the method is usually more reliable for aggregate forecasting than for breakdowns by region, customer groups, or service categories.

Sales Force Opinion. Sales force estimates have the advantage of coming from those individuals who are closest to the marketplace. Because they work in the field, salespeople generally have a fairly good idea of their company's image with travel agents in their territory and the expected business to be generated from these sources. They also have a good feel for the amount of cargo tonnage shipped by freight forwarders and businesses that have been using their services. They are in daily contact with the carrier's major customers and can offer valuable information to the home-office forecaster. Sales representatives are often the first to learn of a competitor's strategy at the local level and may have more knowledge of or better insight into developing trends than any other single group. This grass-roots approach to forecasting can be helpful in breaking down sales by territory, customer, and sales force.

However, forecasting by the sales force is not without its problems. A salesperson's forecast can be biased, and individual salespeople may be overly pessimistic or may go from one extreme to another because of recent revenue setbacks or successes. Also, a salesperson is often unaware of larger economic developments and of company marketing plans that will shape future sales. Consequently, few companies use the salesperson's estimates without some adjustments.

Poll Forecasts. Poll forecasts are based on the expressed intentions of members of the particular target market, who are polled using one of the conventional survey techniques—mail questionnaires or telephone or personal interviews. A poll is a collection of judgmental forecasts from the market sampled in the survey.

Poll forecasts are susceptible to a number of errors, including poor judgment, ignorance, and uncertainty among the respondents. The respondents' judgment, especially with respect to future events such as purchase behavior, can be quite suspect. Further, the respondents may not be the ultimate decision makers regarding the product in question, and plans may change because of company circumstances and general economic conditions.

In the case of polls or surveys of potential business aircraft purchasers, there may be a reluctance to disclose buying intentions. Such a request could be regarded as an invasion of company privacy. Nevertheless, polls are used quite extensively by all aviation firms as a means of developing data for designing new products and services, as well as for forecasting purposes. Polls, if properly designed and used, provide useful estimates about the target market.

Usefulness of Judgmental Methods

The usefulness of expert opinion, sales force opinion, or polls depends on the cost, availability, and reliability of these types of data. For cases in which buyers do not plan their purchases carefully or are very erratic in carrying out their intentions, or in which experts or the sales force are not particularly good guessers, a poll or survey of buyers' intentions is preferable. A poll or survey also is generally more desirable in forecasting the market for a new product or for an established product or service in a new territory.

When a short-term forecast of likely buyer response is desired, an expert opinion may be called for.

KEY TERMS

causal (model) forecast
correlation
forecasting
judgmental forecast
time-series analysis
trend extension
World Health Organization (WHO)

REVIEW QUESTIONS

1 What has forecasting traditionally been based on? How have global events impacted the ability to create forecasts?
2 How does forecasting differ from planning? What is the purpose of forecasting? Give an example of a short-term and a long-term forecast.
3 Describe how forecasts can be used by firms for analysis, planning, and control purposes.
4 What is meant by a *causal*, or *model, forecast*? Define *dependent* and *independent variables* and *correlation*. What are the three characteristics that variables must have to be used in building a model? What are some of the limitations of causal models?
5 How do time-series or trend analysis methods differ from causal models? Define *trend*, *cyclical variation*, *seasonal variation*, and *irregular variation*. What is the purpose of smoothing the data? Describe several methods of smoothing seasonal variations. Why are short-term forecasts generally more accurate than long-term forecasts? Why might a forecast of the GNP be more accurate than a forecast of revenues for a particular model of aircraft?
6 What are judgmental forecasts? Give several examples of forecasts by expert opinion. What are some of the advantages of using expert opinions or sales force observations? What are *poll forecasts*, or *surveys*?

Notes

1 For a good explanation of the factors affecting the selection of forecasting method, see N. K. Taneja, *Airline Traffic Forecasting* (Lexington, MA: Lexington Books/Health, 1978).
2 *FAA Aerospace Forecasts, Fiscal Years 2001–2012* (Washington, DC: U.S. Government Printing Office, 2001).
3 *FAA Aerospace Forecasts, Fiscal Years 2001–2012* (Washington, DC: U.S. Government Printing Office, 2001), p. i.

CHAPTER 10

Airline Passenger Marketing

CHAPTER CHECKLIST • YOU SHOULD BE ABLE TO:

- Define *marketing*, and discuss its importance to carriers in providing air transportation services
- Explain what is meant by the *marketing concept* and how it has changed over the years
- Describe what is meant by *controllable marketing decision variables* (marketing mix) and the so-called *uncontrollable variables*
- Explain what is meant by the *consumer-oriented marketing concept* and how it relates to market segmentation
- Give several examples of three different intensive growth strategies
- Discuss some of the postderegulation marketing strategies used by the major carriers
- Discuss what is meant by *trends* and how they will impact the future of airline passenger marketing

INTRODUCTION

Marketing is certainly one of the most important activities in any company, and the airlines are no different. Approximately one-half of a major or national carrier's employees are engaged in the marketing process. Reservations personnel, ticket and customer service agents, baggage handlers,

DOI: 10.4324/9780429346156-13

flight attendants, food service representatives, passenger and cargo sales representatives, and pricing and market research analysts are involved in marketing the company's product—air transportation.

Marketing is that broad area of business activity that directs the flow of services provided by the carrier to the customer in order to satisfy customers' needs and wants and to achieve company objectives. Marketing is more than selling: it involves a number of business activities, including forecasting, market research and analysis, product research and development, price setting, and promotion, including advertising. Marketing also involves the finance activities such as credit and collection that are associated with ticket sales. Marketing is customer oriented. Creating products and services that fulfill the needs of existing customers and attract new customers is the primary goal. Determining who the customers are or could be and what their needs are is part of the process. Marketing must also assist in achieving the company's objectives: an acceptable return on investment, a reasonable level of profits, and an adequate market share.

Why is marketing so important? Without marketing and sales, airlines would not exist. Marketing is the stimulus that encourages innovation, research, and investment. A carrier can have the latest equipment and the most efficient human and capital resources available, but unless somebody is there to sell the output produced, it is all for naught.

Historically, airlines have not done a good job when it comes to market research concerning route networks which ultimately has an impact on airline passenger marketing. The type or types of passengers the airline serves determines specific routes, therefore determining specific airports the airline will operate at. Many airlines have failed because of the poor quality of their research. In the United States, prior to the U.S. Deregulation Act of 1978, airlines did not have a need to do research because there was virtually no competition. In other words, airlines had a monopoly on certain routes and passengers were forced to fly certain airlines regardless of price or desire. The same applied to many of the European Union (E.U.) countries until the mid-1990s when the Third Package was implemented. The Third Package was the final step of creating a liberalized environment in Western Europe where carriers can fly to any destination, at any price, and compete with other carriers as long as they are operating in a safe environment.

In the 21st century, airlines around the world are finding that extensive research concerning passengers and destinations is required, due to an increasingly competitive environment. Many airlines now spend great portions of their annual budget on market research because airlines have realized for the first time in their existence that passenger loyalty no longer exists. Passengers will fly with the carrier that provides the best price and gets them to their end destination on time. In today's aviation environment, passengers are price sensitive, whereas before passengers were more time sensitive.

Even though extensive market research is necessary, there is no guarantee that the airline will be successful. Forecasting techniques are simply forecasts and the only real way to "test" a market is to operate an actual aircraft on a route. If successful, the airline has virtually no worries. However, if this test is not successful, the airline must have a contingency plan in place to determine how the aircraft will be utilized without it spending time on the ground. The author of this book believes three trends are occurring within the global airline industry. It is important for the developer of the airline business plan to be able to identify future trends and select a specific tier in terms of what category of airline the business plan is to be designed around. The three tiers include: regional/feeder carrier, new-entrant/low-cost/no-frills carrier, and the "megacarrier."

DEVELOPMENT OF THE MARKETING CONCEPT

The carriers' marketing history before World War II was considerably different from what goes on today. In the early years, emphasis was placed on the carriage of mail, not passengers. There was more profit in carrying mail, and besides, the mail didn't complain if it arrived late or was too hot or too cold. Furthermore, people still had a love affair with railroads and automobiles. Market demand for air travel was just sufficient to absorb the available capacity. This era was the **production-oriented period** in airline marketing history—a time when services were so scarce that customers accepted whatever was available.

After the war, airline executives knew much more about how to operate their companies than they knew about how the product they produced—air transportation—should be sold. This was natural in an industry in which the first task had been to develop a product in which the public would have confidence, an industry that after the war was confronted with selling something relatively new, and an industry that basically had to improve its product entirely out of capital, not out of earnings. Furthermore, while many of the newly hired airline personnel in the postwar period brought technical skills acquired in the military, nobody really had any experience in marketing the product.

For hundreds of years, people had traveled by land and water. The airlines in the postwar period had to offer a higher-quality product than consumers demanded at the time. Probably no other product ever offered to the public had to be so perfect, so safe, so convenient, so passenger oriented, and so reliable as did air transportation before public acceptance could be expected.

As the carriers' capacity increased, many companies assumed much more active roles in convincing consumers to purchase the new services offered. At this point, it could be said that the airlines entered their **sales-oriented period**. More often than not, this approach produced services that reflected the operations and selling talents of the company, and only secondarily the needs of the flying public. It was basically a shotgun approach to marketing, convincing people to fly rather than drive or take the railroad. The airlines' success cannot be disputed in light of the tremendous growth during the two decades following the war, combined with the demise of passenger rail service in the United States. By the late 1960s, market demand had outstripped available capacity, and so the wide-bodies were developed to alleviate this problem.

Unfortunately, the airlines have been plagued with excess capacity ever since the introduction of the wide-bodies in the early 1970s. Since that time, many carriers have focused on the marketing concept, which stresses shaping services to meet consumer needs rather than molding consumer needs to fit the available services. This concept has played an important part in the emergence of the **consumer-oriented period** in the airline business, with its many tests and new-product surveys designed to discover what consumers really want. We have moved from the shotgun approach of marketing air transportation to the target market approach—that is, identifying the specific groups of customers to whom the company wishes to appeal with its services. Once this is determined, the next step involves the selection of the appropriate blend of marketing activities—the kind and amount of activities necessary to reach the target market. Let's take a look at these marketing activities, which many analysts refer to as the *marketing mix.*

THE MARKETING MIX

The **marketing mix** consists of the types and amounts of controllable marketing-decision variables that a company uses over a particular time period. Commonly referred to as the "four Ps," these variables are:

1 **Product.** The right product (or service) must be developed for the target market
2 **Price.** A price that gives good value to the customer and adequate revenue to the carrier must be set for the product
3 **Promotion.** Personal selling and advertising must be used, both to communicate information about the product to the customer and to facilitate sales
4 **Place.** Appropriate channels of distribution must be found to ensure that the product reaches the target market at the right time and in the right place

These four elements are the controllable marketing factors that should be used to reach the target market. Thus, any discussion of the business activities that direct the flow of services to customers must stress the four Ps. Because all four elements are present to some degree in any marketing situation, the airline marketer's task is not to decide whether to use a particular element, but rather to determine the relative emphasis to place on each element in the final marketing program.

It must be recognized that the marketer must contend with certain **uncontrollable variables**. Unfortunately, the marketing team does not work in a vacuum. Its actions and strategies will be affected by some or all of the following variables:

1 *Cultural and social differences.* These are the traditions and values of various ethnic groups that represent potential customers. Such traits

as eating habits can vary considerably in different parts of our own country, to say nothing of different countries.

2 *Political and regulatory environment.* Political climates are constantly changing. New levels of taxation and government spending can affect marketing strategies set by the carriers. Regulatory requirements, such as allocations of landing quotas at certain airports because of extreme peaking in the number of flights, can undermine the best of marketing plans.

3 *Economic environment.* A good marketing program might be a flop if the economy is going through a recession or rapid business downturn. Airlines are very sensitive to changes in the economy.

4 *Existing competitive structure.* The number and types of competitors the marketing team must face in its target markets may vary considerably.

5 *Resources and objectives of the company.* Top management really controls these variables, and the marketing team must work within the restraints imposed on them. For example, if management has placed great emphasis on short-term profits and less emphasis on long-term market share on a particular route, the marketing team must develop a strategy consistent with the company's goal.

Although the marketing team can do little or nothing about these uncontrollable variables, it certainly must recognize them and be in a position to respond to them by altering its marketing strategy. The term *marketing strategy* is used to describe the process by which the marketing mix is changed.

Now let's take a closer look at the four Ps.

Product

To the average consumer, a product is simply a physical item with certain uses and a particular appearance. In terms of the marketing mix, it is much more than this. A product purchased by consumers encompasses functional, psychological, and aesthetic features as well as convenience, reliability, and so forth. All of these characteristics are simply called the *product.*

The airline product is not a physical item at all, but services that consumers find useful. Safety, on-time reliability, convenience in terms of airport proximity or seat availability, frequency of departures, in-flight cabin services, ground services including ticketing and baggage handling, aircraft type, and even the carrier's image are part of the airline product. This definition is consistent with the airline marketing concept, which stresses the importance of services that satisfy certain consumer needs.

Quite frequently, airline marketing analysts discuss the *product differentiation* that exists in the industry. If we consider the output of an airline to be a seat departure, some analysts will argue that we are basically dealing with an undifferentiated or standardized product. A seat departure on United is the same as one on Delta or American. Or is it? A seat departure from Chicago to New York at 11:30 A.M. and including meal service is not the same as a seat departure at 1:00 P.M. with no meal service. Thus, the product is differentiated. There is some truth to both arguments. If three carriers are serving the same market, all using the same aircraft and providing basically the same cabin service, on what basis do they compete? Generally, the answer can be found in the frequency of service. The carrier with the most frequent service at times consumers wish to fly will generally capture the largest market share. Consequently, each carrier attempts to schedule more flights than its competitors around the popular early morning and late afternoon hours to capture the biggest share of the market. Unfortunately, too much capacity in terms of seat availability will reduce load factors to a point at which no one can earn a reasonable profit. As a result, there is a tradeoff between meeting consumers' needs in terms of seat availability and meeting the company's objectives, including a reasonable return.

In marketing the airline product, certain unique characteristics must be recognized:

1 The product (service) cannot be kept in inventory to match fluctuations in demand. The revenue lost as a result of an unfilled seat when the aircraft departs is lost forever.
2 The service is usually personalized. Two people who take the same flight might come away with completely different opinions about the service, depending on their individual experiences.
3 There is no such thing as replacement of a bad product, as is the case in the sale of other products.
4 It is difficult to check the quality of the service before the final sale. There is no showroom to visit to test the product before purchase.
5 Delivery of the product cannot always be guaranteed, due to mechanical problems or the unpredictability of the weather.
6 The service can be produced only in batches, as opposed to individual units.

These characteristics have prompted the airlines in today's extremely competitive environment to intensify their efforts in two areas: (1) offering better qualitative and quantitative service to passengers, and (2) enhancing their image. *Qualitative service* includes such things as courtesy and efficiency in contacts with passengers. *Quantitative service* primarily includes such subtle additions as wider variety of on-board magazines and entertainment and greater seat-pitch angle. Enhancing the company image is most evident in recent advertising campaigns in which the general theme projects an airline team ready to serve any and all customer needs.

As noted earlier, many airlines are guilty of not doing thorough research when it comes to researching route structures and passenger types. A good business plan incorporates extra effort when it comes to background research. However, finding a point to start can often be a difficult task. One question should be answered before any research is undertaken: "What route(s) do you have in mind?" To investigate this question, the developer should research underserved routes, saturated routes, become familiar with passenger demand (past, today, tomorrow), and also become familiar with destination legalities. The latter factor is most important when dealing with destinations outside the airline's home country.

Many airlines have evolved based on a "hunch." Some have succeeded while others have failed. Starting an airline is a risky business as it is and anything the developer can do to minimize risk is most beneficial to achieving success. Expanding an existing airline by offering new products and services can be just as risky. Having a general idea of what kind of airline one wants to start is good but background research is necessary to make sure the idea is sound. In most cases, the developer will find new opportunities or barriers that weren't known in the preliminary stages, creating a new concept. For existing carriers, the same laws apply.

In the airline industry, there are many different types of services that can be offered and the business plan should be focused on a particular area or niche market. In most cases, the more specialized the airline is, the better the chance of success. Examples of different areas to research are presented below. It should be noted that this is merely a list of examples to get started and not a complete listing of all the areas requiring research. Once a thorough investigation has been done, the developer will have a greater understanding of what type of airline will be designed in the airline business plan. The following discussion directly relates to how airlines market their products and services to the passenger.

Scheduled or Non-Scheduled Service. For the most part, an airline will offer either a scheduled service or a non-scheduled service. A scheduled airline will fly to different destinations using a published time schedule. For example, *X Airways* offers service from *Airport A* to *Airport C* on Mondays, Wednesdays, and Fridays departing at 0700. Depending on the country of registration, the airline will operate under a particular flight certificate authorizing scheduled service. This certificate is issued by the government (civil aviation authority) of that country. A non-scheduled airline will offer services to different destinations but will not fly according to a published time schedule. For example, *X Airways* offers service from *Airport A* to *Airport D* but the days and times might not be specific. Again, depending on the country of registration, the airline will be issued a specific flight certificate authorizing non-scheduled service.

Luxury, Mid-Range, Low-Cost and No-Frills, Shuttle, and Charter. When building the airline business plan, the developer must know what type of service to operate in terms of the amenities it will offer. Generally, a luxury-oriented airline stands a good chance of failing from the start due to high overhead costs. A good example of this type of carrier was the U.S.-based MGM Grand Air that provided luxury service between New York and Los Angeles. One of the predominant reasons of its failure was the high overhead costs associated with offering first-class seating with extra leg room, china dishes for meal service, exotic food and drink, and aircraft that were expensive to operate and maintain.

A mid-range airline will cater to passengers wanting a reasonable airfare with some in-flight amenities, including food, drink, and entertainment. Generally, mid-range airlines have a reasonable chance to survive as long as the cost structure is well maintained. For the most part, major airlines are categorized as mid-range.

Low-cost carriers cater to passengers wanting cheap airfares with little demand for in-flight services. However, it is important to distinguish between a low-cost and a no-frills carrier. In terms of cost structure, a low-cost airline offers a reasonable airfare resulting from low-cost management strategies. A no-frills airline also offers reasonable or cheap airfare resulting from what might be considered extreme low-cost management strategies. Basically, a no-frills airline offers a seat from point A to point B with limited to no in-flight service. In the United States, Southwest Airlines is considered the leading low-cost carrier while Spirit Airlines is considered a low-cost, no-frills carrier. It can be debated that Southwest Airlines is maturing from a low-cost carrier to a mainstream carrier due to expansion and increasing overhead costs. However, Southwest continues to offer low-cost pricing to customers and is constantly developing innovative logistics solutions to keep costs down. At the time of writing, Spirit Airlines was branded as an "ultra-low-cost" carrier and was focused on market expansion despite the impact of the COVID-19 global pandemic on the airline industry. As of mid-2022, Spirit Airlines was making headlines as Frontier Airlines and JetBlue Airways were in a battle to acquire the budget airline. Regardless of who ultimately acquires Spirit Airlines, assuming a deal is done, there is a great benefit to the new owner, resulting in network expansion and acquisition of a profitable business.

A shuttle airline caters mainly to business travelers seeking movement between two major city centers. The shuttle concept is similar to a conventional bus service offering a reasonable airfare with no reservation. High frequency and easily remembered times are typical attributes of a shuttle.

A charter airline offers services to destinations based on demand without using a published time schedule. In other words, the aircraft might be rented one time or multiple times to transport people or goods to specific destinations. This type of service is referred to as an ad-hoc charter. The more common type of charter caters to passengers seeking leisure-oriented destinations. Most airlines in the charter market operate by a non-published time schedule to specific destinations on a seasonal basis. In the northern hemisphere, many charter carriers operate north and south during the winter and east and west during the summer.

First, Business, Economy. What type of seating should the airline offer? Historically, major airlines offered three types of seating configurations: first, business, and economy. Today, as it becomes more difficult to operate a successful airline from a financial perspective, many airlines are doing away with the three classes and moving toward two classes. First class is being removed and replaced with increased business-class seating and increased economy class seating. The marketing geniuses at many major airlines have renamed the expanded business class first class for psychological reasons. Increasing deck capacity means more revenue is generated for the airline. In short, "putting more butts in the seats" is the new trend. If an airline offers a first-class seat, extra space is occupied by the seat because the first-class passenger demands extra leg room meaning increased seat width and pitch.

Alongside extra room, this particular passenger type demands a costly in-flight service consisting of food, drink, and personal entertainment.

Business-class seating is important to airlines wanting to attract business travelers willing to pay a high airfare. Historically, business travelers have been time sensitive and not price sensitive meaning that the major airlines could offer a last-minute seat and expect to generate a high yield. However, since the events of 9/11, a new trend has occurred.

Economy class seating is more important than ever before. Since 9/11, many corporations have cut down on operating costs by reducing travel budgets for employees. Business travelers who once traveled in business class are being forced to travel in economy meaning that many of the major airlines are no longer receiving the same high yields they previously did. For the first time in aviation history, major airlines are realizing that their "bread and butter" are economy class passengers. Low-cost airlines typically offer a single economy class and generate revenue based on volume rather than by seating class. An aircraft can accommodate more seats with a single seating configuration meaning that airlines operating with maximum deck capacity have lower operating costs, passing the difference on to the passenger and resulting in a reasonable ticket price.

Food and Bar. The airline product seems to be changing as the global airline industry continues to evolve. Some industry experts claim the industry is maturing. In reality, the industry is still young and is anything but mature. Until recently, the airline product was defined as a seat combined with additional services like food, beverage and entertainment. Today, anything other than a seat is considered an add-on. In the United States, most airlines do not serve complimentary food items or alcoholic beverages. Today, passengers are forced to purchase such items. In some cases, even the option of purchasing add-ons is non-existent. Unfortunately, for the passenger, this provides an extra expense on top of the airline fare.

Passenger Seat Weight Restrictions. Some airlines are now charging overweight passengers a fee resulting in purchase of a second seat or upgrade to another class of service. In some cases, if there are no two seats available or an upgrade is not available, the passenger must wait for the next available flight. The issue of overweight people is a growing problem for U.S.-based airlines as space on-board the aircraft is at a premium. Southwest Airlines was the first airline to charge a fee for overweight passengers, and today the airline has a Customer of Size policy in place where the customer can purchase two seats next to each other. In short, the seat armrest acts as the gauge serving as a boundary between seats and if the passenger cannot fit comfortably between the armrests, the second seat must be purchased. In theory, the model works but does cause complications for overweight people not aware of the policy in advance of flying which may result in some passengers being bumped from the flight should it be full. According to the Centers for Disease Control and Prevention, 41.9 percent of Americans are defined as obese which is a significant increase since the last publication date of this book which recorded 34.9 percent in 2015. This is a scary statistic because it indicates Americans are getting larger on an annual basis and interestingly, the prevalence of severe obesity increased from 4.7 percent in 2000 to 9.5 percent in 2022. The increased trend in obesity is impacting aircraft manufacturers and airlines in relation to seating configurations and operations associated with aircraft weight and balance.

Entertainment. Although many aircraft are equipped with various types of in-flight entertainment, offering such entertainment can be a costly decision. The technology associated with offering movies, radio, television, and telephone is very costly and someone has to pay. Historically, such entertainment was complimentary. Just like food and drink, entertainment is now offered by many airlines for an extra charge. Many airlines have realized the profit to be made by selling headsets, live satellite television, and movies to the passenger. The most common trend with airlines is to offer inflight Wi-Fi on a complimentary or charge basis, forcing passengers to utilize their own electronic devices for entertainment purposes including increased shopping opportunities. Interestingly, there is a growing trend to increase more gaming options, including the option to be linked to live esports events. One technology company, Panasonic, is even looking at the idea of partnering with academic institutions to offer in-flight diplomas via e-courses. Interestingly, for airlines seeking to improve the passenger experience, especially in business and first class, new options are being introduced to the market that go beyond entertainment with the focus on improving wellness concentrating on sight, sound, and smell.

Cargo and Freight. If a passenger airline plans to offer cargo or freight service, there are some important factors to consider. Firstly, due to height and weight restrictions, it is important that the transport of such goods does not interfere with the primary revenue generator—the passenger. Also, the type of aircraft operated will impact the amount of cargo and freight that can be hauled. A wide-body aircraft is necessary to offer a pallet and container system but this is becoming increasingly important with narrow-body aircraft as range increases with the advancement of new technology. Prior to any operations, the airline business plan should identify how much involvement with cargo and freight the airline plans for the future. The answer to this could impact the type of aircraft flown, having a significant impact on costs. Current trends indicate that the transport of cargo and freight is beneficial if done on a supplemental basis. A passenger airline cannot compete with the mainstream door to door operators like Federal Express, UPS, TNT, and DHL.

Duty-Free. The offering of duty-free goods only applies to airlines flying on an international basis. For the most part, offering such a service is a positive move because it makes two parties happy. Firstly, the passenger appreciates the opportunity to purchase duty-free goods on board the aircraft. Secondly, the airline benefits by earning a profit on each sale. However, reported data indicates that inflight duty-free sales are on the decline and only one in ten passengers makes a purchase on an international flight. The opposite is happening on the international airport scene where high-end airports like London Heathrow, Singapore, and Dubai are reporting increased annual sales associated with upmarket shopping malls.

Baggage Restrictions. As mentioned previously, many airlines are increasing deck capacity with increased economy and/or business-class seating. Due to increased passenger weight, airlines are finding that they have to limit the amount of baggage a passenger can check in. Passengers checking in baggage beyond the airline's restriction are often charged an excess baggage fee. Many airlines have realized how much revenue can be earned as a result of such a fee. From 2015 to 2019, there was a significant annual increase in baggage fees charged by U.S.-based airlines, ranging from $3,803,742,000 to $5,759,750,000 but there was a significant drop in 2020 ($2,839,304,000) due to the COVID-19 global pandemic (Table 10.1). At the time of writing, the U.S. Bureau of Transportation Statistics did not have reported data for 2021 and 2022.

Interline Agreements. Because the major airlines operate on a hub-and-spoke system, they have the ability to offer interline agreements with other airlines. Although this is positive from a marketing perspective, one of the potential downfalls is that interlining can cause contractual nightmares and baggage transfer headaches. It is also important to note that when interlining passengers, often the passenger is not aware of what airline they are flying on. As a result, bad service offered by one of the interlining airlines can be associated with your airline. On the other hand, a positive experience

Table 10.1 Baggage Fees by Airline 2020

Airlines ranked by 2020 baggage fee revenue, dollars in thousands (000)

Rank	Airline	1Q	2Q	3Q	4Q	2020
1	Alaska	63,687	22,614	38,323	42,715	167,339
2	Allegiant	57,337	19,310	32,115	36,577	145,339
3	American	274,371	62,529	147,069	183,150	667,119
4	Delta	203,528	27,477	88,112	121,875	440,992
5	Eastern	0	130	305	767	1,202
6	Frontier	109,801	17,308	48,433	56,307	231,849
7	Hawaiian	17,277	1,451	2,569	4,729	26,026
8	JetBlue	91,643	6,866	40,875	67,782	207,166
9	Silver Airways	0	288	699	1,157	2,144
10	Southwest	11,588	4,739	8,837	8,895	34,059
11	Spirit	175,074	20,194	99,720	122,695	417,683
12	Sun Country	18,655	2,418	6,806	8,384	36,263
13	United	200,642	35,925	87,439	138,117	462,123
	All	**1,223,603**	**221,249**	**601,302**	**793,150**	**2,839,304**

Source: Bureau of Transportation Statistics, Schedule P-1.2. Updated: Dec. 16, 2013.

may also be associated with your airline. New-entrant airlines are finding it beneficial not to interline with competing carriers in order to keep operations simple. Also, because many new-entrant and low-cost airlines do not utilize hub airports, there is no reason to interline passengers because there is no need for connectivity.

Other Amenities. To increase an airline's chance of success in an increasingly competitive industry, the carrier should be able to offer amenities that competing carriers do not offer. Adding a sense of uniqueness will become more important as the 21st century progresses.

Price

Once a rather docile element in the marketing mix because of its control by the Civil Aeronautics Board, an agency formed by the U.S. Federal Government in 1938 and dismantled in 1985, price has become one of the most volatile areas today. In fact, since deregulation, pricing has become the major competitive variable. This is not surprising in an industry with relatively few companies, each aware of the other's pricing policies and having to match the competition or lose market share. Because of its importance in the marketing process, pricing is discussed in detail in the next chapter. Our discussion of pricing in this section will be general, leaving such items as the types of fares and the theory of demand and output determination to the next chapter.

Basically, two general factors—demand and supply—determine the level of prices in any market. *Demand factors* are the intensities and loyalties that customers bring: how willing and able they are to pay for air transportation. *Supply factors* involve the quantity of seats that a carrier places in a particular market. The major component of supply is the total cost of producing and marketing the seats that are made available. Thus, we will consider here the two major factors that determine price levels: demand, and production and marketing costs.

Demand. The quantity of tickets purchased by customers in a particular market will largely depend on the price. Few customers would be willing or able to pay $5,000 for a flight from Miami to Seattle, regardless of the service provided. Yet if this flight were priced at $300, the number of tickets that could be sold would probably far exceed the number of seats available. This illustrates a fundamental principle in economics regarding the demand for a product: as the price of an item falls, the quantity of that item purchased by customers normally rises.

We can readily see the importance of price in determining the quantity demanded, but there are other factors in or determinants of market demand. Included are the preferences of passengers for one airline over another because of some real or perceived difference, the number of passengers in a particular market, the financial status and income levels of passengers, the prices of competitors and related travel expenses, and passengers' expectations regarding future prices. These factors will all be discussed in detail in Chapter 11.

Production and Marketing Costs. Production and marketing costs also have a bearing on the prices an airline sets. The cost per seat-mile flown must be covered by the price of the ticket. Included in an airline's total cost of operation are its direct operating costs—fuel, crew salaries and expenses, landing fees, and so forth. Indirect operating costs, or fixed expenses, such as maintenance costs, general administrative costs, and the marketing expenses associated with passenger servicing, all must be covered by the revenue generated on flights throughout the system. Thus, in a sense, the production and marketing costs of the carrier represent the floor under the price set for the carrier's product.

Promotion

Promotion is the communication between carrier and customer. This communication can be achieved in various ways, but the two most important forms of promotional communication are *advertising* (sometimes referred to as mass selling) and *personal selling*. Other promotional activities include frequent flyer programs, sweepstakes, raffles, two-for-the-price-of-one air travel, and free giveaway items.

The broad goal of an airline's promotional activities is to increase revenues and profits. To accomplish this, a carrier must engage in activities that inform, persuade, and remind customers in the target market about its services. The principal task in promoting a new item is often simply to inform prospective customers about the existence of the service, to demonstrate its superiority over potential alternatives, and then to encourage customers to try the service and form their own opinions. When a product faces competition from close substitutes, such as competing carriers, the promotional objective is generally to *persuade* customers to buy the carrier's services rather than another carrier's services. If more competition arrives in the marketplace, the promotional effort is directed toward *reminding* customers of their favorable experience with the service and encouraging them to continue to use it or to return to it if they have switched to another carrier.

Advertising is another important element in the promotional scheme of an airline. Other promotional activities include the literature provided to travel agencies to inform them of the latest specials, such as promotional fares and tours, that are available. Much of this activity is carried out by the carrier's sales personnel that service a particular agency.

A major goal of promotion is to let customers in target markets know that the carrier's services are available at the right time, place, and price. This calls for selecting the right blend of promotional activities—the combination that best suits the particular market. This will be covered in greater detail in our discussion of target markets later in the chapter.

Place

For a service to be of value to consumers, it must be available when and where they want it. The place element in the marketing mix includes all institutions and activities that contribute to delivering the product at the times and to the places consumers desire—in other words, convenient facilities or sales outlets where customers can purchase the service.

In the airline industry, there are three basic types of sales outlets: (1) the carrier's own sales offices, including field ticket offices (**FTOs**), city ticket offices (**CTOs**), and centralized reservations offices; (2) other carriers' sales offices; (3) and travel agencies. Several variations of these include joint airline/military ticket offices (**JAMTOs**) and combined airline ticket offices (**CATOs**). A JAMTO, as the name implies, is located at a military base and is staffed by ticket agents from one or more carriers that serve airports close to the military base. A CATO is generally found in a small city; personnel from two or more carriers staff the facility.

An airline's own sales offices can be on-line or off-line. The *on-line sales office* is located in a city served by the carrier. An *off-line sales office* is normally located in a larger metropolitan area; usually only major carriers have off-line sales offices. *Field ticket offices*, as the name implies, are located at the airport in the terminal area or on a major street somewhere near the airport.

Quite often a carrier, or several carriers together, sets up a portable ticket booth in the lobby of an office building in a large city to provide a convenient location for frequent travelers to purchase tickets. An example is the Insurance Exchange Building in downtown Chicago.

The carrier's centralized reservations facility, usually located hundreds of miles from major metropolitan areas, services a whole region through the use of toll-free telephone numbers. A flight from Miami to New Orleans might be confirmed by calling a reservations facility located in North Carolina. In some cases, a passenger might end up speaking to a reservations agent in a different country whose costs are cheaper for the airline (e.g., Philippines, India). The main function of an airline's reservations system is to determine the load status of all future flights. The number of unsold seats can be accessed right up until boarding time.

Other carriers' sales offices can also be very helpful outlets. Tickets sold through this source are referred to as *interline sales*. Millions of dollars in interline sales are processed through the airlines' clearinghouse every year.

The importance of travel agencies grew significantly during the 1980s to the late 1990s. In 1970, there were 6,911 travel agency locations in the United States, which produced $2.3 billion of the industry's $9.3 billion in total revenues, or roughly 25 percent. By 1985, the number had increased to 27,193 agencies, which produced $32.3 billion of the industry's $46.7 billion in revenue, or close to 70 percent. In 1991, approximately 42,000 travel agents booked 80 percent of the flying public. This meant that 80 cents out of every dollar that went through the scheduled airlines' corporate cash registers was generated by a travel agent. Obviously, agents were a very important element in the airline marketing distribution system.

The travel agent operates a supermarket of services in the travel and transportation field, embracing airlines, railroads, cruise lines, buses, and rental automobiles. The agent also arranges hotel accommodations, sightseeing trips, and package vacation tours on an individual or group basis.

The agent's income is derived primarily from commissions paid by carriers, hotels, and other operators for business produced. There is no cost to the traveling public. To be eligible for commissions on sales for domestic or international travel, the travel agency must be approved and appointed by either the Airlines Reporting Corporation or the International Air Transport Association (IATA), after rigid scrutiny of the agent's professional transportation experience and financial resources. Only then does an individual carrier decide if it wants to place its ticket validation plates with the agency.

In many geographic areas where the carrier does not operate, the appointed travel agent is the carrier's sole representative. Travel agents play an important role in the sale of air transportation because they influence customers' decisions concerning destination and carrier. In the postderegulation period, in which promotional fares have proliferated, the travel agent can be an invaluable resource for customers seeking the best buy available.

In many larger cities, the carriers' passenger sales managers hold monthly meetings with travel agents to exchange ideas and information. Travel agents and their employees periodically visit the various carriers' reservations offices to develop a rapport with the carriers' personnel, with whom they are in daily contact. The carriers also host seminars for travel agency personnel to inform them about the latest marketing policies and procedures. A basic course, designed for inexperienced agents, might include the fundamentals of the airline reservations function, including ticketing procedures. An advanced course might include international travel and ticketing.

Evidence of the travel agent's importance can be found in the demise of Eastern Airlines. Travel agents, hearing rumors of Eastern's financial troubles, shifted millions of dollars in business to other carriers to protect themselves and their customers. Unfortunately, this served to hasten the collapse of the carrier.

By the late 1990s and start of the 21st century, the importance of the travel agent had decreased significantly. The use of the Internet, also known as direct selling, in many cases replaced the need for a travel agent, benefiting both the passenger and the airline. The airline is able to eliminate travel agent commissions and pass the savings on to the passenger, resulting in a lower airfare. The Internet also allows passengers from anywhere in the world to book on-line 24 hours per day, 365 days per year, offering a great deal of convenience. In the United States in March 2002, Delta Air Lines was the first airline to eliminate travel agency commissions completely, followed by the rest of the competition. As a result, travel agents throughout the country increased fees to clients by increasing the travel agent fee. In many cases, a $25 per ticket charge became $45 per ticket. Passengers now flock to the Internet for great deals, consulting airline websites and other popular sites, such as Travelocity, Priceline, and Orbitz. Internet bookings will continue to grow rapidly. In 1998, 2 percent of airline ticket bookings were done on the Internet. By late 2002, 12 percent of air travel bookings resulted from the Internet. This figure jumped to 15 percent in 2003. By 2011, according to the Travel Industry Association of America (TIA), this figure was approximately 40 percent. By 2013, this figure was approximately 50 percent, and as of 2022, according to the U.S. Travel Association, this number increased significantly to approximately 85 percent with customers using a mobile app or website. In the U.S. alone, the on-line travel market is estimated to be worth approximately $433 billion with Expedia dominating online ticket sales.

THE CONSUMER-ORIENTED MARKETING CONCEPT

Introduction of wide-body service in the early 1970s marked the climax of the production-sales orientation in the air transportation industry. Excess capacity and a shortage of customers changed the marketing concept to a consumer-oriented approach. According to many analysts, the industry was entering its mature stage after rapid growth in the 1960s. In this stage in an industry's development, many potential customers have already tried the product, weaker competitors have left the industry, the remaining competitors have become well entrenched, and their marketing policies and images are well known. Customer loyalties and market shares become stabilized.

Market research came to the forefront as the carriers began to learn all they could about existing and potential customers for air transportation. The purpose was to design products (services) to meet changing customer requirements as they arose, or preferably before they arose. In other words, the carriers sought to develop services that would be responsive to particular customer needs. To do so, marketing research analysts had to find out who was flying, why they were flying, what income group they belonged to, what they wanted and liked, where they wanted to go, what they could afford (first class or coach), what their personal status was (single, married, stage in their family life cycle), what newspapers and magazines they read, what TV shows they watched and radio stations they listened to, whether they paid with cash or credit cards, and what times of the year they traveled. Moreover, researchers had to learn what was going on at different times in different places and ascertain which activities would be of interest to the company's prospective or existing customers.

Market research became a vital component of the marketing mix during the 1970s and has provided the foundation for the planning and execution of marketing programs to the present day. During this consumer-oriented period, carriers have begun to focus on increased market segmentation and more intensive growth strategies.

Market Segmentation

Market segmentation is the process of dividing potential customers for a product (service) into meaningful consumer groups, or *market segments*, in order to identify a target market. This process involves three steps:

1 Finding relevant characteristics that divide a market into smaller consumer groups. For example, an airline market might be segmented by trip purpose (business, pleasure, personal), traveler characteristics (age, sex, occupation, income, flying experience), trip characteristics (length of haul, peak versus nonpeak, day of the week, season), or length of stay (return same day, overnight, vacation).
2 Using these characteristics to identify all significant market segments and to relate them systematically to the services each segment might buy.
3 Selecting target markets—the collection of market segments most consistent with the company's objectives and capabilities.

Figure 10.1 gives an example of the segmenting process. Because no two travelers are alike, the markets can be segmented and the marketing mix shaped around their differences and needs. We can further grasp the overall trend of finding needs and filling them by taking a closer look at some of the business markets that contribute to the revenue of a typical major carrier.

Mercantile Travel. Retailers, wholesalers, and manufacturers account for a considerable amount of air travel. For example, department store personnel, including buyers, managers, and executives, fly to numerous conferences, trade shows, and special previews of seasonal fashions. Airline marketers view retail establishments as an excellent place to promote travel on their airline, as well as a good target market for air travel. The airline marketing staff assists department store display personnel with various promotions by providing models of airplanes, posters, and so forth.

Religious Travel. In addition to recognizing the particular needs of the members of this market segment, carriers must be aware of the special protocol involved in doing business with the various groups. Included in this segment are members of the clergy as well as laypeople traveling for numerous reasons, including retreats, conferences, and school-related activities.

Funeral Travel. Some airlines have a close relationship with funeral directors because they are among the best repeat customers. Funeral directors account for not only the revenue from the shipment of human remains but also the revenue from the grieving relatives (an average of three) who choose to accompany the deceased or to travel on another flight. Here again, the marketing staff works very closely with the customers because of the critical timing involved.

Some airlines offer bereavement fares for passengers, offering additional flexibility on top of a regular ticket allowing for last minute travel and flexibility with scheduling changes if needed. Generally, bereavement fares are discounted off the normal ticket price by 5 percent to 25 percent depending on the airline. However, fewer and fewer airlines are offering bereavement fares and passengers are forced to pay the same airfare as others depending on ticket class.

Educational Travel. The educational travel market segment includes colleges, universities, secondary schools, and the like. Included are

FIGURE 10.1 Market Segmentation – Groups of Customers Who Share Qualities That Render the Segment Distinct and Make it of Significance to Marketing

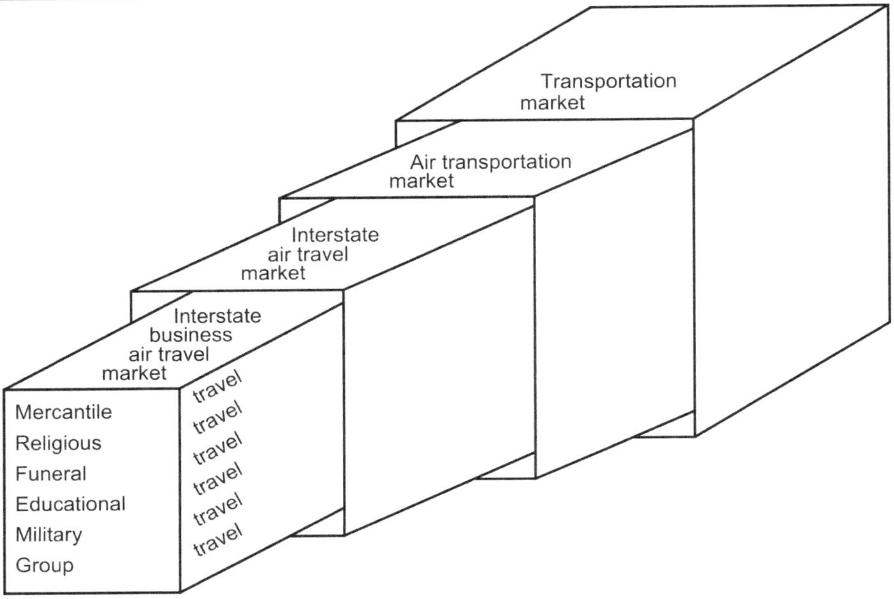

administrative personnel, faculty members, students, athletic teams and their fans, along with others, such as college athletic scouts, members of the news media, and promoters. This is a large market segment that makes repeated use of air travel.

Military Travel. This segment represents a continual flow of travel by personnel on official business, emergency leave, furlough, discharge, and relocation. Some military bases are literally cities unto themselves that provide a significant volume of traffic to carriers servicing nearby airports. Again, the marketing personnel work very closely with the base commander and military staff personnel in developing schedules and services to accommodate the needs of this segment.

Group Travel. An increasingly important segment of target marketing in recent years has been group travel. The opportunities are unlimited, because most everyone belongs to various groups—amateur athletes, teachers, doctors, post office employees, trade associations, and so on. A specially developed package tour might be a group of diabetics accompanied by a physician or a golfers' tour accompanied by a golf pro. One of the reasons airlines have promoted group travel extensively in recent years is the packaging aspect, which generally includes airfare, hotel accommodations, certain meals, various tours, and even rental cars. In this way, they avoid competing with other carriers only on the direct price of airfare.

Intensive Growth Strategies

As the term implies, **intensive growth strategies** involve a concerted effort to (1) penetrate existing target markets, (2) increase product development, and (3) develop new target markets.

Market Penetration. One method of penetrating existing markets more deeply is through the use of *promotional fares*. Promotional fares have been, and still are, an effective way for carriers to fill empty seats with leisure travelers who are being more carefully targeted in specific off-season markets and for off-peak travel periods.

Another approach to greater market penetration is by varying the *classes of service*. In the early years, carriers offered only one-class service. Next came first class and tourist, followed by coach and economy class for domestic travel, and then night coach and day coach, and even deluxe coach and deluxe night coach. Then came standby travel, in which no reservation was held for the passenger. Next came shuttle services, in which passengers did not make a reservation but simply flew based on available space. This was followed by leisure class, in which passengers purchased a regular coach-fare ticket, made a conditional reservation, and showed up 20 minutes before departure time. If a confirmed passenger did not show up, the leisure-class passenger would take that seat, either coach or first class, depending on what was available. If the flight was full, the passenger got a refund or a seat on the next flight out.

The carriers have initiated a number of other promotions in their attempt to achieve deeper penetration of existing markets: frequent flyer bonus awards for mileage accumulated; buy-one-ticket-get-one-free certificates to selected cities; weekender clubs in which travelers, for a nominal membership fee, receive exclusive notice of vacation packages; and upgrading of coach-fare passengers to first class for a small charge.

Product Development. Business travel is not as responsive to changes in the price variable as is pleasure or leisure travel, because businesspeople typically must travel during a particular period because of business needs. It is much easier for pleasure travelers to change their plans to take advantage of price reductions. Consequently, a greater emphasis is placed on *product improvement* when it comes to the business flier. These are also the type of things that build loyalty to a particular carrier.

In an effort to accommodate businesspeople's basic traveling requirements and maintain the conservative environment they may desire, product improvements such as the following have been added to the ground and in-flight service:

1 In-flight Wi-Fi services (Live TV, telephone, Internet, and e-mail access).
2 In-flight reservations for hotel and car rentals.
3 Comfortable seats with increased width and pitch, including personal workspace and life-flat beds.
4 Gourmet meals and complimentary beverages.
5 Enhanced entertainment systems, including direct TV and video games.

6 Reading and writing materials.
7 Larger lavatories with amenities including showers.
8 Impressive duty-free services.
9 In-flight massage services.
10 High-end, full-service airport lounges.
11 Ground transportation services.

Some carriers have shown reruns of the professional football game of the week for business travelers who might have missed it. One carrier distributes a privately circulated newsletter to important business travelers.

Special on-ground services include lounges and meeting rooms for business travelers. Although these facilities are available to the general flying public, there is a membership fee, which tends to make them too expensive for the occasional traveler. Furthermore, they are generally located in out-of-the-way parts of the airport behind unmarked doors.

Carriers have sent special baggage identification tags to known business travelers to make the bags easily recognizable in crowded airport terminals. Special credit cards have been issued to especially frequent business fliers, again to acknowledge the importance of their patronage.

This discussion regarding product development, using the business segment as an example, is by no means exhaustive. Airlines are continually improving existing products (services) and developing new ones directed at particular market segments.

Market Development. Market development is the process of selling current products to new target groups. Market research is continually searching for new target markets based on the traditional method of *demographic segmentation* and the newer *psychographic segmentation*. Demographic segmentation is the process of distinguishing different groups based on age, sex, race, nationality, and so forth. Psychographic segmentation attempts to differentiate groups along lifestyle or personality lines.

Some of the newer, fastest growing airline target markets are the singles market, special interest groups, the athletic market, the women's travel market, and the African American travel market. The increasing size, affluence, and complexity of the singles market is creating new opportunities and challenges for airline marketers. Women are marrying much later, more single men are maintaining their own households, and the number of unmarried persons living together has increased significantly. As of 2022, according to the U.S. Census Bureau, there were 37 million one-person households (28 percent of all U.S. households) compared to the number of single-person households in 1960 which represented 13 percent.

Conventionally, the singles market implies individuals who are unencumbered with responsibilities, who have considerable mobility, and who can spend money on travel that people with traditional family commitments generally cannot. This is particularly true for single people between the ages of 25 and 35. Higher education and income levels and greater amounts of leisure time add up to more travel, both individually and in groups. Ski-weekend packages, theater and other cultural tours, and air-cruise packages are all popular with this demographic group. This group also includes "special interest groups."

The athletic travel market segment includes traffic generated by athletic events and by the transportation of members of the athletic teams. The growing interest in sports at the collegiate and professional level, and increases in amounts of leisure time and family discretionary income, are factors that should produce increased revenues for the carriers during the early 2020s and beyond from this segment. The expansion of professional leagues to additional cities, the creation of new leagues in some sports, and the proliferation of postseason playoff games have added up to increased travel.

Chartering aircraft to professional teams has become a lucrative business for some of the major carriers. Privacy, in-flight service, and dependability (on-time performance) are key ingredients to the success of this growing market for the carriers.

Another growing market segment that the carriers see as having considerable potential is the women's travel market. Although women have traditionally flown primarily for personal and pleasure purposes, many more women are now flying for business reasons as they pursue careers that in the past were primarily open only to men. Airline marketers who are responsive to the particular needs of the female flier will capture the biggest share of this market.

Another fast-growing market segment, according to the carriers' marketing staffs, is the African American travel market. A great deal of research is presently under way to determine the air travel needs of this market, whose economic status has improved since the 1960s. African Americans represent 14 percent (2022) of the total U.S. population, a 29 percent increase since 2000, and account for more than 30 percent of the population of major metropolitan areas. This fact helps explain the interest of the major carriers in attracting this market, which is located on their prime routes.

MARKETING STRATEGIES SINCE DEREGULATION

Now that the marketplace determines profits, airlines have moved aggressively to expand market share and to hold down costs. The tremendous growth in air travel has been achieved through price competition, expansion of service into new markets, and adjustment of service to meet consumer demands. Deregulation has dramatically changed the methods by which airlines market their services. In the competition for passengers, the major carriers have invested heavily in computerized reservation systems (CRSs), developed aggressive techniques to recruit and reward travel agents, built brand-name loyalty through frequent flyer programs, and established affiliations with commuter airlines to provide feeder traffic to their hubs. These strategic moves by the majors—spurred in part by the competitive environment introduced by deregulation—have strengthened the competitive advantages of large carriers.

Behind many of the strategic moves of air carriers since deregulation has been an effort to develop and exploit **economies of scope**. Economies of scope in the airline industry are achieved as a function of the number of points served by a carrier and should be distinguished from *economies of scale*, which are achieved as a function of size (see Chapter 7). Economies of scope are generated as a result of traveler demand for service in more than one city-pair market. For example, a large carrier can enjoy an economy of scope by advertising on television because the carrier serves many markets, unlike a carrier that serves only a few city-pairs. In addition, once travelers obtain information about service quality, cost, and convenience in one city-pair market, they form an impression about that carrier's service in other markets. Economies of scope also result from the generation of information through CRSs, reward structures for travel agents, incentives built into frequent flyer programs, and service patterns made possible by hub-and-spoke networks. Economies of scope confer competitive advantages to large air carriers, even in the absence of economies of scale.

Computerized Reservation Systems

Computerized reservation systems/global distribution systems (CRSs/GDSs) display airline schedules and prices for use by agents in making reservations. The economies of producing and distributing information in the airline industry are fundamental to postderegulation airline competition. Airfares and service patterns have become much more complex and change much more often than in the past, contributing to the importance of CRSs and the advantages that these systems confer on their owners. Although CRSs create opportunities for the smallest carriers to have their flights and fares displayed for travel agents nationwide, they also provide important marketing advantages to the carriers that own them.

The main systems are: AirCore, Abacus, ACCELaero, Amadeus, ameliaRES, Avantik PSS, Crane, KIU, Mercator, Navitaire, Radixx, Sabre, SkyVantage, Takeflite, TravelSky, and Travelport (Apollo, Galileo, Worldspan). CRSs have been expanded to make other types of reservations, such as hotel rooms and rental cars. Fees from sales made using the systems are sources of substantial revenue and profit for their owners.

Because a CRS is programmed to select flights based on published schedules, airlines find tremendous economic advantages in developing schedules that show flights to major cities arriving and departing during the early morning and evening peak hours. For example, to compete for lucrative business travel, airlines bunch arrival times at major airports at 8:30 or 9:30 A.M., in time for morning meetings. The DOT's requirement that airlines report on-time performance was designed in part to prevent airlines from underestimating their actual flying time to gain a more favorable position on the CRS.

CRSs are potent marketing tools because travel agents, who rely heavily on them, are a central part of the commercial air travel system, currently booking more than 70 percent of all tickets, compared with less than 40 percent before deregulation. It is estimated that about half of leisure travelers and one-fourth of business travelers do not have a preference for an airline; thus, travel agents can play a major role in influencing consumer decisions. CRS owners, well aware of the importance of agents in influencing consumers, offer several incentives to influence their behavior and, through frequent flyer programs, offer incentives to travelers even when lower-cost flights might be available. Interestingly, the global CRS market is forecasted to be worth more than $3.75 billion by 2026, driven by economic development, political prosperity, tourism promotions, high disposable income, and leisure time according to Globe Newswire (www.globenewswire.com).

Passenger Service System

In addition to the GDS/CRS discussion, it is important to also understand what a passenger service system (PSS) is as they are becoming increasingly important. Generally, a PSS consists of three systems used by airlines to manage the business efficiently.

The first system is an airline reservation system. This system permits the airline to sell inventory (seats) and contains information like fares, schedules, Passenger Name Records (PNRs), and tickets issued.

The second system is an airline inventory system. This system consists of extensive data related to the airline's flights and seats available. The purpose of this system is to determine the number of seats available on a specific flight by booking class.

The third system is a departure control system (DCS). This system is connected to the reservation system and is used to confirm names of passengers booked on a specific flight and issues boarding documentation. Additionally, the DCS has further applications including links to customs/immigration and border security agencies.

Travel Agents

Travel agents provide an important service to consumers, especially since deregulation, by supplying efficient access to a complex array of travel options. Agents act as brokers of information and sellers of travel services to consumers often closely affiliated with individual air carriers through CRSs and supporting services. Over 90 percent of all travel agencies are automated (by means of CRSs), and most carriers rely on a single CRS to influence agents. Carriers pay commission overrides, which, combined with CRSs, have had much success in causing agencies to shift travelers to favored suppliers.

Some forces at work in the marketplace mitigate the extent to which overrides reduce competition. Most agencies are small, and many do not earn overrides. On the other hand, the travel business is becoming somewhat more concentrated, with firms having revenues of $5 million or more now representing one-third of the industry. These large firms seek out commission overrides.

Another market force that increases competition is the increasing concern of corporate clients with getting the best price. Corporations are more actively monitoring the travel costs of their employees. In addition, a fee system is being developed whereby travel agents earn fees directly from the corporation rather than through a commission. Currently, however, the fee system is limited and available only through some of the larger travel agencies. Some travel agencies even give large corporate clients rebates on the commission overrides that they earn from air carriers, and large corporations increasingly are arranging discount fares directly with airlines. These benefits, however, largely accrue to major corporations able to hire full-time travel managers to oversee their travel agents.

Small-business and leisure travelers have less influence over travel agents, because the incentives for travel agents working with these customers are mixed. Agents may seek out the lowest price for the most acceptable routing in hopes of gaining repeat business. At the same time, the commission system rewards agents on the basis of the total price; thus, there is a disincentive to seek out the lowest fare. In addition, some agents know that the commission will be even larger if they book the flight with a preferred supplier (one from whom the agent has been promised a commission override). However, it is important to recognize that the role of the travel agent, when it comes to booking passengers on the airlines, is decreasing quickly.

Through economies of scope, commission overrides can strengthen the competitive position of large carriers or carriers that serve a large number of city-pairs from the travel agent's home city. From a travel agent's perspective, the airline serving the largest network of cities from the agent's home city provides the agent with the most opportunities to sell tickets or to offer alternatives to consumers considering flying on an airline with a smaller local presence. This advantage in offering incentives to travel agents, combined with frequent flyer programs, reinforces the advantages of size (scope) and thereby makes it more difficult for new entrants to compete, be they major airlines or small, low-cost carriers. It should be noted that the future of the travel agency is in jeopardy with the emergence of technology platforms that replace the need for the travel agent. Companies like Airbnb, VRBO, Skyscanner, Uber, and Lyft are changing the way consumers purchase products and services. While the travel agent provides a personalized service, technology bypasses the need to interact with human beings creating a seamless experience. Consumers are increasingly seeking access to resources that empower them to make on-demand purchases on a timeline that suits them. In other words, consumers support the "do-it-yourself" model, selecting to make their own reservations in the comfort of their own environment 24 hours per day, seven days per week.

Frequent Flyer Programs

Frequent flyer programs have been perhaps the airlines' most successful marketing tool. When American, under a new management team with extensive experience in marketing, first offered its frequent flyer program in 1981, the other carriers dismissed it as a gimmick. The incumbent carriers, who had higher labor costs than the new entrants, soon recognized the importance of retaining business travelers. These travelers are less inclined to take advantage of the discount fares offered by the majors, which usually come with a number of restrictions, but they might opt for the no-restriction low fares offered by their upstart competitors. The importance of offering frequent flyer benefits is heightened by the fact that there are approximately 92 frequent flyer programs in the world with the average member traveling more than 11,000 air miles per year, and it is estimated that more than 300,000 members have earned at least 1 million miles in their respective programs. According to Statista, the leading frequent flier programs in 2022, based on revenue from billings are: American (AAdvantage), Delta (SkyMiles), United (MileagePlus), Qantas Group (Frequent Flyer), Air Canada (Aeroplan), Air China (Phoenix Miles), SAS (Eurobonus), China Southern (Sky Pearl), Azul (TudoAzul), Aeroflot (Bonus), and GOL (SMILES). The use of frequent flyer programs by all of the major carriers is testimony to their importance in building customer loyalty, especially from business travelers. However, gaining and maintaining passenger loyalty is more difficult than ever before. Passengers are more interested in low airfares than they are in frequent flier miles.

Some corporations audit airfares to be sure that employees choose low-cost fares, and some firms try to reclaim frequent flyer benefits for the company. However, most companies concede that employees see frequent flyer awards as compensation for having to travel extensively and, concerned about employee morale, are unwilling to try to reclaim awards for themselves. Unquestionably, a particular program influences a frequent flier's choice of airline, but many frequent fliers also consider flight frequency and on-time performance as important factors in selecting an airline. Consequently, many frequent fliers belong to more than one program. This practice is becoming more problematic, however, because some programs impose expiration dates, thereby making it harder to win awards while participating in multiple programs.

Large carriers with extensive route networks will naturally have the most attractive systems because they can offer travelers more trip choices with which to earn mileage and more exotic vacation possibilities as rewards. Cooperative arrangements between small carriers, who are sometimes competitors, tend to be short-lived. The economies of scope enjoyed by larger airlines build consumer loyalty, particularly among business travelers, who are less concerned about price. Frequent flyer programs confer advantages to size that cannot be offset by a smaller airline that is attempting to compete only on the basis of price.

Business-Class Service

Another program designed to attract business fliers was initiated in 1979 by Pan American World Airways. **Business-class service** is aimed primarily at international business travelers to overcome the regulatory restraints on increasing normal economy (coach) fares in long-haul international markets. Initially, the service consisted of not much more than a few on-board amenities: free drinks, movies, and so forth. It has since become a major element on international routes for most carriers, partly because corporations frequently prohibit, or severely limit, employees from traveling at first-class fares. Most international carriers have now progressed to eight-abreast seating in business class on a wide-body aircraft, compared to the normal ten in economy, and several carriers have extended the concept to six-abreast seating. Most of these seats are as comfortable and provide as much leg room as first-class domestic flight arrangements. At the same time, some carriers have improved first class through provision of "sleeperettes" with leg rests and lie-flat beds or even private suites. For example, Emirates Airlines offers a private suite on the Airbus A380 and Boeing 777 resembling a private jet experience, including fine dining, onboard shower spa, and lounge bar. The price level of business class on international routes was historically in the range of 10 to 25 percent above economy fares. Today, the range is more like 50–100 percent depending on route. Thus far, with the shorter distances involved, business class has not become a major factor in the domestic market, but rather a by-product of some carriers' internationally configured aircraft flying certain domestic sectors. Nevertheless, as carriers attempt to limit the amount of traffic moving at discount fares, some form of business-traffic segregation and pricing must remain one of their options.

Code Sharing

Code sharing refers to two airlines, usually a major and a regional carrier, that share the same identification codes on airline schedules. By code sharing with a regional airline, a major can advertise flights to a much larger market area and expand its market at relatively low cost. The freedom provided by deregulation allowed carrier managers to allocate equipment and personnel in line with costs, and many communities began receiving service by means of turboprop aircraft that carry 60 or fewer passengers. Commuter carriers often provided a low-cost operation, principally because of their use of lower-cost equipment more suited to their specific market characteristics and, to a lesser extent, because of lower overall labor costs. In effect, the commuter carriers began feeding service to the jet carriers at costs below those that the jet carrier could achieve over the same route.

With the development of hub airports, the major carriers soon realized that they could attract passengers traveling beyond their hubs by advertising their affiliations with the commuters serving their hub. Affiliations between carriers of differing sizes, in which schedules and baggage handling are coordinated, predate deregulation, but use of the larger carrier's CRS code by the smaller airline feeding traffic to the larger carrier places these affiliations in an entirely new context.

Listing the commuter with the code of the major in the CRS provides itineraries to travel agents and allows little-known commuter airlines to benefit from the brand name of the major carrier. CRSs also give greater weight to itineraries involving code sharing, which means that they will be listed before other possible interline connections and therefore are more likely to be seen and chosen by travel agents.

Code-sharing agreements became widespread by 1985, and the relationships between the commuters and major carriers became so important that many commuters were acquired in whole or in part by their affiliates. The majors were motivated partly by a desire to control the commuters' low-cost feed to their hubs, but they were also concerned with gaining enough control to ensure levels of quality and safety consistent with their image. As an example of the degree of vertical integration that has occurred in the commuter industry, the top 50 commuter airlines account for about 97 percent of all commuter airline traffic, and all but a few of these top 50 share CRS codes with a major or a national airline.

Consumers may receive some indirect benefits as a result of code sharing. Major airlines entering into code-sharing agreements are likely to impose commensurate service requirements on the commuters, and they may assist them in the purchase of higher-quality aircraft. Efficient, integrated service between large and small carriers, however, predates code sharing, and information about such relationships was displayed in CRSs before code sharing. However, equally convenient connections, and even those that may better meet consumer preferences, may not be as fairly treated in CRSs because of the preference given to online connections. Therefore, consumers may not always benefit from code sharing.

The effects of code sharing on competition are somewhat less direct, but they are still important. Because the commuters provide service on routes with relatively low traffic volume, many routes can be served only by a single commuter. By effectively controlling the commuter traffic arriving at its hubs through CRS listings or outright ownership of the commuter, the major further protects dominance at its hub. Code sharing also makes it difficult for other regional airlines to compete with the code-sharing partner in markets in which demand is sufficient to support more than one carrier, because only one commuter can share the CRS code. This could ultimately lead to reduced competition in the regional airline segment of the industry and higher fares for consumers traveling from small communities. In addition, by extending the service networks offered by large carriers, often at a cost lower than the large carrier could provide directly, code sharing enhances the economies of scope enjoyed by larger carriers.

Interactive Marketing Agreements

Interactive marketing agreements will soon be a common term used in the airline business. Low-cost carriers and point-to-point carriers do not typically participate in code sharing for various reasons, therefore limiting market presence due to simplified route structures. However, as LCCs and point-to-point carriers expand, offering destinations outside the simplified network will increase in terms of importance. Airlines will form "loose" relationships with other carriers that complement the business model. Code sharing involves contractual, liability, connectivity, and accounting issues, whereas interactive marketing agreements simply involve relationships.

An interactive marketing agreement is when two or more airlines develop a relationship where each carrier agrees to promote the other carrier(s). The most simplified form of promotion is use of the airline's website, encouraging passengers to click through to another carrier's website to get to an end destination. When the passenger makes a financial transaction online, the participating carriers are compensated. For example, MAXjet Airways, a now defunct airline that operated between the United States and London, U.K., had the desire of linking up successful LCCs on either side of the Atlantic. Discussions were initiated between easyJet in the U.K. and JetBlue in the U.S. The idea was to cross promote the three airlines using each of the airlines' websites. If a passenger flew from Long Beach, CA, to New York on JetBlue then flew MAXjet from New York to London, the passenger could then fly on easyJet to Geneva. In this hypothetical example, the passenger might not have been aware of the existence of all three airlines but because of cross promotion, the brand name of each carrier was expanded as was the route network. All three airlines would receive financial compensation without the complications associated with a code-share agreement.

As interactive marketing agreements form over time, do not be surprised if global LCC alliances begin to form. Eventually, interactive marketing agreements might mature into code-share agreements among LCCs but, for the time being, this is not likely.

Hub-and-Spoke Service

Airlines have tried to maximize the number of passenger seats filled by eliminating unprofitable routes and concentrating on lucrative high-density routes serving large- and medium-size airports. The **hub-and-spoke system** establishes a number of routes connected to a central hub airport where passengers are collected from feeder flights, transferred to other flights on the same line, and then carried to their ultimate destination. The traffic pattern at a hub airport consists of closely spaced banks of arrivals and departures. Passengers land at the airport and transfer to another flight within 40 to 50 minutes. However, due to increased infrastructure challenges, the length of the transfer period in today's environment usually extends to 60 minutes or more. In some cases, the transfer time can be multiple hours. Although Delta used Atlanta as a hub long before deregulation, most of the other majors adopted this practice during the 1980s, because it permits service between more origin and destination points. Moreover, passengers can be retained by the airline for longer distances, raising the average revenue per passenger. In most cases, carriers choose a busy airport as a hub so they can offer passengers a wide variety of possible connections and capitalize on already heavy origin and destination traffic. About three-quarters of the passengers at Atlanta and one-half at Chicago, Denver, and Dallas–Fort Worth arrive merely to change planes for other destinations.

Hub-and-spoke networks are appealing to air carriers for several other reasons. Most noteworthy, they allow carriers to provide service to a larger number of city-pairs, without a commensurate increase in cost, than do point-to-point networks. For example, a carrier needs a minimum of ten flights to serve ten city-pairs in a point-to-point route system. If operated through a hub, however, those same ten flights can serve as many as 100 city-pairs. Also, by concentrating the flow of passengers toward a central point, hubs make possible service between city-pairs that do not have sufficient passenger flows to support nonstop service in a point-to-point system. Passenger demand for nonstop service also gives the carrier an opportunity to charge higher-than-average fares on a route that it monopolizes. Finally, as a result of the extensive networks made possible by hubbing, carriers are able to attract passengers and, with tight scheduling, to meet passengers' preference for single-carrier service. This also gives the hub carrier a marketing advantage.

The freedom to enter new markets also allowed carriers to adjust their route systems to balance their traffic flows. For example, United, which operated primarily in east–west markets, added more Sunbelt cities to take advantage of increased demand for travel to those cities during the winter.

Because hub-and-spoke operations rely on tightly scheduled arrivals and departures, congestion and delay can occur during peak hours, especially at the airports in Chicago and Atlanta, which serve as hubs for several major airlines. Moreover, the slots at these airports are on half-hour time periods. To maintain their position on CRSs, airlines tend to cluster arrivals and departures in the first ten minutes of their slots, intensifying demands on an already full air traffic control system. Bad weather, requiring instrument flight rules, can make delays much worse. The additional costs attributable to congestion and delay, such as fuel, missed connections, and customer dissatisfaction, have caused some airlines to establish hubs at less busy airports.

Although the hub-and-spoke system has traditionally been very successful for the major airlines, new cost-cutting strategies implemented after September 11, 2001, have altered this success. Airlines have been forced to reduce frequency to many destinations and, in some cases, to drop services altogether. This has resulted in less connectivity taking place at the hub airports, meaning passengers are spending more time in airports waiting to transfer to the end destination. To a certain degree, major airlines are going back to the point-to-point system, and this phase is defined as the "dehubbing" process. As of 2022, it is difficult to determine if dehubbing will be a short- or long-term measure to reduce costs.

Advertising and Sales Promotion

Before deregulation, clever advertising and sales promotion material, extolling the service virtues of one carrier over others, tended to be the prime basis of most advertising. Ads focusing on schedule, frequency, and equipment also were run. The principal difference between carriers, however, was

Table 10.2 Current Trends Impacting Airline Marketing

Ancillary Revenues	Globesity	Storytelling
Authenticity	Green Skies	The Attention Economy
Brand Spaces	Gulf Gullivers	The Conversation Economy
BRICS (emerging economies: Brazil, Russia, India, China, and South Africa)	Hi-Speed Rail	The Expectation Economy
BYOD (Bring Your Own Device)	Hometrotting	The Experience Economy
Business Class-only	Local	The New Normal
Co-Branding	Long-haul, Low-cost	The Next-11
Co-Creation/Crowdsourcing	Mass Globetrotting	The Social Flight
Connected Crew	New Frontiers	The Third Screen
Connectivity	Newbie Travellers	Trading Up and Down
Corporate Social Responsibility	No-Frills Chic	Transparency
Customer Experience Mgt	Perkonomics	Transumers
Democratic Travel	Personalization	Travel 2.0
Digital Natives	Prosumers	Tryvertizing
Digital Nomads	Real-Time	(Un)bundling
Diversity Feeder Businesses	Right Sizing	Upgradia
Female Flyers	Self-Service Nation	Value Players
Flying Families	Signs of the Economic Times	Virtual Connecting
Format Competition	Short-haul Convergence	FST TRCK
Social Media	Sustainable Travel	Future: Tense

Source: Adapted from Airlinetrends.com.

the level and standard of service on the ground and in the air. Pricing was a secondary feature under the relatively tight rein of regulation. Today, most airline advertising has changed considerably. The emphasis has shifted from service to a combination of price, destination, and frequency.

THE FUTURE OF AIRLINE MARKETING

The marketing "industry" continues to evolve, and many experts believe that the industry is in age of disruption and acceleration based on the emergence of trends that are constantly taking on new shapes. Such trends are based on changing cultural, technological, and economic factors that directly influence the airline's ability to offer diverse products and services that ultimately attract passengers. Table 10.2 highlights current trends impacting airline marketing.

Today's airline passenger is more educated than ever as a result of access to different technologies, social media, etc. No longer can airlines dictate to the traveling public what they want. In today's modern environments, it is the customer base or potential customer base telling airlines what types of products and services they demand and how much they are willing to pay for them. As a result, airlines are reinventing the ways in which they market to the customer base by investing in tools to handle the digital marketing environment they now operate in.

As of the 2020s, airlines must focus on innovative technology in order to stay ahead of the competition as the consumer market is driving innovation which ultimately leads to the **passenger experience (PaxEx)**. At time of writing, airlines are focused on the following trends and developing marketing initiatives to address concepts such as: "me-centric" passengers; self-service and real time information; passenger-centric airline business models; airlines as retailers; quiet zones, virtual classes, social flights; onboard hospitality (flight crews as concierges); airlines as cultural ambassadors; branded amenities (teaming up with consumer brands); inflight entertainment (IFE); learning from other business sectors; and eco-friendly airlines.

It is important to note that trends are often interpreted as fads and this can have a large impact on an airline's success both positively and negatively. On the positive side, if an airline is taking advantage of current trends, the opportunity to attract a customer base is good. However, on the negative side, the infrastructure costs associated with trends is extensive and an airline must have access to the required resources to take full advantage. Trends often make future planning a difficult process.

The future of airline passenger marketing is unpredictable and successful models will be developed and implemented with adaptations from other industries. For example, the author of this book will not be surprised if airlines of the future adapt the Amazon.com business model for marketing. Seattle-based Amazon.com is the world's largest online retailer with strong merchant partnerships and exclusive marketing arrangements in place. Although the marketing model cannot be duplicated 100 percent, there are many successful tools and strategies that can be applied in an airline environment.

KEY TERMS

business-class service
city ticket office (CTO)
code sharing
combined airline ticket office (CATO)
computerized reservation system
consumer-oriented period
departure control system
economies of scope

field ticket office (FTO)
frequent flyer program
hub-and-spoke system
intensive growth strategies
interactive marketing agreement
joint airline/military ticket office (JAMTO)
market segmentation
marketing
marketing mix
passenger name records
passenger service system
passenger experience (PaxEx)
place
price
product
production-oriented period
promotion
sales-oriented period
uncontrollable variables

REVIEW QUESTIONS

1 Define *marketing*. What is meant by the *production-oriented period* in airline marketing? The *sales-oriented period*? The *consumer-oriented period*?
2 Briefly describe the uncontrollable variables in the marketing process. Why are they uncontrollable? How might they conflict with marketing plans? Give an example.
3 How would you define the airline *product*? How is it different from other products? In what sense do airlines basically sell the same products? What are some unique characteristics of the airline product? What effect do these have on marketing?
4 It can be said that price was an inactive element in the marketing mix before deregulation. Why? Do you think that the carriers would prefer to compete on the basis of the other three Ps alone, as in the good old days? Why or why not?
5 What are the basic factors that affect price? What is *promotion*? Give some examples of how promotion is used to inform, persuade, and remind. What is the main function of an airline's reservation system?
6 Why did the number of travel agencies increase so significantly during the 1980s? What are some advantages to the consumer of using a travel agent? To the airline? What are some disadvantages to the individual airline? What does the future of the travel agency model look like? How will emerging technology platforms impact the travel agency business model and what does this mean for airlines and consumers?

7 Under the consumer-oriented marketing concept of the 1970s and 1980s, market research has played an important role. Why? What is meant by *market segments* and *target marketing*? How can an airline market be segmented? (*Hint:* Consider trip purpose.) Give some examples of segmented business-travel markets. What methods are generally used by the carriers to penetrate existing markets more deeply? Give some examples of in-flight and ground-product development.
8 What is meant by *selling present products to new target groups*? Discuss the newer target markets in terms of their marketing potential and the marketing mix needed to service their individual needs.
9 How do *economies of scope* differ from *economies of scale*? What are *computerized reservations systems*? How have they become an important marketing tool? What is the purpose of frequent flyer programs and how does this impact the airline and the passenger?
10 What are the differences between code sharing and an interactive marketing agreement? What is the primary purpose of the hub-and-spoke system vs. the point-to-point system? Why are such systems appealing to the carriers? How has advertising and sales promotion changed since deregulation?
11 What are the differences between a CRS/GDS and a PSS? Explain the three systems that comprise a PSS.
12 Discuss the future of airline passenger marketing. What is meant by "trends" and how do they impact an airline's ability to market to customers?

CHAPTER 11

#Mastering the Art of Airline Social Media

Revised and updated by Dr. Benedikt Badanik, Air Transport Department, University of Zilina, Slovakia

CHAPTER CHECKLIST • YOU SHOULD BE ABLE TO:

- Define *social media*
- Discuss how airlines master the art of social media
- Explain reasons why airlines are "flying a social media course"
- Describe objectives of airlines' presence on social media
- List major aspects of airline social media campaign development
- Discuss potential of social media for revenue boosting
- Give several examples of airline best practices in crisis management through social media
- Recognize successful crisis communication in the age of connected travelers
- Give several examples of airline best practices in driving customer service and revenue
- Outline the future of airline social customer care

INTRODUCTION

Before diving into the world of social media and explaining how this world is conquered by airlines, one should define what **social media** means in general.

Social media could be defined as any platform offering exchange of thoughts or feelings. Examples of social media include e-magazines, Internet

DOI: 10.4324/9780429346156-14

forums, social blogs, social networks, podcasts, photographs, applications for direct (social) messaging, etc. Social media may incorporate computer-based technology into the definition as it facilitates the sharing of ideas, thoughts, and information through virtual networks and communities.

The definition of social media is very simple when it comes to the younger generations. Young people usually say that you do not even exist without a Facebook or Twitter account. To put this definition in an everyday perspective, social media is an intangible (virtual) network for sharing thoughts, feelings, and other personal information that could have major influence on the tangible (real) world. Social media is frequently used for sharing even very personal feelings and thoughts. In addition, it is becoming more and more popular among masses of users.

Wikipedia suggests that social media is the interaction among people in which they create, share, or exchange information and ideas in virtual communities and networks. And it depends on mobile and web-based technologies creating highly interactive platforms through which individuals and communities share, co-create, discuss, and modify user-generated content.

The world simply communicates through social media. For masses of users, particularly travelers, social media is the first "stop" on their way to the desired customer care. So, one can pretty much see that offering excellent online service is business critical for every airline. Translated to an everyday perspective, providing outstanding online services assists keeping the airline flying on-course. Passengers like to be connected through every stage of their journey and appreciate being kept up to speed regarding flight updates. Social media enables them to be part of this virtual world and this is the reason why airlines should not ignore it. In addition, passengers expect to be able to get in touch with customer support 24/7/365 in their preferred communication platform.

Why Airlines Are "Flying a Social Media Course"

Social media is no longer considered to be a toy that only serves youngsters for sharing their feelings or what they are doing. Presence on social media and status updates are becoming increasingly important for many companies and institutions, and airlines are no exception.

Siobhán Creaton, author of the book *Ryanair: How a Small Irish Airline Conquered Europe*, explains that the term "Doing a Ryanair" became a generic expression for buying cheap air travel to some out-of-the-way destination over the Internet (in the U.K.). "Doing a Facebook", "tweeting," or "riding a social media wave" could then become the terms for making airlines more visible (and even more appealing) online with a view to turning this virtual presence into real-world relationships with passengers. Airlines use social media much more frequently than in the past. When airlines are cruising on social media, they focus on brand development and product marketing. On top of that, airlines also use social media for improvement of passenger service and for improvement of the overall passenger experience. They do all of this through swift updates and responses to passengers' feedback.

The presence of some airlines on **social media** is big. Air France-KLM group has 34 million fans and followers on Facebook and Twitter. Qatar Airways is followed by 27.8 million followers on Facebook. Southwest Airlines has almost 9 million followers, Delta Air Lines is followed by slightly more than 6 million people, American is followed by more than 5 million followers, and JetBlue is followed by almost 4 million people (cumulated audience of airlines on Facebook, Instagram, and Twitter). AirAsia (through its AirAsia Super App) is followed by 3.2 million followers on Twitter. Lufthansa is also heavily present on social media (followed by more than half a million followers on Twitter). The airline runs several different official profiles on Twitter targeting different world regions like India, U.S.A., and Indonesia. There are also dedicated Lufthansa profiles for different market segments like Lufthansa Technik, Lufthansa Systems, Lufthansa News, and Lufthansa InTouch (the official Twitter account connecting its more than 1.8 million followers with Lufthansa topics and informing them about vacancies). Some specialists say it is better to stay concentrated and instead of spreading the efforts on many social media profiles, airlines should run one official channel. However, Lufthansa is not the only company following this multi-profile policy

With an increasing numbers of followers, airlines are turning employees into social media reporters whereby specific personnel are charged with posting specific "stories" online which assists in recruiting and retaining the customer base. With a view to fostering their presence on social media, airlines are actively growing their social media teams by engaging experts from marketing, passenger service, e-commerce, corporate communications, and other departments.

However, diving into the virtual world of social media could become a very difficult experience for some airlines, especially when they are frightened by incidents on social media that put them into the large public view—for example, the YouTube video "United Breaks Guitars". The video exploded on social media channels, recorded 21 million views on YouTube, and devastated the airline's reputation and even its market value. The case is discussed in more details in the section, "Best Practices in Providing Airline Customer Service Through Social Media".

The above is the reason why many airline CEOs are not sure whether they should step into this virtual world and the process of proceeding with the initiative.

According to Bill Marriott, CEO of Marriott Hotels, "Social Media is not going away. It is not a passing fad. If you do not start playing now, then you are going to be playing catch up and falling further behind as it moves more mainstream."

Shashank Nigam, founder and CEO of SimpliFlying—a leading aviation marketing consulting firm—says that it can be difficult to dive in, but the repercussions can be terrible if airlines choose not to use social media. Maureen Kahonge, Senior Manager of Business Development & Communications at the African Airlines Association, suggests that the studies show the reasons why these airlines are "flying a social media course." To put it in a business perspective, the objectives of airlines' presence on social media could be listed as follows:

1 *To Build a Relationship with Passengers.* If an airline is capable of handling responses to air travelers' queries in a timely manner, it would naturally be able to build positive perceptions of the airline brand. Passengers always want somebody to be listening to them and they feel comfortable when airlines take their feedback seriously. Maintaining a good relationship with passengers over social media could also help airlines to overcome negative perceptions of their brand when they adopt new features of their business model (for example: the airline will move from operating point-to-point, low-cost services to operation of a higher-fare, service-minded network of routes). Social media could also serve as a promotional channel when airlines need to demonstrate their long-term efforts for sustainable operations (in July 2022, sustainable aviation fuel was uplifted onto Singapore Airlines and Scoot departing flights at Changi International Airport via the airport's hydrant system). On top of that, airlines maintaining their presence on social media enjoy an excellent opportunity to establish so called two-way relationships with their travelers. It is a type of relationship in which airlines continue to develop their social media content on one hand, but on the other hand they also allow their followers to create additional content on their own.
2 *To Listen to What Passengers Say and to Respond in Real-Time.* This business objective has something to do with keeping passengers posted on their flight updates in real-time. It is of vital importance for passengers to be updated on flight changes, especially when the flight is late or there are other operational disruptions or irregularities such as unpredictable delays caused by volcanic eruptions. If flight updates are delivered properly and updated in real-time, passengers receive information that is accurate. That is something passengers require all the time. If an airline is able to provide this information, passengers will perceive the airline as a respectful, reliable, and proactive partner that is worth flying with again in the future.
3 *To Drive Traffic.* Airlines keep trying to create and offer attractive online content because they feel this can bring huge competitive advantage. The airline industry is a typical sector in which companies compete to attract more passengers. An online presence is seen as a tool that helps airlines become more attractive and creates better value for more passengers. Another aspect that helps airlines drive traffic is a sense of community between the airline and its passengers. Once the sense of community has been established (using social media) the airline benefits from closer relationships with its passengers leading to increased demand for its air services. A good example of how social media drives traffic is the case of Virgin America and JetBlue airlines. Both carriers recorded an increased number of clicks on their home websites after they ran interesting social media campaigns.

4 *To Increase Awareness About the Airline Brand.* Shashank Nigam (SimpliFlying) says that an airline brand is not what you say it is, it is what they say it is. Therefore, it is of vital importance for the airline to create and to support positive perception of its brand. If an airline examines passengers' needs and wants properly and in detail, if it keeps its promises, reacts quickly and properly on passengers' queries, and if it is eager to innovate, passengers will more likely continue considering the airline for their future travel arrangements.
5 *To Engage and to Interact with Passengers.* Social media enables effective interaction between airlines and passengers. Airlines can handle "tons" of passengers' queries in a short time. Passengers feel comfortable because the airline pays attention to what they think, and the airline values their opinions. On top of that, operation of social media channels is inevitably cheaper than operation of traditional communication platforms. Passengers can also enjoy promotional offers of flights that are available only on these virtual channels.
6 *To Be Transparent in Operations.* There are some airlines that let passengers have a look at how the airline is managed and operated. Southwest Airlines created an interesting online show named "Airline" that offered passengers a look "behind the scenes." This allowed passengers to see how the airline product is designed and how particular operational problems are tackled. This kind of transparency in operations could then be "sold" to passengers as, "You know Southwest because we share details with you." The outcome of such a campaign could potentially be increased loyalty of passengers because they feel they are more connected with the airline.

The presence of airlines on social media should be treated as a tool that helps airlines engage with their passengers and potential prospects (customers with no previous contact with the airline). It should also be treated as a response to ever changing trends in the airline industry, in which the trend of following social media accounts is becoming increasingly important. The presence of airlines on social media enables them to be responsive to public opinion. It could also help airlines to stay ahead of the competition thanks to innovation in passenger service (that the airline discussed with passengers through social media), strong engagement with their passengers, and swift response to passengers' queries (experience of Virgin Atlantic, JetBlue, and Southwest). The presence of airlines on social media should facilitate good communication with passengers and it should also support airlines' service quality assurance. In addition, the presence of airlines on social media should be properly developed and managed. These aspects play a key role in social media campaigns of airlines trying to win travelers' attention and get passengers back in the air postpandemic.

The Importance of Social Media in Getting Passengers Back Onboard Postpandemic

The marketing consulting company SimpliFlying revealed a number of airline campaigns that were helpful in getting passengers back onboard after the COVID-19 global pandemic, and these particular campaigns all succeeded because they were carried out in a creative and unexpected way. Three areas that were articulated most in the campaigns were travelers' peace of mind, comfort, and familiarity.

Singapore Airlines, for instance, recorded success with its Elevated Experience campaign, trying to lift the anxieties of travel off of passengers' minds. The campaign, Repromoting the integration of robust health and safety measures at all touchpoints, recorded more than 21 million views on YouTube and helped the airline to get many passengers onboard again.

Air Canada bet on the smiling faces of its own employees: pilots, baggage handlers, cabin crew, and back-office staff. The Air Canada "People Are Ready for Us" video said that the only thing the airline was missing more than flying . . . were passengers.

The campaign of Saudia reflected the fact that the airline used to be frequently flown by Saudis. That is why it was targeted to locals taking off with the airline again. The airline selected five unique patterns for passenger masks and amenity kits, each of them representing one of five Saudi Arabian regions with its own arts and culture. The video recorded more than 2 million views on YouTube and helped the airline to stress a sense of familiarity to passengers.

The "I Want to Fly the World" campaign produced by Emirates might appear strange at first sight. Initially, one could potentially think of it as something completely at odds with what would usually be expected from an airline. But that is the trick. It's attention grabbing, with dancing flight attendants and catchy music ensuring the campaign will be remembered for quite some time. The campaign is an example of out of the box creativity. A more classic example of an Emirates campaign is "We're on Top of the World," which encourages people to reconnect with their loved ones or take a fabulous vacation. Both campaigns together recorded almost 8 million views on YouTube and helped the airline stay "on top of the world" in terms of the number of returning passengers onboard their aircrafts.

Another example of a successful campaign was WestJet's "The Escape," promoting the airline with the idea they were ready for passengers again. The video is reminiscent of the latest James Bond movie, *No Time to Die*, with WestJet positioning themselves as the airline ready to help passengers escape.

British Airways reshot and recast the famous photograph "Lunch atop a Skyscraper," so that all the construction workers in the image appear to be looking up to the sky at a plane overhead. The campaign was to encourage travelers to get back onboard and to cross reopened borders between the U.S. and the U.K.

As articulated in the section above, social media has become an important tool for airlines seeking a way of getting passengers back onboard after the COVID-19 global pandemic. Additionally, social media remains an important communication channel, helping airlines to maintain an excellent relationship with customers. Using social media, airlines can react instantly to customers' comments and are able to engage with them. Some airlines limit their use of social media activity to providing feedback to customers comments, and there are others that are unlocking the full potential of social media, including **revenue boosting**.

Unlocking the Potential of Social Media as a Revenue Booster

It might seem that airlines need a miracle to earn money on social media but that is not the case for WestJet. Its "Christmas Miracle" video is a brilliant example of how airlines make their name online with a view to turning this promotion into an action that drives revenue.

The idea of the airline was to take departing passengers' Christmas wishes, then to buy the gifts they wished for before surprising the passengers at the carousel belt at their destination where they found their "Christmas wishes fulfilled." There were more than 14 million views of the video recorded on social media within three days of being uploaded and more than 35 million people viewed it within a month (more than 50 million views across social media platforms as of July 2022). The success of the first "Christmas Miracle" video produced by WestJet in 2017 was truly mind-blowing, and that is why the company decided to continue with the Christmas campaigns in the following years, even uploading a video in 2020—one of the most dramatic years in the airline industry ever with its full of lockdowns, in-house activities, postponed family reunions, etc. That year, WestJet wanted to shorten the distance Christmas 2020 created for everyone. It did this by granting Christmas wishes that mattered the most – connecting travelers with their loved ones. The airline titled the campaign "WestJet Christmas Miracle: A Wish Come True" and uploaded it to YouTube. This campaign, together with previous Christmas campaigns by WestJet, generated more than 12 million views on YouTube.

Some argue that the potential of social media for revenue generating is weak compared to the potential of onboard advertising. However, the example of the "Christmas Miracle" video and following WestJet campaigns show how successful online presence is translated into real business. Those 50 million views of the first "Christmas Miracle" campaign, and an additional 12 million people who viewed the other WestJet campaigns, can also be treated as a group of potential customers who will think of WestJet first when they plan a flight trip in Canada.

Videos like those produced by WestJet are a very powerful way of making an airline brand attractive and engaging, but social media is more than videos—it is about staying in touch with customers and keeping them "connected" to an airline. Engagement via social media creates opportunities for experiences resulting in short-, medium-, and long-term gains including passenger loyalty and expanded revenue flow as examples.

Ryanair also sees social media as the opportunity for generating additional revenue. The airline joined Twitter in September 2013, but its presence keeps growing. As of mid-2022, the airline has amassed more than 569,000 followers on Twitter. The airline uses its account primarily for customer care and marketing activities. It allows its customers to chat with different members of its senior management team (hour-long Twitter chats take place every week). Ryanair also offers one-hour, one-route flash sales that have become the most popular feature of its site, securing additional revenue generation.

Another great example of how Ryanair makes good use of social media and translates it into real business is its presence on TikTok. The official TikTok account of Ryanair has grown to 1.7 million followers, which makes it the biggest airline on TikTok. Ryanair's success on the platform is mainly due to its creation of short "meme" videos featuring the airline's Boeing 737 aircraft with a moving cartoon face and moving lips. For many, particularly those born earlier, the memes may look bizarre. However, they are not the target audience. The presence of the airline on TikTok is oriented towards the so-called Millennials and Zoomers, who regularly consume content like this and who exist as a valuable target market to Ryanair with its cheaper fares. Thanks to its presence on TikTok, the airline recorded increased popularity as far away as the U.S.A. and Far East, generating demands for Ryanair to open offices across the Atlantic.

KLM demonstrates another great example of positive return on investment and revenue driving through social media. The airline has publicly shared that every €1 investment in social media generates the airline €1.2 in direct revenue and €1.8 in indirect revenue. That is three times the rate of return (Airline Social Media Outlook Report, 2019). This success is thanks to the fact that KLM is very well focused and organized on social media. The airline offers the passenger a tailor-made feature on every social media channel on which it is present. For instance, the airline offers real-time assistance for travelers via its 24/7 social media service, allowing travelers to contact the airline via their preferred social media channel. On top of that, the airline offers its services and assistance on an additional 11 social media channels accessible by 14 different platforms/apps. KLM says they receive over 200,000 mentions every week, 35,000 of which are questions or remarks. These are personally answered by more than 350 service agents, who form the largest social media team in the world (KLM social, 2022).

Even if some airlines can calculate their return on investment through social media, there are others that say the return is more intangible. This is very well illustrated in the example of LATAM Airlines' call center agents. Each of the agents can reply to six queries on social media in the same time it takes to address one customer over the phone—a potential six-fold cost reduction.

For American Airlines, presence on social media means the opportunity to influence choice of airline in domestic as well as international markets. American Airlines sees a direct correlation between its flash sales and increased bookings and finds the other returns on investment not as easy to quantify. The airline's social media model is focused on doing things in a less complicated way for customers. The airline reacts promptly to passengers' comments and the passengers feel comfortable that the airline "is listening" to what they think. Passengers will therefore be more likely to continue considering the airline for their future travel arrangements.

DEVELOPMENT OF AIRLINE SOCIAL MEDIA CAMPAIGNS

The presence of airlines on social media cannot be turned to success overnight. Social media expert Dave Evans, CEO of Navitaire, suggests that presence on social media is not just about creating a page, making a blog post, posing a question, or tweeting. You cannot just leave "your mark" and expect success. Unlike all the media hype surrounding how great social media is, it certainly is not that quick or easy. Launching a Facebook account is the only simple and fast part of an airline's **social media campaign development**. All the rest requires constant effort and planning.

Major Aspects of Airline Social Media Campaign Development

There are several aspects that airlines need to pay attention to throughout the development of their social media campaign. They need to make sure that they engage with the audience and maintain good customer service. Passengers do not necessarily need to "fall in love" with the airline but the connection that an airline builds up with passengers on social media needs to be emotional. Other principles that airlines should be looking at when they design their campaign are as follows:

1 *The Airline Should Keep Control Over Its Message.* The presence of airlines on social media does not create positive responses only. Passengers react in many ways, some of which are not very pleasant (maybe even negative) for the airline. That is why airlines should prevent giving bigmouth promises of something that the brand simply cannot deliver. Airlines should instead be aware of their strengths and weaknesses so they can highlight their strengths and take full control over the message that it delivers to passengers using social media. There are plenty of online tools available (Instagram Hashtag Generator, All Hashtag, Ritetag, #HashMe, Tagboard, Tagdef, etc.) that can help airlines with their research on which hashtags will be more acceptable and more attractive to passengers.

2 *Airline Should React to Negative Responses/Complaints.* Reacting to negative responses is very similar to dealing with customer complaints in every other business. Proper and prompt reaction on customers' complaints is a must to win the customer back. It is no different when it comes to airlines. It is even more visible when this all happens publicly on social media. So, airlines should place greater emphasis on acting on social media complaints. The goal is to provide passengers with a response that is as timely and helpful as possible. To fulfill

these requirements, airlines need to monitor all social media channels constantly. It is excellent if an expert on social media is part of the customer care team. By proper interaction with passengers, an expert can turn negative feedback into a positive win passengers back to an airline brand. Airlines may sometimes face chronic complainers. They should simply bear in mind that the virtual anonymity that social media offers to these people will keep on making them brave enough to continue their "business."

3 *Social Media Staff Should React Instantly When Something Goes Wrong with Their Airline.* Airlines always do their best to avoid occurrence of operational disruptions, but sometimes they cannot prevent them from happening. What airlines can do is to plan their reaction for when something of this nature happens. This is very important. In a social media world, comments and reactions on any disruptions pop up quickly and every mistake can be discussed in detail. If an airline is in trouble, people will probably get to know it much earlier than when the official statement comes out, because many users share information on social media instantly. That is why airlines are advised to have a well-trained social media staff that will be able to communicate the crisis on social media and prevent negative comments from escalating.

4 *Airline Social Media Staff Should Make Sure That Social Media Strategy Is "Owned" By Every Department.* The social media strategy should not be treated as a "confidential document" of the airline marketing department. It should, instead, be an outcome of brainstorming across the airline so every department will "own" it. The result is a coherent and unified social media strategy that will prevent an airline from running more "official" social media channels. The airline will only give coherent messages to the public. To fulfill the requirement of running a coherent social media strategy, the airline will need to appoint a person who will be responsible for creating such a strategy. This "social media person" will also need to involve an entire team who can help to define the way in which the airline appears online. The more personable and witty the appearance, the better. The appearance could potentially, but not necessarily, be supported by a mascot. Passengers tend to react more frequently and more positively to something that is personalized and to something that they could "fall in love" with. One should also bear in mind that the creation of a good online personalized appearance of an airline takes time, and it also requires expertise. Many airlines try to create content that their passengers want. And they are certainly doing the right thing because passengers will more likely share the content they like and will recommend it to others. In addition, their friends will be following the shared content, which supports positive perceptions of the airline brand.

5 *Airline Social Media Staff Should Build Communities of Airline Brand Ambassadors.* There are two types of social media strategies that are applied by different businesses. The first strategy is focused on

attracting as many followers as possible on social media. The other one concentrates primarily on building communities that share good perceptions of the brand. Compared to the first strategy, the latter one usually attracts slightly fewer passengers, but airlines enjoy much stronger engagement from the passengers as they become **brand ambassadors**. Airlines should preferably concentrate on the latter strategy as it promises the building up of a community of followers that perceives and shares the airline brand in a very positive way. Given each person who is engaged has 245 friends on social media (shared by the Pew Center's Internet and American Life Project study), the airline will be able to spread the message of its brand to a great extent if it gets these people to share a few positive words about their business.

6 *Airline Should Post High-quality Content Only.* Once you have created the content you are satisfied with, you are invited to check whether everything is perfect. It means you should check it for grammar, spelling, and punctuation errors. Publishing excellent content will ensure that your brand looks professional. This is of utmost importance in a world in which there is a great deal of top-quality electronic content available.

7 *Airlines Should Use Their Social Media Accounts Actively or They Should Not Create Them.* If the most expensive aircraft is the one that sits on the ground, then the most pointless social media account is the one that airlines don't use actively. Creating an account for an airline that is not used is simply a waste of time and effort. Airlines should bear in mind that every single message that pops up on a social media account will be part of their brand image. That is why only selected (social media experienced) employees should be granted access to official social media accounts of airlines.

Development of a social media campaign is a constant process that requires the active involvement of airlines. Often this process is connected with trials and errors, but there is a real chance for the airlines who keep on trying to retain the loyalty of their passengers and ensure they identify better with the airline, even becoming brand ambassadors.

There are many examples available that prove this. Some of them are included in the next section. The section shares airline best practices in **crisis management** as well as in driving customer service and revenues. The section also offers a few cases in which communication on social media was not handled properly by airlines.

AIRLINE BEST PRACTICES IN CRISIS MANAGEMENT THROUGH SOCIAL MEDIA

To put the general definition of crisis in an airline perspective, a crisis is a situation resulting from a major internal or external event which impacts upon the airline in the context of public safety, airline staff safety, airline service continuity, or airline reputation and related public confidence. Examples include the terrorist attacks of September 11, 2001, and the COVID-19 global pandemic which impacted the airline industry in 2019–2022. Usually, the crisis comes unnoticed and literally out of the blue. Marco Serusi, former author at SimpliFlying, claims that crises in the air transport industry come in many shapes and forms, but they usually have three things in common: (1) no prior notice or warning signs, (2) they create a need to inform large numbers of people with information in a very short time, and (3) they result in a large number of (increasingly digital) angry/distressed people. He suggests that regardless of whether the crisis is something the airline did to itself, an uncontrollable natural phenomenon, or a strike, there is always a need to reach large numbers of people as quickly as possible, providing information, answering their questions, and avoiding the spread of false rumours.

Professor Hamish McLean, Director of the New Centre of Planetary Health and Food Security, Griffith University, suggests that each crisis shares common themes—surprise, uncertainty, danger, reputation, and relationship. He continues that crisis can impact on individuals, families, organizations, communities, and even nations. It is often the case that crises lead many organizations to collapse. It is because the crisis finds them completely unprepared and they suffer from lack of information, lack of time, and lack of resources. McLean suggests that an effective response to a crisis requires precise, timely, and trusted information. Social media is a far quicker platform compared to traditional mass communication channels. It is therefore considered to be the number one choice when it comes to quick information sharing.

Bearing in mind that some airlines are heavily present on social media, attracting millions of followers, social media again seems to be an ideal tool for handling crisis situations, partly thanks to its global reach, allowing for effective mass communication, and thanks to increasing numbers of people that follow airlines' social media sites for different reasons, such as complaining or simply seeking information.

The next part of the text is dedicated to best practices and lessons learned from different airline crisis management cases that were handled through social media.

Before diving into the recent examples of how airlines handled communication of crises on social media, here comes one case considered to be an exemplary response by an airline to a crisis using traditional media channels (social media did not exist at this time).

The former chairman of British Midland Airways, Michael Bishop, made excellent use of the media to calm nerves of passenger relatives and the public after a crash that killed 47 people in 1989. He mastered the use of the media to de-escalate situation down and explain what had happened to the plane that came down short of East Midlands Airport. Even today, many communication experts consider this case an excellent example of how airlines are expected to respond to a crisis using available (preferably digital and social) media.

British Airways IT System Failure. Back in May 2019, passengers of BA experienced huge delays and flight cancellations after IT system failure. The airline was forced to cancel over 100 flights from both Heathrow and Gatwick airports. It experienced an issue with its check-in systems which led to an additional 200 flight delays. *International Airport Review* shared the information that passengers booked onto short-haul flights from Heathrow Terminal 5 were told to "make their way home" as the delays continued to mount. According to *Financial Times*, the airline was blamed for under-performance on information channels and the poor PR response to the IT failure. The newspaper continued that the airline failed to provide swift updates about the situation to the media and to inform customers on social networks. Public comments, provided by management of the airline days later, did not prevent the crisis from escalating.

Passenger Dragged Out of United Express flight 3411. The incident of Dr. David Dao, who was dragged out of United Express Flight 3411 in 2017, is one that will be remembered for quite some time. As of today, the video of the passenger with a bloodied face being forcibly dragged out of the plane has been seen 5 million of times on YouTube. The airline's official response to United Express Flight 3411 tried to calm the situation down, describing what happened as "re-accommodating the customers". Sarah Shearman from the *Financial Times* commented that the response to the crisis became the story, rather than the crisis itself. A blog by RockDove Solutions suggested that this case was a perfect illustration of the need for speed. It continued that it took United a day to respond, and even then, their response was inadequate, betraying any understanding of the role of social media in reporting and magnifying failures in company customer services. The blog concluded that it took United several days to finally respond in a way that acknowledged the seriousness of what had happened and how it made the airline look in the eyes of customers and regulators.

The *Financial Times* pointed out that in both communication cases, BA and United will be used as communication case studies on how not to handle crises.

Loss of Flights MH370 and MH17. Malaysia Airlines suffered two serious deadly incidents in the same calendar year. The flight MH370 disappeared from radars after it left Kuala Lumpur and headed for Beijing with 239 passengers and 12 crew members onboard. Circumstances of the loss of flight MH370 remain unknown. Months later, flight MH17 was shot down over eastern Ukraine.

For Malaysia Airlines, the loss of MH370 flight was a "black swan" event. The event came as a surprise and had a major effect.

Some criticised the airline for sharing incorrect information on social media. However, positive lessons that can be learnt from the disaster include the immediate reaction of the airline's senior management, who released the passenger list early after the crash and worked closely with the search and rescue teams.

The airline appeared to have learned from the mistakes it made in communicating the first incident on social media. When the airline was hit by the second loss (flight MH17), it subcontracted an agency to assist with sharing detailed information about the incident on social media and updating the public.

When it comes to social media, airlines should react quickly to rumors. No matter if the airline ensures that family and friends are informed about developments well before the media, speculations pop up on social media quickly. The airline should therefore prevent rumours by taking control of the communication agenda on social media. McLean suggests airlines adopt the communication model used by former New York Mayor Rudolph Giuliani in the days following 9/11: This is what we know. This is what we do not know. This is what we are doing. This is what you can do. It is better for the airline if it shares "unknowns" in a crisis early enough. This also prevents people from doubting the transparency of an airline.

Airlines need to provide a constant flow of information during a crisis situation and the following case study, provided by SimpliFlying, outlines how social media channels can be utilized. In this particular case study, a number of organizations are involved, including airlines and Eurocontrol—the pan-European, civil-military organization dedicated to supporting European aviation.

Ash Cloud Crisis. The eruption of the Eyjafjallajökull volcano in 2014 led to the disruption of some 100,000 flights and 10 million passenger journeys. The main period of the crisis lasted a week, though the effects started earlier and continued later, especially in Scandinavia and Iceland. A total of 104,000 flights were cancelled during the crisis. There were as many as 10 million passengers unable to board their flight.

Many airlines did a very good job in keeping passengers posted on recent flight updates, but Eurocontrol delivered an outstanding service through its social media presence, providing passengers with the most up-to-date information. Its Twitter account became a major source of information for airlines and airports during the entire crisis. After the ash cloud crisis, Eurocontrol's Twitter account became a trusted and valuable source of information, serving as a major source of information during other crises that followed: strikes of air traffic controllers in Spain, Greece, Italy, and Portugal, the Italian volcano (Mount Etna) crisis, and airspace closures resulting from North African revolutions.

Asiana Flight 214 Crash in SFO. Krista Seiden, a Google employee, had the unfortunate experience of watching the crash of flight 214 live in 2013. She immediately took a photo of it and uploaded it to Twitter. It took her an incredibly short 20–30 seconds from the moment the plane hit the ground. What followed could be described as social media madness.

In the next few moments, more photos and news about the crash became available on social media. Seiden explained that people kept asking her if it was real because none of the news channels were reporting anything yet.

The Asiana crash is a perfect example of how social media can be used to communicate information in real time. Since the Asiana crash in 2013, social media technology has improved significantly, providing new ways to communicate information to the world instantly.

The most memorable and influential tweet of the day came from David Eun (@Eunner), a Samsung executive, who reported the crash by saying: "I just crash landed at SFO . . ." and tweeted a picture of the wreckage from only a few feet away.

Asiana Airlines updated its status a long eight hours after the crash, thanking people for their concern and support.

Even if there were no impacted travelers at all, airlines simply have to react promptly. Prompt reaction from the airline side is even more important in the era of digital and mobile-Internet passengers.

The case of Asiana shows that the crisis hit the airline as a big surprise and found it unprepared. It is impossible to completely prevent these situations from happening, but it is surely possible to prepare for them. Airlines could be much better prepared if they incorporated their social media communication strategy into their crisis management procedures.

Airlines can prevent situations from happening in which a crash (or crisis) witness shares incorrect information (as it was in the case of Asiana flight 214). For instance, Seiden shared incorrect information about the origin airport of the flight. She stated Taipei as the airport of origin, but the flight departed from Incheon International Airport near Seoul, South Korea. If the airline had been present online, it could have quickly corrected the information.

The case of Asiana also shows that it is important to know where information is shared. Given that most of the passengers aboard Asiana flight 214 were Chinese or Korean, it would have been most useful for information to be posted on major platforms in their home countries, like Weibo and WeChat. The lesson to be learned from this case is that a crisis needs to be communicated on the same channel as the one used by those who seek answers or who wish to comment.

It is necessary for an airline to plan its crisis communication ahead of time. If the airline can act promptly, providing useful facts, it could save its brand from damage.

Successful Crisis Communication in the Age of Connected Travelers

In the world of social media, everything happens fast and the airline needs to be prepared, meaning it must be proactive as well as reactive. The airline's crisis management team must be positioned to communicate the crisis professionally and accurately as it happens. A toll-free number could also help to mitigate the first onslaught of passengers seeking help at the time of crisis. Another aspect that could help airlines to turn crisis communication into success are people who influence social communication to an airline's advantage. It is good if the airline can "cultivate" influencers or even advocates through social media.

At the time of a crisis, it is very important for the airline to identify the type of crisis it is facing. SimpliFlying refers to three possible types of crises:

(1) sudden (it is an expected crisis, but not now); (2) smouldering (ongoing, blowing up); and (3) bizarre (unexpected, never thought of) (www.simpli flying.com). No matter the type of crisis, the communication team needs to start searching for social communications referring to the crisis and it needs to start addressing these communications immediately. In the meantime, the team should activate a hotline. The next step to successful crisis management for an airline is integration with traditional media with a view to driving awareness. Key channels help to target employees, media, customers, and influencers. The more transparent messages an airline transmits in this stage, the more successful it is in elimination of rumors. An airline can also join forces with other airlines, airports, and authorities to provide greater coverage for the public. At the end of the crisis, it is important to evaluate the crisis communication strategy and adjust it for future use.

Leveraging different social media technologies for aviation crisis management and emergency response provides stakeholders with expansive roles in managing and preparing for a crisis. Social media has unique characteristics, such as connectedness, clarity, collectivity, completeness, and collaboration. These features have expanded the use of social media increasingly in supporting different crisis management and emergency response functions in the aviation industry. As a result, airlines can respond to crises through disaster training and planning, information dissemination, information gathering, and collaborative decision-making and problem-solving.

One of the most vital things in responding to a crisis is speed. One could argue that it is difficult to respond if there is a limited amount of information available. The airline will not necessarily need all the details to let the passengers and public know that it is working on the issue. In the very first moments, it is more important to keep regular communication with passengers, rather than providing details that might not be known or are considered speculation.

Airlines are expected to be proactive rather than reactive on social media. It is much better to drive the conversation than to be driven. Providing no information or providing information late leaves enough room for speculations, rumors, and frustration of all those seeking any kind of information or reassurance that the airline is doing its best to solve the issue.

The CEO of the airline should be immediately visible and is expected to provide trusted information and show understanding along with empathy across all media platforms, including social media.

As previously presented, airlines must have a crisis communication strategy in place, and it must be "owned" by all departments. Early stages of the crisis might require additional resources so that unexpected escalations of the crisis, that might pop up literally out of the blue, can be properly tackled.

Airlines should focus on resolution of the crisis within the first 48 hours. Of course, it is not always possible, but the longer the crisis drags on, the more harm it causes.

Best Practices in Providing Airline Customer Service Through Social Media

Historically, social media has been heavily dominated by airline marketing teams. Even nowadays, this continues to be the case at many airlines, but the presence of other airline departments running social media channels is rising. The most visible change is increased involvement of customer care teams in running airline social media channels. This is in accordance with the fact that airline passengers have transitioned from traditional telephone-based customer service to social media. Per SimpliFlying's, Airline Customer Service Social Media Study, the share of airlines that are shifting their resources from call centres to social media is constantly rising.

It is important for airlines to have a deep understanding of the need for a strong social media presence combined with a high level of customer service. The following case study provides an example of why this combination of factors is important.

Hong Kong Airlines' Accidentally Low Business-class Fare. The airline accidentally promoted a very low business-class airfare from Los Angeles to number of cities in Asia. The "faulty fare" was $560. Previously, airlines who accidentally promoted faulty fares tried either to refute the fares or to conditionally accept the fares. Hong Kong Airlines, however, uploaded a message to Twitter, not even 48 hours from the moment the faulty fare was published, that they would sell business-class tickets for the promoted low fare. The reason was that the airline thought it was the right thing to do and it wanted to keep the promise it had given to passengers. Additionally, the airline continued online chat with a number of customers on Twitter, sharing the details about its mistake. More importantly, the airline shared that it was very much looking forward to welcoming all passengers. The lesson learned from this case is that the way in which the social media team dealt with the situation resulted in an increased number of satisfied customers. Additionally, there is a real chance that happier passengers become airline advocates as they tend to spread positive words about the airline.

Iberia's WhatsApp Business API. This example shows a success story from Spain's largest airline which offers passenger and cargo flights to over 139 destinations. At the beginning of the COVID-19 outbreak, the Spanish airline recorded an increased number of customer service inquiries, leaving them unable to help people find answers to their questions and handle their bookings right away. The airline decided to improve its WhatsApp-powered digital assistant to deal with the rapid increase of customer queries and implemented the WhatsApp Business API. The reason for this choice was the popularity of WhatsApp in Spain and its integration capabilities with third-party services to improve cohesion. The airline expanded the overall functionality of its existing virtual assistant, IBot. The customers could use WhatsApp to contact the digital assistant 24/7. As of today, IBot is serving people in 50 countries. The Iberia WhatsApp Business API case study says that it helped the airline to record a quadruple increase in messaging activity (recorded between March – May 2020), 77 percent monthly average first contact resolution rate, and 41 percent increase in return on investment for IBot in Q1 2020 (compared to Q4 2019).

The following case can hardly be considered an example of best practice in providing airline **customer service through social media**. Rather, it is the opposite case, where a low level of customer care by an airline turned into a social media disaster.

Dave Carroll's "United Breaks Guitars." Harbrooke Group's case study, "United Airlines Breaks Guitars", explains how Dave Carroll, a musician, saw his $3,500 guitar being thrown by airline baggage handlers on a stopover in Chicago. He tried to alert airline personnel, but they did not listen. The damage was confirmed when he arrived at his destination, but he did not file a formal complaint until his return trip one week later. After arguing with United for approximately one year, Carroll produced a music video and uploaded it to YouTube. By the time of writing, the video had recorded more than 21 million views. There were also two more "United Breaks Guitars" songs produced by the musician with 2.4 million views (song 2) and 1.2 million views (song 3) on YouTube.

Consequences of the songs were manyfold. Alastair Jamieson from *The Daily Telegraph* reported on the huge success of the song and the public relations humiliation for United Airlines. United Press International shared that United's managing director of customer solutions telephoned Carroll to apologize for the incident and to ask for permission to use the video for internal training. CBC News reported that United claimed that it "hoped" to learn from the incident and to change its customer service policy accordingly.

Airline Best Practices in Driving Revenue Through Social Media

Max Kingsley-Jones, senior consultant at Ascend by Cirium, says that making money by the use of social media is not proving to be very easy. However, many airlines have already recognized that, whatever it costs, they cannot afford not to play in the space—be it on Twitter, Facebook, or LinkedIn as examples. Anyone who joins the social throng must be prepared to constantly innovate. Dusting off "a great idea" from last year for another Facebook competition is exactly that: "so last year." Treating it as a hard-sell channel will be a guaranteed turn-off.

Many of the pay-offs airlines get from their social media presence are of an intangible nature. For instance, loyalty of passengers, ability to respond to passengers' queries quickly, or ability to respond to criticism in the proactive way. Social media presence also helps airlines to reduce costs that would otherwise be invested in costly operations of customer care centers.

Kingsley-Jones also suggests that social media delivers airlines another, and simply the most dynamic, way to communicate with customers through every phase of their journey, from booking to arriving back home. Therefore, social media opportunities for revenue earning and up-selling should be literally endless, particularly if consumer data is harvested and put to good use. If airline social media presence is to deliver significant revenue, the airline should view its social media activity as a marketing function, a public relations function, and a sales channel.

The next part of the text provides a few examples of airlines **driving revenue through social media**. The airlines were able to drive revenue thanks to good use of passengers' data, such as habits of passengers, passengers' needs and wants, or preferences of passengers. The following example of KLM shows it was the first of the airlines to deploy artificial intelligence in their customer relationship management tool.

Social Listening of KLM. Thea Sokolowski, director of marketing at Outside Insight, says KLM is a prime example of the airline turning social customer service into cash. The airline does it by the application of the social listening strategy. The strategy is based on tracking social media platforms for mentions and conversations related to the KLM brand. The team of KLM agents, dedicated to client service on social media, analyses them for insights to discover opportunities to act. The agents offer worldwide service on Facebook, Messenger, WhatsApp, Twitter, WeChat, and KakaoTalk 24/7. The success of turning the presence of KLM on social media into cash lies in the fact that KLM agents do more than respond to complaints. The airline uses Twitter, Facebook, and other social media to manage passengers' bookings and thus turns social listening to revenue. This is where social media managers shine, and by attending to these customers and their needs, such as helping them book tickets manually, they are assisting to retain customers and generating revenue at the same time.

AirAsia "10 Cent Big Sale." Air Asia with its "10 Cent Big Sale" started the whole campaign with a question: Can one buy a flight with a coin? SimpliFlying shares that rumors swamped social platforms well before the campaign was officially launched. AirAsia also let its fans share the sale, so it accumulated a great deal of attention. The airline kept passengers eager to get new information about the sale by adding photos of various destinations (from sunbathing, through historical sightseeing up to sea and surf) that were included in the sale. The airline promoted it as if there was something for everyone.

As a consequence of the campaign, the airline recorded an increased number of tickets sold and a significant increase of Facebook fans. SimpliFlying says the total number of the "10 Cent Big Sale" was a whopping 8.7 million views (www.simpliflying.com).

Route Launches with No Money Spent on Traditional Advertisements. Airlines usually spend a lot of money on advertising new routes. The money goes towards TV or radio commercials or is spent on billboard campaigns. Airlines usually ask for airport incentives as well. Incentives should cover initial advertising costs of a new route and they should also support operations to new destinations. Airports offer various marketing incentives for airlines in return for opening a new destination: welcoming services when a new airline starts its operations at a particular airport, a press conference for the inaugural flight of a new airline, promotion of a new route in the airport magazine, advertising at various locations around the airport, commercial space on the airport website, or even marketing materials in the local language.

Some of the services are offered for free while others cost additional money. The following example from Virgin America shows how the airline promoted its new route using social media and did not spend on traditional advertising. The Toronto route-launch campaign was based on a 50 percent discount offered to the first 500 fans who booked tickets using their Twitter account.

The airline applied a similar approach when it announced the new Chicago O'Hare to San Francisco and Los Angeles to San Francisco routes. The traveler paid $7 and got a $77 coupon that was good for a round-trip airfare purchase of Virgin America's new routes on Groupon.[1] As the campaign turned out to be a great success, the airline repeated it for the Dallas–Fort Worth routes with minor changes to the price.

Another successful campaign was run by Virgin America which focused on the collection of passenger needs and desires in order provide a travel experience (www.simpliflying.com). The airline used the Chrome web application and prompted users to input their gender, as well as where, when, and the kind of trip in order to get suggestions for what to pack and where to go. The application then built trip inspiration for the person based on criteria the traveler entered.

The campaigns of Virgin America helped the airline to drive revenue by selling seats that would otherwise be flying empty. The airline was also able to increase awareness of new routes while paying no extra through traditional advertising channels. On top of that, the campaigns helped the airline increase and strengthen engagement with its followers and fans.

The above case studies show that airlines can manage crisis through social media to a great extent. The same applies to ability of airlines to drive revenues and customer care through social media. Airline presence on social media could even become a tool that differentiates airline services. At a time of connected travelers, it could become a very important part of a passenger's choice of airline, simply because passengers may favour an airline that helped them online and managed their queries through social media in a timely and efficient manner.

Airline Social Customer Care of the Future

There have been many changes witnessed in the way airlines care about their customers on social and digital platforms. In addition to traditional communication social channels, like Facebook and Twitter, private messaging platforms are quickly becoming strong players in the social media arena. For example, WhatsApp is becoming one of the preferred communication channels, attracting more than 2 billion users worldwide while Facebook Messenger has attracted 1.3 billion, and WeChat has attracted 1.2 billion users (Statista, 2022).

Travelers have shifted most of their specific interactions with airlines, including customer care issues or complaints, to private messaging channels. Airlines are expected to pay much greater attention to private messaging. The reason is that messaging provides a number of positive elements such as: real-time feedback (airlines can see that the message has been read, they can even see that the person is typing), asynchrony (the person can go away and continue the conversation later), the whole conversation can easily be linked to a customer record, and it can be connected to smartphone notifications. Combining all these features, private messaging applications are excellent for the so-called in-the-moment service that is extremely convenient for modern travelers and efficient for airlines. On top of that, messaging has the potential to reduce a significant number of phone calls and therefore reduce operational costs of airlines.

Looking at information technologies and the future of digital customer care of airline passengers, one must see it connected with bots and other automated systems. There is an increasing number of airlines introducing bots in sales and customer service but the ways airlines deploy them differ. The Airline Social Media Outlook Report by SimpliFlying shows that Mexico's Volaris introduced chatbots to provide initial response to passengers with a view to reducing the workload of airline employees. To put it in an everyday perspective, chatbots filter conversations that don't require assistance from an airline employee from those that do. The same report provides the example of KLM taking a rather different approach in deploying chatbots—they are used to create initial responses to passengers and airline employees make final adjustments and post them. In this way, chatbots reduce the workload of the customer care team but, on the other hand, there is still some room left for "human touch" and customization.

Another area that could potentially grow in the future is integration of chatbots in the airlines' reservation systems enabling automated check-in features for passengers, including additional flight sales and updated flight information. In this way, airlines would reach out to passengers who do not have an airline application installed on their mobile phones. For airlines willing to go the extra mile in customer care, the next step in mastering the digital experience of their customers would potentially be the transition of the automation capabilities into the visual interactive voice response system. The system would help to identify the type of issue the passenger is facing while collecting all the details of the query and would route the passenger to an agent. It is expected that the introduction of such a system could translate into huge savings in agent time as well as accelerating the resolution process for the passenger.

There is one challenge connected to the successful deployment of chatbots: travelers don't like them very much. A study of the customer support company Pidas, however, shows that almost 89 percent of customers are interested in digital conversations with chatbots provided they are helpful. For the deployment of chatbots into the airline communication system to be successful, airlines need to pay attention to ensuring that their bots understand the customer rather than programming them to solve specific tasks or to guide passengers on specific paths of conversation. Simultaneously, the system needs to make sure that passengers are not re-routed too early so that airline agents are not inundated with an increased workload. To prevent passengers from having a "rocky" experience with automated communication systems, airlines will be expected to answer two questions: when to transfer passenger to a human airline representative and how to communicate that.

KEY TERMS

brand ambassador
crisis management
customer service through social media
driving revenue through social media
hashtag
revenue boosting
social media
social media campaign development
social media profile

REVIEW QUESTIONS

1 How would you define social media? How can airlines exercise their presence on social media?
2 What do airlines focus on when they are cruising on social media? Why could a presence on social media become a very difficult experience for some airlines?
3 What is the main objective of an airline in having an active presence on social media platforms?
4 What are some examples of airlines driving revenue through social media? What are the principles of driving revenue through social media?
5 What are the principles the airlines should be looking at when they design their social media campaign?
6 What are the basic characteristics of crises in the air transport industry (try to explain the things that crises have in common)? What should airlines do in order to communicate a crisis properly through social media? Describe some best practices in crisis management through social media and provide examples.

7 Describe airline best practices in driving customer service and revenue. Do these practices have something in common?
8 How have social media platforms assisted airlines gaining back passengers post COVID-19 global pandemic? Provide some examples.
9 What is the future of airline social customer care? Give some examples.

Note

1 Groupon (derived from "group coupon") is a deal-of-the-day website that features discounted gift certificates usable at local or national companies.

CHAPTER 12

Airline Pricing, Demand, and Output Determination

CHAPTER CHECKLIST • YOU SHOULD BE ABLE TO:

- Describe the trend in domestic passenger airfares during the three decades after World War II, and discuss some of the reasons for this trend
- List the determinants of demand, and explain how each can affect the position of the demand curve
- Distinguish between a *change in demand* and a *change in the quantity demanded*
- Define *elasticity coefficient, elastic demand, inelastic demand,* and *determinants of elasticity*
- Describe the four basic types of airline passenger fares
- Summarize several promotional fare actions initiated by air carriers
- Recognize some of the common rules and regulations used by air carriers in conjunction with fare actions
- Distinguish among *direct operating costs, indirect operating costs,* and *nonoperating costs and revenues*
- Describe the profit-maximizing level of output
- Understand cost-cutting trends imposed by airlines for the 21st century

DOI: 10.4324/9780429346156-15

INTRODUCTION

The policies and practices of U.S. airlines with respect to air travel demand and pricing are both interesting and significant. As they have been implemented over time, they illustrate the importance of the relationships among economics, business, managerial judgment, and governmental regulatory policy.

During the pioneer days of airline development, the airlines tested the responsiveness of **demand** for passenger service by adjusting prices so that the resulting volume of passenger traffic, combined with mail revenues, would produce the maximum net return. Airline management had to use keen judgment to fix fares that would develop traffic, counter existing competition, and yield revenues that, together with other sources of income, would meet operating and other expenses and generate a reasonable return. At first Congress, and later the Civil Aeronautics Board (CAB), was responsible for regulating passenger and freight rates of airlines engaged in interstate commerce so as to ensure that consumers paid fair prices and the airlines earned adequate revenues. Air mail compensation was used by the Post Office Department before 1934 to direct the development of domestic airline services.

THE TREND IN DOMESTIC PASSENGER AIRFARES

During the pioneer years of air passenger transportation, the cost of aircraft operation precluded the air carriers from seeking passenger traffic at rates on a price-competitive basis with other forms of transportation. Before the awarding of air mail contracts, most carriers engaging in passenger transportation operated in the red, without hope of balancing revenues and expenses. Even in the years following the awarding of the air mail contracts, high passenger fares discouraged the growth of traffic, and light traffic caused the costs of operation to be spread over fewer passengers. The airlines were caught in a vicious spiral of fares and operating-costs distribution for which a solution was imperative, because despite the fact that prices increased from 1926 to 1929, passengers were better able to pay the fares than they were after 1929.

Following the autumn of 1929, drastic reductions were made in air passenger transportation fares until the airlines, operating in direct competition with railroad passenger services, established fares at the approximate level of standard railroad passenger fares plus Pullman charges. Airlines not in direct competition with railroad service also reduced their fares in many cases, but not so drastically as the lines in competition with railroad services. The awarding of mail contracts to air carriers enabled these lines to distribute their costs of operation over mail and passenger traffic and thus reduce the amount of cost borne by the passenger traffic. Some of the air transport lines also developed air-express traffic, and this additional revenue made it possible to stimulate passenger traffic by reducing rates.

The trend in air passenger fares for domestic airlines is shown in Table 12.1. These figures reflect a sharp downward trend from 1929 to 1941. A 5 percent federal transportation tax was introduced in 1941; this was raised to 10 percent in 1942 and to 15 percent in 1943. Faced with the problem of too much traffic and too little capacity during World War II, the carriers eliminated all special fares and discounts, such as round-trip fare reductions, reduced fares for children, and reductions in fares for those who traveled under the Universal Air Travel Plan (an air travel credit card). After the war, as a result of various CAB **show cause orders**, carriers began to reduce passenger fares and bring back the prewar discounts. In addition, carriers introduced a number of innovations into their fare structure, including computing fares on a uniform mileage rate. The basic fares between the points served by each airline were developed by multiplying the base rate per mile by the aeronautical miles flown. For example, if the basic rate was 6 cents per mile, and the distance between A and B was 323 miles, the basic one-way fare was $19.38, rounded to the nearest 5 cents, for a fare of $19.40.

Carriers also experimented with a no-show penalty that was 25 percent of the unused portion of the ticket or $2.50, whichever was greater. And most carriers introduced domestic coach service, with fares set at an average of 4 cents per mile, compared to almost 6 cents for regular first-class service.

Average fares climbed again during the Korean conflict in the early 1950s, in response to the increased demand for military airlift capacity. In 1952, the major carriers introduced a $1 per ticket fare increase. This fare increase was unique in that the rate of increase per mile decreased as the trip length increased. This philosophy laid the foundation for fare structures in the years to come, notably that the fare per mile should decline with distance at a rate generally consistent with the behavior of unit costs.

Table 12.1 Average Air Passenger Fares for Domestic Airlines, 1926–2020

Prejet Era		**Jet Era**	
1926–1960	**Passenger Revenue (in cents per passenger mile)**	**1961–1996**	**Passenger Revenue (in cents per passenger mile)**
1926–1930	12.0, 10.6, 11.0, 12.0, 8.3	1961–1965	6.1, 1, 5.9, 5.8, 5.7
1931–1935	6.7, 6.1, 6.1, 5.9, 5.7	1966–1970	5.7, 6, 5.6, 5.9, 6.0
1936–1940	5.7, 5.6, 5.7, 5.1, 5.1	1971–1975	6.3, 6.4, 6.6, 7.5, 7.7
1941–1945	5.0, 5.3, 5.5, 5.1, 4.5	1976–1980	7.8, 8.2, 8.5, 9.0, 11.6
1946–1950	4.5, 5.0, 5.7, 5.8, 5.6	1981–1985	12.8, 12.8, 12.1, 12.7, 12.2
1951–1955	5.6, 5.6, 5.5, 5.4, 5.5	1986–1990	11.0, 11.4, 12.3, 13.1, 13.4
1956–1960	5.3, 5.4, 5.7, 5.9, 6.0	1991–1995	13.2, 12.9, 13.7, 13.1, 13.5
		1996	13.8
		1997	13.97

(Continued)

Table 12.1 *Continued*

Prejet Era		Jet Era	
1926–1960	**Passenger Revenue (in cents per passenger mile)**	**1961–1996**	**Passenger Revenue (in cents per passenger mile)**
		1998	14.1
		1999	14
		2000	14.6
		2001	13.2
		2002	12
		2003	12.3
		2004	12.1
		2005	12
		2006	12.73
		2007	12.98
		2008	13.75
		2009	16
		2010	17.2
		2011	18.9
		2012	19.3
		2013	17.03
		2014	198.9
		2015	19.2
		2016	18.3
		2017	18.3
		2018	18.5
		2019	18.6
		2020	15.3

Source: For 1926–37, Aeronautics Branch of the U.S. Department of Commerce; Statista

Also in 1952, the CAB eliminated the cents-per-mile limits previously used in establishing fares for coach services and instituted a policy that coach fares should not exceed 75 percent of the corresponding first-class fares. The objective of this policy was to encourage the use of coach services—and it worked. By 1955, first-class travel constituted only 59.9 percent of the traffic mix, falling to 45.3 percent by 1960 and to only 21.8 percent by 1965. It has continued to decline ever since.

Air carrier profits plummeted during the recessionary period 1957–1958, and the CAB approved an increase of 4 percent plus $1 in the domestic passenger rates on August 1, 1958. In addition, the board permitted the airlines to reduce family-fare discounts from 50 percent to 33.3 percent and eliminate round-trip discounts and free stopover privileges.

The years from 1962 through 1968 saw the price of an average airline ticket decline by more than 13 percent—probably the most significant cost reduction in the history of passenger transportation. The reason, of course, was the tremendous growth in airline traffic and productivity, largely as a result of new jet aircraft, which was so great that it absorbed costs and made lower fares possible. By 1968, productivity gains began to be outpaced by rising labor costs, landing fees, and interest charges, among other expenses. Clearly, fare reductions could not continue. In 1969, a couple of small fare increases were approved by the CAB, but airline profits continued to fall. In 1970, the CAB was engaged in a domestic passenger fare investigation and denied additional general fare increases pending completion. The result was that in 1970, the industry recorded the largest loss in its history up to that time.

Airfares almost doubled during the 1970s, largely due to the tremendous increase in fuel costs, which rose from an average cost per gallon of 11 cents in 1970 to 90 cents by 1980. Fuel expenses represented close to 13 percent of airline operating expenses in 1970 but approached 31 percent by 1980.

This rise in fuel prices and the 1981 air traffic controllers' strike severely affected airline costs and, subsequently, fares. The mid-1980s brought lower fuel prices and continued efforts by deregulated airlines to control costs, especially by revising labor agreements and improving worker productivity. From 1982 to 1987, average costs per seat-mile declined by about 10 percent, which stimulated further reductions in fares. Discounted fares became available, particularly in the longer-haul, high-density markets. Moreover, this general decline in fares took place when the economy was recovering from recession (in 1980 and 1982) and when many new-entrant airlines and holdover carriers were trying to expand their market share.

By 1987, most of the new entrants had either failed or merged with the surviving incumbent carriers, and since then, average yields have increased steadily. The late 1980s and early 1990s saw further contraction in the industry with the demise of Eastern Airlines and Pan Am. Additional upward pressure on fares was brought about by the Iraqi invasion of Kuwait, as three separate fuel surcharges were initiated in the months that followed. Domestic fare levels were affected by the imposition of passenger facility charges and further concentration in the industry.

From the mid-1990s to 2014, passenger airfares, on average, decreased because of increased competition between new-entrant low-cost carriers and increased competition between the majors. As a result of the terrorist attacks on September 11, 2001, air carriers suffered record-breaking financial losses. In early 2010, airlines were still recovering from such losses (direct and indirect), forcing the airlines to provide incentives to stimulate air travel. Seat sales and enhanced frequent flyer programs were marketed to the public to increase passenger load factors and revenues. By 2014, U.S. average passenger revenue per passenger-mile hit an all-time high of 19.9 cents, and from 2015 to 2019, revenue per passenger-mile remained high but steady with little fluctuation. In 2020, revenue per passenger-mile

Table 12.2 Average Fare in 1995–2020 ($)

1995	444
1996	409
1997	415
1998	440
1999	450
2000	456
2001	420
2002	402
2003	397
2004	375
2005	365
2006	378
2007	364
2008	373
2009	335
2010	357
2011	375
2012	378
2013	379
2014	392
2015	377
2016	349
2017	348
2018	350
2019	355
2020	292

Source: Bureau of Transportation Statistics.

decreased to 15.3 cents per mile which was last experienced in 2002. The large decrease was due to the COVID-19 global pandemic and at the time of writing, no data had been reported but all forecasts indicated a substantial decrease was to be expected.

By the end of the fourth quarter of 2002, the airlines in the United States had lost a combined total of approximately $8 billion since the fourth quarter of 2001. More money was lost in the airline industry in this short period of time than in the entire history of aviation combined. As a result of the COVID-19 global pandemic, U.S. airlines lost $35 billion in 2020 and the global aviation industry was forecasted to lose $201 billion between 2020 and 2022. Table 12.2 shows average airfare for the U.S. from 1995–2020. The figures indicate a trend in the cost of airfares where there were years of steady increases, and from 2003 to 2019, there was a trend of decreases combined with small peaks and troughs. In 2020, there was a significant decrease in average fare as a result of the pandemic due to low demand for air travel and the need for airlines to generate revenue.

PRICING AND DEMAND

Of all the marketing variables that influence the potential sales of airline seats and cargo capacity, price has received the most attention since deregulation. For over 200 years, economists have emphasized the price variable in describing the level of demand for products and services. Pricing remains a very complex issue in many industries. In the case of air transportation, it is even more complex because of the transition in recent years from a highly regulated industry to a deregulated environment.

Economists have developed a simple yet elegant model of how to set a price. The model has the properties of logical consistency and optimization, but it represents a severe oversimplification of the pricing problem as it exists in practice. There is value, however, in examining the model, because it provides some fundamental insights into the pricing problem and because its very limitations help bring out the complex issues involved in pricing.

Demand is defined as the various amounts of a product or service that consumers are willing and able to purchase at various prices over a particular time period. A demand schedule is simply a representation of a series of possibilities that can be set down in tabular form. Table 12.3 is a hypothetical demand schedule for a particular air carrier route.

This tabular portrayal of demand reflects the relationship between the price or fare and the estimated number of passengers who would be willing and able to purchase a ticket at each of these prices.

A fundamental characteristic of demand is that as price falls, the corresponding quantity demanded rises; alternatively, as price increases, the corresponding quantity demanded falls. In short, there is an inverse relationship between price and quantity demanded. Economists have labeled this inverse relationship the **law of demand**. Upon what foundation does this law or principle rest? Basically, common sense and simple observation.

Table 12.3 An Individual Air Carrier's Demand for Air Transportation Per Month Between Two Cities (hypothetical data)

Price	Estimated Number of Passengers
$75	1,000
70	1,150
65	1,275
60	1,400
55	1,550

People ordinarily will fly more at lower prices than at higher prices. To passengers, high price is an obstacle that deters them from buying. The higher this price obstacle, the less they will buy; the lower the price obstacle, the more they will buy. Passengers will drive instead of fly; businesspeople will turn to telephone conference calls and the like as fares rise.

This inverse relationship between price and number of passengers purchasing tickets can be presented on a simple two-dimensional graph measuring estimated number of passengers on the horizontal axis and price on the vertical axis (see Figure 12.1). The resulting curve is called a demand curve. It slopes downward and to the right because the relationship it portrays between price and estimated number of passengers ticketed is inverse. The law of demand—people buy more at a low price than they do at a high price—is reflected in the downward slope of the demand curve. What is the advantage of graphing our demand schedule? It permits us to represent clearly a given relationship—in this case, the relationship between price and estimated number of passengers—in a simpler way than we could if we were forced to rely on verbal and tabular presentation.

Determinants of Demand

In constructing a demand curve, a forecaster assumes that price is the most important determinant of the amount of any product or service purchased. But the forecaster is aware that factors other than price can and do affect purchases, in our case, of tickets. Thus, in drawing a demand schedule or

FIGURE 12.1 An Individual Air Carrier's Demand for Air Transportation Per Month Between Two Cities (hypothetical data)

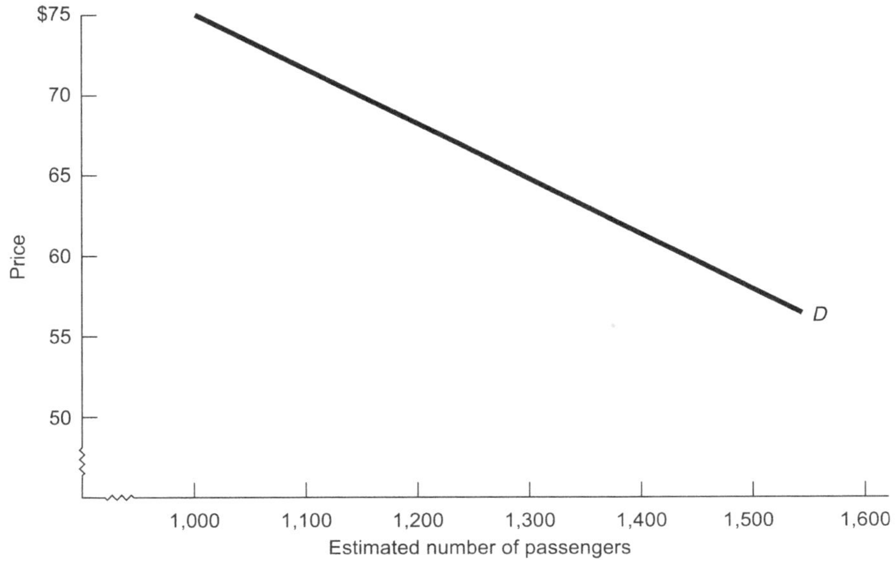

curve, the forecaster must also assume that other factors remain constant; that is, the nonprice determinants of the amount demanded are conveniently assumed to be given. When these nonprice determinants of demand do in fact change, the location of the demand curve will shift to some new position to the right or left of its original position (see Figure 12.2).

The major nonprice determinants of demand in the air travel market are: (1) the preferences of passengers, (2) the number of passengers in a particular market, (3) the financial status and income levels of the passengers, (4) the prices of competitors and related travel expenses, and (5) passenger expectations with respect to future prices.

Changes in Demand

What happens if one or more of the determinants of demand should change? It will change the demand schedule data and therefore the location of the demand curve. Such a change in the demand schedule data, or, graphically, a shift in the location of the demand curve, is called a shift in demand. For example, if passengers become willing and able to buy more tickets, at each possible price over a particular time period we have an increase in demand. An increase in demand is reflected in a shift of the demand curve to the right, for example, from D_1 to D_2, as shown in Figure 12.2. Conversely, a decrease in demand occurs when, because of a change in one or more of the determinants, consumers buy fewer tickets at each possible price than was

FIGURE 12.2 Effect of Changes in Demand

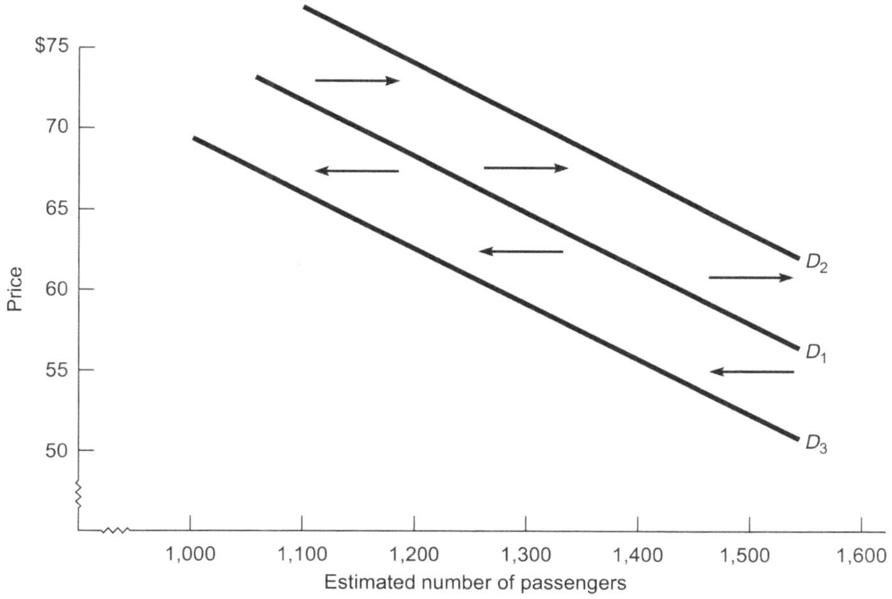

forecast. Graphically, a decrease in demand entails a shift of the demand curve to the left, for example, from D_1 to D_2, as shown in Figure 12.2.

Let us now examine the effect on demand of changes in each of the aforementioned nonprice determinants, using the same hypothetical example.

1 *Preferences of Passengers.* A change in passenger preferences favorable to an airline—possibly prompted by advertising—will mean that more tickets will be demanded at each price over a particular time period, shifting the curve to the right. An unfavorable change in passenger preferences will cause demand to decrease, shifting the curve to the left. The airline sells fewer tickets than forecast at all prices offered during that time period. Preferences can include a number of factors, including an airline's image (United's "friendly skies," Delta's "professionalism"), perceived safety record, ontime reliability, in-flight and ground services afforded, gate position, type of aircraft flown, frequency of departure, and many more either real or perceived differences that relate to a passenger's preference for one airline over another.
2 *Number of Passengers.* An increase in the number of passengers in a market—brought about perhaps by improvements in connecting flights or by population growth—will constitute an increase in demand. Fewer potential passengers will be reflected by a decrease in demand.
3 *Financial Status and Income levels of Passengers.* This nonprice determinant relates to the state of the economy and the level of such things as personal income, disposable income, and profits (in the case of businesses). Air transportation is very sensitive to fluctuations in the economy. If the economy is in a recessionary period, with higher than normal unemployment and decreased factory orders, both business and pleasure travelers will be flying less. Conversely, when the economy is booming, businesspeople are traveling extensively and workers are not hesitant to make air travel plans.
4 *Prices of Competitors and Related Travel Expenses.* An increase in a competitor's price, all other things being equal, will normally prompt some passengers to switch to your airline. The reverse is also true: if you raise your prices and your competitor doesn't, all other things being equal, you will lose some business. An increase in the competitor's price will normally shift your demand curve to the right, and, assuming your prices hold and your competitor's prices drop, your demand curve will shift to the left. Economists refer to these as substitute or competing goods.

   There are other related travel expenses that complement one another. For example, if motel and rental car rates are falling and these items make up 70 percent of the proposed expenses for a trip, the airfare price on a particular trip may be insignificant, relatively speaking. Thus, if a planned $1,000 vacation is unexpectedly obtainable through a package costing $550, the fact that the airfare went from $150 to $165, a 10 percent increase, becomes insignificant.

5 *Passengers' Expectations with Respect to Future Prices.* Passengers' expectations of higher future prices may prompt them to buy now in order to beat the anticipated price rises. Conversely, expectations of falling prices will tend to decrease the current demand for tickets.

A *change in demand* should not be confused with a *change in quantity* demanded. A change in demand is a shift in the entire demand curve, either to the right (an increase in demand) or to the left (a decrease in demand). The passenger's state of mind concerning a ticket purchase has been altered because of a change in one or more of the determinants of demand. As used by forecasters, the term *demand* refers to a schedule or curve; therefore, a change in demand must mean that the entire schedule has changed or that the curve has shifted its position. In contrast, a change in the quantity demanded is the movement from one point to another point—from one price–quantity combination to another—on a fixed demand curve. The cause of a change in the quantity demanded is a change in the price of the ticket under consideration.

Decide whether a change in demand or a change in the quantity demanded is involved in each of the following illustrations:

a. Airline B lowers its price on a particular flight, with the result that Airline A, with a flight departing 15 minutes later, loses passengers.
b. Airline C lowers its price on a particular route segment and experiences an increase in the number of passengers carried.
c. Passengers' incomes rise as a result of a turnaround in the economy, resulting in more vacation traveling.

Elasticity of Demand

The law of demand tells us that consumers will respond to a price decline by buying more of a product or service. But consumers' degree of responsiveness to a price change may vary considerably. Economists, forecasters, and airline price analysts measure how responsive, or sensitive, passengers are to a change in the price by **elasticity of demand**. The demand for some air travel is such that passengers and shippers are relatively responsive to price changes; price changes give rise to considerable changes in the number of passengers carried. This is called **elastic demand**. For other air travel, passengers are relatively unresponsive to price changes; that is, price changes result in modest changes in the number of additional passengers motivated to fly. This is known as **inelastic demand**.

Pricing analysts and others measure the degree of elasticity or inelasticity by the elasticity coefficient, or E_d, in this formula (Δ = change):

$$E_d = \frac{\text{Percentage change in passenger demand}}{\text{Percentage change in price}} = \frac{\%\Delta Q}{\%\Delta P}$$

One calculates these percentage changes by dividing the change in price by the midpoint between the prices and the change in passenger demand by the midpoint between the demands. Thus, we can restate our formula as

$$E_d = \frac{\text{(Change in passenger demand)}}{\text{(Midpoint between passenger demands)}} \div \frac{\text{(Change in price)}}{\text{(Midpoint between prices)}}$$

We use the midpoints to determine percentage changes to avoid the discrepancy that would occur if we went from one price, say \$100, to \$120, which would result in a 20 percent increase changing from \$100 to \$120, but a 16 percent decrease changing from \$120 to \$100. By using the midpoint, \$110, and dividing it into the change, we arrive at a compromise percentage change of 18 percent whether we go from \$100 to \$120 or \$120 to \$100. Similarly, if the original number of passengers carried at a price of \$100 was 220, and 180 passengers were carried at a price of \$120, the percentage change using the midpoint would be 20 percent.

Now let us interpret our formula.

Elastic Demand. Demand is elastic if a given percentage change in price results in a larger percentage change in passengers carried. For example, demand is elastic if a 7 percent decrease in price results in a 12 percent increase in the number of passengers carried or if a 4 percent increase in price results in a 10 percent decrease in the number of passengers. In all such cases, where demand is elastic, the elasticity coefficient will obviously be greater than 1. Another way of determining the elasticity is to see what happens to total revenue as a result of the price change. If demand is elastic, a decline in price will result in an increase in total revenue, because even though the price per passenger is lower, enough additional passengers are now being carried to more than make up for the lower price. This is illustrated in Figure 12.3.

Total revenue is price times quantity. Thus, the area shown by the rectangle $0P_1AQ_1$, where P_1 = \$50 and quantity demanded Q_1 = 200 passengers carried, equates with total revenues of \$10,000. When price declines to P_2 (\$40), causing the quantity demanded to increase to Q_2 (400 passengers carried), total revenue changes to $0P_2BQ_2$ (\$16,000), which is obviously larger than $0P_1AQ_1$. It is larger because the loss in revenue caused by the lower price per unit (P_2P_1AC) is less than the gain in revenue caused by the larger sale in dollars (Q_1CBQ_2) that accompanies the lower price. The reasoning is reversible: if demand is elastic, a price increase will reduce total revenue, because the gain in total revenue caused by the higher unit price (P_2P_1AC) is less than the loss in revenue associated with the accompanying fall in sales (Q_1CBQ_2). That is, if demand is elastic, a change in price will cause total revenue to change in the opposite direction. Figure 12.4 may be helpful in remembering this rule.

Obviously, when airlines reduce prices, they anticipate that consumers will be responsive (elastic). In other words, they assume that the price drop will be more than offset by a larger percentage increase in consumers, thereby filling seats and cargo capacity and increasing total revenues. If they raise prices and consumers are responsive (elastic), the rise in price

FIGURE 12.3 Elastic Demand

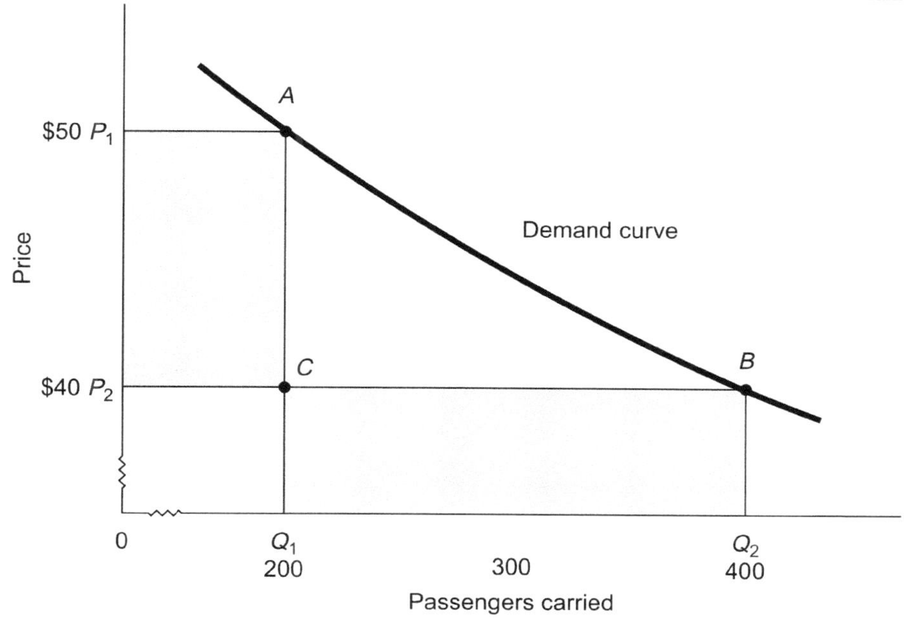

Note: When demand is elastic, a decrease in price results in an increase in total revenue, and an increase in price results in a decrease in total revenue

FIGURE 12.4 Basic Rule of Elastic Demand

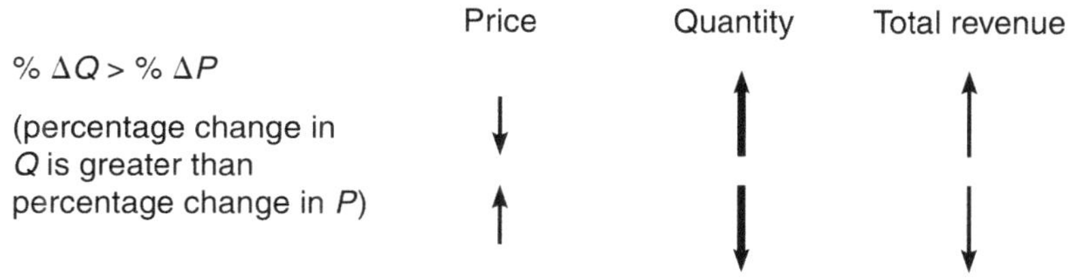

will be offset by a larger percentage decrease in consumers, and total revenues will fall.

Inelastic Demand. Demand is inelastic if a given percentage change in price is accompanied by a relatively smaller change in the number of passengers carried. For example, if a 10 percent decrease in price results in a 5 percent increase in the number of passengers carried, demand is inelastic. If an 8 percent increase in fares results in a 3 percent decrease in the number of passengers, demand is inelastic. It is apparent that the elasticity coefficient will always be less than 1 when demand is inelastic. If demand is inelastic, a price decline will cause total revenue to fall. The modest increase in sales that will occur will be insufficient to offset the decline in revenue per passenger, and the net result will be a decline in total revenues. This situation exists for the $70–80 price range shown on the demand curve in Figure 12.5.

Initially, total revenue is $0P_1AQ_1$ = \$24,000, where price P_1 = \$80 and the number of passengers carried Q_1 = 300. If we reduce the price to P_2 (\$70), the passengers carried will increase to Q_2 (325). Total revenue will change to $0P_2BQ_2$ (\$22,750), which is less than $0P_1AQ_1$. It is smaller because the loss in revenue caused by the lower fare (area P_2P_1AC) is larger than the gain in revenue caused by the accompanying increase in sales (area Q_1CBQ_2).

Again, our analysis is reversible: if demand is inelastic, a price increase will increase total revenue. That is, if demand is inelastic, a change in price will cause total revenue to change in the same direction. Figure 12.6 may be helpful in remembering the rule.

FIGURE 12.5 Inelastic Demand

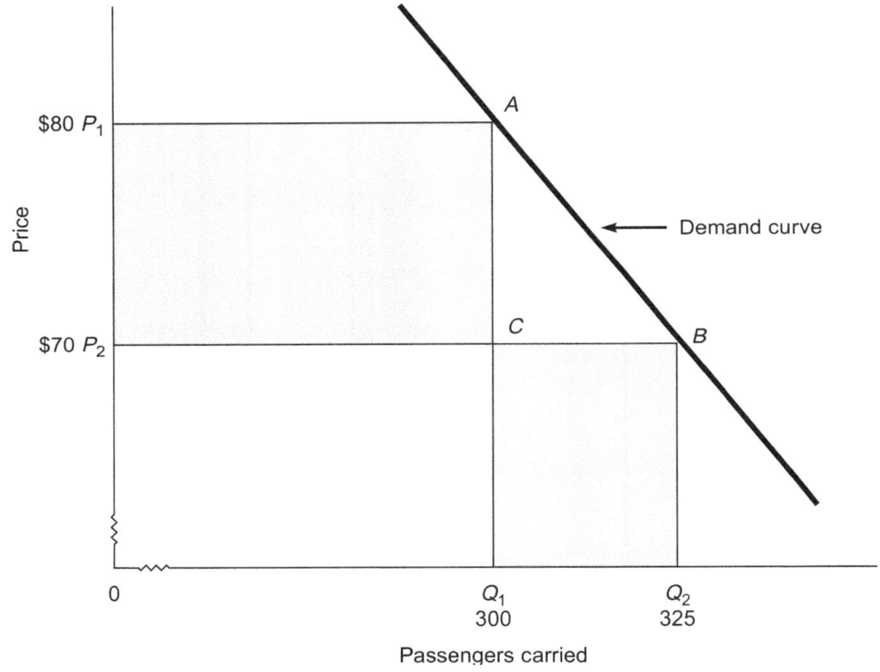

When demand is inelastic, a decrease in price results in a decrease in total revenue, and an increase in price results in an increase in total revenue

FIGURE 12.6 Basic Rule of Inelastic Demand

	Price	Quantity	Total revenue
% Δ*P* > % Δ*Q* (percentage change in *P* is greater than percentage change in *Q*)	↓	↑	↓
	↑	↓	↑

The borderline case that separates elastic and inelastic demand occurs when a percentage change in price and the accompanying percentage change in number of passengers carried are equal. For example, a 5 percent drop in price causes a 5 percent increase in the number of tickets sold. This special case is termed *unit elasticity*, because the elasticity coefficient is exactly 1, or unity. In this case, there would be no change in total revenue.

Determinants of Elasticity

Competition. Generally speaking, the more competition there is (the more substitutes and alternatives), the more responsive (elastic) consumers will be. For example, if four carriers are operating flights within 15 minutes of one another to a particular city and one offers a lower fare, a passenger will likely fly with that carrier, all other things being equal.

Distance. Long-haul flights tend to be more elastic than short-haul flights. Thus, vacationers will be responsive to a fare reduction of $100 on a $500 fare even if they have to leave between Tuesday and Thursday. Short-haul fare changes tend to be inelastic. A 10 percent increase on a $30 fare is only $3. A carrier will generally not experience a 10 percent or greater decrease in passengers for such a small amount.

Business Versus Pleasure. Business flyers tend to be less responsive to price changes than vacationers or individuals on personal trips. Why? Most businesspeople are on expense accounts and have to make their trips within a certain period of time. Nor are they generally willing to take a late-night flight to take advantage of a discount. Vacationers can arrange their schedules and be much more elastic (responsive) to price changes if it is worth it to them.

Time. Certainly, if we have time, we can be much more responsive to price changes than if we do not. On the other hand, if we have little time and must be at a certain place at a particular time, we generally will be very inelastic with regard to price changes. For example, fares to Los Angeles may be going up by 20 percent next week, but if niece Kellie is getting married there next month, we cannot be responsive by flying out there now to save the extra 20 percent.

NO-FRILLS AIRFARE AND SURVEY WARFARE

The following illustration is based on a true case that happened several years ago when a new "no-frills" airfare was introduced.

As the recession made inroads into the passenger traffic loads of the major airlines, Airline A attempted an experiment with a discount of 35 percent from normal coach fares on a certain number of its regularly scheduled routes. In an effort to build up its load factor, Airline A tied its discount fare proposal to the offering of no-frills service during the flight, including doing away with complimentary meals, snacks, soft drinks, and coffee, so as to reduce costs and partially offset the lower-priced fares. However, passengers using the no-frills plan could selectively purchase these items in flight if they wished. The no-frills fares were offered only Mondays through Thursdays.

Airlines B and C, both competitors of Airline A on some of the routes on which Airline A proposed to implement no-frills fares, went along with the discount fares. Airline A claimed that 56 percent of the 133,000 passengers who used its no-frills fare from mid-April through June 30 were enticed to travel by air because of the discount plan. According to Airline A, the new passenger traffic generated by discount fares increased its revenues by $4 million during that period. Airline A said that its figures were based on an on-board survey of 13,500 passengers and represented one of the most exhaustive studies it had ever conducted.

J. Smith, vice-president for marketing for Airline A, was quoted at a news conference as saying that the fare had been an "unqualified success," had created a new air travel market, and had generated more than twice the volume of new passengers required to offset revenue dilution caused by regular passengers switching to the lower fare. He said that the stimulus of the fare gave Airline A a net traffic gain of 74,000 passengers during the initial two-and-a-half-month trial. He also cautioned that the success claims he was making for the no-frills fare did not mean that low fares were the answer to the airline industry's excess capacity problems. Yet Smith did go so far as to state that "what no-frills has proved is that a properly conceived discount fare, offered at the right time in the right markets with the right controls, can help airlines hurdle traditionally soft traffic periods."

Airline B reported a different experience. Its studies showed that only 14 percent of the 55,200 passengers who used its no-frills fare between mid-April and May 31 represented newly generated traffic, with the remaining 86 percent representing passengers diverted from higher fares who would have flown anyway. It said that the effect of the fare in the six major markets it studied was a net loss in revenue of $543,000 during the initial one-and-a-half months. At the same time, Airline B attacked the credibility of Airline A's survey, noting that its own data were based on an exhaustive and scientific blind telephone survey among persons who did not know the purpose and sponsor of the survey. Airline B claimed that this type of study was more apt to produce unbiased results than Airline A's on-board survey.

Other airlines joined Airline B in challenging Airline A's survey results. Airline C, for example, claimed that the no-frills fare did not even come close to offsetting the dilution it experienced in revenues. Other airline officials observed that, although Airline A might have succeeded through its heavy promotion of the no-frills fares in diverting some business from other carriers, they felt that Airline A's claims of generating many passengers who otherwise would not have flown were "preposterous."

Those airlines in direct competition with Airline A on the routes on which the discount fares were tried were vehemently opposed to continuing the discounts. In their view, the no-frills approach constituted "economic nonsense." They announced a policy of matching Airline A's discount fare only when forced to for competitive reasons.

Some Questions for Discussion

1 Does Airline A's experiment suggest that the demand for airline service at discount prices is elastic or inelastic? Do Airline B's results indicate that demand is elastic or inelastic?
2 Which of the two studies, Airline A's on-board survey or Airline B's telephone survey, do you think would yield the most reliable estimate as to the true elasticity of demand? Is it possible or likely that the elasticity of demand for Airline A is different from the elasticity of demand for Airline B? Why? How would you account for the differences in the experiences of Airline A and Airline B with discount fares?

TYPES OF PASSENGER FARES

Several types of fares are included in the passenger fare structure. **Normal fares** (also called standard or basic fares) are the backbone of the fare structure in that they apply to all passengers at all times (without restriction) and are the basis for all other fares. Separate normal fares are provided for each class of service: first class, coach, and economy.

Common fares are an unusual application of **normal fares** in that they apply a specific fare to points other than the points between which the fare is determined. An example of a common fare is shown in Figure 12.7.

Joint fares are single fares that apply to transportation over the joint lines or routes of two or more carriers and that are determined by an agreement between them. Joint fares are becoming very popular between the major and national carriers and commuter (regional) lines.

Promotional fares are discounted fares that supplement the normal fare structure. They are always offered with some kind of restriction, such as minimum length of stay, day of the week, or season. Restrictions serve to minimize the risk of diverting full-fare traffic and maximize the generative

FIGURE 12.7 Common Fare

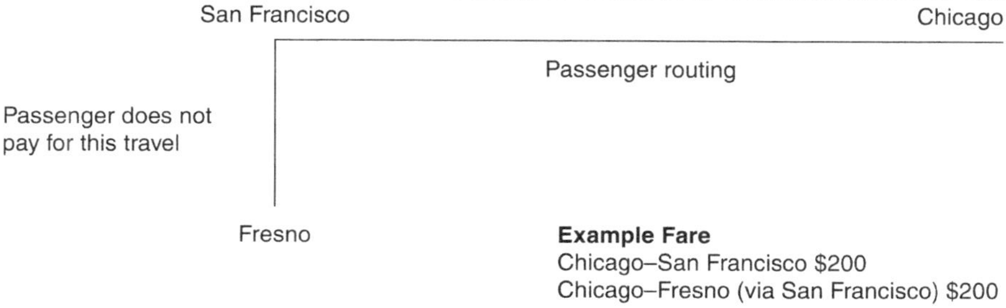

Note: Passengers in this example pay the same fare whether they are flying from Chicago to San Francisco or to Fresno

benefit associated with the fare reduction. Examples include family-plan fares, excursion fares, group fares, and standby fares.

Promotional fares are normally used where load factors are below the optimum level. (Where load factors are above the optimum level, full-fare passengers would be displaced by discounted-fare passengers, thereby reducing revenue.) These discounted fares, because they are lower than normal fares, do reduce revenue yield per passenger. However, this reduction in yield is only undesirable, as we discussed in the section on elasticity, when the additional traffic generated is not enough to offset the price reduction.

THE PRICING PROCESS

The basic twofold responsibility of airline pricing analysts appears to be simple and straightforward. They must: (1) monitor, analyze, and respond to hundreds, sometimes thousands, of daily fare changes implemented by competitor airlines, and (2) routinely develop pricing initiatives to strengthen and/or fortify their company's position in the marketplace. In moving from conceptual responsibility to real-time practice, however, airline pricing becomes quite complex. In broad terms, the pricing process can be characterized as being heavily dependent on automation, having many different fare levels subject to change as a competitive response.

All major airlines participate in the fare filing process via the **Airline Tariff Publishing Company (ATPCO)**, which is jointly owned and funded by 17 U.S. and foreign carriers. The ATPCO serves as an electronic clearinghouse for fare information and changes. Seven days a week, ATPCO accepts fare changes submitted by all participating airlines, consolidates and processes the changes overnight, then transmits and displays these changes to all carriers by 0600. The ATPCO was established in the 1940s, at a time when airline pricing was still regulated by the CAB. The ATPCO's role in pricing was quickly heightened with the advent of airline deregulation, which spawned intense price competition among carriers. Its importance has also grown with the increased role of automation, particularly of computerized reservations systems, which now serve as the source of automation for most of the nation's 42,000 travel agency locations.

At any point in time, because carriers collectively serve tens of thousands of origin and destination (O & D) city-pairs, with each O & D having several different fare levels, the total fare inventory managed by the ATPCO exceeds 2 million individual fares. Any single airline's share of the ATPCO's database may amount to several hundred thousand fares. Each year, the ATPCO processes millions of domestic fare changes. An average day may involve over 130,000. For each carrier, this could mean several thousand each workday, which requires some degree of analysis and, in most cases, some type of competitive response.

It is against this backdrop of fast-paced change, fueled by continuing advances in automation, that the pricing staffs of the nation's airlines formulate, and regularly reformulate, their basic pricing strategies and craft daily tactical maneuvers that are part science, part art.

Pricing Strategies and Objectives

The current literature on pricing describes several different strategies or objectives that a firm might pursue, from simple survival pricing for cash, to fighting for market share, to pricing at a premium over competitors to complement a superior product or service quality. Applying these textbook strategies to the airlines is complicated, because carriers don't charge only one price for their services. Instead, they offer a hierarchical array of fares designed to appeal to both price-sensitive leisure travelers and less price-sensitive business travelers. Further complications arise from various other factors that characterize the market for airline services. These include: (1) the predictable seasonal pattern of demand, especially for leisure travel; (2) the influence of override commissions that many airlines pay to travel agencies; (3) the dynamic nature of airline schedules and the strong relationship that exists between schedule frequency and passenger demand; and (4) the tendency for individual carrier pricing strategies and objectives to vary by market and over time.

Despite the difficulties (and subjectivity) of fitting these general strategies to individual airlines, the exercise can be a meaningful one, particularly if a fixed and relatively brief time frame is defined and if strategies are identified for each carrier. American Airlines, for example, tends to be a profit-focused premium pricer and a price leader in most markets, whereas United tends to be a quick follower rather than leader. Southwest Airlines represents the extreme case of a low-fare pricer, strongly focused on obtaining and maintaining market share and on diverting traffic from auto, bus, and rail travel. Also, some of the financially distressed airlines operating under the protection of Chapter 11 bankruptcy laws clearly have priced primarily for survival. It is noteworthy as well that, despite the differences among airlines, all carriers tend to maintain price parity with their rivals. This is due to the commodity nature of airline service, which may be diminishing somewhat as the supply of air service is controlled by fewer more financially stable airlines.

Although identifying the fundamental strategies of competing carriers is an essential part of airline pricing, it is every bit as important, and perhaps more so, to understand and execute effectively the day-to-day tactics of pricing.

Pricing Tactics

Pricing tactics can be broadly categorized as: (1) fare actions and (2) adjustments to fare rules and/or restrictions. Normally, daily pricing activity involves both tactics. The following discusses some of the more common actions within each category.

Fare Actions. For the most part, fare actions involve changes—increases or reductions—to actual fare levels, in contrast to the rules, restrictions, and/or footnotes that accompany most fares. Changes can be market specific, regional, or mass market in scope.

Introductory fares. When a carrier begins service in a new market, it typically offers unrestricted low fares for a period of 30 to 45 days. Key competitors normally match these fares, with restrictions. Provided that introductory fares are not extended beyond the conventional time frame, they usually don't lead to any sort of "upping of the ante" by competitors (for example, extending the period of availability or discounting the fare even further).

System excursion-fare sales. During seasonally weak traffic periods, carriers frequently offer a systemwide sale of excursion fares. Sales are conducted, on average, for a period of seven to ten days, with travel allowed two to four months into the future. As a rule, provided that the carrier isn't conducting a "fire sale" simply to generate cash, the volume of seats offered in such a sale is limited and controlled on a flight-by-flight basis. American's SuperSaver and MaxSaver fares are some of the more prominent examples.

System business-fare sales. This type of sale is similar to the system excursion-fare sale, except that it involves higher-level business fares. Common motives are to stimulate demand and brand switching and to provide added value. The typical approach in this case is to introduce a one-way or round-trip fare, between 15 and 30 percent less than the full coach (Y-class) fare, with the requirement that the fare be purchased at least three to seven days before travel. Seats offered at this fare tend to be plentiful.

Connect market sales. In markets where an airline offers multiple nonstop flights, the carrier will tend to limit the number of seats sold at discounted fares, because its flights represent a higher-quality service than, for example, connecting-flight service. In these instances, a competing carrier offering only connecting service may periodically attempt to gain increased market presence and steal market share by introducing a low fare in its markets. The business risk faced by the connecting-service carrier is that the competition may attempt the same strategy in the initiator's own nonstop markets.

Target segment pricing. These special fares are lower than normal published fares and are aimed at a well-defined target audience, such as military personnel, senior citizens, or students. For passengers to take advantage of these fares, some form of identification is usually required. Because the audience for these fares is small, the risk of diluting current revenues is minimal.

Flight-time-specific fares. To shore up a particularly weak flight in a market or as a basic competitive maneuver, carriers will sometimes offer lower time-specific or flight-specific fares. A common example is "night-flight" fares (for example, after 8pm) that are 20 to 40 percent below comparable fares on earlier flights with higher demand. There is a risk in offering this kind of fare, because the improvement in the night flight's load factor and the increase in revenue may come at the expense of earlier, stronger flights in the same market as passengers alter their normal travel patterns to obtain the lower fare. When such cannibalization occurs, total market revenue may actually decline.

Mileage-based pricing. Although there are almost always aberrations due to competitive pressures, carriers generally attempt to relate price to distance flown, consistent with some price/mileage curve or mathematical function.

Zone pricing. This is a somewhat more streamlined variation of mileage-based pricing. From Chicago, for example, destinations might be grouped into one of several regions (for example, Midwest, East Coast, Florida/South, West Coast), with each regional group carrying the same price. Logically, longer-distance regions are priced higher than shorter distance ones.

Value-added pricing. Because fares can be matched so quickly through the ATPCO system, carriers sometimes seek a value advantage rather than an outright price advantage. Examples of value-added tactics are an offer of first-class seating for coach fares and extra frequent flyer credits for the purchase of higher-level fares. Ultimately, value-added price offerings also tend to be quickly matched by all competing carriers.

Adjusting Rules and Restrictions. This second set of tactics involves the periodic adjustment of rules and restrictions that accompany most fares rather than the dollar amount of the fares. Common rules and restrictions tactics include the following:

Advance Purchase Requirements. Airlines routinely adjust advance purchase requirements on excursion and discounted business fares. Advance purchase cutoffs are one of the key "fences" airlines erect to prevent business travelers from taking advantage of excursion fares. The advance purchase restriction on the lowest excursion fares tends to range from seven to 30 days, while three to seven days is the norm for business fares. The advance purchase restriction can be likened to a demand throttle: in periods of strong demand, longer advance purchase requirements prevail on the presumption that higher-fare traffic will materialize as the departure date approaches. Conversely, in times of weak demand, advance purchase requirements are less restrictive; that is, shorter.

One-way Versus Round-trip Purchase Requirements. Excursion fares are usually designed to require a round-trip purchase, primarily because their dollar value is so low. Conversely, higher-price business fares are usually offered on a one-way basis and typically can be combined with lower one-way fares, if available, to complete an itinerary. In an effort to maximize revenues, airlines will convert one-way business fares to round-trip purchase fares when three conditions exist: (1) the carrier offers a round-trip schedule pattern that will satisfy the passenger; (2) there is a high probability that any resulting fare increase (as passengers are unable to combine a higher one-way fare with a lower one) will more than offset an associated impact on demand; and (3) there is a strong likelihood that key competitors will match the move.

Minimum or Maximum Stays. Most lower excursion fares carry restrictions such as "requires a minimum three-day or Saturday night stay." The objective is to erect yet another purchase "fence" that business travelers cannot clear.

Fare Penalties. These penalties apply to lower excursion fares and are triggered when a passenger cancels a reservation. Common examples are penalties of $25, $50, 50 percent of the ticket value, or even total forfeiture or nonrefundability if it involves the lowest excursion fares. The objective is to impose these penalties as a revenue offset to the low fares and, more important, to shift seat inventory risk to the passenger. Carriers will periodically try to gain a secondary pricing advantage over one another by relaxing these types of penalties, but competitive matching is usually the end result.

Directional Pricing. If an airline's sales are not appropriately balanced at either end of an O & D city-pair, perhaps because it lacks schedule strength in one of the cities, the carrier may attempt to lower fares on a directional basis from the weaker city.

Peak and Off-peak Pricing. Depending on the seasonality of demand in particular markets, as well as time-of-day and day-of-week patterns of demand, airlines will define certain days of the week and/or times of the day as "peak," which carry a $20 to $30 premium over "off-peak" prices.

Sales, Ticketing, and Travel Windows. As carriers periodically introduce low "sale" fares, they strive to craft a delicately balanced combination of sale, ticketing, and travel periods. They want a sale period that is long enough for the advertising message to be heard but short enough to create a sense of purchase urgency—seven to ten days is the norm. They also want a "ticket by (date)" defined to ensure a degree of control over the pricing initiative, as well as appropriate travel periods for the sale fares. Allowed travel periods usually span 60 to 120 days, during seasonally weak times of the year (for example, January–February and September–October). Travel periods that are too short don't generate the volume of traffic the airlines are seeking. Travel periods that are too long risk dilution of stronger, higher-yield traffic periods.

Pricing Analysis

The decision to use any one, or a combination, of the tactics described is essentially a decision to raise or lower a fare. For example, increasing the advance purchase restriction from three to seven days on a discounted business fare will force a certain number of passengers to buy the next highest fare. Correspondingly, by relaxing the advance purchase requirements on excursion fares from 21 days to seven days and/or allowing for more off-peak days during the week, more passengers will be able to take advantage of a lower fare.

The proper economic analysis supporting the decision to change fares will differ, depending on whether it involves a fare reduction or an increase. In both instances, elasticity expectations are critical, but so are other factors, especially in the case of a fare decrease.

Steps in Analyzing a Fare Decrease. The pricing analysts first calculate the expected revenue gain (or loss) attributable exclusively to elasticity and then do the following:

1 *Subtract Dilution.* Dilution results from those passengers purchasing the proposed lower fare who would have traveled anyway at the prior higher fare.
2 *Subtract Refunds.* Airlines normally obligate themselves through the so-called guaranteed-fare rule to refund the dollar difference between a fare or ticket that has already been purchased and a proposed lower fare in the same fare class, provided that the passenger will still be able to travel on the date and flight originally reserved and meet the travel restrictions of the new lower fare (for example, advance purchase and minimum stay requirements).
3 *Subtract Advertising.* To the extent that previously unbudgeted funds are dedicated to a particular pricing initiative, such an expenditure should be deducted as a step in calculating the net revenue gain, or loss, realized from the fare initiative.
4 *Subtract Additional Variable Passenger Costs.* Certain costs vary directly with passenger volume. Traffic liability insurance, food, and reservation fees are the expenses most commonly identified as truly variable costs. As a final step in estimating the net revenue generated from a fare reduction, the additional variable passenger costs incurred should also be deducted, particularly if the traffic increase is expected to be large.
5 *Add spill.* When a newly introduced fare is especially low and is matched by all major competitors in the market, it has the potential to stimulate primary demand to such a high level that certain carriers may benefit by picking up traffic that is "spilled" to them by other carriers that cannot accommodate all of their potential traffic due to excessively high load factors.
6 *Add rejected demand by other airlines.* At times, certain airlines will tightly restrict the number of seats sold at a particular discounted-fare level on the assumption that they can fill the same seats with higher-fare passengers. This can result in a "rejected" demand by the restrictive carrier, which can be absorbed by another carrier that is less restrictive in controlling its own discount seat inventory.

Steps in Analyzing a Fare Increase

In the case of a fare increase, there are fewer factors to consider in estimating the net economic impact. The formula becomes simply: revenue gain or loss from elasticity plus passenger variable costs avoided. With the introduction of a fare increase, spin and rejected demand are irrelevant. Likewise, there is no potential for refunds, and it is highly unlikely that a carrier will choose to advertise a fare increase. The one important nuance is that passenger variable costs will be lowered as a function of each passenger who, facing a higher fare, chooses not to fly or selects an alternate mode of transportation.

According to Airlines for America, the cost breakdown of a \$300 domestic roundtrip ticket in the U.S. is as follows: \$61.49 Federal Government taxes (20 percent), \$63.47 fuel costs (21 percent), \$51.52 labor expenses (17 percent), \$123.11 non-labor/fuel operating and other expenses (41 percent), and \$0.41 airline profits (0.1 percent).

The Role of Inventory Management

The objective of **inventory management** is to maximize individual flight revenue. In the simplest terms, inventory analysts face the task of selling as many seats as possible at the highest possible fares. This usually means making available an adequate number of lower-fare seats far in advance of the departure date in order to accommodate price-sensitive business travelers. It's a tricky balancing act that requires a keen understanding of the competitive dynamics and traffic composition of individual markets and flights. Additionally, it is the analyst's responsibility to overbook the flights just enough to make up for the number of passengers who can be expected not to show up for their flight.

What makes the inventory management job especially difficult is that bookings for any particular departure may begin to materialize months before the time the flight actually departs, and it's not unusual for an individual analyst to be responsible for 50 to 100 daily departures. As eight or more fare classes are multiplied across the extended control time frame of weeks or months, and as these factors are multiplied again over the workload of 50 to 100 daily flight departures, the job of inventory management can become quite complex.

Ultimately, inventory analysts are evaluated on their ability to do the following simultaneously: (1) minimize "low-yield revenue spin" (the unnecessary loss of lower-fare excursion revenue resulting from the allocation of too few discount-fare seats); (2) minimize "high-yield revenue spill" (the unnecessary loss of higher-fare business revenue resulting from the allocation of too few high-fare seats); (3) minimize the cost of "spoiled" seats (seats spoil when demand is sufficient to fill the aircraft but the analyst underestimates the number of no-show passengers and the flight departs with empty seats); and (4) minimize the cost of denied boardings (when a passenger is denied boarding because an analyst has overestimated the no-show rate on a high-demand flight, the airline usually must place the passenger on another carrier, at a relatively high ticket price).

AIRLINE COSTS

Cost is a major determinant in pricing the airline product. The price or average revenue per passenger mile flown must be sufficient to cover average cost per passenger mile flown. Broadly speaking, airline costs can be categorized as operating costs or nonoperating costs.

Direct Operating Costs

Direct operating costs are all those expenses associated with and dependent on the type of aircraft being operated, including all flying expenses (for example, flight crew salaries and fuel and oil), all maintenance and overhaul costs, and all aircraft depreciation expenses.

Flight Operations. The largest category of direct operating costs is for flight operations. It includes the following items:

Flight Crew Expenses. These expenses involve not only direct salaries and traveling expenses but also allowances, pensions, and insurance. Flight crew costs can be calculated directly on a route-by-route basis or, more commonly, can be expressed as an hourly cost per aircraft type. In the latter case, the total flight crew costs for a particular route or service can be calculated by multiplying the hourly flight crew costs of the aircraft being operated on that route by the **block speed** time for that route. Block speed is the average speed of an aircraft as it moves through the air.

Fuel and Oil. Another major cost element of flight operations is fuel and oil. Fuel consumption varies considerably from route to route in relation to the stage lengths, aircraft weight, wind conditions, cruise altitude, and so forth. Thus, an hourly fuel cost tends to be even more of an approximation than an hourly flight crew cost, so fuel consumption normally is computed on a route-by-route basis. In addition to aviation fuel, oil consumption must be determined. However, oil consumption is negligible and, rather than trying to calculate it directly for each route, the normal practice is to establish hourly oil consumption for each type of engine. The oil consumption on a particular route is then calculated from the number of engines on the aircraft flying the route multiplied by the hourly oil consumption for that engine and by the block speed time. Fuel and oil costs include all relevant taxes and duties, such as taxes on fuel and oil levied by governmental units, and fuel throughput charges levied by some airport authorities on the volume of fuel uplifted.

Airport and En Route Charges. Airlines must pay airport authorities for the use of the runway and terminal facilities. Airport charges normally have two elements: (1) a landing fee related to the weight of the aircraft and (2) in some cases, a passenger facility charge levied on the number of passengers boarded at that airport. Additionally, if an aircraft stays at an airport beyond a stated time period, it will have to pay parking or hangarage fees. These are relatively small compared to the basic landing and passenger charges. It should be noted that not all airports use a standardized system for implementing charges. Many airports, especially those seeking increased business, are willing to negotiate charges on an individual basis. This is especially true of secondary or peripheral airports where facilities are underutilized. In many cases, underutilized airports are willing to contribute resources toward the marketing of a new air service as well as to reduce costs for various ground handling charges.

Aircraft insurance costs. The aircraft hull and liability insurance expenses amount to a relatively small part of flight operation costs. The hull premium is generally calculated as a percentage of the value of the flight equipment and may range from 1 to 2 percent, or lower, depending on the airline, the number of aircraft insured, and the geographic areas in which its aircraft operate. Liability premiums are generally based on the estimated number of revenue passenger miles flown. Additional coverages, such as war risk coverage, may be purchased for an additional premium. The estimated annual premium can be converted into an hourly insurance cost by dividing it by the projected aircraft utilization; that is, by the total number of block speed hours that each aircraft is expected to fly during the year.

Other flight-operations expenses. Finally, there may be some expenses related to flight operations that do not fall into any of the preceding categories. These additional expenses may include the cost of flight crew training and of route development. However, if training costs are amortized over two or three years, then they are generally grouped together with depreciation. Some airlines may have to pay rental or lease charges for the hiring or leasing of aircraft or crews from other airlines. These expenses are usually considered part of flight-operations costs.

Maintenance and Overhaul Costs. Total maintenance costs cover a wide range of costs related to different aspects of maintenance and overhaul. Flight equipment maintenance costs are divided into three categories: direct maintenance on the airframe, direct maintenance on the engines, and a maintenance burden. The maintenance burden is basically the administrative and overhead costs associated with the maintenance function that cannot be attributed directly to a particular airframe or engine but allocated on a fairly arbitrary basis. U.S. air carriers must furnish the DOT with these three categories of maintenance costs separately for each aircraft type that they operate. These data are published quarterly and provide an excellent basis for the comparison of maintenance costs among airlines and also among different aircraft types and engines.

Individual carriers, having estimated the total maintenance costs for one particular aircraft type, may convert these costs into an hourly maintenance cost by dividing them by the total number of block speed hours flown by all the aircraft of that particular type operated by the airline.

Depreciation and Amortization. Depreciation of flight equipment is the third component of direct operating costs. Airlines tend to use straight-line depreciation over a given number of years, with a residual value of 0 to 15 percent. Depreciation periods can vary by aircraft, with the period for wide-body jets ranging from 14 to 16 years. For smaller short-haul aircraft, depreciation periods are shorter, generally eight to ten years.

The annual depreciation charge or cost of a particular aircraft in an airline's fleet depends on the depreciation period adopted and the residual value assumed. For example, an aircraft with a purchase price of $90 million and another $10 million for spare parts depreciated over a 15-year period to a 10 percent residual value would carry a depreciation of $6 million per year:

Price of aircraft and spares	$100
less residual value (10%)	*– 10*
divided by 15 years	$ 90
Annual depreciation	$ 6

If an airline chooses a shorter depreciation period, then the annual depreciation cost will rise. The hourly depreciation cost of each aircraft in any one year can be established by dividing its annual depreciation cost by the aircraft's annual utilization; that is, the number of block speed hours flown in that year. Thus, if our example aircraft achieved 3,000 block speed hours in a year, its hourly depreciation cost would be $2,000 ($6 million divided by 3,000). If the annual utilization could be pushed up to 4,000 hours, then the hourly cost would be cut to $1,500 ($6 million divided by 4,000). Clearly, any changes in the depreciation period, in the residual value, or in the annual utilization will affect the hourly depreciation cost.

Many airlines amortize the costs of flight crew training, as well as any developmental and preoperating costs related to the development of new routes or the introduction of new aircraft. In essence, this means that such costs, instead of being debited in total to the year in which they occur, are spread out over a number of years. Such amortization costs are grouped together with depreciation.

Indirect Operating Costs

Indirect operating costs are all those costs that will remain unaffected by a change of aircraft type because they are not directly dependent on aircraft operations, including expenses that are passenger related rather than aircraft related (such as passenger service costs, costs of ticketing and sales, and station and ground costs) and general and administrative costs.

Station and Ground Expenses. Station and ground costs are all those expenses, apart from landing fees and other airport charges, incurred in providing an airline's services at an airport. Such costs include the salaries and expenses of the airline staff located at the airport and engaged in the handling and servicing of aircraft, passengers, or freight. In addition, there are the costs of ground handling equipment, of ground transportation, of buildings and offices and associated facilities, and of communication equipment. Costs also arise from the maintenance and insurance of each station's buildings and equipment. Rents may have to be paid for some of the properties used.

Passenger Service Costs. The largest single element of costs arising from passenger services is the payroll, allowances, and other expenses related directly to aircraft cabin staff and other passenger service personnel. Such expenses include hotel and other costs associated with overnight stops, as well as the training costs of cabin staff where these are not amortized. Because the number and type of cabin staff may vary by aircraft type, some airlines consider cabin staff costs to be an element of flight-operations costs and, as such, a direct operating cost.

A second category of passenger service costs are those directly related to the passengers. They include the costs of in-flight catering, the meals and other facilities provided on the ground for the comfort of passengers, and expenses incurred as a result of delayed or canceled flights.

Reservations, Sales, and Promotional Costs. All costs associated with reservations, sales, and promotional activities, as well as all office and accommodation costs arising from these activities, are included in this category. Staff expenses at retail ticket offices, whether at home or abroad, are also included. In addition, the costs of all advertising and any other form of promotion, such as familiarization flights for journalists or travel agents, fall in this category. Finally, commissions or fees paid to travel agencies for ticket sales normally are included.

General and Administrative Costs. General and administrative costs are usually a relatively small element of an airline's total operating costs, because many administrative expenses can be related directly to a particular function or activity within the carrier, such as maintenance or sales. Consequently, general and administrative costs should include only those expenses that are truly general to the airline or that cannot readily be allocated to a particular activity. Interairline comparison of these general costs is very difficult, because airlines use different accounting systems.

Nonoperating Costs and Revenues

Nonoperating costs and revenues include those expenses and revenues not directly related to the operation of an airline's own air transportation services. Major nonoperating costs and revenues include the following:

1 Gains or losses arising from the retirement of property or equipment, both aeronautical and nonaeronautical. Such gains or losses arise when there is a difference between the depreciated book value of a particular item and the value that is realized when that item is retired or sold off.

2 Interest paid on loans, as well as any interest received from bank or other deposits. For some accounting purposes, some carriers include interest paid on aircraft-related loans as an operating cost.
3 All profits or losses arising from an airline's affiliated companies, some of which may be directly involved in air transportation, such as an owned commuter carrier.
4 A wide range of other items that do not fall into the preceding three categories, such as losses or gains arising from foreign exchange transactions or from sales of shares or securities.
5 Direct government subsidies or other government payments.

Fixed Versus Variable Costs

The traditional classification of costs just described is essentially a functional one. Costs are allocated to specific functional areas within the airline, such as flight operations and maintenance, and are then grouped together in one or two categories, as either direct or indirect operating costs. This cost breakdown is of considerable value for accounting and general management purposes.

To aid in economic analysis and management decision making, variable costs and fixed costs must be distinguished. Clearly, some costs may be immediately avoidable as a result of some management decision. Furloughing employees and eliminating meal service on certain flights would be examples. Other costs associated with mortgage payments on buildings and hangars may not be avoided except in the long run. The most common way of distinguishing between those costs that can be varied in the short run and those that cannot is through the concept of variable costs and fixed costs. Airlines identify those elements of cost generally accepted as being direct operating costs and further subdivide them into fixed costs and variable costs.

Variable costs are those costs that increase or decrease with the level of output, or **available seat-miles (ASMs)**, that an airline produces. (A seat-mile is one passenger seat transported one statute mile.) These costs, for the most part, are avoidable in the short term. For example, if a flight or series of flights is canceled, the airline is no longer responsible for flight crew expenses, fuel charges, landing fees, and the costs of passenger meals. These are fairly self-evident. Less obvious are the engineering and maintenance costs, which should be classified as variable. Certain maintenance checks of different parts of the aircraft, involving both labor costs and the replacement of spare parts, are scheduled to take place after so many hours of flying or after a prescribed number of flight cycles. (A flight cycle is one takeoff and landing.) Because a large part of direct maintenance is related to the amount of flying or the flight cycles, canceling a service will immediately reduce both the hours flown and the flight cycles and will save some engineering and maintenance expenditures, most notably on the consumption of spare parts, and some labor costs.

Fixed costs are those direct operating costs that, in total, do not vary with changes in ASMs. They are costs that are unavoidable in the short term. Having planned schedules for a particular period and adjusted its fleet, staff, and maintenance requirements accordingly, an airline cannot easily cut back its schedules and services beyond a certain minimal level because of its obligation to the public. Thus, fixed operating costs may not be avoidable until the carrier can change its scheduled service.

Although most indirect operating costs are fixed costs, in that they do not depend in the short term on the amount of flying undertaken, others are more directly dependent on the operation of particular flights. This is particularly true of some passenger service costs, such as in-flight catering, and some elements of cabin crew costs. Fees paid to service organizations or other airlines for ground handling of aircraft, passengers, or freight may be avoided if a flight is not operated. Some advertising and promotional costs may be avoidable in the short run. This leaves within the indirect cost category costs that are not dependent on the operation of particular services or routes. Lease payments on flight equipment and maintenance burden security services are clear examples of costs that are fixed in the short term.

Cost-Cutting Trends

Leading up to the early 2000s, airlines commenced application of cost-cutting measures to reduce rising operational costs. Many of the world's airlines had huge deficits that were further increased after the 2001 terrorist attacks in the United States, putting many airlines over the edge. Huge losses forced airlines to implement additional cost-cutting strategies basically overnight.

In the short term, airlines furloughed or laid off employees, with some carriers rehiring employees on a part-time basis. Aircraft fleet sizes were reduced, having a negative impact on frequency. To compensate for reduced frequency, some airlines used larger aircraft on selected routes. Airlines operating on traditional hub-and-spoke systems reduced or eliminated service to selected destinations. Alliances between air carriers were increased, resulting in increased market share and cross-utilization of resources. In some cases, airlines merged or filed for bankruptcy protection. For example, in late 2002, US Airways filed for bankruptcy with the hope of restructuring and reemerging as a successful carrier. Since 9/11, in addition to US Airways, United, Delta and Northwest all filed for bankruptcy. The trends briefly discussed are expected to continue for the foreseeable future. To remain afloat, airlines are being forced to cut pennies wherever reasonably possible while maximizing revenue. For the major airlines, downsizing is a difficult process and, in some cases, next to impossible. However, opportunities are created for smaller airlines, especially those in the low-cost sector.

PRICING AND OUTPUT DETERMINATION

Pricing and output determination for airlines is as much an art as a science. There is no simple or, for that matter, singular way to approach the analysis. We will start our analysis by reviewing the demand side of the picture. As noted previously, the demand curve facing any airline slopes downward and represents an inverse relationship between price and passengers carried: the lower the price, the greater the amount of passenger traffic generated. In addition, passengers are responsive to price changes. At first, they may be very responsive (elastic) to price reductions, and that might stimulate a large percentage change in passengers carried. Unfortunately, at some point, further price cuts will not stimulate additional traffic in sufficient numbers to offset the reduction in total revenue caused by the price cut. In other words, passengers will become unresponsive (inelastic). Columns one and two in Table 12.4 portray this situation. We assume in this particular instance that our hypothetical airline must accept a price cut in order to generate additional **revenue passenger miles (RPMs)**. A revenue passenger mile is one passenger transported one mile in revenue service. Our fare in this case is expressed in dollars per mile, commonly referred to as *yield*. Yield is actually defined as the air transport revenue per unit of traffic carried, or total passenger revenue per RPM. Basically, it is the same as price, average revenue (AR), or fare per mile. Column three represents the total revenue for each level of RPMs generated during this particular period. Column four shows the marginal, or extra, revenue that results from additional RPMs. The data in Table 12.4 are shown graphically in Figures 12.8 and 12.9.

Total Costs in the Short Run

Now let's turn our attention back to the cost side of the picture. The costs an airline incurs in ASMs depend on the types of adjustments it is able to make in the amounts of the various resources it employs. The quantities of many resources used—labor, fuel, and so forth—can be varied relatively quickly in the short run. But the amounts of other resources demand more time for adjustment. For example, acquiring new aircraft or building new hangars can be varied only over a considerable period of time. The *short-term period* refers to a period of time too brief to permit the airline to alter its capacity yet long enough to permit a change in the level at which the existing fleet of aircraft is utilized. An airline's overall capacity is fixed in the short run, but ASMs can be varied by applying larger or smaller amounts of labor, materials, and other resources to that capacity. In other words, the existing fleet can be used more or less intensively in the short run. Through better scheduling and more efficient use of labor, the airline can increase ASMs in the short run, but there is a limit.

As the airline adds resources to a fixed capacity, its output (ASMs) might increase at an increasing rate for a while if it had been underutilizing its existing capacity. However, beyond some point, ASMs would increase at a *decreasing* rate until ultimate capacity in the short run was reached. This economic principle is called the **law of diminishing returns**.

Table 12.5 illustrates the law of diminishing returns numerically. ASMs increase at an increasing rate up to 2.6 and then continue to increase at a decreasing rate up to capacity in the short run. Column three shows

FIGURE 12.8 Total Revenue and RPMs for an Individual Airline Over a Particular Period of Time (hypothetical data)

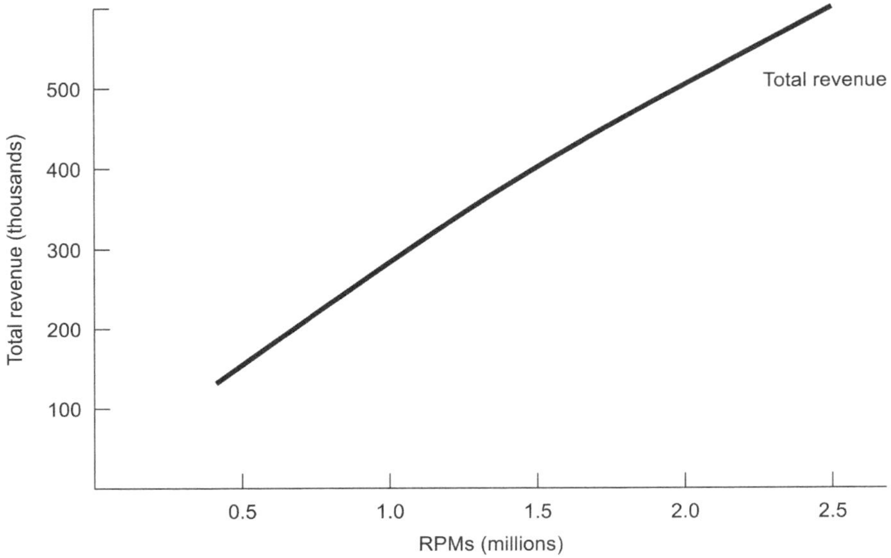

FIGURE 12.9 Yield Expressed in Fare per 1,000 RPMs for an Individual Airline Over a Particular Period of Time (hypothetical data)

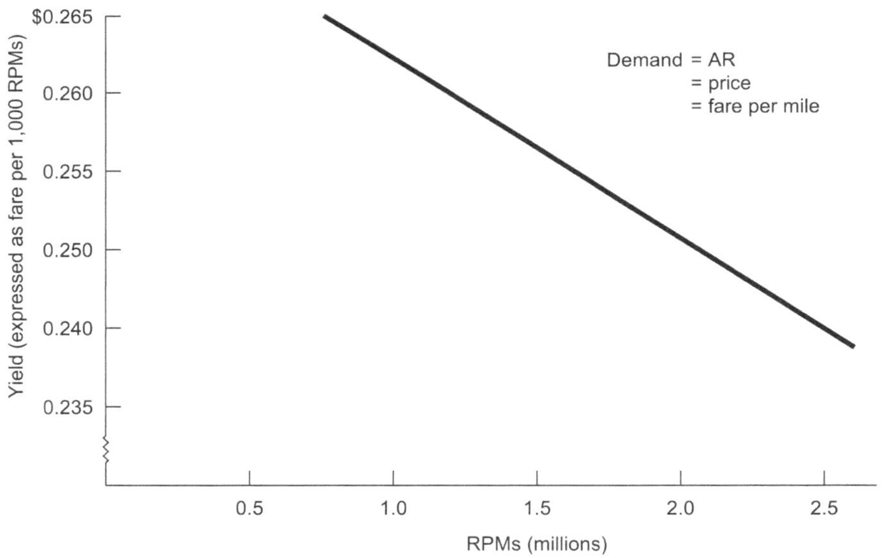

that the total variable costs associated with each level of ASMs flown are not constant. As ASMs increase, variable costs actually increase at a *decreasing* rate from 1.7 to 2.6 million ASMs. Eventually, variable costs increase at an *increasing rate*. The reason for this behavior of variable costs

Table 12.4 Demand and Revenue Schedule for an Airline Over a Particular Period of Time (hypothetical data)

Yield (price or AR) per Mile	RPMs (millions)	Total Revenue (thousands)	Marginal Revenue (thousands)
$0.265	0.800	$212.0	
0.260	1.275	331.5	$119.5
0.255	1.820	464.1	132.6
0.250	2.210	552.5	88.4
0.245	2.400	588.0	35.5
0.240	2.475	594.0	6.0
0.235	2.500	587.5	-6.5
0.230	2.515	578.5	-9.0
0.225	2.520	567.0	-11.5
0.220	2.522	554.8	-12.2

Table 12.5 Total Fixed-Overhead Costs, Total Variable Costs, and Total Costs for an Airline Over a Particular Period of Time (hypothetical data)

ASMs (millions)	Total Fixed Cost (thousands)	Total Variable Cost (thousands)	Total Cost (thousands)	Marginal Cost (thousands)
1.0	$100	$160	$ 260	
1.7	100	170	270	$ 10
2.6	100	240	340	70
3.4	100	300	400	60
4.0	100	370	470	70
4.5	100	450	550	80
4.9	100	540	640	90
5.2	100	650	750	110
5.4	100	780	880	130
5.5	100	930	1030	150

lies in the law of diminishing returns. The total cost shown in column four is self-defining: it is the sum of fixed and variable costs at each level of ASMs. Figure 12.10 shows graphically the fixed, variable, and total costs presented in Table 12.5.

Load Factor

One more piece is needed before we can complete our pricing analysis. In Chapter 7, *passenger load factor* was defined as revenue passenger miles divided by available seat-miles. In developing a demand schedule, a pricing analyst assumes that all of the ASMs produced by the airline company will not be filled by RPMs. (This was discussed in detail in Chapter 7.) Consequently, it is reasonable to assume that a carrier will not experience a 100 percent load factor on all routes or on all flights, during the period of time for which the analyst has made the price and RPM forecast. For purposes of analysis, it is assumed that the load factors shown in Table 12.6 are associated with the ASMs and RPMs previously shown.

Load factors normally increase with reductions in ASMs, because the carrier would cut back on those flights and routes that have experienced the lowest load factors and poorest profits.

Those remaining would be the ones that have experienced the highest load factors and greatest profits—hence, the higher overall average.

As a practical matter, the analyst also realizes that systemwide load factors above 75 percent or below 55 percent are not realistic. To maintain an average of 75 percent is quite an achievement, considering the number of flights and passengers it would take at 90 percent or above to offset the low load factors experienced during off-peak hours and resulting from flights made to position aircraft into large hubs for the morning or afternoon bank of flights. Load factors below 55 percent would also not be practical because profit would not be realized.

Profit Maximization in the Short Run

Given prices, RPMs, total revenues, total costs, and load factors, the airline is faced with the question of what level of ASMs will maximize profits or,

FIGURE 12.10 Total Costs and ASMs for an Individual Airline Over a Short Period of Time (hypothetical data)

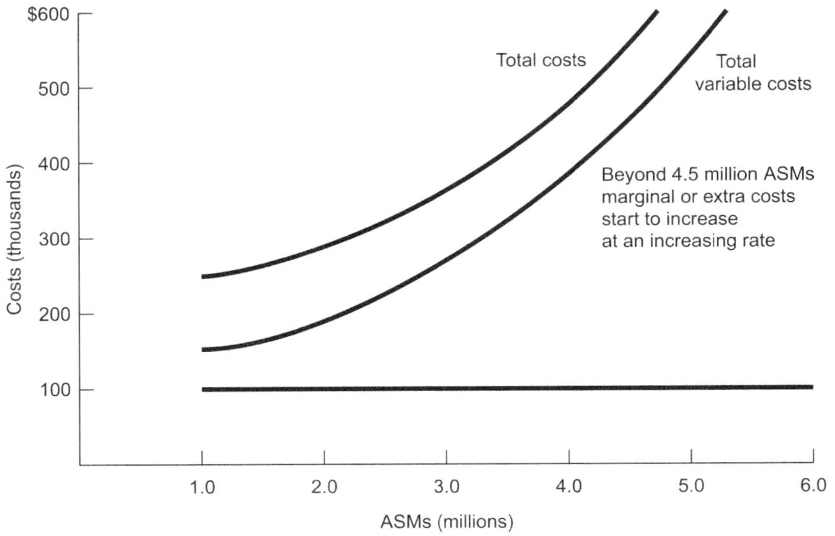

Table 12.6 Systemwide Passenger Load Factor for an Airline Over a Particular Period of Time (hypothetical data)

Load Factor		
ASMs (millions)	*RPMs (millions)*	**Estimated System Load Factor**
1.0	0.800	80%
1.7	1.275	75
2.6	1.820	70
3.4	2.210	65
4.0	2.400	60
4.5	2.475	55
4.9	2.500	51
5.2	2.515	48
5.4	2.520	47
5.5	2.522	46

at worst, minimize losses. Table 12.7 includes the data from both Tables 12.4 and 12.5, plus the profit (+) or loss (-) at each level of output. Assuming that this is a profit-maximizing airline, it should produce 3.4 million ASMs, which will generate 2.21 million RPMs at a price or average revenue (yield) of $0.250 per mile and a total revenue of $552,500. The load factor at this level of output will be an acceptable 65 percent. The 3.4 million ASMs will cost this airline $400,000 to produce, and the airline will experience profits of $152,500. If the airline were more concerned with holding its market share in certain markets by increasing scheduled flights and decreasing load factors to a systemwide level of 55 percent, it could still experience profits of $44,000. Beyond 4.5 million ASMs, it is not generating enough traffic (passengers have become unresponsive to further price reductions) to offset the costs associated with this level of output.

Figure 12.11 compares total revenue and total cost graphically. This airline's profits are maximized at the level of output (3.4 million ASMs and 2.21 million RPMs) at which total revenue exceeds total cost by the maximum amount. Unfortunately, if the RPMs shown in Figure 12.11 do not materialize and if demand decreases at all price levels over this particular time period, revenues will fall, squeezing the profit area shown in the diagram. If prices are in the inelastic range (in other words, if passengers are unresponsive to further price reductions), the only choice for the airline is to reduce capacity (cut back ASMs). In so doing, it will reduce variable and total costs, improve load factors, and, it is hoped, maintain profitability.

Table 12.7 Profit-Maximizing Output for an Airline Over a Particular Period of Time (hypothetical data)

ASMs (millions)	yield (price or AR) per Mile	RPMs (millions)	Total Revenue (thousands)	Total Fixed Cost (thousands)	Total Variable Cost (thousands)	Total Cost (thousands)	Profit (+) or Loss (-) (thousands)
1.0	$0.265	0.800	$212.0	$100.0	$160.0	$260.0	$-48.0
1.7	0.260	1.275	331.5	100.0	170.0	270.0	+61.5
2.6	0.255	1.820	464.1	100.0	240.0	340.0	+124.1
3.4	0.250	2.210	552.5	100.0	300.0	400.0	+152.5
4.0	0.245	2.400	588.0	100.0	370.0	470.0	+118.0
4.5	0.240	2.475	594.0	100.0	450.0	550.0	+44.0
4.9	0.235	2.500	587.5	100.0	540.0	640.0	-52.5
5.2	0.230	2.515	578.5	100.0	650.0	750.0	-171.5
5.4	0.225	2.520	567.0	100.0	780.0	880.0	-313.0
5.5	0.225	2.522	554.8	100.0	930.0	1030.0	-475.2

FIGURE 12.11 Total Revenue and Total Costs for an Individual Airline Over a Short Period of Time (hypothetical data)

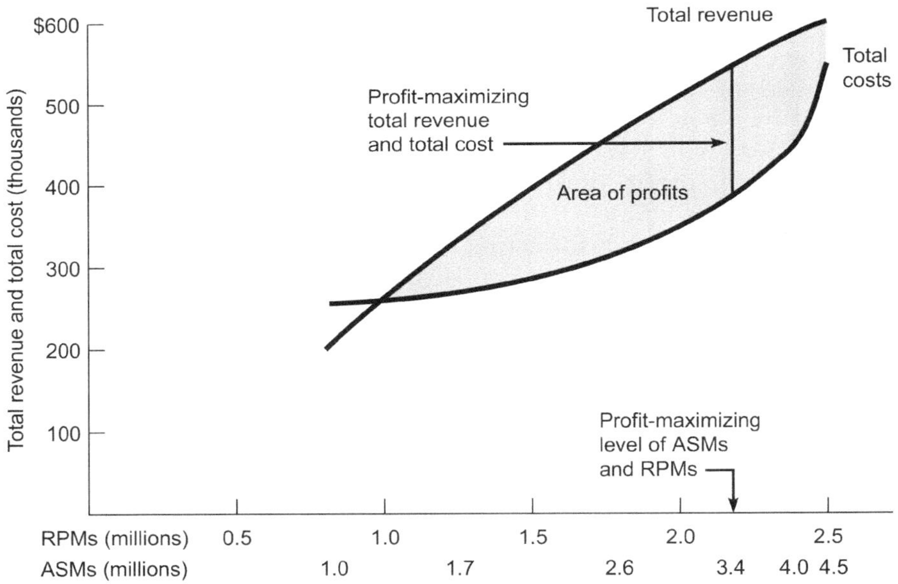

KEY TERMS

Airline Tariff Publishing Company (ATPCO)
available seat-miles (ASMs)

block speed
common fares
demand
direct operating costs
elastic demand
elasticity of demand
fixed costs
flight operations
indirect operating costs
inelastic demand
inventory management
joint fares
law of demand
law of diminishing returns
nonoperating costs and revenues
normal fares
promotional fares
revenue passenger miles (RPMs)
show cause order
variable costs

REVIEW QUESTIONS

1 What was the primary reason for the changes in average air passenger fares between 1929 and 1941, 1950 and 1953, 1960 and 1970, 1973 and 1986, 1987, 2001 and the present?

2 Explain the law of demand as it relates to air travel. What are the nonprice determinants of air travel demand? What happens to the demand curve when each of these determinants change? Distinguish between a change in demand brought about by price and one caused by the nonprice determinants.

3 What effect will each of the following have on the demand for Airline A's passenger traffic?

   a. Competitor B improves its on-time performance.
   b. Competitor B offers a special promotional fare on the same route as Airline A's.
   c. Competitor C increases the number of connecting flights at a particular airport served by Airline A.
   d. A spur line connecting the airport with an interstate highway is completed.
   e. The airport authority requests that a commuter airline share ticket and gate space with Airline A.
   f. Airline A's image is tarnished as a result of a recent wildcat strike.
   g. Competitor D increases its advertising, accentuating in-flight services.

h. Competitor E experiences a serious crash on takeoff.
i. The economy experiences an upturn, unemployment drops, and business expansion is under way.
j. A hotel chain offers a specially priced three-day package, including rental car.

4 What does the coefficient of elasticity of demand measure? What is meant by *elastic demand*? By *inelastic demand*? What effect will the following changes have on total revenue?

a. Fares are reduced and demand is elastic.
b. Fares are raised and demand is inelastic.
c. Fares are reduced and demand is inelastic.
d. Fares are raised and demand is elastic.

5 Determine the elasticity of demand for the following demand schedule (use the total revenue test to check your answers):

Fare	Passengers Carried	Total Revenue	E_d
$160	622		
150	730		
140	782		
130	804		

6 What are the major determinants of elasticity of demand? Use these determinants to judge whether the demand for the following services is elastic or inelastic:

a. Short-haul, primarily business-market flights.
b. Long-haul, primarily vacation flights.
c. Short-haul flights with extreme competition from surface modes of transportation.
d. Mid-week promotional fare directed at the pleasure market.

7 Distinguish between *normal* and *promotional fares*. What is meant by *common fares*? By *joint fares*?

8 What is the primary function of the Airline Tariff Publishing Company (ATPCO)? Why is the application of textbook strategies to airline pricing so difficult? How do introductory fares differ from excursion fares? What are *target segment*, *mileage-based*, *zone*, and *value-added pricing*?

9 Give an example of an advance purchase requirement, a fare penalty, and peak/offpeak pricing. Why is the decision to use any one, or a combination, of these tactics essentially a decision to raise or lower a fare? Describe the steps involved in analyzing a fare decrease. Describe the steps involved in analyzing a fare increase. What is the objective of inventory management? Why is it such a difficult job? Inventory analysts are evaluated on the basis of their performance in four areas. What are those areas?

10 Define and briefly describe five direct operating expenses. What is meant by *maintenance burden*? Give an example of depreciation and an example of amortization. What are indirect operating costs? Give several examples of nonoperating costs and revenues. What is the relationship between variable costs and available seat-miles (ASMs)? Give several examples of fixed costs.

11 Give several examples of direct (variable) expenses and of fixed-overhead expenses. What is the relationship between ASMs and RPMs? Given a fixed fleet of aircraft and other resources in the short run, why do ASMs increase at a decreasing rate up to some maximum limit? Why does the total revenue curve bend, finally reach a peak, and then drop off?

12 Describe in your own words the profit-maximization point (use ASMs, RPMs, total revenue, and total cost in your answer). What is meant by *marginal cost* and *marginal revenue*? How do we determine passenger load factors?

CHAPTER 13

Air Cargo

Revised and updated by Dr. Robert O. Walton, College of Business, Embry-Riddle Aeronautical University Worldwide, USA

CHAPTER CHECKLIST • YOU SHOULD BE ABLE TO:

- Distinguish between air express, air freight, and air mail services
- Discuss the role of the Civil Aeronautics Board (CAB) in the early development of the air cargo industry in the United States
- Describe the concept of overnight air express as established by Federal Express
- Describe the role of air freight forwarders in the air freight business
- Explain why the arrival of jumbo jets in the early 1970s proved to be both a boon and a bane for the cargo business
- Define the four types of air cargo carriers and give examples of each
- Compare and contrast the role of air cargo today and in the future with the carriage of passengers and other modes of transportation
- Discuss the market for air freight in relation to the type of commodity carried and demand and distribution problems
- List some of the special air freight services provided by the carriers
- Discuss several types of air freight rates and factors affecting them

DOI: 10.4324/9780429346156-16

INTRODUCTION

Carrying cargo has been far more important than carrying passengers for almost every mode of transportation ever used by humankind. This was true of beasts of burden, waterborne carriers, and wheeled vehicles, including railroads. The only exception so far has been aircraft. Others believe that aircraft will be carrying more cargo than passengers as the 21st century progresses. But there is no doubt that cargo volume has been increasing more rapidly than passenger volume for the past two decades.

Air transportation tends to be used to move passengers and cargo over long distances. While most people think of airplanes for the movement of passengers, a great deal of cargo is moved on the same aircraft in the cargo compartment. This cargo carried in the cargo compartment is known as **belly cargo**. In addition to belly cargo, dedicated freighter aircraft are also used to move cargo by air. Air transport moves about 1 percent of the global trade by volume but accounts for about 35 percent of the total trade in dollar value. The value of goods moved by air is about $6.2 trillion each year, which is equivalent to about 7.4 percent of the global GDP. This is due to the fact that air transportation of freight is mainly used to move time-sensitive or high-value cargo.

INDUSTRY OVERVIEW

Prior to the COVID-19 pandemic in 2020, the worldwide aviation industry flew almost 9 trillion revenue passenger kilometers. A revenue passenger kilometer (RPK) is a unit of measurement of the volume of passengers carried by an airline. A RPK is recorded when a revenue passenger is carried one kilometer. In the US, the measure typically used is a revenue passenger mile (RPM). In general, an increase in RPM/RPK is a positive sign for an airline since it means that more passengers are using their service which should result in topline growth.

Other than the all-cargo airlines, the aviation industry is heavily reliant on passenger revenue for its financial sustainability. As more wide-body aircraft with longer ranges have entered the market (such as the B777, B787, A330, A340, and A350), more cargo is being carried as belly cargo. In 2019, about 41 percent of **freight-ton kilometers (FTK)**, that is the equivalent of one ton of cargo moved one kilometer, was moved on dedicated freighters whereas the other 59 percent was moved as belly cargo.

Air transportation is typically used to carry time-sensitive or high-value goods, such as perishables (i.e., flowers and fruits), electronics, pharmaceuticals, and racehorses, but is also used to carry time-sensitive items such as repair parts that are urgently needed to keep a factory operational. There is a higher cost to moving goods by air, and air transportation of cargo is the most expensive of the five modes of transportation. However, it does have some key advantages which will be discussed later in the chapter.

In the past, U.S. passenger airlines have viewed belly cargo as only a small revenue stream and it typically accounts for 5 to 10 percent of total revenues. However, the international foreign-flag carriers such as Lufthansa and KLM/Air France can earn up to one-half of their gross revenues from cargo on some international routes.

HISTORICAL OVERVIEW

Air cargo got its start on May 28, 1910, when Glenn Curtiss flew a sack of mail from Albany to New York City for the Post Office Department, covering the 150 miles in two and a half hours. Or you could say it all started on November 10, 1910, when the Wright Company flew 65 miles from Dayton to Columbus, Ohio, with five bolts of silk cloth strapped into the passenger seat of the plane for a department store that wanted to sell strips of the cloth as mementos of "the first air shipment."

These were interesting events, but they did not mark the start of any regular air cargo service. Actually, there are three separate elements of air cargo services—air mail, air express, and air freight—and therefore three histories to trace. "Air mail" has taken on new definitions over time and eventually became known as "air express". Today, "air mail" has evolved to become known as "air freight" with the introduction of all-cargo aircraft. Today, **air express** refers to small packages that usually have a higher priority of carriage than air freight. Until the mid-1970s, air express was also distinguished from air freight by the fact that it was a cooperative effort among airlines, using a separate ground operator—the Railway Express Agency (REA). The REA accepted shipments from customers and distributed them over the available routes of the associated carriers so as to give the customer the most expeditious service.

Air freight, on the other hand, has always been marketed independently by airlines in competition with one another. In recent years, the lines of distinction between air express and air freight have become less clear. In 1989, Federal Express (FedEx), the pioneer of overnight small-package air service and now the largest carrier in that business, acquired Flying Tiger, the world's largest all-freight carrier. FedEx was a pioneer in the hub-and-spoke methods to move air cargo and this allowed them to dominate the overnight cargo market. In 2021, FedEx flew 14,186 million freight tonne-miles (according to USDOT). The weight limit on express shipments was removed, causing some industry analysts to conclude that the boundaries between freight and express are blurring and may soon disappear.

Air mail service, the first of the air cargo services, was an important factor in the formation of air transportation in the United States (see Chapter 3). The first air mail service, which its founders hoped would be permanent, started with an experimental service between Washington, D.C. and New York. During the three-month test, the Post Office Department moved 193,021 pounds of mail, collected $159,700 from the sale of its 24-cent air mail stamp, and showed a profit of $19,103. This experiment marked the real beginning of air mail service because it convinced the Post Office Department that air service was feasible.

For the next nine years, the Post Office Department completely controlled air mail service—even the operation of the airplanes—using both Army Air Corps and civilian pilots. In 1925, Congress ordered the government out of the business of flying the mail and established procedures for contracting with private operators. By 1927, the government had ceased aircraft operations for mail services completely. Air mail began to grow more rapidly after the Post Office Department turned operations over to private contractors. It is difficult to overemphasize the importance of air mail to the early aircraft operators. The first commercial aircraft were built primarily to transport mail, and mail was the principal revenue source for the operators for many years. Air mail was responsible for the beginnings of the U.S. airline system as we know it today. Mail continued to be the dominant revenue source for the airlines until the arrival of the DC-3 in 1935. This aircraft could carry 21 passengers across the country in 15 hours, but more important, it was the first aircraft that could be operated profitably on passenger revenues alone. The introduction of the DC-3 began to shift the focus away from air mail and toward passenger operations. Although air mail would continue to be a significant revenue source to the airlines, it would gradually slip in relative importance. Today, mail accounts for less than 3 percent of the airlines' revenues.

Meanwhile, in Europe the first official air mail flight in Germany was completed on June 10, 1912—although there were limited cases of the air transportation of newspapers in both France and Germany before this date. In other parts of the world the transportation of mail was also being tried around the same time, with the first postal flight conducted in Japan being completed on June 1, 1912, and in Egypt in January 1914.

Air Express

Whereas mail had its greatest impact on air transportation in the early days of the industry, air express has only recently begun to fulfill its promise. Air express service was inaugurated at Hadley Field near New Brunswick, New Jersey, on September 1, 1927, by National Air Transport, a predecessor of United Airlines, created specifically for the purpose of carrying air express, and by the REA. Three other carriers joined the effort to provide a comprehensive express service: Colonial Airlines, Boeing Air Transport, and Western Air Express.

The carriers affiliated with the REA tried to persuade other air carriers to join them in this enterprise, but American, Eastern, TWA, and several others were concerned over the choice of the REA as the ground operator. They were afraid that the REA's rail operations would be in conflict with the air service and preferred a more neutral operator. These airlines decided instead to organize General Air Express. Established in August 1932, General Air Express claimed to provide "the largest and most complete air express service in the world," serving 125 cities directly by air and offering connections to Canada, Mexico, the West Indies, and Central and South America. But the REA's head start was too much for General Air Express to overcome; General Air Express folded at the close of 1935, and the REA became the sole express agent for the U.S. air carrier industry.

Even with the REA acting as coordinator for all the carriers, air express was a small part of the airlines' income. When the mail contracts were cancelled in 1933, United Airlines was earning almost 60 percent of its revenues from the carriage of mail and 40 percent from passengers. Its express business accounted for only a little over 1 percent of the gross revenue —some $133,000 a year.

Air express did not become the important revenue source the carriers hoped it would. While airline managements concentrated on winning passengers away from the railroads, the REA and the airline cargo staffs struggled with air express, often at odds over who should control the product and how revenues should be shared. On November 12, 1975, the REA declared bankruptcy. In place of the coordinated joint effort, each carrier introduced its individual air-express service, preceding the nationwide coverage they were able to provide with the REA.

Overnight Air Express

On April 17, 1973, Frederick W. Smith began his Federal Express operations at 13 airports. Smith's concept was to provide a door-to-door overnight service for small packages. The key new element was the overnight feature. Up until then, air-express service relied almost entirely on passenger flights that operated during daylight hours. Packages tendered after the close of business generally sat at the origin airport until the next morning and were not delivered until the second day. By flying dedicated aircraft, FedEx was able to fly at night and deliver packages the next business day.

Operationally, Fred Smith revolutionized the air industry by introducing the hub-and-spoke system, routing all packages and aircraft through a hub in Memphis. A large portion of FedEx's workforce was made up of college students who performed the sorting and loading functions at Memphis each night.

In 1975, its third year of operation, FedEx was grossing $173 million in revenues but still losing money. What helped turn FedEx profitable was the demise of the REA. By then, Smith's company was big enough to enable it to pick up the pieces from the REA, his fleet having grown to 30 Falcon-20 mini freighters, each with a capacity of 350 to 400 packages.

And so the banner was passed from the passenger carriers to FedEx. And FedEx has carried it very high indeed. From an average of fewer than 500 packages handled per night in 1973, FedEx has grown at a phenomenal rate, to garner half of the express traffic in the United States and become a significant factor in international service.

In the U.S., the United Parcel Service (UPS) is the main competitor to FedEx. UPS is larger than FedEx, however this is due to more international traffic carried by UPS.

Air Freight

If we accept the original definition of air freight as traffic carried in all-cargo aircraft, then the birth of air freight operations would date back to 1931 when Transcontinental and Western Air began overnight air freight service between New York and Kansas City. It used "specially constructed freight planes cruising over 100 miles per hour." The planes were unscheduled; they departed in the evening whenever a full cargo load became available. They made six intermediate stops—in Philadelphia, Harrisburg, Pittsburgh, Columbus, Indianapolis, and St. Louis. Customers could ship between any two of the points served for the same "astonishingly low price" of $11 per 100 pounds. Adjusted for inflation, this would be the equivalent of $190 today (in 2022). As part of the promotion for "the first air freight service," TWA introduced a new shipping document, the air freight waybill, and offered a souvenir copy to any customer who requested one.

The first regularly scheduled all-cargo service was started by United Airlines in 1940 between New York and Chicago. The flight left New York at 11:30 P.M. and arrived in Chicago at 3:40 A.M.

While passengers and cargo were being transported in these early years, it really was not until after the end of World War II in 1945 that both markets started to take off. During the war, aircraft were shown to be reliable over long distances and had been used by the military to move both passengers and freight. However, in the U.S. both cargo and passenger transportation was heavily regulated until deregulation occurred in 1977 for cargo, and shortly afterward in 1978 when passenger transportation was deregulated.

Air freight received a big boost at the end of World War II with two landmark decisions by the Civil Aeronautics Board (CAB). The first, in April 1948, legitimized air **freight forwarders** as middlemen between shippers and airlines, giving them the right to consolidate individual shipments and tender them to the airlines at the carriers' volume rates. Although opposed by most of the air carriers, the official recognition of the forwarder added a new dimension to air freight, greatly increasing marketing and sales efforts and stimulating new traffic.

The second CAB decision gave operating rights to three all-cargo carriers: Slick, U.S. Airlines, and Flying Tiger. The last-named airline had been formed by Bob Prescott in 1945 under the name National Skyway Freight Corporation. But it soon came to be known by its slogan, "The Line of the Flying Tigers," because it was equipped with surplus military transports and flown by pilots who had served with Prescott under General Chennault, defending the Burma Road during World War II. It was the first of the three all-cargo carriers to be certificated, on September 21, 1949.

The halcyon days of air freight began in the 1960s. In October 1962, American Airlines ordered its first Boeing 707 freighter, and United followed suit in 1964 by ordering 727-QCs (for "quick change"). These planes had removable passenger seats so that they could be flown in the daytime as passenger aircraft and at night as freighters. By 1969, American was operating a fleet of 39 of the 707 freighters; United had 15 DC-8 freighters plus 30 QCs; and TWA was flying 12 of the 707s and 8 QCs. Even with all this dedicated lift, however, cargo still accounted for only 10 percent of the revenues for these carriers.

The Arrival of Jumbo Jets

In January 1970, the Boeing 747 jumbo jet began operating as a passenger liner. The 747 proved to be both a boon and a bane for the cargo business. The 747s were a boon because as an all-cargo aircraft they provided the capacity to carry containers as big as 8 × 8 × 40 feet and to lift over 100 tons per trip. In November 1971, Boeing finished the construction of the first 747 freighter. Delivered to Lufthansa on March 9, 1972, it was put into service on the Frankfurt–New York route. On February 21, 1974, Sabena World Airways marked another important first in the jumbo-jet era by introducing the 747 combi in scheduled service—an aircraft that divided the main deck so that 8 × 8 × 10 foot cargo containers could be carried aft of the passenger compartment on the main deck. KLM was the final operator of the 747 combi aircraft but retired the last one in 2020. Two were shortly afterward brought back into service to support increased cargo demand during the COVID-19 crisis, however by 2022 all KLM combi aircraft had been retired.

The jumbo jets were also a bane, however, because the bellies of passenger aircraft could accommodate most of the air cargo tonnage available, and—by virtue of the by-product nature of the space—at considerably less cost than dedicated freighter aircraft. The combination of expanded belly capacity and lower air freight rates permitted under the CAB's liberalized pricing policies following deregulation in 1978 proved to be the death knell for freighter operations by the U.S. passenger airlines. TWA operated its last freighter in December 1978, and in subsequent years, American, United, and Pan Am all got out of the business. Northwest was the last of the originally certificated combination carriers to operate freighter aircraft in the U.S. Flying Tiger, acquired by Federal Express in 1989, was the only surviving all-cargo carrier from those originally approved by the CAB in 1948.

After most U.S. certificated carriers phased out their operation of freighters, the promotion of air cargo devolved upon the freight forwarders, who had been the airlines' best customers. Only about 10 percent of all air freight is sent directly from the shipper, the other 90 percent of air cargo is handled by forwarders. The air freight forwarders receive the goods and consolidate the shipment then work with the airlines to arrange transportation and customs clearance. Figure 13.1 provides a basic schematic of the cargo flow from shipper to consignee either through an integrated carrier or forwarder channels. Integrated carriers are full-service firms that transport goods door-to-door, such as DHL, UPS, and FedEx.

Foreign-flag carriers, which continue to operate cargo services with dedicated freighters, have been far more aggressive than U.S. carriers in

FIGURE 13.1 Cargo Flow Through a Freight Forwarder or Integrated Carrier

Forwarder vs. Integrator

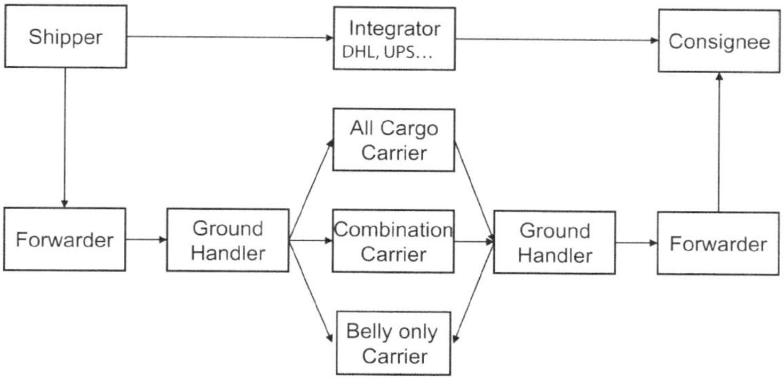

promoting air cargo. In recent years some of the U.S. passenger airlines have started to expand their cargo operations to include operating dedicated freighters again, such as United.

Types of Carriers

The air cargo industry includes four types of carriers: integrated carriers, combination carriers, belly-only carriers, and conventional all-cargo carriers. **Integrated carriers**, also called express carriers, operate door-to-door freight transportation networks that include all-cargo aircraft, delivery vehicles, sorting hubs, and advanced information systems. These carriers operate their own aircraft to ensure adequate capacity and service reliability, although they also use the belly cargo space of passenger aircraft to supplement their own capacity and to provide international service. The U.S. express carriers include FedEx and United Parcel Service (UPS). DHL also provides express carrier service in the U.S. but is mainly focused on express service outside of the U.S. As FedEx and UPS are clearly the dominating players in the U.S. air freight market, the oligopolistic market characteristics discussed in Chapter 7 apply even more to this market.

A second major type of cargo carrier is the **combination carrier**, which carries passengers and cargo and operates both passenger aircraft and freighters. These carriers primarily offer point-to-point service on a wholesale basis, relying on freight forwarders for pickup and delivery, sales to shippers, and customer service. Because the passenger plane belly space that represents much of their cargo capacity is a co-product of passenger service, combination carrier cargo services have a low marginal cost and thus usually offer much lower prices than express carriers. Although virtually all passenger airlines handle some cargo, the importance of the cargo business varies substantially from airline to airline. Many large Asian and European carriers, including Korean Air, Cathay Pacific Airways, Lufthansa, KLM, and Air France, operate fleets of freighter aircraft to supplement their belly cargo capacity. Cargo accounts for a large share of total revenue for most major non-U.S. air carriers, but it plays a much less prominent role for many other airlines, including most major U.S. passenger airlines.

The third type of cargo carrier is the **belly-only carrier**, which transports passengers and belly cargo only, but does not operate any freighters. These carriers only transport cargo within their existing passenger networks. Newer passenger aircraft coming onto the market have larger carrying capability so the belly-only carriers have been able to capture more of the cargo market with only a marginal cost increase. Like the combination carriers, belly-only carriers rely on freight forwarders for sales and pickup and delivery services. Both Delta and American Airlines in the U.S. are examples of belly-only carriers since neither airline operates freighters.

The fourth type of cargo carrier is the **all-cargo airline**, which operates a variety of cargo services. Some, including Kalitta Air and Polar Air Cargo, provide point-to-point service for air freight forwarders, either as common carriers or under guaranteed-space agreements. Others, like Atlas Air and Air Transport International, primarily operate aircraft on a contract basis for other airlines. Two of the conventional carriers, Atlas and Polar, specialize in international 747 freighter service, however with the ending of production of the 747 in 2022, they are shifting towards other freighters such as the B-767 and B-777. It should be noted, Atlas Air and Polar Air Cargo are owned by Atlas Air Worldwide Holdings.

By volume, belly cargo capacity accounts for 54 percent of the total world cargo capacity, with the rest being carried on freighters. However, about 90 percent of air cargo based on revenue is carried on main-deck freighters. Figure 13.2 shows the 2019 air cargo revenue by type of carrier.

FIGURE 13.2 Air Cargo Revenue by Type of Carrier (2019)

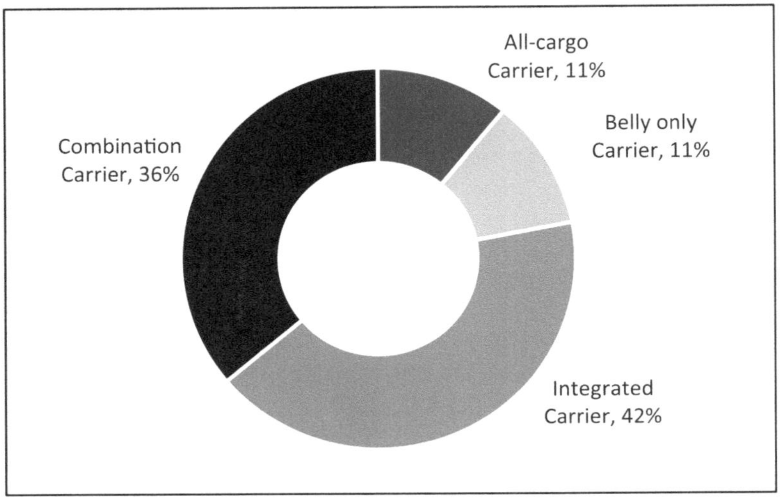

Source: Boeing

AIR CARGO TODAY

Air cargo traffic continues to grow at a healthy rate, but it has not yet achieved the status envisioned by the air cargo pioneers of the 1930s and 1940s. They fully expected that air cargo would, in time, be the most important revenue source for the airlines. After all, every known form of transportation had earned more money from the carriage of freight than of people. Thus, the only real question for the airlines was how soon air freight would overtake passenger revenues. Most experts thought it would happen within five years, or ten at most.

So what has happened? Why is it that the time frame for the ascendancy of air cargo keeps being pushed into the future? And why do many experts suspect that air cargo may never be the top money-maker?

A fundamental reason for air cargo's inability to surpass passenger revenues is that air is a premium-cost transportation mode compared to other surface transportation modes. It costs far more to operate an airplane than to run a truck, ship, or railroad car. Thus, there has to be a compelling reason for customers to use air services. Electronic producers regularly ship by air, for example, because the added cost of air transportation is more than offset by getting the product to market and to consumers earlier. Shippers of perishables—such as fresh fruits, flowers, and fish—use air transport because they have no other way to reach their worldwide markets. But shippers of most commodities find surface delivery times acceptable and therefore choose the lower transportation costs associated with surface modes.

The unprofitable operations of freighter aircraft through the years also took a toll on air cargo's reputation. The fact that freighters lost money somehow translated to the belief among senior management of the leading U.S. carriers that air cargo was an unprofitable business—certainly not a valid conclusion when you look at the profits that are made by the carriage of cargo in combination aircraft. In any event, the perception that cargo was a loser has convinced many passenger airline managements not to invest their scarce capital in any more freighter aircraft. This is not the case with international carriers where a number of the international passenger carriers also operate a robust freighter fleet (e.g. Qatar, Emirates, Cathay Pacific Airways, Korean Air, Turkish Airlines, etc).

Although air cargo has failed to achieve the preeminent position that was expected of it, and in spite of the limitations imposed by the marketplace and the design of aircraft, air cargo is alive and well. More and more companies are using air cargo services as they experience the inventory reduction benefits that air transportation can provide.

Air cargo has grown very rapidly over the past 20 years, as shown in Figure 13.3. However, after a strong recovery from the global financial crisis in 2008/09, revenues flattened for a few years, before starting to climb in 2014. During the COVID-19 pandemic revenues again declined. Between 2009 and 2019, global air cargo revenue tonne-kilometers (RTK) grew at a rate of about 4.3 percent annually, and this rate is projected to stay around

4 percent over the next 20 years. Note: a **revenue ton-mile (RTM)** or a **revenue tonne-kilometer (RTK)** is one ton of revenue cargo carried for one mile or one kilometer.

Although cargo accounts for only 5 to 10 percent of total revenues for most of the combination carriers in the United States, it is a considerably more important revenue source for many of the foreign-flag carriers, which continue to operate jumbo freighters on international routes. Some of them—such as Lufthansa, Japan Airlines, and Air France—earn as much as one-third to one-half of their gross revenues from cargo on some routes.

The four largest markets—the Asia-Pacific, North America, Europe, and the Middle East—account for nearly 90 percent of air cargo shipments (based on RTK), with the Asia-Pacific region being the largest bloc at 34 percent.

The composition of the U.S. domestic market changed dramatically during this time, as the integrated all-cargo carriers captured virtually all of the growth and became the industry leaders. Between 2009 and 2019, the international express market grew at an annual rate of 8.5 percent, and this trend is expected to continue as the e-commerce industry continues to expand. However, the share of combination carrier cargo RTMs is still substantial. Hence, belly hold cargo operations and the concept of economies of scope are still of importance to the airline industry.

The integrated carriers have successfully followed the strategy of offering superior service at a premium price. By providing time-definite,

FIGURE 13.3 Freight and Mail Carried by U.S. Airlines in Cargo Revenue Ton-Miles (millions)

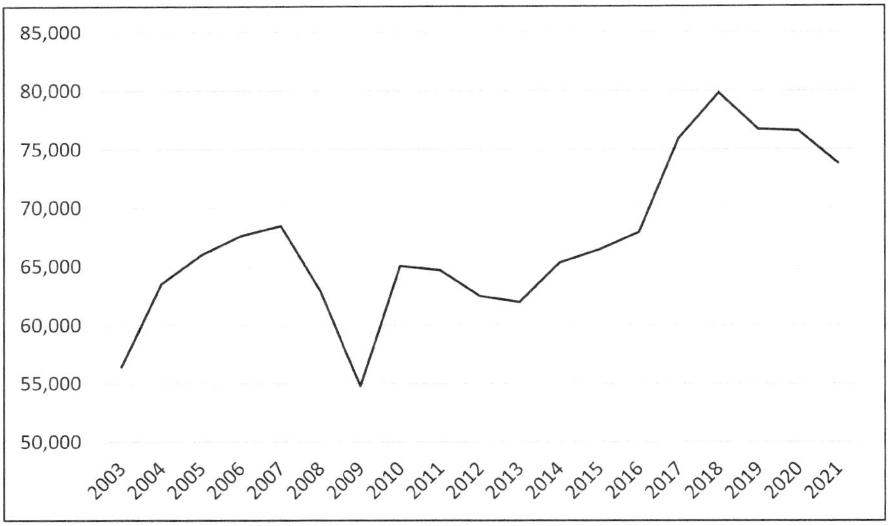

Source: BTS (through Oct 2021)

guaranteed door-to-door service supported by a real-time shipment tracking service, they are able to generate a yield of about $1.20 to $1.40 per pound for domestic shipments and $1.93 for international priority. Their leading competitors, the combination carriers, supply airport-to-airport service primarily on a space-available basis, usually provide no service guarantees, offer little or no tracking capability, and typically earn $0.30 to $0.40 per pound for domestic freight. It should be noted that during the COVID-19 pandemic yields on air freight were higher.

The combination and belly hold carriers appear to have little chance of reversing the trends of the past 30 years and capturing a larger share of the domestic freight market. By offering a consistently high level of service, the integrated carriers have raised the expectations of freight shippers. The passenger airline freight product has changed little over the past 30 years, and the gap between the level of service they can support and the level demanded by the market is widening. Recent changes designed to improve the profitability of passenger service, including grounding wide-body aircraft and scheduling faster turn times, further limit cargo opportunities for combination carriers. In addition, the integrated carriers have developed a variety of lower-cost second-day and deferred service options through increased use of trucking. These services options reduce the combination carriers' price advantage while preserving shipment tracking and other integrated carrier service advantages.

The most important competitive response by U.S. combination and belly hold carriers is the trend toward contracting out airport cargo services. This may increase airline cargo profitability by reducing labor costs, but it will not help the combination carriers regain market share and may cause a further drop in share if it lowers their service quality.

If current trends continue as expected, the volume of domestic traffic handled by the integrated carriers will continue to grow rapidly. This will have important implications for U.S. airports. Because almost all integrated carrier domestic traffic moves in all-cargo aircraft, the number of all-cargo operations will rise. This will increase the demand for cargo aircraft parking positions, particularly at spoke airports, where many cargo aircraft remain parked from early morning until late evening. Integrated carriers have more flexibility in locating cargo warehouses than do combination carriers, which need access to passenger aircraft, so the demand for on-airport cargo warehouse space will grow less rapidly than the demand for cargo aircraft parking. Parts of the airport that do not have good access to passenger terminals and are not well suited for combination carrier freight warehouses may be suitable for integrated carrier facilities. The noise impacts from cargo may also increase because most integrated carrier flights are operated at night, although the shift to quieter Stage 3 aircraft will offset the increase in the number of cargo operations in many cases.

The growth in U.S. airport freighter activity primarily reflects the development of integrated carrier flight routings. Most of the airports with the greatest activity and growth are the integrated carrier hub/gateway airports: Memphis Super Hub, Indianapolis, Miami, Greensboro, Anchorage, Oakland, Newark, and Dallas–Fort Worth for FedEx; Louisville Worldport, Columbia Metro, Chicago Rockford, Dallas–Fort Worth, Miami, Philadelphia, and Ontario California for UPS; Internationally, DHL has hubs in Cincinnati, Leipzig in Germany, and Hong Kong. Because the integrated carriers have established major facilities, cargo usually receives sufficient attention at these airports. Where cargo may not always receive enough attention, and where the increase in freighter activity makes it an important issue, is at the large airports that are not integrated carrier hubs, such as Atlanta, Chicago, Denver, Honolulu, Phoenix, and Boston.

THE MARKET FOR AIR FREIGHT

A review of the major commodities shipped by air, according to data supplied on an annual basis by the Air Transport Association, gives a good idea of the major markets for air cargo. These commodities include the following:

- Auto parts and accessories
- Machinery and parts
- Printed matter
- Electronic/electric equipment and parts, including appliances
- Fashion apparel
- Footwear
- Tools and hardware
- Televisions and radios
- Computers and software
- Fruits and vegetables
- Sporting goods, toys, and games
- Live animals
- Chemicals, elements, and compounds
- Machines for electronic data storage and processing
- Metal products
- Photographic equipment, parts, and film
- Cut flowers and nursery stock
- Plastic materials and articles
- Medicines, pharmaceuticals, and drugs
- Instruments—controlling, measuring, medical, and optical
- Food preparations and miscellaneous bakery products
- Other e-commerce products

While the list above provides good examples of the types of cargo transportation by air, these commodities can be grouped into six major categories. Figure 13.4 provides a general breakout by percentages of the general types of commodities carried.

FIGURE 13.4 Types of Commodities Carried by Air

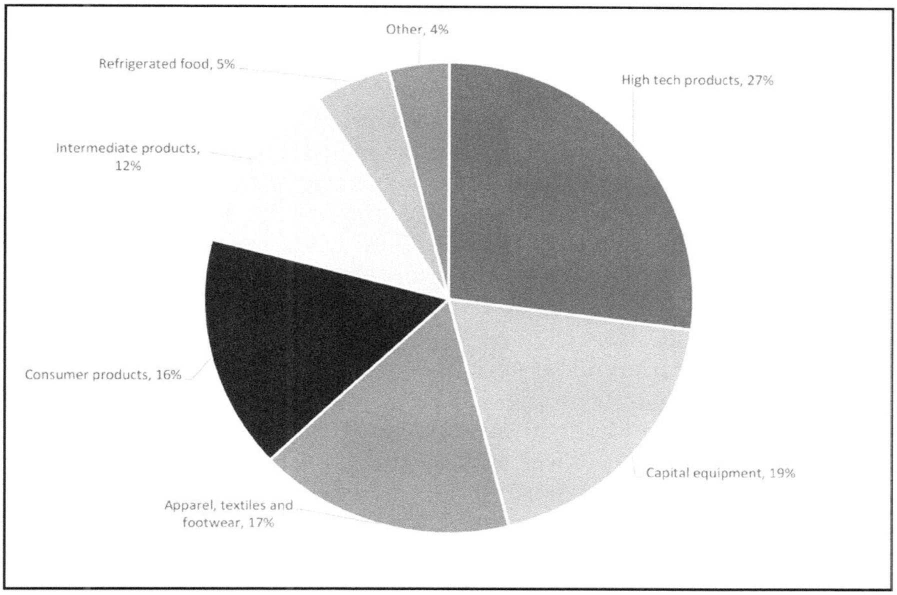

Source: Moving Boxes by Air (Morrell, P. S.)

Shipping commodities by air is the most desirable form of distribution when one or more of the following characteristics is present:

1 When the commodity is:

   a. Perishable
   b. Subject to quick obsolescence
   c. Required on short notice
   d. Valuable relative to weight
   e. Expensive to handle or store

2 When the demand is:

   a. Unpredictable
   b. Infrequent
   c. In excess of local supply
   d. Seasonal

3 When the distribution problems include:

   a. Risk of pilferage, breakage, or deterioration
   b. High insurance costs for long in-transit periods
   c. Heavy or expensive packaging required for surface transportation
   d. Need for special handling or care
   e. Warehousing or stocks in excess of what would be needed if air freight were used

For commodities that are perishable, subject to quick obsolescence, or required on short notice, the speed of air transportation becomes advantageous. Timing is important for products such as fashion apparel, novelty items, and electronics. When the market is seasonal or when demand fluctuates for any reason, air freight allows an immediate response without the penalty of costly fixed overhead—being out of stock or overstocked. A manufacturer that offers a wide selection of styles, sizes, colors, or accessories in a product line and whose market covers a wide geographic area is usually faced with the dilemma of carrying costly inventory and risks obsolescence or long delays in filling orders. Air freight can eliminate the cost of carrying inventory. Customers can select freely from the entire line of products and they can be assured of delivery from a central warehouse as quickly as from a local warehouse.

Air freight is a premium service. It projects an image of a premium product and company progressiveness. The retailer who advertises "flown in from . . ." and the salesperson who assures the client that "we'll fly it in from our main office" understand the value of such an image. The various modes of transport represent great differences in quality. Air freight can add a new competitive edge to the marketing effort. Superior service adds value to any product and generates a quality image for the shipper.

Air freight can stimulate growth in existing markets, and it allows firms to enter new markets without making a commitment to large, fixed investments in warehousing and inventories. Test markets supplied overnight by air allow adjustment to market response as readily as to the demands of a local market.

The risk of pilferage, breakage, or deterioration is minimized through the use of air transportation because of the lack of en-route handling and exposure of goods to long periods under minimum security. Insurance charges tend to be substantially lower for air freight than for surface freight, because there is less risk by air and because the transit time is shorter. Insurance represents a considerable expenditure for many companies.

Packaging for air freight is usually of minimal cost (apart from medical equipment and pharmaceuticals which usually require temperature-controlled air freight containers). Because air transport reduces the risk of jolts and shocks, cardboard cartons usually will suffice, whereas heavy wooden crates may be required for surface transportation. Ground handling is done on a more individual basis than is the case for most other modes of transportation. The risk of exposure to the elements is slight, and for commodities for which containerization is used, there may be no need to package at all.

The total costs associated with carrying inventory are high; it includes the cost of capital tied up in warehouse facilities and in stock, insurance, and taxes. In addition, stocked items may become obsolete, and the cost of labor and multiple handlings is a major consideration. With each handling, loss and damage is a factor. Air freight can often bring about drastic reductions in the cost of carrying inventory. Businesses that use regional warehousing supplied by surface transportation can reduce safety stocks and perhaps eliminate some warehouses. Even when air freight costs more than surface freight, the trade-off in reduced costs has made it profitable for many businesses to substitute overnight distribution by air from a central warehouse.

TYPES OF AIR FREIGHT RATES

General Commodity Rate

The air freight rate structure is similar to the passenger fare structure in that there is a normal or basic price applicable to all commodities in all markets. This is called the **general commodity rate**. General commodity shipments are rated by weight. Dimensional weight is used if the shipment is of very low density; this will be discussed shortly. As the weight of a shipment increases, the per-pound rate decreases, as Figure 13.5 illustrates. There is generally a minimum charge, depending on the city-pairs between which the shipment takes place.

Dimensional weight is computed by finding the cubic measurement of a shipment (length × width × height) and charging the rate for one pound for each 194 cubic inches. There are exceptions. For example, cut flowers and nursery stock being transported to domestic cities take a charge of

FIGURE 13.5 General Commodity Rates Vary by Weight of the Shipment. The Greater the Weight, the Lower the Rate (hypothetical example)

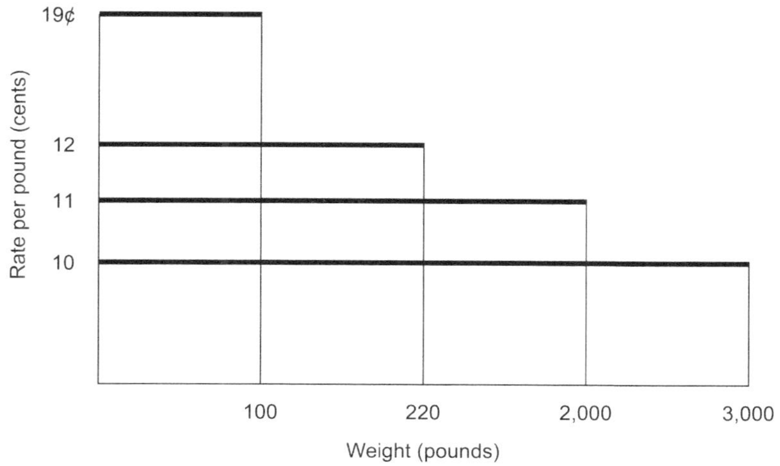

1 pound for each 250 cubic inches. In this way, if a cargo compartment were filled with, say, 20 pounds of Styrofoam cups, the charge would be based on a weight that represented a minimum density in relation to the space occupied.

Specific Commodity Rate

Specific commodity rates are established for unusually high-volume shipping of certain products between certain cities, such as fish from Anchorage, Alaska, to certain points in the continental United States; athletic goods, or musical instruments from Denver to San Francisco; and flowers, decorative greens, furs, fruits, and vegetables between Seattle–Tacoma and Minneapolis–St. Paul. In most cases, the specific commodity rate is lower than the general commodity rate to reflect the benefit to the carrier of regular high-volume shipments.

Exception Rate

Exception rates are higher than the usual air freight rates and apply to certain types of shipments that require special handling. For example, live animals and uncrated furniture take exception rates. A dog travels at 110 percent of the applicable general commodity rate on interstate routes within the continental United States. In some cases, an exception rate does not apply on certain routes.

Joint Rate

For domestic shipments transported on two or more airlines between origin and destination, a published rate, called a **joint rate**, often applies. The joint rate is usually the same as the rate for direct service. Where a joint rate is published, the shipper has the advantage of the availability of a number of different routings at the same rate. This is especially advantageous if direct service is limited.

Priority Reserved Air Freight

Priority reserved air freight is designed to serve shippers of heavy or bulky freight who need the advantage of reserved space on a specific flight. For example, if an oil-drilling company has stopped production because it needs some drill bits, space can be reserved on the next flight. Knowing exactly when the drill bits will arrive, the drilling company can plan accordingly. Because special handling is required for this type of service, the rate is higher than the normal general commodity and specific commodity rates.

Speed Package Service

Speed package service is a small-package fast-delivery service, airport to airport, with certain carriers on their own systems. Packages are accepted at the airport passenger terminal, at the passenger baggage check-in position, or at the air freight office. They are delivered to the baggage claim area at the destination. Speed package service is handled like passenger baggage, but because there is no accompanying passenger, the sender must make arrangements for someone to pick up the package on arrival.

Speed package service is designed for situations in which even a few hours are important. For example, critically needed small machinery parts often are shipped by this method. There is generally a flat rate based on the distance between city-pairs for any speed package service shipment.

Container Rate

Container rates are low rates charged by the carriers to shippers using containers to ship air cargo. There are many types of containers designed for air freight, suitable for shipping quantities from 400 pounds to 5 tons. Some types are owned by the airline and made available to the shipper on request. Other types are purchased by shippers for regular use or rented from various sources (see Figures 13.6 and 13.7). There are many advantages to containerizing air freight shipments:

1 Transportation charges are lower when a shipper has a large enough shipment to fill, or nearly fill the container used. This is true even when the airline supplies the container
2 Packaging costs can be reduced because the container provides protection against handling mishaps
3 Shippers can seal containers to prevent pilferage
4 Shipments arrive as one complete unit; there are no delayed or missing parts
5 Counting and checking the pieces of the shipment at the destination is simplified
6 Transportation costs for high-density freight shipments in containers often are lower than for surface transportation

Shippers can use carrier-owned containers, for which they are generally charged a flat fee that includes both the use of the container and the transportation of its contents. Sometimes, the weight of the contents allowed at the flat fee is a specified maximum. An excess pound rate is applied to the weight that exceeds the amount allowed at the flat rate. The weight of the container is not considered in these calculations. In many cases, there are different rates for day and night. Airlines can also provide one or more containers for the shipper that has many items going to the same city and charge the shipper less for the total shipment while reducing packaging costs and providing the benefits of decreased handling and protection from the weather. Carriers have specially built containers for heavy items, such as machinery parts.

Shippers often purchase their own containers or else rent them. These containers also qualify for special rates that are lower than the general commodity rate. Most shipper-owned containers are small enough to be moved through factory assembly lines. Thus, goods can be loaded and the container sealed at the plant. An airline normally will charge a container rate to a shipper that can stack its boxes on a pallet and secure them with a cargo net, provided that the overall dimensions do not exceed the dimensions for the type of container on which the rate is based.

FIGURE 13.6 Containers Provided by Airlines

TYPE: A1 Dom. /SAB-UAB Intl.
Int. Capacity: 393 Cu. Ft.
Ext. Dimensions: 88x125x87 In.
Max. Gross Weight: 13,300 Lbs.
Cube Displacement: 425 Cu. Ft.

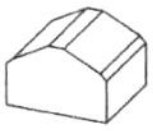

TYPE: A2,A3 Dom. /AAA-SAA Intl.
Int. Capacity: 440 Cu. Ft.
Ext. Dimensions: 88x125x87 In.
Max. Gross Weight: 12,500 Lbs.
Cube Displacement: 475 Cu. Ft.

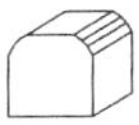

TYPE: FTC Dom. /=
Int. Capacity: 151 Cu. Ft.
Ext. Dimensions: 81x60.4x62.75 In.
Max. Gross Weight: 4,500 Lbs.
Cube Displacement: 174.5 Cu. Ft.

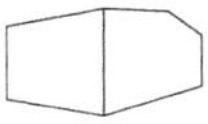

TYPE: LD2 Dom. /APA Intl.
Int. Capacity: 120 Cu. Ft.
Ext. Dimensions: 47x60.4x64 In.
Max. Gross Weight: 2,700 Lbs.
Cube Displacement: 134 Cu. Ft.

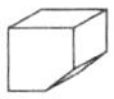

TYPE: LD3 Dom. /AVE-AKE Intl.
Int. Capacity: 150 Cu. Ft.
Ext. Dimensions: 79x60.4x64 In.
Max. Gross Weight: 3,500 Lbs.
Cube Displacement: 166 Cu. Ft.

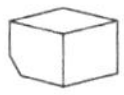

TYPE: LD4 Dom. / DLP-DLF Intl.
Int. Capacity: 193 Cu. Ft.
Ext. Dimensions: 96x60.4x64 In.
Max. Gross Weight: 5,400 Lbs.
Cube Displacement: 215 Cu. Ft.

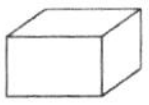

TYPE: LD5, LD11 Dom. /AWB-AWD Intl.
Int. Capacity: 265 Cu. Ft.
Ext. Dimensions: 125x60x64 In.
Max. Gross Weight: 7,000 Lbs.
Cube Displacement: 265 Cu. Ft.

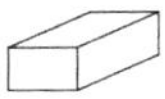

TYPE: LD6 Dom. /AWC-AWF Intl.
Int. Capacity: 316 Cu. Ft.
Ext. Dimensions: 25x60.4x64 In.
Max. Gross Weight: 5,680 Lbs.
Cube Displacement: 339 Cu. Ft.

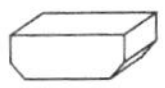

TYPE: LD7,LD9 Dom. /AAP-AAR Intl.
Int. Capacity: 355 Cu. Ft.
Ext. Dimensions: 125x88x64 In.
Max. Gross Weight: 13,300 Lbs.
Cube Displacement: 401 Cu. Ft.

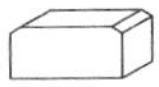

TYPE: LD8 Dom. /ALE Intl.
Int. Capacity: 253 Cu. Ft.
Ext. Dimensions: 196x60.4x60 In.
Max. Gross Weight: 5,400 Lbs.
Cube Displacement: 280 Cu. Ft.

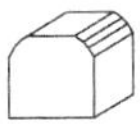

TYPE: LD10 Dom. /AWR-AWS Intl.
Int. Capacity: 246 Cu. Ft.
Ext. Dimensions: 125x60.4x64 In.
Max. Gross Weight: 5,680 Lbs.
Cube Displacement: 257 Cu. Ft.

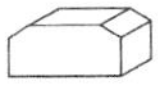

TYPE: LDW Dom. /=
Int. Capacity: 70 Cu. Ft.
Ext. Dimensions: 98x42.2x41.6 In.
Max. Gross Weight: 1,700 Lbs.
Cube Displacement: 76 Cu. Ft.

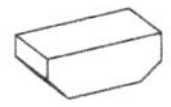

TYPE: M1 Dom. /ARA Intl.
Int. Capacity: 572 Cu. Ft.
Ext. Dimensions: 125x96x96 In.
Max. Gross Weight: 15,000 Lbs.
Cube Displacement: 666 Cu. Ft.

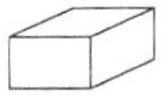

TYPE: M2 Dom. /ASE-ASG Intl.
Int. Capacity: 1,077 Cu. Ft.
Ext. Dimensions: 240x96x96 In.
Max. Gross Weight: 25,000 Lbs.
Cube Displacement: 1,286 Cu. Ft.

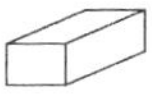

Note: These containers are owned by the airlines and are certified as an integral part of the aircraft. These units are available from the carrier for shipper use. The specifications may vary slightly by owner; this information is provided as a guide only

Source: Air Transport Association of America, *Air Cargo from A to Z* (Washington, DC: Air Transport Association, 1988)

FIGURE 13.7 Containers Offered by Shippers

TYPE: B Dom. /Intl. =
Int. Capacity: Varies (Insert for A)
Ext. Dimensions: 84x58x76.45 In.
Max. Gross Weight: 5,000 Lbs.
Cube Displacement: 197.7 Cu. Ft.

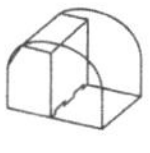

TYPE: EH Dom. /=
Int. Capacity: Varies
Ext. Dimensions: 35.4x21x21 In.
Max. Gross Weight: 250 Lbs.
Cube Displacement: 9.03 Cu. Ft.

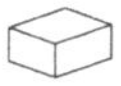

TYPE: B2 Dom. /=
Int. Capacity: Varies
Ext. Dimensions: 42x58x76.45 In.
Max. Gross Weight: 2,500 Lbs.
Cube Displacement: 98.85 Cu. Ft.

TYPE: LD-N Dom. /=
Int. Capacity: Varies (LD-3 insert)
Ext. Dimensions: 56x55x57 In.
Max. Gross Weight: 3,160 Lbs.
Cube Displacement: 1,016 Cu. Ft.

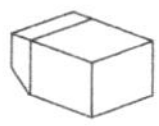

TYPE: D Dom. /=
Int. Capacity: Varies
Ext. Dimensions: 58x42x45 In.
Max. Gross Weight: 2,000 Lbs.
Cube Displacement: 63.44 Cu. Ft.

TYPE: Q Dom. /=
Int. Capacity: Varies
Ext. Dimensions: 39.5x27.5x21 In.
Max. Gross Weight: 400 Lbs.
Cube Displacement: 12 Cu. Ft.

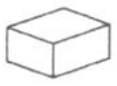

TYPE: E Dom. /=
Int. Capacity: Varies
Ext. Dimensions: 42x29x25.5 In.
Max. Gross Weight: 500 Lbs.
Cube Displacement: 17.97 Cu. Ft.

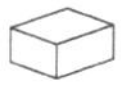

These containers are shipper owned and are available from many commercial sources and from the airlines. Most carriers offer container incentive rates when used. Specifications may vary slightly; this information is provided as a guide only

Source: Air Transport Association of America, *Air Cargo from A to Z* (Washington, DC: Air Transport Association, 1988)

FIGURE 13.8 Assembly Service Charge by Total Shipment Weight Over a 24-Hour Period (hypothetical case)

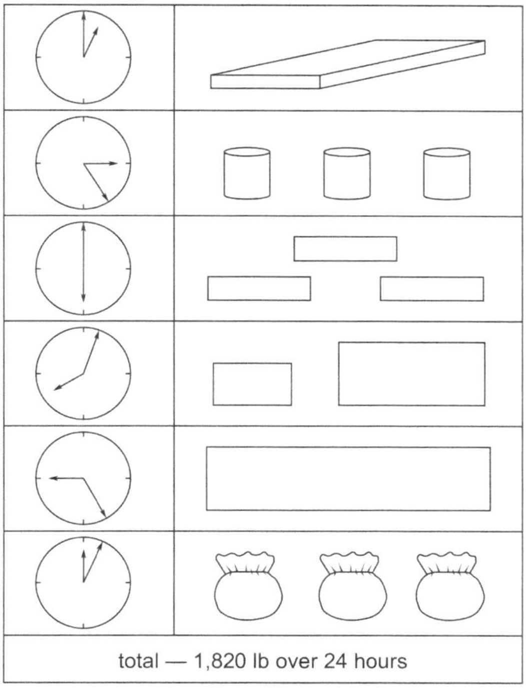

SPECIAL AIR FREIGHT SERVICES

Assembly Service

Airlines will consolidate packages from a shipper, or group of shippers, and base the transportation charge on the total weight of all the pieces, which allows a price break on heavy shipments. When numerous shipments are sent to the same address, the use of assembly service can result in real savings to the shipper. The assembly time can begin at 12:01 A.M. and end the following day at 12:00 A.M. (midnight). During the 24-hour period, a shipper that asks for assembly service can dispatch any number of packages to the carrier's air freight office and the airline will assemble the parts until the shipment is complete or the assembly time has expired (see Figure 13.8).

Distribution Service

Another service provided by airlines that fly air cargo is accepting one shipment from a shipper and, at the destination, separating it into its parts and distributing them to different customers. The advantages are the same as those for assembly service in that a shipper with many customers in the same city can take advantage of the rate break for heavy shipments. However, carriers generally do not provide assembly and distribution services on the same shipment. A variation of this service is for the carrier to deliver a shipment to the main post office at the destination city, where the shipment is sorted by zip code. Rather than ship thousands of items from the home office, large retailers and wholesalers who mail catalogs, magazines, and so forth frequently use this service because of the substantial savings involved.

Other Specialized Services

Airlines provide a number of other specialized air freight services, including armed guards for shipments of highly valuable goods, such as furs, precious gems, watches, jewelry, negotiable securities, bills of exchange, bonds, and currency. Generally, such items are not accepted by the carrier until three hours before the scheduled departure time of the flight on which they are to be transported, nor can they be held for more than three hours after arrival at the destination. Because many of these items are small, carriers generally require that a minimum size container be used. For example, coins must be shipped in a 1,500-cubic-inch container.

Shipments of human remains are arranged for by a mortuary and are consigned to another mortuary at the destination city. The shipping mortuary must provide a death certificate and burial certificate to accompany the shipment.

Commodities called restricted articles range from those that are accepted without limitation but that must have an identifying label (magnetized materials, for example) to such things as poison gas, which cannot be made safe enough for commercial air transportation under any circumstances. Most restricted articles are materials that can be shipped safely when packaged according to DOT specifications for hazardous materials and that are limited in terms of allowable quantities per container and per aircraft. All restricted-article shipments must be conspicuously labeled by the shipper, using authorized labels, so that all airlines participating in the routing can observe special loading arrangements and advise flight crews of any potentially hazardous materials on board. Accurate labeling is also essential so that the carrier can deal appropriately with leakage or spillage of materials that are hazardous to humans and animals, to the aircraft structure, or in combination with other materials being shipped in the same cargo compartment. Most restricted-article shipments require a shipper's certificate.

Many products have various degrees of hazard, depending on their components. Aerosol products, for example, may be classified as an inflammable gas or as poison or may have no restrictions, depending on both the contents and the propelling agent used. Paint is another product classified in various ways, depending on its composition.

Some airlines accept certain restricted articles not accepted by other airlines. Some restricted articles may be carried on all-cargo aircraft but not on the passenger-carrying aircraft of any carrier. And, again, some highly dangerous materials cannot be made safe enough to carry on commercial air carriers under any circumstances.

FACTORS AFFECTING AIR FREIGHT RATES

Air cargo freight rates tend to be 10–15 times those for sea transport. Therefore, only higher value to weight items typically move by air. Products need a value to weight ratio of greater than $7.30 per pound before it becomes cost-effective to consider air movement.

Passengers (except for business travelers) tend to be sensitive to changes in price. However, due to the time-sensitive nature of most air cargo, demand is more inelastic. That is a small change in price will not cause many shippers to look elsewhere for transport. However, if the price change is too great, then there may be a modal shift to another mode of transportation, normally truck or sea shipment.

Costs of the Service

A basic consideration in rate making is that the rates should cover the costs of service and yield a reasonable profit. In air transportation, where air freight is carried in the cargo compartments of passenger aircraft as well as in all-cargo aircraft, the costs that must be covered generally are the same as those of an all-cargo aircraft operation. This approach is usually followed for two reasons: (1) the allocation of costs in a combination aircraft is difficult, and (2) the maximum development of an air cargo industry requires the operation of all-cargo aircraft whose costs must be met. As was pointed out earlier in the chapter, freight rates have considerably less profit potential than passenger fares because the advantages of air over surface modes of transportation are less apparent.

Volume of Traffic

Numerous pricing considerations affect rates. One of these is the volume of new traffic a carrier can achieve at any particular rate. Volume is significant because traffic potential is a key factor in determining the maximum net revenue that can be derived from any commodity. Thus, the rate structure contains reduced rates for larger shipments.

Directionality

Whereas most passenger travel is round-trip, freight traffic is all one-way. Historically, domestic air freight has tended to move in larger volumes in a westbound direction than eastbound, and in larger southbound than northbound volumes within the eastern United States. Consequently, rates have been set at lower levels in the off-direction as a means of filling up space to equalize the flow of traffic and put aircraft to more efficient use. Internationally, freight traffic is larger outbound from Asia towards the U.S. and Europe so these rates are higher.

Characteristics of the Traffic

Air carriers also consider the transportation characteristics of the commodity as an important element in the rate-making process. The major transportation characteristics are the density of the commodity (the relationship of weight to measurement), the size (weight or volume) per average piece, and the average weight of the shipment (whether 10, 20, 40, 100, 1,000, or 10,000 pounds makes up one shipment at one time).

In cargo aircraft, utilization of available space and available lifting capacity must be optimized. The density of the load must be related to the capability of the aircraft in determining freight rates. A cargo aircraft fully loaded with a particular commodity should produce sufficient revenue to cover the full cost of operation and earn a profit. For example, suppose that an all-cargo aircraft has a practical volume capacity of about 7,700 cubic feet and a lifting capability of almost 92,000 pounds. The optimum density for traffic is therefore:

$$\frac{92{,}000}{7{,}700} = \text{About 12 lb per cubic foot.}$$

When individual shipments are loaded on an aircraft, unavoidable losses in the utilization of space occur due to the irregular shapes of the shipments. These are called stacking losses. To achieve the optimum density, the average density of shipments tendered to our example aircraft must be greater than 12 pounds per cubic foot to compensate for stacking losses. If the loaded density of the commodity is 12 pounds or more, the revenue-producing load will be 92,000 pounds in this aircraft. Basically, the total cost of the operation plus the profit margin, divided by the pounds of the commodity on board, will give the approximate air freight rate for that commodity.

The character of the commodity also includes whether it is dangerous, hazardous, perishable, or susceptible to damage or pilferage; what packing and packaging is needed; whether it is easily loaded and stowed aboard aircraft; and whether it will readily ensure safe transportation with ordinary care in handling. When unitized or containerized shipments are involved, the importance of some of these rate-making factors may be reduced.

Value of the Service

Value of service is frequently an important factor in establishing a specific commodity rate. In theory, a specific commodity rate should allow the commodity to move in a volume that yields the maximum revenue in excess of the added costs of carrying the commodity. Taking revenue dilution into consideration, the principal factors that reflect value of service include the speed and reliability of air freight service, the value of the commodity, and the profit margin of the consignor or consignee. The consignor, usually the shipper, is the party that designates the person to whom goods are to be sent. The consignee is the person named as the receiver of a shipment—one to whom a shipment is consigned.

Market demands, possible obsolescence of stock, cost of inventory, the necessary lead time in placing orders for surface shipments, and the possibility of reduction of warehouse expenses are all factors that may influence the shipper's acceptance of a rate level for an air shipment.

Competition

Competition is, of course, also a major factor in determining air freight rates. Where capacity exceeds demand, there is considerable pressure to lower rates. Rate reduction can be introduced by the least successful competitor to improve its market share or possibly by the principal carrier to generate new traffic.

As air freight rates increase, a modal shift to surface transportation typically occurs. Competition from other modes of transportation, especially trucks and railroads, may help determine the rate that can be charged on any commodity. The competitive impact of shipping via other routes, shipping via non-scheduled air carriage, or using shipper-owned vehicles also may be pertinent.

SECURITY

Following the attack on the U.S. on September 11, 2001, the Aviation and Transportation Security Act was signed into law and established the Transportation Security Administration (TSA). The TSA falls under the Department of Homeland Security and is responsible for aviation security within the U.S. The TSA not only screens passengers entering the airside (secure side) of an airport, but they also deal with a threat to air transportation security in general, including cargo security.

Due to air cargo's time-sensitive nature, it is key that an efficient and speedy cargo screening system is in place. In the U.S., cargo screening has been delegated to the air carrier or an approved agent, so the airport has no role in the screening of cargo. As both the airline and the approved agent are part of the air cargo supply chain, they both have an incentive to ensure a safe and speedy clearance of cargo moving through the system.

In addition to the U.S. and foreign authority's security rules, both IATA and ICAO have issued security best practices for air carriers.

Owing to the high-value cargo typically moved by aircraft, there is a risk of pilferage during movement, however, most of the pilferage is relegated to the warehouse or while in transit to or from the airport.

THE FUTURE

The COVID-19 pandemic accelerated growth in the express and e-commerce market. While the passenger market was severely disrupted during the pandemic, the express market expanded and this expansion is expected to continue in conjunction with the e-commerce market. In addition, as the globalization of the supply chain continues to expand so will the demand for air cargo.

The globalization of the world economy—the production of parts and the assembly of products half a world away from where they will be placed in service—will also provide a major stimulus to air freight. Rather than rely on ocean transportation, which can take as much as two or three weeks, shippers can transport the goods by air within a couple of days. For products with a short shelf life—be they magazines or fashion goods or fresh fish—air freight is the only real choice shippers have, and they are realizing it more and more.

Both Airbus and Boeing are projecting that the demand for air cargo will grow at about 4 percent over the next 20 years. This means that the air cargo fleet will need to expand by 60 percent over the next two decades. Express carriers are expected to have an even higher growth rate.

As with passenger aircraft, sustainability will become a more important issue in future years. The most pressing issue is the need to switch from carbon emitting fuel engines to a more sustainable fuel option. However, other strides can be made in ground handling operations also to reduce the environmental impact of the industry.

As demand for air cargo increases, there will be a need for specialized aircraft. Currently, there is a lack of cargo-specific aircraft throughout the global fleet. Most airplanes used to transport air cargo are converted passenger aircraft. In most cases, those aircraft are old, costly to operate, and at the end of their life span. As these aircraft retire, aircraft manufacturers are realizing the need to produce aircraft that are geared toward air cargo transport. In addition, with the cessation of production of the Boeing 747, in the future there will be demand for a nose or tail loading aircraft to take over the mission of transportation of large outsized cargo. Currently, in addition to the 747, only the AN-124 has this capability—however, the AN-124 is also no longer being produced.

KEY TERMS

air express
air freight
air freight forwarder
air mail
all-cargo airline
belly cargo
belly-only carrier
combination carrier
container rate
exception rate
freight-ton kilometers/miles
general commodity rate
integrated carrier
joint rate
priority reserved air freight
revenue ton-miles/kilometres
specific commodity rate
speed package service

REVIEW QUESTIONS

1 What is the difference between air express, air freight, and air mail service? Why was the early air mail service so important in establishing the U.S. airline system?
2 Describe the flow of air cargo from the shipper to the consignee as it travels through the freight forwarder system.
3 Distinguish between integrated carriers, combination carriers, belly carriers, and all-cargo airlines, and give examples of each.
4 Describe the types of commodities shipped by air and what typical characteristics these commodities have in common.
5 List and briefly describe the six factors affecting air freight rates.

CHAPTER 14

Principles of Airline Scheduling

CHAPTER CHECKLIST • YOU SHOULD BE ABLE TO:

- Describe the major internal and external factors that affect the scheduling process
- Define and explain *maintenance efficiency goals*, *flight-operations factors in schedule planning*, and *facility constraints*
- Understand the role of the scheduling department in developing and coordinating the schedule planning process
- Describe such unique problems facing schedulers as traffic flow, sensitivity to schedule salability, operational difficulties of adjusting schedules, and the financial leverage of load factors
- Explain the four basic schedule types
- Discuss the advantages and disadvantages of hub-and-spoke scheduling and point-to-point scheduling
- Explain the impact COVID-19 has had on the airline scheduling process

INTRODUCTION

"Anyone without the mind of a computer, the patience of Job, or the ability to compromise need not apply." This sign should be on the door of

DOI: 10.4324/9780429346156-17

every airline's scheduling department. Schedules represent one of the primary products of an airline and certainly the leading factor in a passenger's choice of a particular carrier. Scheduling may also be one of the most difficult jobs in any airline. Scheduling is one of the most vital functions in the business—as important as forecasting, pricing, fleet planning, or financing. As we shall see, a schedule can make or break an airline as the process is full of complexities encompassing route networks, aircraft types, air traffic control, airport operations, personnel, payment structures, and environmental regulations as examples. Additionally, there are numerous charges impacting the balance sheet at the end of the day including, but not limited to, runway (landing fee), passengers (per on-board person), security (personnel and equipment), airport infrastructure (terminals, check-in desks, baggage equipment, air bridges), parking (aircraft), terminal navigation (airport-controlled airspace), en-route navigation (controlled airspace), environmental (noise and emissions), and government taxes (per passenger).

THE MISSION OF SCHEDULING

What is the mission of scheduling? It is as broad as the mission of the airline itself. An airline has the responsibility to provide adequate service to the cities it serves; an airline must also, of course, operate efficiently and economically. Therefore, in its scheduling practices, airline management must continually search for the balance between adequate service and economic strength for the company. Airline **scheduling** can be defined as the art of designing systemwide flight patterns that provide optimum public service, in both quantity and quality, consistent with the financial health of the carrier.

The public service and economic aspects of scheduling must be balanced with other factors, including:

1 *Equipment Maintenance.* A separate maintenance-routing plan must be drawn up for each type of aircraft in the fleet. All routing plans must be coordinated to provide the best overall service. Maintenance of airplanes requires that certain stations be provided with facilities and personnel for periodic mechanical checks. Concentration of maintenance at only a few stations is desirable, and it is likewise desirable to utilize fully the facilities provided by planning an even flow of maintenance work.
2 *Crews.* Assuming that all pilots, flight engineers, and flight attendants have had adequate training on each type of airplane and over the routes to be flown, there are always considerations of utilization and working conditions. Certain crew routings must be followed to maintain efficient monthly utilization; crew routings that would require excessive flying without proper rest cannot be used.
3 *Facilities.* Gate space on airport ramps must be adequate. Terminal capacity, including ticket counters, baggage-handling areas, and waiting rooms, must be expanded to meet growing market requirements.

Access roadways to and from airports must be adequate. Airport capacity, including runways, taxiways, and navigational aids, establishes an upper limit on operations.

4 *Marketing Factors.* Marketing factors are numerous, including such characteristics as market size, trip length, time zones involved, and proximity of the airport to the market served.

5 *Other Factors.* Seasonal variations in wind patterns require differences in summer and winter flying times on certain routes (usually east–west); however, some airlines use constant year-round flying times on routes where variations in wind components are negligible (usually north–south routes). In addition, on many segments, variable times are used to allow, to some extent, for anticipated delays during periods of heavy air traffic.

External factors must be taken into consideration by the scheduling department. Air freight shippers and the U.S. Postal Service have schedule preferences. Airport authorities, seeking a smooth flow of traffic to optimize utilization of facilities, will discourage peaking; in recent years, certain large airports have assigned quotas (flight slots) to carriers during certain time periods. Local communities near an airport will voice strong opposition to flight departures before 7:00 A.M. and after 11:00 P.M. Hotel and motel operators generally prefer that all guests check in and check out between 11:00 A.M. and 1:00 P.M. Figure 14.1 is a conceptual framework for the scheduling process that shows all these elements.

Picture a city with a large metropolitan airport, another airport with short runways and a terminal handling only one flight at a time, and another airport bustling with multiple connections. Envision a maintenance base geared to accept aircraft at prescribed time intervals for various maintenance checks, from routine inspection to major overhaul.

As the picture begins to unfold, you see scheduling as a vital and complex function that cuts across every aspect of an airline operation. It is so vital, in fact, that scheduling is performed by top management collectively. There is a chief architect, to be sure—the **scheduling department**, headed by a vice-president or director, depending on the size or organizational makeup of the company. With the exception of some of the major carriers, which include scheduling as part of the corporate economic planning administration, most scheduling departments are under the marketing administration because of the overriding importance of service to the public. In developing a system flight pattern or *schedule plot*, as it is sometimes referred to, the scheduling department works closely with all other departments and with all field stations.

In addition to its own continuing review, the department continually receives suggestions and proposals from local-station personnel and the public. With knowledge of traffic volumes and patterns, numbers and types of aircraft on hand and to be delivered, maintenance requirements, operational factors, and scores of other considerations, the scheduling department, after weeks and often months of planning, develops a proposed system schedule. This is then submitted to all appropriate departments for study.

FIGURE 14.1 Conceptual Framework for the Schedule Development Process

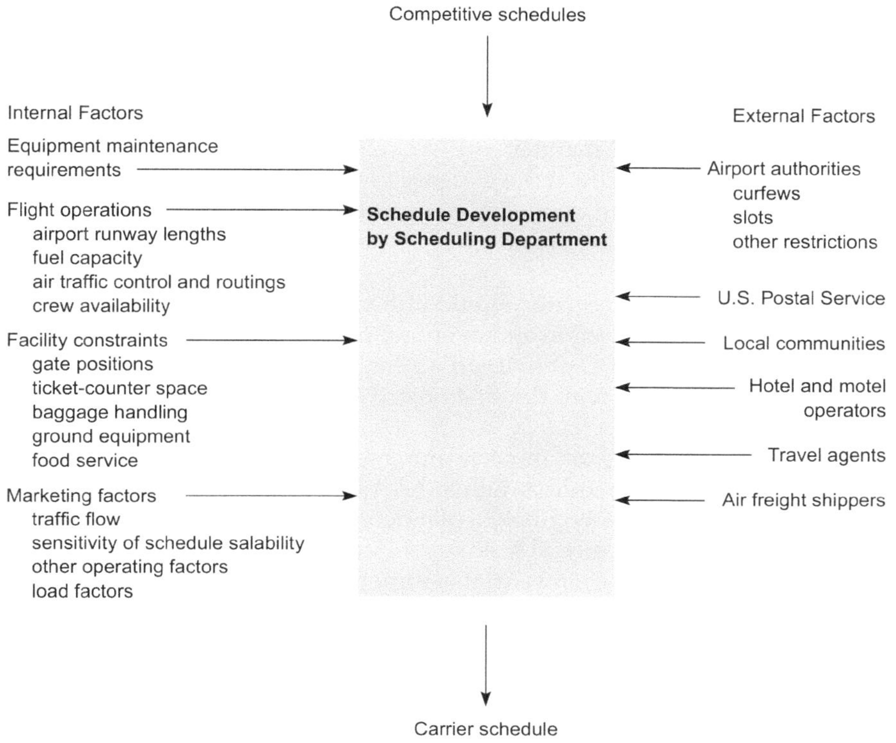

Many airlines use the **committee system**, in which officials from all operating departments meet to analyze the proposed schedule, make suggestions, and resolve conflicts between departments. Whether the committee system or some other method of interdepartmental coordination is employed, the result is the same: a schedule that meets the combined goals of public service, sales and competitive effectiveness, profitability, and operational dependability and efficiency.

EQUIPMENT MAINTENANCE

The primary purpose of the maintenance organization of an airline is, of course, to provide a safe, salable aircraft for every schedule. This would be simple if the carrier had an unlimited number of airplanes, unlimited facilities, and unlimited personnel—all located at every point on the system. But it does not, and so it must strive for a number of **maintenance efficiency goals**: (1) minimize aircraft out-of-service time, (2) use up time allowable on aircraft and parts between overhauls, (3) seek optimum utilization of personnel and even workload, and (4) maximize utilization of facilities. These goals do not affect safety, of course—safety can never be sacrificed to meet a schedule. You can see, however, the implications these goals have for the schedule planner. Let's examine them closely.

1 *Out-of-service Time.* Because the profitability of an aircraft depends to a large extent on its daily utilization or availability, the carrier must do everything it can to design a maintenance system that provides a high standard of maintenance yet minimizes out-of-service time. If this can be done only at the expense of safety and dependability considerations, the airline must either reduce planned aircraft utilization to allow adequate maintenance or improve the product until it meets the goals.
2 *Allowable Time.* The carrier should utilize the maximum time allowable in the various inspection and overhaul programs. This item represents a very large cost variable in an airline's operation. Again, however, this must be done with the first objective in mind—minimum out-of-service time.
3 *Personnel and Workload.* In performing any inspection, repair, or overhaul, the carrier requires either FAA-licensed personnel or highly trained specialists—engineers, planners, inspectors, and a host of others. Because the overhaul base payroll for a major air carrier runs into millions of dollars each year, it is important to keep costs down if the carrier is to achieve maximum utilization of its people. An airline also must maintain an even work flow, because these specialists and technicians require a high degree of training and experience and are not readily available in the open labor market.
4 *Use of Facilities.* The carrier must utilize facilities to the maximum extent possible, because of its substantial investment in buildings, tooling, and specialized equipment.

Let's examine a hypothetical maintenance system and some of the problems of maintenance scheduling. Table 14.1 lists the various inspection and overhaul periods used today for a large jet aircraft, including the time between inspections, the hours required to accomplish the work, the elapsed or out-of-service time required, and the work performed. Here, we have assumed a normal amount of nonroutine, unscheduled work. In order to provide maximum flexibility for aircraft routing and to keep the maintenance system as simple as possible, the maintenance department attempts to schedule all new or revised maintenance needs into these maintenance inspection periods. The only exceptions are the engines and other expensive components, such as the turbo-compressor or auxiliary power unit. In these cases, the time is monitored on each unit and the unit is overhauled when it reaches the specified time. Note that these numbers are never static, because maintenance continually revises the work to be accomplished and the work is periodically evaluated, based on service experience as well as the experience of other operators.

Figure 14.2 shows the maintenance capability of the various stations on a major carrier's system. A similar setup exists on every major airline.

Table 14.1 Maintenance System for a Jet Aircraft (hypothetical example)

Inspection	Time Between Inspections	Labor	Duration	Work Performed
En route service	Each stop	1 hour	1/2 hour	"Walk-around"—visual inspection to ensure no obvious problems, such as leaks, missing rivets, or cracks
Overnight	8 hours	Varies	Up to 8 hours	Ad hoc repairs—work varies
A-check	125 hours	60 hours	8 hours	Primary examination—fuselage exterior, power plant, and accessible subsystems inspected
B-check	750 hours	200 hours	Overnight	Intermediate inspection—panels, cowlings, oil filters, and airframe examined
C-check	3,000 hours	2,000–12,000 hours	5 days	Detailed inspection—engines and components repaired, flight controls calibrated, and major internal mechanisms tested
D-check	20,000 hours	15,000–35,000 hours	15–30 days	Major reconditioning—cabin interiors removed, flight controls examined, fuel system probed, and more

On this map, the blocks indicate the type of work or inspection that can be performed at the various stations. There are two items to consider: (1) any station accomplishing service or maintenance checks requires not only hangars and tooling but also millions of dollars in spare parts (for a major carrier), and (2) each station also requires highly skilled mechanical and technical personnel. As Figure 14.2 shows, there are eight stations capable of accomplishing B-checks and three stations capable of doing C-checks. In addition, the overhaul base is located at San Francisco.

To further illuminate the problems involved in maintenance routing, Figure 14.3 shows the planned routing pattern for a 737 on a major carrier's system, including the various points at which the necessary inspections can and will be conducted. Because the inspection periods allowed are maximum times, the aircraft router must have the airplane at an inspection station before its time expires, or the carrier must obtain a **special flight permit (SFP)** from the FAA to move the airplane to the correct station. As defined by the FAA, an SFP is also referred to as a **ferry permit** and may be issued to any U.S. registered aircraft that may not currently meet applicable Airworthiness Requirements but is capable of safe flight.

This pattern, which is ideal, shows the problem that exists if the airplane has a mechanical breakdown, for example, in Des Moines (DSM) or is affected by weather at that point. The router must then substitute another aircraft for the airplane in question. Moreover, a tied-up airplane is now off the track that was designed to allow the carrier to accomplish all required

FIGURE 14.2 Maintenance Facilities (hypothetical case)

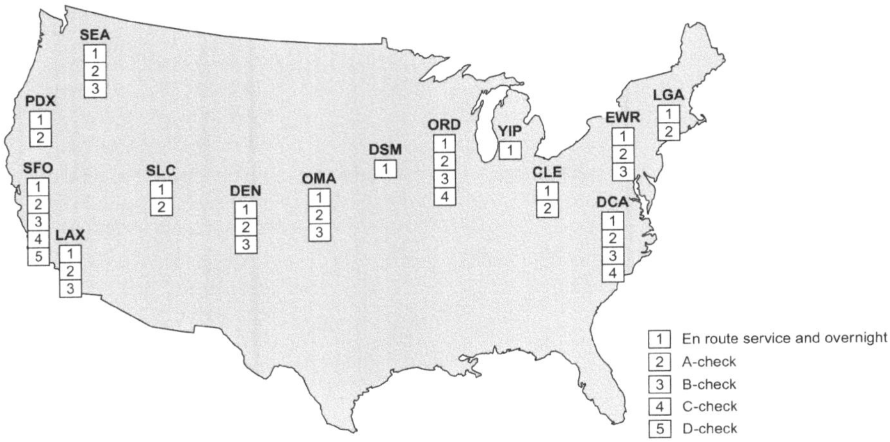

FIGURE 14.3 Boeing 737 Routing Pattern (hypothetical case)

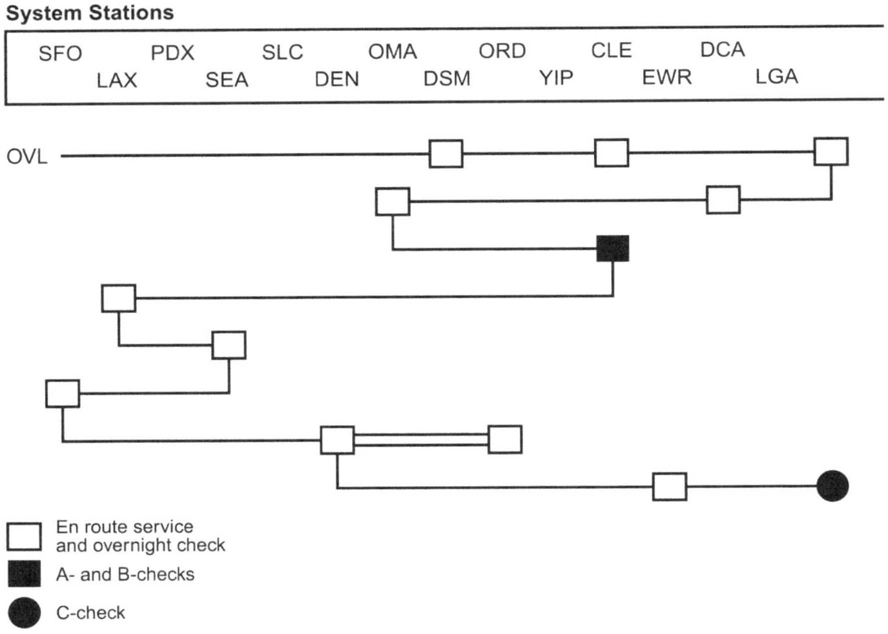

inspections and component replacements and to time engine changes with maximum utilization of the overhaul period.

Schedule planners must take into account the maintenance department's plans and systems for efficiency. Of course, this is a two-way street. When the maintenance organization makes certain changes in the way it does things, this, too, can affect the scheduling department. Therefore, the maintenance people and the scheduling planners in any airline maintain a close, day-to-day relationship.

FLIGHT OPERATIONS AND CREW SCHEDULING

Because airline schedules, once published, must be flown by the company's flight crews, the flight-operations department must ensure that flights are scheduled in a fashion that will permit them to be safely and efficiently operated. The following **operational factors** are important in schedule planning:

Airport runway lengths
Aircraft fuel capacity
Habitual adverse weather
Air traffic control and routings
Crew availability and time limits
Employee agreements
Marketing factors (market size, trip duration, time zones)

Obviously, airport runway lengths, aircraft fuel capacities, and so forth affect scheduling decisions. Other less obvious but equally important factors in drafting schedules include weather, aircraft routings, and flight crew scheduling.

In this sense, the term *weather* is used to describe the type of condition that occurs ordinarily at a specific locale during certain times of the day or seasons of the year. For example, in winter months weather may make it inadvisable to overnight an aircraft in a particular northern city where hangar facilities are not available. Although overnighting might facilitate the operation of a desirable late-evening arrival and early-morning departure, the need to remove snow and ice from the aircraft after a storm might make such an operation impractical. Certain areas of the country, such as the Gulf Coast, do not lend themselves to dependable on-time or safe operations because of the likelihood of fog from shortly after midnight until sometime before noon. Often, flights scheduled during this period must be delayed or canceled or, if operated, restricted in load because of the excess fuel reserves required for safety.

A second operational factor concerns air traffic control (ATC). ATC routings often dictate longer flight times between two points than normal. In addition, certain flight segments are subjected to route closures and resultant time-consuming and costly diversion by military actions.

One of the most important and complex factors affecting flight operations is that of crew assignment to specific flights. The working limitations that govern flight crews are found in both the Federal Aviation Regulations (FAR) and employment agreements. The FAR limits are as follows:

1 There is a daily limitation of 16 hours maximum flight duty time for pilots on a two-person crew, unless, prior to exceeding 16 hours, a rest period is provided of no less than ten hours. Therefore, an increase of only a few minutes to a schedule, or the addition of one extra station, might force a crew break and layover not otherwise necessary. Duty time includes planned flight time, taxi time, known delays, and debrief time. After push back, the pilot must return to the gate if extended ground delays would cause duty to exceed 16 hours at the estimated release time.
2 Flight crew members must have had at least eight hours of rest in any 24-hour period that includes a flight time.
3 Flight crews may not exceed a maximum of 40 flight hours during any seven consecutive days. Release from all duty for 24 hours must be granted to each flight crew member during any seven-consecutive-day period.

Employment contracts compound the difficulties. Most airline contracts provide that one hour of flight pay must be paid for every four hours a pilot spends away from the domicile. This time is frequently not flown; therefore, pilots are frequently paid for time not flown. These contracts also require that the airline bear the expense of training otherwise unneeded crews. And most airline agreements provide a maximum of 80 hours flight time during any month for their pilots.

An operations manager's dream is to be handed a schedule that permits all crews to operate flights on a direct turnaround basis with no layover problems or expense. This is manifestly not possible, but every attempt must be made in the interest of crew utilization and economy to minimize layovers. Average flight crew utilization for some of the major carriers with intricate route structures goes as low as 55 hours per crew member per month.

Seniority, labor's most valued asset, is management's biggest headache when it comes to training and assigning flight crews. The newer, faster planes generally are flown by the most senior crews, who earn the highest wages. Therefore, moving down through the ranks, the most junior captains and first and second officers fly the smaller, slower planes.

Were all crews based at a single location, the job of scheduling would be much easier. This is not, however, physically or economically practical, and so the majority of airlines assign crews to fly from one of several individual crew bases. A typical major carrier may base crews at only seven of the 40 cities serviced. Which flights are to be flown by crews from which bases is determined by the company, but many factors influence such decisions. The equipment qualifications of the crews already assigned to each base, the crew expenses incurred if the flight is flown from that base, the seniority of the crews compared with those at other bases on the flight route, the likelihood of crews requesting reassignment if trips are not to their liking—all of these factors enter into a decision. An airline has to take a good hard look before implementing a schedule that will require additional crews to be trained when sufficient numbers already exist to meet the maximum utilization of the available equipment.

GROUND OPERATIONS AND FACILITY LIMITATIONS

Ground service can be arranged in any conceivable schedule pattern, provided that there is no limitation on the gate positions, ground equipment, passenger service facilities, and personnel. But, of course, there are limitations. First, it is physically impossible to obtain adequate facilities in many instances within a reasonable period of time. For example, additional gate positions at Fort Lauderdale/Hollywood International Airport are virtually impossible to obtain. Second, there is the matter of cost. The schedule planner must do the utmost to avoid excessive flight congestion, in view of such cost items as these:

$400,000–$500,000 for ground support equipment at an intermediate station, and approximately double this figure for two jet flights at the same time

$2 million for construction of each added gate position, including the loading bridge, at a typical major airport

The objective of ground service, then, becomes to accommodate as many flights as possible and as efficiently as possible, consistent with physical limitations and prudent utilization of personnel and equipment. The schedule planner must consider all of the following at every station for every proposed schedule:

1. Are there enough gate positions for the number of planes on the ground simultaneously, including a cushion for early arrivals or delayed departures?
2. Is there adequate ticket-counter space to handle the passengers expeditiously?
3. Is sufficient time provided for on-line or interline transfer of passengers, baggage, mail, and cargo?
4. Can the planned flights be handled efficiently by the present level of ticket-counter, ramp, and food service personnel? If not, will additional revenue from the new flights or the new connection be sufficient to more than offset the cost of additional personnel?
5. Will the proposed schedules introduce a second or a third personnel shift? Conversely, will a minor flight adjustment permit the reduction of one shift?
6. Is there ground equipment of the right type: aircraft starter units, baggage vehicles, cargo conveyors, forklifts, tow tractors? If not, is there sufficient lead time to purchase them, and can they be economically justified? Should the carrier contract these services from another carrier because of the small number of flights into a particular station?
7. Does the proposed schedule overtax food service facilities?

These and many other questions must be answered for every station on the system for every schedule change. Any corrective action—and there is always a need for flight adjustments to meet ground service requirements—must be rechecked to determine its effect on the delicate balance worked out to accommodate sales, maintenance and operational needs, and to make sure that corrective adjustments at one station are not creating complications at another.

Normally, the scheduling department measures the physical and personnel requirements with a visual layout of the schedules at each station. All flights are plotted on a **station plotting chart** that documents sequence and schedule time of operation using certain standards and codes (see Figure 14.4). It shows precisely the amount of time an aircraft requires to maneuver into a gate position, the scheduled arrival time, the period of time it is at the gate, its scheduled departure time, and the length of time needed to clear the gate. The chart also shows whether it is an originating flight, a through trip, a terminating flight, or a turnaround. Figure 14.4, a section taken from a schedule pattern, illustrates peak and valley periods at the hypothetical All-American Airport (AAA). It illustrates clearly one of scheduling's biggest headaches—peaking, or multiple operation. Such peaks must be reduced wherever possible to achieve the goal of optimal utilization of personnel and equipment without sacrificing service or revenue.

After posting proposed flight times on this chart, the scheduling department must first determine that it has not exceeded the gate capability. Therefore, the first adjustments are those necessary to bring schedule times into line with available physical facilities. At AAA, for example, the carrier has four gate positions. At around 8:00 A.M., they are all full. Obviously, any additional flight would have to be scheduled either before or after this peak period. On the other hand, if the additional flight is more important than the existing flights, then the carrier must consider moving an existing flight earlier or later.

Scheduling is sometimes restricted by ticket-counter space. For example, if a carrier had only four ticketing positions at a major location and one ticket agent could check in about 20 passengers an hour, the four ticket

FIGURE 14.4 Station Plotting for the Hypothetical All-American Airport (AAA)

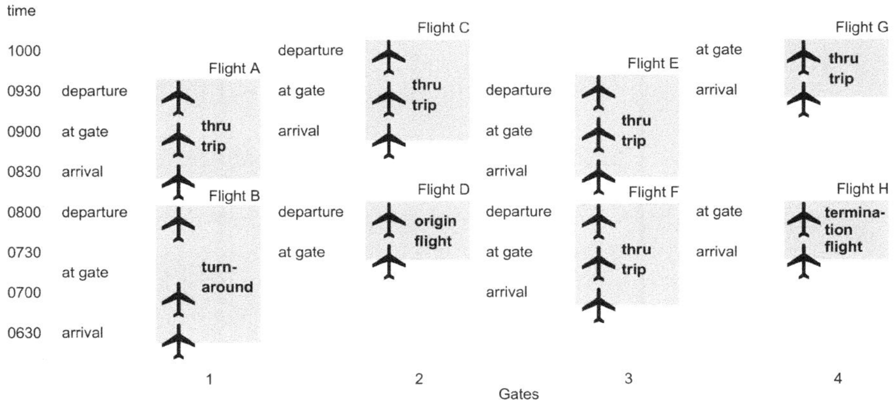

positions could handle one 757 flight. But if the carrier wanted to schedule three jet departures within a 45-minute period, it would have several alternatives. The carrier could, of course, go ahead and schedule these three flights, at considerable inconvenience to the passengers—forcing them to stand in line much too long—as well as at risk of jeopardizing on-time departures. The preferred solution would be not to schedule the two added trips until the carrier had expanded its ticket-counter facilities.

Station staffing is determined by application of time-study standards and formulas. These have been developed and are applied much the same as any manufacturer's production line time and workload standards. Schedulers use separate standards and formulas for ticket counters, ramp and load control, ramp cargo handling, food service, and freight facilities.

Like personnel staffing, flight peaking presents a major problem for the efficient utilization of ground equipment. Ground equipment costs to handle peak traffic can run into the millions of dollars at any one location. Understandably, carriers are anxious to reduce these requirements if they can do so without affecting other costs or revenues or service. Whenever a carrier changes schedules or adds flights, adequacy of ground equipment must be checked closely, not only because of expense but also from the standpoint of lead time.

In conclusion, the schedule planner contends with a variety of challenges in the ground operations area, many of them conflicting. Scheduling is literally hemmed in by space limitations. Yet planners must find gate positions for the essential flight complexes. They must keep personnel costs at a minimum but at the same time staff for flight connection opportunities to maximize service to the public. And they must avoid new capital outlays for expensive ground equipment yet do everything possible to enable flight peaking at times when passenger demand is greatest.

Every situation has to be studied separately at each of the carrier's stations, with every item of added cost weighed against the estimated added revenue. No decision can be made without carefully assessing its consequences.

SCHEDULE PLANNING AND COORDINATION

Thus far, we have discussed the particular problems faced by maintenance, flight operations, and ground operations. Each offers a multitude of requirements for the schedule planner to take into consideration. The responsibility for schedule development is the province of the scheduling department, which is generally within the marketing administration and which oversees the entire system. This department must pull together all of the factors discussed so far, plus many more. Just how a carrier goes about this task is the focus of this section.

Nothing is more basic to an airline than the schedule pattern it operates. All productive resources—planes, trained personnel, and ground facilities—have the one essential function of operating the schedule safely and dependably. All selling resources—the carrier's ticket offices, reservations offices, sales representatives, marketers—have the one essential function of getting passengers and shippers to use the schedule. Let's take a look at some of the problems and complexities of developing a sound overall schedule pattern in these hectic postderegulation times.

At the outset, let us recognize the sheer impossibility of developing a schedule pattern that will simultaneously satisfy all desirable objectives. Many of these objectives are inherently in conflict. For example, a carrier must provide enough time on the ground for maintenance and servicing operations while at the same time keeping aircraft in the air as much as possible for economical utilization. It must build up complexes of connecting flights at major gateways while at the same time avoiding excessive peaking of station activity. It must maintain schedule stability for the convenience of passengers and the optimal utilization of employees while at the same time displaying the flexibility needed to adjust rapidly to new competitive threats or other developments. It must recognize that public service obligations will sometimes work against strictly economic considerations while at the same time remembering that it could not provide any service without a sound financial position.

Probably the schedule planner's most important function is to evaluate all of these varied and partially conflicting objectives and come out with the optimal balance between these several goals. Some of the problems faced by a schedule planning department are comparable to those that many other industries face in their own respective product planning:

1 Determining the size of a given market and projecting its future growth
2 Estimating the effect of planned product changes on the size of the total market and on the carrier's own share of the market
3 Attempting to forecast what the competition may do and developing a plan of action to meet such competitive thrusts
4 Estimating the costs and revenues of the alternative plans of action to determine which will be profitable

But the complexities of airline scheduling extend far beyond these problems. Many airline marketing problems are unique, stemming from the special nature of the business. Principal among these are: (1) the problem of traffic flow; (2) the sensitivity of schedule salability to even minor differences in departure times or other factors; (3) the operational difficulty of accomplishing schedule adjustments as desired, because of problems of time zones, station personnel, equipment turnaround, and the chain reaction effect; and (4) the financial leverage of load factors.

Traffic Flow

The concept of **traffic flow**—or the number of originating and connecting passengers on a particular route—is widely recognized; the degree of its importance is not sufficiently understood. Smooth traffic flow helps to

FIGURE 14.5 Traffic Flow (hypothetical data)

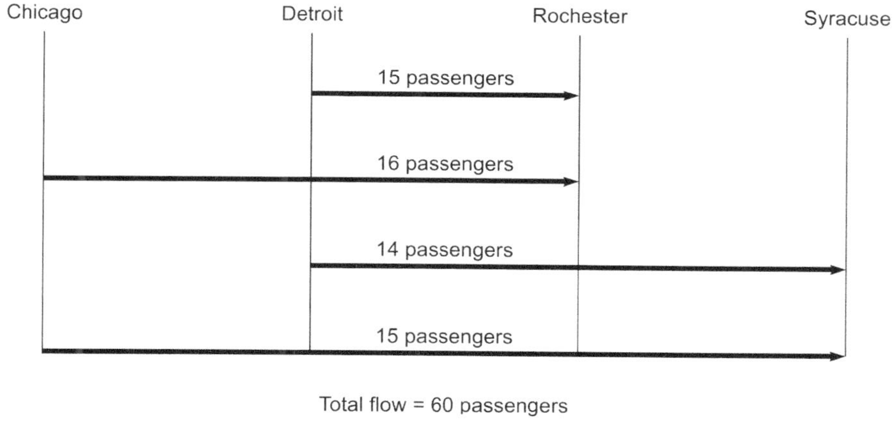

explain schedules that seem quite excessive in relation to origin-destination traffic. Let's take a hypothetical example of a 737 operating from Chicago to Detroit, Rochester, and Syracuse (see Figure 14.5).

This flight averages about a 60 percent load factor on the leg from Detroit to Rochester, but this is possible only because of four separate, and almost equal, traffic flows. No single traffic flow, or combination of two traffic flows, would be adequate to support economical service. By the same token, this flight could not economically overfly Detroit or Rochester, as there would not be enough traffic flow remaining.

The schedule planner must take advantage of traffic flow opportunities but cannot wave a magic wand to create such opportunities. By its very nature, traffic flow varies from case to case, depending on geography, route structure, and alternative service available. Some cities, because of favorable geography, obtain maximum benefit from traffic flow; others do not. An airline cannot change this, and a carrier cannot generalize that City A can support a certain type of service simply because City B receives such service.

Years ago, a route such as Chicago–Los Angeles received traffic flow support from the Los Angeles-bound passengers coming from major points in the northeast, including New York, Boston, Philadelphia, Cleveland, and Washington, D.C. Today, direct nonstop service from these other points to Los Angeles has drained away much of the traffic flow that formerly moved over the Chicago gateway. And this same development is taking place continuously throughout the air transport system.

This constitutes another reason for the impossibility of generalizing about traffic flow and about the type of service a community can economically support. Not only does traffic flow vary from city to city because of geography and route structure, but even for a single city the flow varies from year to year, depending on the type and volume of nonstop service that may be bypassing that city.

Schedule Salability

The second of the special complexities of airline scheduling is the fact that schedule salability is highly sensitive to even minor differences in departure time or other factors. Quite often, several key personnel will spend several days trying to work out a change of just 15 minutes or half an hour in the departure time of a transcontinental jet. This is not time misspent; experience has shown that even such minor adjustments can significantly affect the success of a flight.

The reason is that schedule convenience ranks high among the competitive elements affecting the traveler's choice of an airline. Loyalty to a particular airline will not normally cause a passenger to sit around an airport an extra hour or to miss a business appointment or to wake up earlier than usual if a competitor offers a viable alternative.

The speed of today's jet aircraft has intensified the importance of specific departure times. The difference between a 5:00 P.M. and a 6:00 P.M. departure was of minor consequence for a traveler confronted with a three-day transcontinental train trip. Nor did it make much difference when the industry was dealing with DC-3s that took 20 or so hours to fly coast to coast. But the same one-hour difference becomes vastly important with today's jets, when New York and Los Angeles are separated by less than five elapsed hours and by less than three hours on the clock.

The continual extension of nonstop service has also increased the importance of specific departure times. Thirty years ago, Boston–Los Angeles service involved one-stop schedules through Chicago. Those schedules were not entirely dependent on Boston–Los Angeles traffic, and if departure times were not ideal for such through traffic, they might nevertheless have been quite good for local Boston–Chicago or Chicago–Los Angeles passengers.

Let us consider some examples showing the sensitivity of schedules to differences in departure times. An Embraer 190 operates from Chicago to New York at 7:00 P.M., 8:00 P.M., and 9:00 P.M. But the 9:00 P.M. flight carries only about two-thirds of the load of the flight that departed one hour earlier and only half the load of the flight that left two hours earlier (see Figure 14.6).

Let's take another example. An airline flying from Louisville to New York is forced to shift a flight 20 minutes later, from 5:15 P.M. to 5:35 P.M., due to equipment routing. The city manager in Louisville advises that this will cause the airline to lose an average of about ten passengers per day to a competitor's 4:45 P.M. flight. However, the carrier has no practical option but to make the change (see Figure 14.7).

To make schedule planning even more complicated, schedule salability not only varies by time of day and by route but also has a different pattern of variation between the two directions on the same route. For example, between Hartford and New York, an airline might obtain a much higher volume of traffic on a late departure northbound out of New York than it does on a late trip southbound out of Hartford (see Figure 14.8). Nor does

FIGURE 14.6 Schedules Are Time Sensitive to Departure Time (hypothetical data)

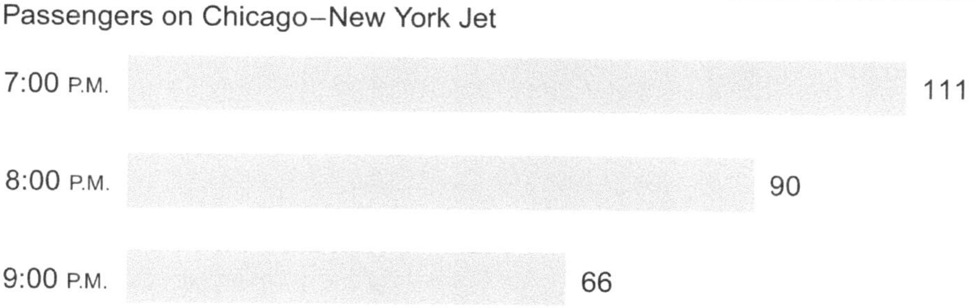

FIGURE 14.7 Schedules are Sensitive to Changes (hypothetical data)

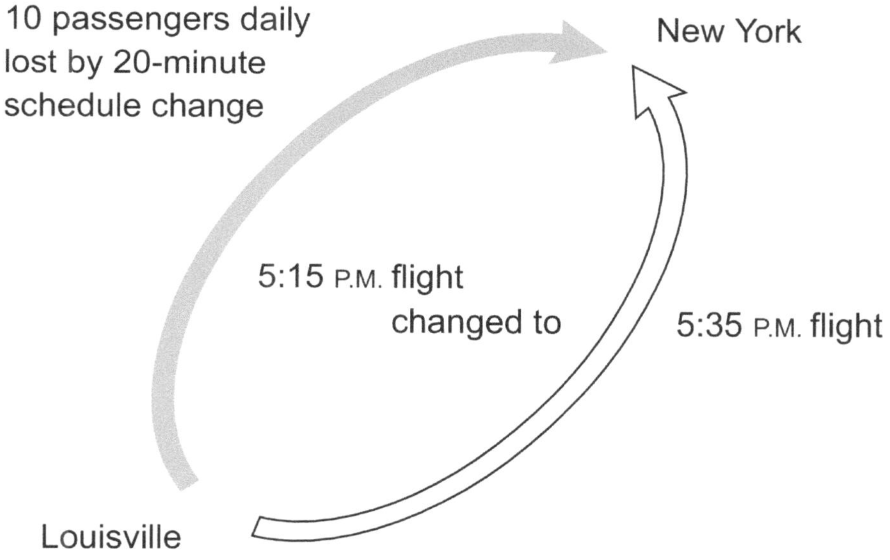

the sensitivity of schedules stop with the matter of departure time. Schedule salability also varies with airport. An airline might have a 4:40 P.M. flight from Newark to Boston, followed 15 minutes later by a departure from another New York-area airport, La Guardia, to Boston. The load factor on the Newark trip might be about 20 to 30 percentage points below that of the La Guardia trip (see Figure 14.9).

By now, one important point should be emerging from this discussion. Although there is often a tendency to think broadly of airline capacity in terms of total seat-miles, a carrier actually deals with a highly varied product line. Every schedule an airline operates is a separate product, having

FIGURE 14.8 Schedule Salability Varies with Direction (hypothetical data)

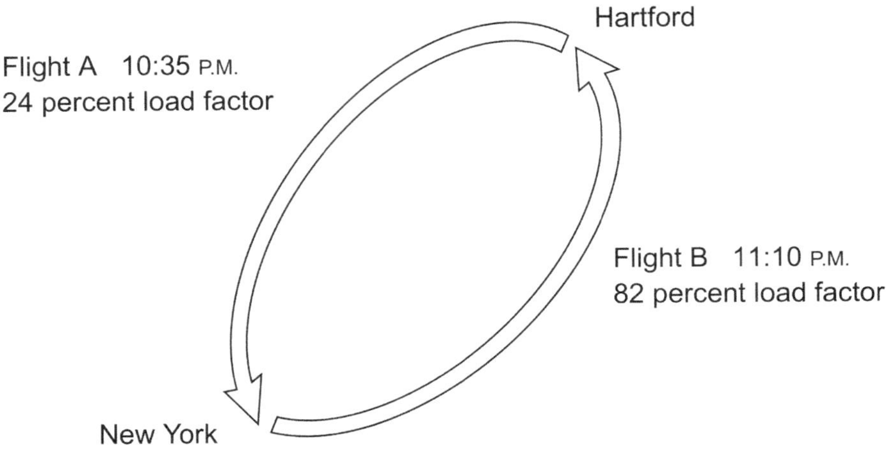

FIGURE 14.9 Schedule Salability Varies with the Airport (hypothetical data)

its own special market and salability. And as competition gets ever more intense, the importance of even minor schedule changes becomes correspondingly greater, making the job of scheduling more complicated.

At this point, the question may arise as to why it should be particularly complicated to adjust schedules to achieve maximum salability. If a 15-minute or 30-minute change in departure time would significantly improve the salability of a schedule, why not simply make that minor change? This question is a logical one, and it leads to a discussion of the third of our general complexities of airline scheduling: the operational difficulty of accomplishing schedule adjustments as desired, even when the adjustments seem minor.

Schedule Adjustments

An airline's total schedule pattern represents a tightly woven, highly interrelated structure. Many aspects are rigidly governed by specific regulatory or contractual requirements, such as those relating to maintenance of equipment, and working conditions of flight crews, as discussed earlier in the chapter. Moreover, almost every schedule is intertwined with other scheduled flights because of connections, equipment routing, or other factors. These other flights come from, or go to, such scattered points as Buffalo, Chicago, Hartford, Washington, Charleston, and Dallas, and more often than not, the ability to reschedule these other flights is limited and a change would create new problems elsewhere. Let's look at some hypothetical examples of the limiting factors at La Guardia Airport:

1. Flight A is our 5:00 P.M. departure to Chicago and is part of our hourly pattern of service on that route.
2. Flight B operates on the New York–Cincinnati–Indianapolis–Chicago route. If this flight were moved back, a gate-congestion problem would develop at Cincinnati.
3. Flight C is part of our hourly pattern of service from New York to Boston.
4. Flight D is a multistop coach from Dallas and Memphis. If it operated later, gate congestion would develop at Memphis.

Obviously, these limiting factors do not mean that it is impossible to move a hypothetical Flight E by 15 minutes. They do indicate, however, that even seemingly minor adjustments have a way of setting off chain reactions, which, in this case, might affect Flights A, B, C, and D.

Time Zones. An important factor affecting schedule actions is the **time zone effect**. The fact that we gain three hours on the clock going westbound and lose three hours coming eastbound has a major impact on scheduling a jet fleet. An eastbound nonstop jet from Los Angeles to New York takes eight hours "on the clock": five hours of flight time plus three hours lost crossing time zones. Most passengers do not like to arrive at their destination close to or after 11:00 P.M. They would usually prefer to fly overnight and arrive early in the morning.

With the eight-hour clock time, any Los Angeles departure at or after 4:00 P.M. means a New York arrival at or after midnight (see Figure 14.10). For all practical purposes, therefore, the period from 3:00 P.M. on is unusable for salable eastbound nonstop departures. Then, beginning at about

FIGURE 14.10 Time Zone Effect on Schedules

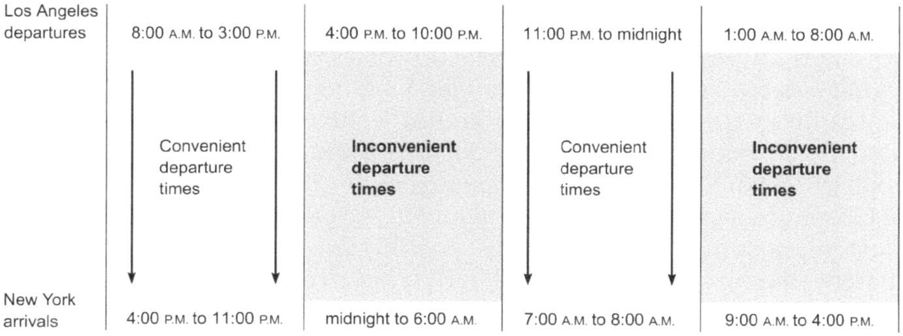

11:00 P.M. Los Angeles time, the carrier can schedule the overnight flights. And after that, it will again have an unusable period, lasting until about 8:00 the next morning. Thus, the carrier's choices of salable eastbound departure times are effectively limited to the period from about 8:00 A.M. to about 3:00 P.M. and then at about 11:00 P.M.

But one other fact must be noted. Equipment starts arriving at Los Angeles from New York's morning schedules shortly after noon. Allowing time to service and turn the equipment, the planes become available for return trips at about 2:00 P.M. This, coupled with the other factors, determines the pattern of service that can economically be operated: early morning service with equipment that terminated in Los Angeles the night before; then service at around 2:00 P.M. with equipment that came from the east the same morning; finally, the 11:00 P.M. departures with equipment that came from the east in the afternoon.

Station Personnel. Still another factor that affects scheduling is the need to minimize the peaking of personnel and ground equipment. An extra ground crew for a jet operation requires 10 to 12 people and an annual payroll of $500,000 or more. Wherever the carrier can feasibly avoid having two operations scheduled simultaneously, and thus can gain use of a single ground crew for two schedules, the carrier will naturally try to do so. This objective is, however, inherently in conflict with a marketing goal of maximizing connections. The carrier therefore has to find the balance between these two conflicting objectives.

The scheduling department staff cannot always tell at a glance from its own schedule plans whether it is creating an inefficiency of personnel utilization. Figure 14.11 shows the station activity chart used by local-station management to translate the impact of a given schedule pattern into staffing workload, by hour of day. This particular example shows the cabin service workload at a local station. Through split shifts and other arrangements, such as part-time personnel, local-station management can frequently handle what looks like a schedule peak without actually incurring a personnel peak. Unfortunately, the reverse situation also occurs: a schedule pattern looks like a smooth workload but in fact involves a peaking requirement of station personnel. In such cases, the station will ask to move Flight A by 15 minutes or Flight B by a half-hour in order to avoid inefficient use of personnel. Then, of course, this adjustment of Flight A or B may create new problems for other stations, which may require still other flights to be adjusted, and so on.

This situation becomes especially problematic at stations where the carrier has only a limited volume of jet operations and where it would be especially inefficient to have this limited volume peak at one particular time. As an example, consider the departure and arrival times of an afternoon jet scheduled into St. Louis (see Figure 14.12). There presently is a gap of 27 minutes between the departure of Flight A and the arrival of Flight B. Now, suppose that for some reason—possibly gate congestion at some other station—the carrier had to move Flight C up a half-hour. To do so would create simultaneous jet operations at St. Louis, making it no longer possible to handle the station with a single jet ground crew.

FIGURE 14.11 Local-station Activity Chart for Airplane Cleaners (hypothetical case)

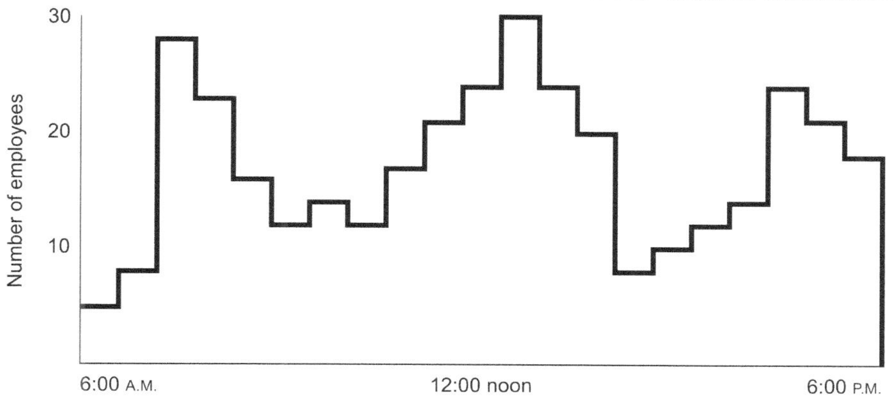

FIGURE 14.12 Staggered Arrivals and Departures of Afternoon Jet Service Avoid Costly Duplication of Ground Crews and Ground Equipment (hypothetical case)

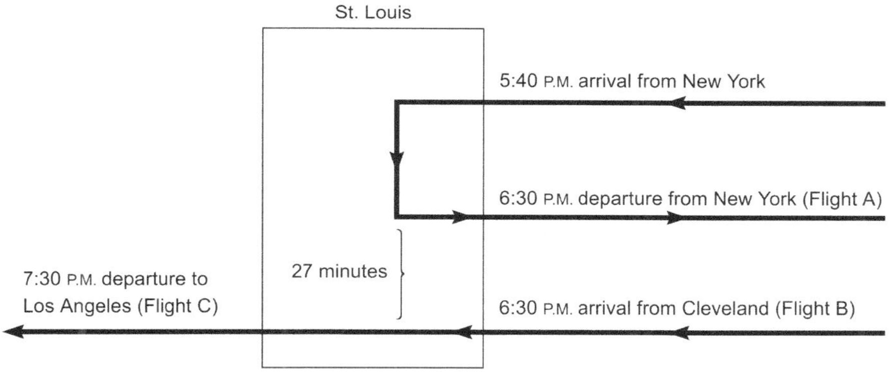

Equipment Turnaround Time. Let's now touch on one more factor affecting scheduling flexibility—**equipment turnaround time** requirements. At the end of every trip, certain operations must be performed, such as cabin cleaning, refueling, and catering. Standards have been established for the *turn time* required for different planes on different-length hops. On top of these minimum requirements, the scheduling department must build in another factor as a cushion for the possibility of late arrival.

Quite often, an airline will find itself in the frustrating position of having equipment sitting idle on the ground at a station, with enough time available to fly the plane to some other point and back, but without enough time on the ground at the other point for adequate turn time. Lacking this extra hour or so, the carrier has no alternative but to leave the plane sitting on the ground, possibly for several hours.

FIGURE 14.13 Chain Reaction Effect (hypothetical case)

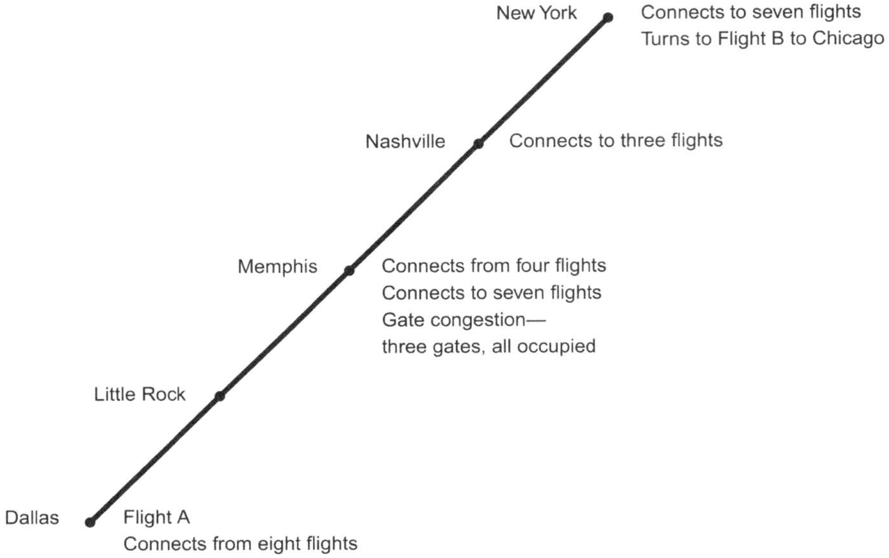

Chain Reaction Effect. Thus far, we have discussed each of these operational marketing factors as separate and independent variables. Actually, however, several of them are usually present in a single schedule situation, thereby increasing the complexities in geometric proportion. Because of the interrelationship between gate congestion, maintenance routing, and other factors, a single schedule action frequently sets up a **chain reaction effect** requiring many other schedule changes. As an example, let's look at Flight A, a 737 operating from Dallas to New York via Little Rock, Memphis, and Nashville (see Figure 14.13).

At its Dallas origination, this flight receives connections from eight inbound flights in the Dallas gateway. When it gets to Memphis, it receives connections from four flights of other carriers and also delivers connections to seven other flights. In addition, its arrival and departure times at Memphis tie into gate occupancy with other flights going through that station at about the same time. When it gets to Nashville, the flight delivers connections to three other flights. Finally, when it gets to New York, it delivers passengers to seven flights, and the equipment then turns back out as scheduled Flight B to Chicago. If the carrier had to change this flight schedule at any point, it would potentially mean making many changes in other flights to preserve connections, avoid gate problems, and so forth.

Load-Factor Leverage

Now let's turn to the last of the special complexities of airline scheduling: the problem of load-factor leverage. One of the unfortunate facts of the airline business is that the carriers produce revenue passenger miles but sell available seat-miles—hence the importance of load factors. In other industries, a manufacturer can estimate the probable market for each individual product and then gear production accordingly. And, if overestimation has occurred, the manufacturer can add the surplus to inventory and dispose of it, perhaps at a reduced price.

An airline has no similar opportunity. It may be convinced that, say, a given nonstop jet to Los Angeles will average only 80 to 90 passengers per day. Nevertheless, if it operates the schedule, it must fly a seat-mile including 230 seats. And, of course, once it produces the empty seat-miles, they are irretrievably lost.

Costs of operating a schedule vary only slightly as load factor changes, whereas revenue varies in direct proportion to changes in load factor. Thus, a shift in load factor of only a few percentage points can make all the difference between a money loser and a profitable trip.

There is another way to dramatize this point. The sensitivity of schedules to even minor changes in departure times has been mentioned. Let's assume that we were unable to accomplish one of the desired changes in the departure of a Chicago–Los Angeles jet and as a result lost a daily average of ten passengers per trip, most of whom would probably be lost in the opposite direction as well. These ten daily passengers would represent an annual revenue of over $1 million:

One economy-class passenger	$300
Ten economy-class passengers	$3,000
Ten daily economy-class passengers	$90,000
Ten daily economy-class passengers	$1,095,000

Because costs would not be materially changed, it can also be said that these ten daily passengers would represent a reduction of over $1 million in operating profits. This, then, may start putting into focus why airlines will go to such lengths to work out schedules to maximize their salability and why they do not take lightly requests from city managers for even a 10- or 15-minute change in a schedule.

We can look at the financial implications of our schedule action in still another way. Let's consider the total cost of operating a transcontinental jet schedule. In a year, a single daily round-trip between New York and Los Angeles costs over $1.5 million. Assume that the carrier adds such a trip that is not really required and that is not likely to get any significant amount of new business to help pay its way. In that case, this cost becomes straight operating loss and a sheer economic waste. The economic waste involved in an unnecessary airline schedule is rarely appreciated, possibly because the waste in an airline schedule does not leave tangible physical evidence. At the end of the year, the unused seat-miles cannot be seen gathering dust in a warehouse.

Referring to the scheduling process, a planner was once overheard to say that "our job is like trying to put together a jigsaw puzzle, constructed in three dimensions, while the shape of key pieces is constantly changing." The fact that salability of an airline's product is sensitive to even minor changes would be no serious problem if the carrier had the flexibility to make these changes readily. Or carriers could live with the dual problems of sensitivity of schedules coupled with the difficulty of adjusting schedules without too much strain were it not for load-factor leverage. Then it would be possible to adjust capacity on any given schedule to the level of traffic the carrier thought it might get for that particular trip. But when all of these factors are taken together—the sensitivity of schedules to even minor changes, the difficulty of adjusting schedules, and the tremendous financial impact of losing even a few passengers—the full measure of the difficulty becomes apparent.

Putting Together the September Schedule

Normally, a carrier publishes a new schedule six or seven times a year, generally on a bimonthly basis. During an average year (the last several have been anything but average), the spring and fall schedules are the primary ones.

Schedule building never really starts from scratch. Data are continuously fed into the scheduling department from regional sales and services, as well as from the other major operating departments. These new data are added to the basic body of knowledge that the scheduling department has about the airline's scheduling patterns and the numerous factors involved. The schedule that emerges is the product of continual refinement.

Let's take a look at an example of a carrier attempting to put together a schedule for September 1, 20XX. The compilation and meshing of data begin around April 1. In our hypothetical case, a number of major marketing considerations have to be looked at by the scheduling department in preparing the September schedule:

1 The addition of two A320s
2 The need to return service to the point it had reached before the terrorist attacks of September 11, 2001, which had necessitated schedule cuts
3 Creation of a fourth connecting bank of flights in Buffalo
4 Addition of new hourly service between Pittsburgh and Chicago, based on more single-plane service through Pittsburgh
5 Restoration of Boston–Philadelphia and Pittsburgh–Philadelphia hourly frequencies

These are but a few of the objectives that top-level marketing management has set for scheduling in preparing the September schedule.

The scheduling department generally submits its proposed schedule to all operating departments 60 days before the effective date. About a week after the distribution, the interdepartmental meetings begin. The conference room adjoining the scheduling department, where the meetings are generally held, looks like the war room from a World War II movie. Station charts with the proposed schedule are taped on every spare inch of wall space. A typical meeting in the early stages of negotiation might include 10 to 20 management personnel representing all of the operating departments.

The scheduling department may make concessions when suggestions by other departments are backed up with the realities of operational requirements. But, in general, the scheduling department must remain firm. If it does not, the entire schedule—the results of months of planning—may suffer. Problems might involve such things as sufficient turnaround time or separation between flights. For one reason or another, including personnel, gate availability, or vehicles required, customer services or line maintenance might argue that they need more time between flights. Often, calls will be made to field personnel during the meetings to get their input: "Can you handle it? If not, what do you need?"

Another major factor in setting the September 1 schedule might be the goal of increasing the carrier's on-time performance. Economic planning might have performed a special study to determine what was causing delays. Late-arriving passengers, weather, cargo loading, maintenance, and other factors all play a role. The results would be integrated into the September 1 schedule.

At this stage, the scheduling department cannot afford to give away large chunks of time. It tries to take into account the peculiarities of each station's operational capacity and to trade in no larger than five-minute increments. Customer service gives a little, line maintenance backs off on its demands, and scheduling adds a couple of minutes along the aircraft's route. Flight operations agrees.

Another problem at one of the departmental meetings might involve a joint marketing program with one of the international carriers. Let's suppose the carrier has a flight to Kennedy Airport in the September 1 schedule that connects with a flight to London, whose time was to revert to standard after the schedule was published. Scheduling might have to change this flight at a later date.

Other problems might include the time required by maintenance for an aircraft en-route check, an additional five minutes needed to accommodate a bus transporting commuter passengers at O'Hare Airport, or a 737 wingspan too wide to accommodate two planes simultaneously at La Guardia Airport's Gates 20 and 21, as the schedule calls for.

The meetings go on until a general consensus is reached. Even then, most schedulers admit that the final product is a compromise at best—the best possible under the marketing and operating criteria set forth.

As a carrier grows, the scheduling process becomes more complicated. Computer models are used quite extensively by the major carriers, but they have not eliminated the meetings that scheduling must have with the operating units to work out specific problems.

EQUIPMENT ASSIGNMENT AND TYPES OF SCHEDULES

The scheduling department will generally refer to aircraft throughout the system as being operated in either *in-service* or *out-of-service use*. In-service use refers to those aircraft being flown (1) on scheduled service, (2) as an extra section, or (3) as a charter flight. An *extra section* is an additional aircraft assigned to handle a particular flight because of an unusually large number of passengers. Out-of-service use refers to those aircraft temporarily assigned for major overhaul, maintenance checks, flight training, special projects, such as installing different seats, or line reserves. *Line reserves* are extra airplanes stationed at major terminals to be called on in the event of a problem with a scheduled flight. It should be noted, in today's economy, few airlines have spare aircraft "sitting" on reserve. In most cases, airlines revise aircraft fleet schedules using the existing operating fleet. Unfortunately, because of the need to use all the assets, schedule delays often result.

Airlines use four basic schedule types in assigning their equipment: (1) skip-stop, (2) local service, (3) cross-connections (hub and spoke), and (4) nonstops. *Skip-stop* scheduling refers to the practice of providing service to points A, B, C, D, E, F, G, and so forth by scheduling flights in the following manner: A–C–E–G or A–D–G, or similar combinations in which one or more of the intermediate stations are "skipped," with service being provided by other flights. The principal advantage of skip stopping is to provide fast service to intermediate stations; the principal disadvantage is in not providing service between consecutive cities.

In *local-service* schedules, shorter-range aircraft make all stops on a segment and connect at larger intermediate stations with long-range aircraft. The principal advantage of local service is that it provides fast service between small intermediate stations and terminal points; the principal disadvantage is the change of planes involved.

Cross-connections (hub and spoke) are frequently used in schedule planning by all airlines. An example of a route over which this can be accomplished is the United Airlines route serving the principal cities shown in Figure 14.14. When a Washington–Chicago–San Francisco flight, a New York–Chicago–Seattle flight, and a Boston–Chicago–Los Angeles flight arrive at Chicago essentially at the same time, traffic can be transferred from one to another, thereby providing more daily service between points in the east and those in the west. This is the principal advantage, particularly if one of the flights is the only one to serve one or more of the stations; principal disadvantages are the change in planes and the congestion of traffic. (The next section discusses hub-and-spoke scheduling in more detail.)

Nonstops are being used more frequently than ever by the major and national carriers. The principal advantage is provision of fast service between terminal points; there is no real disadvantage, although, of course, no intermediate stations receive service on these flights.

Actually, all airlines have used and will continue to use all four major schedule types with variations to fit their individual needs. The types most adapted to a fleet of same-range airplanes are skip stopping and cross-connections; for a fleet of at least two general types of airplanes, all four schedule types can be used, with perhaps more emphasis on local service and nonstops.

From the passenger's viewpoint, the goal is safe, speedy, dependable, and comfortable service from point A to point Z. Safety is the overriding and controlling factor in all airline operations. To gain the other three in

FIGURE 14.14 Cross-connection (Hub-and-Spoke) Service (hypothetical case)

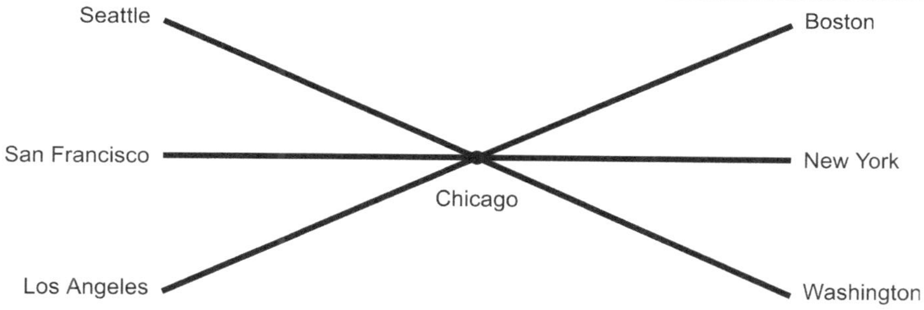

the greatest possible measure, the passenger naturally prefers: (1) a nonstop flight from point A to point Z, or (2) if that service is not available at a convenient time, a through flight, or (3) if the journey can be accelerated, a connecting flight with adequate connecting time to ensure dependability and with fast equipment and as few stops as possible.

From an airline standpoint, the desire to meet every individual passenger's needs must be weighed against profitability. A nonstop flight costs less to operate from point A to point Z than one on the same type of equipment that makes intermediate stops. If sufficient traffic demand is not available to justify nonstop operation, through service means that each passenger is handled only once and therefore costs are lower than they are on a connecting service.

HUB-AND-SPOKE SCHEDULING

Deregulation has led to significant changes in the routings and schedule patterns of the carriers. A catalyst for these changes has been the greatly increased emphasis on hub-and-spoke scheduling. Deregulation eliminated airlines' incentive to dissipate their added revenues through wasteful expenditures on extra (and underutilized) flights along the route structure mandated by the CAB. In addition, deregulation allowed carriers to create new schedule patterns that lowered the costs of providing new flights.

In the past, there was constant pressure (from communities and from the CAB) for more and more direct point-to-point nonstops. If a carrier did not exercise its franchise of nonstop operations in a particular market, it risked having that community induce another airline to seek the unused authority from the CAB. This concept of nonstop obligation was carried right into the Airline Deregulation Act, which classified "dormant authority" as any route segment not then actually served nonstop and, as the first step toward liberalized route grants, provided for the transfer of dormant authority to other carriers.

Many city-pair markets, however, could not support nonstop service in terms of their own origin and destination traffic. Economic viability frequently depended on adding traffic flows from backup markets on either end of a nonstop route. In CAB route cases, cities often were added to a carrier's route system specifically for the purpose of providing enough traffic to make nonstop service viable. Because of the protection afforded by a regulated route franchise system, the backup markets for some nonstop routes could be expected to remain relatively stable over long periods of time.

In this framework, the airline route structure evolved gradually into many "linear" patterns, in which one city would mainly serve as backup to some specific route segment, while other cities would back up other routes, and so forth. With deregulation, carriers could no longer regard their backup traffic markets as stable or secure. There were, of course, some hub-and-spoke connecting operations, but their scope was limited by the route franchises then in effect.

In response to competitive pressures following deregulation, carriers rapidly replaced the old structure with a **hub-and-spoke system**. In hub-and-spoke systems, several points of departure are fed into a single airport (the "hub"), from which connecting flights transport passengers to their various destinations (along the "spokes").

Advantages of Hub-and-Spoke Systems

The main advantage of the highly developed airline hub-and-spoke operation is that it provides an enormous "multiplier" effect as to the number of city-pairs an airline can serve with a given amount of flight mileage. This is demonstrated in Figure 14.15. The top portion of the chart shows eight hypothetical cities, linked in pairs with direct nonstop service. The number of city-pairs receiving air service in this pattern is four. The middle portion of the chart shows what happens if, with approximately the same amount of mileage flown, each city is linked to a centrally located hub.

With the permutation of routings possible via the hub, there would now be a total of 24 city-pairs served (the 16 city-pairs obtained by the connection linkage of each of the four eastern cities with each of the four western cities, plus the linkage of the four eastern and four western cities to the hub city itself). Obviously, this multiplication of traffic greatly increases the chances of obtaining strong load factors. Full airplanes result in lower costs, which permit lower fares, and these savings have also allowed the airlines to increase the frequency of flights.

Once a carrier establishes itself with a solid network of spokes at a particular hub, it becomes difficult for any other carrier to challenge it competitively, unless the other carrier has the resources to undertake a similar feed network. To attempt to compete on only one or two of the individual spokes into that hub becomes difficult, because the challenging carrier in this situation must rely mainly on just the local O & D traffic on those few segments while the hub operator can support a much broader pattern of service with the support of all of the "feed" traffic. By dominating a hub, an airline can

FIGURE 14.15 Multiplier Effect of Hub Connections

Point-to-Point Service Without Hub

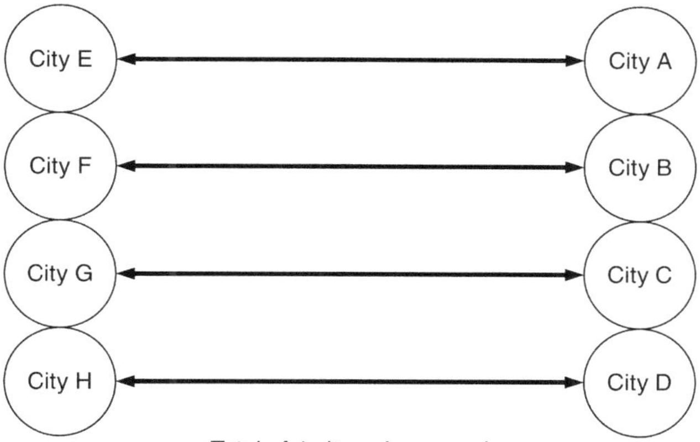

Total of 4 city-pairs served

Service via Cross-Connection (Hub)

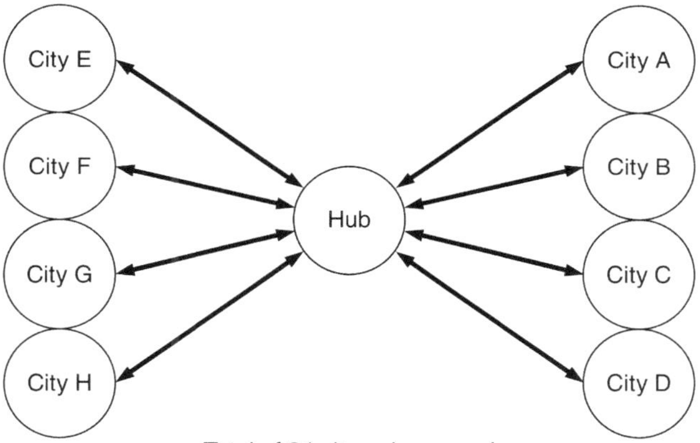

Total of 24 city-pairs served

Growth in the Power of a Hub

n Spokes	$n(n-1)/2$ Connecting Markets	*n* Local Markets Terminating at the Hub	Total Markets Served
2	1	2	3
6	15	6	21
10	45	10	55
50	1,225	50	1,275
100	4,950	100	5,050

Source: Dennis and Dogaris (1989)

also charge higher airfares to passengers originating from the hub region, thus achieving a greater potential for profits.

Hubbing also offers advantages to travelers. Passengers flying in low-traffic markets might not enjoy low airfares or fly in large jets if the airlines were to fly them nonstop between the end cities. Small planes cost more per seat-mile to operate and may require multiple stops for refueling. In fact, through multiple-hub systems, passengers from small cities can fly to any small or large city in the world with relatively low airfares. By connecting at a hub, passengers can also enjoy the convenience of frequent flights to and from that hub. This usually results in lower *schedule delay,* which is defined as the waiting time between a passenger's most desirable departure time and the actual scheduled flight. The use of large jets also increases travelers' chances of finding a seat on their desired flight.

Disadvantages of Hub-and-Spoke Systems

Although hubbing seems to benefit airlines and offers some advantages to travelers, the extent of excessive concentration at the hub can result in some negative economic impacts, namely, congestion delay. As aircraft volume approaches the capacity of the hub airport, congestion delay increases rapidly, which may outweigh some of hubbing's benefits to both airlines and passengers. This additional delay increases passengers' total travel time and adds to the airlines' operating costs (for example, wages for the crew and fuel and maintenance expenses for the airplane). Congestion during peak periods also puts a tremendous strain on airport and airline personnel. It requires maximal staffing for each 45-minute peak-staffing at the gate, on the apron, at the ticket counter, and at curbside. Moreover, for each city feeding into the hub, a separate gate is required, and adding more cities requires more gates.

On the tarmac, the launching of 30 aircraft within a five- to ten-minute period can cause excessive taxi waits, forcing schedulers to build additional minutes into block times. During bad weather, delays at one hub airport create delays systemwide. The requirement that aircraft arrive at the hub at the same time is costly. Airplanes serving the shorter spokes must sit on the ground at the out-stations, often for hours, to compensate for those airplanes on the longer segments. Also, because scheduling into the hub is based on the times of the connecting complexes, actual departure times at the out-stations may not be the most convenient for the communities. Some portion of the potential local O & D market is at risk of being left unsatisfied. To compensate for this, some carriers have increased the use of the regional jet (RJ) concept. Consumer demand in out-station markets continues to grow rapidly as more and more passengers are flown from secondary locations through hubs and on to secondary locations.

Still another problem is baggage. Most complexes provide between 30 and 45 minutes for passengers to make their connections. When flights are late, however, there is very little leeway for the baggage to make the same connection. Passengers simply walk from one gate to the other and board their new flight. Baggage, on the other hand, must be off-loaded, sorted, transferred, and loaded aboard the new aircraft. When off-schedule operations occur, the 30- to 45-minute connecting time guarantees a high mishandled-baggage expense. Congestion delay also creates additional work for air traffic controllers and increases their stress levels. It may require upgrading the ATC facilities and adding more personnel at the ATC centers and airport towers. Finally, excessive aircraft concentration at the hub can have adverse environmental impacts, such as noise and pollution. These negative economic effects of aircraft concentration must be taken into account when conducting cost-benefit analyses into building or expanding major hubs.

The Future of Point-to-Point Systems

The hub-and-spoke system, generally speaking, has been a positive tool for legacy-based air carriers due to increased network access and increased load factors. Low-cost carriers (LCCs) have traditionally preferred the point-to-point network. Interestingly, as LCCs mature in various regions of the world, many have found cities within the network now overlap creating a form of a hub-and-spoke but not in the traditional sense. The purpose of the "new" hub-and-spoke is not necessarily meant to connect passengers on a single itinerary like the traditional hub-and-spoke. Some LCCs now offer passengers the ability to embrace the hub-and-spoke network by providing direct connection options and guarantees but it is up to the passenger to self-connect. This saves the airline both time and money while the carrier's ever-increasing network with naturally banked scheduling provides a good amount of connection opportunities. Air Asia, Air Asia X, easyJet, FlyDubai, and Ryanair are good examples of LCCs pursuing this path. As LCCs, and airlines using the **point-to-point system**, grow in terms of network ability, it is very likely some of these companies will not only grow the "new" hub-and-spoke concept but connect with airlines they now compete with. In terms of logical stages of growth, it is very possible that LCCs, for example, form regional and global alliances similar to what the legacy carriers have done with the current alliance relationships.

DATA LIMITATIONS IN AIRLINE SCHEDULING

Since the early 1980s, sophisticated computer programs, which use complex mathematical algorithms, have been developed to address the complete scheduling task. The most widely used are those programs that assist with the mechanical complexity of assembling up to 1,000 flights, efficiently routing aircraft across flight segments, and assisting the carrier in meeting constraints imposed by such factors as maintenance requirements, flight operations and crew scheduling, ground operations and facility limitations, and passenger service needs. However, airline scheduling remains a function that involves as much art as science.

Although detailed traffic data are available on-line, historically, airline scheduling has been performed with limited sources of traffic data. Station managers observe competitor enplanements, and many carriers participate in informal information exchanges with one another. The problem with this type of information is that its accuracy is questionable and it is only available on an aggregate basis. The DOT forms 41, T-100, and ten percent surveys of domestic and international traffic are basic schedule planning and route analysis tools, and although the information they provide is beneficial, there are problems concerning data accuracy and level of detail. For example, these sources provide limited information on flight numbers and passenger origins and destinations, and are typically not available from the DOT until three to six months after the flight date.

The availability and presentation of these data by commercial information service organizations has improved significantly in recent years. The DOT data are available by accessing the DOT website (https://data.gov).

Current data regarding international carriers are more difficult to obtain. Organizations such as the IATA and ICAO collect highly aggregated information that is generally not available for years. Not only is the information dated, it is often incomplete because of the reluctance of many carriers to share data for competitive reasons.

Advances in telecommunications and computer science are providing better information sources for the airlines. Along with better information, more sophisticated analytical tools are being developed using electronic data sources. However, even with new information resources and more sophisticated analytical tools, airline scheduling will continue to be a complex and challenging task.

Airlines rely on historical data to assist forecasting the future and, under normal circumstances, this is a relatively slow process providing a fairly realistic view, and last-minute decisions are generally only made due to operational challenges. However, there are times throughout history when historical data flies out the window and the ability to forecast the future is more than challenging. The COVID-19 global pandemic forced the airline industry to think and act differently as no one planned for such a catastrophic event.

In 2001, the events of 9/11 brought the industry to a halt but, fortunately, this tragic event was a short blip on the radar screen as the industry continued to generate revenue despite the short stoppage in operations. From 2019–2022, airlines suffered greatly as historical data became irrelevant and the need to plan focused on real-time operations, resulting in massive scheduling changes in order to stay afloat financially. At the time of publication, airlines had not fully recovered from the impact of COVID-19, and although the law of supply and demand still exists, scheduling departments have been forced to think more strategically than ever as booking curves are short and erratic meaning data is not necessarily reliable. New challenges that did not exist previously include shutdown of country borders, reduced bookings, and passenger no-show rates increasing. Has the airline industry changed forever? Some experts say yes and operators must rethink the business model in order to survive and thrive while other experts look at the COVID-19 crisis as a "short" piece in history that had a negative impact on the industry but all will return to "normal." Is the airline industry operating in what many define as the "new normal"?

KEY TERMS

chain reaction effect
committee system
equipment turnaround time
hub-and-spoke system
maintenance efficiency goals
operational factors
point-to-point system
scheduling
scheduling department
Special Flight Permit (SFP)
station plotting chart
time zone effect
traffic flow

REVIEW QUESTIONS

1 What is the mission of scheduling? Discuss some of the external factors that schedule planners must take into consideration. Why do many airlines use the committee system to analyze a proposed schedule?
2 What is the primary purpose of engineering and maintenance and line maintenance with regard to scheduling? Discuss the four maintenance efficiency goals. Name several of the inspection and overhaul periods for a jet as it is routed throughout a system. Why are there different levels of maintenance capability throughout an airline system?
3 If an aircraft experienced a mechanical breakdown in Cleveland, how might that affect passengers expecting to board a flight in Youngstown?
4 Flight operations is concerned with a number of operational factors in schedule planning. Discuss three of them. How do crew time limits and employee agreements affect flight scheduling? How does the fact that crew members are based at various localities complicate flight scheduling? How do seniority and crew qualifications at a specific location present challenges in the scheduling process? Why is so much emphasis placed on reducing crew layovers and deadhead flights?
5 What is the objective of ground handling in the scheduling process? What are some of the facility limitations imposed on schedulers? What is a schedule plotting chart? Why is personnel planning so difficult and costly when there is extreme peaking of flights into a particular station? Why is it so expensive for a major carrier to service a small airport with only two or three flights per day? (*Hint:* think about equipment and personnel.)
6 "You can please all of the people some of the time and some of the people all of the time, but you can't please all of the people all of the

time." How does this relate to scheduling? Why is it important to build up complexes of connecting flights at major gateways?

7 Discuss some of the problems faced by an airline scheduling department that are similar to problems of other industries and some problems that are unique to the airline industry. Discuss three marketing related problems. What is meant by *traffic flow*? *Sensitivity of schedule salability*? Give one example of the latter.

8 How do other operating factors, such as time zones, station personnel, and equipment turnaround time, affect the scheduling process? Why might a jet flight scheduled to depart Los Angeles at 11:35 P.M. be popular? What is meant by the *chain reaction effect*?

9 Airlines produce revenue passenger miles but sell available seat-miles. What does that mean? Why do the costs of operating a flight vary only slightly with additional passengers?

10 What are the three basic in-service equipment assignments? The five out-of-service assignments? Discuss the advantages and disadvantages of skip-stop, local service, cross-connection, and nonstop service.

11 What was meant by *dormant authority* before deregulation? How did it affect scheduling? What is the purpose of hub-and-spoke scheduling? Discuss the advantages and disadvantages of hub-and-spoke scheduling.

12 What are the main differentiators between a hub-and-spoke system and a point-to-point system? What might the future point-to-point system look like and why?

13 Airline scheduling is dependent on historical data that is used to forecast the future impacting routes served and aircraft operated as examples. Explain how the COVID-19 global pandemic has impacted airlines and how they address new challenges associated with scheduling. Compare and contrast the impact of COVID-19 with the events of 9/11. What are the similarities and what are the differences?

CHAPTER 15

Fleet Planning

The Aircraft Selection Process

CHAPTER CHECKLIST • YOU SHOULD BE ABLE TO:

- Understand the importance of fleet planning, and describe its long-range implications
- Describe the industry changes since deregulation that have affected the fleet-planning process including new aircraft technology
- Discuss the major factors an aircraft manufacturer must take into consideration in designing and developing a new jetliner including the aging process
- Identify the four inputs in the fleet-planning process and explain what each one means
- Understand the Fleet Optimization Model
- Define *system constraints* and *constrained operating plan*
- Discuss the five areas that must be considered by an individual carrier in evaluating a particular aircraft
- Understand the importance of emerging technologies like supersonic travel and how this will change the airline business model

INTRODUCTION

One of the most difficult decisions airline managements must make is whether to buy new or used aircraft and what type. Alternatively, they must

DOI: 10.4324/9780429346156-18

consider whether it makes better financial sense to modernize older aircraft already in their fleet or to acquire aircraft from the outside. Many additional factors, including the costs associated with engineering and maintenance, must be weighed. The factors are constantly changing, and their relative importance at each airline depends on the carrier's individual situation.

FACTORS IN FLEET PLANNING

Purchasers of new aircraft can generally get by for seven to ten years without having to make any major structural repairs. Furthermore, maintenance costs as a percentage of total costs have been steadily decreasing since the 1960s. However, percentages do not necessarily present a true picture. If one set of costs, such as for maintenance, rises less steeply than others, its percentage of the total may drop although the cost in absolute dollars may be rising. In this context, a set of figures from American Airlines is worth noting. Over the 20-year life of a 707, American found that maintenance costs rose 10 percent but that improvements in reliability more than compensated for the rise. This was in terms of current dollars. When translated into constant dollars, which take inflation into account, the situation was even better: maintenance costs actually dropped. Today, the same can be said with the utilization of modern aircraft with airlines around the world. In most cases, depending on the region of the world and type of aircraft operated, maintenance costs are usually one of the top three highest costs in addition to fuel and labor. **Aging**, which includes technical aging, economic aging, and financial aging, is a complex process due to the number of factors that must be considered in the equation. Routine maintenance, non-routine maintenance, airworthiness directives (AD), and service bulletins (SB) are the primary elements affecting aging and all are strongly associated with data, which can also be a challenging process.

It would be quite simple if maintenance were the only, or the most important, factor to consider in fleet decisions. But besides maintenance costs, many other factors must be balanced against one another: the price of fuel; the availability and price of used aircraft; resale value; the price of new aircraft; terms of purchase; cash flow; debt/equity ratio; the availability of money from lenders; the receptivity of Wall Street to the issuance of stocks, bonds, and debentures; interest rates; route structure; competitive situation; strategy; and labor costs. All are even more important than before in today's deregulated environment.

The Prederegulation Era

Before deregulation, the airlines constituted a fairly stable business, and fleet decisions were much simpler, usually based on technical considerations. The airframe and engine manufacturers came up with improved models, and the airlines bought them on about a five-year re-equipment cycle. In the prederegulation world, the carriers would buy up the new aircraft coming on the market despite their high prices. The highly efficient and reliable engines, digital avionic cockpits, outstanding performance, and improved maintainability of these aircraft seemed to make them irresistible. But the reality is very different.

In the old days, overall costs could be predicted with some degree of confidence. Traffic kept growing and routes were protected by the CAB. Lenders were secure in the knowledge that loans would be repaid on time. Even the weaker carriers could get the financing they needed, because under the "failing carrier" doctrine, the CAB would, if necessary, find them a stronger airline as a merger partner. Northeast Airlines was merged into Delta under this doctrine in the early 1970s when the former ran into financial difficulty.

Before deregulation, there were excellent technical reasons for massive replacement of aircraft. The advent in the 1960s of the turbine engine, and in the 1970s of the wide-body airframe, permitted quantum jumps in productivity. Technical progress since then, although impressive, has been more in the nature of step-by-step advances. Today, there has to be a much more careful analysis of costs versus benefits before fleet decisions can be made.

Deregulation changed the rules of the game. New nonunion carriers, usually flying relatively inexpensive used aircraft, invaded traditional markets with low fares. Other low-cost carriers, such as Southwest Airlines, expanded their systems into new markets. To make matters worse, the price of fuel soared to over $1 a gallon. The old, established trunk carriers, whose fleet philosophy had been to prepare themselves to meet peak demands, were stuck with fleets of three- and four-engine aircraft flown by cockpit crews of three or four and with power plants designed at a time when a gallon of fuel cost only 10 to 15 cents. The new carriers, on the other hand, flew twin-engine aircraft with only two pilots in the cockpit. To put the cost of fuel into perspective, at the time of writing this book, the average price of jet fuel was $4.15 per gallon in 2022 which was an increase of 150% compared to 2021.

With deregulation, the established airlines had to find ways to reduce the operating costs associated with aircraft already in their inventory that were not as efficient as the newer generation of equipment. The incumbent carriers began to focus on new equipment that generated the lowest operating costs and were available in sufficient quantities and at the right times to meet their fleet and market-planning requirements. The strong market for used aircraft enabled many of the incumbent carriers to upgrade their fleets more rapidly and, even with higher labor costs, to compete successfully with the start-ups.

The Hub-and-Spoke System

In the quest to achieve the lowest possible unit cost, U.S. airlines have come to exhaust hub-and-spoke route systems where practical. This, too, has had a profound influence on new aircraft requirements. Lift capacity has tended to be greater in smaller aircraft with shorter full-payload ranges.

Hub-and-spoke networks have influenced airlines in other ways. Although the air carrier community has long recognized economies of scale (as reflected in the preference for a large number of identical aircraft), it has also come to appreciate that, with deregulation, economies of scope are perhaps as important as economies of scale. This has led carriers to serve not only more city-pair markets but more varied markets than ever before. This, in turn, has caused the largest airlines to require a wider variety of aircraft than ever before. Indeed, the range of attributes embodied in such aircraft appears to be broadening as economies of scope are pursued, partially through airline consolidation.

Hubs have also influenced carriers' decisions with regard to larger aircraft, such as the Boeing 767 and Airbus A330. As the hubs become increasingly congested and slot limitations more constraining, there is a natural tendency to schedule larger aircraft rather than smaller ones through the hub, especially during periods of peak activity. This, too, has led to a proliferation of certain types of aircraft in the fleets of the larger carriers reliant on hub-and-spoke networks. Here, also, there has been a happy conjunction of events: changes in the so-called two-engine rule have increasingly enabled airlines to operate larger twin-engine aircraft intercontinentally and internationally as well as on shorter hauls.

Technical Aspects

During the early years following deregulation, most major carriers were reducing, and even liquidating, whole staff departments, including, in some cases, all their engineering personnel. Under such circumstances, the physical aspects of aircraft to be acquired have been left increasingly in the hands of the manufacturers of aircraft, engines, and associated equipment. Indeed, with the economics of aircraft having become the most critical issue, not surprisingly, the aircraft purchasing decision has become simpler again. Typically, an air carrier's senior executive concerned with financial and market performance of the airline dominates the aircraft acquisition decision process, and those engineering personnel that remain, as well as the operating staff (including pilots), play a much more reactive than proactive role.

In part, this can be seen by the relative ease with which the heavily innovative Airbus A320 is being sold to major airlines. Here is an aircraft that embodies a number of truly innovative concepts and much new hardware and software. In a former age, this would have given pause to most airline engineering departments, which would have preferred to see much more incremental technological steps because of their typically conservative approach to fundamental changes in aircraft technology.

For example, the total fly-by-wire concept in the A320, together with its sidestick controls, represents a substantial departure from past practice, and surely most airline engineering departments would caution their managements to go somewhat slower. This is not to suggest that the A320 is an unwise choice or poses any threat to safety. But the aircraft is being acquired primarily because it promises lower-cost production of the airline product, not because of its inherent differences—which most passengers will not recognize in any case.

Until the mid-1990s, the A320 was originally purchased with little airline engineering input. This was best reflected in the fact that the A320 incorporated components in its vital avionics system that were supplied by manufacturers with little or no previous success in the air transport market. Given the nature of the A320 (and a growing number of modern aircraft types such as the Boeing 787 Dreamliner and the Airbus A350), avionics installations are integral to the aircraft. The fact that many airlines purchased the A320 with critical components from suppliers with whom they had never previously done business showed strong support for the contention that airline engineering departments were substantially out of the loop so far as decisions to purchase new aircraft were concerned. Today, the A320 is an aircraft with a proven history, and airline engineering departments are able to provide important input in the fleet-planning process. Interestingly, the Airbus A320 is highly regarded and often referred to as the "workhorse of short-haul flying" by the industry with an incredible performance and safety record. As of 2022, the A320 had a 99.7% operational reliability with more than 280 million flight hours and more than 152 million flight cycles since entry into service according to Airbus.

Fleet Rationalization

Consolidation of the industry during the 1980s as a result of mergers has led to a proliferation of specific aircraft types operated by any particular carrier. No doubt, much of this proliferation will be reduced as fleet rationalization becomes both practical and possible. Although fleet rationalization may well be a first order of business for consolidated airlines, such carriers still need to acquire new aircraft not only to address new markets but also to enable them to enjoy the benefits of maximum practical fleet commonality in the long run. What will influence the acquisition process involving new aircraft is the economic organization of the airline industry as consolidation proceeds. The issue is the behavior of the airline industry under conditions of oligopoly.

Economic theory suggests that as airlines become fewer in number, there will be tacit understanding with regard to fare levels and structures, even though no formal or strictly illegal agreements are reached. Cost minimization will not be completely disregarded. However, with greater price stability and with the behavior of competitors reflecting their own acquisition of a greater measure of monopoly power, product differentiation through service rather than price will certainly become more important.

With aircraft once more playing a greater role in determining a carrier's market share, coupled with the mild relaxation of cost-cutting pressures that consolidation will induce, airlines can be expected to add staff, especially as consolidation increases and the scale of individual airlines supports specialization of function within the organization. Under such conditions, airlines capable of acquiring significant blocks of new aircraft are likely once more to move in the direction of formalizing the fleet decision-making process. Although that process will necessarily be more concerned with the economies of the aircraft than it was under comprehensive economic regulation, engineering considerations will once again matter.

Consolidation also increases the interdependence between megacarriers on the one hand and the manufacturers of aircraft and engines on the other. Whether such interdependence will be as great as in the period between 1933 and 1960 remains to be seen, but it will be an important factor. For example, with fewer airlines to serve as sponsors and launch customers for a new aircraft type, and with such airlines having requirements for a very large number of such aircraft, these carriers may seek to sew up the production capabilities of a given manufacturer by receiving initial delivery of a large number of aircraft—if not at the beginning of the production run, then somewhat later. The manufacturer, on the other hand, has every incentive to spread deliveries among as many air carriers as possible. As the number of airlines capable of placing launch orders and of becoming sponsors of new aircraft types diminishes with consolidation, the manufacturers will also experience added pressure to lower prices.

Still another anticipated effect of consolidation and subsequent fleet rationalization is that aircraft will tend to stay in the fleets even longer, given that the average operational lifecycle is now approximately 30 years before it is retired. This gives rise to the possibility of far longer depreciation periods than are now being experienced. This will result in the replacement cycles for new aircraft being extended and manufacturers becoming less able to market innovative types of aircraft as frequently as in the past. But if, as expected, airline consolidation does lead to heightened pressure to reduce aircraft prices and to a diminished willingness of the carriers to acquire innovative new aircraft so frequently, this may well serve at least the short-term interests of the manufacturers as well as of the air carriers.

Have you ever wondered what happens to commercial and military aircraft upon retirement? In the U.S., many of these aircraft end up at **Aerospace Maintenance and Regeneration Group (AMARG)** located at Davis-Monthan Air Force Base—"the world's biggest boneyard" located in the Arizona desert near Tucson. Additional boneyards exist in Arizona, California, New Mexico, and Texas. The desert is an ideal location to store aircraft short-term or permanently due to the dry heat which ultimately protects the aircraft from rusting. The AMARG desert location consists of more than 2,600 acres of land storing approximately 4,400 jets worth more than $32 billion. The primary active airline boneyards and military aircraft storage facilities are in Arizona, including Kingman Airport, Phoenix-Goodyear Airport, and Pinal Airpark.

But there is another side to this coin. Specifically, manufacturers of aircraft and their components, as well as the airlines, have benefited materially from the ability and willingness of most such enterprises to accept innovation. Were technological change to become less highly prized, there is a real question as to whether airline industry growth could be as vigorous as it would otherwise be.

Perhaps more critical is the question of whether any seriously reduced propensity to innovate on the part of the manufacturers of aircraft and components will delay the advent of such equipment as the projected hypersonic vehicle and, at the other extreme, the tilt-rotor aircraft.

Consolidation means greater control of the market by fewer airlines. If the lessons of other industries are a valid guide, such consolidation inevitably will lead to a reduced propensity to accept innovation from manufacturers. In turn, this will influence the latter's own propensities to implant advanced technology.

The extent and character of the pace and direction of technological change in aircraft and components may well be substantially determined by the extent to which airline consolidation becomes a global phenomenon. If consolidation is constrained in some nations, the intercarrier competition that remains may nevertheless be enough to enable the waning number of aircraft producers to continue to pursue innovation as a means of product differentiation and cost reduction.

Fleet Commonality

One of the main reasons for aircraft purchases in large numbers is fleet commonality. The Boeing 757 and 767 have common type-rating requirements—a distinct advantage to the carriers operating both types, as well as a strong inducement for airlines that are operating either model. However, the Boeing 757 went out of production in 2004 with different versions of the Boeing 737 and Boeing 767 replacing this part of the market. The new generation of the 737 family provides various models with identical cockpits and seating from 100 to 180 passengers, which offers airlines using such models greater flexibility for planning new routes. Commonality is also apparent in the Airbus series. The A320/321 and the A330/340 share many of the same component parts and flight deck instrumentation.

Engine choice is offered on almost all new transports having 200 or more seats—an important factor in decisions to buy a particular type. Usually, the selection is based on power plant commonality with other aircraft in the operator's fleet. Sometimes, it is a politically motivated decision, especially when the air carrier involved is government-owned or heavily subsidized.

Long-Range Aircraft

The Boeing 777, launched in 1990, is aimed at markets between the 767 and 747. It competes directly with the A330/340 series and, at one point, competed with the MD-11 when the aircraft was used in passenger service operations. Today, the MD-11 is only utilized in a cargo configuration with operators like FedEx. The 777 is the first commercial airliner with the option of folding wings, allowing it to fit its otherwise long wings (for required range) in most existing airport gates. However, by the mid-2000s, no aircraft operator had ordered a 777 with this option due to high costs ($2 million per aircraft). With this said, Boeing flew the 777X for the first time in 2020 for test flying purposes and the plane was debuted at the 2021 Dubai Airshow. The 777X is scheduled to go into commercial operation in 2023 and it will be the most rigorously tested aircraft in Boeing's history. The folding wing tip option, designed to increase performance, will be offered on the 777X allowing operators to use this option at locations where there are airport-gate space restrictions. At the time of writing, the 777X had orders placed by All Nippon Airways, British Airways, Cathay Pacific, Emirates, Etihad, Qatar Airways, and Singapore Airlines. In late 2011, Boeing launched the 787 Dreamliner, a mid-sized twin-engine wide-body aircraft that is capable of carrying between 250 and 290 passengers. This aircraft competes against Airbus' 350. The A350 is the first aircraft manufactured by Airbus with fuselage and wing structures made of carbon-fiber reinforced polymer. According to Airbus, the aircraft is more fuel-efficient than the Boeing Dreamliner with operating costs 8 percent lower than the Boeing competitor. Qatar Airways was the primary launch customer of the A350 and is one of the largest operators alongside Singapore Airlines, Cathay Pacific, Delta Air Lines, and Lufthansa.

Because of the hub-and-spoke system's drawbacks, airlines are currently rethinking route structures and are considering new aircraft that can economically bypass hubs and provide point-to-point service. This would certainly win friends among the traveling public. Point-to-point service has always been popular, but the concept has even more appeal for travelers today because of their increasing frustration with air traffic delays and mounting congestion at major hub terminals. Bombardier's Canadair CRJ series and Embraer's E-Jet series are aiming at this market niche. Interestingly, Embraer now offers the E190F and E195F freighter aircraft, allowing operators to increase efficiency with the focus on e-commerce demands and decentralized operations without the need of a hub airport that is reliant on transfer traffic.

Since the events of September 11, 2001, many airlines have refocused on point-to-point services to cut costs. In most cases, the regional jet is used because of efficient operational costs and reduced load-factor requirements compared to other aircraft.

The Trend Toward Leasing

The choice for an airline interested in financing a new airplane is, ultimately, to lease or purchase the aircraft. Before the 1980s, most established airlines chose purchase. Indeed, in 1984, only approximately 20 percent of the world's commercial aircraft were leased. By early 2000, however, leasing had become far more popular, accounting for well over half of all aircraft acquisitions. As of the 2020s, more than 50 percent of the world's commercial aircraft are leased and annual trends predict that this will grow by another 20 percent or more over the next two decades supporting a global aircraft leasing market expected to be worth more than $295 billion by 2029 (Statista).

Two factors in particular explain why leasing tended to be more attractive in the late 1980s. First, the 1986 Tax Reform Act eliminated the investment tax credit associated with purchase. Under the investment tax credit legislation, taxpaying companies could deduct a fixed percentage (7 to 10 percent, depending on the type of asset) of the cost of the asset directly from their tax liability. Such credits constituted an effective reduction in the price of the asset to the acquirer, assuming that taxes were owed. These credits have no value to tax-exempt investors or to firms that are not profitable. Second, the act reduced allowable deductions from taxable income for depreciation. Accelerated depreciation allows firms to depreciate more than the actual depreciation of an asset for tax purposes. This has the effect of postponing taxes over the life of the asset, thereby increasing the rate of return on the asset. For financial reporting (separate from tax reporting), aircraft were depreciated over 12 to 15 years on a straight-line basis to a 15 or 20 percent salvage value. Specifically, Congress passed an alternative minimum tax provision such that profitable companies could not reduce their tax bills to zero with depreciation and other noncash charges. Under the alternative minimum tax, all noncash expense deductions after a certain threshold were disallowed or deferred, thereby reducing their value.

There are two types of leases: operating and financial. An **operating lease** is a noncancelable short-term lease. Other than noncancelability, perhaps the most important characteristic of an operating lease is that at the end of the lease, the lessor retains full title to the asset and bears any market risk as to its value at that time. Also, the lessee shows no debt on its books because operating lease obligations are offered only as a footnote to the balance sheet. Similar to other leases, when an operating lease is signed and the asset is put into service, there is no large initial cash outflow from the lessee.

The other type of lease is a **financial (capital) lease**. With these leases, the financial effect is the same as a loan except that title to the asset remains with the lessor until all lease payments have been made. Under a financial lease, title passes at the end of the lease to the lessee for a preagreed-upon sum. The result is that there is no market risk on the value of the asset borne by the lessor unless there is default. Financial leases are required to be reported in virtually the same manner as loans. That is, the value of the leased asset shows in the assets of the corporation and the present value of the lease payments shows as a liability.

The operating costs of maintenance, insurance, and taxes are normally the same for both ownership and leasing. This occurs because under most operating leases, the lessee is responsible for maintaining the asset in good condition. The nature of the responsibilities of the lessee is revealed in the term "net-net-net lease," signifying that the lease payments are net of maintenance, taxes, and insurance.

Before 1990, default was not perceived as a major cost in the airline leasing business, either because airlines seldom ran out of cash or because in the unusual situations when they did, aircraft could easily be repossessed and placed with other airlines, often with only a quick change in the paint job. Thus, the default risk borne by the lessor was no more or no less than for a normal secured lender. With this said, due to the COVID-19 global pandemic, which impacted the airline industry in 2020, 2021, and 2022, aircraft leasing companies outpaced airlines for the first time in purchasing aircraft with preferential financial terms. Prior to the global pandemic, aircraft leasing companies accounted for 40–45 percent of aircraft deliveries but as airlines were hit financially through the pandemic, leased content increased to 60 percent of deliveries.

The advent of new leasing companies in the mid-1980s added a new dimension to the air transportation industry. Although sales and lease-backs with banks and other financial institutions have been around a long time, organizations such as GPA Group of Shannon, Ireland; International Lease Finance Corporation (ILFC) of Beverly Hills, California; and General Electric's GECAS were suddenly purchasing new airliners in rather spectacular numbers to lease to existing U.S. and foreign carriers. For the smaller carriers that lacked the huge amounts of cash needed to buy a couple of planes, leasing firms provided an attractive avenue to acquisition. Leasing also gave the smaller carrier the flexibility to trade up by exchanging (with its lessor) a smaller model for a larger one, as traffic dictated. By buying in quantity, of course, leasing companies get lower unit prices—a benefit reflected in the relatively reasonable rental rates they charge their customers.

In fact, the leasing enterprise became so successful that the firms engaged in it became the airframe manufacturers' biggest clients. ILFC ordered 130 assorted aircraft in May 1988; then in April 1989, GPA Group bought a staggering 308 transports, valued at over $17 billion—the largest order ever in terms of units. United topped that dollar figure in October 1990 with a $22 billion order (with options) for 68 Boeing 777s and 60 Boeing 747-400s (half of each type being firm orders).

Naturally, these record volume orders obligated large-scale airframe production. As a result, GPA Group and ILFC also created a new market for themselves. Airlines that had previously ordered equipment directly from manufacturers found that they were unable to get deliveries when they needed the planes. To solve their problem, they turned to leasing companies. Indeed, financing has become a significant part of the air transportation business these days.

Moreover, because of the troubled state of the airline industry during the early 1990s, many financial institutions awaited the outcome of the bankruptcy of several major carriers. The aircraft manufacturers offered special incentives to boost sales. Boeing accepted a substantial amount of United stock around the time that United ordered its new aircraft. Airbus Industrie arranged a sizable loan for Northwest Airlines when the carrier converted options for 75 A320s into firm orders. Even the engine manufacturers have helped to arrange financing. In an unprecedented move in 1996, Boeing signed a contract with American Airlines and Delta to become their exclusive supplier of planes.

Why do so many airlines need new equipment? For a number of reasons, not the least of which is the fact that air travel became more accessible to more people in the 1980s. More people were flying, and the airlines simply did not have enough capacity to move them all. Most orders originated to replace the aging aircraft in the world fleet. Once new models were delivered, it soon became clear that the modern aircraft would be supplementing rather than replacing the older jets.

On the other hand, the older Boeing 727s and Douglas DC-9s will not be flying forever. As of 2022, only 38 727s were still in operation with 23 operators and only 26 DC-9s remained active. Ever-increasing maintenance costs and fuel-inefficient turbines make older models much more expensive to fly. Operators of these planes must also contend with the public perception that they are unsafe. Yet it has been shown that an older plane, properly maintained, is as safe as the newest one in service. Ever since the top of the fuselage peeled off an aging 737 in flight in April 1988, the news media have been targeting the "sorry state" of the airline fleet. In this case, the Boeing 737 was operated by Aloha Airlines and was en route from Hilo to Honolulu, Hawaii. At 23,000 feet, the fuselage door became loose, causing an explosive decompression. The aircraft made a successful emergency landing at Kahului Airport on Maui with one fatality and eight serious injuries.

Noise Restrictions

Most early orders for new-generation aircraft were conceived as direct replacements of older planes—usually with models of roughly the same size. But as it became obvious that air travel was increasing beyond early projections, the carriers started looking for larger aircraft with more seats to obviate the need to add more flights. This led to orders for models such as the Boeing 757 to replace the 727s and the McDonnell-Douglas MD-80 to supplant the DC-9s. More than 2,000 new jet transports were on order for delivery during the 1990s, indicating that the days for aging airliners in the fleet were undoubtedly numbered. Higher maintenance costs, higher noise levels, and higher fuel consumption made them candidates for replacement by newer-generation models.

What happened to these planes after serving the public so well for so many years? Most of the old 727s have, in fact, found a new home with Federal Express; hushkits were developed to meet the noise rules. FedEx was able to absorb many of the aircraft and the remainder ended up in places like South America and Africa where noise is not a major issue. As of 2013, FedEx was the world's largest operator of the 727 with 170 in the fleet; the company began retiring the fleet in 2007 with the last flight in 2013. The 727 was ultimately replaced by the 757 and 767. As of 2022, FedEx operated more than 400 aircraft directly and, more approximately, 280 aircraft in the contracted fleet, including the Airbus A300-300F, Boeing 757-200SF, Boeing 767-300F, Boeing 777F, McDonnel-Douglas MD10-30F, McDonnel-Douglas MD 11F, ATR 42-300F, ATR 72-200F, ATR 72-600F, Cessna 208B Super Cargomaster, and Cessna 408 SkyCourier.

Table 15.1 lists the U.S. fleet by manufacturer. The data exists up to 2020.

Table 15.1 U.S. Aircraft Fleet by Manufacturer

Number	Manufacturer	2020	% of Fleet	2019	% of Fleet
1	Boeing	3,342	43.5	3,301	44.3
2	Airbus	1,767	23.0	1,677	22.5
3	Bombardier	1,001	13.0	984	13.2
4	Embraer	972	12.6	804	10.8
5	Cessna	245	3.2	246	3.3
6	McDonnel-Douglas	233	3.0	289	3.9
7	ATR	45	0.6	46	0.6
8	Gulfstream	30	0.4	32	0.4
9	Lockheed	13	0.2	14	0.2
10	Convair	12	0.2	12	0.2
11	Douglas	11	0.1	18	0.2
12	Dassault	9	0.1	12	0.2
13	CASA	3	0.0	3	0.0
14	Hawker	3	0.0	3	0.0
15	Curtiss	2	0.0	2	0.0
16	Pilatus	2	0.0	2	0.0
Total		7,690	100	7,445	100.00

Source: Aeroweb

Many factors must be considered before reaching the critical decision to acquire a specific number of a particular aircraft. All operating departments become involved in determining the number and type of aircraft required to implement the corporate strategy in future periods. This process is referred to as **fleet planning**, or the aircraft selection process. However, before getting into the specifics of the process from an individual airline's standpoint, it is important to look at some of the problems faced by the manufacturer in designing and building a new aircraft.

DESIGN AND DEVELOPMENT – THE MANUFACTURER'S VIEWPOINT

The Boeing Approach

The design and development stages for a new jetliner can take from five to six years. In the case of the Boeing 757 and 767 models, the concept of a more fuel-efficient aircraft was born in the mid-1970s with the skyrocketing price of fuel. When the 757 was being planned, engineers for Boeing, working with the airlines, were hoping for a 10 percent reduction in operating costs compared to the 727 jetliner that the new aircraft was designed to replace. In fact, Boeing had very modest ambitions for the 757. The original plan was essentially to modify the 727 to operate with two highly efficient engines instead of the three less efficient engines used on the 727. But as the months passed, Boeing's engineers kept making changes, and they finally decided to build the airplane more along the lines of the 767. About 60 percent of the parts in the 757 are interchangeable with parts in the 767; only 6 percent of the parts in the 757 are the same as those used in the 727. It should be noted, production of the 757 ended in October 2004 after 1,050 had been built.

Boeing promised a 22 percent improvement in operating costs over the 727—more than double the original estimate. The improvements are based primarily on the fact that a fully loaded 757 is 42 percent more fuel efficient than a full Boeing 727—the most popular commercial aircraft ever produced and the mainstay of the major carriers. The 757 is about the same size as the 727, but design improvements allow it to carry up to 63 more passengers with the 757-300 model. That is one reason for the reduction in operating costs. In addition, Boeing was able to use lighter-weight components, newly designed wings, and more efficient engines manufactured by Rolls-Royce and Pratt & Whitney. Despite the reduced need for fuel, the engines are so powerful that only two are needed to power the 757, rather than the three used on the 727.

The use of electronic monitoring devices and navigational aids allows the 757 to be flown by two pilots, as opposed to three for the 727—another improvement in operating costs. In the 757 cockpit, many of the common mechanical gauges and control systems are replaced by video screens and computers. The flight control systems are so advanced that, beginning shortly after takeoff, the plane can fly and even land by itself. In the 2020s, the 757 is considered an outdated aircraft in terms of technology but many of the existing aircraft in the fleet have received upgrades making the aircraft more relevant as it matures through the lifecycle.

Like the 727, the 757 is a narrow-body aircraft with only one aisle. But passengers will notice many differences. For one thing, interior design changes, including higher ceilings, oversized storage bins, and wider window frames, give the 757 something of a wide-body appearance. For another, the lavatories have been moved to a more convenient location closer to the center of the airplane to help keep flight attendants out of the way of passengers and vice versa.

The 757 represents a compromise product that attempts to meet the basic need for a fuel-efficient aircraft by the major U.S. carriers. Understandably, the different carriers had their own ideas about a replacement for the 727. Some carriers were primarily interested in a medium-size, medium-range aircraft with two engines. Others were primarily interested in an aircraft with transcontinental range, over-the-water capability, and three engines. The problem became even more complicated as more carriers offered their own ideas. Boeing's answer was to develop a family of aircraft—the 757, the 767, and the 777—that attempts to respond to the needs of most carriers. As of the 2020s, the industry is still waiting for a new aircraft to replace the 757

Figure 15.1 Major Characteristics of Competing Commercial Jetliners (hypothetical data)

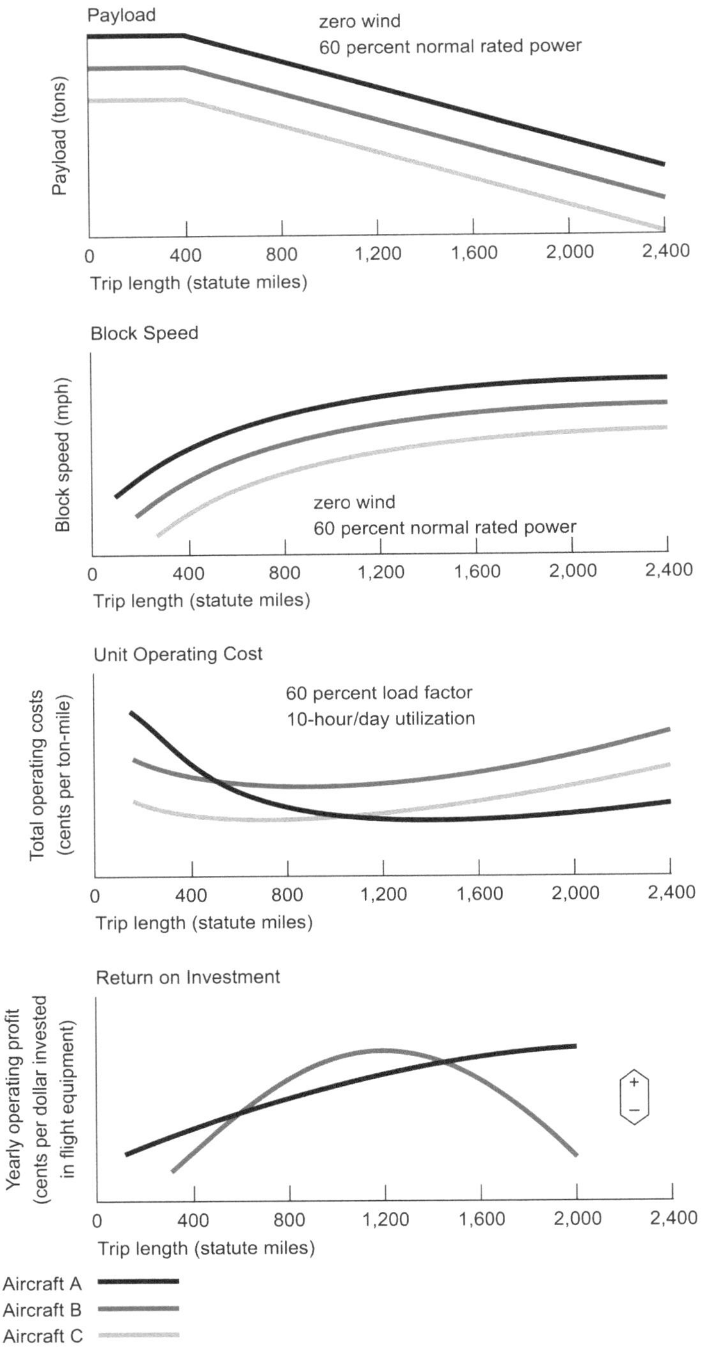

in terms of similar performance characteristics. In the meantime, airlines have acquired Airbus and Boeing products to fill the temporary gap. As of 2022, Boeing was considering development of a new mid-size airplane (NMA/797 project) to replace the 757 and 767 fleets with a seating capacity of 225 to 275 passengers.

Developing a new aircraft type comes with extremely high costs. It is impossible to have a single airplane or even several aircraft tailor-made, even for a major carrier. Because the break-even production point for a manufacturer can be anywhere from 200 to 600 aircraft, depending on the level of technology, a number of carriers must be interested in a particular aircraft before a manufacturer will make the necessary investment. Consequently, manufacturers bring in the airlines at the earliest possible time in order to get their ideas and to begin focusing on generic aircraft categories.

Designing and developing an appropriate family of aircraft to meet a majority of the airlines' needs has become even more difficult since deregulation. With new competition from other established carriers and from the newcomers, most of the large carriers are still in the process of rationalizing their current and future route structures in an attempt to determine where they want to be in five or ten years. The major carriers have been dropping low-density routes and concentrating on their high-density, long-haul routes with more standardized fleets, the motivation being to improve efficiency (load factors and utilization). This specialization among the different levels of carriers presents a problem for the manufacturer that tries to develop an aircraft whose users' needs vary considerably. The custom of prederegulation days, when each carrier had various models of aircraft from different manufacturers, seems to be over.

Another important step in the process of designing and developing a new aircraft is taking an objective look at the company's product in comparison with its competition. It is important to select those characteristics for comparison that are of particular concern to the potential airline customer (see Figure 15.1).

Challenges from Airbus

Before the Boeing and McDonnell-Douglas merger in 1997, Boeing's chief competitors for the 757 and 767 were McDonnell-Douglas's MD-80, MD-90, and MD-11, and Airbus Industrie's A300, A320, A330, and A340. By 1996, the global market share for McDonnell-Douglas commercial airplanes fell to 4 percent of new sales. Boeing's proposal to acquire McDonnell-Douglas drew severe objections from the European aviation community and served to intensify the competition for new-generation aircraft. In 2001, Airbus surpassed Boeing in terms of market share to become the world's largest aircraft manufacturer. Although Airbus is delivering more planes than Boeing, and has won the order battle each year since 2001, many industry analysts believe Boeing ended 2005 in a much better position than its rival, owing in large measure to the sales success of its 787 Dreamliner, which is crushing the Airbus A340 in market share. By 2020, Boeing had suffered in terms of sales compared to Airbus due to major challenges with the 737 MAX grounding in addition to further challenges associated with the COVID-19 global pandemic. In 2021, Boeing delivered a total of 340 new aircraft while Airbus reported delivery of 611. From March 2019 to December 2020, the 737 MAX fleet, consisting of 387 aircraft, was grounded worldwide due to two aircraft disasters that ultimately killed 346 people. In 2018, Lion Air crashed and in 2019, Ethiopian Airlines crashed, forcing the FAA and other civil aviation agencies to stop flying in order to avoid future accidents.

Airbus is determined to correct what its officials see as the abnormal situation of U.S. manufacturers dominating sales to the Western world. The founding partners, France and Germany, each had a 37.9 percent interest in the Airbus Industrie consortium. British Aerospace held 20 percent and Spain the remaining 4.2 percent. Airbus Industrie was originally co-owned by European Aeronautic Defense and Space Company (EADS), with 80 percent interest, and BAE Systems PLC, with 20 percent interest. Today, the company is called Airbus SE with the "SE" meaning Societas Europaea which permits Airbus to be registered as a European corporation instead of a national corporation employing more than 126,000 personnel. The ownership structure has changed over the years and as of 2022, Airbus was owned by SOFEPA (France) with 11 percent, GZBV (Germany) with 10.9 percent, Capital Group Companies with 10.1 percent, SEPI (Spain) with 4.1 percent, The Vanguard Group with 2.19 percent, PRIMCAP Management Company with 2.1 percent, Invesco with 1.1 percent, and "other" with 58.51 percent.

Three huge transport planes, whale-like aircraft known as SuperGuppies, continually ferry German fuselages, British-made wings, and other airliner sections to Toulouse, France, where the assembly plant is located. Many smaller parts and components are manufactured in the United States and shipped to Europe. Europe has obviously learned that one company or one country alone cannot make it in aviation manufacturing. In the 1960s and 1970s, there were a lot of good European aircraft—the Caravelle, the Mercure, the Trident, the BAC One Eleven, and the Concorde—but none was able to broaden its market significantly beyond Europe. Airbus Industrie receives no subsidies from member countries, and although participating governments contribute funds for research and development, all such assistance is paid back out of aircraft sales. But the European venture undoubtedly benefits from some of its political connections. The Airbus has been ordered by several state-owned airlines, and top management is sprinkled with former political leaders.

Although the Airbus might have benefited from political help, most industry observers attribute its success not to politics, but to timing. The Airbus was the first large twin-engine aircraft on the market, competing successfully against Lockheed 1011s and McDonnell Douglas DC-10s—both three-engine aircraft that consume more fuel.

Airbus Industrie's program for production of the long-range A340 and the medium- to long-range A330 was formally launched at the Paris Air

Show in June 1987. The A340, which took Airbus Industrie into the long-range market for the first time, is available in two versions. The A340-300 carries 295 passengers in a three-class layout a distance of 6,850 nautical miles. The A340-200 carries 262 passengers up to 7,700 nautical miles. Both types have a maximum takeoff weight of 542,300 pounds and are powered by CFM 56-5C-1 engines—a more efficient and more powerful version of the CFM International engine that is used on the A320.

The A330, a two-aisle, twin-engine aircraft, can transport 328 passengers in a two-class layout a distance of 5,000 nautical miles. It has a maximum takeoff weight of 454,100 pounds and can be powered by either General Electric CF6-8OC2 or Pratt & Whitney PW4000 engines. The A330 and the A340 are also offered in passenger/freight combination versions.

The design of the new models continues Airbus' policy of maintaining a high degree of commonality in the systems, power plants, equipment, and structures of all its models. This allows operators to realize many savings in training costs and in spares holdings and investments.

The A330 and A340 have common landing gear and a common fuselage, with the A340-300 eight frames longer than the A340-200. Airframe commonality between the A330 and A340 has been raised to the high overall level of 85 percent.

The two models have an all-new, highly advanced wing, which Airbus claims produces a lift/drag ratio up to 40 percent better than early wide-body aircraft and will allow the aspect ratio to be increased from 26 to 34 percent. The variable-camber wing incorporates automatic load alleviation for maximum structural efficiency, adapting its profile automatically during flight to match changing conditions of weight, speed, and altitude. The only differences between the wings of the A330 and the A340 are those required for installation of the outboard engines on the A340.

The A330 and A340 also share a common two-member cockpit crew similar to that of the A320, incorporating the latest glass cockpit instrumentation and sidestick controls instead of a yoke.

In 1988, Boeing introduced its 747-400, capable of flying 412 passengers more than 7,200 nautical miles, 1,000 more than the 747-300. When it was in operation, Northwest Airlines, the first to use these aircraft, was able to fly nonstop from New York to Tokyo without weight restrictions. The aircraft were transferred into the Delta Air Lines fleet when Northwest merged with Delta in 2008.

The 747-400 represents a natural progression in the 747 family, which began service life in 1970 with Pan Am. Boeing's sales of the 747 reached 1,200 aircraft by the turn of the 21st century, covering the 747-100 and its long-range, short-fuselage variant, the SP; the increased-takeoff-weight 747-200; the stretched-upper-deck 300; and the 400.

In basic design, the latest model is substantially the same as that of the 300, with identical fuselage, flight controls, and wing section (as far as the wing tips). There are, however, three major differences: (1) the wings are extended by 6 feet and have 6-foot-high winglets; (2) an all-digital two-person-crew flight deck is substituted for the three-person, conventionally instrumented original; and (3) the aircraft is offered with new engines—the Pratt & Whitney PW4000, General Electric CF6-8OC2, or Rolls-Royce RB 211-524134a. The 747-400 also has capacity in its horizontal stabilizer for 3,000 gallons of extra fuel, bringing capacity to over 56,500 gallons. In November 2005, Boeing announced a new model called the 747-800. Technology was based on the 787 capable of flying up to 350 passengers in a three-class configuration up to 8,000 nautical miles.

Other changes included the use of new aluminum alloys developed for the Boeing 757 and 767; a change to carbon brakes, saving 1,800 pounds in weight; and a completely redesigned interior, providing greater seating flexibility, larger overhead storage bins, and a wireless cabin entertainment system, in which radio and visual signals are picked up from floor-mounted transmitters, greatly simplifying rearrangement of the interior. The 747 made its first flight in 1969 and after more than 50 years of service to the industry, the final three 747s were built in 2022 as 747-8F models purchased by cargo carrier, Atlas Air.

Other Factors in Design and Development

Another important factor in the design and development stage is the ability of individual carriers to finance the proposed new aircraft. There is a direct relationship between aircraft orders and airline profitability.

Although airline profitability is a key element in the design and development of any new aircraft, forecasting earnings and orders for some future period is a difficult task. Furthermore, forecasting the breakdown of orders by manufacturer and by type of aircraft for each manufacturer becomes an even more difficult task. Yet this important step must be taken before plans can be made to invest millions of dollars in the design and development of a new aircraft.

Finally, manufacturers must be concerned with the proliferation of government regulations regarding the design and development of a new aircraft through the certification stage. These regulations cover everything from safety to noise and emission standards. Consequently, manufacturers work closely with government regulatory agencies, including the FAA, throughout all of the production stages.

THE FLEET-PLANNING PROCESS

From an individual airline's standpoint, the aircraft selection process is an ongoing function coordinated by a generalist group, such as corporate planning, with major help from technical, or specialist, administrations such as finance and property, marketing, line maintenance, engineering and maintenance, and flight operations. The existing fleet of an operator also is a significant factor in an operator's fleet-planning decisions. Substantial savings in terms of training, spares inventories, and operations can be achieved by operating a common fleet of aircraft.

Information Needed

Basically, corporate planning is interested in information on four different areas in the fleet-planning process: the carrier's current resources, corporate objectives, projected industry environments, and marketing strategy.

Current Resources. The carrier's **current resources** include its present fleet inventory by type of aircraft, use, and month (see Table 15.2). Also included are financial and technical data on aircraft on order. Financial data include acquisition costs (purchase or lease), start-up costs (primarily maintenance and flight training), and unit operating costs. Technical data on aircraft currently on order include payload-range figures, cruise performance information, runway requirements, noise levels, parts and service availability, and flight characteristics. Labor resources are also included under current resources. Maintenance capability in terms of type and availability of personnel to be trained on the new equipment must be considered, and lead times must be established. Similarly, flight crews must be prepared in advance of delivery dates of aircraft currently on order. In short, the corporate planning unit must completely analyze the carrier's current resources—what it has now, what it has on order—as a starting point in the aircraft selection process.

Table 15.2 A Carrier's Current Inventory of 737s (hypothetical data)

20XX	Own Plus Leased	Scheduled Service	Charter Service	Other*
January	11	11	0	0
February	14	12	0	2
March	16	12	0	4
April	18	14	2	2
May	21	14	3	4
June	22	14	4	6

Note: *Other assignment: maintenance, training, overhaul, line reserve, new aircraft in preoperational assignment.

Corporate Objectives. Top management's objectives for the company, or **corporate objectives**, include forecasted profitability (operating revenues and expenses, operating income, net earnings, earnings per common share, and return on investment), systemwide load factors, acceptable levels of cash on hand, market share on prime routes, debt/equity ratio, and general guidelines regarding new-aircraft acquisition. Other objectives include labor productivity, improvement targets and cost-saving goals. Corporate objectives are broad and emphasize what is to be achieved, but not necessarily how it is to be done.

Projected Industry Environments. **Projected industry environments** include the outlook for the national economy, the outlook for the industry, and the carrier's performance within the industry. First and foremost, corporate planning is concerned with the national economic outlook: the gross national product, national income, personal income, disposable income, and level of consumer income in the next one-year, five-year, and ten-year periods. Next to be considered is the air transport industry forecast within the overall economy, including such items as revenue passengers and cargo tonnage, RPMs, ASMs, cargo ton-miles, revenue block hours, and so forth. This is followed by a forecast of the carrier's traffic statistics within the industry. In addition, the carrier makes certain assumptions regarding passenger traffic mix (business versus pleasure), cargo directionality, and price elasticity of demand in selected long- and short-haul markets.

Marketing Strategy. This is a key piece of information, requiring considerable interplay among corporate planning and other administrations, primarily marketing. Given the company's current resources and corporate objectives and the projected industry environments, how is the carrier to implement its plan, or marketing strategy? Significant items to be considered include how much service to provide between key city-pairs, how much emphasis to place on long-haul or short-haul markets or both, which weak markets to penetrate now or later or to eliminate, and in which markets to trade off profit for market share or vice versa. A critical area of consideration is fare and rate structure levels in various markets for both passenger and cargo service.

The Fleet-Planning Model

Computer models have been developed to translate this information into a fleet-planning model that is used in determining future aircraft acquisition requirements, aircraft assignment requirements, financial requirements, and operating conditions over various planning periods (two and three years ahead for order versus option decisions, four and five years ahead to ensure that the purchases made in years two and three were consistent with long-term developments, and possibly seven to ten years ahead to ensure consistency and to gain insight into financial and facility needs in the long term). This fleet-planning model is commonly referred to as the *unconstrained operating plan*, because it ignores system constraints in order to ensure a full range of opportunities to be considered.

Computer-generated fleet-planning models provide corporate planning with the basic output—the number and type of aircraft to be acquired, the times of acquisition, and the timing of trade-in or phaseout of existing fleet. But they also allow management to assess the impact of altering the information fed in, primarily corporate objectives, industry environment, and marketing strategy.

System Constraints

The next step in the fleet-planning process is the application of **system constraints** to the model output that has been derived. Generally, system constraints become more amenable to relief as lead time increases. In other words, over a ten-year period, the normal period for a fleet-planning model, the original constraints might be eliminated. Some constraints are external to the airline, such as facility requirements at airports into which the airline flies, including runway capacity, gate capacity, terminal capacity (parking, ground access, passenger processing), and community noise. Government regulatory bodies may impose constraints on the airline's operating strategies, with consequences for the aircraft designed to implement that strategy. For example, the State Department might decide after negotiations with another country that there is enough service between selected cities in that country, despite the fact that a carrier wants to expand its service. Airplane availability can also impose an external constraint, as can environmental considerations.

There are a number of internal constraints, including such economic realities as the airline's profitability or lack thereof. Suppose the model called for the acquisition of seven wide-body jets. If the funds cannot be raised to make the purchase, the company might want to consider leasing. Other internal constraints include maintenance facility requirements, crew-training facilities, and capability of existing personnel to implement the fleet-planning model.

After the system constraints have been applied to the fleet-planning model, corporate planning is left with a **constrained operating plan**, or *optimization model*. Basically, the airline has now broken down aircraft types needed to implement its plan according to characteristics such as range (long, medium, short), passenger or cargo capacity, and direct operating costs.

Aircraft Evaluation

The aircraft evaluation process can be broken down into five areas: consideration of design characteristics, physical performance, maintenance needs, acquisition costs, and operating economics. The data provided is primarily focused on the Boeing 747, which is now considered to be old technology compared to new offerings in the market. However, the content serves as a good resource for discussion and the data could easily be replaced with a more modern aircraft.

Design Characteristics. **Design characteristics** include such factors as the aircraft's dimensions, weight profile (including maximum zero-fuel weight and operator's empty weight), fuel capacity, type of power plants, systems (electrical, hydraulic, and environmental), seating configuration, containers and pallets, bulk volume, and total volume.

It is difficult to compare these various characteristics for competing aircraft, and the problem is compounded by the many options available on each aircraft. For example, Boeing's high-cruise-speed 747-300 with the upper-deck extension has many seating arrangements. In the upper deck, on the economy side, with seats at 34-inch pitch, 69 passengers can be carried. At the same pitch, so can 81, 85, or 91. At 32-inch pitch, the maximum number of economy passengers is 96. Either 42, 52, or 63 business-class passengers can be carried at 36-inch pitch. On the first-class side, 38 passengers at 40- or 42-inch pitch or 26 first-class sleepers at 62-inch pitch can be carried. Varied lower-deck-forward arrangements include 18 first-class sleepers at 62-inch pitch plus 63 business passengers, or 41 first-class sleepers at 57-inch pitch. There are also arrangements for 40 first-class sleepers at 60-inch pitch or 36 first-class sleepers at the same pitch.

A high-density all-passenger-configuration 747-300 could carry as many as 624 people. By comparison, the 747-300 combi (combination passengers and freight) can carry 278 passengers and 12 pallets, or 360 passengers and 6 pallets. A choice of engines from Pratt & Whitney, General Electric, or Rolls-Royce is available.

Physical Performance. The technical parameters normally considered under this area are referred to as the **physical performance factors**. These include such items as payload-range diagrams, takeoff and landing data, cruise and approach speeds, runway requirements, and noise performance. *Payload-range diagrams* demonstrate the relationship between payload (passengers and cargo) and the distance an aircraft can fly. For each aircraft under evaluation, there is a maximum payload that can be carried over a particular range. Beyond that point, payload must be reduced to accommodate more fuel. Also, for routes over mountains, there must be consideration given to the maximum altitude that the aircraft can fly.

Flight test results with Pratt & Whitney's JT9D-7R4G2 turbine engines show that the 747-300's long-range cruise speed is Mach 0.01 faster than that of the 747-200; its Mach 0.85 fuel mileage is within an average of 0.5 percent at typical cruise weights. On climbout, fuel consumption is 3 to 5 percent better than that of the 747-200. On a 5,000-nautical-mile mission, at a speed of Mach 0.85, the 747-300 takes 35 minutes less trip time than a DC-10-30 flying at Mach 0.82. Carrying 496 passengers, fuel burn is 10 percent less per passenger than that of the 747-200B carrying 452 passengers and flying at Mach 0.84. The 747-300 has the same range as the 200B, and its holding fuel flow is 3 percent better at 20,000 feet, 2 percent better at 15,000 feet, and 5 percent better at 1,500 feet. Adding to the fuel efficiency of the 747-300 is the Boeing/Delco 747 performance management system. Economy cruise mode, cranked into its computer, advises pilots of the minimum-cost cruise based on the airline's specified fuel and time costs. Another item basic to the 747-300 is the improved Autoland system, which is said to give better lateral performance during localizer beam capture, approach, and landing; better longitudinal performance in flare and go-around; and better Category III A success rate. (Airport weather minimums for Category I are a runway visual range [RVR] of 2,400 feet and decision height [DH] of 200 feet; for Category II, RVR of 1,200 feet and DH of 100 feet; and for Category III A, RVR of 700 feet and no DH.)

Runway requirements are another important physical performance factor in the selection of an aircraft for those airlines operating out of airports situated well above sea level or in extremely hot climates. Finally, aircraft noise requirements continue to change airline priorities with respect to equipment decisions.

Maintenance Needs. **Maintenance needs** include such considerations as spare parts availability, aircraft compatibility with the rest of the fleet, product support, technical record keeping, and training support in terms of visual and audio aids. Maintenance cost comparisons over the expected service life of the equipment must be studied. These expenses are influenced by a number of factors, including stage lengths flown and amounts paid for outside services.

The corporate planning department works closely with the engineering and maintenance and flight-operations administrations in evaluating the technical factors (design characteristics, physical performance, and maintenance considerations). Contacts are also made with other airlines that have ordered or are considering similar equipment. And the airline's technical personnel make extensive on-site inspections.

Having narrowed the choice of aircraft on the basis of these technical factors, the airline must consider the final two: the acquisition costs, including payment terms and financing, and the operating economics of the aircraft.

Acquisition Costs. **Acquisition costs** include the cost of the aircraft itself plus spare parts, ground equipment needed, maintenance and flight training required, and the cost of the money itself if the aircraft is to be financed through debt financing (borrowing from various financial intermediaries, such as insurance companies or commercial banks) or equity financing (sale of bonds or stocks). The manufacturer's warranties and prepayment schedule must be closely examined. Although the actual price of one aircraft may be less than that of another, the total cost, taking these other factors into account, may be more. For example, one manufacturer may require more money in the form of *progress payments*—payments the airline makes to the manufacturer while the aircraft is under production. Another manufacturer's total costs may involve higher start-up costs. Consequently, it is important for the corporate planning department, working with finance and property people, to examine the cumulative capital investment requirements thoroughly.

The availability of new aircraft is another important consideration. The manufacturers, not wanting to experience the same tremendous layoffs that occurred back in the early 1970s when they were geared up to turn out a considerable number of the early wide-bodies, have chosen to spread out their production and add names to a waiting list that might extend to three years for some aircraft.

Airlines must also consider the possibility of trade-ins and compare the potential advantage of leasing versus purchase. The option of purchasing used aircraft cannot be overlooked. Finally, consideration must be given to any tax benefits if the decision is between a new and a used aircraft.

Operating Economics. **Operating economics** is perhaps the most difficult area to evaluate. It includes the potential aircraft's contribution to the company's profitability. Revenue potential and direct operating costs in terms of airplane miles and seat-miles must be examined. However, these items depend on and are related to a number of other factors, including the carrier's route structure, traffic flow and composition, existing traffic volumes, potential future growth, seating density, load factors, and utilization. Caution must be exercised, because there is really no one direct operating cost per seat-mile. For a particular aircraft, operating costs will vary with range. Furthermore, although the airplane under consideration might have a low direct operating cost per seat-mile, the seats must be filled with paying passengers for the airline to experience the low cost per mile. Consequently, the wide-bodies, with their higher seating capacities, are normally scheduled on high-density routes.

Flight crew expenses and fuel costs represent a significant portion of direct operating expenses, and the new-generation aircraft (Boeing 787 and Airbus A350) were built with this in mind. The 2-plus-2 concept (two pilots and two power plants) represents a significant improvement in direct operating costs over older models that rely on larger crews and more engines.

Tentative Fleet Planning and Financial Evaluation

After the aircraft evaluation, corporate planning prepares a projected earnings statement and cash flow for the expanded fleet. Then it makes recommendations for specific aircraft additions to and retirements from the fleet over a given time period, generally up to ten years. Included with the recommendations is an order-option-plan mix. *Orders* include proposed firm orders; *options* (to purchase) permit the acquisition of relatively favorable delivery positions but provide flexibility to meet changing circumstances. Options enable the carrier to change its plans without as severe a financial penalty as might otherwise be the case in the event that the option is cancelled. *Plan* aircraft are long-range future aircraft acquisitions that permit activation of long-lead-time items, such as facility renovations, while permitting further study of shorter-lead-time elements. Also included with the recommendations are a forecast of new funds to support the fleet purchase and a preliminary appraisal of the alternative methods of financing (equity, debt, lease, mix).

Presentation and Management Approval

Progress reviews are done periodically during the fleet-planning process, which not only ensures the full input of management's views but also minimizes the amount of new material to be covered during the final presentation. Major capital commitments normally must be cleared by the board of directors. Upon approval of the plan (in adjusted form if necessary), negotiations with the manufacturers and finance community move into their final phases. The fleet plan also becomes a key source of other planning data, including personnel and facilities.

FLEET OPTIMIZATION MODEL

Figure 15.2 provides an example of a fleet optimization model. The concept of such a model is to select the "right" aircraft at the "right" time. The aircraft fleet planning process is very in-depth and if followed correctly, should provide the best results for the air carrier. Fleet optimization is part of the fleet-planning process and concentrates on modeling fleet selection and composition and fleet development, estimating the effects of commonality on fleet planning; analyzing differences in fleet planning; and analyzing the impact of changes in the economic, ecologic, and technological environment. A Fleet Optimization Model can be useful for air carriers, aircraft manufacturers, technology developers, and government institutions.

THE DECISION TO UPGRADE OR REPLACE

In late 1995, a major U.S. carrier faced the problem of how to replace its fleet of older, late-1960s and 1970s vintage twin jets with newer, more efficient, and more noise-compliant 110-seat jets. A number of factors unique to that airline were influencing its fleet decision making. The aircraft in question, a fleet of DC-9-30s, were operating largely on short segments, averaging 500

Figure 15.2 Fleet Optimization Model

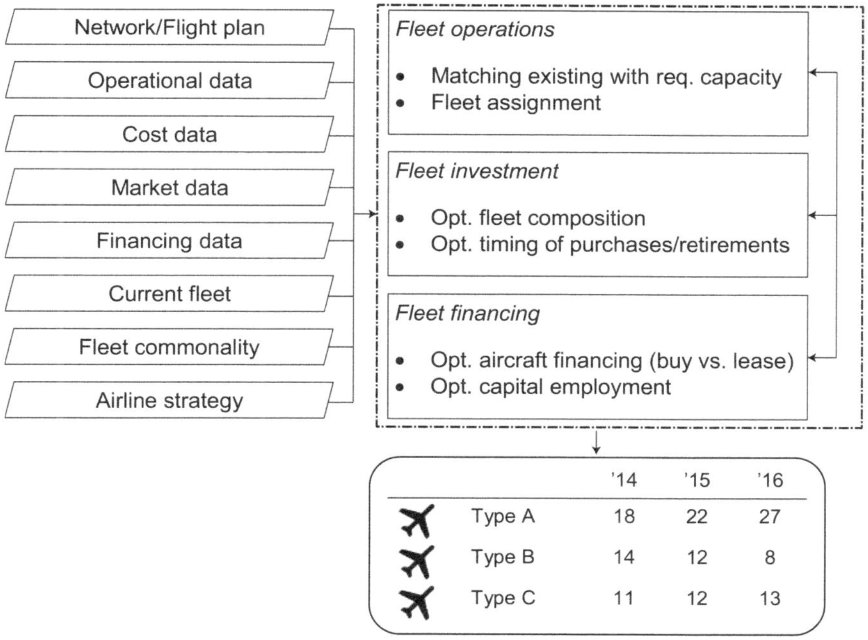

Source: Adapted from Institute of Air Transportation Systems

miles. The nature of these routes was twofold. First, the point-to-point service portion of the route was highly competitive, even hypercompetitive. Fares were determined by intense competitive pressure, and therefore, setting fares was largely outside the control of the airline. Second, a portion of the traffic represented highly valuable feed between the origination point and major hubs, where it would interconnect with longer-haul, less competitive, and higher-profit service provided by the airline beyond the hub. Although the connecting, or feeder, traffic was viewed as having strategic importance to the airline, overall, profit margins on the routes were very thin.

The airline also had to begin replacing the DC-9-30s because they did not meet Stage III noise compliance standards. The DC-9s could be replaced with newer, noise-compliant model(s) or, alternatively, be retrofitted with hushkit devices that would bring the aircraft into compliance with the more stringent noise regulations. If the engine retrofit were performed, the airline could also, at additional investment, perform a number of heavy maintenance procedures to refurbish the aircraft and extend their useful life. Included in this work could be a major cosmetic overhaul, replacing the seats, galleys, sanitation facilities, and passenger comfort items, which would create the impression of a new aircraft from a passenger's perspective. The total investment was estimated at about $5 million, in addition to the airline's existing book investment of less than $1 million. Retrofitted and refurbished, the fleet of DC-9s would be certified for more than 100,000 lifetime cycles (a cycle is one takeoff and landing). Because the fleet had, on average, an age of about 50,000 cycles and an estimated use of 2,900 cycles per year, these refurbished aircraft conceivably could operate another eight to 12 years. The downside included higher and harder-to-forecast maintenance expenses compared with new aircraft and the adverse impact of higher fuel prices (translated into higher fuel expenses), because the older, now hushkitted aircraft would burn more fuel than new models.

The airline narrowed its choice of replacement new aircraft to a single alternative, and then it began, with the assistance of an outside consultant, to choose between replacement or retrofit. In this analysis, the data were compared on a cost-per-block-hour basis; because the aircraft were operated on numerous and varied routes, a route-by-route comparison was not appropriate.

The DC-9s had close to a 20 percent operating cost disadvantage ($1,450 versus $1,200 operating cost-per-block-hour) compared with the new aircraft. However, the estimated capital cost-per-block-hour favored the DC-9s ($400 versus $1,100 capital cost-per-block-hour). The DC-9s also had a much lower ownership cost compared with the new aircraft, which cost four times as much. The net overall cost-per-block-hour was nearly 20 percent lower for the old aircraft versus the new because the capital or ownership costs were less than half the new aircraft's cost on a block-hour basis.

The original description of the routes on which these aircraft operate noted that the operating margins are very thin. The airline concluded that, whatever its long-term needs might prove to be (the implication being that the retrofit represented only an intermediate-term solution), the basic economics of these hypercompetitive routes would not support new aircraft with an overall block hour cost much higher than the estimated block hour costs of the refurbished DC-9s. The difference for the airline meant literally flying or not flying the routes.

In modern times, there are some tradeoffs and risks involved. The most important risk is the likelihood that some of the operating expense components may differ in actual experience, compared with the forecasted assumptions made in the analysis. Fuel remains a real vulnerability, although in this case the airline concluded that fuel prices would need to rise sharply and remain high over a sustained period to offset the ownership cost differential. Maintenance also remains a vulnerability; however, the airline's experience with the aircraft (in its fleet for nearly a quarter of a century) enables it to have an adequate level of confidence in the aircraft's maintenance requirements. There always remains the risk of a major price/performance breakthrough in similar new-manufacture aircraft development. This is actually the largest risk in the analysis. However, the payback period on the retrofit is so short (about three and a half years) that the attractiveness of refurbished aircraft is hard to resist. It is important in all of the analyses to distinguish between efficiency and the cost of necessary levels of efficiency.

Even today, many valuation methods would give little credence to this particular aircraft because they often fail to take into account the value-in-use or revenue-generating capacity of a specific type of aircraft, with specific operating economics, operating on a specific mission. It is the specificity of the fit, the definition within context, that gives rise to value. Obviously, not every aircraft and every mission show similar results. Also, the economics of one aircraft size cannot necessarily be extrapolated to other classes of jets.

SUPERSONIC AIR TRAVEL

The world is in an age of acceleration and disruption at the foothills of the fourth industrial revolution which is focused on intelligence, and the next two decades will bring many changes to the aviation industry. Manufacturers are constantly looking at emerging technologies to design, build, and test new forms of power that make air travel more seamless, efficient, and faster. New technology includes aircraft powered by alternative fuels and electricity powered by batteries as examples. Ever since the Concorde, which was in commercial service from 1976 to 2003, **supersonic** travel has been a dream, but no manufacturer has been able to perfect the technology and make it affordable while also acknowledging infrastructure challenges associated with airport operations and noise.

In 2022, Bombardier announced creation of a small private jet called the Global 8000 capable of flying at supersonic speeds at a cost of $78 million per aircraft. In 2014, Boom Supersonic was founded to design and build a commercial supersonic aircraft called the Overture. As of 2022, the Overture is more than just a vision and the company hopes to be flying in the commercial sector by 2029. The Overture will have a seating capacity of 65 to 88 passengers and will be capable of flying just under twice the speed of sound at an estimated cost of $200 million per aircraft. The Overture is expected to have a range of 4,250 nautical miles, capable of cruising at Mach 1.7 at 60,000 feet. United Airlines and Japan Airlines have expressed interest in being launch customers for the Overture. As of 2022, United Airlines had a signed agreement in place with Boom to purchase 15 aircraft with an option for 35 additional. Imagine flying between London and New York in only three hours and thirty minutes compared to today's option which averages six hours and thirty minutes. Boom!

KEY TERMS

Aerospace Maintenance and Regeneration Group (AMARG)
acquisition costs
aging
constrained operating plan
corporate objectives
current resources
design characteristics
financial (capital) lease
fleet optimization model
fleet planning
maintenance needs
operating economics
operating lease
physical performance factors
projected industry environments
supersonic
system constraint

REVIEW QUESTIONS

1 Discuss the importance of the fleet-planning process to both short-term and long-term management decision making in an airline. How is this process in a sense betting on the future? What effect has deregulation had on the fleet-planning process? Discuss the implications of the hub-and-spoke system and industry consolidation on fleet planning.
2 What are some of the advantages of fleet commonality? Why has there been a trend toward leasing? Distinguish between an operating and a financial lease. How will noise restrictions affect future aircraft purchases?
3 What are some of the factors an aircraft manufacturer has to take into consideration during the design and development stage of a new commercial jetliner? What is meant by "designing and developing an

appropriate family of jets for the airlines"? What is the aircraft aging process and what factors must be included?

4 Describe what is included in each of the four basic inputs (informational needs) to the fleet-planning process. Marketing strategy was referred to as the "how-to" function. What does that mean? And why is this such a key piece of information?

5 Describe the Fleet Optimization Model. Who benefits from such a model?

6 What is meant by the *unconstrained operating plan*? What are the basic purpose of and data derived from fleet-planning models? Give several examples of external and internal system constraints. Define the *constrained operating plan*.

7 Give some examples of items to be considered under the following areas in the aircraft evaluation process: design characteristics, physical performance, maintenance needs, acquisition costs, and operating economics. Give some examples of difficulties encountered by airline management in comparing aircraft. What are some of the difficulties in examining a single model aircraft? The new-generation jetliners were designed with what primary consideration in mind?

8 What are some of the items included in corporate planning's recommendations of a fleet plan to top management? Why is top management apprised of developments as the fleet-planning process progresses?

9 What happens to commercial and military aircraft at the end of the lifecycle? Where do these aircraft go to be stored and why?

10 Is supersonic air travel going to be a reality? When is the first supersonic aircraft forecasted to be in commercial operation? What airline will be the launch customer?

APPENDIX: FLEET PLANNING AT AMERICAN AIRLINES

The following content on fleet planning at American Airlines is to be used as a case study. The different types of aircraft presented in the case study reflect older models and could be replaced with modern aircraft in terms of manufacturer, type, and model.

It has been said that airline executives never know for sure whether they have bought the right airplane until they have used it for ten or 15 years. The purchase decision, whipsawed by the same variables that rob executives of early affirmation of their judgments, is clearly the largest and one of the longest-term commitments an airline ever makes. It determines much of the operational flexibility, risk, cost structure, and related investment for the company.

The first step in the American aircraft selection process is defining the airplane's mission, including such particulars as general descriptions of size, range, and passenger/cargo loads. An additional element of this step at American, and at other airlines with two-tier crew pay scales, is deciding whether the aircraft is for expansion or for replacement of older aircraft.

If the answer is replacement, then the aircraft cannot be credited with the benefits of growth economics, since the employees necessary to fly it and support it will merely be moved from an old aircraft to a new one. A growth aircraft, on the other hand, can be staffed fully with new employees at market rates. Such agreements make it in the airline's best interests to expand, for by expanding and bringing in new employees at lower wages and zero seniority, the airline's average wage burden decreases. This, too, was the point of the 1985 United strike as management delayed what was expected to be a massive expansion until a critical two-tier wage agreement was in place.

The decision on approximate aircraft size has to take into account the big versus small issue. In boom times, carriers with large airplanes have the opportunity to make a great deal more money than carriers whose capacity is constrained with small units. The leverage in large aircraft is tremendous. On the other side of the issue, you cannot lose money operating small aircraft with high load factors. The balance is between opportunity and caution. However, since deregulation, the vast majority of new orders have been for small- to medium-size aircraft.

Once the mission is defined and a decision made on whether to credit the purchase with growth economics, American examines the airframe and engine alternatives in a conventional manner using, for example, the type of information often seen on charts plotting seat-mile and aircraft-mile costs versus capacity.

The engine selection process is more influenced by engineering assessments than by financial analysis. Competition among manufacturers with engines on the same aircraft is intense and helps keep the overall price down. This competition is not surprising when one considers that over 15 to 20 years the purchaser will spend three to six times an engine's original worth on spare parts.

When the engine and airframe alternatives are understood, American factors in the revenue impact and operating costs of each alternative applied to the defined mission. The decision process, on generally secure, empirical grounds until now, definitely gets into some very speculative areas as future traffic and yields are predicted. It requires defining the overall size and competitive shape of the industry at some future date.

Once that difficult judgment is made, American applies a number of models and formulas to determine the revenue impact of a particular aircraft type operating in its route system.

First of these models is called *spill*, which calculates the increase in passengers that can be accommodated if a larger aircraft is bought to place on a densely traveled route, or, on the other hand, how many more passengers will be "spilled" off a flight if a smaller aircraft is purchased. For example, with a 142-seat Super 80, when the load factor reaches 60 percent, some passengers, at some times of the year, on some flights, on some days are not being accommodated. Clearly, if you substitute a 124-seat 737-300, additional passengers would be lost. The value of that lost contribution must be used to offset the benefit of lower operating costs on the smaller airplane.

But a passenger bumped off one flight is not necessarily lost to the airline, so another model is used to forecast how many passengers are *recaptured* by another American flight. If, for example, a passenger is bumped off one of American's four flights between Cities A and B, he or she has a choice of the other three American flights or, let's say, eight offered by competing airlines. The chances of holding the passenger might be expressed simply as three out of 11, or 27 percent. High load factors on the other flights would decrease the chance of recapture, but the brand loyalty created by a frequent flyer program would increase the capture rate.

Examination of revenue impact does not end with spill and recapture. The industry concentration on hub-and-spoke systems gives added importance to up-line and down-line factors affecting route traffic. There is a high probability that a person gained or lost has come up-line from, or will go down-line to, another American Airlines flight. Thus, a revenue impact analysis must include an examination of the contribution of the capacity of an aircraft on a hub-bound route to other routes onward from the hub (up-line) and, conversely, the contribution of the other routes feeding the route through the hub (down-line). If American loses a passenger on the first segment because the aircraft is too small, there is a high probability they will lose that passenger on the connecting segment even if the aircraft on that up-line or down-line segment has seats available.

The final route revenue impact factor to be examined is *pushdown.* When a new aircraft enters the fleet, it is assigned to high-pressure routes flown by smaller aircraft or low-pressure routes flown by bigger aircraft, in both cases increasing the efficiency of the operation. For example, American's new Boeing 767s were used on dense 727-200 routes where load factors were close to 88 percent. This load factor on the 144-seat 727 translated into a 62 percent load factor in the 204-seat 767. However, use of the larger aircraft decreases the spill from the highly loaded 727s, pushing the actual load factor on the 767s closer to 75 percent.

All the fleets below the 767 in size are pushed down progressively onto lower and lower demand routings, with the smallest and/or oldest aircraft in the fleet—the 727-100 in American's case—pushed onto the marginal routes or onto the block for sale. Meanwhile, as more and more 767s arrive, there are fewer high-pressure 727 routes to take over, so the overall 767 fleet load factor drops. Looked at another way, the revenue value of the first five 767s is greater than the revenue value of the last five. This forces American to get to grips with the issue of optimal fleet size—too many units may force deployment on routes where the incremental seats have little, if any, value.

The fleet size issue is a question of balance. In order to closely match airplanes to the markets to be served, a number of different types of airplanes are needed. Of course, each new type purchased brings along with it certain support, equipment, and training costs. While the costs of having to maintain a support infrastructure for a few airplanes may be seen by some to be too high a price to pay, others note the benefits of closely keying aircraft capabilities to the market, regardless of the fleet size.

The challenge is to find the right balance between fleet complexity and market fit. American has generally concluded that unless it can see a clear need for 15 to 20 units, the costs of fleet proliferation far outweigh the benefits of better market sizing.

Forecasts must be made about the operating environment of the future, and no matter how sophisticated, a forecast is still a forecast. To lessen the risk of making fleet decisions today based on forecasts about the future, American compares aircraft under a variety of future scenarios using a matrix approach and calculating the point at which the decision would change. For example, at what fuel price would American prefer a higher-priced new-technology airplane? This allows the decision makers to assess the degree of risk associated with each alternative.

Intangibles are those factors in the purchase decision process covering such items as the perception that passengers prefer wide-bodies, new airplanes, and no crowds. Also, some aircraft are more adaptable than others. But some of these intangibles have lost their pull in the deregulated environment, where the herd instinct is sharply diminished and an airline does not buy an aircraft just because a competitor bought it.

Once all the preceding questions have been answered, the candidate airplanes are compared in terms of a *defined service life*. It is a relatively simple matter to calculate the net present value of the future cash flows associated with each airplane under consideration, and this permits American to rank the various alternatives and establish an acceptable all-in price for each airplane. With an acceptable price established, manufacturer negotiations begin.

This appendix was adapted from a speech given by Robert E. Martens, American Airlines Vice-President of Financial Planning and Analysis, in New York in May 1985, at a Lloyd's of London conference.

CHAPTER 16

Airline Labor Relations

CHAPTER CHECKLIST • YOU SHOULD BE ABLE TO:

- Discuss some of the reasons labor is such an expensive resource
- Describe the basic purposes of the Railway Labor Act of 1926, and explain the role of the National Mediation Board
- Discuss the collective bargaining process under the Railway Labor Act
- Describe some of the criticisms of the process
- Explain how airline union activity has changed over the years
- Distinguish between *industrywide bargaining* and *pattern bargaining*
- Compare and contrast labor relations in the prederegulation and postderegulation periods
- Discuss future human resource challenges in the 21st century

INTRODUCTION

The aviation industry has a major impact on the U.S. economy contributing more than $1.6 trillion in annual economic activity and supporting over 11 million direct and indirect jobs.

In 2008, the U.S. scheduled airline industry employed approximately 560,000 persons, of whom roughly 525,000, or approximately 94 percent, were pilots, flight attendants, mechanics, and other aircraft- and traffic-servicing personnel. In 2009, the number of jobs decreased due to the U.S. financial recession and from 2010 to 2019, the number of jobs increased annually. By 2021, U.S. scheduled airlines employed approximately 412,000 persons with the massive decrease due to the COVID-19 global pandemic. Of the 24 scheduled service passenger airlines operating in 2021, four

DOI: 10.4324/9780429346156-19

network airlines provided 62.2 percent of jobs (American Airlines, Delta Air Lines, United Airlines, Alaska Airlines), six low-cost airlines provided 21.4 percent of jobs (Southwest Airlines, JetBlue Airways, Spirit Airlines, Frontier Airlines, Allegiant Air, Virgin America), and ten regional airlines provided 14.5 percent of jobs (SkyWest Airlines, Envoy Air, Piedmont Airlines, Republic Airlines, Endeavor Air, PSA Airlines, Horizon Air, Mesa Airlines, Air Wisconsin Airlines, GoJet Airlines). The remaining jobs were supported by niche carriers (Hawaiian Airlines, Sun Country Airlines, Silver Airways, and Eastern Airlines) (Bureau of Transportation Statistics) (see Table 16.1).

Table 16.1 Airline Employment, 1990–2021

Year	Total
1990	461,204
1991	429,673
1992	446,097
1993	439,873
1994	425,387
1995	430,491
1996	440,852
1997	454,783
1998	477,264
1999	502,925
2000	527,577
2001	497,024
2002	471,944
2003	428,951
2004	439,218
2005	412,810
2006	402,907
2007	417,777
2008	394,173
2009	377,975
2010	379,154
2011	386,595
2012	382,291
2013	381,178
2014	384,700
2015	399,928
2016	415,979

Year	Total
2017	430,232
2018	442,744
2019	452,352
2020	365,053
2021	412,844

Source: Bureau of Transportation Statistics.

Compared with the labor force of many other industries, airline workers are highly skilled and assume a high degree of responsibility. Strict standards in employee selection and training are essential. The nature of airline service requires 24-hour operations every day of the year and location of employees throughout the country. Wage settlements must reflect the nature of the operations and complexity of the jobs.

Over 300,000 employees of the airline industry are members of unions, and union officers administer noteworthy assets and have available executive jets to travel to meetings around the country. Airline labor unions are **craft unions**. That is, there is no single union that represents the entire labor force of an airline; rather, one union represents pilots, another mechanics, another flight attendants, and so forth. A disadvantage of this arrangement is that a strike by a single craft union may cause a shutdown of the entire airline. There may also be disputes as to what constitutes a craft and which jobs actually belong to which craft. Furthermore, airlines, like other transportation modes, are likely to be particularly hurt by strikes, because, unlike manufacturing firms, they cannot store their product. An airline, anticipating a strike, cannot stockpile its inventory, as a manufacturer can, and unions are aware of this. The seasonality of demand for airline travel may also augment labor's bargaining position, in that a union can select an approaching seasonal peak at which to press for its demands.

A typical major carrier may have a dozen or more labor contracts in force, all with different renewal dates. The percentage of employee membership varies among the established carriers, but active union membership in this labor-intensive field has ranged from 60 percent of the employees of some airlines to over 90 percent of others.

In 2021, over 30 separate unions were certified within the airline industry, although several, such as the Air Line Pilots Association (ALPA), the **Association of Flight Attendants (AFA)**, the **National Air Traffic Controllers Association (NATCA)**, the International Association of Machinists and Aerospace Workers (IAM & AW), and the Transport Workers Union (TWU), hold broad certification embracing numerous carriers. The major and national carriers alone had several hundred individual contracts in effect in the early 2020s, though some are negotiated on a group basis by a single union. This fragmentation of representation has increased the potential for strikes over the years. The average two- or three-year contract period produces continual labor negotiations for most airlines.

THE RAILWAY LABOR ACT AND THE AIRLINES

Labor relations in the airlines are regulated under a special federal law applicable only to them and to the railroads—the Railway Labor Act (RLA). This act was passed to provide a series of steps for the settlement of transport labor disputes. The reason for its passage was the serious economic implications of widespread strikes against the railroads, which, like the airlines, are a heavily unionized industry.

The Origin and Provisions of the Railway Labor Act

Congress had tried to avoid such disruptions as early as 1888 and had enacted various pieces of railroad labor legislation over the years, but it had not been able to produce a highly effective measure. Finally, in an unusual display of unity, a joint committee of railroad labor and management leaders in 1926 drafted and presented to Congress a bill they could agree on. Congress overwhelmingly passed the legislation, and the **Railway Labor Act** went into effect on May 20, 1926.

The statute's basic purposes, as spelled out in Section 2 of the act, are the following:

1. To prevent interruption of service
2. To ensure the right of workers to organize and bargain effectively
3. To provide complete independence of organization by both parties
4. To assist in the prompt settlement of disputes or grievances arising out of interpretation or application of existing contracts

The law carefully laid out a complicated system of "adjustment" boards, arbitration procedures, and other machinery that, while not wholly satisfactory to all parties, worked well enough that the RLA was viewed in the late 1920s as a model labor law.

Three important amendments were adopted by Congress in 1934 to greatly strengthen the act. The amendments, proposed by a number of major railroad unions, established the current three-member **National Mediation Board (NMB)** to administer the law and facilitate settlement of major disputes. The board consists of three individual members appointed by the president, each serving a three-year term. The board has jurisdiction over disputes involving rates of pay or changes in rules and working conditions in those instances in which the parties to an agreement have been unable to reach a settlement. The primary task of this board is to institute mediation and attempt to help both parties find a common ground for contract agreement. The board does not decide issues or make awards. Either party may invoke the service of the board, or it may intervene without request.

Other amendments sharply restricted company-sponsored or -dominated unions and outlawed "yellow dog" contracts. (A yellow dog contract, as defined by the NMB, is "one in which a worker disavows membership in and agrees not to join a labor union during the period of his or her employment.")

By this time, the fledgling ALPA, founded in 1931, had begun to lobby Congress to bring the airlines under the Railway Labor Act. The new law had obvious applications to airline pilots struggling for basic union rights with the carriers, and the ALPA's founders pressed for its extension to the airline industry.

The ALPA's lobbying efforts were successful, and a bill to place airlines under the RLA was passed on April 10, 1936. As with the railroads, the major policy consideration favoring coverage of the air carriers was concern over disruption to service.

Today, the RLA still applies only to the railroad and airline industries. Its influence is felt well beyond those two industries, however, because it served as the model for the 1935 National Labor Relations Act (NLRA), whose provisions apply to the rest of the nation's workers.

The RLA is based on the principle of freedom of contract and maximum self-determination. Under the law, employees have the right not only to form and join a union but to bargain collectively with their employer as well. Also, under the law, an employee has the right to be protected against any coercion or pressure by an employer of his or her choice of representative. The employee has the right to expect that the employer will negotiate with the employee's union in good faith and make every effort to reach an agreement and carry out that agreement. If the employer does not carry out the agreement, then the employee has the right to expect that certain procedures will permit him or her to process grievances and have them fairly resolved by a neutral arbitrator if necessary.

There are several major differences between the RLA and the NLRA, but perhaps the main distinction is the mandatory mediation control that the NMB has over the collective bargaining process in the railroad and airline industries. Under the NLRA, mediation is purely voluntary, never binding upon the parties to a dispute unless they agree beforehand that it will be. Mediation under the RLA, however, is mandatory subject to the direction and control of the NMB.

Another important distinction is that under the RLA, unfair labor practices are not spelled out and parties are required to seek court action for relief. The NLRA specifically prohibits certain activities in labor relations and provides for an administrative enforcement procedure. Despite the lack of stipulated unfair labor practice provisions in the RLA, however, a body of law has sprung up that is very much analogous to many things prohibited under the NLRA. And both acts tend to feed on each other. Many rights that workers have under the NLRA are carried over into the RLA, and similarly, the kind of restraints that are part of the RLA are applied more and more under the NLRA.

Mandatory mediation under the RLA does not mean mandatory settlement. The compulsion underlying the mechanism is its requirement that the parties keep searching for a possible solution to their differences through the mediation process, sometimes even long after the parties have given up. During mediation, the NMB does not decide how the dispute must be settled. It tries instead to guide the parties through an examination of the facts and alternative considerations that would lead to a mutually acceptable settlement.

Although the RLA has applied to the airline industry over the years, there is some question as to whether the labor problems of the two industries are really similar. Because the railroad industry is highly integrated (a large proportion of freight is interchanged among the carriers), a strike against one or a few carriers can bring the whole system to a halt. In contrast, a strike against a few major air carriers may not have national emergency implications. Even the IAM's strikes against seven carriers in 1966 (see Table 16.2) were not considered by the president to cause a national emergency. Furthermore, much of the RLA machinery is oriented toward railroad needs and has been criticized over the years as not being responsive to airline needs.

Although each step under the RLA is not clearly defined or provided under the law, there are various steps in the mechanics of labor–management conflict settlement, depending on whether the dispute is a minor or a major one. A "major dispute" arises in the formation of a collective agreement or the lack of one, while a "minor dispute" arises in the proper meaning or application of an agreement. The RLA's process differs for each dispute. Minor disputes, for which there are not strikes, are settled by system boards of adjustment. Resolution of major disputes follows a formalized procedure. These procedures rely on the RLA's philosophy of collective bargaining, along with the NMB's mediation and optional arbitration.

The Collective Bargaining Process

The RLA has an enormous emphasis on stability. Most important, the status quo—specifically, prohibition against unions striking or carriers unilaterally changing pay, rules, or working conditions—is preserved throughout the long and involved collective bargaining process. That process lasts until the NMB, in its sole, virtually unreviewable discretion, determines that the parties should be released to use self-help. Self-help usually means, for a carrier, a lockout or unilateral implementation of new wages, hours, and working conditions, and, for the union, a strike.

Collective bargaining under the RLA is a rather insular process. It limits the disputes to the parties involved and it avoids the kind of litigation that is characteristic of the NLRA and other labor relations statutes. Two of the NMB's central functions, resolving representation disputes and aiding collective bargaining through mediation, allow the board virtually unreviewable discretion. Complaints challenging the representation and collective bargaining activities of the board are seldom successful because the federal courts largely defer to the board.

The processes of the RLA increase the likelihood of settlement, which avoids shutdowns. The act requires the parties to meet, to talk, to mediate, to "exert every reasonable effort to settle all disputes." The process keeps the parties working on resolving their disagreements and limits the involvement of the courts and their endless appeals processes. The length of time during which the parties are required to negotiate also may be long and drawn out to encourage the parties to make the accommodations necessary for settlements.

At the same time, NMB election rules tend to preserve continuity of union representatives. This also provides stability and makes agreements more obtainable.

Step 1: Collective Bargaining. The mechanics of settlement assume that contracts will normally be reached by use of the traditional methods of free collective bargaining. Disputes over contracts, interpretations, and grievances presumably will usually be settled by conferences between carriers and employees. These two devices, it is hoped, will handle the majority of problems, and no other procedure will be necessary. Unfortunately, however, the mere existence of additional procedures sometimes seems to jeopardize the effectiveness of earlier steps, and neither side makes any great effort to settle issues at the lower levels.

The process starts with the union and company exchanging opening proposals. The two sides have ten days to agree on a time, place, and date to begin the collective bargaining talks. Both sides must begin talks within 30 days following the exchange of openers. The talks continue with only the union and company representatives involved. There is no time limit, and if both sides come to an agreement, a new contract is voted on by the union members.

Step 2: National Mediation Board. If the collective bargaining is unsuccessful and the talks deadlock, the union or company requests, or the NMB offers, mediation. This step must begin within ten days of both sides declaring a deadlock in the talks. The NMB assigns a mediator, and mediation talks begin. There is no time limit as to when the talks start, or how long they must continue. These decisions lie with the NMB. If mediation is successful, a new contract is reached.

Step 3: Voluntary Arbitration. If the NMB fails in its effort to bring the parties together on common ground, the law requires it to work for voluntary arbitration. Both sides must agree to abide by the results of arbitration before a temporary arbitration board is established to hear the dispute. One-third of the arbitrators are chosen by the carriers, one-third by the labor organizations, and one-third by the carrier–labor arbitrators together. In cases of disagreement concerning the choice of the neutral arbitrators, the NMB chooses them. Although arbitration itself is voluntary, once the parties agree to it, the arbitration decision is legally binding on both parties.

Step 4: Emergency Board. If arbitration is refused, the NMB notifies the parties that its mediatory efforts have failed, and for 30 days thereafter, unless the parties agree to arbitration in the interim or an **emergency board** is created, no change can be made in the conditions that prevailed at the time the dispute arose. At the same time, if in the NMB's opinion a strike could lead to a national emergency, it is required to notify the president, who may create an emergency board, which has 30 days to investigate the dispute and report its findings to the president. The recommendations of the emergency board are not enforceable, but they have been accepted in a number of instances and it is hoped that public opinion will induce acceptance of the findings. If the recommendation of the emergency board is refused, which has been the case in most instances in recent years, another 30 days must elapse before any change or action can commence. Thus, it is often said that the appointment of an emergency board postpones any work stoppage for a 60-day cooling-off period. After the cooling-off period, the company may change work rules, rates of pay, and so forth, or it may institute a lockout. The union must decide whether to accept the company offer or go on strike.

A Final Option: Presidential Intervention. If all the foregoing efforts fail and the power of public opinion does not induce a settlement, the president may act to avoid disruption of commerce. The president can either allow the strike to occur or ask Congress for emergency legislation to prevent it. This step is not included in the RLA, but it is a real possibility. On several occasions, the president has "seized" the railroads, and on at least one occasion, he recommended immediate congressional action to avoid a nationwide rail strike. However, this has not been the case with the airlines. In fact, President George H. W. Bush refused to participate in the mechanics' strike against Eastern Airlines before that carrier's bankruptcy. However, President Clinton did call American Airlines president Robert Crandall to avert a strike by that carrier's flight attendants in 1993.

Criticism of the Process

Where a carrier is weak and a concessionary agreement is clearly appropriate, the process might delay the carrier from obtaining vitally needed cost savings and, therefore, make the carrier more vulnerable to financial collapse. Although this may be true, the NMB has great discretion to operate quickly to make sure carriers stay afloat, for the benefit of the employees and the carrier, as well as for the traveling public.

Nonetheless, the NMB's release of the parties to use self-help does not necessarily result in concessions that ensure carrier survival. Rather, a devastating strike might take place that would, in fact, lead to the carrier's demise. In addition, companies subject to the NLRA have also entered bankruptcy as a result of a labor dispute.

Critics point to another alleged drawback of the RLA process—that carriers even in good times are insulated from challenging unions to rationalize excessive costs and inefficient work rules. Of course, one person's excessive costs and inefficient work rules are another person's decent living wage and tolerable working conditions. But in terms of the process, the trade unionists' counterargument is that unions are often, in fact, worn down by the elongated processes of the act and not allowed to use their greatest weapon, the strike, as readily as they would and do under the NLRA and that, therefore, they settle more cheaply than they might otherwise. It is almost a truism that in good times, when the carriers are making money, unions who expect to make wage gains criticize the RLA process, while in bad times, carriers who need quick relief criticize it.

Another criticism is that the delays in collective bargaining occasioned by the workings of the RLA breed bad labor–management relations. Of course, if a carrier does not survive, good labor relations are irrelevant.

Given the relative security of the unions in the industry, they can and do make concessionary agreements and other accommodations where needed for the survival of a carrier. But as a practical matter, substantial delays in reaching collective bargaining agreements are not good for labor relations. Delays are sometimes necessary, however, to permit good-faith bargaining and a thorough review of issues in a serious attempt to find solutions that both parties can live with. In those situations, delays have a much more beneficial than harmful effect, particularly in an industry that can ill afford shutdowns at any time.

In a particularly vulnerable industry like the airlines, having a system that encourages an adversarial situation whenever a dispute arises is bad labor policy.

The general consensus among labor economists is that the process of collective bargaining has benefited the carriers and labor in the postderegulation period and that labor costs have not been the cause of the airlines' financial crises to any significant degree. But analyses have shown just the opposite. Labor productivity has increased tremendously since the 1978 passage of the Airline Deregulation Act, because the airlines have not been able to almost automatically pass on their costs to the traveling public as they were able to do when the CAB regulated them. Also, since deregulation was enacted, the industry per capita compensation has actually fallen. Unit labor costs have also decreased and have represented a decreasing fraction of capacity costs. Labor costs per available seat-mile, which is the standard measure of productivity in the industry, are much lower on U.S. airlines than on foreign carriers, by approximately 15 to 20 percent. Labor costs generally cannot be said to determine an airline's survival or the destiny of the industry.

HISTORICAL OVERVIEW OF AIRLINE UNION ACTIVITY

Since 1936, the year that Congress put commercial airlines under the Railway Labor Act—a period of seven decades that included 42 years of economic regulation and approximately 25 years of deregulation—airline labor–management relations have been overseen by the U.S. government. Over that time span, the goals of collective bargaining have not changed much, nor have the objectives of management and labor.

What has changed is the economic, social, and business environment, and the result has been a new industry structure and tremendous advances in technology and in the economics of operation. These changes are readily apparent when a DC-3, the glamour plane of the 1940s, is compared to a modern-day Boeing 777.

The Prejet Age

In the early years of the airline industry, during its air mail service phase and into the early years of the New Deal of the 1930s, airlines, like railroads, were viewed as common carriers vested with a public interest—a kind of private-public utility to be regulated by means of the control of predatory competition, market entry, wages, and fares. In this fledgling stage of commercial air transportation, economic stability of the airline industry was a high government priority, as the nation endeavored to pull itself out of the Great Depression of the 1930s. Concern for workers' rights and standards of living was part of the social and political philosophy of the period. This was quite unlike the period of deregulation after 1978, when government viewed the airline industry as mature enough to weather any kind of competition. This outlook was based on a belief that the market, not the government, could more efficiently allocate resources.

Industrywide bargaining became a reality in 1934 through Decision 83 of the National Labor Relations Board, which was established under the National Recovery Act. **Industrywide bargaining** occurs when unions and management of the major firms in an industry agree to bargain collectively to reach contract terms that will apply to all the firms and their employees, wherever they are located. One purpose is to take wages out of competition.

Decision 83 established minimum wages and maximum hours for pilots across the industry. It also attempted to compensate pilots at least partially for technological changes by relating pay to increasing aircraft speed. Though the decision protected wages and hours only of pilots employed by airlines carrying mail under contract to the Post Office Department, it established de facto industrywide protection. It was the byproduct of a protected infant industry in which no company could hope to survive without government support through mail pay—a form of subsidy. Mail compensation covered total costs (including losses on passenger business), not merely the cost of carrying the mail.

As important as Decision 83 was, it was limited to a small portion of the airline industry—namely, airline pilots. A more important event dealing with labor–management relations in the entire airline industry took place in 1936 when Congress, largely at the behest of labor, placed the airline industry under the RLA and its mandatory mediatory dispute settlement procedures administered by the NMB. This protection of labor's and management's rights had not been secured by collective bargaining.

The wage formula (Decision 83) was later included in the Air Mail Act of 1934 and the Civil Aeronautics Act of 1938. By that time, however, collective bargaining had increased wages and fixed hours so that the wage formula and hour rules had become meaningless. And with the passage of the Airline Deregulation Act of 1978, they were formally abolished.

Since passage of the Railway Labor Act as amended in 1936, the major type of bargaining in the airline industry has been **pattern bargaining**. Pattern bargaining occurs when each airline negotiates its own agreement with a labor union. Because agreements are negotiated over different time periods with different expiration dates, each employee group seeks to better the most recent agreements signed by other airlines. Thus, a "pattern" is established in which the unions are said to "piggyback" and "leapfrog" contract benefits, one over another, to ensure ever-increasing wage rates and benefits. Managements use the term *whipsaw* to describe how they are forced to accede in successive negotiations to wages and/or benefits that some other airline has given.

In the early days, airline pilots were the only effectively organized group, and their relationships with management were usually handled by operations personnel. There were no industrial relations departments as we know them today. Instead, the personnel departments handled everything, and in most cases, personnel specialists were ignored by top airline management. All too frequently, the advice and counsel of personnel were neither wanted nor sought and, when offered, went unheeded.

This situation began to change in late 1946, and by 1948, many of the employee groups in the airline industry were organized. Companies began to realize that they had to upgrade their personnel departments and their methods of handling employees to deal with these newly organized groups and the problems that were developing. Industrial relations departments started to crop up, and the opinions of personnel and industrial relations directors began to hold some weight. As these experts and their departments grew in stature within their companies, their titles were upgraded and their economic positions improved.

During this same period, labor unions began to recognize the potential membership that existed among unorganized employees in the aviation industry, and many unions began to jockey for position within the industry. By 1955, class and craft lines were becoming well defined, and not only pilots but also flight attendants, mechanics, stock clerks, communication employees, flight engineers, and dispatchers were organized. There was, however, practically no unionization among the white-collar ground employees, including clerical, reservations, and ticketing personnel and station agents.

Although great progress had been made in organizing airline employees by 1955, the industry was still small enough for most workers to be on first-name terms, and most problems were handled on a personalized basis. This could be termed phase 1, or the prejet age, in the airline industry.

The Jet Age

With the introduction of the jet into commercial airline transportation in the late 1950s, the entire picture changed. Suddenly, the airlines became the number-one means of transportation. The jet age brought speed, luxury, comfort, and a host of other advantages to the airline industry—and it also brought with it literally hundreds of new problems for airline employees. Old ways of doing business had to be replaced by more efficient and safer ones. More skills and training were needed, and labor requirements exploded overnight. Not only did pilots have to be retrained to handle the new jets, all ground personnel had to be retrained in servicing techniques, and new systems had to be developed to handle the increasing flood of travelers. These problems, and others that developed with the advent of the jet age, produced considerable labor unrest, a feeling of insecurity among employees, and a developing resistance to change, especially to automation, which was and is necessary to run an efficient jet airline industry.

The jet age brought with it unexpected profits, and the employees' natural desire to share in these profits often caused head-on conflict with management, which resisted what it considered unreasonable demands or an invasion of management prerogatives by the unions. This was a period of strained labor–management relations, as the frequent strikes suggest (see Table 16.2). Both management and labor were unprepared for some of the changes brought about by the jet age.

In an effort to improve their bargaining power with the unions, in 1958 a group of the major carriers drew up the so-called **mutual aid pact (MAP)** whereby they agreed that if one of them was struck, the others would pay the struck carrier the windfall revenues they realized from the strike minus the added expense of carrying the additional traffic. Precise calculation of these revenues was not possible, but formulas were agreed on that attempted to measure the added revenues of each nonstruck carrier and to deduct the added costs of moving this traffic. The struck carrier agreed to make every reasonable effort to provide the public with information concerning air service offered by other carriers in the pact.

The MAP was a form of strike insurance, and the unions naturally opposed it on the grounds that the carriers were not bargaining in good faith when they brought carriers that were not party to the dispute into it and thereby forced the union to accept their recommendations. In the spring of 1959, the CAB approved the MAP, rejecting the unions' position on the grounds that there were other important factors that would stop a carrier from prolonging any strike. The CAB cited such factors as the long-term losses associated with resuming service, lost market share, and the fact that payments under the MAP did not cover the entire cost of the strike.

Several amendments were made between 1958 and 1970 to increase payments under the MAP. In 1970, the pact was broadened when the CAB approved the participation of the regional carriers, six of which subsequently joined.

Over the years, labor tried unsuccessfully to have the courts set the MAP aside or to have Congress outlaw it. Finally, in 1978, with the passage of the Airline Deregulation Act, all existing mutual aid agreements were

Table 16.2 Duration of Airline Strikes Between the Fall of 1958 and 1970 (the first 12 years of the jet age and the mutual aid pact (MAP))

							Total	
Year	**Carrier and Union**	**Days**	**Year**	**Carrier and Union**	**Days**		**Before MAP**	**MAP 1958–1970**
1958	Capital, IAM	37	1965	Pan Am, ALPA	10	Number of strikes	38	59
	West Coast, IAM	3	1966	SFO Helicopter, TWU	8			
	TWA, IAM	16		Eastern, IAM	43	Total duration in days	575.5	2,198
	Lake Central, ALSSA	13		National, IAM	43			
	Eastern, FEIA	38		Northwest, IAM	43	Average	15.1	35.5
	Eastern, IAM	22		TWA, IAM	43	Total duration in days		
	American, ALPA	22		United, IAM	43			
1959	Pacific, ALDA	3		Pacific, IAM	8			
	Southern, ACMA	65		Mohawk, IAM	54			
1960	Flying Tiger, TWU	27		West Coast, ALEA	8			
	Mohawk, ALLA	18	1967	Airlift, ALEA	24			
	Southern, ALPA	117		Qantas, IAM	60			
	Continental, FEIA	105	1968	Standard, SAFEA	46			
	Eastern, ALPA	11		Reeve Aleutian, IAM	76			
	Braniff, BRAC	10	1969	National, IAM	4			
	Pan Am, FEIA	1		American, TWU	21			
	Northwest, IAM	137		Air Canada, IAM	30			
1961	American, FEIA	7		Piedmont, ALPA	30			
	TWA, FEIA	7		Western, IBT	19			

(Continued)

Table 16.2 *Continued*

						Total	
Year	Carrier and Union	Days	Year	Carrier and Union	Days	Before MAP	MAP 1958–1970
	Eastern, FEIA	7		Pan Am, IBT	4		
	National, FEIA	7		Los Angeles Airways, ALPA	187		
	Pan Am, FEIA	7	1970	National, ALEA	116		
	Flying Tiger, FEIA	7		Ozark, AMFA	5		
	Western, FEIA	82		World Airways, IBT	51		
	National, IAM	6		Northwest, BRAC	160		
1962	Eastern, FEIA	82		TWA, ALSSA-TWU	2		
	Pan Am, FEIA	1		Mohawk, ALPA	154		
1963	United, IAM	1					
1964	National, ALEA	1					
	PanAm, TWU	1					
	BOAC, IAM	42					
	Trans Caribbean, IBT	3					

Source: *Airline Management*, June 1972

Airline unions and abbreviations: ALDA, Air Line Dispatchers Association; ALEA, Air Line Employees Association; ALPA, Air Line Pilots Association; ALSSA, Air Line Stewards and Stewardesses Association; AMFA, Aircraft Mechanics Fraternal Association; BRAC, Brotherhood of Railway, Airline and Steamship Clerks, Freight Handlers, Express and Station Employees; FEIA, Flight Engineers International Association; IAM & AW, International Association of Machinists and Aerospace Workers; IBT, International Brotherhood of Teamsters; TWU, Transport Workers Union declared void. During the 20-year history of the MAP, over half a billion dollars in mutual aid was paid out. Although the Airline Deregulation Act's provisions wiping out all existing mutual aid pacts appeared to be a victory for labor, they left the door open for new agreements, but under severely limiting conditions:

> All new agreements continued to be subject to CAB approval until the board's expiration, at which time this function was turned over to the Department of Justice. The department shall not approve any such agreement unless such agreement provides (a) that any air carrier will not receive payments for any period which exceed 60 per centum of the direct operating expenses during such period, (b) that benefits under the agreement are not payable for more than eight weeks during any labor strike, and that such benefits may not be for losses incurred during the first thirty days of any labor strike, and (c) that any party to such agreement will agree to submit the issues causing any labor strike to binding arbitration pursuant to the Railway Labor Act if the striking employees request such binding arbitration.[1]

Airline union negotiators were quite successful in gaining above-average increases for their members up to the time of deregulation. The average annual percentage increase in compensation per employee was 9.9 percent for the airline industry from 1969 to 1979, compared with an 8.1 percent average for all U.S. industry. This differential added $1.5 billion to total airline labor costs in 1979 alone.

The disparate gains in wages and fringe benefits for the U.S. scheduled airlines in the 1970s are shown in Table 16.3. Basic wages are of fundamental interest to any worker and are usually a straightforward payroll calculation

Table 16.3 Increase in U.S. Scheduled Airline Wages and Fringe Benefits Compared to Consumer Prices (Index 1970 = 100)

Year	Wages	Fringe Benefits	Consumer Price Index*
1970	100.0	100.0	100.0
1971	108.8	113.1	104.3
1972	120.0	134.0	107.4
1973	127.5	157.4	114.5
1974	137.0	175.1	127.0
1975	149.0	201.2	138.6
1976	162.7	239.2	146.6
1977	180.0	276.3	156.0
1978	197.1	313.0	168.0
1979	207.8	336.6	186.9

Note: *Based on U.S. Bureau of Labor Statistics.

Source: Air Transport Association of America, *ATA Annual Report*, 1970–1979. Used with permission.

Table 16.4 Fringe Benefits as a Percentage of Wages for Selected Workers, U.S. Scheduled Airlines, 1970–1979

Year	Flight Deck Crew	Mechanics	Flight Attendants	Total Work Force
1970	22.3%	10.8%	10.8%	13.8%
1971	21.8	12.0	11.6	14.3
1972	22.9	13.3	12.6	15.4
1973	24.7	15.2	14.0	17.0
1974	25.3	15.2	14.9	17.7
1975	26.3	16.3	16.0	18.6
1976	28.0	18.1	17.5	20.3
1977	30.6	18.5	17.5	21.2
1978	32.3	19.9	17.7	21.9
1979	30.7	21.3	18.9	22.3

Source: Air Transport Association of America, *ATA Annual Report*, 1970–1979. Used with permission.

applying rates negotiated in a labor contract. Fringe benefits cover a multitude of added concessions of value that are partially or fully paid by the employer. There has been a distinct union emphasis on stressing such benefits in recent years, particularly because they are generally tax-free to the employee. The main areas of fringe benefits vary by airline, but they usually include medical and dental plans (basic and major), life insurance, accidental death and dismemberment coverage, retirement plans, vacation-accrual provisions, and sick-leave coverage.

Additional benefits are regularly proposed by the unions, including increased company contributions to employee retirement programs and increased retirement benefits. Free air transportation is also a fringe benefit available to airline employees and certain members of their family, but this advantage does not usually produce a cost outlay by the carrier. Not all crafts obtain fringe benefits of the same proportion of their average wages, but fringe benefits of all workers increased appreciably as a percentage of overall wages during the 1970s, as shown in Table 16.4.

In spite of continuing wage escalation during the 1970s, fringe benefits became an increasingly large proportion of total employee compensation, the expense of which continued in the 1980s to inflate the operating costs of the established carriers. Further-more, flight crews on most major airlines have other financial advantages. For example, their contracts usually provide them, while away from home base, with company-paid ground transportation to hotels, single-occupancy rooms, and in-flight meals, while their pay scales also include liberal allowances per hour away from home. The result of these developments has been a steady gain in the average employee compensation within the airline industry that outpaced the rise in the Consumer Price Index during the 1970s.

Summary: Prederegulation Labor–Management Relations

Between 1936 and 1978, the range of labor–management relationships among the airlines had been remarkably consistent compared with those in U.S. industry in general. Nonetheless, those relationships ranged from outright hostility toward unions, to arm's-length dealing (some refer to this as armed truce), to accommodation, to cooperation, or some combination thereof. In the prederegulation period, the most common posture of airline firms was arm's-length dealing, with accommodation running a bit behind. There were few, if any, examples among the major airlines of the extremes of outright hostility toward or cooperation with unions. Although there were, from time to time, new-entrant airlines, there was no dramatic growth of unions that threatened to upset the existing dynamics of union–management relationships.

Moreover, at that time, powerful moderating forces were at work. The first was government regulation of airline routes, prices, competition, and operations. Second, dispute resolution procedures under the RLA were in place and available to the parties. Third, collective bargaining existed in a general political environment that favored accommodation or problem solving over hostility, as labor and management were learning to live with each other under both the NLRA and the RLA. Fourth, on both sides of the table were people who had grown up in the airline industry and knew one another's problems.

As time passed, and up to the late 1970s, what had started out as multi-employer bargaining gradually evolved into coordinated bargaining of unions followed by pattern bargaining. Later still, efforts to return to coordinated bargaining by employers, epitomized by the mutual aid pact, failed.

Unions in the United States reached their membership peak by 1953, boasting some 34 percent of the nonagricultural labor force, but by 1995 membership had declined to 15 percent. In general, the postderegulation era began with evident weakness in membership of the U.S. labor movement. Union weakness was compounded by the increased diversity of union membership and by sometimes conflicting interests. By the late 1970s, the attitude of industry toward unions was less than welcoming, much like in the 1920s, before the passage of the RLA, or during the period leading up to passage of the NLRA.

LABOR RELATIONS SINCE DEREGULATION

Compared with the postderegulation era, prederegulation bargaining was more orderly. The major destabilizing element that had affected collective bargaining during deregulation had been intense competition from numerous new-entrant carriers that immediately began to bite into the market share of the major airlines. A host of new unorganized carriers emerged in the early 1980s to provide scheduled service on selected routes in direct competition with the established operators, and more entrants are expected to appear over time. These carriers included Midway Airlines, People Express, New York Air, Muse Air, and Jet America, to name a few. Others with longer histories, such as Air Florida, Southwest, Capital Airlines, and World Airways, all expanded their routes. During the first five years of the 1980s, more than 100 new airlines entered the industry, and in that decade, as many or more exited—an indication of unparalleled industry instability. This instability was accompanied by periodic fare wars that have continued to the present, along with bankruptcies or threatened bankruptcies of major airlines, greater competition from surviving new-entrant airlines, frantic efforts to gain competitive advantage, and massive and costly investments in planes and airline hubs designed to monopolize passenger traffic from start to stop.

Most of the new airlines started service with smaller twin-engine jets on short- to medium-length routes with high traffic density. The fledgling airlines benefited from minimal employee seniority, which produced low unit wage costs, because most union pay scales are based on longevity of service. In addition, they were generally nonunion companies, which enabled them to obtain greater employee productivity without restrictive class and craft groupings that result in costly work rule limitations. Furthermore, these point-to-point operators did not offer the same level of passenger service (such as interline ticketing and baggage checking) provided by the mature airlines. Another cost advantage was their greater flexibility to contract out ground handling services at many stations to existing carriers on a per-flight-handled basis. This obviated high fixed expenses to maintain staff and facilities at secondary terminals with only minimal operations per shift. In addition, these airlines controlled costs by employing part-time workers to a degree not possible in the case of unionized airlines.

The result was that these new entrants enjoyed appreciably lower unit wage costs than most old-line operators. The new entrants were further aided by their selection of smaller 2-plus-2 jet aircraft (two engines and two pilots), which were more efficient and better sized to maintain flight frequencies in markets fragmented by increased competition under deregulation. The Boeing 737-200 and the DC-9-30 twin jets were especially popular with the newer airlines, and these planes had an average seat-mile cost around 25 percent below that of the Boeing 727-100, then the smallest aircraft operated by many major airlines. Part of this cost advantage stemmed from an ability to use high-density coach seating on such aircraft restricted to selected markets. Thus, the new point-to-point airlines were able to offer lower fares than their established competition while still generating profit.

Ironically, start-up airlines sometimes purchased smaller twin jets second-hand from established carriers and used them in low-fare services in direct competition with the original owners. This unit operating cost differential between new and mature airlines eroded the market shares of the entrenched incumbents by skimming some profitable traffic beyond the break-even level and forced the higher-cost operators to lower their fares competitively to nonprofitable levels. The profitability of the established carriers was impaired to the point that their services were eventually cut back, with a consequent reduction of the employee workload and level of take-home pay. At the least, it hampered the ability of these airlines to generate adequate earnings for financing of capital expansion to purchase the more cost-efficient aircraft necessary to remain competitive.

More complexities and competition were introduced by mergers, combinations, buyouts, and various restructurings of airlines, either to grow, to enter the market, or to survive the fallout from the cost of debt. These came in the form of wage and benefit cuts, bankruptcies that resulted in lost jobs, two-tier pay systems and even second-tier airlines that produced second-tier wages, and outsourcing of work to contractors. The goal was to average down wages and further cut costs—a practice familiar to the automobile industry, which had long outsourced production and services to achieve lower wages and higher productivity.

Elimination of the Automatic Labor Cost Pass-Through

Before deregulation, the CAB set allowable fare levels based on actual industry costs. As a result, the added expense of each carrier's new labor agreement was eventually embedded in the overall rate structure that established full-fare price levels approved by the CAB and generally charged by all domestic scheduled airlines. Of course, the unit operating costs of individual airlines did vary around the rate-making norm, and there were also discount fares.

Nevertheless, there was very little incentive for one company to resist excessive union demands to the point of a potentially expensive strike, because the settlement costs could eventually be passed through to the adjusted general fare level. This attitude produced the stair-step approach to industry labor negotiations by nationwide unions, under which major concessions gained from one carrier (often a financially weak carrier) became the basis of escalating labor demands for the next open contract.

There was also widespread airline preoccupation with protection of market share from competition under the franchised route structures that existed. This concern often caused carriers to accept unrealistic union demands. The now-defunct mutual aid pact provided some incentive toward hard bargaining, but of the trunk lines, only National and Northwest showed any strong inclination to accept protracted strikes during the 1970s.

Now it is a different story. Under the free-entry system that has evolved, there are no true franchises to protect domestic routes, no mutual aid programs to compensate for strike losses, and no basic fare structure charged by all participants. But there are new low-cost, nonunion competitors. The underlying problem is an inability to pass on directly to passengers any abnormally high unit cost increases, whether caused by more generous contract settlements or use of inefficient aircraft.

Of course, competitive fares were part of Congress's basic intent in passing the deregulation law. Today, a low-cost airline, whether a new entrant or an established carrier, with efficient jets and a relatively flexible labor situation can unilaterally set its fare structure (both full fare and discount) at a profitable level that can seriously harm any competitor with appreciably higher unit operating costs.

A Period of Labor Unrest: The 1980s

Labor has always been an important part of the cost structure of the airlines, representing on average over one-third of total operating expenses and over two-thirds of "controllable" costs. It became quite clear shortly after deregulation that there was room for substantial savings in this area. Employees at the established carriers were making considerably more than they could outside the industry, particularly true for certain jobs, such as airplane cleaners and baggage handlers. The new entrants made the most of this potential advantage, with their average compensation during the early 1980s being more than one-third below the industry average.

The disparity still existed in 1986 at carriers such as American, Delta, and United, where wages and benefits ranged from 36 to 39 percent of operating expenses. In the same year, labor accounted for only 20 to 24 percent of total operating expenses at Continental, Southwest, and some of the newer carriers.

These enormous differences inevitably result in price and cost differences, and the established carriers must eventually meet the price of any significant competitor. Past and future competition has created enormous pressure to reduce labor costs.

Equally important for potential cost savings, though less quantifiable, were the work rules, built up over many years, that hindered productivity improvements. Work was divided along craft lines, making cross-utilization of workers almost impossible. The use of part-time employees to cover peak-load periods was sharply restricted. Pilots and flight attendants had won complex limits on the number of flying hours, plus many extras involving duty time and expenses incurred away from base.

Actually, labor began deregulation on an upswing, with wages and benefits continuing to rise on average until 1981. In that key year, a severe economic recession, compounded by the firing of the striking air traffic controllers, restricted traffic and wiped out carriers' ability to spread costs through expansion. Meanwhile, fuel prices soared, and all carriers engaged in fierce price competition.

The incumbents were forced to reduce costs to afford the lower fares needed to match the lower fares of this new competition. Cost reduction affecting employees took the form of layoffs, two-tier pay systems, the beginning of the outsourcing of work to lower-cost providers, and the establishment of lower-cost second-tier airlines as subsidiaries. Pilots, because of their specialized, not easily transferrable skills and higher pay, were particularly affected. Blaming many of their problems on past strategic mistakes by top management, mistakes in which they had no input, employees mounted a counteroffensive not previously used. For example, pilots at United Airlines, the industry's largest and most successful major carrier, concluded that their management not only was bent on destroying the union but also was shifting its corporate strategy from that of airline growth to a bottom-line objective. The pilots also believed that United was creating a conglomerate that included nonairline enterprises (rental car and hotel properties) that seemed to make the airline (and their jobs) secondary and dispensable. When the pilots struck, top management departed.

The first union concessions appeared at Braniff, Western, and Pan Am, but these were followed shortly by concessions at Continental, Eastern, and Republic, as those labor groups engaged in "survival bargaining." The cost cuts at those carriers gave healthy competing airlines the leverage to drive their own costs down, continuing the spread of concessions to the carriers. In some cases, the need for wage cuts led to a search for cooperation. In exchange for cooperation, the unions sought three things: (1) adequate information to persuade them that the cuts were necessary, (2) a voice in future strategic decisions, and (3) equality of sacrifice among workers, managers, and shareholders. These conditions led to a deep involvement of unions in the "managerial" realm, through representation on company boards, worker participation programs, and extensive employee stock ownership.

Eastern Airlines was the best-known example of this approach. Labor cost savings, exchanged for employees' sharing in decision making and equity, helped propel it to the most profitable first half in its history in 1985. Republic, Frontier, and Western Airlines also adopted many of the same tactics. In 1981, the Air Line Pilots Association (ALPA) directed its ire toward what it called "runaway airlines." A prime example was the ALPA's attempt on behalf of Texas International (TI) pilots, flight attendants, mechanics, and ticket agents to obtain an injunction against TI's holding company, Texas Air Corporation, for establishing a new nonunion subsidiary (New York Air), claiming that existing contracts required union membership within this offshoot of the company. Of course, the crux of this dispute was the fact that New York Air captains were being paid about $30,000 per year for a 75-hour month, whereas Texas International captains earned approximately $62,000 annually for flying only 55 hours per month on the same type of aircraft. The ALPA had requested release from mediation with Texas International in order to begin the statutory 30-day cooling-off period, but the union withdrew this request from the National Mediation Board before a ruling was given.

During the summer of 1981, the Professional Air Traffic Controllers Organization (PATCO) illegally called on its membership to walk off the job. Eleven thousand FAA controllers followed the order and were subsequently fired by President Reagan. Legislation had been introduced in Congress (and was subsequently passed) calling for top pay of $73,420 per year for air traffic controllers, cost-of-living raises one-and-a-half times the rate of inflation, a 32-hour work week, and retirement at 75 percent of a controller's top pay after 20 years.

The year 1982 saw the first bankruptcy of a major carrier with the demise of Braniff Airlines. Despite several major pay cuts incurred by Braniff union members and other employees, the carrier's cash flow reached a point at which it could not expect to make a dent in its outstanding debt, despite several restructuring attempts, and it finally threw in the towel.

By 1983, it became quite clear to labor unions, with an estimated 33,000 of their members either furloughed or permanently let go, that the ailing carriers held the trump cards and were successfully playing their hands, gaining substantial labor concessions that represented millions of dollars in operating-cost savings. In March 1983, four out of five major unions dealing with Pan American World Airways ratified agreements extending current labor concession contracts. The Teamsters Union, representing 6,629 ground employees, ratified a wage reduction agreement on March 3, 1983. The Independent Union of Flight Attendants agreed to a similar pact on the following day.

Continental Airlines took quite a different approach to cutting labor costs. In September 1983, Continental chairman Frank Lorenzo attempted to reduce wage costs by temporarily going out of business. Lorenzo's plan was to close down the ninth largest U.S. airline and reopen a smaller carrier with lower labor costs, along the lines of the newcomers. He claimed that Continental had been unable to win enough voluntary wage concessions from its unions.

True to Lorenzo's aim, Continental re-established service to 25 of the 78 cities it had served within 54 hours after filing petitions for reorganization under bankruptcy laws in Houston. Lorenzo defended his strategy, saying that the airline's union contracts were "vestiges of another era." He added that the bankruptcy maneuver would create for Continental the "opportunity to compete in a very challenging and potentially rewarding marketplace." He had fired all 12,000 employees and then invited 4,000 back at barely half their former wages. Senior Continental pilots, who used to average $83,000 a year, could return, but at salaries of $43,000. Flight attendants who had worked their way up to $35,700 per year were cut back to $15,000. Senior mechanics saw their wages shrink from $33,280 to $20,800. Lorenzo also reduced his own annual salary from $267,000 to that of a senior captain, $43,000.

The sharp wage drops brought on by survival bargaining and its ripple effects were altered in late 1983 by American Airlines' benchmark two-tier wage scales—a term airline management since has abandoned in favor of "market rates." In the two-tier system, new employees are hired on a "B" pay scale considerably lower than that of established employees (the "A" pay scale). With the successful implementation of this approach at American, managements introduced the system into every U.S. airline.

From a labor relations standpoint, the years from 1982 to 1985 were the worst of times for the unions. In the aftermath of the PATCO strike and the recession, unions had no public support and were beset by internal dissension and disunity. Moreover, the availability of ample replacements for strikers doomed the chances of waging a successful strike. The realization that a strike was no longer an effective bargaining tool profoundly altered the balance of power in the collective bargaining process.

Against the backdrop of the Braniff reorganization, the American settlement in August 1983, and the imposition of emergency work rules at Continental in September 1983, management approached the bargaining table with enormous strength and an agenda to match. In most instances, the issue was no longer how much management would give, but how much it would get back. Management's principal bargaining goals were more flexibility through cross-utilization and the use of part-timers, increased productivity, reductions in fringe benefits, and an overall reduction in compensation.

The bargaining objectives of financially sound carriers included wage freezes or small percentage increases, lump-sum payments in lieu of pay increases, and the establishment of a two-tier pay system. All these methods limited the roll-up cost of fringe benefits. Financially troubled carriers sought a decrease in A-scale rates and related fringe benefits, the establishment of B scales for future use, and the establishment of variable compensation schemes, including profit-sharing and stock plans. Temporary concessions that snapped back at a future date to previously higher levels were no longer acceptable. Management wanted long-term, permanent concessions so as to establish a lower fixed-cost base for developing their long-range planning.

Management used whipsaw bargaining techniques to achieve concessions. Each time a carrier received concessions, employees at other carriers knew that similar or deeper cuts would be demanded. Midterm negotiations became commonplace. Threats of shutdowns, partial liquidations, lockouts, or massive furloughs were heard everywhere. With little risk of confrontation, management increasingly adopted a "take it or leave it" attitude at the bargaining table.

Increasingly, management used its leverage to gain concessions from its unions and to undermine the employees' faith in labor's strength. Although labor gave significant relief to many carriers during this period, much of it was used by management to subsidize the ongoing fare wars and to continue the corporations' diversification strategies rather than to improve airline operations.

Labor's goals shifted dramatically as well. Unions and employees began to question management's actions and to resist further concessions in wages and working conditions. Labor argued that concessions without concrete changes in operating procedures, and in some instances in management, would not restore a carrier to profitability. As such, employees began to demand a return for their concessions. The "return" took the form of profit-sharing plans, employee stock ownership plans (ESOPs), employee and management coalitions, representation on company boards of directors, job security provisions, and, in some cases, replacement of top management. The national economy, and with it the airline industry, began its recovery in 1984. Airline employment rose from 329,000 in 1983 to more than 400,000 in 1986. A pilot surplus became a severe shortage, and 5,465 pilots were hired by the commercial carriers in 1984 and another 7,872 in 1985. Consequently, with the new demand for pilots, management was forced to review its position on entry-level pay rates and even its willingness to undertake a strike.

During this time, labor unions also were successful in obtaining legislative reform of the Bankruptcy Code. The new amendments prevented a company like Continental from unilaterally imposing terms and conditions of employment (the emergency work rules) on employees without review and approval.

An example of the effect of this increased coordination can be seen in the ALPA's handling of the B-scale issue after the American settlement in 1983. Although the ALPA was unable to prevent two-tier pay systems for other pilots, by acting in concert it restricted their parameters. Under all the two-tier systems negotiated by the ALPA, pilot B-scale compensation merged at some point, usually after five years, with the A scale.

In response to the United strike in 1985 and to the potential for others to follow the same confrontational course of action, a special meeting of the ALPA board of directors was convened in June 1985 to establish and maintain a major contingency fund of $100 million. This fund was established to ensure the financial ability of the union to combat future major threats to pilots.

Although the Continental bankruptcy and strike were the low points in this period, from a union perspective, the strike by United's pilots and the TWA–Icahn agreements were key events that slowed down the negative trend in collective bargaining for airline unions. Both events reflected the renewed ability of unions to fashion strategies to cope with difficult and potentially devastating situations. If strikes or negotiations were handled properly, unions could once again engage in self-help and effectively shut down a major carrier. Likewise, unions could enter the financial world and make arrangements that would enable airline employees to determine ownership of their companies.

Unusual measures were required to meet the challenges of deregulation and the current operating environment. No one foresaw that unions would become experts in corporate takeovers, leveraged buyouts, and employee stock ownership plans (ESOPs). The activities at Trans World, Frontier, Transamerica, Texas Air, United, Republic, Eastern, and other airlines, however, demonstrated the need to develop such strategies and to apply them to the collective bargaining process. Nor had anyone foreseen before deregulation that airline unions would engage in massive communications programs involving coalitions of employees, corporate campaigns, family-awareness seminars, and satellite teleconferencing to deal with management actions.

Despite the tremendous number of mergers and acquisitions during 1985 and 1986, 6,341 pilots were hired in 1986, and the trend was continued throughout the remainder of the 1980s. Tighter labor markets, especially for pilots, contributed to the negotiation of higher pay scales for new hires than were originally conceded and to reductions in the number of years before pay scales merged. The unions had also learned how to intervene in airline merger activities, using concession offers as major bait. They prevented a Texas Air takeover of TWA by facilitating Carl Icahn's acquisition. United's pilots, unhappy with the policies of holding company Allegis Corporation, offered to purchase United for $4.5 billion and were instrumental in effecting a change in corporate management. A Pan American union coalition, seeking a change in top management, offered significant cost concessions in return.

The Consolidation Period: 1986–2011

Airline analysts agree that to guarantee profitability and survival, an airline needs access to three vital components. First, it needs a strong balance sheet. This includes not only a strong cash position but also a strong debt/equity ratio. Second, an airline must have a route structure that includes dominant hubs, a regional feeder system, and international routes. Maintaining dominance at these hubs has proven to be a strong protection against new airlines and against competition from existing carriers. Third, an airline needs at least an ownership interest in a computer reservations system.

Few airlines entered 1986 with all three components essential to future viability. In fact, only three airlines—American, United, and Delta—had strong balance sheets, hub dominance, and ownership in computer reservations systems. Those airlines lacking in these elements realized that the best way to obtain them was by merging with an airline that had them. Even the three airlines just mentioned believed they needed to strengthen certain aspects of their structure and acted accordingly.

The bargaining trends of the preceding years continued after 1986. Management still approached negotiations from a position of strength, seeking overall cost reductions to remain competitive with new airlines and such low-cost carriers as Continental. Management's key objectives were pay freezes or small percentage increases, lump-sum payments, containment of fringe benefits, B scales, increased productivity, and relief from scope clauses restricting the development and ownership of regional carrier networks. Long-term settlements were sought to establish a base for expansion and consolidation.

In the case of financially unhealthy carriers, demands were made or imposed for substantial permanent concessions. At Eastern and TWA, permanent cost reductions of 20 percent or more, with additional productivity gains, fringe-benefit reductions, and "deep" merging B scales, were agreed on after bitter negotiations during which unions were threatened with bankruptcy, liquidation, or sale of substantial assets. Also at TWA, the pilots gained an equity interest in the company and job security provisions, including protection of the pilots in future mergers or sales and restriction on the sale of an airline's assets in partial exchange for permanent concessions. In 1986, even Delta requested mediation for the first time in its history and had difficult negotiations with its pilots before reaching a settlement.

The $2 billion net industry profit in 1988 was encouraging, but by 1989 there were signs that the economy was slowing down. The bubble burst in 1990 as the economy slid into recession and the airline industry suffered $4 billion in losses, due mostly to the rise in fuel costs precipitated by the Persian Gulf crisis. The war and its accompanying recession caused the first decrease in air travel in a decade. Losses amounted to $2 billion in 1991. The airline industry was indeed in a financial crisis. The $6 billion loss in 1990 and 1991 was more than all the profits the airline industry had earned throughout its entire history. Of the 12 major carriers that existed in the industry at the beginning of 1991, only American, Delta, Federal Express, Southwest, and United remained with strong balance sheets at the end of 1992. America West, Continental, and TWA were in bankruptcy; Northwest and USAir were in financial difficulty; and Eastern and Pan Am had gone out of business.

In 1980, labor costs accounted for 37 percent of total operating costs. By 1992, employee salaries and benefits had fallen below 30 percent of total operating costs for the major carriers, and only 22 percent for national carriers. Despite this decline, many carriers, in their struggle to survive, requested further wage and benefit concessions from labor.

In October 1992, ailing TWA reached agreement with its three unions for wage and benefits concessions and announced that $24 million would be cut from nonunion and management compensation. Under the agreement, workers received a 45 percent ownership stake in the airline in exchange for employee concessions worth $660 million. Pilots were promised a 5 percent pay raise on the second anniversary of their contract, but only if verifiable cost savings resulted from specified work rule changes. TWA emerged from bankruptcy reorganization in November 1993 and was eventually purchased by American Airlines in 2001.

In 1994, Northwest Airlines narrowly avoided bankruptcy when its unions agreed to wage concessions in return for an ownership stake. The troubled carrier lost more than $1 billion in 1992. Burdened by an enormous debt load as a result of its $3.65 billion buyout in 1989, Northwest had been pruning its work force in an attempt to return to profitability. The wage cuts proposed by management were 30 percent for pilots, 20 percent for flight attendants, and 18 percent for mechanics. Management and union representatives finally agreed to $886 million in employee concessions over the next three years in return for three seats on Northwest's 15-member board of directors and 37.5 percent equity interest in the company.

In 1993, USAir (now US Airways) announced plans to lay off another 2,500 workers by mid-1994, in addition to the 7,000 employees terminated since 1990. The airline indicated that further cost-cutting measures were necessary despite previous worker concessions slated to save the carrier $60 million in 1993. The prior wage cuts and work rule concessions were negotiated with the International Association of Machinists and Aerospace Workers following a five-day walkout by union members.

Delta Air Lines, reversing a no-furlough policy in existence for 36 years, began furloughing an estimated 600 of its 9,400 pilots in 1993. Senior vice-president Thomas J. Roeck blamed "uneconomic fare programs" for damaging revenues. Roeck stated that the additional traffic generated by the fares had fallen "significantly short" of making up for the lower fares. The pilots, Delta's only unionized labor force, agreed in 1991 to a 16-month extension of their current contract and a 2 percent raise, well below former Secretary of Transportation Samuel K. Skinner's critical prediction of 10 percent annual raises for flight crews.

In 1993, American Airlines slashed approximately 1,700 jobs in order to cut costs. Despite such measures, chairman Robert Crandall announced that an additional 5,000 workers would be terminated by the end of 1994.

American Airlines, which in 1983 had parlayed a cost-reducing two-tier pay system into a record expansion, by the 1990s found that its employees, particularly its pilots and flight attendants, had become fed up with the company's two-tier scale and its later strategy of shrinking the airline and outsourcing work. In response to Crandall's call for further work rule and wage concessions, American's 21,000 flight attendants walked off their jobs during the busy Thanksgiving holiday in 1993. The five-day dispute, the shortest U.S. airline strike since deregulation, was brought to an end by President Clinton's recommendation that both sides agree to binding arbitration. Another threatened strike occurred in 1997 when the decision was made to allow American Eagle to fly jets on many of American's shorter-haul routes; the pilots saw this as a further erosion of their jobs.

United Airlines lost $1.5 billion between 1990 and 1992. In 1993, the company implemented a sweeping cost-reduction program designed to save $400 million a year by eliminating 2,800 jobs and grounding 40 aircraft. As a result, shareholders began putting pressure on chairman Stephen Wolf to make some changes. His response was a proposal either to dismantle the airline into several regional carriers staffed with nonunion labor or to give employees an ownership stake in return for sweeping concessions. Pilots and mechanics reacted by offering to take significant wage and benefit cuts in order to gain some corporate leverage. Specifically, they agreed to take a 15.7 percent pay cut and lose 8 percent of their pension benefits for the next five years. In exchange, the company agreed to invest 53 to 63 percent of its stock in a special employee pension fund and give workers three seats on the 12-member board of directors. The good news for the employee owners was that they would be given "supermajority" voting rights on key issues such as acquisitions, mergers, and the sale of assets. The bad news was that employee ownership would be allowed to decline over five years as retiring workers were issued pension stock. Once the employee ownership stake falls below 50 percent, workers may find themselves right back where they started. This **employee stock ownership program (ESOP)** took over seven years of effort and represented the largest ESOP transaction in U.S. business history. Upon completion in 1994, several top officers, including Wolf, left the company.

Many carriers have adopted profit-sharing and/or employee ownership options as a means of enticing workers into granting wage or benefit concessions. Previously, such plans were generally initiated by financially unstable carriers, and few workers actually benefited. At America West, employees were induced to work for less than their industry counterparts based on the assurance that their short-term sacrifices would reap long-term profits. Some type of employee ownership is now also in place at US Airways, Northwest, and Southwest Airlines.

The profit-sharing plan at Southwest Airlines is one of the employees' most lucrative benefits. Southwest has managed to consistently show a profit since 1973. This is due in no small measure to its unique approach: it shuns the use of hub-and-spoke routes, operates no computer reservations system, serves no meals, and treats its employees like an extended family. Employees cannot collect from their profit-sharing plan until they leave Southwest. The company is 84 percent unionized, but its exemplary labor–management relations are demonstrated by the fact that the carrier's employee turnover rate during the 1990s was only 7 percent. Southwest would appear to be a perfect example of how an airline can be profitable without demanding concessions from labor.

On March 26, 2001, Comair pilots walked off the job, resulting in an 89-day strike over such issues as retirement, scheduling rules, job security, and compensation. Cincinnati-based Comair, a subsidiary of Delta Air Lines, was forced to suspend its operations between March 26 and July 1, 2001. Flights were partially restored on July 2, 2001, and fully restored by January 2002. Comair's pilots refused to accept a proposal by management that would have resulted in the best pay offered to any pilots in the regional airline industry. Mediation attempts by the NMB failed, and the NMB released pilots and management into a 30-day cooling-off period. The NMB released the parties from federal mediation on the condition that the pilots' union (ALPA) submit the management's settlement offer to the pilot membership for a vote. More than 99 percent of the pilots refused to accept the settlement, and strike action commenced. The result was a grounded airline and approximately $680 million in revenue losses for Delta for 2001. Before the strike, Comair served 95 cities and carried an average of 25,000 passengers per day with a fleet of 119 aircraft. After the strike, pilots agreed to a five-year contract that gave them pay raises and a company-paid retirement plan.

Since 2001, U.S. airlines have faced numerous challenges as a result of union action. As noted earlier in the text, major airlines have entered into bankruptcy situations causing increased friction between employees and management. The legacy carriers, United, American, and Delta for example, will continue to face union issues especially over the topic of pilot pension plans. By 2011, some pilots, active and retired, feared that pension payments would be reduced or even eliminated. New-entrant and low-cost carriers, at least for now, do not have to deal with the same union issues as the legacies, as such carriers are not typically unionized. However, as such companies grow in size, union formation is likely. As of the early 2000s, virtually all of the legacy carriers were faced with picket situations by pilots and in some cases mechanics and flight attendants. Management teams at all the major carriers have been forced to reduce costs in order to save the airlines from failure. Typically, the three main costs for an airline are fuel, labor, and maintenance. Unfortunately, for employees, labor is the area management has the most control over in terms of cutting costs.

In 2014, the U.S. economy was in a positive upswing and many of the financial woes airlines faced in the few years leading up to 2014 disappeared, partly as a result of consolidation among the legacy carriers. In terms of labor relations, most issues were resolved, allowing the airlines to concentrate on restructuring and growth strategies. In the foreign scene, the only notable news story at the time focused on Germany's largest airline, Lufthansa, where management cancelled 600 flights in anticipation of a ground staff, baggage handler, and maintenance worker walk-out over pay. Flights in Germany and Europe, along with long-haul connections at Frankfurt and Munich, were severely disrupted.

From 2014 to 2019, the airline industry experienced an uptick, meaning the industry was doing well financially for the most part and there was not a lot of major headlines associated with union activity. With this said, there were peaks and troughs related to news stories primarily focused on pilot and flight attendant compensation. By 2020, some interesting trends occurred due to the COVID-19 global pandemic, causing airlines and unions to better align around themes related to vaccination of employees (vaccinated and non-vaccinated) and isolation times as examples. The COVID-19 crisis had a severe negative impact on staffing levels resulting in shortage of staff, flight delays and cancellations, and economic challenges for operators. At the time of writing, the global pandemic was not over and numerous challenges continue to exist for the airline industry with an unknown date of when the industry will have full recovered. By the end of 2020, American Airlines reported a record financial loss of $8.9 billion, Delta Air Lines $12.9 billion, and United Airlines $7.1 billion. According to IATA, the airline industry was expected to lose more than $200 billion for 2020–2022. In terms of regional losses, Europe has been the hardest hit followed by Asia-Pacific, Middle East, Latin America/Caribbean, North America, and Africa.

Future Collective Bargaining Strategies

The goals of collective bargaining include provisions for resolving the conflicting interests of management and labor—protection of the rights, dignity, and worth of workers as industrial citizens, and, based on the first two goals, preservation of collective bargaining as a bulwark of the private enterprise system.

Since the onset of deregulation in 1978, the objectives of airline unions and managements have changed because of intense competition. This has affected the ability of unions to preserve and strengthen themselves as organizations, to gain "more" for their members, to participate with management in making decisions that affect jobs and employment, and, more recently, to preserve health benefits. Some unions have, in fact, believed that they had to get to the top of the firm through ownership (profit sharing) in order to participate at all. Social goals seem not to have assumed much importance for labor and certainly not for management.

In contrast, management's prederegulation objectives were mainly profit oriented, within the parameters of government regulation of entry, fares, wages, and routes. After deregulation, objectives were shaped instead by the plethora of low-fare, low-cost, low-wage new-entrant competitors and by the major airlines' attempts to survive the fierce contest for passengers and revenues. At the same time, airline managements were driven by the demands of the financial markets—lenders and investors—to pay interest on debt, often acquired at peak interest rates in the 1980s, or to increase the return on stock shares held by the financial markets, or else to be merged, taken over, or bankrupted. These experiences were not unknown to the industrial sector, but they were new to the airline industry. Certainly, this was unlike anything that had occurred before deregulation.

Stress from the financial markets, pressure from disgruntled passengers, predatory fare competition, expensive new technology—all these factors contributed to the turbulent industry environment. Although both management and unions were concerned with preserving their interests, they were not in agreement that workers should shoulder the costs of financing growth, takeovers, and mergers, or increasing productivity to pay the costs of debt financing.

Out of this experience, two sets of solutions emerged, one from unions and another from firms in the airline industry. Early in their efforts to cope with massive debt and the consequences of predatory competition (for neither of which the airline industry had an answer, except Chapter 11 bankruptcy), management embarked upon wide-ranging cost cutting. This had been tried in other industries and falls under the rubric of averaging down wages.

The practice of averaging down wages included implementing two-tier pay systems that started new employees in a craft—pilots, mechanics, flight attendants—at lower wages for a period of years (or, in the case of a 1983 flight attendant contract, forever) than longer service craftpeople, even though both perform the same tasks and work together. A recent variation of this two-tier pay system was the invention of the two-tier airline, with separate units (same union) and with lower pay for the second-tier crew, along with generally lower costs. Another variation was the outsourcing, or contracting out, of such items as nonunion ticketing, business services, and maintenance to independent organizations that pay their employees less than the airlines. These may consist of two or more tiers at lower levels of pay. Each of these averaging-down strategies sponsored by management has been accompanied by reductions in health benefit costs, in tandem with either lower wages or lower benefits derived from lower wages.

Unions, in turn, have begun to pursue four strategies. First, they organized activity specifically to promote workers' interests, particularly at airlines with a nonunion status or distaste for unions. Second, the unions challenged the business and staffing strategies of the airlines that they believed threatened workers' security of employment and income, as well as contributed to the obsolescence of the skills workers had acquired over many years. Third, in the case of the Allied Pilots Association (APA), the union sent a petition to the NMB to declare American Eagle and American Airlines to be a single carrier for bargaining purposes. The union feared that the growth of American Eagle, with its lower wages, could be a prelude to reducing pay and benefits of the top-tier American pilots or to increasing American Eagle employment at the expense of employment at American. Fourth, unions obtained a financial interest (via an ESOP) in a major airline in order to influence its policies. Buying control of an airline, popularly known as profit sharing, meant that an increasing share of the income that workers received from their employers came from stock ownership and thus became a more flexible and manageable cost during business downturns.

In brief, union strategies during deregulation have been directed, as during past periods of rising prices and recession, to preserving the industry itself and the jobs and skills associated with its crafts, even if individual income becomes more variable because of profit sharing. Employers, on the other hand, tried, as they have in the past, to improve the efficiency of workers in the system by tinkering around the edges to average down wages and thereby some costs.

HUMAN RESOURCES IN THE 21ST CENTURY

Aviation organizations should realize that people are the biggest asset. "I am convinced that companies should put their staff first, customers second, and shareholders third," noted Sir Richard Branson, of Virgin Atlantic Airways.

As the 21st century progresses, airlines and other aviation organizations will have to cope with new trends and challenges for the future. Perhaps one of the biggest challenges for such organizations will be managing the **Millennial generation**. Typically, this employee will be outspoken, expectation driven, and self-motivated. Organizations will have to learn Millennials' language and be able to supply such workers with the proper tools to get the job done. Interestingly, one American sociologist, Kathleen Shaputis, referred to Millennials as the "Peter Pan" generation because of the perceived tendency for delaying some rites of passage into adulthood.

Employers must create conditions that attract the best people for the job, meaning that organizations will rethink the role of the core group. Organizations will learn the benefits of building and using a large and diversely skilled talent pool, where employees will be trained quickly to increase their value to the company. Employees at all levels will be taught career-effectiveness skills. Perhaps most important, managers will be taught to manage instead of acting as liaisons or enforcers of rules. Efficiency will be enhanced through the support of education and training, creating an organizational environment where personal growth and development are stimulated.

Aviation organizations must learn to identify human resource needs through the formulation of objectives, policies, and budgets. Strategies should be related to human resource needs temporarily and permanently. Specific jobs should be outlined with specific job descriptions, and only qualified candidates should be recruited to fill positions. Modern recruitment methods include industry contacts, professional recruiters, employment agencies, colleges and trade schools, and various forms of advertising.

In terms of training, employees should be trained specifically in the area for which they are hired. Such training should permit for more advanced functions within the organization and should be able to address social and economic changes that affect the way the organization must operate. All training programs should have some sort of evaluation process to measure performance of the employee and the benefits received by the organization.

There are some barriers or challenges airlines will face in terms of human resources during the course of this century. These include:

1 *Skills.* Many of the skills used by the airline industry are exclusive to aviation. Such skills are costly and time-consuming to acquire. There is a need for constant refinement of regulatory, technological, and market developments. The airline industry is highly cyclical, which leads to overcapacity in human skills and tangible resources.
2 *Need for New Skills.* Increasingly competitive environments generate the need for new skills. To be successful in today's airline industry, workers will need specific skills. For example, multilingual, culturally sensitive, and responsive customer-contact staff will be in demand.
3 *Finding the Right Staff.* Airlines have realized that finding the right staff is no longer sufficient. The delivery of high-quality service is based on attitudes and values of employees. For example, much of Southwest Airlines' success is based on a unique corporate culture that promotes positive attitudes.
4 *Labor Trends.* Airlines of the future will find it beneficial to use more part-time and fixed-term staff. Charter airlines have been doing this for years, but it is a relatively new phenomenon with the scheduled airlines. This creates a challenge for mold-acculturated, committed team members.
5 *Multiskilling and Flexibility.* The focus of discussion at many airlines is changing from why to how and to in return for what? Encouragement of productivity growth through multiskilling (the application of multiple skills by one person) and more flexible work practices in highly unionized environments will create a challenge for the airline industry.
6 *Control of Labor Costs.* Airline passengers are becoming more knowledgeable and demanding, creating a challenge of how to control labor costs without disrupting customer service. There is a strong argument to place greater emphasis on productivity improvement rather than on salary and benefit cuts.

7 *Cross-utilization of Human Resources.* There will be increased cross-utilization of human resources within global alliances. The challenge is that variables relevant to the attraction, utilization, and motivation of talented employees differ widely between cultural settings. Some unions think that a global labor pool will create a threat to work conditions and job loss.
8 *Making Human Resource Strategies Adaptive.* This is the least specific challenge of those introduced, but it is the most significant. Human resource strategies should be as adaptive as corporate and competitive strategies have to be in the face of increasingly complex and turbulent environments.

In the 2020s, the need for qualified and skilled talent has never been more important especially given the impact of emerging technologies impacting all industry sectors. There is increased demand for new skills, reskilling, and upskilling and there is a large gap between the need for talent and the resources to recruit such talent. The argument can be made that talent is officially the number one commodity impacting how human resource departments will be forced to restructure including the need to create new types of positions not commonly known. According to Forbes, the following positions will become the norm in order to establish a more diversified workforce resulting in culture transformation: manager of employee engagement, director of learning, diversity officer, mindset coach, talent and repertoire manager.

As indicated, human resource departments are very important to the success or failure of an organization. Paying close attention to the challenges presented will help aviation organizations achieve efficiency and success in the future.

KEY TERMS

Association of Flight Attendants (AFA)
craft union
emergency board
employee stock ownership program (ESOP)
industrywide bargaining
Millennial generation
mutual aid pact
National Air Traffic Controllers Association (NATCA)
National Mediation Board (NMB)
pattern bargaining
Peter Pan generation
Railway Labor Act (RLA)

REVIEW QUESTIONS

1 From 2008 to 2021, what trends were occurring related to employment with the U.S. scheduled airlines? What event transpired

in 2020 resulting in a negative impact on the global airline industry and how did this impact employment figures?

2 In what sense are airline labor unions organized on a craft basis? What significance does this pattern of organization have in airline operations?

3 Why is the airline industry subject to the Railway Labor Act? How are airline strikes different from railway strikes? What are the basic purposes of the act? Describe several major differences between the RLA and the National Labor Relations Act.

4 What are the steps involved in the collective bargaining process under the RLA? What is the role of the National Mediation Board? Discuss some of the criticisms of the process.

5 Distinguish between *industrywide bargaining* and *pattern bargaining*. What was Decision 83?

6 Describe the labor–management scene before 1958. What happened in the early 1960s to change that scene? What was the result of this situation for the period from 1958 to 1970? What was the mutual aid pact? Why did the unions oppose it? What was the CAB's position? Why was airline labor so successful in raising wages and fringe benefits during the 1970s? Summarize labor–management relations before deregulation.

7 What has been the most important effect of deregulation on airline labor relations? What are some of the newer carriers' advantages over the established lines regarding payment and utilization of labor?

8 What is meant by the *elimination of the automatic labor cost pass-through*? How did labor–management relations change in the 1980s? Give some examples. Why was the period between 1982 and 1985 so difficult from labor's standpoint? Discuss some of the bargaining objectives of management during this period. How did things change during the mid-1980s? What is the purpose of profit sharing and/or employee ownership? Describe the labor–management environment during the 1990s and early 2000s. Summarize the objectives of management and labor in recent years.

9 What challenges will industry face as a result of the Millennial generation?

10 Human resource departments are being forced to restructure due to the need to attract qualified and skilled talent to meet the demands of the workforce. Describe why this is important. What types of new roles are being created to support this change?

Note

1 Airline Deregulation Act of 1978, Section 412(e).

CHAPTER 17

Airline Financing

CHAPTER CHECKLIST • YOU SHOULD BE ABLE TO:

- Describe the airlines' major sources of internal funds
- Define *debt financing* and *equity financing*, and discuss the airlines' primary sources of external funding
- List the advantages and disadvantages of leasing
- Compare and contrast *operating leases* and *capital leases*
- Define *balance sheet*, and describe the major items appearing under *assets* and *liabilities*
- Discuss the major uses and sources of funds for the U.S. scheduled airlines from 1960 to the present, and compare the cycles of business activity during this period
- Define *current ratio, long-term debt/equity ratio*, and *return on investment (ROI)*
- Summarize the general financial climate in which the U.S. scheduled airlines find themselves during this decade
- State which carriers might have the most difficult time generating funds in the money market in the future
- Discuss the importance of cash management and financial planning
- Discuss how airlines around the world finance aircraft

INTRODUCTION

Financing billions of dollars in flight and ground equipment in the new century presents a tremendous challenge to the airline industry. Airline

DOI: 10.4324/9780429346156-20

earnings tend to be cyclical, and industry returns on investment generally have been poor (see Table 17.1). With a few notable exceptions, airline cash flows over the long run have been inadequate to meet capital requirements. At the same time, the ratio of debt to equity for many carriers has increased to levels that have had a negative impact on their creditworthiness. Not only has this limited access to these airlines to external funds, but it has also led to larger option fees and progress payment requirements from the manufacturers—as much as 25 percent of the aircraft price in a three- to four-year period before delivery.

The advent of deregulation changed the basic rules of the game for air carriers. Deregulation has increased the demands on management for marketing skills, strategic planning, cost control, and competition with other firms. Deregulation stemmed in part from a belief that airlines, like other firms, should earn their own way in the market, not look to a public body or policy to guarantee it. It might then be appropriate to ask why, in a deregulated environment, one should be concerned with the financial condition of the airlines.

The financial condition of the industry directly affects individual firms' behavior in the short run and, ultimately, their structure and performance in the long run. In the short run, failing firms may resort to less-than-compensatory fares to generate sufficient cash to cover their fixed short-term commitments but not their long-term costs. This may threaten, in turn, the profitability and survival of other carriers in the long run. Although passengers benefit from low fares in the short run, for well-operated carriers to survive, fares must be raised eventually to recoup losses and provide a sufficient return to keep capital in the industry. Furthermore, the disruption to air service caused by the failure of a particular carrier imposes real costs on passengers, both business travelers and pleasure travelers.

In the long run, whereas the survival of any one firm is not important on a national policy basis, the failure of a significant number may lead to increased concentration and too few firms in the industry. The minimum number of firms necessary to ensure a competitive industry has been widely debated. As important as that number, however, is the degree to which the existing airlines serve the same markets and the vigor with which they compete on price and service. A small number of nationwide firms that compete with one another at all the large commercial airports may provide much stronger competitive pressure to hold down costs and fares than a large number of carriers competing in less extensive networks. The fewer the number of firms, however, the easier it is for them to form and enforce a tight oligopoly in which industry output is lower and fares are higher than would be the case in a competitive market.

SOURCES OF FUNDS

Internal Sources

Basically, the only true internal source of funds is **net earnings**, or *profits*, which are the funds left after taxes are paid to local, state, and federal governments and tax credits are taken. The company board of directors decides how much of the earnings should go to the owners (stockholders) in the form of dividends and how much should be retained in the company for investment purposes.

Two other internal sources of funds are depreciation and deferred taxes. **Depreciation** represents the airlines' largest single source of internal funds.[1] It is the allocation of an asset's cost over its estimated useful life. The provision for depreciation of fixed assets is an allowable expense of doing business. Unlike most expenses, however, it does not represent a cash outlay and so is referred to as a *noncash expense*. As a result of this accounting procedure, the company has funds in an amount equivalent to the depreciation provision. The purpose is to provide for the ultimate replacement of the depreciating asset. To the extent that this is not done immediately, the

Table 17.1 Net Income (In Thousands of Dollars $000) All U.S. Carriers, All Regions

Year	Quarter	DOMESTIC	LATIN AMERICA	ATLANTIC	PACIFIC	INTERNATIONAL	TOTAL
2000	1,2,3,4	1,991,496	12,581	311,761	137,623	79,238	2,532,700
2001	1,2,3,4	-7,234,855	10,499	-182,509	-768,656	-90,989	-8,266,509
2002	1,2,3,4	-9,329,102	-436,783	-1,029,513	-491,717	-78,369	-11,365,484
2003	1,2,3,4	-1,469,581	285,808	116,463	-651,702	3,543	-1,715,469
2004	1,2,3,4	-9,906,154	313,825	407,530	-71,523	151,897	-9,104,424
2005	1,2,3,4	-19,747,536	-720,181	-2,109,279	-4,833,816	190,916	-27,219,896
2006	1,2,3,4	9,043,659	1,464,063	3,188,145	4,352,204	138,042	18,186,112
2007	1,2,3,4	2,995,875	1,135,327	2,048,328	1,321,476	190,398	7,691,404
2008	1,2,3,4	-18,173,970	-415,249	-3,276,511	-1,662,522	-221,582	-23,749,834
2009	1,2,3,4	-2,252,074	404,667	-634,577	-213,634	169,340	-2,526,277
2010	1,2,3,4	1,176,134	635,210	447,673	1,102,857	304,122	3,665,995
2011	1,2,3,4	1,440,558	912,402	-1,167,311	222,501	-15,962	1,392,188
2012	1,2,3,4	2,212,176	-104,970	-1,130,016	-419,991	-193,468	363,732
2013	1,2,3,4	10,521,844	512,433	1,446,741	159,239	70,956	12,711,213
2014	1,2,3,4	8,645,383	-239,780	543,413	-637,981	129,598	8,440,634
2015	1,2,3,4	21,211,902	1,002,854	2,898,451	1,161,633	105,091	26,379,931
2016	1,2,3,4	13,354,439	1,050,005	630,002	478,968	96,330	15,609,744
2017	1,2,3,4	17,021,453	750,471	-227,796	-841,730	102,083	16,804,481
2018	1,2,3,4	14,109,503	1,033,398	1,118,450	-1,007,124	174,844	15,429,071
2019	1,2,3,4	15,705,970	1,549,883	378,323	-950,769	-250,885	16,432,523
2020	1,2,3,4	-24,627,764	-1,894,543	-3,538,667	-1,756,279	884,860	-30,932,394
2021	1,2,3,4	4,621,535	-1,879,774	-2,197,715	-184,949	781,882	1,140,979
2022	1	-2,331,375	-774,464	-1,252,818	42,428	132,284	-4,183,945

Source: Bureau of Transportation Statistics

company has the use of the cash generated for such purposes as it sees fit. In the case of airlines, with their heavy investment in flight equipment, the amount of these funds can be quite substantial.

Deferred taxes refer to certain taxes that companies are required to collect for various taxing authorities, including federal excise and state sales taxes and payroll withholding of employee income taxes. These taxes are paid to the government after periods varying from one month to three months from the time of receipt of the income on which they are calculated. Thus, the company has the use of these funds in the interval, and it acknowledges its obligation by an *accrual* for taxes, or a reserve. In accounting, an accrual is an expense (such as taxes) that is recognized when it is incurred but before cash is actually disbursed. Considering the tremendous cash flow of airlines, this source of funds can represent millions of dollars.

Currently, most airlines are unable to generate sufficient reserves from their depreciation charges and retained earnings to finance aircraft acquisition. Cash flows have also been affected by reductions in depreciation allowances and elimination of the 10 percent investment tax credit with the Tax Reform Act of 1986. Industrywide, cash reserves might normally provide almost a quarter of future aircraft investment needs, but these reserves are not evenly distributed among airlines, and, for some, the availability of cash for investment is virtually negligible.

Another internal source of funds in recent years has been the conversion of existing assets. This relatively new way of obtaining cash for financing aircraft is linked to the development of leasing and has some advantages when the secondhand market is buoyant. It can take the form of an outright sale of equipment or a sale and lease-back. The latter type of transaction allows airlines to use the generally appreciated value of aircraft to finance additional aircraft, to remove older aircraft from balance sheets while values are still high, to finance investment in other airlines, or to finance their own internal operations (in the case of undercapitalized airlines).

Many leasing companies have generated business through sale and lease-back transactions. Some airlines have even created their own leasing companies to which they sell their aircraft, leasing the same aircraft back from these companies. However, the current cycle of high residual value for secondhand aircraft seems to have passed its peak, and this source of financing might be much more limited in the future.

External Sources

Required funds that are not generated internally must come from outside sources; that is, the competitive money market. The nature of the business, its earnings, its financial structure, and the money market environment all have a bearing on what external sources are used. In obtaining outside funds, the airline industry must compete for the investable funds of the country (both debt and equity) with all other industries. **Debt financing** refers to the borrowing of funds from commercial banks, insurance companies, and other sources. **Equity financing** refers to the sale of stocks, bonds, and other equity in the company to the public. The *debt* portion of these external funds will be attracted, generally speaking, into situations in which the greatest relative security exists, in terms of both assets and ability to repay. The *equity* portion will be attracted into situations in which the foreseeable yield (in dividend income, capital appreciation, or a combination of both) is relatively large in relation to the risks taken. *Dividend income* refers to the distribution of earnings to stockholders (owners) of a corporation, and *capital appreciation*, as used here, refers to the value of capital stock. Thus, to succeed in the race for funds in the competitive money market, the airlines must be at least as strong as the other competing industries.

In practice, however, equity financing is available almost exclusively to "financially strong" airlines, and most airlines today remain undercapitalized. Therefore, they are unlikely to be able to raise enough in the way of equity to finance substantial orders for aircraft.

Investments today are more often debt financed than equity financed. Depending on the financial viability of a company and the perceived risk involved, debt may be either unsecured or secured by the assets concerned—hence the term *asset-based financing*. In practice, increasing debt/equity ratios and occasional bankruptcies have led to a shift toward asset-based financing in the airline industry; debt bonds and related asset-linked securities are the only public offerings that still attract much attention. The debt market is large in the United States, where insurance companies and pension funds have strong cash assets to place, but it is sensitive to the general economic environment.

Commercial Banks. Although loans can be structured to fit almost any need, they basically fall into two categories—**short-term loans** for seasonal needs and working capital and **long-term loans** to finance new or used equipment. Commercial banks have historically been primarily in the short-term credit business, because they obtain their funds from checking accounts and so their investments are made to conform to the pattern of their liabilities. Data are lacking to measure accurately the part played by commercial banks as a source of long-term funds. However, it has been well established that they have become a major factor in long-term lending in recent years.

How a loan is priced, structured, and presented depends on the bank's perception of a borrower's condition, as well as on the bank's perception of its exposure to risk. For example, a short-term loan (90 days) may be easy to negotiate on an unsecured basis, but a long-term loan needed to finance a significant fleet expansion may require extensive negotiations and complex documentation.

A bank will want the borrower to show that the reason for the loan request has been clearly conceived and makes sound business sense. This can be a simple task, as in the case of demonstrating seasonal cash flow variations, or it can be more complex, as in proving the need for new or additional aircraft. **Cash flow** refers to the receipt or payment of an amount of money. For accounting purposes, cash flow equals net earnings (profits after taxes) plus depreciation charges. The tenor of a loan should match its purpose. If the loan is to be used to cover seasonal cash flow variations, then it should be paid off before the next seasonal cash flow cycle starts. Repayment terms should be matched to the purpose of the loan and to the airline's best projections of its ability to repay. How much a bank charges for its loans depends on many factors, ranging from external factors, such as the bank's willingness to be competitive in a certain market or perceived risk, to internal constraints, such as the bank's loan portfolio management policy.

The usual practice is for an airline to establish a **line of credit** with a commercial bank before the time the funds will be needed. Establishment of a line of credit does not bind the bank legally to make a loan at the time requested, if conditions have changed. But the bank seldom fails to honor its agreement unless circumstances have changed drastically. Under normal arrangements, the line of credit establishes the amount and the terms on which the bank will advance funds as required. The amount may vary from several thousand dollars to several million, depending on the size of the airline and its credit status. Whatever the amount, the arrangement is a highly desirable one for the airline's corporate management, because it provides funds when needed, quickly and without complicated financial procedures.

Most banks require collateral when they lend to airlines, because of the sensitivity of the industry to general economic cycles and the high debt/equity burdens carried by most airlines. However, most bankers are not willing to make their credit decisions strictly on the basis of *collateral* value (the value of the assets pledged in the event of default). Most will want to make sure that their primary source of repayment is the cash flow stream generated by the company's operations. Collateral value and guarantees of repayment are viewed as secondary sources, because they are more difficult to convert into collections than cash flow is.

Aircraft equipment loans in recent years primarily have been in the form of equipment trusts. With **equipment trust financing**, a bank, or more likely a group of banks, lends the required money for the purchase of new equipment, but the title for the equipment remains with the banks, who are the trustees of the series of certificates issued with the equipment as security. The equipment trust certificates are owned by the banks doing the financing and are held by them or sold to investors, who hold them until maturity. The airline operating the equipment pays enough each year to retire a series of the certificates and to pay interest on them, as well as on those certificates in the hands of the remaining banks or investors. Maturities run from ten to 20 years.

The big advantage to investors of equipment trust financing is security. Airline equipment does not depreciate as fast as other types of capital goods because of rigid FAA maintenance requirements. It is not unusual for a carrier to sell the equipment five or ten years later and still get 75 percent of its original value. Also, as each annual payment is made, the equity behind the remaining certificates becomes greater, because the entire value of the equipment is security for the entire issue of certificates until all are paid off. In other words, the airline does not own any of the equipment until all of it is paid off.

Finance and Life Insurance Companies. Other sources of debt financing include finance and life insurance companies, which come in all sizes and have widely varying capabilities. Most of the finance companies that have been active in the airline field offer a selection of loan and lease packages. The basic finance company services include equipment financing, leasing, and, occasionally, short-term loans. In many cases, the credit packages offered by finance companies are similar to those offered by banks, as are their pricing and credit evaluation policies.

Life insurance companies became a major source of airline investment funds in the early 1970s, when the industry turned to other competitive sources in search of dollars to finance the jumbo jets. In many respects, life insurance companies are the most singularly fitted of all financial institutions to provide for the long-term capital needs of the airline industry. Because the bulk of the funds placed with life insurance companies are for extended periods of time, life insurance companies are in an ideal position to extend credit that synchronizes with their own liabilities.

Investment Banks. Investment banks provide the most formally organized machinery for the raising of funds. Indeed, it is their primary function. In a sense, they are not a source of capital, but rather serve mainly as intermediaries between investment outlets and the industry. In addition, they often serve as advisers or consultants in the development of various types of transactions, such as mergers and the placement of private loans.

Investment bankers provide private debt placement and public equity offerings. A *private debt placement* is similar to a bank loan, except that the funding source of the loan is a private party, such as an investor group, an insurance company, or another concern that is looking for long-term investments. As with bank loans, covenants and financial tests are required. These usually can be renegotiated with the lender if the company's circumstances change during the course of the loan.

Although investment banking firms are not technically sources of equity, they are experts at tapping the public equity source. The benefits of a *public equity offering* are considerable. A public offering may be the lowest-cost capital available for continued airline growth, and a successful offering is a means of reducing some of the leverage burden often associated with growth. In addition, the issue can create a market for the airline's stocks or bonds. This has two uses. First, given further corporate development and success, a market for future offerings has been created. Second, the owners of the airline have a means of valuing or selling their holdings—an important point in terms of financial planning.

An investment banking firm will usually agree to accept the responsibility for finding buyers for the stocks and bonds it plans to underwrite (select and market). In order to commit itself to the underwriting task, an investment banking firm must be confident about the airline's condition and plans. The firm will scrutinize the airline closely and base its decision to make an offer on the quality of management and the company's financial position. Once the bank has made an affirmative decision, it will provide direction for the preparatory work, which takes months to complete.

Even when everything is ready and all of the accounting, legal, and printing tasks are complete, the timing of the offering is largely up to the investment banker. The bank knows the strengths and weaknesses of the market. Consequently, an airline's top management generally develops a close working relationship with the investment banking source.

An airline that needs to supplement its capital funds by borrowing or selling stock in the open market ordinarily consults its investment bankers, who investigate the corporation's needs and recommend methods of financing. These include the following:

1. *Common Stock (equity).* The ownership of the corporation is divided into a specified number of shares of **common stock**, each representing equal participation in the affairs of the firm. The owners of the company, called *common shareholders* or *common stockholders*, receive certificates of common stock or shares in proportion to their participation in the firm.
2. *Preferred Stock (equity).* Like common stock, **preferred stock** is a share in the ownership of the company, but instead of equal participation in the profits, preferred shares carry fixed annual dividends that must be paid before dividends can be declared on common stock.
3. *Bonds (debt).* In formal, legal terminology, a **bond** is a promissory note under seal. However, we commonly use the word *bond* to mean a long-term debt obligation, particularly one issued to the general public.

Leasing. Leasing has become one of the most widely accepted financing tools for equipment acquisition. An important advantage to leasing is that an airline can get the use of aircraft without having to put out any of its own equity funds. Leasing conserves working capital. It also avoids **progress payments** to the manufacturer, or money payments that a carrier advances to a manufacturer on a regular schedule while the aircraft is under production. These payments can be as much as 30 percent of the cost of the aircraft.

Leasing makes it easier to replace and modernize equipment. Ownership of equipment tends to foster a make-do philosophy. When equipment is capitalized, it often becomes awkward for a company to replace it before obsolescence. If the equipment has a long life, such as airplanes, many companies continue depreciation before replacement to avoid a heavy write-off. The result could be a loss of competitive advantage, due to not having the latest equipment, or a reduction of profits through costly maintenance.

The major disadvantage associated with leasing is the high cost. Other financing forms or outright purchase do cost less, on the surface. However, when the present value of cash flow is taken into consideration, leasing can actually be the least expensive form of financing. Another disadvantage is the loss of residual values in many cases. If the equipment is marketable at the termination of a lease, then any residual value normally goes to the lessor, not the lessee. To lessen the impact of this disadvantage, lessors frequently offer reduced rentals after lease termination. Many leasing companies can provide assistance in evaluating specific lease versus purchase options.

Leasing consists of both operating leases and capital, or financial, leases. **Operating leases** are short term (generally not more than five years) and have varying degrees of flexibility for cancellation by the airline. They generally convey no residual value in the aircraft and, from an accounting standpoint, are considered strictly as an operating cost. **Financial (capital) leases** are long term, generally 12 to 25 years. Because of restrictions on termination, their long term, and the contractual commitment to pay the total value of the lease payments, they are considered a form of capital financing. The total cost of the lease payments is amortized over the life of the lease, and a portion of the rental payments is attributed to the implicit interest cost of the financing.

Both forms of aircraft financing have become important since the mid-1970s, or roughly since deregulation. Whereas virtually 100 percent debt financing and internal financing of aircraft typified the 1960s and early 1970s, current estimates are that 51 percent of the aircraft of major carriers is under lease and that this figure might reach 70 percent over the next decade. Of particular interest here is the effect that operating leases have on carriers' financial performance.

Capital leases appear as long-term liabilities on carriers' balance sheets, and the interest expense and the amortization of principal are treated in a manner similar to interest and depreciation on debt-financed aircraft. The principal advantage offered by capital leases is the lower financing costs that arise from the difference in the ability of lessors and lessees to use depreciation and other tax benefits. In leases under which the airline does not retain the residual value of the plane at the end of the lease, the opportunity for long-term capital gains may be sacrificed, especially if the expectations of the lessor (reflected in the lease terms) and the lessee differ.

Operating leases, on the other hand, do not appear on balance sheets and are sometimes criticized for providing off-balance-sheet financing of essential capital goods. The implication is that fixed capital costs are hidden, thereby presenting a rosier balance sheet picture of debt to equity investors. Nevertheless, the substitution of operating leases for other forms of financing offers advantages as well as disadvantages.

On the positive side, operating leases may provide a method of lowering the air carrier's overall cost of capital. Equity, debt, capital leases, and operating leases all have differing direct costs, risk premiums, depreciation and tax benefits, and degrees of flexibility. Relying too heavily on one source of financing likely would result in capital costs greater than those achievable with a mixed portfolio of capital sources.

Part of the lower cost that operating leases may provide to an airline's financing derives from the flexibility offered by their relatively short term. The best way to describe this aspect is by way of an admittedly oversimplified example. Suppose that an airline puts 30 percent of its operating fleet on equally staggered five-year noncancelable leases. In this case, 6 percent of its fleet is up for renewal each year. In the event of a falloff in traffic, these aircraft can be returned to the lessor and a new lease delayed until after the downturn. To the extent that equity financing of aircraft is supplanted by the contractual commitments of debt and leases (both operating and capital), the flexibility and cushion of carriers in a downturn are reduced. In this example, if that 30 percent of the fleet were equity financed, the earnings requirements of these aircraft (essentially, dividends and retained earnings) could be totally avoided in a downturn (though eventually, in an upturn, the aircraft would have to provide a return to compensate shareholders in the long run).

In summary, the move to operating leases by carriers may assist in balancing a debt portfolio. However, when changes in individual carriers and industry leverage are examined over time, specific terms of operating leases must be taken into account, because apparent leverage may be reduced by operating leases but the financial risk of the airline may not drop proportionately.

Vendor Financing. Manufacturers increasingly are offering financial support as an inducement in the competitive environment of aircraft marketing. Traditionally, aircraft manufacturers have granted support to customers through various means, including the arrangement or provision of equity financing, purchase of stock options, and guarantees for debt financing to financial institutions. With the increasing sophistication of financing techniques, manufacturers are becoming involved in complex leasing and other arrangements.

In early 1983, American was the first airline to make what was termed an "innovative arrangement" with McDonnell-Douglas and Pratt & Whitney by leasing 20 MD-80s. TWA followed shortly thereafter with a 15-aircraft order. American had studied other aircraft and had data on the MD-80 from other carriers and performance guarantees from the manufacturers that aided in the purchase decision. American planned to replace their 111-seat Boeing 727-100s with the MD-80s, with their 142-passenger seat configuration, on certain routes that were experiencing continual heavy load factors and actually turning some prospective passengers away.

Because American had $1.5 billion in outstanding long-term debt on its balance sheet and did not want to add to it, an innovative arrangement had to be devised. The lease was for only five years; however, an option to extend the lease was provided that could run 13 extra years, bringing the total to 18 years, the traditional term for new-jet financing. The unique feature in the arrangement between American and McDonnell-Douglas and Pratt & Whitney was profit sharing. If the operating costs of the MD-80s, with their two JT8D-200-series engines, fell below an agreed-on point, then American would share that increase in operating profit. In effect, McDonnell-Douglas and Pratt & Whitney assumed joint ownership of the $20 million aircraft. Pratt & Whitney would provide all engine overhauls.

TWA, like American, found the terms of the agreement very attractive—a way to acquire new airplanes without extending its heavy debt obligation. But the TWA arrangement did not include the profit-sharing feature. In any case, McDonnell-Douglas was anxious both to make its first sale of an MD-80 with the JT8D-200-series engines to a major carrier and to stretch out its production line, which was at risk of closing down without an order like American's and TWA's.

Venture Capital. **Venture capital** is money invested in business enterprises that generally do not have access to the conventional sources of capital previously discussed. Many of the newer regional carriers have used venture capital to get started, and some established airlines also have tapped this source in search of new funding.

The key ingredient of venture capital firms is an entrepreneurial team. The entrepreneurs generally prepare a detailed business plan that describes the nature of the proposed business and forecasts future activities and incomes. This business plan is used to attract venture capital. Venture capital investors will invest only in situations that will ultimately produce sizable capital gains. Because the investments are made in unproven situations, venture capital investing is risky and depends on the ability of the entrepreneurs (new carriers) to turn their ideas into a successful company. The investment in the enterprise is made by buying stock (generally from the treasury), by lending money, or by combinations of both.

People Express, the innovative airline that served the eastern part of the United States with Boeing 737s, was launched when two men took their idea for a new low-cost airline to Citicorp Venture Capital and asked for a hearing. At that time (late January 1980), People Express was only the name on a business plan; no aircraft were owned, no routes were being served, and no approvals had been requested from the FAA or the CAB.

Within two months, however, Citicorp Venture Capital was sufficiently impressed to invest $200,000, thereby launching People Express. A short time later, $400,000 was added. Although the $600,000 put forth by Citicorp Venture Capital was not even close to what was needed to create an airline, it was sufficient to pull together a management team and to formulate detailed plans for People Express. By November 1980, the airline was enough of an entity that management was able to raise $27 million in the public market by selling equity in what had been nothing but an idea less than a year before.

One of the most successful airlines today, Federal Express Corporation, got its start in July 1973 when it approached a New York venture capitalist, New Court Securities. This company, a division of Rothschild's, was a merchant banking operation that managed massive amounts of capital. Some $52 million was subsequently raised—the largest private placement up to that time.

Until a few decades ago, the primary sources of venture capital were wealthy families or partnerships of affluent individuals looking for capital gains. For example, the Rockefeller family has funded several venture capital pools. It was Laurance Rockefeller who backed Eddie Rickenbacker to launch Eastern Airlines in the 1930s. J. H. Whitney supported Juan Trippe's first Pan American flights between Florida and Cuba. Since the mid-1960s, a number of professional managers of venture capital have formed firms to invest funds provided by wealthy families and insurance companies and other institutional investors. Since 1978, there has been a flurry of activity in this type of financing as major corporations, labor unions, pension funds, and even universities have allocated portions of their investment funds to venture capital management firms to locate entrepreneurs and participate in the management of new companies.

The venture capitalist's involvement with management is an essential element in agreeing to finance a start-up situation. The backer usually insists on a position on the board of directors. In this way, the venture capitalist can act quickly to effect changes in the event that business conditions shift. The majority of venture capital investments are made by purchasing equity (stocks) or debt convertible to equity (bonds) in the start-up firm. Pure debt is generally secondary to equity, because such financing does not provide the opportunity to share in future growth. Furthermore, the young firm probably would not produce sufficient cash flow to service the debt.

Some venture capital firms specialize in start-up investments, while others prefer to wait until a second, third, or later round of private financing. Venture capitalists are successful only if the companies they back succeed. Then they can sell the stock they hold to the public at a higher multiple of the original purchase price or to whatever larger company acquires the now-successful operation.

Some venture capital groups have affiliated themselves with investment banking firms (or in some cases, with large commercial banks). These are generally the groups with the greatest resources. In philosophy, they are similar to private venture capitalists. In terms of capabilities, they often bring with them the management and financial resources of their affiliated companies, which makes access to debt and equity markets much easier. The principal advantages of both the private venture capital groups and the affiliated venture capital groups lie in their flexibility and ability to take risks. Unlike most other funding sources, venture capitalists will give start-up ventures serious consideration.

SOURCES AND USES OF FUNDS BY THE U.S. SCHEDULED AIRLINES

The following analysis of the sources and uses of funds by the U.S. scheduled airlines is based on data from the income statements and balance sheets provided by Airlines for America (A4A) Passenger Airline Cost Index with source data coming from the U.S. DOT Form 41. The industry has grown significantly since 1960 following passage of the Federal Aviation Act of 1958, basically within a highly regulated environment. The twilight period of regulation began in 1978, and the 1980s ushered in a new era for the industry. During the period from 1960 to 1981, the industry experienced a complete transition in the fleet, with the first jets appearing in the early 1960s, the stretched versions in the late 1960s, and the wide-bodies in the early 1970s. By the late 1970s, the major carriers were placing their orders for the fuel-efficient equipment that began appearing in the early to mid-1980s. In the period, the airlines experienced four distinct business cycles that closely followed the overall economy's performance. The data in Table

17.1 evidence the cyclical performance reflecting the upward and downward swings of the cycle in earnings and return on investment. From 2010 to 2019, the industry showed signs of positive growth but took a major negative hit in 2020 and 2021 due to the COVID-19 global pandemic.

Industry Balance Sheet

A **balance sheet** is merely a statement of assets and claims that summarizes the financial position of a firm—or, in this case, the U.S. scheduled airline industry—at some specific point in time. By definition, it must balance, because each and every known asset, as something of value, will be claimed by someone. It balances because assets equal claims (liabilities and net worth). In this context, **assets** are things of value that are owned—cash, property, and the rights to property. **Liabilities** are monetary debts or things of value that are owed to creditors. **Net worth**, or owner's equity, is the difference between assets and liabilities.

The claims shown on a balance sheet are divided into two groups: (1) the claims of the owners of a firm against the firm's assets, called *net worth*, and (2) the claims of nonowners, called *liabilities*. Thus:

Assets = Liabilities + Net worth.

Table 17.2 shows financial results for U.S. passenger airlines from 1977 to 2021. Previous editions of this book published annual balance sheet information for air carriers leading up to 2004 but unfortunately, this data is no longer published.

Table 17.2 Financial Results, U.S. Passenger Airlines

Year	Total Operating Revenue	Fuel Expense	Labor Expense	Other Expense	Total Operating Expense	Operating Profit	Pre-Tax Profit	Net Profit
1977	19,423	3,618	7,481	7,450	18,549	874	888	669
1978	22,245	4,040	8,569	8,315	20,924	1,320	1,354	1,176
1979	26,411	6,267	9,975	9,960	26,203	209	148	325
1980	31,950	9,443	11,301	11,395	32,140	-189	-157	51
1981	34,390	10,180	12,124	12,534	34,839	-448	-700	-257
1982	34,820	9,643	12,348	13,575	35,566	-747	-1,005	-906
1983	37,124	8,959	13,113	14,764	36,836	289	-83	-152
1984	41,998	9,322	13,545	17,178	40,044	1,954	1,278	645
1985	44,537	9,283	14,351	19,605	43,238	1,299	986	846
1986	44,867	6,951	15,127	21,898	43,976	891	122	-122
1987	50,957	7,530	16,398	25,187	49,115	1,842	692	163
1988	56,657	7,479	17,845	28,532	53,857	2,800	2,568	1,314

(Continued)

Table 17.2 *Continued*

Year	Total Operating Revenue	Fuel Expense	Labor Expense	Other Expense	Total Operating Expense	Operating Profit	Pre-Tax Profit	Net Profit
1989	60,577	8,501	19,437	31,400	59,338	1,239	793	-85
1990	65,817	11,639	21,543	35,090	68,272	-2,455	-4,345	-4,114
1991	64,688	9,558	21,751	35,672	66,981	-2,293	-2,509	-2,056
1992	67,308	9,124	23,086	37,895	70,105	-2,797	-3,836	-4,681
1993	72,801	8,781	23,930	39,146	71,857	944	-1,789	163
1994	74,632	8,213	24,744	39,715	72,671	1,961	-679	-682
1995	79,081	8,436	25,457	40,043	73,936	5,145	3,144	2,001
1996	84,733	10,311	26,477	42,578	79,366	5,367	4,048	2,422
1997	90,143	10,301	27,931	44,461	82,693	7,450	7,095	4,779
1998	91,949	8,342	29,425	46,141	83,908	8,042	7,360	4,425
1999	96,163	9,020	31,394	48,802	89,216	6,948	7,954	4,686
2000	105,311	14,099	34,490	51,020	99,609	5,702	4,776	2,238
2001	92,012	13,120	36,261	52,996	102,377	-10,365	-10,656	-8,008
2002	84,255	10,959	35,653	47,186	93,799	-9,544	-14,578	-11,762
2003	92,950	12,853	34,148	48,998	95,999	-3,049	-2,025	-2,088
2004	106,734	18,713	33,848	57,549	110,109	-3,375	-8,575	-10,046
2005	119,010	27,221	31,159	62,635	121,015	-2,005	-27,605	-28,647
2006	130,961	31,539	30,338	64,049	125,926	5,035	16,570	16,527
2007	138,221	33,877	31,045	66,625	131,547	6,675	7,909	6,306
2008	146,392	47,945	30,798	73,246	151,989	-5,597	-26,155	-24,500
2009	123,455	27,419	31,026	63,988	122,433	1,022	-3,440	-2,821
2010	138,642	32,314	32,276	65,760	130,350	8,292	3,088	2,245
2011	153,049	42,712	33,334	71,733	147,779	5,270	847	525
2012	156,374	43,987	35,630	70,720	150,337	6,037	548	131
2013	161,595	41,663	35,787	72,837	150,287	11,309	5,179	12,183
2014	169,277	42,473	38,289	73,914	154,676	14,601	9,850	7,383
2015	168,874	26,174	42,642	72,064	140,881	27,994	23,886	24,794
2016	168,129	21,672	46,708	74,653	143,033	25,096	21,826	14,224
2017	175,553	25,268	50,306	78,355	153,929	21,624	19,324	15,666
2018	187,474	33,620	52,660	83,548	169,828	17,646	15,163	11,775
2019	196,215	31,990	56,771	86,685	175,446	20,768	19,221	14,763
2020	77,298	11,876	47,036	64,875	123,786	-46,488	-45,232	-35,047
2021	130,010	22,297	49,772	75,292	147,361	-17,351	-3,356	-2,786

Source: A4A's Passenger Airline Cost Index and U.S. DOT Form 41

Sources and Uses of Funds: 1960–Present

The airline industry has experienced defined cycles of upward and downward growth from 1960 to the present day. In previous editions of this book, air carrier data was published showing balance sheets, income statement, and operating expenses but, as previously mentioned, this data is no longer published. However, historical data and new data has been accessed from a variety of sources to assist with a discussion on the defined cycles.

Upward Side of the First Cycle: 1960–1966. Bolstered by strong earnings during this period, particularly from 1963 to 1966, increases in owned and leased property were largely financed through internal sources. Depreciation and retained earnings represented significant sources of funding during this period. Profitability during the mid-1960s also was instrumental in securing debt financing which played an important role during these years. New-stock issuance played a minor role as a funding source.

Downward Side of the First Cycle: 1966–1971. It was during this period that the industry placed billions of dollars in new orders for wide-bodied equipment, which arrived on the scene in the early 1970s. However, this commitment was made before the industry followed the economy into a tailspin that started during the last half of 1969 and continued through 1971. Many of the newly produced wide-bodies were parked in the Arizona desert because of lack of demand for air transportation during the early 1970s. Low profits, an uncertain future concerning earnings, inflation, and declining airline stock prices resulted in a tight supply of money for the airline industry.

Equity has supplied less outside funds for the airlines ever since they reached their high-water mark in mid-1967. The general lack of confidence on the part of investors has also affected the attitudes of the lenders who make up the debt market.

Capital in the form of debt or equity was difficult to obtain during these years, and with earnings drying up, the industry had to turn to new sources. Commercial banks had provided the greater portion of debt financing up to this point. Now the industry had to turn to different and more expensive instruments to finance its capital needs, including convertible debenture financing, largely with life insurance companies, and lease financing.

The insurance companies, in particular Prudential, Metropolitan, and Equitable, were not particularly interested in straight lending. In general terms, a **debenture** is a debt. However, financial practice has restricted the meaning of *debenture* to only those bonds that are not secured by any specific pledge of property. The debenture bond is a widely accepted mode of corporate financing. It appealed to the airlines at this time because the absence of a specific lien gives greater freedom to management and permits the reservation of secured obligations for periods of emergency. In the event of default on interest or principal payments, the bondholders are unable to bring foreclosure proceedings to have the property sold by the court.

From the investor's point of view, the debenture bond is appealing because the general credit or financial position of the corporation constitutes the primary basis of safety. As the name suggests, *convertible debentures* give the holder the privilege of exchanging holdings for securities of a different type, usually common stock. The use of convertible debentures as a means of raising new capital depends in large measure on conditions in the capital market and the financial appeal of the issuing corporation. Stock prices were still reasonably buoyant during this period, which made the conversion privilege attractive to the insurance companies, which looked upon the airline industry as attractive in terms of long-term growth.

During the 1966–1971 period, a substantial portion of the capital required was financed through long-term debt. Financing through commercial banks was expensive because of higher short-term interest rates and shorter loan periods (generally eight to ten years) that required renegotiation.

Leasing flight equipment came into vogue during this period of poor earnings and considerable extension of debt. The general financial position of the carriers at the end of 1970 looked very poor indeed.

Upward Side of the Second Cycle: 1971–1976. Following massive layoffs in the early 1970s (industry employment dropped from 311,922 in 1969 to 289,926 by the end of 1975) in response to a sagging economy, excess capacity, and an increase in operating costs, most notably fuel prices, the industry rebounded slightly in 1971, and profits rose through 1976. A great deal of the success during this period is attributable to the severe cost-cutting measures launched by the carriers. Capital requirements during these years were met largely through depreciation, increases in current liabilities, and, to a lesser degree, retained earnings.

Downward Side of the Second Cycle: 1976–1983. Growth in traffic and earnings continued through 1978, despite ever-increasing fuel costs. A number of factors boosted traffic a record 17 percent in revenue passenger miles (RPMs) during 1978. A weak dollar abroad attracted record numbers of Europeans to the United States, and substantial price cutting stimulated an elastic market for air travel. Profits of $1.2 billion were posted, and the carriers responded by ordering $9.4 billion in new planes. Traffic fell off in 1979 but still showed a 12 percent increase in RPMs.

Depreciation provided the major source of funding during this period, followed by debt financing and retained earnings resulting from the profitable years from 1976 to 1979. Leasing became so important that the capitalized leased-property dollar amount is now broken down in the Air Transport Association annual reports. Severe financial losses totaling $1.4 billion for the industry from 1981 to 1983 were largely the result of a recessionary economy, high fuel costs, severe competition, and the extended effects of the air traffic controllers' strike in August 1981.

Upward Side of the Third Cycle: 1983–1988. The economy rebounded in 1983, and an upswing in airline earnings resulted in significantly improved financial performance in 1984 and 1985.

A record 418 million passenger enplanements were recorded in 1986, undoubtedly stimulated by the greatest ever decline in airfares. By 1986, the year of the mergers, almost 90 percent of passengers were flying on some form of discount. Average discounts (percentage off full fare) reached a high of 61 percent.

Industry earnings fell during 1986. Although such carriers as American, Delta, Northwest, Piedmont, and USAir reported significant net profits, Eastern, Pan Am, TWA, and United experienced large losses.

Improved earnings enabled many of the carriers to tap both the debt and equity markets for equipment financing during this period. However, leasing continued to play an important, and growing, role in meeting carriers' equipment needs. Tax reform and repeal of the investment tax credit in 1987 caused an upsurge in aircraft orders during 1986. One-third of the total jet orders in 1986 were by leasing companies. Similarly, one-third of the U.S. major airlines' fleets were leased, compared with about 21 percent in 1980.

Bolstered by a strong economy, airline revenues increased by 13 percent between 1987 and 1988. Hub-and-spoke systems grew, and net profits rose from $593 million to $1.7 billion. The major carriers placed significant orders for new jet equipment, and employment remained strong.

Downward Side of the Third Cycle: 1989–1994. A greatly overexpanded economy began to show signs of slowing down in 1989, precipitated by the failure of many savings and loan associations. Fuel prices rose, and Eastern Airlines faced a long, difficult strike. The collapse of the United Airlines leveraged buyout in October 1989 and the shutdown of Braniff a month later scared away a lot of potential investors in the airline industry. Braniff's failure released 48 jets into the market and, for the first time, placed a large number of new Stage 3 Airbus A320s into the market. These factors all had a depressing effect on domestic air travel. The result was that, although several airlines had a good year financially, the industry's overall net profit was $128 million, with a net profit margin of only 0.2 percent, compared to 5.5 percent average for all U.S. industry.

The U.S. airlines lost close to $4 billion in 1990, virtually all in the fourth quarter, when the cost of fuel doubled as the result of the Iraqi invasion of Kuwait. Losses continued through 1991, as the effects of a deepening recession in the United States and a steep decline in travel abroad brought on by the Gulf War took their toll. Huge losses forced a number of carriers to cut back service severely; to sell major assets, including international routes, aircraft, and airport gates; to postpone aircraft orders; and to furlough workers. Close to 40,000 employees were laid off, including 18,000 Eastern workers when that carrier closed down in January. The depressed economy continued into 1992, which took its toll on two more carriers: Pan American, the pioneer international carrier, and Midway Airlines, a new entrant since deregulation. Thousands more airline employees were left without jobs. Three other major carriers, America West, Continental, and TWA, were operating under Chapter 11 bankruptcy by the end of 1992. USAir and Northwest Airlines were also experiencing financial difficulties.

In response, Standard and Poor's (a major bond rating agency) downgraded the debt ratings of just about all of the large U.S. carriers not already in bankruptcy. The shortage of affordable capital prompted many observers both inside and outside the industry to call for relaxation of foreign investment rules to make it more attractive for foreign airlines to acquire ownership interest in the U.S. airlines, thus providing much-needed capital infusion. Foreign ownership of U.S. airlines is currently limited to 25 percent of voting power and 49 percent of equity.

Between 1990 and 1994, the industry lost close to $13 billion. Losses dwindled in 1994 to $344 million, in large part due to lower fuel prices and the sacrifices that airline employees and airline stockholders made during industry restructuring.

Upward Side of the Fourth Cycle: 1995–1997. When the industry was losing billions of dollars in the early 1990s, the airlines took on additional debt in order to sustain their operations and remain in business. The profits earned during 1995 and 1996 were used to reduce the level of debt in the industry. Total long-term debt decreased from $17.6 billion in 1994 to $16.5 billion in 1995 and to $14.8 billion in 1996. The percentage of capital coming from debt and long-term capital leases in the airline industry in 1996 was 50.4 percent. This is a very high level of indebtedness when compared to U.S. industry overall, in which the percentage of capital coming from debt and capital leases averages only 40 percent. Because of the high level of indebtedness, airlines have high fixed charges for interest expenses. In an economic slowdown, these fixed charges do not drop with reduced operations and expose the industry to higher levels of risk as earnings decline. For this reason, most airline debt has not yet regained its investment-grade rating, preventing many banks, insurance companies, and pension funds from investing in airline securities. As additional debt is repaid, rating agencies will likely reconsider these ratings.

Some of the carriers' earnings were being used to acquire additional aircraft. Industry capacity has been growing slowly for the past several years. Airlines have been very cautious about adding capacity following the losses of the early 1990s. At the end of 1996, ATA U.S. member airlines, which carried more than 95 percent of domestic passenger and freight traffic, had 575 new aircraft on order, at a total cost of $34.3 billion. This was the lowest number of aircraft on order in many years and demonstrated a continuation of the trend toward reducing the growth rate of new capacity. Furthermore, many of the aircraft on order were used to replace older Stage 2 aircraft, rather than to add new capacity. The relatively low number of aircraft orders suggested that capacity for the U.S. airline industry was anticipated to grow at a slow pace for several years. At the beginning of 1997, the gross book value of aircraft assets reached $67.3 billion, including capitalized leases. Aircraft were the largest category of the airlines' $95 billion in total assets.

Funding Sources in the 1990s and at Present

The balance sheet gives a picture of the financial position of a particular company or an entire industry at a certain date. To bankers and the investment community in general, it became the crucial yardstick by which funding decisions were made in the 1990s. Before deregulation in 1978, the U.S. airline industry represented limited risks for the investment community. With routes protected by the CAB and costs passed on to the flying public through higher prices approved by the same agency, there was little to fear from an investment standpoint. Where low liquidity levels (cash reserves) and a large outstanding debt were once accepted, the financial community now demands a better balance sheet and better asset management by airlines.

Many members of the financial community increasingly are concerned with the gap that seems to be growing in many airlines between operating cash and the burdens of interest expense and cash needs based on required capital expenditures.

One of the primary indicators of a company's ability to meet its current liabilities—and, as such, its ability to seek funding in the money market—is the **current ratio**. The current ratio is a measure of liquidity obtained by dividing current assets by current liabilities. The higher the number, the more cash there is on hand for short-term needs. A low current ratio would be a signal of concern to the financial community, particularly if accompanied by an operating loss. A carrier in a weak liquidity position may experience difficulty paying its day-to-day bills. If the current ratio is low, it may be compared with prior years to evaluate the extent of deterioration.

Another prime indicator is the **long-term debt/equity ratio**, which reflects the company's long-term borrowing power and long-term stability. It is obtained by dividing long-term debt by stockholder equity. The higher the number, the less able a company is to borrow money. Airlines that have financed their growth primarily with long-term debt (warrants, debentures, equipment loans, capital leases, and so forth) rather than equity are referred to as being highly leveraged. Furthermore, they incur substantial fixed-interest costs because of the high debt. A study of the larger U.S. carriers shows, in general, that their ratio of leverage parallels their profitability. Highly indebted firms are typically unprofitable. For example, Eastern and Pan Am were highly leveraged and consistently unprofitable. Thus, highly leveraged carriers represent a high risk because they are burdened by having to service high debt. Under these conditions, there is little equity available to absorb losses, and further borrowing is difficult and must be undertaken at an even higher rate. On the other hand, carriers like Southwest and Delta are not highly leveraged and are consistently profitable.

If the debt/equity ratio increases over a period of time, it indicates that the airline is taking on more debt to grow, entering new markets, or encountering losses. A debt/equity ratio of 2.5:1 or more indicates a highly leveraged airline and raises a red flag in the financial community. Such a ratio is particularly worrisome if operating losses are anticipated. When the ratio is moving upward and operating losses are expected, highly leveraged airlines find additional funding not only difficult to acquire but, if available, very expensive and often accompanied by restrictive provisions.

Basically, there are three tiers of major carriers in terms of balance sheet strength:

1 The few carriers in the first tier have sufficient financial strength, either through internally generated funds or favorable balance sheets, to go to the money markets for replacement aircraft. These carriers also tend to have a current fleet mix that allows them a period of time before they must refurbish their fleets.
2 Airlines in the second tier, the largest part of the industry, are either capital constrained or capital short.
3 The third tier won't have to go out of business (like Eastern and Pan American, which found themselves short of current assets and with an

abnormally high long-term debt/equity ratio), but they must reassess their business and improve profitability to attract capital. They might also have to reassess their route structures and consider shrinkage. This should improve profitability and at the same time reduce equipment requirements. It is hard for anyone in the financial community to envision any long-term viability for this group in the absence of profitability and route restructuring.

Significant concern about the financial health of the airline industry revolves around its level of leverage. In particular, if a firm is already highly leveraged, it may not be able to finance operating losses during recessions or periods of reduced demand. The striking dichotomy between the strong carriers and the weak ones is quite apparent. Previously strong carriers are not necessarily strong in today's environment. The demise of Eastern, Pan American, and Midway was tied directly to the high cost of carrying debt. Similarly, the bankruptcies of Continental, America West, and TWA were partly a consequence of their debt structure. Certainly, the high leverage of the weaker carriers makes them vulnerable in a recession and, if they survive, makes it difficult for them to renew their fleets in the re-equipment cycle.

Return on investment (ROI) is a key measure of an industry's and individual firms' abilities to attract capital for continued growth and replacement of existing assets. It is the ratio of net profit to total assets. Whereas high leverage can kill a firm quickly when operating losses arise, continual low returns on invested capital can also lead to its demise, though generally more slowly. Eventually, access to equity markets would be lost, forcing a reliance on debt and the subsequent potential for an inability to cover fixed charges.

The industry's ROI has never been strong and consistently has underperformed the average of all manufacturing industries except for the strong years of 1978 and 1988 and the expansion years of the mid-1960s. As is the case for operating results and leverage, ROIs on an industrywide basis hide the large discrepancy between a group of relatively strong airlines and a group of weaker carriers. The strong carriers have achieved, both before and since deregulation, ROIs much closer to those seen in all manufacturing industries and ones that should leave us less concerned with their future ability to attract equity investment. For the weaker carriers, the poor operating results of the last decade are reflected in the large losses to equity, primarily because of their high leverage in recent years.

In late 2019, the global airline industry took a turn in a negative direction, suffering the impact of the COVID-19 global pandemic which resulted in the greatest financial losses since the beginning of the industry in 1914. At the time of writing, the industry was not able to measure the true impact of the pandemic and data was still being collected and analyzed for 2020, 2021, and 2022. The pandemic has potentially changed the industry forever more and historical data that was previously used to forecast future trends has been skewed, creating a new set of challenges for the industry. There is no doubt that a fifth cycle is transpiring that will most likely cover 2019 to 2025 when the industry is expected to recover. As the industry evolves, funding sources will be increasingly concerned about contingency planning efforts focused on business model sustainability due to increased risks.

Putting It All Together

We can summarize the discussion of funding sources and their implications as follows:

1. Demand for capital funds will remain strong as carriers recycle their fleets into more fuel-efficient aircraft.
2. Some carriers are in a much better financial position than others (in terms of liquidity and balance sheet) to secure funding sources in the money market.
3. Some carriers will have to retrench by selling assets and reducing their route structures to remain competitive.
4. Operating results have been somewhat weaker on an industrywide basis, though they were hardly robust before deregulation.
5. In the early 1990s, the carriers were not in a position to raise cash through their common stock. The industry needs earnings before the investment community will look at common stocks, and it needs more than just one or two years of earnings.
6. For individual firms, the industry can be divided into a group of strong performers whose results have slipped only slightly since deregulation and a larger group of weaker performers whose results have brought their continued existence into question.
7. Some increase has occurred in industry leverage, though this has tended to be concentrated in certain firms.
8. ROIs are as bipolar as operating results, with the group of strong carriers achieving returns much more in line with those of other industries.
9. Interest rates will fluctuate depending on the world economy. When interest rates are high, borrowing is costly even for those who are in a position to do so. When interest rates are low, aircraft are easier to acquire, assuming the organization is in good financial standing.
10. Insurance companies are not as eager to join in the new round of lending as they were in the early 1980s. First, they haven't been paid in full for previous loans. Second, they, like other members of the financial community, were generally opposed to deregulation, because there was no CAB to keep the airline industry financially healthy. Competition may eliminate some carriers, and no long-term lender will lend unless it is reasonably sure that the airline will survive and pay back its loans.
11. Banks are in a slightly different situation than insurance companies, because on a short-term loan they can renew and re-renew. If the outlook is not good, they can recall the loan.
12. Leasing will continue to grow steadily, and airlines will be concentrating on a fleet balance of purchase and lease with an emphasis on lease.

13 Lenders and carrier management will be looking for employee commitments to their company in the form of investment programs.
14 Global events like the COVID-19 pandemic will continue and lenders will be increasingly interested in how airlines develop continency plans to weather the storm.

The situation can be interpreted in various ways. The weak performance of the industry as a whole can be viewed as evidence of a drastic decline that is still under way and that is leading to the collapse of the industry and the concentration of airline service in the hands of a few carriers. Or the weak performance can be viewed as the necessary shaking out of weak carriers, with the result that the industry will emerge with fewer but stronger carriers that are capable of competing vigorously nationwide and, indeed, worldwide. Deregulation was meant not to improve or aid the performance of all carriers in the industry but to reward the best-managed ones.

Clearly, the industry is still in transition from the regulatory period. The demise and bankruptcies of airlines can be traced without much difficulty to the operating and structural adjustments that have been continuing since deregulation. The industry apparently is moving toward an equilibrium of a small number of large nationwide carriers and an uncertain number of significant smaller ones. The industry's financial performance in such a world may end up on any point of the spectrum. On the one hand, a loose oligopoly could form in which fares and service remain fairly stable and remunerative but at levels close to or equal to competitive returns. On the other hand, a tight oligopoly could arise, leading to higher than normal profits, reduced service offerings on routes, and efficiency losses to the economy.

From a financial standpoint, it is difficult to predict what the recent financial history portends. Thin operating margins offer little pricing room to avoid slipping below fares that are sustainable in the long run. The level of leverage in the industry may work in both directions. Highly leveraged firms will have incentives to control costs and produce efficiently; at the same time, the exigencies of meeting debt service may encourage initiation of or acquiescence to oligopolistic pricing behavior.

Another concern often expressed is whether the industry has the financial capacity for the re-equipment and expansion of its fleet in the foreseeable future. The ability to attract capital and provide service depends on the strength of the underlying demand for an industry's output. Few doubt that airline service will continue to be in high demand in the long run. Undoubtedly, capital will be available at some price to meet that demand. Returns in the industry may have to increase to pay that price.

Deregulation has provided firms with the ability to respond rapidly to changes in their costs and the fares offered by their competitors. In the end, the profitability and strength of airline firms will depend on how well they use those freedoms. Whether the emerging capital structure of the airlines will be a source of additional strength and profitability or will add costs from inefficient structures, excessive risks, or costs of adjustment from bankruptcies and disruptions of service cannot be predicted with the available evidence. Conceivably, some reduction in the number of carriers will reduce excess capacity in the industry and thereby improve the financial performance of the remaining carriers. The lackluster financial condition of some of these carriers, however, which might be further weakened by a recession and an increase in fuel prices, gives reason to be concerned about the number of carriers that will survive and the effect this might have on competition.

HOW THE WORLD AIRLINES FINANCE AIRCRAFT

Much of the content of this book focuses on the United States and for the most part, airlines around the world function the same way as U.S. carriers, including the different ways to finance aircraft. With that said, it is important to provide a brief overview of the different options that exist as applied on a worldwide basis. Some of this content may overlap with content already provided in this chapter but this section presents more of a generic overview of the different options available to finance aircraft. There are eight main ways for an airline to finance aircraft and in most cases, airlines select more than one option depending on their needs.

Cash

Few airlines have access to surplus cash but in some cases, if available, airlines will opt for this method to finance aircraft. The next section of this chapter better explains the advantages and disadvantages to using cash for finance purposes.

Operating Leasing and Sale/Leasebacks

This method of financing aircraft provides flexibility for the airline because it can be done on a short-, medium-, or long-term basis. Such an arrangement is not much different than renting a car. Simply, the lessor orders the aircraft from a manufacturer or purchases the aircraft from an airline and leases it back. The lessor leases the aircraft to the airlines, also known as the lessee.

Bank Loans/Finance Leases

In this scenario, a bank lends capital to an airline and the loan is guaranteed by the aircraft also known as the asset. Most banks offer an average loan term of 12 years for commercial aircraft.

A finance lease is similar to a bank loan except in this scenario, the bank purchases the aircraft from the airline and the airline is responsible for making monthly lease payments. At the end of the lease payment term, the airline owns the aircraft. In most cases, the bank finances approximately 85 percent of the aircraft's value based on the airline's ability to cover the remaining amount with cash.

Export Credit Guaranteed Loans

The aircraft manufacturing industry is a major economic contributor to the country(s) in which the aircraft is manufactured. As a result, governments support and promote manufacturing companies by assisting with the export process, often providing loan guarantees for customers. For example, Overseas Country X seeks to purchase a Boeing 777 but no financial institution will provide a loan for the transaction due to the risk involved. The U.S.-based Export–Import Bank will guarantee the loan in order to maximize the positive impacts of the export process.

Tax Leases

Taxes are often a financial burden for companies and many businesses fail due to the related costs. Because of this, many governments provide tax breaks and/or tax incentives so that "their" companies can compete with companies in other countries. For example, an airline seeking to purchase an aircraft may have an opportunity to avoid paying taxes as an incentive, with the benefit coming in the form of a depreciation allowance.

Manufacturer Support

Aircraft manufacturers tend not to favor financing aircraft as their main business is to make them. However, due to increased global competition, aircraft manufacturers find it beneficial to assist financing aircraft for customers if it results in a sale. There are many different forms of manufacturer support but the main examples include leasing the aircraft on a finance or operating lease, or guaranteeing the aircraft's value at the end of the contracted term. In other cases, the manufacturer may assist with pilot training costs or provide "free" maintenance in some form or fashion. In the case of Canada 3000 Airlines, a former successful scheduled-charter airline that operated both Boeing and Airbus aircraft, both manufacturers competed for the airline's business. Since Canada 3000 was the primary launch customer of the Airbus A320, the manufacturer provided an incentive whereby the airline only paid for the aircraft when it was flown (for a pre-determined period of time).

Enhanced Equipment Trust Certificates (EETCs)

Airlines issue EETCs, also known as bonds, to cover the cost of acquiring aircraft. Simply put, the airline forms a special purpose company (SPV) and issues bonds to the investor(s). The SPV uses the cash acquired from the bonds to purchase aircraft via a sale/leaseback. Lease payments are made to the SPV by the airline and the SPV forwards bond interest to the investor(s).

Islamic Leasing

In Islamic countries, the law prevents lenders from charging interest, providing a somewhat challenging environment for foreign organizations conducting business in these countries. In most Islamic countries, the common aircraft finance tool is known as Ijarah (leasing). Under an Ijarah, the owner/lessor enters into an arrangement to transfer the right to utilize an asset to another person in exchange for rental payments. This type of arrangement is similar to a conventional lease agreement.

CASH MANAGEMENT AND FINANCIAL PLANNING

At several points in this chapter, we have mentioned the importance of cash holdings as part of working capital. Certainly, one of the primary reasons for the demise of Eastern Airlines was the fact that it became cash starved and simply could not pay its bills. Airlines take in and spend millions of dollars daily. Apprehensive about Eastern's financial problems, travel agencies diverted millions of dollars in ticket sales to other carriers in order to protect their customers, despite assurances from Eastern management almost up to the day they called their fleet home.

In many respects, cash is the most important item in the operation of an airline. It is both a means to and an end of the enterprise. Return on investment takes the form of a payment of cash dividends, and in the event of liquidation, cash becomes the final medium by which claims are discharged. Cash is one of the most important tools of day-to-day operation, because it is a form of liquid capital that is available for any use. Cash is often the primary factor in the course of an airline's destiny. The decision to expand may be determined by the availability of cash, and the borrowing of funds, as was stated earlier, may be determined by the carrier's cash position. There is never a time in the life cycle of an airline that cash, or the ready access to it, is not important. However, it is of particular importance for a fledgling carrier to have an adequate supply of cash. Payrolls must be met; contracted maintenance sources must be paid; fuel suppliers will not tolerate an extension of credit in today's environment. Unexpected costs incurred as a result of poor weather and many other events require cash on hand. Lacking cash, a carrier's operations are slowed, if not paralyzed. Creditors press the collection of their claims. If payments cannot be made or adjustments effected, bankruptcy and failure follow.

Even after a company has overcome its initial financial growing pains, the daily cash position continues as a key factor in its operations. Some major carriers maintain large liquid cash balances in excess of their immediate needs and prefer to borrow little, if at all, on their current account. But other carriers are not in this position and must frequently borrow their seasonal working capital requirements. Some companies deliberately plan their financing and operations to provide their seasonal requirements from bank loans. In such cases, they must plan carefully so as to provide adequate cash to repay the current loans when due. Credit must be maintained by promptly meeting all obligations as they become due.

As learned throughout this book, access to cash is frequently difficult and a rare option for airlines on a worldwide scale. Fortunately, for profitable airlines, or state-owned airlines with wealthy owners, assuming cash is available, this is the most economical way to finance aircraft. However, if one thinks logically about using surplus cash to finance aircraft, it makes more sense to use such money in other areas where the return is much greater. One large issue to think about when financing aircraft with cash, is that when an economic downturn hits, and the airline needs to release cash, the terms of financing may not be desirable.

Las Vegas-based Allegiant Air is a good example of an airline that is consistently profitable on an annual basis. The Allegiant model allows access to cash for large expenditures like aircraft. Allegiant is one of the few airlines in the world with the ability to purchase aircraft on an all-cash basis. Many financial analysts are stumped by the success of this company but in truth, the business model, which focuses on low costs and high fees, is straightforward and makes a lot of sense, particularly in an industry with excessively high fixed costs. While other airlines focus on acquiring new aircraft at high costs, Allegiant sticks to the second-hand market, only purchasing older aircraft that are refurbished. Of course, operating older aircraft can have disadvantages when it comes to things like maintenance, sometimes resulting in delayed operations, but in the case of Allegiant, the model works well partly due to limited to no competition. Allegiant does not go head-to-head with other airlines and seeks to operate in markets with no air service. Now, if Allegiant decided to enter competitive markets using the existing business model, the likely result would be failure.

There is no easy formula to determine the amount of cash a company should maintain. It depends on many factors, including the business cycle, revenues produced, seasonal requirements, and current maturing debt. Management policy toward the carrying of cash in excess of immediate current needs also plays a role. The general economic outlook and the financial and banking situation are always important considerations. The matter of expansion or contraction in operations is frequently a factor. Finally, prices—their level and direction of change—influence management's judgment as to the amount of cash that should be maintained.

Cash Flow

Some financial analysts regard cash flow as a better measure of corporate success and dividend-paying ability than net income in itself. It must be remembered that noncash expenses, of which depreciation is the largest, are determined in large part by management policy. Over the period of time representing the average useful life of an airline's assets, depreciation must equal the amounts invested, or the costs of operation will be understated. Similarly, if depreciation is overstated, income will be understated and taxes reduced (at least temporarily).

The important consideration in the cash flow concept is a measure of flexibility. A large cash flow means that a carrier can fly new routes or adopt new strategies without as much (or perhaps any) new financing.

Cash flow analysis assesses a carrier's ability to generate cash from internal sources relative to the level of claims against that cash. Cash flow may be defined as funds from operations (the sum of net income, depreciation and amortization, and any change in noncurrent deferred taxes) or cash from operations, which takes into account changes in the current accounts. Current assets and current liabilities are typically a small part of the balance sheet for airlines, so the difference between the two defined values is not great. As with earnings measures, however, extraordinary items are excluded.

The key analytical ratio is cash flow divided by total debt. This shows, in theory at least, how quickly a carrier could repay debt if all cash flow were applied to that goal. Indeed, it is the mathematical inverse of a debt payback period. Examination of the debt maturity schedule is an additional and important part of this analysis.

The current ratio and working capital balances are less useful in judging an airline's liquidity than they would be for many industrial companies. Most airlines routinely run working capital deficits, because they take advantage of the fact that airline tickets are usually paid for before they are used. The cash generated is thereby offset by an account called "air traffic liability" under generally accepted accounting principles. In contrast to most industries, a growing airline's cash flow from operations will therefore often be greater than its funds (working capital) from operations. Instead of investment in working capital, airlines generate cash from working capital when they expand. Of course, the reverse is true when an airline contracts—a situation that is most dangerous when a strike halts operations and passengers return their unused tickets.

Comparison of cash flow to capital expenditures gauges a company's ability to finance capital programs with internally generated funds. Unfortunately, reported capital spending often understates the true level of outlays, because most facilities and many aircraft are leased. If aircraft are financed using a sale and lease-back, their cost will show up in capital expenditures, but if they are leased directly, no such amount appears.

Cash Budgeting

The key to good airline cash management and financial planning is the cash forecast, or, more specifically, the **cash budget**. On a short-term basis, it is extremely important that the airline manage its finances in a manner that will permit it to make maximum use of its available cash. On a long-term basis, financial planning must be conducted in a timely and effective manner if the corporation is to achieve its long-range objectives.

Let's take a look at the nature and purpose of both short-term and long-term cash forecasts. *Short-term forecasts* generally cover a period of up to one year. For the first two or three months, estimates are normally provided on a daily or weekly basis. These can usually be made with considerable accuracy and have many day-to-day applications. This forecast is used to accomplish several things:

1 *Determine Operating Cash Requirements.* In other words, the cash forecast ensures that cash receipts meet cash operating expenses. Such

information is vital to airlines with a tight cash position. With the aid of an effective short-term cash forecast, certain expenditures, such as inventory and capital expenditures, can be timed to coincide with the availability of cash.

2 *Anticipate the Need for Short-term Financing.* The forecast enables an airline to minimize borrowing costs (by avoiding borrowing more or borrowing for longer periods than needed) and provides the bank with reliable forecasts of the company's requirements, thus enabling the company to obtain more liberal loans.

3 *Manage the Investment of Surplus Cash.* An accurate cash forecast helps companies select securities with appropriate maturities, avoid over- or underinvesting, and maximize profits from investments.

4 *Maintain Good Bank Relations.* The forecast helps optimize relationships with banks by indicating the highs and lows of cash and the timing of its flow into and out of the company coffers. With this information, the company treasurer can take steps to ensure that bank balances become neither too low (to the dissatisfaction of the banks) nor too high (so that cash is lying around idle).

5 *Provide a Basis for Monitoring Many Items on the Balance Sheet.* This ensures achievement of goals and prudent financial administration.

Long-term cash forecasts show the effect of proposed long-range plans, new equipment requirements, debt retirement, and long-range growth on the company balance sheet five or even ten years in the future. The long-range forecast is used primarily to do the following:

1 *Appraise Proposed Capital Projects.* The forecast shows whether enough cash will be generated internally to support the working capital requirements of future operations and investments. It indicates when the company will probably run out of cash, and why. It also shows how much must be borrowed and for how long it will be needed. It thus helps management evaluate and approve, defer, change, or abandon various equipment programs or projects in light of the company's anticipated cash and invested-capital position.

2 *Provide Information Needed to Establish a Financing Plan and Arrange for Long-Term Financing.* The financing plan, of course, must include careful consideration of capital structure, dividend policy, and the company's obligations to existing lenders and equity investors. Once a decision has been reached to pursue a course of action that will require long-term financing, the long-range cash projection is valuable in obtaining a satisfactory loan. A detailed long-range cash plan that shows how much money will be required, when it will be needed, and at what rate it will be repaid not only provides the lender with important information but also, if it is realistic, indicates competent financial management and helps to obtain the loan on more liberal terms.

It should be noted in closing that any forecast, whether short range or long range, must be updated periodically and monitored continually. Nothing is permanent but change, and the value of cash forecasting depends on keeping abreast of change.

KEY TERMS

assets
balance sheet
bond
cash budget
cash flow
common stock
current ratio
debenture
debt financing
deferred taxes
depreciation
equipment trust financing
equity financing
financial (capital) lease
liabilities
line of credit
long-term debt/equity ratio
long-term loan
net earnings
net worth
operating lease
preferred stock
progress payment
return on investment (ROI)
short-term loan
venture capital

REVIEW QUESTIONS

1 Discuss the relationship between profitability and financing capital needs during the 1990s and 2020s. What is meant by *depreciation*? By *deferred taxes*? How does one distinguish between *debt financing* and *equity financing*?
2 Why have commercial banks traditionally been in the short-term lending market? What is a *line of credit*? What is an *equipment trust*? What is its major advantage?
3 Why did the life insurance companies in particular become a major lending source in the early 1970s? What are investment banks? What is the difference between common stocks and preferred stocks? How do they differ from bonds?
4 Why has leasing become such an important source of funding for the airlines? Give four advantages of leasing. What is its major disadvantage? Distinguish between *operating leases* and *capital leases*.

5 What is meant by *venture capital*? Why has this source of funding become particularly important to the newer carriers? Who provided the backing for the earlier venture capital groups?
6 Define *balance sheet*, *assets*, *liabilities*, and *net worth*. What is included under the assets portion of an airline's balance sheet? Under the liabilities portion?
7 What were the major sources and uses of funds according to the industry's balance sheets during the four cyclical periods highlighted? What is a *convertible debenture*?
8 In light of the demand for capital funds by the airlines during the 1990s and early 2000s to 2020s, how does the financial community view the industry as a whole? Why was the financial community generally against deregulation? Define *long-term debt/equity ratio*, *current ratio*, and *return on investment (ROI)*.
9 Classify the major carriers in terms of their ability to finance their capital needs in the 2000s. What are some of the alternatives for capital-constrained carriers? Summarize several of the major points regarding airline funding sources.
10 In your opinion, does the industry have the financial capability for fleet replacement and expansion in the early 2000s and beyond?
11 Why is having too much cash on hand almost as bad as not having enough? Why is the financial community concerned about the cash position of the carriers? How much cash should an airline have on hand? What is meant by *cash flow*? Give several applications of short-term and long-term cash forecasts.
12 When looking at the global tools available for aircraft finance, what are the eight main options? Describe each.
13 Given the impact of the COVID-19 global pandemic, will lenders have different needs in terms of what airlines need to produce related to contingency planning and risk management? Explain in detail.

Note

1 Nawal K. Taneja, *The Commercial Airline Industry* (Lexington, MA: Lexington Books/Heath, 1976), Chapter 5.

PART FOUR

The International Scene

CHAPTER 18

International Aviation

CHAPTER CHECKLIST • YOU SHOULD BE ABLE TO:

- Define *sovereignty of airspace*, and distinguish between the two principal theories held by early international jurists
- Discuss the major provisions of the Paris Convention
- Understand the purpose of international air law
- Explain the importance of the Warsaw Convention
- Discuss the major articles of the Chicago Conference, and describe the major purpose of ICAO
- Discuss the nine freedoms of the air
- Describe the *Chicago standard form*
- Discuss some of the major changes in international aviation over the past three-plus decades
- Explain current U.S. policy on international aviation
- Discuss some of the factors underlying the movement toward globalization in international aviation, including airline alliances and airport alliances
- Understand the need for new airline business models and describe recent attempts

DOI: 10.4324/9780429346156-22

INTRODUCTION

Today, approximately 120 years after a frail craft made of metal, wood, and fabric struggled into the air and carried a single passenger 120 feet, the world is enveloped by a network of air routes. In 1945, 9 million passengers travelled by air, which represented less than one-half of 1 percent of the world's population at that time. Air traffic has doubled every 15 years since 1972 (Airbus, 2019). The International Civil Aviation Organization (ICAO) estimated that airlines of its 193 member states handled 4.5 billion passengers in 2019, with Europe representing 26.8 percent of world traffic, Africa 2.1 percent, Middle East 9.1 percent, Asia and Pacific 34.7 percent, North America 22.2 percent, and Latin America/Caribbean 5.1 percent. Unfortunately, in 2020, the global aviation industry was negatively impacted by the COVID-19 global pandemic, experiencing the greatest decline since World War II and outpacing the data collected from the 9/11 terrorist attacks in the United States. Despite the ups and downs of the global aviation industry, it is a well-known fact that air has literally become a highway for world commerce, linking regional economies to the global economy. This development of the airplane into a major instrument of transportation has brought with it international problems—the coordination of operational techniques and laws and the dissemination of technical and economic information—far beyond the ability of individual governments to solve. The need for safe, reliable air transportation involves building airports, setting up navigation aids, and establishing weather reporting systems. The standardization of operational practices for international services is of fundamental importance so that no error is caused by misunderstanding or inexperience. The establishment of such standards or rules of the air, of air traffic control, of personnel licensing, and of the design of airplanes and airports, as well as other considerations of prime importance to the safety and economic viability of international aviation, all require more than national action.

THE QUESTION OF SOVEREIGNTY IN AIRSPACE

As the airplane developed during the first decade of the 20th century, the **sovereignty of airspace** above nations became an issue. Should airspace above a nation be considered within the sovereignty of each nation, or should airspace, like the high seas, be considered international? Should each nation have sovereignty over the airspace above it for a limited distance from the surface of the earth, and should the airspace above this limit be considered free airspace? Should there be complete freedom in airspace?

Two principal theories of national sovereignty of airspace were advocated by international jurists. One held that the air is free and therefore that individual states have no authority over it, either in time of peace or in time of war, except when necessary for self-preservation. The other held that the individual states indeed have a right of sovereignty over the airspace above their soil. They claimed that aircraft flying only a few miles over the land are in a position to observe, photograph, and otherwise obtain data that might be used to the disadvantage of the nation over which the aircraft are flown.

The advocates of the freedom of airspace contended that their approach would promote international air commerce and peace throughout the world. The opponents of the free-air theory argued that the concept of free airspace above nations was incompatible with national sovereignty and would threaten national interests and security.

At the close of World War I in November 1918, the problems of international air control became important subjects of negotiation at the peace conference. The secretary of the Inter-Allied Aviation Committee proposed that the committee be constituted as an organization for international air regulation. This action was approved by the representatives of the allied nations at the peace conference.

The Paris Convention of 1919

Representatives from the allied and associated nations met in Paris in 1919 and formed the International Commission for Air Navigation and enacted the International Air Navigation Code, usually referred to as the Paris Convention of 1919. The drafting of the convention was undertaken exclusively by the allied and associated powers. The war experiences and the unity of the allies tended to promote agreement among them and made possible the reconciliation of the divergent views regarding the question of sovereignty of airspace.

The International Commission for Air Navigation drew up a list of principles to govern the drafting of the convention that included the following:

1 The recognition of the principle of the full and absolute sovereignty of each state over the air above its territories and territorial waters, carrying with it the right of exclusion of foreign aircraft and the right of each state to impose its jurisdiction over the air above its territories and territorial waters
2 The recognition of the desirability of the greatest freedom of international air navigation subject to the principle of sovereignty, insofar as this freedom is consistent with the security of the state and with the enforcement of reasonable regulations relative to the admission of aircraft of the contracting state and with the domestic legislation of the state
3 The recognition that the admission and treatment of the aircraft of the contracting states was to be governed by the recognition of the principle of the absence of all discrimination on the ground of nationality
4 The recognition of the principle that every aircraft must possess the nationality of the contracting state only and that every aircraft must

be entered upon the register of the contracting state whose nationality it possesses

The following provisions were recognized as desirable from an international point of view to ensure the safe conduct of air navigation:

1 The requirement of a compulsory certificate of airworthiness and licenses for wireless equipment, at least of aircraft used for commercial purposes; mutual recognition of these certificates and licenses by the contracting states
2 The requirement of compulsory licenses for pilots and other personnel in charge of aircraft; mutual recognition of these licenses by the contracting states
3 International rules of the air, including international rules for signals, lights, and the prevention of collisions; regulations for landing and for procedures on the ground

Among the principles adopted to guide the convention were the following:

1 Special treatment for military, naval, and state aircraft when they are in government service
2 The right of transit without landing for international traffic between two points outside the territory of a contracting state, subject to the right of the state transversed to reserve to itself its own internal commercial traffic and to compel landing of any aircraft flying over it by means of appropriate signals
3 The right of use, by the aircraft of all contracting states, of all public airports, on the principle that charges for landing facilities should be imposed without discrimination on the grounds of nationality
4 The principle of mutual indemnity between the contracting states to cover damage done to another state
5 The necessity of a permanent international aeronautical commission
6 The obligation of each contracting state to give effect to the provisions of the convention by its domestic legislation
7 The principle that the convention does not affect the rights and duties of belligerents or neutrals in time of war

These principles served as guides to three subcommissions—one on technical problems, another on legal problems, and a third on military affairs—that drafted the text of the convention and its annexes. On October 13, 1919, the convention, with its annexes, was finally agreed upon, adopted, and opened to signature by the representatives of the 32 allied and associated powers represented at the peace conference.

The rules and regulations incorporated in the International Convention for Air Navigation were adopted by the principal European nations. The 34 articles covered the reservation of the sovereignty of airspace by the contracting nations; each nation's registry of aircraft; the issuance of certificates of airworthiness and competence by each contracting nation; the flight of aircraft across foreign territory; international aircraft navigation rules;

prohibition of the transportation of arms, explosives, and photographic equipment by aircraft; and the establishment and maintenance of a permanent commission for air navigation.

The supplementary annexes dealt with technical matters and other subjects apt to require more frequent changes, because of changing conditions in air navigation, than the articles of the convention. The annexes covered such issues as regulations for certificates of airworthiness, logbook regulations, light and signal rules, pilot and navigator license regulations, international aeronautical maps and ground markings, the collection and distribution of meteorological information, and national customs regulations.

The Havana Convention of 1928

At the Fifth Pan-American Conference in 1923, an Inter-American Commercial Aviation Commission was appointed to draft a code of laws and regulations, the adoption of which was recommended to all the nations in the Americas. These rules dealt with commercial aviation, the determination of air routes, the establishment of special customs procedures for aviation, the determination of adequate landing policies, and recommendations with respect to the places at which landing facilities should be established.

The Commercial Aviation Commission met in May 1927, at the Pan-American Union in Washington, and prepared a draft of the code, which was revised by the director-general of the union and submitted to the Sixth Pan-American Conference, which met in Havana in 1928. The Havana Convention included most of the basic tenets established by the Paris Convention. The draft was adopted, with some minor modifications, and signed by representatives of the 20 states of the Pan-American Union.

INTERNATIONAL AIR LAW

With the expansion of commercial aviation after World War I, the need to draft an international code of regulations to govern commercial aviation became apparent. Commercial aviation, like all other means of transportation, involves many difficult legal problems, including the rights and duties of shippers and carriers and the questions of carrier liability. These questions were handled at the outset by applying the laws of the several nations, but the lack of uniformity among the commercial laws of different countries constituted a formidable obstacle to international commerce and transportation by air. In response to this need, several important international organizations sponsored movements seeking the international codification of commercial aviation law.

The first organized demand for the promotion of an international conference to draft a code of private international aviation law was made by the

International Chamber of Commerce. In its conferences in 1923 and 1925, this organization adopted a resolution calling the attention of the public to the need for the establishment of a uniform code of international control over private commercial navigation.

The need for international private law was recognized by the French government as well. France issued a call to the nations of the world to meet for the purpose of considering a convention that would regulate the carriers and shippers in international air traffic and codify the private international law of the air, comparable to the Paris Convention of 1919 in the sphere of public international law. This proposal of the French government was accepted, and representatives of 43 nations met in Paris in 1925.

The conference made several amendments to the draft convention prepared previously by the French government. It did not adopt the draft as amended, but left it for further study by the representatives of the respective governments and final discussion at a second international conference, to be convened later. At the same time, the conference established the International Committee of Technical Experts on Air Jurisprudence (Comité International Technique d'Experts Juridiques Aeriens), with headquarters in Paris, to oversee the conference proceedings, and especially the study of the possible codification of aerial law.

The committee, popularly called CITEJA, made a valuable contribution to the final codification of the private international air law as it was adopted in a convention by the conference in Warsaw, Poland, in 1929. The committee carefully drafted the projects of the convention that had been proposed by the experts representing many nations and studied and criticized by the various governments. The views of the various governments were exchanged, and the text of the convention was modified to meet the divergent views. During the next four years, the committee proceeded steadily toward the goal of codification. After four sessions held between 1926 and 1929, the final draft of the codified private international air law was adopted at the Second International Conference on Private Air Law, which met in Warsaw in 1929.

The Warsaw Convention of 1929

The convention for the unification of certain rules relating to international air transportation applies to any international transportation of persons, baggage, or merchandise by aircraft for compensations. It is commonly called the Warsaw Convention of 1929. The United States has been a party to it since 1934.

The convention defined international transportation as any transportation between two points in different contracting countries, irrespective of an interruption of the transportation or transshipments, and also as any transportation between two points in the territory of one state when a stop is made in another country or countries en route.

The Warsaw Convention provided that an air carrier was liable for damages in the event of: (1) death or injury to passengers, (2) destruction or loss of or damage to baggage or goods, or (3) loss resulting from delay in the transportation of passengers, baggage, or merchandise. The limit of liability with respect to passengers on international flights was set at $8,300. The convention also set standards for passenger tickets, cargo waybills, and other air travel documentation.

Signed on October 12, 1929, the Warsaw Convention has become one of the most important documents in international commercial air transportation. The convention was amended on September 28, 1955, in The Hague, Netherlands, where a diplomatic conference was held primarily to discuss the limits of liability. The Hague Protocol to the Warsaw Convention, as it is called, doubled the monetary limit to $16,600 as a maximum recovery for death and extended to agents of the carrier the limit of liability provided to the carrier.

A diplomatic conference, held in Guatemala City in 1971, adopted a far-reaching revision of the provisions of the Warsaw Convention and the Hague Protocol. Among other things, the Guatemala City Protocol provided for absolute liability (no proof of negligence) on the part of the air carrier; an unbreakable limit to a carrier's liability of a maximum amount of $100,000 per person; a domestic system to supplement, subject to specified conditions, the compensation payable to claimants under the convention with respect to the death of or injury to passengers; a settlement inducement clause; conferences for the purpose of reviewing the passenger limit; and an additional jurisdiction for suits pertaining to passengers and baggage.

The Chicago Conference of 1944

World War II had a tremendous impact on the technical development of air transportation. A vast network of passenger and freight carriage was set up, but there were many problems, both political and technical, to which solutions had to be found to benefit and support a world at peace. There was the question of commercial rights—what arrangements would be made for airlines of one country to fly into and through the territories of another? Other concerns centered on the legal and economic conflicts that might arise with peacetime flying across national borders, such as how to maintain existing air navigation facilities, many of which were located in sparsely settled areas. Before World War II, the negotiation of international routes was left to the individual carriers.

The difficulty of negotiating for each new route was among the many reasons the United States and some other nations were anxious for a modification of the international law of civil aviation. In early 1944, the U.S. government issued invitations to the International Conference on Civil Aviation, often called the Chicago Conference. Representatives of 52 nations assembled in Chicago in November 1944. Although invited, the Soviet Union did not send representatives to the conference.

The preamble to this conference stated that its purpose was to foster development of international civil aviation "in a safe and orderly manner" and to establish international air transport service on the basis of equality of opportunity and sound and economical operation. The first of the 96 articles of the agreement made the usual grant to each state of complete and exclusive sovereignty over the airspace above its territory. The right of transit over the contracting sites and the right to land in a foreign state was made available to aircraft on nonscheduled flights, while scheduled services were required to secure prior authorization. Each state was granted the right to reserve to its own airlines' aviation traffic exclusively within its own borders.

The conference established the application of customs regulations and national traffic rules to aircraft in international flight, bound the states to take effective measures to prevent the spread of disease by air, and granted to each nation the right of reasonable search of arriving and departing aircraft. Among the measures provided to facilitate air navigation were rules for avoiding delays in "immigration, quarantine, customs, and clearance." Aircraft in transit and their normal supplies of fuel and oil were exempted from local duties or charges, and aircraft and supplies were made safe from seizures on patent claims. Each state undertook, "so far as it may find practicable," to adopt such standard procedures on airport control, radio services, navigational facilities, use of signals, publication of maps, and similar matters as it was contemplated would be recommended under the terms of the conference.

The conference specified that an aircraft engaged in international flight must carry certain documents, including certificates of registration and airworthiness, licenses for crew members, a logbook, and passenger or cargo manifests. The carriage of munitions was prohibited, and it was specified that a state might restrict the carriage of other articles if these regulations were applied uniformly to the aircraft of all other states.

The contracting states were required to undertake to secure the highest degree of uniformity in complying with international standards and practices, as might from time to time seem appropriate, with respect to the following:

1 Communications systems and air navigation aids, including ground marking
2 Characteristics of airports and landing areas
3 Rules of the air and air traffic control practices
4 Licensing of operating and mechanical personnel
5 Airworthiness of aircraft
6 Registration and identification of aircraft
7 Collection and exchange of meteorological information
8 Logbooks
9 Aeronautical maps and charts
10 Customs and immigration procedures

11 Aircraft in distress and investigation of accidents, and other matters concerning the safety, regularity, and efficiency of air navigation

Formation of ICAO. The Chicago Conference established the International Civil Aviation Organization (ICAO), composed of "an Assembly, a Council, and such other bodies as may be necessary" to foster the planning and development of international air transport in accordance with certain enumerated principles. Permanently headquartered in Montreal, ICAO is charged with the administration of the articles drawn up at the conference.

The ICAO assembly is composed of one representative from each contracting state. At its annual meetings, it may deal with any matter within the scope of the organization not specifically assigned to the council. It also elects the council and initiates amendments. There are close to 200 members today.

The council members, originally composed of 21 contracting states, are elected by the assembly for three-year terms. The council is charged with the establishment of an air transport committee and an air navigation commission, the collection and publication of information on international air services, the reporting of infractions, and the adoption of international standards and practices to be designated as annexes. The air navigation commission acts mainly in technical matters, considering modifications of the annexes and collecting useful information. The general expenses of ICAO are apportioned among the various states, and each state pays the expenses of its own delegation to the organization.

The Chicago Conference of 1944 specifically stated that it superseded the Havana and Paris conventions. It also stipulated that all existing aeronautical agreements and those subsequently contracted should be registered with the council of ICAO and that those that are inconsistent with the terms of the convention should be abrogated.

Disputes may be settled by reference to the Permanent Court of International Justice or a special arbitration tribunal. Enforcement is founded on the power to suspend an airline from international operation or to deprive a state of its voting power. However, states may not be deprived of their freedom of action in the event of war.

In addition to making the rules governing international aviation, ICAO also recommends general principals and policies on a wide range of issues. For example, the first draft of the "ICAO Policy on Assistance to Aircraft Accident Victims and their Families" was issued in 2013 (Doc 9998 AN/499), which required that "The provision of family assistance requires the commitment of resources in several areas . . . information regarding the progress of the accident investigation should also be provided to accident victims and their families in a timely manner." Such a policy provided timely guidance in the search for the Malaysian flight MH370, which lost contact with air traffic control on March 8, 2014, during its flight from Kuala Lumpur to Beijing.

The Two Freedoms and Five Freedoms Agreements. The Chicago Conference produced two other significant documents: the International Air Services Transit Agreement, which became known as the **Two Freedoms Agreement**, and the International Air Transport Agreement, or the **Five Freedoms Agreement**.

Figure 18.1 The Nine Freedoms of the Air

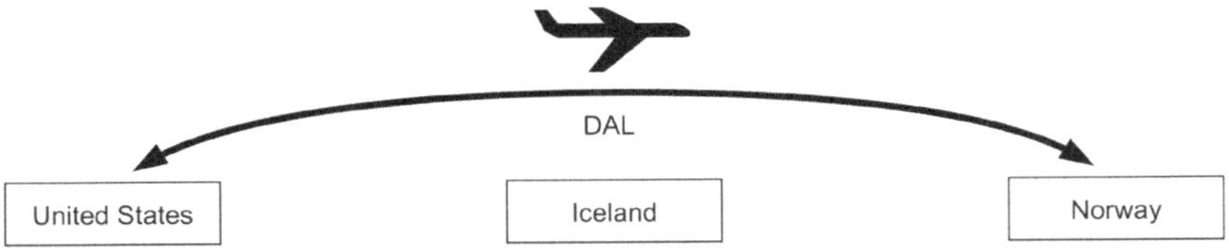

First freedom: A carrier may fly over the territory of another nation without landing. *Example:* Delta (DAL) flies from the United States over Iceland to Norway.

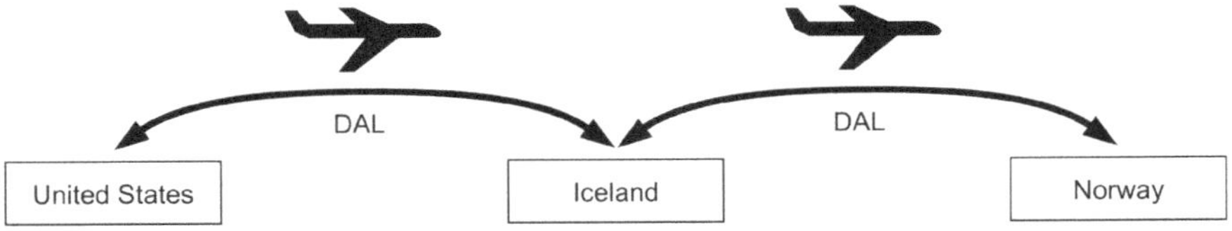

Second freedom: A carrier may land in another nation for non-traffic-related purposes; i.e., only for a crew change or refueling. *Example:* DAL flies from the United States to Norway but lands in Iceland for fuel.

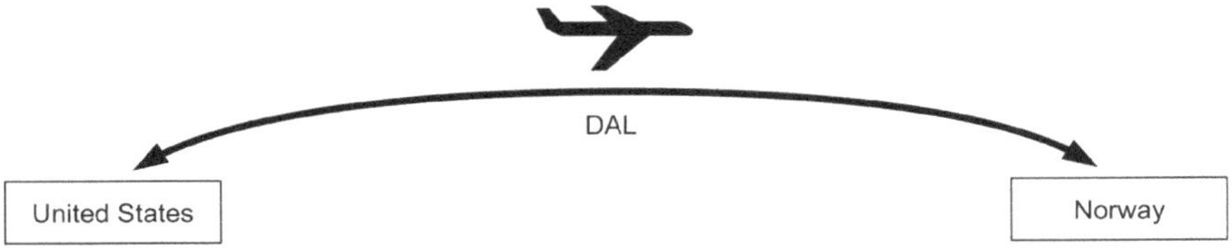

Third freedom: A carrier may drop off passengers from its own country in another nation. *Example:* DAL flies passengers from the United States to Norway.

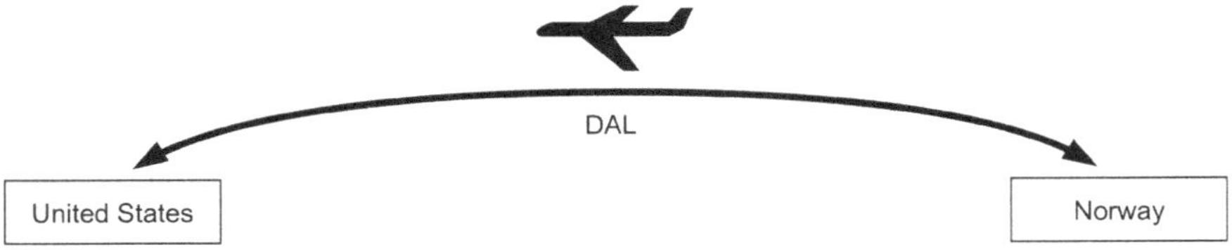

Fourth freedom: A carrier may pick up passengers in another nation and carry them back to its own country. *Example:* DAL flies passengers from Norway to the United States.

Figure 18.1 Continued

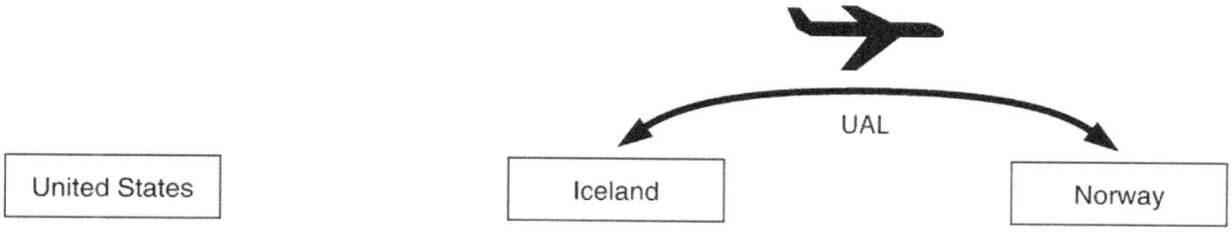

Fifth freedom: A carrier may pick up passengers from a state other than its own and deliver them to a third state, also not its own. *Example:* UAL picks up passengers in Iceland and drops them off in Norway.

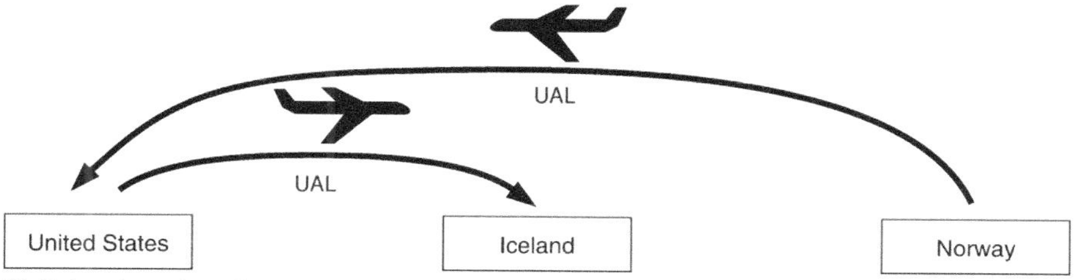

Sixth freedom: A carrier may carry passengers from one state through its home country to a third state. *Example:* UAL flies from Norway to the United States and then on to Iceland.

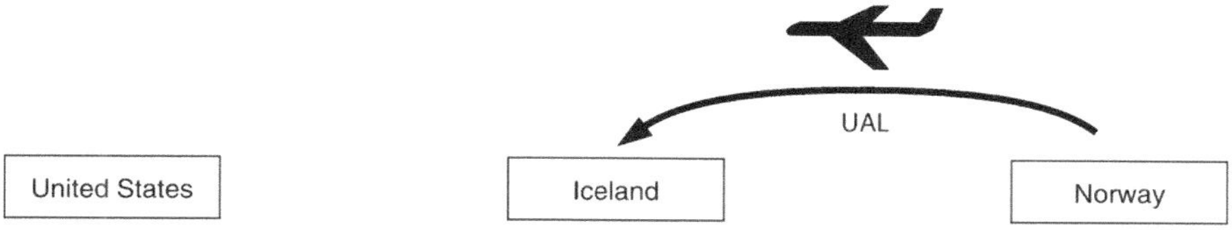

Seventh freedom: A carrier may carry passengers from one state to a third state without going through its home country. *Example:* UAL flies from Norway to Iceland without stopping in the United States.

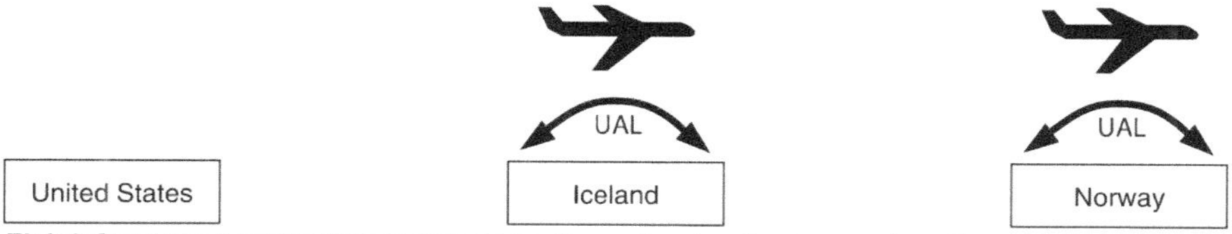

Eighth freedom: A carrier may operate domestic services in a foreign country with continuing service to or from one's own country (also known as cabotage) *Example*: UAL flies between two cities in Norway or between two cities in Iceland.

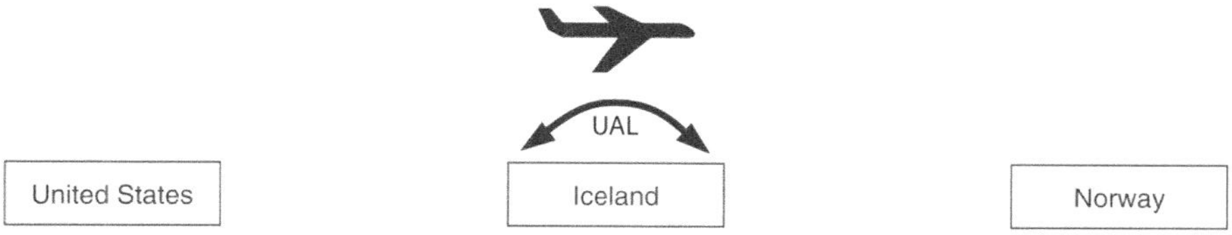

Ninth freedom: A carrier may operate within a foreign country without continuing service to or from one's own country (sometimes known as stand alone cabotage). *Example*: UAL flies between two cities in Norway.

The Two Freedoms Agreement provided that each contracting state grant to the other contracting states the following freedoms of the air with respect to scheduled international air services: (1) the privilege of flying across its territory without landing and (2) the privilege of landing for nontraffic purposes. The additional freedoms set forth in the International Air Transport Agreement were: (3) the privilege of putting down passengers, mail, and cargo taken on in the territory of the state whose nationality the aircraft possesses, (4) the privilege of picking up passengers, mail, and cargo destined for the territory of the state whose nationality the aircraft possesses, (5) the privilege of picking up passengers, mail, and cargo destined for the territory of any other contracting state, and (6) the privilege of putting down passengers, mail, and cargo coming from any such territory.

These additional freedoms, in effect, would have eliminated the need for special negotiations in the conduct of international air transportation. Unfortunately, the Five Freedoms Agreement did not receive support from the representatives. The United States was among the original signers of the Five Freedoms document, but the State Department subsequently gave notice of U.S. withdrawal. The Two Freedoms Agreement, on the other hand, received fairly wide acceptance by various nations. Today, there are a total of nine freedoms (see Figure 18.1).

An important achievement of the Chicago Conference was the adoption of a standard form of air transport agreement that has influenced all subsequent bilateral negotiations conducted. Since the Chicago Conference, the United States has concluded arrangements with a number of countries for the operation of international American-flag services. Most of these are **bilateral agreements**, some based on the so-called Chicago standard form and others on the so-called Bermuda principles (to be discussed shortly).

On October 15, 1943, the Department of State and the CAB issued a joint statement relative to the development of American-flag air services in the international field. This stated that the CAB would certificate new American-flag air services to foreign countries, that corresponding air rights would be negotiated by the State Department in close collaboration with the CAB, and that the airlines would be certificated by the board.

Bilateral Agreements. The Chicago Conference resulted in various agreements and recommendations to facilitate the extension of world air routes through intergovernmental agreements. Among the documents was the Chicago standard form, which has been adopted by the United States and many other countries as a basis for arrangements. In addition, by virtue of the International Air Services Transit Agreement, U.S. airlines may exercise the rights of transit and nontraffic stops in certain other countries with which bilateral agreements have not been concluded.

The formal bilateral agreements negotiated by the United States achieve the primary purpose of obtaining satisfactory operating and traffic rights to be exercised by certificated U.S. airlines on their foreign routes. No two of these agreements are identical, but their basic similarities are summarized in the provisions of the Chicago or Bermuda types of agreements.

Agreements concluded on the Chicago standard form have the following provisions:

1 Intergovernmental exchange of air rights to be exercised by designated airlines of the respective countries
2 Equality of treatment and nondiscriminatory practices with respect to airport charges
3 The imposition of customs duties and inspection fees
4 The exemption from such duties and charges in certain cases
5 Mutual recognition of airworthiness certificates and personnel
6 Compliance with laws and regulations pertaining to entry, clearance, immigration, passports, customs, and quarantine regulations
7 Regulations pertaining to ownership and control of each country's air services
8 Registration of pertinent agreements with ICAO
9 Termination of agreement on one year's notice
10 Procedures for amending the annexes to the agreement

Although the bilateral agreements vary, they all cover three fundamental issues: (1) the number of carriers that each government can designate to provide service between the countries, (2) the routes that each carrier can serve, and (3) the government's role in approving fares. Some agreements limit carrier capacity, but most do not explicitly restrict the number of flights or the type of equipment used by the designated airlines. The DOT has the primary responsibility for administering international regulations and assists the State Department in negotiating bilateral agreements. As of 2011, the United States has agreements with over 90 countries.

Today, most of the routes awarded by a bilateral agreement are the so-called third- and fourth-freedom rights that entail transportation of passengers and cargo between a city in one signator's country and a city in the other signator's country. Some agreements also provide fifth-freedom rights that enable a carrier to continue an international flight that originated in (or is destined for) the carrier's home country to another foreign country and to carry local passengers on the flight between the two foreign countries. An example would be a flight by a U.S. carrier from New York to London that continues to Paris and transports London–Paris passengers in addition to New York–London and New York–Paris passengers. The New York–London flights would be third and fourth freedoms, and the London–Paris flights would be a fifth freedom. A carrier must secure the necessary operating rights from its home country, as well as from both foreign governments, in order to operate fifth-freedom service.

Many of the bilateral agreements that governed U.S. international aviation through the 1970s were products of the post-World War II environment. The agreements gave the United States broad authority to designate carriers to serve major cities in foreign countries from any point in the United States; several of the agreements also awarded the United States extensive fifth-freedom rights. In contrast, foreign governments generally could designate carriers to serve only a few specified U.S. cities on the coasts, and any beyond service was very limited. Under these agreements, carriers needed approval of both governments to offer a fare, and fares were generally established in cartels sponsored by the International Air Transport Association (IATA). The U.S. carriers participated in these fare-setting conferences under a grant of antitrust immunity.

The WTO Secretariat (World Trade Organization, 2006) identified seven Air Service Agreement (ASA) regulations as relevant openness indicators for scheduled air passenger services:

1 Grant of rights (air freedoms allowing airlines to provide services over designated markets)
2 Capacity clause (regulation of the volume of traffic, frequency of service and/or aircraft types)
3 Tariff approval (whether fares must be approved before they are applied)
4 Withholding (which defines the conditions for the foreign carrier to operate, such as ownership and effective citizen control requirements)
5 Designation (which governs the number of airlines allowed to serve the market between two countries and on specific routes)
6 Statistics (requiring the exchange of operational statistics between countries or their airlines)
7 Cooperative arrangements (which regulate the cooperative marketing agreements between airlines)

Piermartini and Rousová (2008), Fu and Oum (2014) reviewed the existing ASAs and concluded that the most frequently used regulations are those on pricing, capacity, and cooperative arrangements.

THE FORMATION OF IATA

In the spring of 1945, representatives from 31 scheduled carriers, many of whom had attended the Chicago Conference, assembled in Havana to organize the International Air Transport Association (IATA). Its broad aims were

> to provide a means for collaboration among air transport enterprises engaged directly or indirectly in international air transport service; to promote safe, regular, and economical air transport for the benefit of the people of the world; to foster air commerce and to study the problems connected therewith; and to cooperate with ICAO and other international organizations.

Its principal purpose was to address one of the problems that Chicago had failed to deal with—that of fares and route structures.

IATA has a director general and an executive committee made up of airline executives and a president who presides at the annual meetings. There are two classes of air transportation enterprises in the association: the voting members, who are active in international flying, and the nonvoting members, who are not. When nonvoting members become active in overseas routes, they acquire a vote.

There are four permanent committees of IATA: (1) the Traffic Advisory Committee, which has jurisdiction over the fixing of tariffs, rates, schedules, and other related issues; (2) the Technical Committee, which is responsible for operations, safety and efficiency of flight, standardization of equipment, and related issues; (3) the Financial Committee, which serves as a clearinghouse for insurance, international monetary documents, and other similar functions; and (4) the Legal Committee, which has the responsibility for international conventions on public and private air law, arbitration, and the like.

Both IATA and ICAO have their headquarters in Montreal, but the former association is divided into three traffic conferences: (1) the Western Hemisphere, Greenland, and the Hawaiian Islands; (2) Europe, Africa, and the Middle East, including Iran; and (3) Asia, Australia, and the islands of the Pacific. IATA works closely with ICAO and is permitted to have a representative at the meetings of the latter organization and its committees.

THE BERMUDA AGREEMENT OF 1946

Although a number of countries were willing to conclude bilateral arrangements with the United States based on the Chicago standard form, there were fundamental differences of opinion among some of the countries represented at the Chicago Conference as to how international air transportation should be developed. The United States and certain other countries favored a relatively liberal approach to the problem, without any arbitrary restrictions or predetermined formulas on capacity of aircraft, flight frequencies, carriage of so-called fifth-freedom traffic, and fixing of rates. Another group of countries, led by the United Kingdom, was not prepared to go this far and wanted these matters regulated to such an extent that, in the opinion of the United States and other countries, the full development of air transportation would be hampered.

However, as the airlines of the United States, Britain, and other countries became better prepared to offer services to one another's territories, it became obvious that these fundamental differences in air policy should be reconciled. Accordingly, in 1946, representatives of the United States and Britain met in Bermuda and negotiated a bilateral understanding that is generally known as the Bermuda Agreement.

In addition to incorporating the Chicago standard clauses, the Bermuda Agreement provided that disputes that could not be settled through bilateral consultation were to be referred to ICAO for an advisory opinion. It also stipulated that the agreement should be revised to conform with any subsequent multilateral air pact that might be subscribed to by both countries.

In contrast to the agreements concluded by the United States before Bermuda, this agreement not only described the extensive routes and traffic points involved but also set up a comprehensive procedure for determination of rates to be charged by airlines operating between points in the two countries and their territories. Procedures for rate making and for the establishment of traffic rules were assigned to IATA. These rates were subject to review by the respective governments having jurisdiction. Provisions were also made for the manner in which route changes would be made. And one section dealt with *change of gauge*—that is, with the carrying onward of traffic by aircraft of a different size from that employed on the earlier stage of the same route and connecting services.

In addition, the Bermuda Agreement included a number of collateral understandings on the operation and development of air transportation services between the two countries. No arbitrary restrictions were placed on capacity, flight frequencies, or fifth-freedom traffic, but it was stipulated that the airlines of one country would not treat the airlines of the other unfairly. The Bermuda Agreement was generally regarded as a satisfactory reconciliation of the differences that existed on international air policy between the United States and the United Kingdom after the Chicago Conference. At the time of its conclusion, there was no specific understanding that either government would insist on this type of arrangement in its subsequent negotiations with other countries. However, in a joint statement, both governments agreed that experience had demonstrated that the Bermuda principles were sound and provided a reliable basis for the orderly development and expansion of international air transportation. It was further agreed that the Bermuda type of agreement presented the best form of approach to the problem of bilateral arrangements until a multilateral agreement could be adopted. As a means of furthering acceptance of the Bermuda principles, the joint statement also mentioned that each government was prepared, upon the request of any other government with which it had already concluded a bilateral pact that was not deemed to be in accordance with those principles, to make such adjustments as might be found necessary. The agreements concluded by the United States with other countries since Bermuda include all the important Chicago and Bermuda provisions. These agreements total over 70 today.

THREE DECADES LATER: FROM BERMUDA TO DEREGULATION

Had one looked back at the Bermuda Agreement in, say, 1963, one would have had to be pleased with its results—not in every detail, but in overall effect. European (and other) airlines had been able to catch up with U.S. airlines, but not really at the latter's expense. The lack of capacity controls had enabled the optimism of the U.S. carriers and government to prevail over the skepticism of the Europeans. Bigger and better aircraft were continually joining fleets, and there was a general downward pressure on fares (compared to other prices) as the purchasers of the new planes sought, for the most part successfully, to fill them.

Challenges to the Established Order: The Early 1970s

By 1975, in the context of economic stress, the Bermuda compromise looked very different. The first assumption to be tested was that the scheduled carriers in IATA could control fares indefinitely. In the spring of 1963, there was a showdown of sorts between IATA and the U.S. government when IATA, backed by the European governments, increased fares (or rather, reduced the round-trip discount) at a time when the CAB thought fares should remain stable. IATA stood firm and won that fight, but at a heavy cost. The CAB's response, though never explicitly stated, was to give a big boost to a new class of airlines that had not been considered in the original agreements—the nonscheduled or supplemental carriers. First, the CAB, with the support of Congress, granted permanent certificates to many supplementals, enabling them to receive financing for the purchase of jet aircraft. Second, it permitted so-called split charters, whereby groups as small as 40 were allowed to charter part of an airplane. Third, from 1966 on, the CAB permitted so-called inclusive tour charters, whereby tour operators could market vacation travel to the public at bargain prices, without requiring that the passengers belong to any club or preexisting group. Supplemental transportation attracted millions of travelers to Europe from the United States, especially from the west coast. The CAB, using the same approach that it developed in domestic regulation, tried various distinctions between scheduled and charter services, such as requirements for affinity groups, requirements for ground services and multiple stops in package tours, and advance booking and down-payment conditions, all designed to encourage creation of new markets and to discourage diversion from the scheduled carriers.

After a while, the CAB realized that the public did not particularly care for any of the distinctions: all kinds of arrangements were made to circumvent the requirements. But as long as the overall market continued its straight-line growth, only sporadic enforcement was undertaken, accompanied by frequent tinkering with the rules. By the time the growth began to level off, just as the wide-bodied jets arrived, the market had changed, probably irreversibly. A side effect was that, although the share of international traffic carried by scheduled U.S. carriers kept declining, the overall share of traffic carried by U.S. carriers began to rise again, because the supplementals were predominantly American.

Among the European countries, several considered limiting or controlling charters, which were not provided for in the postwar agreements, but as long as all the European countries were not united, only those countries that could count on a separate and distinct market, such as Israel, were able to avoid the charter problem. Another basic assumption of the international air transport system had been shattered: much of the tourist market, it turned out, was not a point-to-point market at all, but rather a region-to-region market. If one wanted to tour Europe in a rented car, for instance, or with a Eurail pass or by hitchhiking, it did not matter very much whether one flew to Paris or Brussels or Amsterdam. And within limits, it did not matter very much whether one flew on Friday the 31st or Thursday the 30th, or returned from the first gateway or from another one.

The response of the major airlines was interesting. After arguing unsuccessfully to the CAB that air travel was all one big market and therefore that expanded charter authority would be largely diversionary, the scheduled international carriers took the opposite approach in their own pricing policy. From a basic two-class fare structure, they developed in the late 1960s and early 1970s a schedule of fares so complicated that hardly anyone—carriers, travel agents, or government regulators—could keep up with it. Excursion fares, peak and directional fares, "group-inclusive tours" (which were neither inclusive nor tours), and various fares calling for advance booking or payment proliferated, again with cheating almost universal and not perceived as wrong and with virtually no relation between the fare paid and the cost of providing the service. The objective was to treat demand elasticities differently, on the theory that business travelers, who had to travel on short notice, would be prepared to pay more than vacationers with a fixed holiday schedule, who, in turn, might make down payments or otherwise commit themselves several months in advance. The result was often a reduction in yield per passenger not made up for by a corresponding increase in the number of passengers carried.

In a sense, one might say that price competition had come to international aviation, and specific countries and airlines became increasingly sensitive to the prospects of attraction or "diversion" of potential tourists as the result of any given new fare proposal. But under IATA rules, it was not possible for any single carrier or group of carriers to experiment with promotional fares to see whether they created new traffic or simply diluted the yield from the same passenger who would have traveled anyway. IATA rules provided that if one carrier could offer a special fare, all could, and unless all would do it, none could. By the early 1970s, the basic economy fare on which the system in theory rested was paid by less than 20 percent of travelers across the Atlantic, not even counting the widespread rebates to travel agents that became ever more widespread as the ratio of fixed to variable costs of air services kept rising. Ironically, just as IATA finally decided to invite the supplemental carriers to join, Pan American became the largest international charter carrier; TWA was close behind, and many of the major European airlines either took up chartering themselves or developed subsidiaries to do so.

As load factors fell on scheduled services, profits declined and then disappeared altogether. The advent of the wide-bodies increased capacity, while traffic failed to increase at anything like the rates that had been predicted and assumed within the industry at the time the decision was made to move to the new generation of larger aircraft.

All these trends were most acute in the critical North Atlantic routes, which account for over one-third of international air traffic but which provide, for almost all the major airlines of the world, the make-or-break margins of profit and success.

In the face of the trends that were evident from 1970 on, one might have supposed that the airlines would move to curtail their services drastically and comprehensively. But no major airline was prepared to do this on its own, lest its competitors capture a greater share of the traffic. From time to time in the early 1970s, carriers tried to fashion joint capacity–restraint agreements. But these agreements—for example, New York–London, New York–Rome, or United States–Switzerland—were ad hoc, short-term arrangements without any consistent formula. The CAB gave its approval, but with a bad conscience and in the expressed hope that overcapacity was a temporary phenomenon that would soon pass. The prevailing doctrine in Washington still held to the Bermuda Agreement—no predetermination and no interference by governments in matters of capacity.

Thus, even before October 1973, the basic Bermuda structure was under severe stress, and international aviation was a sick industry. The rise in oil prices in late 1973 simply dramatized and made far more acute the underlying situation. Pan Am, long the pioneer and pacesetter in routes and equipment, lost over $80 million in 1974, its sixth straight year of massive financial setbacks.

Meanwhile, fares, which had gone down overall between 1960 and 1970, rose in the early 1970s almost as fast as the Consumer Price Index—in 1974 alone up 30 percent on some routes. U.S. travelers saw, to their surprise, that Pan Am had withdrawn from Paris and much of the Mediterranean, and TWA from Frankfurt and the Pacific. Foreign airlines were making similar retreats, giving up, for example, hard-won routes to the U.S. west coast. As not only the United States but also most of the non-Communist world experienced for the first time the combination of inflation and recession, as well as fuel shortages, price increases, and unemployment, an industry geared largely to the discretionary consumer seemed to be facing a situation quite different from that which its founders in the 1940s had in mind.

The key elements of the Bermuda Agreement, as we have seen, were that fares would be controlled but capacity would be essentially unrestrained. Three decades later, it appeared that the reverse solution might be appropriate.

New U.S. Policy in International Aviation: The Late 1970s

As early as 1975, President Ford called for regulatory reform in international aviation. While his steering committee was reviewing the necessary changes in U.S. aviation policy, the British announced their intention to terminate the Bermuda Agreement with the United States, effective in June 1977. The primary problem that the British had was the excessive capacity offered by U.S. carriers on the North Atlantic route. A compromise agreement was signed by the two countries on July 23, 1977, which provided for: (1) some new carriers to enter the market with the understanding that their schedules would be prescreened by their governments, and (2) government approval of proposed fares and routes after review by IATA. It was this agreement that permitted Laker Airways to enter the market, which gave the impetus for the intense competition for the next several years over the North Atlantic.

In 1978, President Carter's administration began to review the Bermuda II Agreement, as it was commonly referred to, as being excessively protectionist and providing an unfair advantage for the British carriers. Encouraged by the CAB's deregulation of the domestic airline industry and the initial success of Laker's Skytrain service in the London–New York market, the Carter administration pushed for a U.S. policy based on free-market competition in the international arena. In a terse statement, the administration threw out the concept of regulated competition in international markets by pledging to work to achieve a system of international air transportation that placed its principal reliance on actual and potential competition to determine the variety, quality, and price of air service. An essential means for carrying out our international air transportation policy will be to allow greater competitive opportunities for U.S. and foreign airlines and to promote new low-cost transportation options for travelers and shippers.[1]

In implementing its new policy, the Carter administration issued a new policy statement regarding the conduct of the United States in international aviation. Seven specific goals would be sought in all future negotiations of international agreements:

1 A more innovative and competitive approach to pricing that would meet the needs of different travelers and shippers
2 Elimination or greater liberalization of restrictions on charter operations and rules
3 Elimination of restrictions on capacity, route, and operating rights for scheduled carriers
4 Elimination of discrimination and unfair competitive practices experienced by U.S. carriers in international markets
5 Designation of additional U.S. airlines in international markets that could support such service
6 Authorization of more gateway cities and improved integration of domestic and international service
7 Greater development of competitive air cargo services

These policy goals were established to provide U.S. negotiators with guidelines in formulating their negotiating objectives. Clearly, the intent of U.S. international aviation policy was to give consumers the most competitive service available.[2]

THE PURSUIT OF OPEN SKIES

Predictably, a fight against the policy's implementation ensued. But the policy, unlike its predecessors, was issued independent of any immediate crisis in international markets or financial performance of U.S. carriers. The introduction of change while the industry was financially strong actually facilitated the process. Implementation proceeded at a rapid pace for at least a couple of years as so-called liberal bilateral agreements were negotiated with Korea, Thailand, Singapore, Taiwan, Israel, The Netherlands, Belgium, and, to a lesser degree, Germany.

The International Air Transportation Competition Act of 1979

The International Air Transportation Competition Act of 1979, which was enacted by Congress on February 15, 1980, amends the Federal Aviation Act of 1958 to provide competition in the international market. Basically, the act is the international counterpart to the Airline Deregulation Act of 1978 and implements U.S. policy in international aviation. The act's primary objectives are:

1 To strengthen the competitive position of U.S. carriers to at least ensure equality with foreign air carriers, including the attainment of opportunities for U.S. carriers to maintain and increase their profitability in foreign air transportation
2 To give air carriers (U.S. and foreign) the freedom to offer consumer-oriented fares and rates
3 To place the fewest possible restrictions on charter air transportation
4 To provide the maximum degree of multiple and permissive international authority for U.S. carriers so that they could respond quickly to shifts in market demand
5 To eliminate operational and marketing restrictions to the greatest extent possible
6 To integrate domestic and international air transportation
7 To increase the number of nonstop U.S. gateway cities
8 To provide opportunities for foreign carriers to increase their access to U.S. points if exchanged for benefits of similar magnitude for the U.S. carriers or passengers and shippers
9 To eliminate discrimination and unfair competitive practices faced by the U.S. carriers in foreign air transportation, including excessive landing and user fees, unreasonable ground handling requirements, undue restrictions on operations, and prohibitions against change of gauge
10 To promote, encourage, and develop civil aeronautics and a viable, privately owned U.S. air transport industry

The 1980s

By early 1981 the new president's policy staff was being barraged with criticism of the previous administration's policies from incumbent operators, who were less than enamored of the relentless pursuit of pure competition. At the same time, the economy moved into a recession, oil prices again spiraled upward, the air traffic controllers' strike drastically disrupted the domestic market, and the airline industry slipped into a period of financial loss. These losses, and the first demise of a U.S. trunk carrier in 1982 (Braniff Airlines), lent credence to the cries of havoc in the international aviation policy arena. Implementation of the procompetitive policy came to a halt in the early 1980s.

However, many factors gradually converged to support the conviction that free trade in international aviation should progress over time. Carrier management, much of which was also changing, appeared to like being unfettered, although it may not always have welcomed or thrived on unbridled competition. There was some political support from a presidential administration that viewed free trade and deregulation of industry as basic tenets of its economic policies. At the same time, the domestic market was showing a tendency toward lackadaisical growth, while international travel was burgeoning. As U.S. carriers again introduced new and more efficient aircraft, they looked to international markets for expansion. Finally, the economic boom of the mid- to late-1980s resulted in higher profits and ambitions to expand.

From the regulator's perspective, evidence began to emerge that markets that had been liberalized were growing faster than those that remained closed. Liberalized markets were those markets open to U.S. carrier competition, while restrictive markets were those in which U.S. carrier designation and/or capacity was limited, either by negotiated agreements or by practice. In the case of the United Kingdom, which could be classified as "other," entry and capacity were restricted, but negotiations and provisions in the agreement allowed some increases in capacity. Also, the pricing provision in the agreement was interpreted liberally by both the United States and the United Kingdom, permitting a substantial amount of price competition.

In every instance, between 1978 and 1983, the liberal markets demonstrated a stronger traffic growth rate than the restrictive markets. By 1988, this disparity was even greater, with the only exceptions being France and Japan. The growth in United States–France traffic reflected the fact that the Bermuda Agreement with the United States, which permitted multiple designation and unlimited frequencies, had been honored by France as U.S. carriers moved to introduce new services. This expansion by U.S. carriers was stopped when France served notice in 1992 that it would terminate its agreement with the United States. In the case of Japan, new services by incumbent carriers were permitted to some extent in order to accommodate the boom in traffic that was largely driven by the Japanese economy.

Thus, although most of the liberal markets were not large, the decision to trade open access in the foreign country for expanded access in the United States appeared to be a good one for the traveling public.

Nevertheless, the continuing efforts to liberalize aviation agreements were hampered for a number of reasons. First, the countries that were the most likely candidates for such agreements had already been approached by the U.S. government. In these instances, the foreign-flag carriers were anxious to expand into the United States and willing to make a generous offer to the U.S. government to do so. Where the foreign-flag carriers had no, or very limited, expansionary ambition, there was no interest in liberalizing the relationship with the United States. Thus, there was no clear path as to how to handle the remaining countries.

Second, disruption within the U.S. domestic industry was continuing apace, with bankruptcies and mergers becoming commonplace. These changes lent political credence to the arguments being made in some quarters that deregulation of the domestic industry had been too abrupt and that the U.S. government should again become more concerned about the health of its industry.

Third, U.S. carriers, often competing against one another and seeing international markets as the ticket to expansion, fought harder than ever to strengthen their market presence, and the infighting around negotiations became increasingly brutal. The U.S. government was unwilling and unable to take risks by negotiating arrangements that could not be well justified to Congress in terms of their constructive effect on U.S. air carriers.

As the economy strengthened in the mid-1980s and fuel prices stabilized, the United States tried to find opportunities for liberalization of international aviation agreements. Accordingly, the most effective way to create a more competitive environment was to negotiate a new bilateral agreement. To get other governments to grant carriers the greater pricing and operating flexibility it sought, the United States often had to give foreign carriers the right to operate more international routes to the United States. Smaller nations generally found such offers to be more appealing than larger ones did. The United States entered into agreements with countries like The Netherlands and Belgium, although it recognized that U.S. carriers would gain little from the greater operating flexibility. In part, the United States viewed less regulation as an end, in and of itself, but it also saw the agreements with smaller countries as a means of putting pressure on larger nations. For example, KLM's expanded service to the United States placed competitive pressure on Lufthansa, the carrier of The Netherlands' larger neighbor, Germany.

None of these early agreements represented what has become known as an **open-sky agreement**. Under an open-sky agreement, carriers of both countries can fly any route they wish between the countries and can continue those flights into third countries, although **cabotage** is still not permitted. Cabotage is a foreign operator carrying passengers between two domestic points of another country.

Although the United States was the most vehement proponent of increased international competition, its carriers' share of international traffic declined in the early 1980s. Although U.S. carriers' international traffic grew, their share fell from 50.7 percent in 1979 to 47.4 percent in 1986. In addition, both U.S. and non-U.S. carriers were registering losses on many international routes despite the growth in traffic. As a result, the United States relaxed its pursuit of the deregulation of international markets.

The picture began to change in the mid-1980s. Carriers with large domestic systems expanded international service from their hubs and acquired outstanding route authority from other carriers. For example, United, a very large domestic carrier with no international service in 1982, acquired Pan Am's Pacific division in 1983. By 1994, United's share of U.S. international traffic was larger than its share of domestic traffic. Most international routes operated by U.S. carriers have become an integral part of a domestic route system, and carriers with large domestic route systems now control a large share of international traffic.

In late 1992, concerned with the horrendous financial losses in the industry, Congress created the National Commission to Ensure a Strong Competitive Airline Industry. Once again, given the circumstances of the time, the commission was faced with the choice of competition versus protectionism. Throughout the commission's discussion of international policy, its ambivalence was evident. On the competitive side, there were statements to the effect that "air service agreements should be competitive" and recognition that bilateral agreements were "resulting in agreements or de facto relationships either markedly more rigid or protectionist than before, or seriously out of balance." The remedy, as far as the commission was concerned, was to be the negotiation of liberal multinational agreements. However, at the behest of a small number of U.S. carriers, the commission perpetuated old-style concepts of comparability and equivalency of market size and opportunities: "Because of our country's geographical size and population, bilateral agreements can result in the U.S. granting foreign carriers greater access to the immense and diverse U.S. air travel market without corresponding competitive opportunities for U.S. carriers." The commission either did not recognize or did not want to acknowledge that these concepts, based on views of "our" traffic versus "their" traffic, are inescapably protectionist and are increasingly outdated and irrelevant as markets become global.

Late 1990s' Policy

Given the conservative nature of the commission's report, it was surprising that a year later, in November 1994, the Clinton administration issued a policy statement that was both perceptive and adventuresome. Reminiscent of the CAB when it realized that the domestic industry had essentially grown beyond the bounds of the regulators' ability to keep up, the DOT focused on the fundamental and dramatic structural changes in the industry:

> As a direct result of the Chicago Convention, an air transport system has developed that consists primarily of national carriers offering point-to-point services, with international connections principally provided through interline arrangements between those airlines. Although such operations continue to be important components of international air transport, major changes

> have occurred during the past few years that are challenging traditional notions of these services. Airlines are becoming increasingly global. Route networks are now being linked in alliances consisting of carriers from different nations, with international hub-and-spoke networks that offer passengers on-line services to cities around the world.

The document also contained a precise "Plan of Action." The first step in this plan was to "extend invitations to enter into open aviation agreements with a group of countries that share our vision of liberalization and offer important flow traffic potential for our carriers *even though they may have limited Third and Fourth Freedom traffic potential*" (emphasis added). This was the first time that the U.S. government implicitly acknowledged that its previous attempts to implement its free-trade policies had, in fact, been discriminatory and inconsistent. With the exception of the United States–Netherlands service, the United States had focused since the early 1980s on trading access for U.S. and foreign air carriers only if the foreign market was relatively large.

This acknowledgment marked a giant step forward in government thinking because it fundamentally rejected the notion that international aviation markets between countries must be "comparable" or "equivalent" in size before they should be opened. As basic as this concept is to most other areas of trade, it has eluded the international aviation industry since bilateralism and freedoms of traffic were invented. The DOT also acknowledged political reality when it stated that "we will offer liberal agreements to a country or group of countries if it can be justified economically or strategically." Subsequently, despite the opposition of some U.S. carriers and some members of Congress, the government began negotiations with a group of countries and reached agreements with nine small aviation partners in Europe.

At the same time, the U.S. government expressed a willingness to construct a phased-in open agreement with Canada. This agreement, which was a major breakthrough in a market that had grown extraordinarily slowly under a highly restricted regime, demonstrated the benefits to the public and to the two countries' carriers as the market expanded through increased services and greater flexibility in setting prices.

Today, carrier networks seem to be at least as important to success in international markets as they are domestically. International services generally involve substantially longer distances than domestic services, and most can be served efficiently only with wide-bodied aircraft. There are only a handful of international routes, therefore, that have sufficient local traffic to make point-to-point service economically viable. Regulation created a segmented industry in which carriers had to supplement their local traffic on international routes with interline connecting traffic from other airlines. The growth of international service from carrier hubs has changed that and has made it increasingly necessary for carriers to generate on-line connecting traffic from their own networks.

The Early 2000s

On March 30, 2008, the European Union (E.U.)–United States (U.S.) Open Skies Agreement went into effect allowing any airline of the E.U. and any airline of the U.S. to operate between any destination in the E.U. and any destination in the U.S. The **Open Skies Agreement** also allows U.S. air carriers to operate between destinations in the E.U. Interestingly, E.U. air carriers are not permitted to operate between destinations in the U.S. However, air carriers of the E.U. are allowed to operate between non-E.U. destinations and the U.S. The main advantage to the agreement is that it replaced established open skies agreements between the U.S. and specific E.U. countries. As per the U.S. Department of State, Office of Aviation Negotiations, Bureau of Economic, Energy and Business Affairs, open skies agreements establish liberal ground rules for international aviation markets and minimize government intervention with the following key provisions: free market competition, pricing determined by market forces, doing business protections, cooperative marketing arrangements, provisions for consultation and arbitration, liberal charter arrangements, safety and security, and option seventh freedom all-cargo rights. A second-stage agreement was reached between the U.S. and E.U. in 2010, which dealt with environmental areas such as noise and emissions. In 2011, the agreement was further extended to include Iceland and Norway.

The Open Skies discussion became more active leading up to 2018 after the U.K. made its intention known to withdraw from the E.U., which officially took place on January 31, 2020. This move became known as **Brexit** (British Exit) and resulted in the U.K. becoming the only sovereign nation to leave the E.U.—it had been a member state of the European Communities (E.C.) since 1973. As a result of Brexit, numerous discussions took place to determine what consequences the U.K.'s departure from the E.U. would have on Open Skies, including air carriers operating between the U.K. and U.S., with the understanding the U.K. would depart from the E.U.–U.S. Open Skies Agreement. In 2018, the U.S.–U.K. Civil Air Transport Agreement was formed.

GLOBALIZATION OF AIRLINES AND AIRLINE ALLIANCE MODELS

Globalization of the world economy, which is being so profoundly evidenced in myriad manufacturing and service industries, as well as the airline business, will most certainly press the United States and other governments away from protectionist posturing and toward open markets. Yet under existing laws and agreements, it is difficult for U.S. carriers to establish hubs outside the United States, and foreign carriers cannot establish hubs in the United States. First, governments throughout the world both prohibit cabotage and limit nonresident ownership of domestic carriers. In addition, fifth-freedom rights tend to limit a carrier's flight frequency and therefore its ability to compete for local traffic. Although fifth-freedom rights often have only limited value in establishing an international hub, there are exceptions. For example, U.S. carriers have had some success in fifth-freedom markets and have, in effect, established hubs in Japan. Both United and Northwest continue their Tokyo flights to beyond destinations such as Manila, Singapore, and Malaysia. These routes are relatively long hauls, and their frequency limitations are not as much of a problem as they are on shorter-haul routes. Probably of greater significance, however, are the slot restrictions at Tokyo's Narita Airport, which limit the ability of third- and fourth-freedom carriers to increase their services in these markets.

While still actively seeking expanded third- and fourth-freedom service, the United States and other governments are increasingly addressing carrier desires to create global route networks. There are two approaches. Under one option, countries can negotiate a new international regulatory regime multilaterally. Such an agreement conceivably could provide a forum to address not only fifth-freedom rights but also cabotage and foreign ownership issues. Independent commissions in both the United States and Europe have advocated such multilateral negotiations, yet the negotiation of such agreement is likely to be a very difficult process.

An alternative approach is to continue to negotiate bilateral agreements and to permit carriers to expand their route networks through the use of code-sharing agreements with other carriers. Such code sharings are most commonly used for connecting service and permit carriers to market interline transportation as though it were on-line. Although multilateral agreements may ultimately be negotiated, the United States is pursuing the development of global networks bilaterally. A carrier can offer a code-sharing service only in markets where it has the underlying authority, and so the United States is attempting to negotiate open-sky agreements that give both U.S. and non-U.S. carriers broad operating authority. The United States, however, still prohibits cabotage and limits foreign ownership of U.S. carriers; both restrictions are legislated and can only be changed by an act of Congress.

Despite the trend of liberalization in the past decades, the airline industry still has some of the most restrictive regulations on international ownership and control. The ownership and control regulations are difficult to remove in the international sector partly due to its linage to the systems of bilateral ASAs. The 1944 Chicago Convention requires that in order to serve the international markets, an airline should hold: (1) an Air Operator's Certificate (AOC), (2) an operating license, and (3) a route license or permit. Yet, an operating license is only issued to an airline if it is majority owned and effectively controlled by a country's own nationals. This implies that ownership and control requirements are an integrated part of the bilateral agreement system. The UK Civil Aviation Authority (CAA, 2006) reviewed the history of ownership and control in various countries. In the United States, the 1926 Air Commerce Act required that at least 51 percent of an airline had to be owned by Americans and that the president and two-thirds of the board had to be U.S. citizens. Later this requirement was revised to requiring that at least 75 percent of the voting shares needed to be owned by U.S. citizens. In addition, "actual control" of the airline had to belong to Americans. In the U.K., there are no requirements on the share ownership or board composition. However, an airline has to show that it is effectively controlled by U.K. nationals. This involves the examination on whether any non-qualifying third party had indirect influence, such as provision of services upon which the airlines could be dependent. The control regulations are superseded by European legislation. At European level, since 1993 the ownership and control has been under the regulation on all European Economic Area members including all E.U. countries. An airline has to be majority owned and effectively controlled by qualifying nationals.

With an open-sky agreement and a code-sharing partner, a non-U.S. carrier can form an alliance with one or more domestic carriers and gain access to virtually the entire United States. Most foreign countries are much smaller than the United States, and therefore, a single bilateral agreement, in and of itself, does not provide U.S. carriers with similar opportunities. An open-sky agreement does permit a U.S. carrier to incorporate cities in other countries into its network through code sharing, but each such service requires the acquiescence of a third country. These countries can provide that acquiescence by also signing an open-sky agreement, so the United States has sought a critical mass of countries to accept such agreements. Future open-sky initiatives may depend on how U.S. and non-U.S. carriers divide the traffic generated by these agreements.

Under some code-sharing arrangements, the partners make a concerted effort to coordinate both flight schedules and ground operations to mimic on-line service. In some cases, one carrier, and perhaps both, in the cooperative venture invests in the other. Such investments can demonstrate a good-faith commitment by the carriers and reduce the risk of opportunistic behavior. Governments, however, restrict the share of an airline that can be owned by a foreign citizen. In the United States, foreign ownership of domestic airlines is limited to 49 percent with a maximum of 25 percent of the voting rights.

Some code-sharing agreements, however, provide little in the way of service enhancements and are simply the carrier's same interline services marketed under a different name. In these cases, an important part of the marketing advantage stems from computerized reservations system practices. Frequently, both of the carriers participating in code sharing will market the service as their own, and thus, a given service is displayed three times in a CRS: under each carrier's code and on an interline service. Governments may come under increasing pressure to determine whether these CRS practices distort the information provided by travel agents and, if necessary, to design a regulatory solution.

A more fundamental question, however, concerns the impact that these code-sharing agreements have on competition. An agreement that leads to less capacity than would otherwise be provided will likely yield reduced service and increased airfares, which is not in the public interest. For example, instead of servicing a particular route, a carrier might rely on its code-sharing partner, and other carriers may be reluctant to enter. On the other hand, by expanding the size of its network and generating increased traffic, code sharing can prompt a carrier to institute new services. For example, by increasing feed, code sharing may make service on a route economically viable. Code sharing can also stimulate traffic by providing more frequent service and better connections, and by increasing traffic, it can reduce costs and fares.

A code-sharing agreement gives carriers the authority to serve markets jointly; it does not give them the right to set fares jointly. Before carriers serving the United States can set fares jointly, they must receive antitrust immunity from the DOT. In some cases, a code-sharing agreement with antitrust immunity may produce lower prices than an agreement without antitrust immunity.

With an efficient code-sharing arrangement, a carrier faces essentially the same cost of providing the service as it would if it provided the same service on-line. In most code-sharing agreements, however, one carrier charges the other for traffic it carries in its aircraft, and that charge is likely to be the cost of transporting the passengers plus some markup. Because of this markup, each carrier faces a higher cost for transporting passengers under the code sharing than it would for a similar service it provided on-line.

With antitrust immunity, carriers are free to establish some mechanism by which fares can be based on incremental costs, and then the profits generated by the sale can be divided. In that case, the carriers will perceive the cost of transporting an additional passenger to be lower than the cost each carrier would face from a typical joint-fare agreement. If two carriers have a large share of the relevant markets, however, the reduction in competition could dominate any efficiency gain. A decision about antitrust immunity should be based on an analysis of both the affected markets and the impact of the joint-fare agreement. As the web of global alliances and code sharing increases, the United States will clearly be mindful of the competitive effects and the possible impact of antitrust immunity. There are incentives for the United States to be relatively liberal in awarding grants of immunity, because the prospect of antitrust immunity is a valuable bargaining chip in negotiating liberal agreements with foreign governments.

The airline and airport industries are facing continuous change on a global scale and recent trends show that as both industries continue to expand, globalization will increase in importance.

Globalization of Airlines and Airline Alliance Models

Global alliances will continue to expand among airlines because passengers demand travel to destinations beyond a single airline's network. Alliances are necessary to drive down the costs of airline operations.

There are three main factors influencing the development of airline alliances: marketing advantages, nationality and ownership rules, and competition. The marketing advantages of airline alliances were identified in the United States during the 1980s in a deregulated environment. Major U.S. airlines were able to survive in a competitive market through mergers and acquisitions, thus increasing the size of networks.

Nationality and ownership rules limit the power of airlines to purchase a foreign carrier, thus restricting competitive advantage over other carriers. Bilateral regulations state that airlines must be substantially owned and controlled by nationals of the state in which they are registered. The only way to get around these rules is to enter airline alliances that may incorporate code sharing, franchising, joint frequent flyer programs, combined sales outlets, and so on.

Finally, competition plays a large role in the development of alliances because mutual agreements among airlines eliminate the need to compete with each other. For example, routes that were previously flown by two competing companies may result in reduced fares because there is no need to compete against each other once an alliance has been formed.

As of 2022, three major global alliances (Star Alliance, SkyTeam, OneWorld) jointly controlled more than 80 percent of the key routes linking Europe—Asia-Pacific, North America—Asia-Pacific, and Europe—North America (Table 18.1).

Formation of airline partnerships expands existing route networks through code-sharing agreements, provides new products for consumers, creates a high brand of service for business travelers, and creates global recognition for priority passengers. Concentration of airline activity will take place at hub airports and priority will go to airports providing a flexible structure. However, a large number of secondary airports will increase in terms of importance as LCCs and point-to-point carriers make a stronger presence without the need for connectivity. As a result of transfer traffic, minimum connecting times will be important, but this will be a challenge as airports become more congested as hub-and-spoke network carriers constrain themselves with somewhat limited time schedules. Specific targets will be made to decrease aircraft and luggage delays. For an airport to be successful, it must understand the needs of the airlines and be able to meet those demands.

As previously mentioned, the rise of the low-cost airline has resulted in a connected world, meaning a passenger can fly around the world on multiple itineraries and it is only a matter of time before the low-cost sector creates a model to transfer traffic, including passengers and cargo. It is expected that the traditional airline alliance model will remain the same for years to come, recognizing that airline partners will come and go. The big disruptor will most likely be the growth of the low-cost airline alliance which will compete head-to-head with the main existing alliances like Star Alliance, SkyTeam, and OneWorld. For example, the first three low-cost airline alliance models have spawned in the Asia-Pacific and Indian Ocean region and it is only a matter of time before other regions, including North America, Latin America/Caribbean, Middle East, Europe, and Africa, get in the game. The first low-cost airline alliance was the Vanilla Alliance,

Table 18.1 Airline Alliance Comparison

Alliance	Members	Passengers Per Year (millions)	Countries Served	Destinations	Fleet
Star Alliance	26	642	195	1,360	5,000
SkyTeam	19	665	175	1,062	3,937
OneWorld	14	557	161	1,016	3,560

Source: Wikipedia

designed to promote tourism in the "Vanilla Islands" and operating in the Indian Ocean region, serving states that are members of the Indian Ocean Commission or French overseas territories in the Indian Ocean. Current alliance members include Air Austral, Air Madagascar, Air Mauritius, Air Seychelles, and Int'Air Îles. The second low-cost airline alliance model is the U-FLY Alliance consisting of airlines representing Hong Kong, Mainland China, and South Korea (Eastar Jet, Lucky Air, Urumqi Air, West Air). The interesting part of the U-FLY Alliance is that all of the associated airlines were originally part of the HNA Group and the concept behind the model was to launch a number of small airlines under the HNA Group flag with the goal of creating a powerful network. The third low-cost airline alliance to emerge was the Value Alliance, claiming to be the first pan-regional model in the world. The Value Alliance consists of Cebu Pacific, Cebgo, Jeju Air, Nok Air, and Scoot.

Airport Alliances

Airports, like any other business, try to reduce costs wherever possible and maximize their profits. One way of doing this is to join an airport alliance. This is a relatively new concept, but it is becoming more important as airport operators realize the benefits. Airport alliance members can reduce costs through the joint purchasing of equipment, joint marketing, joint training, and the centralization of corporate office functions. This type of alliance is especially beneficial for small airport operators, because they can take advantage of the large airport's management and expect to increase profit at the same time.

Airports located close to one another may choose to join an airport alliance in order to control runway and terminal capacity or to control future development. This may lead to the joint marketing of the member airports, resulting in less competition. In other words, such alliances decrease the friction of transition.

Frankfurt International Airport would like to promote the concept of airport alliances in Germany, but as yet, it has not been able to convince other German airports that this move would be beneficial for all concerned. An airport alliance would bring operational benefits for aviation and nonaviation business, increase the catchment area, promote intermodal transport, simplify operational procedures, coordinate communication systems, and provide a good quality product to all.

In recent years, airport groups have been playing increasingly important roles in the aviation industry. Some airport groups are created by governments to manage airports in a country. For example, the Airports Authority of India (AAI) manages and operates 126 airports in India, the Aeroportos de Portugal manages major airports in Portugal. In other cases, an airport group may operate as an ordinary business and provide management services to other airports. Such services can be accompanied with shareholding and investments. For example, the Aéroports de Paris (ADP) group not only operates the Paris Orly Airport, Paris Charles de Gaulle Airport and Paris Le Bourget Airport, it also owns shares in the Amsterdam Airport Schiphol and the Istanbul Atatürk Airport. In addition, it owns 38 percent of the Tepe-Akfen-Ventures Investment Holding (TAV), which manages several large airports in Europe. Apparently, it is more likely for airports managed or affiliated to the same airport group to form an airport alliance. With airport groups and airport alliances expanding globally, airport operations and ownerships are expected to become more international over time.

Airline–Airport Vertical Arrangements

Airports provide essential inputs to airlines. To promote healthy development of international aviation, it is important to ensure that quality service and sufficient capacity are available at airports. Most of the international air traffic takes place between hub airports that serve as international gateways. Airbus found that 50 percent of the world's 100 fastest-growing city pairs are among the 32 global hub cities, and almost all of the remaining city pairs have a hub at one end or the other. However, many international gateway airports are approaching their capacities, thus airlines may not be able to schedule more flights even if they have been rewarded the necessary air freedoms. Major airport expansion projects in metropolitan regions can be very expensive. If costly airport infrastructures are not well utilized, it may impose financial risks to airports. However, Fu and Oum (2014) found that liberalization and airlines' expansions into overseas markets could lead to dynamic changes in airline competition and network configuration. As a result, airport traffic volumes may experience great uncertainty and fluctuation. To reduce financial risks, an airport may choose to commit capacity investments only when the traffic volume is sufficiently high. On the other hand, the planning and construction of a runway or a new airport terminal can easily take decades. Late investments will lead to severe congestion over an extended period before new capacities are available. These challenges have led airlines and airports to enter into various vertical arrangements. For example, Starkie (2008) found that liberalization of international aviation has given airlines greater freedom to change routes and switch airports. Airlines also need to secure essential inputs from airports at reasonable prices. Therefore, both airports and airlines have the incentive to establish long-term contracts to reduce risk and uncertainties.

FUTURE CHALLENGES

Most liberalization packages have been implemented by developed countries, notably the United States. In 2003, there were 87 liberalized agreements involving 70 countries, 59 of which were U.S. open-skies agreements. By 2012, there were over 400 liberalized agreements involving 145 states. By 2022, there more than 410 liberalized agreements involving approximately 150 states, of which more than 100 were U.S. open-skies agreements (ICAO).

The challenges are hardly over for the United States in the international arena. It must continue to retain the courage of its convictions and pursue liberalization of international aviation markets. To do so, it must apply its convictions consistently and ignore the arguments of those who would have the United States revert to traditional concepts about balancing benefits and seeking equivalencies. These mercantilist concepts believe the fact that aviation trade, like all other trades, should be based not on the ability of one country to produce as much as the other or the fact that one country's market for a product is as large as its partner's market, but on the willingness of countries to open their markets to free trade.

The United States will also have to continue to undertake additional major policy changes. Just as it had to break down entrenched ideas about the need to regulate competition in international markets, so, too, it must reexamine the rationale for many of the tenets on which the scheme for regulating competition in international aviation markets was originally based. Clearly, times have changed dramatically since the infancy of the industry, and what seemed natural and right at the time of the Chicago Convention may be irrelevant at best, and harmful at worse, to the interests of both the traveling public and U.S. carriers and their employees.

Specifically, requirements for national ownership, reservation of domestic traffic for domestic carriers (cabotage, Fly America, government-reserved traffic), and various means of propping up the financial state of domestic carriers (state aids and subsidies, Chapter 11 bankruptcy laws) should be questioned on a worldwide basis. The United States should take the lead in this debate, but it cannot do so if it is uncertain about its own commitment to unregulated markets.

At this stage in its development, it is unclear why the U.S. international aviation industry should be treated differently than any other industry. Right now, the industry is a strong international competitor, and it should be among the beneficiaries of a reduction in trade barriers. The United States must continue to use the muscle of its large domestic and international market to beat down trade barriers. But it must also be dedicated to genuinely open markets in the purest terms. This will require taking some risks, but only by leading the way, as it has recently done in its negotiations with Canada and the smaller European countries, will the United States reap the benefits of an unrestricted market in international aviation services.

Australia provides a good case study of an aviation environment currently facing change. Qantas, the "official" airline of Australia, has been one of the most important airlines in the history of aviation and has been able to survive the trials and tribulations impacting aviation. However, Qantas' fate is more important than ever before as the airline faces continuous competitive pressure in both the domestic and international markets.

In theory, Australian aviation operates in a deregulated environment and yet, many restrictions still apply, particularly in the area of foreign ownership. Qantas is a legacy carrier plagued by legacy characteristics. The business model was developed during a time of regulation and like airlines in other markets forced to adapt to liberalized or deregulated environments, Qantas has not had the opportunity to reinvent itself and take advantage of a new platform like many of its competitors. The Qantas Sale Act of 1992 put serious restrictions on the airline's ability to optimize performance due to the associated foreign ownership restrictions.

The Australian domestic and international markets are faced with excess capacity issues, meaning there is too much supply for demand and this circumstance provides a good case study for global awareness. As noted in Qantas' 2014 (Q1) announcement of a $235 million loss, both the domestic and international markets were suffering as airlines competed for business. Unfortunately, for Qantas, the competition was fierce as Virgin Australia, backed by three state-owned airlines at the time, was fighting for market share. Both Qantas and Virgin Australia posted financial losses in 2014 and the battle for supremacy continued despite this. In the world of globalization and deregulation, the airline industry is an "eye for an eye, tooth for a tooth" business.

Due to the current foreign ownership restrictions put on Qantas, the airline must have 51 percent Australian ownership. Access to "cheap" capital is very difficult for Qantas due to this restriction set forth by The Qantas Sale Act. However, its main competitor, Virgin Australia, had a major advantage over Qantas as it had access to "cheap" capital, via the three state-owned airlines (Singapore, Etihad, Air New Zealand). In 2020, Virgin Australia Holdings was negatively impacted by the COVID-19 global pandemic resulting in the airline entering voluntary administration (bankruptcy), and later that year Bain Capital acquired the company.

Australia has always had a sense of pride and is a nationalistic society. Qantas has traditionally been supported as the official flag carrier of the country and this continues to be evident with the current foreign ownership restrictions discussion. There seems to be a belief between government and the citizens of Australia that reducing foreign ownership restrictions will result in loss of pride and loss of the nationalism associated with the name Qantas. In reality, if foreign ownership restrictions were lessened, and foreign monies were invested into the airline, it is very doubtful Qantas would lose its identity. The solution to the identity issue is a well-planned marketing and branding strategy.

Qantas' Alan Joyce has argued for the need for government support, essentially subsidized assistance for the airline, while Virgin Australia's former CEO, John Borghetti has argued against. In a deregulated environment, government assistance should not be permitted as it creates an unfair competitive advantage to airlines operating in the same deregulated environment.

As Qantas and Virgin Australia run head-to-head, it is only a matter of time before access to resources disappears. In this particular case, Virgin Australia has greater resources but even this powerful brand, backed by strong ownership, has limitations.

It is possible for both Qantas and Virgin Australia to survive and operate successfully long-term. And it is important for the Australian government to understand this perspective, as competition is best for the market because it keeps airline fares reasonable and expands market share in terms of route network. However, in order to accomplish the task of having an efficient airline industry, changes are necessary both externally and internally.

Externally, the Australian government must revise the rules associated with The Qantas Sale Act removing the current 51 percent ownership restriction. Such a change will permit Qantas to seek access to cheaper capital, most likely in the form of equity relationships with airlines in the Oneworld Alliance (i.e., Cathay Pacific, Qatar). Internally, Qantas has a lot of work to do in terms of restructuring. The domestic and international operations should be split into separate businesses, resulting in a new business model for each entity including new leadership. The Qantas brand would continue to survive and both business models, though different, would complement each other. The physical size of Qantas should be reduced as the current fixed costs are high. Unfortunately, one of the negative impacts is a reduction of the employee base. The airline is overstaffed. Additionally, Qantas must restructure its aircraft fleet by simplifying it.

The notion of building a smaller airline is a good thing as costs will be significantly reduced and by splitting the business into two air carriers (domestic and international), management can focus on opportunities, including enhanced partnerships with the Oneworld Alliance that can essentially offer the world in terms of network. Air New Zealand, although primarily government owned (approximately 75 percent), is a good case study for Qantas to research. Air New Zealand restructured the company by developing and implementing a successful strategy. The end result was a decrease in capacity, a focus on long-haul travel, a simplified aircraft fleet, strong alliance relationships, and a positive track record of profitability. Interestingly, the government of New Zealand has been selling off shares of the airline as part of a partial-privatization plan.

One of the key strategies for airlines worldwide is to "shrink" the physical business but "grow" the network through strong partnership opportunities. In other words, airlines, within alliances, should strive to complement one another rather than compete.

NEW AIRLINE BUSINESS MODELS

As previously mentioned in this book, air carrier business models continue to evolve and will do so until the "perfect" business model has been developed. Many industry experts will agree that seeking perfection is impossible due to the internal and external forces impacting the industry, especially as they relate to the ever-changing economic environment. Perhaps the newest business model to evolve concentrates on the long-haul, low-cost market. The final section of the book defines and discusses three types of new business models: network specialists, product specialists, and price specialists.

The content of this section was adapted from an academic journal paper published by the author of this book (J.G. Wensveen and R. Leick (2009). "The Long-Haul, Low-Cost Carrier: A Unique Business Model." *Journal of Air Transport Management*. Elsevier Science. Vol./Issue 15/3 103–105).

Does the Long-Haul, Low-Cost Model Work?

The airline industry is a risky industry in which to invest, statistically second only to the hospitality industry, and yet investors are continuously attracted to it regardless of its economic state. Airlines are considered "sexy." One of the main reasons it is attractive to investors is that it is one of a few industries that can provide a large payback if things work out well.

The airline industry is often unstable and unpredictable, forcing airlines to frequently restructure and, in particular, to create flexible strategies that can respond as external operating environment changes. New airlines have an advantage over existing carriers in terms of implementing such strategies because they are devoid of legacies of indebtedness or an out-of-date business model. A new low-cost, long-haul carrier would be in such a position.

Van der Bruggen (2008) examines the pros and cons of the low-cost application to long-haul travel. At first glance, there are clear competitive advantages to the low-cost model in long-haul markets. For instance, no direct substitute exists for long-haul air travel. The captive market allows legacy carriers to excessively inflate fares in premium cabins. The result is high yielding, long-haul routes subsidize less profitable short-haul routes in legacy carriers' networks and expose the carrier to higher overall cost structures.

The higher fares associated with long-haul travel make price a more critical criterion in the purchase decision. However, long-haul economy fares are already competitive and there is little evidence that lower airfares will translate into increased demand in long-haul markets as it has in short-haul. More opportunity for competitive products exists in the premium cabin where price is less of a factor for business and affluent leisure passengers. The challenge is now in finding opportunities for cost advantages that apply to the long-haul environment.

Most secondary markets have no existing long-haul service and provide little competition for point-to-point demand. However, existing long-haul aircraft are designed for a high-density configuration, which makes profitability more difficult when applied to medium- and small-sized long-haul markets. Few routes have the potential to support point-to-point frequencies and secondary airports often do not have the infrastructure to support large aircraft and around-the-clock operations. Operational efficiencies from secondary airports are minimized for long-haul networks while hub connectivity becomes more critical. Long-haul flights operate at lower frequencies and achieve higher utilization through longer stage flights. Less congested secondary airports do not necessarily translate into quicker ground turn times. Fewer landings mean that landing fees are a smaller percentage of operating costs. High frequency connectivity to short-haul markets becomes more critical to long-haul operations since many passengers connect on either or both ends of their long-haul flights.

Many of the competitive advantages enjoyed by short-haul, low-cost airlines do not apply to long-haul operations. Legacy carriers already achieve low seat-mile costs and high load factors. Further increasing aircraft utilization is difficult due to the long stage lengths and minimal number of turns. Cutting frills on long-haul flights would only alienate passengers who find more value in in-flight entertainment, meals, and seat pitch on longer flights. Overall, the cost advantage of long-haul, low-cost carriers is expected to be 20 to 25 percent compared to 40 to 60 percent for their short-haul counterparts (van der Bruggen, 2008).

The core fundamental in operating long-haul flights is rather simple. As distance increases, operating costs rise while unit costs decrease. This is particularly true when it comes to fuel burn, crew cost, maintenance cost, passenger services and over-flight. Incumbent carriers primarily make up this difference through substantially higher premium fares, not economy fares.

It is very difficult to achieve a fare advantage with an all economy seating configuration in long-haul markets. Economy fares increase slowly with distance. Airlines trade fare advantage for limited market applications with a wide-body aircraft. Narrow-body, long-haul aircraft also have limited applications. Despite the factors limiting the application of the existing low-cost, short-haul strategy to long-haul operations, great opportunities still exist. The key is to concentrate on developing a new business model which capitalizes on opportunities and accounts for limitations of the long-haul market.

Network Specialists

A network specialist operates as a corporate shuttle catering mainly to business passengers and executives on high-yield routes. PrivatAir, previously based in Geneva, Switzerland and operated from 1977 to 2018, was the pioneer of this business model and was able to survive successfully while other airlines failed. However, PrivatAir ultimately fell into economic hardship and ceased operations on December 5, 2018. The network specialist often has contracts with major corporations for the transport of executives between locations. In the case of PrivatAir, the airline offered business-class seating on trans-Atlantic flights, utilizing a mixed fleet of aircraft including Airbus A319-100, A319-100LR, Boeing B737-700BBJ, B737-800, B757-200, B767-300ER, and had orders in for the B787-8 Dreamliner. The key differentiators for the network specialist are the ability to operate as a corporate shuttle, aircraft crew maintenance and insurance (ACMI) operator for existing airlines and tailored or customized services for a wide range of clients. Both

Lufthansa and KLM utilized PrivatAir in their network for all business-class service from Düsseldorf and Amsterdam, respectively. The historical success of PrivatAir can be attributed to limited competition and lucrative corporate contracts, and it is unfortunate the company was not able to survive.

Product Specialists

A product specialist is an all business-class, all first-class seating configuration, or a combination of both, with a primary focus on large and small business and affluent leisure travel. Scheduled services are offered on routes with high load factors and premium fares. The product specialist competes on the strength of legacy yields in premium cabins on long-haul flights. Pioneers in this market include Eos Airlines, MAXjet Airways, Silverjet, and L'Avion. Unfortunately, the first three carriers listed have all gone bankrupt. The fourth, L'Avion, was acquired by British Airways and the airline was most likely never profitable either. L'Avion has since merged with OpenSkies and is a wholly owned subsidiary of British Airways.

Eos Airlines (United Kingdom) operated a 48-seat first-class configuration utilizing the Boeing 757-200 between London Stansted and New York JFK. The airline closed operations in April, 2008. MAXjet Airways (USA) operated a 100-seat business-class configuration utilizing the Boeing 767-200 between London Stansted and New York JFK, as well as between London Stansted and Las Vegas. The airline closed operations in December, 2007. Silverjet Airways (United Kingdom) operated a 100-seat business-class configuration which utilized the Boeing 767-200 between London Luton and Newark, as well as between London Luton and Dubai. The airline closed operations in May, 2008. L'Avion (France) operated a 90-seat business-class configuration by utilizing the Boeing 757-200 between Paris Orly and Newark. British Airways now operates the aircraft under their OpenSkies subsidiary with 24 lie-flat beds, 28 premium economy, and 30 economy seats from airports within continental Europe to the U.S.

The key differentiator for the product specialist is the ability to offer low airfares with flexible tickets in a premium cabin. Given the recent history of the four product specialists, it is evident that this business model has not yet been mastered. Of the three recent bankruptcies, all reported the same reasons for failure, including rising fuel and oil prices, undercapitalization, and newly created competition by legacy carriers offering premium cabins on similar routes. Despite these failures, there do not appear to be any inherent problems with the model; however, aggressive competition from legacy carriers and an ever-difficult operating environment make initial success difficult. Nevertheless, although business- and first-class travellers are usually not price sensitive, there are limits on the prices they are willing to pay. Singapore Airlines had been offering a 19-hour all business-class flight between Singapore and New York Newark airport for many years. However, due to surging fuel price, the carrier terminated the service in 2013. Passengers have since then been routed to JFK via Frankfurt, adding five hours to the journey.

Price Specialists

The price specialist incorporates low-cost strategies to compete on price. They offer long-haul flights against lower fares than legacy competitors and therefore require large aircraft with high-seating configuration to be profitable. Essentially, the price specialist has attempted to duplicate the successful short-haul, low-cost business model and apply it to long-haul. The pioneers of the price specialist market are Oasis Hong Kong, Zoom, Jetstar, Viva Macau, and AirAsia X.

Oasis Hong Kong (China) operated a 359-seat mixed business and economy configuration utilizing the Boeing 747-400 between Hong Kong and Vancouver, as well as between Hong Kong and London Gatwick. The airline closed operations in April, 2008. Jetstar (Australia) operates three aircraft, including the Airbus A320-200 with a 177-seating configuration, the A321-200 with a 213-seating configuration, and the Airbus A330-200 with a 303-seating configuration. The airline operates domestic flights in Australia with additional services to Cambodia, Hong Kong, Indonesia, Japan, Macau, Malaysia, Myanmar, New Zealand, Philippines, Singapore, Taiwan, Thailand, U.S.A., and Vietnam. Jetstar's Australian operation is owned by Qantas Airways.

The key differentiators of the price specialist are the ability to offer low fares by utilizing high-density cabins in high demand markets. The price specialist model offers more flexibility than the two models mentioned previously and more opportunity to expand into new markets. Oasis Hong Kong and Zoom went bankrupt while the others appeared to be growing successfully. Based on the mixed result of price specialists, there appear to be no inherent problems with the model. The bankruptcy of Oasis Hong Kong and Zoom can both be attributed to failures in airline business planning. However, it remains to be seen how sustainable the price specialists' cost savings are over the long term.

Low-Cost, Long-Haul Opportunity

For the foreseeable future, network specialists will secure and capitalize on opportunities, fitting the corporate shuttle profile on thin, long-haul routes producing high yield. The markets are somewhat limited, allowing only a small number of air carriers to tap into such opportunities on point-to-point networks linking a major business centre with another major business centre. The main advantage to this type of operation is the increased cost savings and increased productivity for executives. Network specialists with sound business models will be able to secure agreements to operate on behalf of an airline. In other words, an operator who specializes in this area can offer a service that makes financial sense when the actual airline is not able to. This arrangement ultimately results in a "win–win" situation for the operator, the airline, and the passenger. To date, there is limited competition in this sector.

Given the history of the product specialist carriers, it is evident the product specialist model must continue to evolve. In July 2007, British Airways announced it was purchasing L'Avion with the idea of folding the company into OpenSkies, British Airway's new luxury carrier on the trans-Atlantic. Rising fuel and oil prices combined with low yields resulting from high competition in limited markets ultimately led to the downfall of MAXjet, EOS, and Silverjet. In terms of opportunities for product specialists, future business models will have to capitalize on the relative strength of legacy yields in premium cabins on long-haul flights while at the same time developing an operation that reduces high fixed costs. Whether or not this is even possible remains to be seen.

Of the three types of emerging carriers discussed, the price specialist has the greatest number of potential opportunities. Success will be based on the ability to identify high-density markets where legacy competition exists and yet allows the price specialist to survive. Such markets will tap into point-to-point operations as well as hub-and-spoke operations. This means that some passengers will make transfers on other carriers using separate itineraries. The price specialist entrants use seating density to capture lower-yield traffic profitably. In the longer term, the authors expect such airlines will be able to establish connections with short-haul price specialists in specific markets with the ultimate goal of creating a global network. Depending on specific situations, such partnership arrangements may be in the form of IATA agreements but for simplicity and ease of efficiency, most relationships will probably be non-IATA agreements that eliminate the burden of legal and financial responsibilities established in such contracts.

The Future of the Long-Haul Air Carrier

Success in the airline industry can be measured by one's ability to show up at the office and turn the lights on. Why? Traditionally, airlines are short-term thinkers and have been forced to make decisions impacting "today" with little regard for "tomorrow." However, things are beginning to change as airlines, particularly new start-ups with no "excess baggage," are run as real businesses rather than as "airlines."

Predicting the future of how long-haul air carriers will differentiate themselves is a difficult undertaking due to the continuously challenging and evolving nature of the airline industry. The internal makings of an airline are challenging enough without even thinking about the vast external challenges airlines are plagued with.

It can be argued no air carrier has perfected the airline business model and this is perhaps the largest challenge faced today. Is there such thing? Can it be accomplished? In the long-haul market, there have been many failures over the past decade, including product differentiators like MAXjet, Silverjet, and EOS. In each of these cases, the airline attempted to market business- or first-class seating, pre/in/post-flight amenities, and high-end service, at reasonable fares, often falling at the high end of economy prices. In theory, the business models were sound but external factors killed them. These airlines competed on dense, competitive routes served by the "big boys" who had greater access to resources and the ability to strategically undercut fares while improving passenger loyalty programs. Additionally, the new airline business models launched during a period of record-breaking fuel and oil prices adding increased pressure and quickly changing the way of thinking from innovative to survival mode.

The long-haul airline of the future will experience many face lifts as a result of the need to remain competitive with other air carriers. Today, from the perspective of a passenger, all long-haul airlines seem to be the same. The only real difference is the color of the livery on the tail. New planes with multi-class seating configurations, lie-flat beds, and high-tech inflight entertainment (IFE) systems are the norm. Is this really the future?

Social, mobile, and the cloud are trendy buzz words today, and it's only a matter of time before long-haul airlines implement marketing and branding strategies to essentially exploit new product and service offerings associated with each. In the short-term future, this will be a reality but if one looks further ahead, there will be another period of change in the evolution of the long-haul business model.

Rather than concentrate on what the competition is doing to differentiate itself, it is important to determine the future needs of passengers and how the long-haul air carrier can tap into this by being at the forefront. The answer is Asia!

The world can be defined by six geographic regions including: North America, Latin America/Caribbean, Asia-Pacific, Europe, Middle East, and Africa. Despite the ups and downs of the world economy, Asia continues to grow and it is the Asian passenger that will greatly assist in determining what the future of long-haul air carriers look like. Between the two main aircraft manufacturers, Airbus and Boeing, the former gets it and is developing new product lines, succumbing to the needs of the passenger of the future.

Traditionally, price and time have been the instigators behind demand for travel followed by "luxury" amenities often available in a smorgasbord environment. Although still important factors, the future long-haul model will be about comfort, sleep, wellbeing, relaxation, and productivity.

Asia is an emerging market with an increasingly affluent population (ages 18–34) and a high propensity to fly variable that is expected to increase dramatically. First time career people combined with established mid-career people, are likely to travel more frequently for business and personal as the need for "me" time becomes a more dominant factor in Asian society. One of the end results for the "new" type of passenger will be the demand for a specific type of seat. The challenge, and the opportunity, for the long-haul provider is to be able to offer an environment that meets the needs for the passenger beyond price and time.

Sleep, wellbeing, and relaxation equal productivity and this is the future opportunity for the long-haul air carrier model. The challenge is being able to tap into each of these factors in a cabin configuration that must cater to a diverse range of passengers (low fare to high fare). The future cabin will offer increased width, pitch, and legroom combined with adjustable seating, quiet zones, and more arm room. In other words, it's all about real estate! Every seat occupies space and the greater the space, the more valuable the property.

The long-haul cabin of the future will be complimented by high quality service from the inflight crew, communication technology that is available 24/7 for increased business productivity, and perhaps 3D or 4D IFE offerings. As aircraft manufacturers strive to produce better aircraft in the future, factors like improved air quality and mood lighting will become important aspects of improving the wellbeing of the passenger.

At the end of the day, all airlines, no matter what type or size, need "butts in seats." Long-haul air carriers have the added challenge of long routes, meaning less aircraft rotations compared to short- and medium-haul carriers resulting in a decreased opportunity to generate seat revenue. The big challenge, for the long-haul air carrier, will be catering to the passenger of the future while fine-tuning the economics of how the business can be run profitably.

Real estate—almost always a good investment! Who will get it right?

The content of this section was adapted from an article authored by Dr. John Wensveen on Runway Girl Network (www.runwaygirlnetwork.com).

A New Era is Coming: Crowdfunding and Cryptocurrency

An interesting new **airline business model** was created in 2021 and it is an adaption from the low-cost airline business model. Northern Pacific Airways, based in Anchorage, Alaska, seeks to operate transpacific flights serving North America and Asia utilizing Anchorage as the stopover and providing an accelerated connection time. In 2022, the airline made global headlines with Northern Pacific Airways' CEO, Rob McKinney, announcing the company was raising capital on Wefunder, an online **crowdfunding** service, to accelerate growth. At the time of writing, the company had some success securing funding from the general public which would ultimately allow the airline to serve Asia, Alaska, New York, Florida, California, and Nevada. The company also made headlines when it announced they would establish a "cutting edge" loyalty program called FlyCoin. The interesting component to this model is that passengers will receive rewards in the form of **cryptocurrency** and the benefit is that it never expires and will be accepted as a future form of payment, including with concessions at airports, within the network. Northern Pacific Airways' business model is similar to that of Icelandair with the exception of the crowdfunding and cryptocurrency options. Is the future of the airline business model? Time will tell!

Market Characteristics: Independents

The non-legacy, long-haul airlines operating in today's environment can be characterized in terms of the network model that includes the frequency model and the destinations model. The former, also referred to as Scale Model, provides service for large corporate clients in markets with strong catchment areas. The target market often consists of affluent leisure and VIP traffic operating sub-nine-hour stage length with a once daily aircraft rotation. The latter model, also referred to as the Scope Model, consists of a mixture of affluent leisure and movable business with broad regional catchment areas. There is a seasonal and economic balance combined with availability of peak-time slots operating seven- to 12-hour stage lengths.

Market Characteristics: Network or Legacy Airlines

The legacy long-haul airlines operating in today's environment can also be identified by certain characteristics in terms of network model, including the hub complement and the hub bypass. The former allows the route network to build from hub infrastructure with strong corporate demand, lean leisure, frequent flyers, and cargo demand. Typically, stage length is up to nine hours. The latter leverages product superiority versus competition attracting incremental corporate business combined with a lower-cost competitive response.

Conclusions

A new competitive environment is emerging in the international air transport market. Long-haul, low-cost carriers bridge the networks of short-haul, low-cost carriers allowing LCCs to compete with the mega-alliances of the international network carriers. Interactive marketing agreements allow low-cost carriers around the world to form loose alliances for interlining and frequent flyer programs. At the same time, changes are taking place between the established worldwide alliances. Liberalization has reduced the need for alliances but the benefits of a shared network still hold much value. Consolidation is taking place within the global alliances resulting in three evenly distributed network alliances.

An ad hoc fourth global alliance is forming with low-cost carriers around the world linking networks in order to compete with the legacy alliances. Low-cost carriers have always been restricted by their inability to satisfy the demand for transcontinental travel. Long-haul, low-cost carriers represent an opportunity for LCCs everywhere to join forces and compete with the global alliances. The long-haul point-to-point model integrates well with the similar point-to-point focus city model of the short-haul carriers. There are several examples where long-haul and short-haul carriers have entered into interactive marketing agreements to promote cross-selling, integrate websites, and advertise cooperatively. These agreements permit passengers to fly to and from small markets in any region of the world via low-cost carriers.

If long-haul, low-cost carriers are to survive and adapt in the evolving air transport environment, they must continue to innovate. Opportunities should not focus on low-cost, long-haul models but instead focus on the three types of emerging carriers: network, product, and price specialist. The keys to future success of the model include a solid business plan that demonstrates a sustainable competitive advantage, flexibility, the right management team, steady and moderate growth.

KEY TERMS

airline business model
airline strategy
bilateral agreement
Brexit
cabotage
crowdfunding
cryptocurrency
Five Freedoms Agreement
long-haul
low-cost carrier
Open-Skies Agreement
rights of freedom
sovereignty of airspace
Two Freedoms Agreement

REVIEW QUESTIONS

1 What were the two principal theories regarding the national sovereignty of airspace? Which theory prevailed?
2 Discuss several of the principles governing the drafting of the Paris Convention. What provisions were designed to ensure the safety of air navigation? Discuss several of the principles that were adopted by the convention. What was the primary purpose of the Havana Convention?
3 Why is there a need for international air law? What were the major agreements resulting from the Warsaw Convention? How did the Hague Protocol and the Guatemala City Protocol affect the provisions of the Warsaw Convention?
4 Discuss some of the reasons for the Chicago Conference of 1944. What was the purpose of this convention? Describe some of the important articles under this convention. What were some of the areas in which the contracting states agreed to develop "the highest degree of uniformity"?
5 What is the purpose of ICAO?
6 How many rights of freedom are there? What was the Two Freedoms Agreement? The Five Freedoms Agreement? What is meant by *bilateral agreement*? Discuss some of the provisions under the Chicago standard form.
7 What is the broad aim of IATA? What is the function of the four permanent committees of IATA?

8 What were some of the factors leading up to the Bermuda Agreement? What was the position of the United States? Discuss some of the principles established under the Bermuda Agreement.

9 Discuss some of the major changes that took place in international aviation during the three decades following the Bermuda Agreement. How would you describe the CAB's position toward IATA during the 1970s? What was the problem that the British had regarding the Bermuda Agreement in the late 1970s?

10 What major event prompted the new U.S. policy on international aviation in the late 1970s? Describe some of the goals enumerated under the U.S. policy statement. Discuss some of the objectives of the International Air Transportation Competition Act of 1979. How was traffic affected during the early 1980s? Why were continuing efforts to liberalize aviation agreements hampered?

11 What is an *open-sky agreement*? *Cabotage*? What was the purpose of the Commission to Ensure a Strong, Competitive Airline Industry? In 1995, the commission outlined a "Plan of Action" regarding future open-aviation agreements. Explain.

12 Why did the U.K. exit from the E.U.? How did this impact discussions related to open skies?

13 Describe globalization as it applies to the airline industry. Why is it so difficult for U.S. carriers to establish hubs outside the United States? Why are bilateral agreements between the United States and many foreign countries to the disadvantage of U.S. carriers? How would an open-sky agreement improve this situation? Describe how code-sharing agreements operate. What is the impact on competition? How does the airline industry differ from other industries with regard to globalization?

14 Describe the emergence of new types of airline business models. Discuss whether or not the long-haul, low-cost model works. Define a network specialist. Define a product specialist. Define a price specialist.

15 Describe how the low-cost airline alliance model is emerging. What region(s) of the world was the first to launch this model? How many low-cost airline alliances exist? How will this impact the future of the traditional airline alliance?

16 As new airline business models evolve, how will new trends related to crowdfunding and cryptocurrency impact the industry?

Notes

1 United States Policy for the Conduct of International Air Transportation Negotiations, 1978, p. 1.

2 For an excellent discussion of the pros and cons of current U.S. international aviation policy, see Nawal K. Taneja, *U.S. International Aviation Policy* (Lexington, MA: Lexington Books/Heath, 1980), Chapter 3.

APPENDIX

Career Planning in Aviation

Introduction
Choosing and Getting Your First Job in Aviation
Cover Letters and the Résumé
The Interview

APPENDIX CHECKLIST • YOU SHOULD BE ABLE TO:

- Make a self-assessment of your talents, abilities, and preferences in preparing for career choices
- Identify the various aviation and aerospace industries and career paths and jobs with firms in those industries
- Describe the primary sources of information available in locating job openings
- Prepare a cover letter and résumé
- Prepare for a successful interview with prospective employers

INTRODUCTION

Career opportunities in aviation are quite extensive and diversified. Among the most visible occupations are pilot, mechanic, flight attendant, and air traffic controller. Less visible are thousands of other flight- and nonflight-related career paths in aviation, including flight dispatcher, crew scheduler, market analyst, manufacturers' sales or technical representative, aviation insurance underwriter, and consultant.

Aviation offers career opportunities for people with varying educational backgrounds. An associate's or bachelor's degree is generally required for most management or supervisory positions with the major carriers. A master's degree in business administration is increasingly necessary for research or consulting positions in the industry or with federal or state aviation agencies. Frequently, aviation consultants, industry analysts, and aviation educators have earned PhDs in transportation or related subjects.

An aviation background can also train a person to operate their own business. Among the entrepreneurial opportunities available are careers as fixed-base operators (FBOs), consultants, insurance agents, and freelance writers for the numerous aviation publications.

CHOOSING AND GETTING YOUR FIRST JOB IN AVIATION

The decision that you want to be "in aviation" is a major breakthrough in itself. However, aviation can mean many different kinds of careers. The decisions you make about your career will affect you for the rest of your life. The time spent on planning now may make the difference between a satisfying career or a series of job mistakes later. The following are suggested steps for choosing a career and finding that first job.

Making a Self-Assessment

Self-assessment is one of the most important steps in the job search. In order to choose a career that will satisfy you, you must first decide on your priorities and your needs. Honesty is critical to this self-assessment—you cannot afford to deceive yourself about what you want. The goal here is to understand your talents, abilities, and preferences so that you can maximize them by choosing an appropriate career path. You should make some tentative decisions about your own objectives—what you want out of a job and out of life. At the very least, you should decide whether you are simply looking for a job or whether you want to build a career. Do you want the position to be personally satisfying, or is money the key concern? How much financial return do you need—or are you willing to work for? How much are you willing to sacrifice in leisure activities and money to achieve success in a career? A career-oriented individual must establish short-term and long-term objectives. For example, your long-term objective might be to become a captain for a major airline. Reaching this objective will require putting in a considerable number of hours, earning many certificates and ratings, and working at several intermediate lower-paying positions. If, however, your objective is to get a job that pays well in the short term, one that is personally satisfying but might not pay as well in the long term, you will need different kinds of training and job experiences.

Because of the great variety of aviation jobs, it is difficult to generalize about what aptitudes you should have, ideally, to pursue a career in aviation. Different jobs attract people with different interests and abilities. Self-assessment is largely a process of clarifying and articulating ideas you may already hold in a fuzzy or ambiguous form. To assist in self-assessment, you might look at the following books, which raise many questions you should consider:

What Color Is Your Parachute?, by Richard N. Bolles
Self-Assessment and Career Development, by James G. Clawson et al.

Making Vocational Choices: A Theory of Careers, by John L. Holland
Life Plan: A Practical Guide to Successful Career Planning, by Louise W. Schrank

Also avail yourself of the counseling service at your school. Tests such as the Strong–Campbell Interest Inventory will help profile your interests and aptitudes.

Examining Career Fields and Job Descriptions

The next stage is moving from an abstract list of your skills, strengths, and priorities to actual job descriptions. You must translate your self-assessment into an actual job that suits your needs. The first step is to find a field, such as flying, maintenance, management, marketing, computers, or a combination of these fields, that requires your talents. The second step is deciding what aviation or aerospace industry you want to apply your particular skills to. Airlines, aviation insurance companies, aircraft leasing and financing companies, FBOs, consulting firms, airports, government agencies, and airframe, engine, and systems manufacturers—all look for people with varied technical and nontechnical, flight and nonflight backgrounds. Aviation jobs and career paths can be found everywhere; you should consider the widest possible variety of employers who could use your skills. Probably the most comprehensive listing of organizations and personnel within all of the aviation and aerospace industries can be found in the *World Aviation Directory*, which is published quarterly by News Group Publications. Table A.1 gives a broad overview of these industries.

Use some basic research techniques to investigate career paths and jobs that appeal to you. Your goal is to learn enough about the field to decide whether you would be happy in it. There are many different sources of information available.

Consult Published Materials. Your school library or the local public library may have a special career information section. Even if it does not, the library's holdings will certainly include many valuable references.

First, check the federal government publications. Each year, the U.S. Department of Labor publishes the *Occupational Outlook Handbook*. This book provides up-to-date and detailed information about hundreds of careers. It describes the nature of the work, working conditions, the number of people in the field, prospects for advancement, the job outlook for the coming decade, and average earnings. Another government publication, the *Dictionary of Occupational Titles*, categorizes every job in our economy. Tables A.2 through A.8 (which can be found at the end of this appendix) contain detailed, but not exhaustive, listings of job titles in several aviation industries. For up-to-date articles on changes and trends in the job market, including emerging occupations and occupational outlooks, look through recent issues of the *Occupational Outlook Quarterly*.

Table A.1 Aviation and Aerospace Industries Listed in the World Aviation Directory

Types of Firms	Listings
Air transportation firms	
Major and national air carriers	U.S. major and national air carriers and Canadian air carriers providing scheduled passenger service and operating aircraft seating more than 60 passengers; designated flag carriers are also listed
Regional air carriers (scheduled)	U.S. regional and Canadian air carriers providing scheduled passenger service and international air carriers providing scheduled passenger service and operating aircraft seating fewer than 60 passengers
Charter and commercial operators (nonscheduled)	Nonscheduled air services, including air taxi, contract, and charter
Specialty air services	Specialty air services, including air ambulance, agriculture, and aerial surveying/photography
Air cargo carriers and air and freight-forwarding firms	Scheduled and nonscheduled carriers specializing in all-cargo operations
Manufacturers	
Airframe/engine/systems manufacturers	All companies that manufacture airframes or engines. Also listed are major aviation/aerospace systems manufacturers employing more than 10,000 people and achieving aviation/aerospace sales in excess of $100 million
Component/equipment/supplies manufacturers	Aviation/aerospace component/equipment/supplies manufacturers and companies involved in machining or planting processes
Fuel and oil companies	U.S. firms manufacturing, trading, marketing, or transporting aviation gas, jet fuel, or oil
Computer hardware/systems manufacturers and software developers	Computer/microprocessor-based systems manufacturers and software developers with end-user civil and military aviation/ aerospace applications
World helicopter services	Scheduled and unscheduled helicopter services and specialty air services; airframe/engine/systems manufacturers; component/equipment/supplies manufacturers; equipment distributors, suppliers, and modifications; overhaul and repair; consultants and special services; heliports, flight schools, organizations, and publications
Aviation services	
Insurance companies	Companies involved in aviation insurance, claims, and insurance brokerage
Aircraft leasing, finance, and sales	Companies leasing, financing, and/or selling aircraft
Distributors/suppliers	Companies involved in aircraft/aerospace equipment distribution or supply

(Continued)

Table A.1 (Continued)

Types of Firms	Listings
Modifications/completions/overhauls/FBOs	All companies involved in aircraft ground handling, maintenance, overhaul and/or completions, including fixed-base operators (FBOs)
Consultants and special services	All companies providing special aviation-related services, such as engineering, R & D, management, consulting, legal, and planning
Organizations	Organizations that represent groups of active participants in the aviation/aerospace industry worldwide
Publications	Qualified aviation/aerospace periodicals published with established frequency
Airports and airport services	
Air carrier airports and regulating agencies	Airports serviced by scheduled air carriers and the geographically specific agencies and commissions that regulate them. Fixed-base operators and Part 139 certification are indicated
General aviation airports	General aviation airports (U.S. only) with lights and paved runways that are open to the public year-round
Aviation training schools	Schools specializing in training for all ratings (including airframe and powerplant licensing) and in training airport personnel, travel agents, air and ground personnel, and flight engineers
Catering and in-flight services	Companies involved in food, music, and related in-flight services
World government and military organizations	Government/military agencies, divided into U.S., Canadian, and international subsections. U.S. listings include civil and military agencies involved in aviation. Canadian and international listings include embassy, civil, and military categories
World space organizations	Spacecraft/launch vehicle manufacturers; ground station/tracking, telemetry, and control equipment manufacturers; space systems, subsystems, component, and equipment manufacturers; orbital research and materials processing; space insurance, consultants and special services, space organizations, and publications

The Internet has become the primary source for job seekers. Virtually, most companies seeking to recruit employees have an "Employment" section on their website. Larger companies tend to post specific jobs while smaller companies often do not post specific job opportunities but welcome résumé uploads. When seeking employment using the Internet, search for specific organizations of interest but also search for online employment firms or media companies with recruiting tools. Some examples include the following websites: Aviation Employment (www.aviationemployment.com), Aviation Week (www.jobs.aviationweek.com). Social media sites are also good resources for seeking employment opportunities. Some examples include the following: LinkedIn (www.linkedin.com), Facebook (www.facebook.com).

The mass media, including both local and national newspapers and trade publications, provide some of the most current information available. Periodicals such as *Business and Commercial Aviation*, *Airline Executive*, *Commuter Air*, *Air Transport World*, *Flight International*, and *Airline Pilot* have classified sections that list job opportunities.

Professional organizations publish a variety of helpful source materials. The Air Transport Association, Aerospace Industries Association, American Association of Airport Executives, and General Aviation Manufacturers Association are just a few examples. Some organizations have put together publications devoted to career development, such as NASA's *Limitless Horizons: Careers in Aerospace*. Arco Publishing Company publishes a number of excellent career guides, including *Directory of Employment Opportunities in the Federal Government* and *The Aerospace Careers Handbook*. A U.S. Government Printing Office publication that is particularly good is the *Federal Career Directory: A Guide for College Students*.

Finally, a wealth of information can be found in various encyclopedias, dictionaries, handbooks, manuals, bibliographies, statistical compendiums, indexes, and guides devoted to various industries. For a bibliography of many of these miscellaneous sources of information, arranged by industry, see the section titled "Sources of Information on Selected Industries and Career Opportunities" in *Self-Assessment and Career Development*, by James G. Clawson et al.

Contact People in Industry. Talking with people working in the field is often more revealing than reading books. This process does not have to be extremely formal. Using a source such as the *World Aviation Directory*, identify people holding jobs that you want to know more about. You can also talk with friends, acquaintances, and family members who hold similar jobs. Don't be reluctant to approach people—most people are flattered to be asked and like to talk about their work. Just be explicit that you are *not* asking for a job, but only for information.

Arrange an interview by phone or letter, and then come prepared with questions. Some basic questions include the following:

1. What are your responsibilities?
2. What is an average working day like? Is there much variety from week to week or month to month?
3. What are your greatest satisfactions and deepest frustrations with your job?

4 What kind of people do well in your line of work? Are any special qualifications or training needed?
5 How do you feel about future job opportunities in the industry?
6 What are typical entry-level jobs and typical career paths?
7 What salary does the average person make after 5, 10, and 15 years in the field?
8 Do you have any suggestions for other people to whom I should talk?

Learn from Direct Experience. You can learn most about a job by trying it out. If you're really serious about a career, try to find a paid part-time or summer job, volunteer work, or a post in a school group that will expose you to the field. For example, working for an FBO, volunteering to help out at a local air show, or serving as an officer in a school organization such as the flying club or Alpha Eta Rho will enhance your experience and résumé.

These kinds of opportunities allow you to test your inclinations. At best, you may get experience and develop skills that will eventually help you land a job. Even if your responsibilities are limited, you can observe the full-time employees and see the organization from the inside. At worst, you may find that you dislike your career choice. This will at least allow you to switch career goals before you have invested much time or training.

Collecting Information

Once you have found a job that interests you, use the sources previously mentioned to research the career area. Develop a file that includes the following material:

1 Sources of information on the career area, including published materials, interviews, and experience
2 Job titles in the career area
3 Nature of the work
4 Working conditions (hours, physical surroundings, fellow employees, travel, pressures and rewards, locations, and so on)
5 Qualifications for the job (education, experience, skills, licenses, ratings, hours, type of equipment, and so on)
6 Compensation (salary range for entry-level jobs and for more advanced jobs, and benefits)
7 Career paths (common routes for advancement, transferability of skills to another field, average rate of advancement)
8 Future prospects (projected growth of field, industry problems, competition for jobs)
9 The match between the career and your self-assessment
10 Additional sources of information for further investigation

Finding Job Openings

Once you have decided on the type of job you want, the next step is locating actual job openings. Many sources of information are available to you.

Academic Leads. Both your professors and the campus placement office may have leads about job openings. Tell them about your interests and abilities. Attend any job fairs that the placement office sponsors. In addition, it is helpful to talk to campus recruiters. Even if such interviews do not lead to a job, you can check whether your expectations are realistic.

Business and Community Organizations. Professional, civic, and other organizations sometimes maintain job banks and give advance notification of job opportunities to members or other people who are signed up. Check with alumni organizations, professional groups, chambers of commerce, and similar groups.

The Media. Most job openings are not advertised. However, classified advertisements in major newspapers, professional periodicals, trade journals, and social media sites do list a lot of job opportunities.

It is also helpful to follow up on news stories about the planned expansion or relocation of a company in your area. The change is likely to create jobs. You can follow up on the lead by contacting the company directly.

Employment Agencies. Private employment agencies have contacts that can reduce the time it takes to find a job, but there are often fees involved and other strings attached. It is usually in the agency's interest to place you as fast as possible, not to find your ideal job. The agency's loyalty is to the employer, because employers pay the bills and may be steady customers. It has been estimated that private agencies place less than 5 percent of the people entering the job market and about 15 percent of people changing jobs. The state and federal governments also sponsor employment services.

Networking. The majority of all jobs, perhaps as many as 90 percent, are never formally advertised. Instead, they are filled by word of mouth. People hear about the job opening from their personal contacts and apply to the employer directly. Obviously, there is less competition for these jobs, and they may offer the greatest rewards. Studies indicate that people who get jobs through this hidden job market stay with them longer and tend to do better financially.

How do you go about tapping into these jobs? You must establish a growing network of personal contacts. Eventually, you will hear about unadvertised jobs and will meet the people who make decisions about hiring. You have already begun the process by talking to people in order to learn about their jobs. Each person you talk to will refer you to more people. The process continues until you get a job lead.

It is important to keep a record of everyone to whom you talk or are referred. In this way, you can keep track of all the details needed to follow up on every lead and to make an appropriate introduction in every interview. Your records should document every contact, including letters and telephone conversations and interviews.

COVER LETTERS AND THE RÉSUMÉ

Preparing a cover letter and résumé is the next step in the process. Your library will include a number of good sources to use in preparing these important items. Two particularly good books you may want to consult are:

The Résumé Builder, by John Komar
High Impact Résumés and Letters, by Robert Krannich and William Banis

Cover Letters

The cover letter acts as a substitute for a personal introduction to a potential employer. It should convince the reader to look at your résumé and consider seeing you in person.

Try to address the letter to the person who has the power to make the hiring decision for the job in which you are interested. You can call the company directly to find out the names of the people who head specific departments or divisions. Try to learn the name of the individual who would be your boss if you got the job. A form letter directed to a title rather than an individual is likely to receive little attention.

Begin the letter with a reference to the person, their department, or their company. Prior research may have turned up a recently published article about the company. By mentioning this, you demonstrate the fact that you have done your homework, and you capture the reader's interest.

In the body of the letter, you must explain why you are interested in this particular organization and show how you can contribute to it. The key is to tie your skills, experience, education, and motivation to the particular position you are seeking. The goal is to convince the reader that you are worth interviewing.

Close the letter by requesting an interview. Express your eagerness for a discussion of the possibilities and mention that you plan to call in a week or two to set up an appointment. This naturally leads to a follow-up phone call. Even if you do not get the interview, send a thank you letter for the call. Keep reiterating your interest in the organization.

The Résumé

A résumé is a brief summary of your education, work history, career goals, and interests. You should submit a copy of your résumé with every letter expressing interest in a company, with every job application, and at every interview. Employers get their first impression of job candidates from their résumés and use them to screen applicants. You need a good résumé to sell yourself to employers and convince them you're worth talking to. An employer often gets hundreds of responses to an advertisement but will probably interview only five or six candidates.

When writing your résumé, always remember that people spend very little time looking at any one résumé. Someone sorting through a pile of résumés might glance at each one for 10 or 15 seconds. That is how long you have to persuade the employer that your résumé deserves to be followed up on. You cannot afford to include anything that gives a negative impression. Therefore, the way the résumé looks (typing, paper, spelling mistakes, layout) can be as important as the actual content. For all these reasons, you should devote a lot of time to crafting your résumé.

You may be tempted to use a résumé service because their products may seem more professional to you. However, résumé services produce a standardized, recognizable product, when the intent of your résumé is to set yourself apart from the crowd. You know yourself—both your goals and your past—better than anyone else in the world. That makes you the best person to produce a complete, honest, and representative résumé.

To save space and allow the reader to grasp the material quickly, you should write any descriptive items in concise phrases rather than complete sentences. Use action verbs such as *created*, *developed*, or *designed* to lead off these phrases. Make descriptions clear and easy to understand. Do not be too technical. Be specific and use numbers if possible.

Consider the potential employer as you decide what to include in your résumé. Stress those skills and accomplishments that the employer needs. If you are applying for different kinds of jobs, it may be best to make several versions of your résumé.

In trying to create the most impressive document possible, you should highlight your strong points and downplay your weaknesses. For example, a recent graduate typically will list their schooling first, because that is more impressive than a sparse work history. An older worker with lots of experience would normally put education credentials last. You can also choose different formats for your résumé in order to stress your strengths.

Once you have developed a final version of your résumé, check it against these criteria:

1. Is the résumé one page long? If you have used a second page, is there a compelling reason for it?
2. Are there any spelling, typing, or grammatical errors?
3. Have you presented the information accurately and honestly?
4. Have you included any irrelevant information that might distract the reader?
5. Have you left out any important information?
6. Have you accounted for each period of time? Are your accomplishments listed in reverse chronological order, starting with the most recent?
7. Does the résumé stress your strengths and your accomplishments? Is the content tailored to support your career objective?
8. Is the writing concise and easily understood?
9. Is your format consistent throughout? Are your indentations, underlinings, and use of capital letters the same for every entry?
10. Is it attractive to look at? Does it appear professional?

Once you have prepared the final version of your résumé, you may wish to have a professional typist or word-processing service prepare copies to be sent to prospective employers. These are more expensive options, but in some cases, a more impressive looking résumé is worth the additional cost.

THE INTERVIEW

A strong résumé may get you an interview, but only a good interview can get you a job. Employers make their final decisions based on how you impress them in person. During an interview, you are judged not only on your experience but also on your social skills, your ability to think on your feet, your personality, and many other items. Therefore, you must always remember that you are trying to demonstrate more than your job competence during an interview. You also want to convey your honesty, enthusiasm, motivation, responsibility, ability to follow instructions, and all the other intangibles that the employer is looking for. To make the best possible impression, you must be aware of your appearance, your body language, and the way you treat the secretaries, as well as what you say in response to the interviewer's questions.

The Questions

Interviewers routinely ask the same types of questions, although the order and phrasing vary widely. Typical questions include these:

1. Why do you want to work for our company?
2. What would you like to be doing ten years from now? Do you think you will achieve your goals?
3. Why did you choose the particular college you attended? What did you enjoy most about school? What were some of your favorite courses?
4. What is the accomplishment of which you are proudest?
5. What are your strengths and weaknesses?

Answer the questions positively, stressing your accomplishments wherever possible by giving examples from your past. Try to keep some particular job in mind, and tailor your answers for that job. The goal is to convince the interviewer that you can make a contribution to the company.

When you respond to questions during an interview, answer them completely, but do not dominate the conversation to the exclusion of the interviewer. Try to be a good listener as well as a talker. Use examples from your experience to show how you can be of value to the employer. In general, the best job candidates are the ones who know about the company, have specific career goals, ask good questions, are articulate, and have good social skills.

Always address the interviewer by name during the interview. Try to project enthusiasm, sincerity, honesty, and a sense of humor. Always thank the interviewer for their time and help in answering your questions.

Finally, never leave an interview without getting a commitment about when you will hear from the employer. Find out what the next step in the employment process is and how long it usually takes.

After the Interview

After each interview, write a letter thanking the interviewer. This will demonstrate basic courtesy, help you be remembered, and show a little extra enthusiasm for the job. In addition, it will provide an opportunity to add any information that you forgot to mention in the interview, to correct a wrong impression, or to re-emphasize your qualifications.

Table A.2 Selected Flight-related Job Titles with the Airlines

Job Title	Description
Captain	Commands the aircraft and is responsible for the safety of its passengers, crew, and cargo. Normally requires an Air Transport Pilot rating from the FAA. With the assistance of the first officer, the captain must run a check on all instruments, controls, and equipment. After clearance from air traffic control, the captain must follow the established takeoff pattern until cruising altitude is attained. Once airborne, periodic position reports are made with the appropriate air traffic control route center, as are frequent navigational changes. The captain must have a thorough knowledge of operational policies and regulations, aircraft systems, engines, instruments, radio equipment, routes, airports, and weather conditions to effectively plan a flight. In addition, the pilot-in-command must be highly skilled in the takeoff, landing, and airborne operation of the aircraft, as well as the methods of navigation.
First officer (co-pilot)	Assists the captain in the operation of the aircraft by monitoring the flight instruments, handling radio communications, watching for air traffic, and taking over the flight controls when directed by the captain. At a minimum, the co-pilot normally will have a Commercial Pilot license with an instrument rating.
Second officer (flight engineer)	Given the advancement of aircraft technology, there are fewer flight engineers today than there were in previous decades. However, there are still many aircraft operators requiring flight engineers. Makes a walk-around inspection of the aircraft, checking approximately 200 items. Oversees fueling operations, reviews mechanics' reports, and assists the captain and first officer with the preflight cockpit check. The second officer also monitors engines, fuel consumption, and the heating, pressurization, hydraulic, electrical, and air conditioning systems. Flight engineers or second officers troubleshoot and, if possible, repair faulty equipment in flight, check and maintain aircraft log books, report mechanical difficulties to the maintenance crew chief, and make a final postflight inspection of the aircraft. This position requires the same licensing requirements as the first officer, including a Flight Engineer license from the FAA. Smaller carriers do not fly this position.

(Continued)

Table A.2 (Continued)

Job Title	Description
Flight instructor	Primary responsibility is to instruct pilot personnel undergoing classroom, simulator, and in-flight training in the carrier's aircraft. Flight instructors develop and present courses, as may be required, on such topics as meteorology, navigation, and airplane systems, performance, and operations. They prepare progress and grade reports on assigned trainees, evaluating their ability to perform in accordance with company and FAA standards. In addition to performing the duties of a ground instructor, a flight instructor is responsible for training pilots in normal and emergency operating procedures, system troubleshooting, and crew coordination for new-hire flight engineers, second officers, and other flight officers. This training is conducted in flight simulators and in aircraft in flight. Flight instructors must maintain FAA Flight Engineer licenses and fly on-line as instructor/observers to retain current qualifications.
Flight dispatcher	In cooperation with the pilot, furnishes a flight plan that enables the aircraft to arrive at its destination on schedule with the maximum payload and the lowest operating cost. The flight dispatcher considers en-route and destination weather, winds aloft, alternative destinations, fuel requirements, altitudes, and traffic flow. The flight dispatcher's signature, along with that of the pilot, releases the aircraft for flight. This individual maintains constant watch on all flights dispatched and is the go-between for the pilot and ground service personnel. The flight dispatcher keeps all personnel informed concerning the status of the flight and must be familiar with navigation facilities over airline routes and at airports, as well as with takeoff, cruising, and landing characteristics of all types of aircraft operated by the airline. An FAA Flight Dispatcher license is required.
Meteorologist	Analyzes weather data and prepares weather reports for the flight dispatcher, pilots, and other airline personnel concerned with weather information. This individual also assists the flight dispatcher in preparing flight plans.
Flight attendant	Role revolves around two major responsibilities: safety and service. The safety of passengers might involve emergency procedures necessary because of an aircraft accident during takeoff or landing; this would include guiding passengers to exits in a calm, professional manner. It might also mean simple first-aid procedures or rescuing a victim from choking. It always includes instructing passengers in the emergency use of oxygen, in the location of emergency exits, and in the use of life vests if the aircraft flies over water. Service is an extension of the flight attendant's role in marketing. This includes such customer relations activities as soothing nervous or irritated passengers and responding to customers' needs and concerns. Flight attendants provide food and beverage services—from a modest snack service on short-haul flights to a full-course meal on long-haul flights.
Flight operations coordinator	Monitors the progress of aircraft and crews en route; receives and relays reports of delays due to weather and mechanical problems; notifies operations personnel regarding delays or changes; and gives orders for substitution of aircraft when required. The coordinator is involved with diversions of flights to alternative airports and monitors weather factors affecting air traffic, turnarounds, estimated time of arrival, and unscheduled stops. This individual also works closely with schedule planning personnel in developing the system schedule plan and with crew scheduling personnel in considering pilot availability to meet schedule changes.

Table A.3 Selected Maintenance-related Job Titles with the Airlines

Job Title	Description
Avionics technician	Tests, maintains, and produces aviation electronics, including jet engines and flight-control circuitry.
Power plant mechanic	Maintains the aircraft engines, including dismantling, inspecting, assembling, and testing. A jet aircraft can be completely overhauled in less than a week at a large carrier's overhaul facility. The airplane is stripped of all removable units, which are then refurbished, reassembled, checked, tested, and inspected on an around-the-clock schedule. Jet engines are broken down and all parts are cleaned and inspected. If suitable for reuse, parts are thoroughly reconditioned. After being reassembled, engines are tested in test cells to ensure their complete functional reliability before they are put back on the line. An FAA Airframe and Powerplant license is required.
Accessory overhaul mechanic	Responsible for overhauling and testing hydraulic, pneumatic, fuel, and water components, mechanical activators, and landing gears. Mechanics work on major systems, such as hydraulic units used to power landing gear and cabin air compressors. An FAA Airframe and Powerplant license is required.
Sheet metal mechanic	Responsible for a wide variety of aircraft components, from simple clips and brackets to oil cooler and heat exchanger units; from trim tab devices to complete control surfaces such as ailerons and rudders. These individuals also overhaul jet engine pod parts, maintain all pressure vessels, and make patterns and cast dies for stamping contoured parts. Line sheet metal mechanics perform structural repairs, both in overhaul duties and in the repair of airframes and their component parts. Shop mechanics in sheet metal perform such duties as template layout, set-back, heat treatment, normalizing, annealing, and fabrication. An FAA Airframe and Powerplant license is required.
Electrical mechanic	Responsible for the repair, overhaul, and testing of electrical units ranging from generators, motors, valves, activators, relays, thermo switches, fire detectors, and harnesses to coffee makers. Line electrical mechanics maintain working systems, fuel quantity calibration checks, lighting, and power components. An FAA Airframe and Powerplant license is required.
Instrument technician	Installs, tests, repairs, and overhauls all aircraft, engine, and navigational instruments. These include gyro horizons, altimeters, air speed and rate-of-climb indicators, tachometers, fuel flow meters, temperature indicators, compasses, pressure gauges, and other types of instruments. An FAA Airframe and Powerplant license is required.
Radio technician	Installs, maintains, repairs, and tests all avionics (airborne electronics) equipment, such as transmitters and receivers, weather-mapping radar, navigational radio (VOR) and radar (Doppler), distance measuring equipment (DME), inertial guidance equipment, elements of the autopilot system, and in-flight entertainment systems. An FCC Second Class Radio license is required.

Table A.4 Selected Management- and Non-management-related Job Titles with the Airlines

Job Title	Description
Reservations agent	Handles telephone inquiries from travel agents, other carriers, and the general public regarding flight schedules, fares, and connecting flights and reserves seats and cargo space for customers. Using computerized reservations equipment, this individual keeps records of reservations and must be able to recommend services that fit customers' requirements and be familiar with routes and schedules of other airlines.
Customer service agent	Generally specializes in one or more of the two following areas. (1) Ticket counter—has contact with the traveling public, issuing tickets and answering inquiries regarding fares, schedules, and all aspects of international and domestic air travel. The agent also handles the check-in procedure for all customers and checks tickets before boarding the aircraft. (2) Operations—receives and transmits messages between the aircraft in-flight and terminal personnel; works with airport personnel in assigning gate positions; advises the flight crew of weather conditions, altimeter settings, and clearances; announces arrivals and departures; coordinates the activity of other personnel receiving and dispatching aircraft; and prepares important reports and charts concerning the weight, balance, and fueling of the aircraft.
Air freight agent (cargo agent)	Receives air freight shipments, weighs them, prepares shipping orders, and sends shipments on the way to their destination. The agent also audits domestic carrier freight bills, furnishes rate and route information, handles loss and damage claims, compiles statistics for monthly reports, and prepares correspondence to obtain correct freight rate classifications.
Sales representative (account executive)	Calls on travel agencies, commercial accounts, and government accounts to promote passenger travel and shipment of cargo. In this capacity, the sales rep explains the carrier's marketing plan, including current promotions, advertising strategy, and sales literature.
District sales manager	Administers the city ticket and reservation offices and promotes and develops airline passenger and cargo traffic in the district in accordance with the company's marketing goals and policies.
Accountant	Helps to prepare financial statements and corporate annual reports. Internal audit provides opportunities to conduct field audits of the carrier's expenditures. Revenue accounting has full responsibility for cash sales, credit, and interline sales transactions. Accounts payable is responsible for meeting the carrier's financial obligations to suppliers, and cost accounting allocates expenses to various departments. The budget department provides planning and analysis of the corporate financial position.
Budget analyst	Monitors actual expenditures against the budgeted figures. Specifically, this would include the design, implementation, and control of the company profit plan, capital, operating, and personnel budgets.

Job Title	Description
Marketing research analyst	Duties include traffic forecasting and analysis of company sales and marketing data research, as well as of competitors' marketing programs. This position is also involved in the development of marketing objectives and analysis of passenger preferences through the use of consumer research techniques.
Facilities offices	Participates in the planning and layout of airline facilities such as shops, hangars, planner and terminal facilities.
Industrial engineer	May be called upon to define and solve problems related to passenger and cargo service, aircraft maintenance and overhaul, material distribution, and management systems. Studies may deal with facility layout, material handling and control systems, equipment analysis, improved productivity, and cost reduction. Industrial engineers are often involved in studies to determine staffing needs at particular stations or within various departments.
Programmer	Applies modern electronic data-processing techniques to areas of airline operations ranging from flight scheduling, reservations, accounting, and payroll control to parts inventory, purchasing and inventory control, and scheduling of personnel and aircraft equipment.
Employment representative	Selects and hires new employees in all job classifications. Duties include recruiting, interviewing, application analysis and test interpretation, control of employment requirements, and frequent contacts with outside agencies and user departments. Representatives must have a thorough knowledge of company employment policies and procedures.
Instructor	Conducts workshops or classroom training for airline personnel on current procedures, regulations, methods, or equipment. Some management instructors teach courses in supervision or leadership, while others teach in technical programs directed toward aircraft and ground support equipment. Marketing instructors teach courses in sales, customer service, and public relations.
Buyer	Develops vendor sources in a particular area, such as aircraft materials, supplies, and services. There are fuel buyers, aircraft parts buyers, and uniform and office supplies buyers. These individuals work closely with the user departments in determining their needs and then solicit bids from suppliers and negotiate contracts. Buyers work closely with sales representatives to determine the quality of their products and ability to deliver. Buyers also need to analyze the inventory required and then establish reasonable, economical ordering procedures.

Table A.5 Selected Flight-Related Job Titles in General Aviation

Job Title	Description
Flight instructor	Teaches students to fly. The instructor demonstrates and explains two basic principles of flight—aerial navigation weather factors and flying regulations—both on the ground and in the air. The instructor demonstrates operation of aircraft and equipment in dual-controlled planes. He or she observes solo flights and determines each student's readiness to take examinations for license ratings. The instructor also assists advanced students in acquiring advanced ratings, such as commercial, instrument, multi-engine, and air transport ratings.
Corporate pilot	Flies aircraft owned by business and industrial firms, transporting company executives on cross-country flights to branch plants and business conferences. The pilot arranges for in-flight passenger meals and ground transportation at destinations and is responsible for supervising the servicing and maintenance of the aircraft and keeping aircraft records.
Air taxi pilot (charter pilot)	Flies fare-paying passengers "anywhere anytime" but usually for short trips over varying routes in single-engine or light twin-engine planes.
Commercial airplane or helicopter pilot	Performs a variety of flying jobs. If piloting a fixed-wing plane, the pilot may engage in such flying jobs as aerial photography, aerial advertising, sight-seeing, geological survey, fish and game census, highway patrol, or checks on federal airways and navigational aids. Helicopter pilots may fly on a regular schedule carrying workers and supplies to offshore oil rigs or may fly accident victims to a hospital heliport, lift heavy loads to tops of buildings or to remote mountain sites, rescue people stranded by floods, carry smoke jumpers to fight forest fires, or deliver Santa Claus to shopping center parking lots.
Patrol pilot	Flies cross-country at low altitudes along pipelines or power lines, checking for signs of damage, vandalism, and other conditions requiring repairs. Patrol pilots radio to headquarters the location and nature of repair jobs.
Agricultural pilot (aerial applicator)	Flies specially designed aircraft (including helicopters) to apply herbicides, insecticides, seeds, and fertilizers to crops, orchards, forests, fields, and swamps. Some jobs require doing aerial surveys of cattle and crops or fighting forest fires by dumping fire-retardant materials.
Ferry pilot	Flies new and used aircraft from manufacturing plants, aircraft leasing facilities, and other storage facilities to dealers and to private customers' home airports.
Test pilot	Flies newly designed and experimental aircraft to determine whether they operate according to design standards and makes suggestions for improvements. Production test pilots fly new planes as they come off assembly lines to make sure they are airworthy and ready to turn over to customers. Commuter airline test pilots flight-test airliners after major overhauls before the planes are put back into service. They also flight-test new aircraft to be sure they are up to airline standards before the airline accepts them from the manufacturer. Test pilots for the FAA fly FAA planes with experimental equipment aboard to test the performance of the equipment, or they fly FAA planes to test new kinds of ground-based navigational aids such as radar or runway lighting.
Line person	Employed by an FBO and responsible for meeting arriving aircraft, assisting pilots in tying down their aircraft, and performing other important duties in serving general aviation and airline customers. These duties include fueling and servicing aircraft. Line persons are usually young people who are interested in aviation and begin their aviation careers by building experience with aircraft under the guidance of a fixed-base operator.

Table A.6 Selected Job Titles in Airport Administration

Job Title	Description
Airport director	Responsible for the overall day-to-day operation of the airport. This individual directs, coordinates, and reviews, through subordinate supervisors, all aircraft operations, building and field maintenance, construction plans, community relations, financial matters, and personnel matters at the airport.
Assistant director, finance and administration	Responsible for all matters concerning finance, personnel, purchasing, facilities management, and office management.
Manager of community relations	Acts as the chief liaison officer between the airport and the surrounding community. In this capacity, he or she is responsible for all public relations activities, including the development of advertising and publicity concerning the airport. This individual is also responsible for handling all noise and other environmental matters.
Facilities chief	Establishes criteria and procedures for the administration of all airport property. In this capacity, the facilities chief is responsible for inventory control of all equipment and facilities. This individual also evaluates and makes recommendations concerning the most efficient use of airport property and coordinates with purchasing and legal staff concerning tenant and concessionaire leases.
Director of operations	Responsible for all airside and landside operations, including security and aircraft rescue and fire-fighting operations. This individual recommends and implements all operational rules and procedures; supervises investigations of violations of airport regulations; prepares the annual operations budget; and participates in all programs relating to airport operations, such as height limits around airports and noise control.
Chief accountant	Responsible for financial planning, budgeting, accounting, payroll, and auditing. This individual administers all of the general accounts and is responsible for all receipts and disbursements.

Table A.7 Selected Job Titles with the Federal Aviation Administration

Job Title	Description
Air traffic control specialist (airport control tower)	Directs air traffic so it flows smoothly and efficiently. Controllers give pilots taxiing and takeoff instructions, air traffic clearances, and advice based on information received from the National Weather Service, air route traffic control centers, aircraft pilots, and other sources. They transfer off aircraft on instrument flights to the air route traffic control center (ARTCC) controller when the aircraft leaves their airspace and receive from the ARTCC control of aircraft on instrument flights flying into their airspace. They must be able to recall quickly registration numbers of aircraft under their control, the aircraft types and speeds, positions in the air, and the location of navigational aids in the area.
Air traffic control specialist (air route traffic control center)	Gives pilots instructions, air traffic clearances, and advice regarding flight conditions along the flight path, while the pilot is flying the federal airways or operating into airports without towers. The controller uses flight plans and keeps track of the progress of all instrument flights within the center's airspace. They transfer control of aircraft on instrument flights to the controller in the adjacent center when the aircraft enters the center's airspace. The controller also receives control of flights entering his or her area of responsibility from adjacent centers. They monitor the time of each aircraft's arrival over navigation fixes and maintains records of flights under their control.
Air traffic control specialist (flight service stations)	Renders preflight, in-flight, and emergency assistance to all pilots on request. Gives information about actual weather conditions and forecasts for airports and flight paths, relays air traffic control instructions between controllers and pilots, assists pilots in emergency situations, and initiates searches for missing or overdue aircraft.
Aviation safety inspector (operations)	Applies knowledge and skills acquired as an aviator (pilot, navigator, flight instructor, and so on) to develop and administer the regulations and safety standards pertaining to the operation of aircraft. Their primary duties include: (1) examining aviators for initial certification and continuing competence, (2) evaluating aviator training programs, equipment, and facilities, and (3) evaluating the operations aspect of programs of air carriers and other commercial aviation operations.
Aviation safety inspector (airworthiness)	Applies knowledge and skills acquired as repair person of aircraft and aircraft parts or avionics equipment to develop and administer regulations and safety standards pertaining to the air worthiness and maintenance of aircraft and related systems. Their primary duties include: (1) evaluating mechanics and repair facilities for initial certification and continuing adequacy, (2) evaluating mechanics training programs, (3) inspecting aircraft and related systems for airworthiness, and (4) evaluating the maintenance aspects of programs of air carriers and other commercial operators, including the adequacy of maintenance facilities, equipment, and procedures; the competence of personnel; the adequacy of the program or schedule for periodic maintenance and overhauls; and the airworthiness of aircraft.

Job Title	Description
Aviation safety inspector (manufacturing)	Applies knowledge and skills pertaining to the design and production of aircraft, aircraft parts, and avionics equipment to develop and administer regulations and safety standards pertaining to the original airworthiness of aircraft, aircraft parts, and avionics equipment. Their primary duties include: (1) inspecting prototype or modified aircraft, aircraft parts, and avionics equipment for conformity with design specifications, (2) inspecting production operations, including equipment, facilities, techniques, and quality control programs for capability to produce the aircraft or parts in conformance with design specifications and safety standards, and (3) making original airworthiness determinations and issuing certificates for all civil aircraft, including modified, import, export, military surplus, and amateur-built aircraft.
Airspace system inspector pilot	Conducts in-flight inspections of ground-based air navigational facilities to determine whether they are operating correctly. This individual pilots multi-engine, high-performance jet aircraft with specially installed, ultrasophisticated computerized equipment to serve as a flying electronic laboratory on day and night flights, under both visual and instrument flight rules, recording and analyzing facility performance and reporting potential hazards to air navigation for correction. The pilot assists in accident investigations by making special flight tests of any FAA navigational aids involved. They maintain liaison with aviation interests regarding the installation, operation, and use of their navigation facilities but are mostly involved with the FAA personnel who maintain the navigational aids.
Flight test pilot	Checks the airworthiness of aircraft through inspection, flight testing, and evaluation of flight performance, engine operation, and flight characteristics of either prototype aircraft or modifications of production aircraft and aircraft components that are presented for FAA-type certification. The flight test pilot supervises FAA-designated flight-test representatives and participates in investigations of accidents and violations of the federal air regulations.

Table A.8 Selected Job Titles in Manufacturing

Job Title	Description
Pricing analyst specialist	Knowledgeable about pricing techniques, cost estimating, cost proposal development, and negotiation. Pricing analysts must have the ability to evaluate major cost proposals and prepare an estimating rationale.
Specifications	Plans, estimates, and performs uniform specifications efforts for military and commercial programs and proposals. A talent for engineering writing is called for, as well as the ability to compile accurate specifications. The specifications specialist receives input from various sources and is responsible for organizing, editing, and developing formats for reports, proposals, and manuals from rough draft to final publication.
Product training specialist	Aids in the formulation of requirements for large-scale military training programs. Designs textbooks, visual aids, and training films. Product training specialists prepare and deliver formal lectures in the operation and maintenance of large-scale data-processing and sensor systems in the aerospace field or in the operation of various guidance and control systems for aircraft or spacecraft.
Aeronautical engineer	Designs, develops, and tests aircraft, missiles, rockets, space vehicles, and the parts and components of these vehicles or weapons. These individuals do technical sketching, test equipment, and interpret information from reports and statistical data. They construct and evaluate aircraft and spacecraft engines and develop fuel systems and avionics equipment. Aeronautical engineers evaluate the effects of stress on aircraft, spacecraft, and missiles during flight.
Applications programmer	Writes codes for engineers who use computers to perform calculations and simulations. Encodes detailed instructions for processing data in various computer languages. Applications programmers program robots to assemble aircraft parts and components. They work closely with aeronautical engineers in designing engineering applications to computer programs.
Performance analyst	Studies aerodynamic configuration to forecast variations in performance. Predicts operation of systems and calculates performance characteristics of space and air vehicles, including lift, drag, speed, altitude, and atmospheric conditions. The performance analyst interprets propulsion and weight information and determines effects of design parameters.
Sales manager (airline)	Requires in-depth experience in marketing aircraft, from determining airline requirements to coordinating sales activities. Responsibilities include preparing and executing aircraft sales presentations after evaluating a customer's financial and related data, providing market support staff with relevant market research for critical and comprehensive analysis, and developing and maintaining close ties with key airline management personnel.

Job Title	Description
Technical sales manager	Responsible for the production of all technical presentations and evaluation studies and assists in the development of sales strategies. This individual is also required to provide input during detailed negotiations and to assist in customer demonstrations.
Aircraft analyst	Provides supporting data in the preparation of technical proposals and presentations. Researches competitive data, performs customer-requested analysis and comparisons of a variety of aircraft products, maintains and updates competitive aircraft and performance data, and often accompanies sales representatives on selected presentations to answer customer inquiries regarding technical aspects of aircraft.

GLOSSARY

This glossary includes all Key Terms appearing at the ends of the chapters, as well as many other terms used in the text and others of significance in air transportation. The definitions are meant to be brief and straightforward rather than technically precise and all-inclusive.

AAM Advanced Air Mobility helps emerging aviation technologies to safely move people and cargo in an air transportation system.

Accounts payable the unpaid balance of amounts collected for transportation, furnished by other collections as agent, and other open accounts payable.

Accrued federal income taxes accruals for currently payable federal income taxes.

Acquisition costs the cost of an aircraft itself plus spare parts, ground equipment needed, maintenance and flight training required, and the cost of the money itself.

ADMA (Aviation Distributors and Manufacturers Association) a trade organization composed of large fixed-base operators and manufacturers of aircraft components.

Administration a major functional area, such as marketing, flight operations, or personnel. Individual departments fall under a major administration.

Aerial application those activities that involve the discharge of materials from aircraft in flight for food and fiber production and health control.

Aeronautical Radio, Inc. see **ARINC**.

Aeronautics the art and science of operating aircraft.

Aerospace employment an annual average calculated as one-twelfth of monthly estimates of the total number of persons employed during a designated pay period by the aircraft and missile and space industries, plus estimated aerospace-related employment in the communications equipment and instruments industries and in certain other industries.

Aerospace Industries Association of America see **AIA**.

Aerospace industry the industry engaged in research, development, and manufacture of aerospace systems, including manned and unmanned aircraft; missiles, space launch vehicles, and spacecraft; propulsion, guidance, and control units for all of the foregoing; and a variety of airborne and ground-based equipment essential to the testing, operation, and maintenance of flight vehicles.

Aerospace Maintenance and Regeneration Group (AMARG) the world's largest boneyard for retired commercial and military aircraft located at Davis-Monthan Air Force Base near Tucson, Arizona.

Aerospace sales the AIA estimate of aerospace industry sales, developed by summing (1) the Department of Defense (DOD) expenditures for procurement of aircraft and missiles, (2) estimates of DOD expenditures for research and development of aircraft and missiles, (3) NASA expenditures for research and development, (4) outlays for space activities by the DOD and other U.S. government departments and agencies, (5) net sales of aerospace products to nongovernment sources, including civil aircraft products (domestic sales and exports), commercial sales of space-related equipment, and exports of missiles and military aircraft, and (6) nonaerospace sales of major aerospace companies. (See also **Sales, aerospace**.)

AFA Association of Flight Attendants is a union representing flight attendants in the U.S.

Affinity group a group of travelers with similar interests, such as bridge players, alumni from a particular school, members of the clergy, college professors, or members of a horticultural society.

Aging refers to the life-cycle of the aircraft including technical, economic, and financial aging.

AIA (Aerospace Industries Association of America) a trade association of the major manufacturers of aerospace systems and components (formerly Aircraft Industries Association).

Airborne speed the average speed of an aircraft while airborne, in terms of great-circle airport-to-airport distance. It is calculated by dividing the airport-to-airport distance, in statute miles, by the number of actual airborne hours. Often called *wheels-off, wheels-on speed*.

Air cargo the total volume of freight, mail, and express traffic transported by air. It includes freight commodities of all kinds, including small-package counter services, express and priority reserved freight and express services, and all classes of mail transported for the U.S. Postal Service.

Air Cargo, Inc. a service organization owned by the scheduled U.S. airlines to provide local air freight pick-up and delivery, air/truck and container pick-up and delivery, and loading and unloading.

Air carriers the commercial system of air transportation, consisting of domestic and international certificated and charter carriers.

Air commerce the carriage by aircraft of persons or property for compensation or hire, the carriage of mail by aircraft, or the operation or navigation of aircraft in the conduct or furtherance of a business or vocation.

Aircraft all airborne vehicles supported either by buoyancy or by dynamic action. Used in this text in a restricted sense to mean an **airplane**—any winged aircraft, including helicopters but excluding gliders and guided missiles.

Aircraft and traffic servicing expenses compensation of ground personnel for their expenses incurred on the ground to protect and control the in-flight movement of aircraft, to schedule and prepare aircraft operational crews for flight assignment, to handle and service aircraft while in line operation, and to service and handle traffic on the ground after issuance of documents establishing the air carrier's responsibility to provide air transportation, and for their in-flight expenses of handling and protecting all nonpassenger traffic, including passenger baggage.

Aircraft departure, scheduled a takeoff scheduled at an airport, as set forth in published schedules.

Aircraft engine, turbine an engine incorporating as its chief element a turbine rotated by expanded gases. It consists essentially, in its most usual form, of a rotary air compressor with an air intake, one or more combustion chambers, a turbine, and an exhaust outlet. Aircraft engines of this type have their power applied mainly either as jet thrust (turbojet or turbofan) or as shaft power to rotate a propeller (turboprop).

Aircraft grounding a voluntary determination by a carrier or an order from the Federal Aviation Administration to refrain from flying a particular type of aircraft, as a result of suspected or actual malfunction of such aircraft, until the cause can be determined and appropriate corrective action taken. The term is also used to refer to occasional inability of an individual aircraft to operate due to weather conditions or minor mechanical malfunction, or to a voluntary decision by a carrier to refrain from flying certain aircraft for reasons other than mechanical malfunctions.

Aircraft hour, airborne the airborne hours of an aircraft, computed from the moment it leaves the ground until it touches the ground at the next point of landing. Often referred to as *wheels-off, wheels-on time.*

Aircraft hour, block-to-block the time elapsed from the moment an aircraft first moves under its own power for purposes of flight until it comes to rest at the next point of landing. Block time includes taxi time before takeoff and after landing, takeoff and landing time, and airborne time. Also referred to as *ramp-to-ramp hours.*

Aircraft hour, revenue an aircraft's airborne hours in revenue service, computed from the moment it leaves the ground until it touches the ground at the next point of landing.

Aircraft hour, revenue per aircraft per day (carrier's equipment) the average number of hours of productive use per day in revenue service of a reporting carrier's equipment. Determined by dividing aircraft days assigned to the carrier's equipment into revenue aircraft hours minus revenue hours on other carriers' interchange equipment plus total hours by other carriers on the carrier's interchange equipment. (See also **Utilization**.)

Aircraft hour, revenue per aircraft per day (carrier's routes) the average number of hours of productive use per day in revenue service on a reporting carrier's routes. Determined by dividing aircraft days assigned to service the carrier's routes into revenue aircraft hours.

Aircraft industry the industry primarily engaged in the manufacture of aircraft, aircraft engines and parts, aircraft propellers and parts, and auxiliary aircraft parts and equipment. A sector of the aerospace industry.

Aircraft, large an aircraft having a maximum passenger capacity of more than 66 seats or a maximum payload capacity of more than 18,000 pounds.

Aircraft, leased (rental) aircraft obtained from (or furnished to) others under lease or rental arrangements.

Aircraft miles (plane miles) the miles computed in airport-to-airport distances for each interairport hop actually completed, whether or not performed in accordance with the scheduled pattern.

Aircraft operation an aircraft arrival at or departure from an airport with FAA air traffic control service. There are two types of operations—local and itinerant. **Local operations** are performed by aircraft that (1) operate in the local traffic pattern or within sight of the tower, (2) are known to be departing for, or arriving from, a location within a 20-mile radius of the control tower, or (3) execute simulated instrument approaches or low passes at the airport. **Itinerant operations** are all aircraft arrivals and departures other than local operations.

Aircraft Owners and Pilots Association (AOPA) the principal representative of individual aircraft owners and operators before Congress, the administration, and its regulatory agencies, such as the Federal Aviation Administration; has over 200,000 members.

Aircraft, passenger/cargo an aircraft configured to accommodate passengers and cargo in the above-deck cabin.

Aircraft, regular body a generic and commonly used term applied to jet aircraft, especially a turbofan with a fuselage diameter of less than 200 inches whose propulsive power is supplied by turbine engines with a per-engine thrust of less than 30,000 pounds (for example, Boeing 707 and 727, McDonnell-Douglas DC-8 and DC-9).

Aircraft revenue hours see **Aircraft hour, revenue**.

Aircraft, short takeoff and landing see **STOL**.

Aircraft, small an aircraft having a maximum passenger capacity of 66 seats or less, or a maximum payload capacity of 18,000 pounds.

Aircraft, supersonic transport (SST) a transport aircraft capable of a normal cruising speed greater than the speed of sound (741 mph at sea level).

Aircraft, turbine an aircraft with either turbojet, turbofan, turboprop, or turboshaft engines.

Aircraft, turbofan (fan jet) an aircraft powered by a turbojet engine whose thrust is that of a fan-jet aircraft. The turbofan engine has either an oversized low-pressure compressor at the front with part of the flow bypassing the rest of the engine (front fan) or a separate fan driven by a turbine stage (aft fan).

Aircraft, turbojet an aircraft powered by a gas turbine engine incorporating a turbine-driven compressor to take in and compress the air for the combination of fuel, with the gases of combustion (or heated air) used both to rotate the turbine and to create a thrust-producing jet.

Aircraft, turbo-propeller (turboprop, prop jet) an aircraft powered by a gas turbine engine in which output is taken as shaft power to drive a propeller via a reduction gear; it also has a small residual jet thrust.

Aircraft type a distinctive model, as designated by the manufacturer.

Aircraft, vertical/short takeoff and landing see **V/STOL**.

Aircraft, vertical takeoff and landing see **VTOL**.

Aircraft, wide-body a generic and commonly used term applied to jet aircraft (turbofans) with a fuselage diameter exceeding 200 inches whose per-engine thrust is greater than 30,000 pounds (for example, Boeing 747, McDonnell-Douglas DC-10, Lockheed L-1011).

Air express small packages that usually have a higher priority of carriage than air freight.

Airframe the structural components of an airplane, including the fuselage, empennage, wings, landing gear, and engine mounts, and excluding such items as engines, accessories, electronics, and other parts that may be replaced from time to time.

Air freight large packages and cargo that do not have as high a priority as air express.

Air freight forwarder any indirect air carrier that assembles and consolidates or provides for assembling and consolidating property for shipment by air. They are also responsible for the transportation of property from the point of receipt to the point of destination and utilize for the whole or any part of such transportation the services of a direct air carrier.

Airline Clearing House a corporation, wholly owned by the larger certificated airlines, through which the interline accounts of certificated and commuter airlines are settled on a net basis each month.

Airlines see **Air carriers**.

Airline Tariff Publishing Company (ATPCO) an electronic clearinghouse for fare information and changes; jointly owned and funded by 30 U.S. and foreign carriers.

Air mail the first of the air cargo services, and an important factor in the formation of air transportation in the United States.

Air movement airport-to-airport movement.

Air Navigation Service Providers (ANSP) the organization that separates aircraft on the ground or in flight in a dedicated block of airspace on behalf of a state or a number of states. ANSP are either government departments, state owned companies, or privatized organizations.

Airport an area of land or water that is used or intended to be used for the landing and takeoff of aircraft, including its buildings and facilities, if any.

Air shuttle see **Shuttle service**.

Air taxi any common carrier for hire that holds an air taxi operating certificate and primarily operates small aircraft without fixed routes.

Air Traffic Conference (ATC) a part of the Air Transport Association, which represents the U.S. scheduled airline industry. The ATC is made up of a number of committees and subcommittees whose members are representatives from the member carriers. Improved service, streamlined procedures, and reduced costs are all goals sought by the members of the ATC. One of the major functions performed by the conference is the approval of travel agents who do business with the airlines.

Air traffic control a service operated by the appropriate authority to promote the safe, orderly, and expeditious flow of air traffic.

Air Transport Association of America see **ATA**.

Air transportation, foreign the carriage by aircraft of persons or property as a common carrier for compensation or hire or the carriage of mail by aircraft in commerce between a place in the United States and any place outside thereof, whether such commerce moves wholly by aircraft or partly by aircraft and partly by other forms of transportation.

Air transportation industry all civil flying performed by the certificated air carriers and general aviation.

Air transportation, interstate the carriage by aircraft of persons or property as a common carrier for compensation or hire, or the carriage of mail by aircraft in commerce between a place in any state of the United States or the District of Columbia and a place in any other state of the United States or the District of Columbia, or between places in the same state of the United States through the airspace over any place outside thereof, or between places in the same territory or possession of the United States or the District of Columbia, whether such commerce moves wholly by aircraft or partly by aircraft and partly by other forms of transportation.

Air transportation, intrastate the carriage by aircraft of persons or property as a common carrier for compensation or hire wholly within the same state of the United States.

Air transportation, overseas the carriage by aircraft of persons or property as a common carrier for compensation or hire or the carriage of mail by aircraft in commerce between a place in any state of the United States or the District of Columbia and any place in a territory or possession of the United States, or between a place in a territory or possession of the United States and a place in any other territory or possession of the United States, whether such commerce moves wholly by aircraft or partly by aircraft and partly by other forms of transportation.

Airworthiness certificate a certificate attesting to the fact that each airplane conforms to the type certificate and is safe to fly; the ability of an aircraft to fly safely through a range of operations is determined by the Federal Aviation Administration.

All-cargo airline a carrier that operates a variety of cargo services.

American Society of Travel Agents see **ASTA**.

AOPA see **Aircraft Owners and Pilots Association**.

Appropriation (federal budget) an act of Congress authorizing an agency to incur obligations and make payments out of funds held by the Department of the Treasury.

Arbitration the settlement of disputed questions, whether of law or fact, by one or more arbitrators by whose decision the parties agree to be bound.

ASMs see **Available seat-miles**.

Asset property or property rights owned by a business that is valuable, either because it will be converted into cash or because it is expected to benefit future operations, and that was acquired at a measurable cost. A **current asset** is an asset that is either currently in the form of cash or is expected to be converted into cash within a short period, usually one year. A **fixed asset** is a tangible property of relatively long life that generally is used in the production of goods and services.

Assets the items on the balance sheet of a business showing the book value of its resources.

ASTA (American Society of Travel Agents) a trade association of the travel agency industry.

Astronautics the art and science of designing, building, and operating manned or unmanned space objects.

ATA (Air Transport Association of America) a trade association of the U.S. certificated-route air carriers.

ATC air traffic control. (See also **Air Traffic Conference**.)

ATPCO see **Airline Tariff Publishing Company**.

Authority the power to make decisions, command, and delegate responsibility to others.

Automatic market entry under the Airline Deregulation Act of 1978, the right of an air carrier to apply to the CAB for permission to engage in nonstop service between any one pair of points in interstate or overseas air transportation after the first business day of each of the calendar years 1979, 1980, and 1981. However, no air carrier could apply if any other air carrier had filed written notice to the board to preclude any other carrier from obtaining that same authority. An air carrier could protect only one pair of points by precluding all other carriers from obtaining authority between them.

Available seat-miles (ASMs) the total of the products of aircraft miles and number of available seats on each flight stage, representing the total passenger-carrying capacity offered. (See also **Seat miles, available**.)

Available seats the number of seats installed in an aircraft (including seats in lounges), exclusive of any seats not offered for sale to the public by the carrier, and inclusive of any seat sold.

Available seats per aircraft the average number of seats available for sale to passengers, derived by dividing the total available seat-miles by the total aircraft revenue miles in passenger service.

Available ton-miles the aggregate of the products of the aircraft miles flown on each flight stage multiplied by the available aircraft capacity tons for that flight stage, representing the traffic-carrying capacity offered.

Aviation Distributors and Manufacturers Association see **ADMA**.

Aviation gasoline a high-grade (high-octane) gasoline used as a fuel by all piston-engine aircraft, in contrast to the jet fuel (generally kerosene) used in turbine-powered aircraft. This piston-engine fuel is also referred to as *avgas*. (See also **jet fuel**.)

Backlog the sales value of orders accepted (supported by legal documents) that have not yet passed through the sales account.

Balance sheet a statement of assets, liabilities, and stockholder equity (or equivalent interest of individual proprietors or partners) as of a particular date.

Bankruptcy a procedure by which a company unable to pay debts may be declared bankrupt, after which all assets in excess of the exemption claims are surrendered to the court for administration and distribution to creditors and the debtor is given a discharge that releases it from the unpaid balance on most debts.

Barnstormers pilots who toured the country after World War I putting on air shows and giving rides to local people.

Barriers to entry term used in reference to oligopolistic industries to denote the difficulty firms have in entering the industry. The barriers can be in the form of capital requirements, regulatory requirements, technical personnel required, and so forth.

Big Four the four largest major carriers (American, Eastern, TWA, and United). These carriers were first officially termed the Big Four in the 1949 Annual Report of the Civil Aeronautics Board.

Bilateral agreement an agreement or treaty between two nations contracting for reciprocal international air service, such service to be operated by designated carriers of each nation. The agreement may include provisions for the type of aircraft used, intermediate stops en route, aircraft airworthiness, taxation-free fuel, and arbitration procedures. It is usually a standardized agreement used in negotiations for air transport between one nation and many others and allowing for the inclusion of different points and routes.

Blockspeed range diagram a diagram that shows the relationship of the average speed in statute miles per hour of an aircraft, between the time the aircraft first moves under its own power for purposes of flight until it comes to rest at the next point of landing, and the distance the aircraft can fly.

Boarding pass a document issued to a customer that contains their flight number, date, class of service, seat number, and special-services information. It is sometimes issued in exchange for a lifted flight coupon and used as the passenger's actual authority to board a flight.

Board of directors a group elected by stockholders to provide general guidance for a corporation.

Bond a promissory note under seal. In common use, a long-term debt obligation, particularly one issued to the general public.

Book value the dollar value of a company's assets minus its liabilities. Book value per share is the company's book value divided by the number of its common stock shares outstanding.

Break-even point that level of operations at which total expenses equal total revenue.

Brexit the withdrawal of the United Kingdom (U.K.) from the European Union (E.U.) in 2020.

Budget a plan of action expressed in figures. A financial plan indicating expected revenues and anticipated expenses for a specified period, such as a year, that can be used as a means of exercising financial control.

Business aircraft use in reference to general aviation aircraft, any use of an aircraft not for compensation or hire by an individual for the purpose of transportation required by a business in which the individual is engaged (personally flown).

Business-class service transport service aimed primarily at the international business traveler, to overcome the regulatory restraints on increasing normal economy (coach) fares on long-haul international markets; provides fewer amenities than first-class service but more than economy; also provides more comfortable and less congested seating than economy class.

CAB Civil Aeronautics Board.

Cabotage a foreign operator carrying passengers between two domestic points of another country.

CAM routes contract air mail routes. Early air mail routes were designated by the Post Office Department as CAM routes.

Capital money, goods, land, or equipment used to produce other goods or services. **Capital goods** are the tools or other productive agents by which resources are transformed into usable products.

Capital budgeting long-term planning for proposed capital outlays and their financing.

Capital gains or losses (operating property) gains or losses on retirements of operating property and equipment, flight equipment expendable parts, or miscellaneous materials and supplies when sold or otherwise retired in connection with a general retirement program and not as incidental sales performed as a service to others.

Capital lease see **Financial (capital) lease**.

Capital stock the declared money value of the outstanding stock of a corporation.

Capital, total owners' equities plus creditors' equities.

Cargo aircraft an aircraft expressly designed or converted to carry freight, express, and so forth, rather than passengers.

Cargo revenue ton-miles all traffic, other than passengers, times the miles transported in revenue service. Includes freight, express, mail, and excess baggage.

Cash general and working funds available on demand that are not formally restricted or earmarked for specific objectives.

Cash budget a schedule of expected cash receipts and disbursements.

Cash flow the amount of cash flowing in and out of a business in a given period.

CATO (combined airline ticket office) a ticket office staffed by the personnel from two or more air carriers.

Causal (model) forecasts the most sophisticated of the forecasting methods; these forecasts express the relevant causal relationships between variables mathematically. Examples include regression analysis, econometric models, and computer models.

Certificated air carrier one of a class of air carriers holding certificates of public convenience and necessity issued by the former CAB or the DOT authorizing the performance of scheduled air transportation over specified routes and a limited amount of nonscheduled operations. This general carrier grouping includes the all-purpose carriers (the so-called passenger/cargo carriers) and the all-cargo carriers and comprises all of the certificated airlines. Certificated air carriers are often referred to as *scheduled airlines*, although they also perform nonscheduled service.

Certificate of public convenience and necessity a certificate issued to an air carrier under Section 401 of the Federal Aviation Act of 1958 by the former CAB or the DOT authorizing the carrier to engage in air transportation. The certificate may specify certain designated routes and certain designated points or geographic areas to be served and any limitations and restrictions imposed on such service.

Chain of command a hierarchy of managers and subordinates.

Chain reaction effect the interrelationship among gate congestion, maintenance routing, and other factors that are affected by a single schedule change. In other words, one schedule change causes a chain reaction requiring many other schedule changes.

Charter (inclusive tour) the charter of the entire capacity of an aircraft or at least 40 seats (providing the remaining capacity of the aircraft is chartered by a person or persons authorized to charter aircraft) by a tour operator. The inclusive-tour charter is required to be a round trip with a minimum of three stops other than the point of origin and to be a minimum of seven days in duration, and its cost must include all accommodations and surface transportation.

Charter air carrier an air carrier holding a certificate of public convenience and necessity authorizing it to engage in charter air transportation.

Charter revenues revenues from nonscheduled air transport services in which the party receiving the transportation obtains exclusive use of an aircraft and the remuneration paid by such party accrues directly to, and the responsibility for providing transportation is that of, the accounting air carrier. Passenger charter revenues are those from charter flights carrying only passengers and their personal baggage. Freight charter revenues are those from charter flights carrying either freight only or passengers and freight simultaneously.

City-pair the origin and destination cities of an air trip.

City ticket office see **CTO**.

Classes of stations a term used in reference to the level of maintenance service provided at various stations throughout a carrier's route system. In descending order of capability, they include the carrier's maintenance base, major stations, service stations, and other stations.

Class of service the type of accommodations or fares offered on an airplane. Referred to as *reservation booking codes*.

Coach passenger revenue revenue from the air transportation of passengers at fares and quality of service below first-class service.

Coach service transport service established for the carriage of passengers at fares and quality of service below that of first-class service.

Code sharing marketing partnerships between regional carriers and major carriers that create an integrated service linking small communities and the national air transportation system. Both carriers in such a partnership share the same identification codes on airline schedules.

Collision avoidance systems electronic devices that warn pilots directly of potential conflicts with other aircraft and show them how to avoid them. One system presently being developed by the FAA is the Discrete

Address Beacon System (DABS), which is an improved transponder and will provide a data link for use with a ground-based anticollision system.

Columbia route the first major transcontinental air mail route between San Francisco and New York. Boeing Air Transport, the successful bidder on the western portion of the Columbia route, began service on July 1, 1927, between San Francisco and Chicago. National Air Transport, the successful bidder on the eastern portion, commenced operation on September 1, 1927.

Combination carrier an air carrier that provides passenger and cargo services.

Combined airline ticket office see **CATO**.

Commercial aviation in reference to general aviation flying, commercial use includes air taxi/commuter use, rental use, aerial application, aerial observation, and other work.

Commission the payment by airlines to a travel agent of specified amounts of money in return for the agent's sales of air transportation. It is expressed and paid by each carrier as a percentage of the value of the air transportation sold on that air carrier.

Committee system a group of individuals representing various administrations, departments, or regions who are officially delegated to perform a function, such as investigating, considering, reporting, or acting on a matter.

Common air carrier an air transportation firm that holds out its services for public hire.

Common fares an unusual application of normal fares: a specific fare applied to points other than those between which the fare is determined. For example, a passenger flying between Seattle and Milwaukee might pay the same fare as a passenger flying between Seattle and Chicago.

Common stock the ownership of the corporation divided into a specified number of shares, each representing equal participation in the affairs of the company.

Commuter air carrier a class of noncertificated air carriers (air taxi operators) that operate small aircraft (fewer than 66 seats) and perform at least five round trips per week between two or more points; publish flight schedules specifying times, days of the week, and places between which such flights are performed; or transport mail by air pursuant to a current contract with the U.S. Postal Service.

Competitive market any city-pair or pair of geographic areas served by more than one air carrier.

Computerized reservation system (CRS) a system that displays airline schedules and prices for use by agents in making reservations.

Constrained operating plan the system constraints (runway length and capacity, gate capacity, ground access, and so forth) that are placed on the carrier in the fleet-planning process.

Consumer-oriented period the airline marketing period starting in the early 1970s in which the carriers attempted to determine through marketing research techniques exactly what air travelers really wanted and then designed products and services to meet those wants.

Container rates special cargo rates for shippers using containers.

Controlling the evaluation of performance and, if necessary, correction of what is being done to ensure attainment of results according to plan.

Corporate aircraft use any use of an aircraft by a corporation, company, or other organization for the purpose of transporting its employers or property not for compensation or hire and employing professional pilots for the operation of the aircraft.

Corporate objectives major objectives established by the board of directors and senior management. Such objectives might include expected return on investment (ROI), profits after taxes, stockholder dividends, or targeted market share on a major route segment.

Correlation a statistical total that measures the degree of dependency between two or more variables and the average amount of change in one variable associated with a unit increase in another. In simple correlation, the dependent variable is related to only one independent variable. In multiple correlation, the dependent variable is related to two or more independent variables.

Craft union a labor union composed of workers in a particular trade, such as pilots, mechanics, flight attendants, or dispatchers. An "exclusively" organized union.

Cross-utilization the use of personnel in work outside of their normal job description—for example, mechanics used to sort baggage, or flight attendants serving as reservation or ticket agents.

Crowdfunding the use of small amounts of capital from a large number of individuals to finance a new business venture via an online service platform.

CRS see **Computerized reservation system**.

Cryptocurrency decentralized digital money supported by blockchain technology.

CTO (city ticket office) an airline ticket office generally located in the major business district of a large city.

Current assets cash and other resources expected to be realized in cash, sold, or consumed within one year. Includes cash, marketable securities, receivables, and inventories.

Current liabilities obligations the liquidation of which is expected to require the use, within one year, of current assets in the creation of other current liabilities. Includes accounts payable, unpaid taxes, and other debts within one year.

Current notes payable the face value of notes, drafts, acceptances, or other similar evidences of indebtedness payable on demand or within one year to other than associated companies, including the portion of long-term debt due within one year of the balance sheet date.

Current ratio a measure of liquidity obtained by dividing current assets by current liabilities. The higher the number, the more cash is on hand for short-term needs.

Current resources the quantity and quality of human and capital resources available, including present fleet, maintenance facilities, flight crews, mechanics, and so forth.

Customer any person to whom air transportation and related services are to be provided. Technically, a *customer* becomes a *passenger* only when he or she boards an airplane for a flight.

Debenture a type of bond that is generally not secured by any specific pledge of property as collateral. **Convertible debentures** give the holder the privilege of exchanging the holdings for securities of a different type, usually common stock.

Debt current and noncurrent liabilities; equities of creditors.

Debt financing current and noncurrent liabilities (equities of creditors) incurred from borrowing funds from commercial banks, insurance companies, and other sources.

Decentralization an extension of delegation generally from the home office to branch offices; the delegation of responsibility and authority away from a centralized unit.

Decision making the process of choosing between alternative courses of action.

Deferred charge debit balances in general clearing accounts, including prepayments chargeable against operations over a period of years, capitalized expenditures of an organizational or developmental character, and property acquisition adjustments.

Deferred credits credit balances in general clearing accounts, including premiums on long-term debt securities.

Deferred taxes certain taxes that companies are required to collect for various taxing authorities including federal excise and state sales taxes and payroll withholding of employee income taxes.

Deflators (constant dollars) multipliers used to reduce a price level to that comparable with the price level at a given time, offsetting the effect of inflation. The gross national product, in constant dollars, is arrived at by dividing components of the current dollar figures by appropriate price deflators.

De-hubbing strategies implemented to spread flights more evenly throughout the day allowing airlines to use their resources in a more efficient manner.

Delay a lack of timely movement that results in monetary loss to the shipper. It includes, but is not limited to, consequential or special damages and physical deterioration or damage to the goods that results from delay.

Delegation of authority the assignment of authority and duties to others at a lower organizational level.

Demand a schedule that shows the various amounts of a product or service that consumers are willing and able to purchase at various prices over a particular time period.

Denied-boarding compensation compensation paid to a passenger holding confirmed reserved space who arrives for carriage at the appropriate time and place but is denied seating. The passenger must have complied fully with the carrier's requirements as to ticketing, check-in, and reconfirmation procedures and be acceptable for transportation under the carrier's tariff.

Department a grouping of activities. Departments generally fall under administrations (for example, the advertising department falls under the marketing administration).

Departmentalization the practice of subdividing both people and functions into groups within an organization in order to gain the advantages of specialization.

Department of Transportation (DOT) an executive department of the U.S. government established by the Department of Transportation Act of 1966 for the purpose of developing national transportation policies and programs conducive to the provision of fast, safe, efficient, and convenient transportation at the lowest possible cost. The department consists of the secretary, the undersecretary, and the heads of the operating agencies, which include the Coast Guard, the Federal Aviation Administration, the Federal Railroad Administration, and several other administrative units.

Departure an aircraft takeoff from an airport.

Depreciation the general conversion of the depreciable cost of a fixed asset into an expense, spread over its remaining life. There are a number of methods of depreciation, all based on a periodic charge to an expense account and a corresponding credit to a reserve account.

Depreciation of flight equipment charges to expense for depreciation of airframes, aircraft engines, airframe and engine parts, and other flight equipment.

Deregulation the process of removing entry and price restrictions on airlines affecting, in particular, the carriers permitted to serve specific routes.

Design characteristics an aircraft's dimensions; weight profile, including such items as maximum zero-fuel weight and operator's empty weight; fuel capacity; type of power plants; systems (electrical, hydraulic, and environmental); seating configuration; containers and pallets; bulk volume; and total volume.

Determinants of demand those factors that affect demand. Price is generally considered the most important determinant of demand; however, other nonprice determinants include: (1) the preferences of passengers, (2) the number of passengers in a particular market, (3) the financial status and income levels of the passengers, (4) the prices of competitors and related travel expenses, and (5) passenger expectations with respect to future prices.

Determinants of elasticity those factors that change a consumer's responsiveness to price changes, including competition, distance flown, business versus pleasure travel, and time involved.

Developmental and preoperating cost costs accumulated and deferred in connection with alterations in operational characteristics, such as the development and preparation for operation of new routes and the integration of new types of aircraft or services.

Directing the process of assigning tasks and ordering, telling, and instructing subordinates what to do and perhaps how to do it.

Directionality the preponderance of air cargo traffic flowing between city-pairs.

Direct operating cost all expenses that are associated with and dependent on the type of aircraft being operated, including all flying expenses (such as flight crew salaries, fuel and oil, all maintenance and overhaul costs, and all aircraft depreciation expenses).

Diseconomies of scale see **Economies of scale**.

Dividends dividends payable, in cash or in stock, to preferred and common stockholders declared but not necessarily paid during the accounting period. The current liability is created by the declaration— the amount ordinarily being charged to retained earnings.

Division a specialized unit or grouping of activities within a department (for example, cost accounting might be a division of the general accounting department, which falls under the finance and property administration).

Domestic operations in general, operations within or between the 50 states of the United States and the District of Columbia.

DOT see **Department of Transportation**.

Earnings per share net earnings divided by the number of shares outstanding.

Earnings, retained the cumulative increase in stockholders' equity as a result of company operations.

Economies (diseconomies) of scale the decreases (increases) in a firm's long-run average costs as the size of its operations increases. The factors that give rise to economies of scale are: (1) greater specialization of resources, (2) more efficient utilization of equipment, (3) reduced unit costs of inputs, (4) opportunities for economic utilization of by-products, and (5) growth of auxiliary facilities. Diseconomies of scale may eventually set in, however, due to: (1) limitations of (or "diminishing returns" to) management in its decision-making function and (2) competition among firms in bidding up costs of limited inputs.

Economies of scope economies related to the number of points served by a carrier, as distinguished from *economies of scale*, which are achieved as a function of size.

Economy service in domestic operations, transport service established for the carriage of passengers at fares and quality of service below coach service.

Efficient use of capital the utilization of the latest technology available, which brings about economies of scale.

Elastic demand the demand if a given percentage change in price results in a larger percentage change in passengers carried (consumers are responsive). The coefficient of elasticity of demand is greater than 1. When demand is elastic, a price increase will reduce total revenue and a price decrease will raise total revenue.

Elasticity of demand the percentage change in quantity demanded resulting from a 1 percent change in price. Mathematically, the ratio of the percentage change in quantity demanded to the percentage change in price. In general, elasticity may be thought of as the responsiveness of changes in one variable to changes in another, where responsiveness is measured in terms of percentage changes.

Emergency board a special committee set up by the president upon recommendation of the National Mediation Board when, in their opinion, a strike by employees of one or more carriers might lead to a national emergency. The emergency board has 30 days to investigate the dispute and report its findings to the president.

Employee productivity output (in terms of some volume, such as flying hours or departures) versus input (number of employees). Generally, the average total number of employees divided into the indicated traffic and/or financial measures for the year.

Enplanements, passenger see **Passenger enplanements**.

Equipment trust financing a loan by a bank or group of banks to an air carrier for the purchase of equipment in which title remains with the banks, which are trustees of a series of certificates issued with the equipment as security. A number of certificates are paid off annually by the carrier.

Equipment turnaround time the length of time between an aircraft's arrival and departure. Generally, the time needed to prepare an aircraft for departure, including aircraft cleaning, fueling, en-route maintenance check, baggage loading, and food service.

Equity financing the sale of stocks and bonds in the capital market to the public.

Essential air service the threshold number of departures linking a community to the nationwide air transport network. Two round trips per day, five days a week, or the level of service provided on the basis of calendar year 1977 air carrier schedule, whichever is less, is the statutory minimum service.

eVTOL Electric Vertical Takeoff and Landing aircraft use electric power to hover, take off, and land vertically.

Exception rate a rate higher than the usual air freight rate that applies to certain types of shipments that require special handling (animals, for example).

Excess baggage passenger baggage in excess of free allowance. This excess is subject to a charge, which is called *excess baggage revenue*.

Express property transported by air under published air express tariffs filed with the Civil Aeronautics Board. Originally, *express* referred to the priority movement of parcel shipments moving on aircraft in conjunction with an agreement between the various air carriers and REA Express, Inc. Since the cessation of operations by REA Express in 1976, this term refers to the replacement services offered by the various air carriers.

Extra section an additional passenger-carrying flight, usually set up for one day only, to accommodate heavy customer demand.

FAA see **Federal Aviation Administration**.

Facility constraints operating limitations caused by inadequate runway length, gate positions, ticket counter space, and so forth.

Fare the amount per passenger or group of persons stated in the applicable tariff for the transportation thereof, including baggage unless the context otherwise requires.

Fare, coach (tourist) the tariff applicable to the transportation of a passenger or passengers at a quality of service below that of first-class service but higher than or superior to that of economy service.

Fare, discount a reduced fare designed to stimulate traffic volume. Discount fares are subject to one or more travel restrictions, such as minimum length of stay or applicability only on certain days of the week or only during a particular season, and are typically calculated as a percentage reduction from the normal full fare.

Fare, economy a charge for domestic air transportation at a level of service below that of coach service. The significant difference between coach and economy service is that the coach passenger receives a complimentary meal while the economy passenger has an option of purchasing a meal. Seating density in the economy area may be higher than in the coach area. In international air transportation, *economy fare* applies to second-class service or service just below that of first-class. It is synonymous with the term *coach fare* within the United States.

Fare, excursion a type of discount fare.

Fare, first-class the fare applicable to the transportation of a passenger or passengers for whom premium-quality services are provided.

FBO see **Fixed-base operator**.

Federal Aviation Administration (FAA) an independent agency of the U.S. government charged with controlling the use of U.S. airspace (by civil and military operators) to obtain the maximum efficiency and safety. Formerly the Federal Aviation Agency, it became part of the Department of Transportation in 1967 as a result of the Department of Transportation Act. The FAA is charged with regulating air commerce to promote its safety and development; achieving the efficient use of the navigable airspace of the United States; promoting, encouraging, and developing civil aviation; developing and operating a common system of air traffic control and air navigation for both civilian and military aircraft; and promoting the development of a national system of airports.

Feeder routes routes designed to "feed" traffic into the major trunk routes. After World War II, a number of smaller air carriers were established that became known as *local-service carriers* or *feeder lines*.

Field ticket office see **FTO**.

Final report the final accident report issued by the NTSB that cites the probable cause of the accident.

Financial (capital) lease a long-term lease (generally 12 to 15 years) that, because of (1) restrictions on termination, (2) its long term, and (3) the contractual commitment to pay the total value of the lease payments, is considered a form of capital financing.

First-class passenger revenues revenues from the air transportation of passengers at standard fares, premium fares, or reduced fares, such as family plan and first-class excursion, for whom standard- or premium-quality services are provided.

First-class service transport service established for the carriage of passengers at standard fares, premium fares, or reduced fares, such as family plan and first-class excursion, for whom standard- or premium-quality services are provided.

Fitness an applicant carrier's size, financial resources, flight equipment, strategy for conducting proposed operations, and past performance in conforming to various legal requirements.

Five Freedoms Agreement the International Air Transport Agreement that arose out of the Chicago Conference of 1944 proposing two basic freedoms (see **Two Freedoms Agreement**) plus three additional freedoms: (1) the privilege of putting down passengers, mail, and cargo taken on in the territory of the state whose nationality the aircraft possesses; (2) the privilege of picking up passengers, mail, and cargo destined for the territory of the state whose nationality the aircraft possesses; and (3) the privilege of picking up passengers, mail, and cargo destined for the territory of any other contracting state and the privilege of putting down passengers, mail, and cargo coming from any such territory.

Fixed assets the land, plant and equipment, and other physical productive assets of a firm that are expected to have a useful life in excess of one year.

Fixed-base operator (FBO) a free-enterprise business that carries on general aviation sales, service, and support operations.

Fixed costs those direct operating costs that in total do not vary with changes in available seat-miles (ASMs) that an airline produces.

Fixed-wing aircraft an aircraft whose wings are fixed to the airplane fuselage and outspread in flight (nonrotating wings).

Fleet planning the aircraft selection process.

Flight **airborne movement of an aircraft.** Commonly used to mean *scheduled flight*.

Flight dispatch the overall planning of flight operations. Flight dispatch personnel work closely with the flight crew in preparing all details pertaining to the proposed flight, including such factors as the nature and duration of the flight, weather conditions at various flight altitudes, airway routing to be used, and fuel requirements.

Flight equipment airframes, aircraft engines, aircraft propellers, aircraft communications and navigational equipment, miscellaneous equipment used in the operation of the aircraft, and improvements to leased flight equipment.

Flight-equipment cost the total cost to the air carrier of the complete airframe; fully assembled engines; installed aircraft propellers, rotary wing aircraft rotors, and similar assemblies; installed airborne communications and electronic navigational equipment and other similar assemblies; complete units of miscellaneous airborne flight equipment;

and costs of modification, conversion, or other improvements to leased flight equipment.

Flight-equipment expendable parts flight-equipment replacement parts of a type recurrently expended and replaced rather than repaired or revised.

Flight-equipment spare parts and assemblies parts and assemblies of material value that are generally reserviced or repaired and used repeatedly and that possess a service life approximating that of the property type to which they relate.

Flight, scheduled any aircraft itinerary periodically operated between terminal points that is separately designated, by flight number or otherwise, in the published schedules of an air carrier.

Flight service station (FSS) an FAA-operated air/ ground voice communications station that relays clearances, requests for clearances, and position reports between en-route aircraft and the air route traffic control center. In addition, the FSS provides preflight briefing for flights operating under either visual or instrument flight rules, gives in-flight assistance, broadcasts weather once each hour, monitors radio navigational facilities, accepts flight plans for aircraft operating under visual flight rules and provides notification of arrival, and broadcasts notices to air missions (NOTAM) concerning local navigational aids, airfields, and other flight data.

Flight stage the operation of an aircraft from takeoff to landing. (See also **Overall flight stage length**.)

Flying operations expenses expenses incurred directly in the in-flight operation of aircraft and expenses attached to the holding of aircraft and aircraft operational personnel in readiness for assignment to in-flight status.

Forecasting the attempt to quantify demand in a future time period. Quantification can be in terms of dollars, such as revenue, or some physical volume, such as revenue passenger miles or passenger enplanements.

Foreign air carrier permit a permit issued by the former CAB or the DOT to a foreign air carrier authorizing it to conduct air transport operations between foreign countries and cities in the United States, either in accordance with the terms of a bilateral air transport agreement or nonscheduled air service agreement or under conditions of comity and reciprocity.

Foreign-flag carrier an air carrier other than a U.S.-flag air carrier engaged in international air transportation. **Foreign air carrier**, a more inclusive term than *foreign-flag air carrier*, presumably includes those non-U.S. air carriers operating solely within their own domestic boundaries, but in practice the two terms are used interchangeably.

401 carrier an air carrier certificated under Section 401 of the Federal Aviation Act of 1958 by the former CAB or the DOT authorizing the carrier to engage in air transportation.

Freight property other than express and passenger baggage transported by air.

Freight revenues revenues from the transportation by air of property other than express or passenger baggage, predominantly from individually waybilled shipments carried in scheduled service.

Frequent flyer program an air carrier program that allows frequent fliers to earn free tickets after accumulating a certain number of miles flown on the carrier. First introduced by American Airlines, which recognized that roughly 5 to 6 percent of their fliers account for about 40 percent of all trips taken annually. It was a marketing program originally aimed at creating flier loyalty in response to price competition in the early 1980s.

Fringe benefits insurance plans, pensions, vacations, and similar benefits for employees.

FSS see **Flight service station**.

FTO (field ticket office) a ticket office located on airport property.

Fuel tax an excise tax paid by an airline on the aviation gasoline and jet fuel it purchases.

Functions of management the process of achieving an organization's goals through the coordinated performance of five specific functions: planning, organizing, staffing, directing, and controlling.

GAMA (General Aviation Manufacturers Association) a trade organization of the manufacturers of light aircraft and component parts.

General and administrative expenses expenses of a general corporate nature and expenses incurred in performing activities that contribute to more than a single operating function, such as general financial accounting activities, purchasing activities, representation at law, and other general operational administration not directly applicable to a particular function.

General aviation aviation other than military and commercial common carriage, including business flying, instructional flying, personal flying, and commercial flying such as agricultural spraying and aerial photography.

General Aviation Manufacturers Association see **GAMA**.

General commodity rate the basic or normal price applicable to all commodities in all markets. General commodity shipments are rated by weight. As the weight of a shipment increases, the per pound rate decreases.

General-use airport an airport serving as a regular, alternative, or provisional stop for scheduled and nonscheduled air carriers and non-air carriers and offering minimum services, such as fuel and regular attendants during normal working hours; also, airports operating seasonally that qualify under the above definition.

Glider a heavier-than-air aircraft whose flight does not depend principally on a power-generating unit.

Go-team the NTSB accident investigators who are on 24-hour alert to respond to any major accident. The team is generally made up of experts trained in witness interrogation, air traffic control, aircraft operations, and aircraft maintenance records.

Gross profit profit earned on sales after deducting the cost of the goods sold but before deducting other business expenses.

Grounding see **Aircraft grounding**.

Ground movement pickup and delivery and/or connecting or joint motor carrier service pursuant to interline air/ground agreements.

Ground property and equipment property and equipment other than flight equipment, land, and construction work in progress.

Ground transportation surface transportation between an airport and city or between two or more airports. It is provided by private or government operated limousine, bus, cab, or rail, and may include baggage transfer service.

Guaranteed loan see **Loan, guaranteed**.

Helicopter a type of aircraft that derives lift from the revolving of "wings" (engine-driven blades) about an approximately vertical axis. A helicopter does not have conventional fixed wings, nor in any but some earlier models is it provided with a conventional propeller, forward thrust and lift being furnished by the rotor. The powered rotor blades also enable the machine to hover and to land and take off vertically.

Hub, air traffic a city or standard metropolitan statistical area requiring aviation services. Communities fall into four classes, as determined by their percentage of the total enplaned passengers in scheduled and nonscheduled service of the domestic certificated route airlines in the 50 states, the District of Columbia, and other U.S. areas designated by the Federal Aviation Administration. A **large hub** is a community that enplanes 1 percent or more of total enplaned passengers for all air services in the United States; a **medium hub**, from 0.25 to 0.99 percent; a **small hub**, from 0.05 to 0.24 percent; and a **nonhub**, less than 0.05 percent.

Hub-and-spoke system a system that feeds air traffic from small communities through larger communities to the traveler's destination via connections at the larger community.

IAOPA International Council of Aircraft Owner and Pilots Association is a non-profit federation of autonomous, nongovernmental, national general aviation organizations.

IATA (International Air Transport Association) a voluntary organization open to any scheduled air carrier whose home country is a member (or eligible to be a member) of the International Civil Aviation Organization (ICAO). The IATA's main function is the economic regulation of international air transportation—in particular, international rates and fares that are set by one of seven regional or joint traffic conferences and subject to unanimous resolutions of the carriers, provided that the countries do not object.

ICAO (International Civil Aviation Organization) a specialized agency of the United Nations composed of contracting states whose purpose is to develop the principles and techniques of international air navigation and to foster the planning and development of international air transport.

IFR see **Instrument flight rules**.

Incidental revenues, net revenues less related expenses from services incidental to air transportation, such as sales of service, supplies, and parts, and rental of operating property and equipment.

Income before taxes net sales minus the cost of goods or services sold, minus operating expenses, minus nonoperating expenses.

Income, net (after income taxes) net income (before income taxes) less federal income taxes.

Income, net (before income taxes) net operating income plus or minus other income and expenses.

Income, net operating total net sales less total operating costs.

Income statement a statement of revenues and expenses and resulting net income or loss covering a stated period of time, usually one year.

Income taxes for the period provisions for federal, state, local, and foreign taxes that are based on net income.

Indirect operating cost all costs that will remain unaffected by a change of aircraft type because they are not directly dependent on aircraft operations (for example, passenger service costs, costs of ticketing and sales, station and ground costs, and administrative costs).

Industrial/special use any use of an aircraft for specialized work allied with industrial activity, excluding transportation and aerial application (pipeline patrol, survey, advertising, photography, helicopter hoist, and so forth).

Industrywide bargaining agreement between unions and managements of major firms of an industry to bargain collectively to reach contract terms that will apply to all the firms and their employees, wherever they are located. One purpose is to take wages out of competition.

Inelastic demand demand situation that occurs when a given percentage change in price is accompanied by a relatively smaller change in passengers carried (consumers are unresponsive). The coefficient of elasticity of demand is less than 1. When demand is inelastic, a price increase will increase total revenue and a price decrease will lower total revenue.

Instructional flying any use of an aircraft for the purposes of formal instruction with the flight instructor aboard or with the maneuvers on the particular flights specified by the flight instructor.

Instrument flight rules (IFR) rules specified by qualified authority (FAA) for flight under weather conditions such that visual reference cannot be made to the ground and the pilot must rely on instruments to fly and navigate.

Integrated carriers carriers that operate door-to-door freight transportation networks that include all-cargo aircraft, delivery vehicles, sorting hubs, and advanced information systems. Also called *express carriers*.

Intensive growth strategies attempts to more intensively penetrate existing target markets, increase product development, and develop new target markets.

Interest expense interest on all classes of debt, including premium, capitalized interest, and expenses on short-term obligations and amortization of premium discounts and expenses on short-term and long-term obligations.

International Air Transport Association see **IATA**.

International Civil Aviation Organization see **ICAO**.

International operations those operations between the 50 states of the United States and foreign points, between the 50 states and U.S. possessions or territories, and between foreign points. Includes both the combination passenger/cargo carriers and the all-cargo carriers engaged in international operations.

Interstate see **Air transportation, interstate**.

Intrastate see **Air transportation, intrastate**.

Inventory management the strategy of selling as many seats as possible at the highest possible fares. This usually means making available an adequate number of lower-fare seats far in advance of the departure date in order to accommodate price-sensitive business passengers.

Investment bank a bank that serves as an intermediary between investment sources and those who need funds. Investment bankers serve as consultants and advisers regarding private debt placement and public equity offerings.

Investments and special funds long-term investments in securities of others exclusive of U.S. government securities; funds set aside for specific purposes; and other securities, receivable equipment purchase deposits, and applicable capitalized interest or funds not available for current operations.

JAMTO (joint airline/military ticket office) a ticket office located at a military base and generally staffed by personnel from several air carriers.

Jet fuel the kerosene used to fuel turbine-powered aircraft, as opposed to aviation gasoline used in piston-engine aircraft.

Jetway a trade name, used to describe all makes and models of passenger loading bridges. A *passenger loading bridge* is an enclosed, movable walkway that connects the cabin of an airplane with the terminal.

Job description a statement of the objectives, authority, responsibility, and relationships with others required by a person occupying a specific position.

Job evaluation a formalized system for determining the worth, in monetary terms, of all jobs within an organization.

Joint airline/military ticket office see **JAMTO**.

Joint fare a single fare that applies to transportation over the joint lines or routes of two or more carriers and that is made and published by an agreement between the carriers.

Joint rate an air freight rate for domestic shipments transported on two or more airlines between origin and destination.

Judgmental forecasts forecasts based on intuition and subjective evaluation of the future. Normally, they are derived from expert opinion, sales force estimates, and various customer research polls.

Land the initial cost and the cost of improving land owned or held in perpetuity by an air carrier.

Landing area any locality, either of land or water, including airports and intermediate landing fields, that is used, or intended to be used, for the landing and takeoff of aircraft, whether or not facilities are provided for the shelter, servicing, or repair of aircraft or for receiving or discharging passengers or cargo.

Law of demand the inverse relationship between price and quantity. As price falls, the corresponding quantity demanded rises; alternately, as price increases, the corresponding quantity demanded falls.

Law of diminishing returns law stating that as resources (labor, capital equipment) are added to a fixed capacity (number of aircraft, gate positions, hangars), output (ASMs) might well increase at an increasing rate while existing capacity is underutilized. However, beyond some point, ASMs will increase at a decreasing rate, until the ultimate capacity in the short run is reached.

Levels of management the levels of authority and responsibility within an organization. *Top management* is the highest level and includes the company's chief policymakers, including senior officers responsible for major administrations. *Middle management* is responsible for developing operational plans and procedures and includes heads of departments and divisions. *Operating management* is the lowest level and includes managers and supervisors who are primarily concerned with putting into action operational plans devised by middle management.

Liability the equity of a creditor.

Liability, current an obligation that becomes due within a short time, usually one year.

Liberalization is the process of removing entry and price restrictions on airlines but the government still has control over certain matters including, but not limited to, access to domestic and international markets, airline competition, fares, and route selection. It is the step between regulation and deregulation.

Limited-use airport an airport available to the public but not equipped to offer minimum services.

Line departments those areas in an airline that are directly involved in producing or selling air transportation. They fall under the following administrations: flight operations, engineering and maintenance, and marketing.

Line of credit the amount and the terms upon which a bank will advance funds as required. The amount may vary from several thousand dollars to millions, depending on the size of the airline and its credit condition.

Line personnel those employees whose orders and authority flow in a straight line from the chief executive down to lower levels in the organization. Line personnel are directly involved in producing or selling air transportation. Commonly referred to as volume-related people because their numbers are generally determined by some volume such as flying hours or departures.

Liquidity ability to meet current obligations. The ease with which an asset can be converted to cash.

Load factor, revenue passenger the proportion of aircraft seating capacity that is actually sold and utilized. Revenue passenger miles divided by available seat-miles.

Loan, guaranteed an aircraft purchase loan guaranteed by the federal government and administered by the Department of Transportation to assist certain carriers in obtaining suitable flight equipment.

Local-service air carriers a class of air carriers that originally provided service to small and medium communities on low-density routes to large hubs and that were eligible for CAB subsidies to cover operating losses from such service. These carriers have since evolved from their feeder airline origins into medium to large airlines.

Long-term debt the face value or principal amount of debt securities issued or assumed by the air carrier and held by other than associated companies or nontransport divisions, which has not been retired or canceled and is not payable within 12 months of the balance sheet date.

Long-term debt/equity ratio the percentage of the business that is financed by creditors in relation to that financed by owners. It is computed by dividing long-term debt plus capitalized leases by net stockholder equity. The higher the number, the less able a company is to borrow money.

Long-term loan a loan negotiated for long-term capital projects and aircraft purchases.

Long-term prepayments prepayments of obligations, applicable to periods extending beyond one year.

Low-cost carrier (LCC) an airline that generally has lower fares and a low-cost management model. Revenue lost on ticket sales is made up by the sale of ancillary services.

MAC see **Military Airlift Command**.

Maintenance, direct the cost of labor, materials, and outside services consumed directly in periodic maintenance operations and the maintenance, repair, or upkeep of airframes, aircraft engines, other flight equipment, and ground property and equipment.

Maintenance efficiency goals four primary productivity goals: (1) minimize aircraft out-of-service time, (2) use up time allowable on aircraft and parts between overhaul, (3) seek optimum utilization of personnel and even workload, and (4) maximize utilization of facilities.

Maintenance, indirect overhead or general expenses of activities involved in the repair and upkeep of property and equipment, including inspections of equipment in accordance with prescribed operational standards. Includes expenses related to the administration of maintenance stocks and stores, the keeping of maintenance operations records, and the scheduling, controlling, planning, and supervising of maintenance operations.

Maintenance needs maintenance considerations in the acquisition of a new aircraft. Included are such factors as spare parts availability, aircraft compatibility with the rest of the fleet, product support, technical record keeping, and training support in terms of visual and audio aids.

Major air carriers a class of certificated air carriers whose annual gross revenues are over $1 billion.

Management the process of combining and guiding the factors of production to achieve the desired goals of the firm.

Management by objectives (MBO) a process in which employees at all levels are given tangible, usually numerical, goals and held accountable for achieving them.

MAP see **Mutual aid pact**.

Marketing the broad area of business activity that directs the flow of services provided by the firm to the consumer in order to satisfy customers and to achieve company objectives.

Marketing mix the types and amounts of controllable marketing decision variables that a company uses over a particular time period: product, price, promotion, and place.

Market segmentation the process of dividing potential customers for a product or service into meaningful consumer groups or market segments in order to identify a target market.

Market strategy approach used in the fleet-planning process when integrating new aircraft into the fleet. Included are such considerations as the proposed level of service between key city-pairs, emphasis on long-haul or short-haul routes, and fare and rate structures in various passenger and cargo markets.

Merger the acquisition of one firm by another, either through purchase of stock or direct purchase of assets, and the merging of operations.

Mile a statute mile (5,280 feet).

Military activities under charter or other contract with the Department of Defense.

Military Airlift Command (MAC) a major command organization of the United States Air Force that provides air transportation for personnel and cargo for all military services on a worldwide basis. MAC is the contractor for the U.S. Air Force's Logair and the U.S. Navy's Quicktrans.

Misconnection a passenger who, due to late arrival or cancellation of their originating flight, arrives at a connecting point too late to board the connecting flight.

Missile a term sometimes applied to space launch vehicles but that more properly denotes automatic weapons of warfare (weapons that have an integrated system of guidance, as opposed to unguided rockets).

Mixed-class service **transport** service for the carriage in any combination of first-class, coach (tourist), and/or economy (thrift) passengers on the same aircraft. The aircraft could also carry freight, express, and/or mail. Excludes all-first-class, all-coach, and all-economy services.

Model the general characterization of a process, object, or concept in terms of mathematics. A model enables a relatively simple manipulation of variables to be accomplished in order to determine how the process, object, or concept would behave in different situations.

Mortgage a pledge of real estate as security for a loan.

Multilateral agreement an agreement or treaty between three or more nations contracting for reciprocal international air service between the various nations, such service to be operated by designated carriers of each nation. The agreement may include provisions for the type of aircraft used, intermediate stops en route, aircraft airworthiness, taxation-free fuel, and arbitration procedures. It is usually a standardized agreement used in negotiations for air transport between one nation and many others, allowing for the inclusion of different points and routes.

Mutual aid pact (MAP) an agreement between the major carriers during the 20-year period from 1958 to 1978 that provided for mutual assistance in the event that any carrier's flight operations were shut down by a strike. If one or more members of the agreement were struck, the other members of the pact paid the struck carriers windfall revenues they realized from the strike less the added expense of carrying the additional traffic.

Mutual dependence a characteristic of oligopolistic industries: the necessity of each seller to consider the reactions of competitors when setting prices or implementing other competitive strategies.

NAS **(National Airspace System)** is the airspace, navigation facilities, and airports of the United States.

NASA (National Aeronautics and Space Administration) a U.S. government organization established by the National Aeronautics and Space Act of 1958 with the principal statutory functions to: (1) conduct research for the solution of problems of flight within and outside the earth's atmosphere and develop, construct, test, and operate aeronautical and space vehicles; (2) conduct activities required for the exploration of space with manned and unmanned vehicles; and (3) arrange for the most effective utilization of the scientific and engineering resources of the United States with other nations engaged in aeronautical and space activities for peaceful purposes. Many of NASA's research programs have led to findings and developments that are applicable to today's commercial air transportation.

NASAO (National Association of State Aviation Officials) based in Washington, D.C., an organization representing the interests of 47 state aviation agencies and Puerto Rico in promoting and developing air transportation at the local, state, and federal levels.

NATCA National Air Traffic Controllers Association is a labor union in the U.S. and is the bargaining representative for air traffic controllers employed by the Federal Aviation Administration.

National Aeronautics and Space Administration see **NASA**.

National air carriers a class of certificated air carriers whose annual gross revenues are between $100 million and $1 billion.

National Association of State Aviation Officials see **NASAO**.

National Business Aviation Association (NBAA) the leading organization for companies that rely on general aviation aircraft to help make their businesses more efficient, productive and successful.

National Mediation Board three individuals appointed by the president whose primary responsibility is to mediate major labor disputes under the Railway Labor Act. The board has jurisdiction over disputes involving rates of pay or changes in rules and working conditions in those instances in which the parties to an agreement have been unable to reach a settlement.

National Transportation Safety Board (NTSB) an autonomous agency established in 1975 by the Independent Safety Board Act. The board seeks to ensure that all types of transportation in the United States are conducted safely. The board investigates accidents and makes recommendations to government agencies, the transportation industry, and others on safety measures and practices.

Navigable airspace the airspace above the minimum altitudes of flight prescribed by regulations issued under the FAA Act, which includes airspace needed to ensure safety in takeoff and landing of aircraft.

NBAA see **National Business Aviation Association**.

Net earnings (profit or loss) revenues minus expenses, taxes, interest paid, and depreciation. The earnings of a company after allowing for all legitimate business expenses, including taxes.

Net income before income taxes operating profit or loss plus or minus nonoperating income and expenses.

Net operating property and equipment, as a percentage of cost the cost of operating property and equipment less related depreciation and overhaul reserves as a percentage of the total cost of operating property and equipment before deducting such reserves.

Net worth the difference between assets and liabilities for a person, family, or business. If the dollar value of assets is greater than that of liabilities, there is a positive net worth. In a business, net worth might also be known as *partnership share* or *owner's equity*.

NextGen Next Generation Air Transportation System is an ongoing modernization project to improve the U.S. National Airspace System.

Noncurrent liabilities obligations whose liquidation is not expected to require the use, within one year, of current assets or the creation of current liabilities.

Nonoperating costs and revenues income and loss of commercial ventures not part of the common-carrier air transport services of the accounting entity; other revenues and expenses attributable to financing or other activities that are extraneous to and not an integral part of air transportation or its incidental services.

Nonrevenue flights flights and flight stages involving training, testing, positioning for scheduled flights, ferrying, company business, publicity, and forced returns for which no remuneration is received.

Nonroutine maintenance generally the result of an unforeseen event, an accident or random occurrence, or a response to an airworthiness directive (AD). Examples would include corrosion control, cabin upgrading, installation of a hushkit, and repairing damage from a bird strike or a dent from a catering truck.

Nonscheduled freight property carried in charter operations.

Nonscheduled service revenue flights not operated in regular scheduled service—principally contract and charter operations.

Nonstop service between two points on a single flight with no scheduled stops between the points. Authority granted to a carrier, in a certificate of public convenience and necessity, to service two points without additional stops.

Non-volume-related workers see **Staff personnel**.

Normal (standard or basic) fare a fare that applies to all passengers at all times without restriction and is the basis for all other fares. Separate normal fares are provided for each class of service: first class, coach, and economy.

No-show a person who books a reservation or purchases a ticket for a flight and fails to use the reservation or ticket or to notify the carrier of that intent before the flight's departure.

NTSB see **National Transportation Safety Board**.

Official Airline Guide a bimonthly publication of the airlines' scheduled operations and services showing service and fares to one city from all other cities where direct or simple connecting service is available.

Off-peak pricing a promotional fare designed to attract passengers during an otherwise slack period.

Oligopoly a market in which a few firms sell either a similar or differentiated product or service, into which entry is difficult, in which the firm's control over the price at which it sells its product or service is limited by mutual dependence, and in which there is typically extensive nonprice competition.

Open-sky agreement an agreement that permits carriers of different countries to fly any route they wish between the countries and to continue those flights into third countries, although cabotage is still not permitted.

Operating economics an aircraft's contribution to the company's profitability, including its revenue potential and direct operating costs in terms of airplane miles and seat-miles.

Operating expenses expenses incurred in the performance of air transportation, including direct aircraft operating expenses and ground and indirect operating expenses.

Operating income (profit or loss) the profit or loss from performance of air transportation before income taxes, based on overall operating revenues and overall operating expenses. Does not include nonoperating income and expenses or special items.

Operating leases short-term leases (generally not more than five years) that have varying degrees of flexibility for cancellation by the airlines. They generally convey no residual value in the aircraft and, from an accounting standpoint, are considered strictly an operating cost.

Operating profit and equipment land and units of tangible property and equipment used in air transportation services and incidental services.

Operating revenues revenues from the performance of air transportation and related incidental services, including: (1) transport revenues from the carriage of all classes of traffic in scheduled and nonscheduled services, including the performance of aircraft charters, and (2) nontransport revenues, consisting of federal subsidies (where applicable) and the net amount of revenues less related expenses from services incidental to air transportation.

Operational factors factors that must be taken into consideration in the schedule-planning process. Included are airport runway lengths, aircraft fuel capacity, habitual adverse weather, air traffic control and routings, crew time limits, and employee agreements.

Operations, domestic see **Domestic operations**.

Operations, international see **International operations**.

Organization the official relationships or the positions generally shown on an organizational chart and stated in job descriptions. A plan for bringing together resources (capital and labor) into the position of greatest effectiveness, or productivity. The plan consists of the grouping of operations (labor and equipment) to achieve the advantages of specialization and a chain of command.

Organizational chart a diagram showing positions and their relationships to one another in an organization.

Organizing the grouping of component activities that assigns each grouping to a manager and establishes authority relationships among the groupings.

Origin and Destination Survey a domestic (also international) origin–destination survey of airline passenger traffic, a 10-percent sample of passengers' origins and destinations in air transportation based on an analysis of selected flight coupons.

Other accrued taxes accruals for taxes, exclusive of federal income taxes, constituting a charge borne by the air carrier.

Other aerospace products and services all conversions, modifications, site activation, other aerospace products (including drones) and services, basic and applied research in the sciences and in engineering, and design and development of prototype products and processes.

Other current and accrued liabilities accruals for liabilities against the air carrier for personnel vacations, dividends declared but unpaid on capital stock, and other miscellaneous current and accrued liabilities.

Other current assets prepayments of rent, insurance, taxes, and so forth, which if not paid in advance would require the expenditure of working capital within one year, and other current assets not provided for in specific objective accounts.

Other deferred charges unamortized discounts and expenses on debt; unamortized capital stock expenses; and debits not provided for elsewhere, the final disposition of which must await receipt of additional information.

Other deferred credits an unamortized premium on debt and credits not provided for elsewhere, the final disposition of which must await receipt of additional information.

Other investments and receivables notes and accounts receivable not due within one year and investments in securities issued by others except associated companies.

Other noncurrent liabilities liabilities under company-administered employee pension plans and for installments received from company personnel under company stock purchase plans, advances from associated companies, and noncurrent liabilities.

Other nonoperating income and expenses net capital gains or losses or retirement of nonoperating property and equipment and investments in securities of others, interest and dividend income, and other nonoperating items except capital gains or losses on operating property and interest expense.

Other paid-in capital premiums and discounts on capital stock, gains or losses arising from the reacquisition and the resale or retirement of capital stock, and other paid-in capital.

Other temporary cash investment securities and other collectible obligations acquired for the purpose of temporarily investing cash, other than those issued by the U.S. government or associated companies.

Other transport revenues miscellaneous revenues associated with the air transportation performed by the air carrier, such as airline employees, officers and directors, or other persons, except ministers of religion who travel under reduced-rate transportation; reservation cancellation fees; and other items not specified in other transport revenue accounts.

Overall aircraft revenue hours, scheduled service the airborne hours computed from the moment an aircraft leaves the ground until it touches the ground at the end of the flight.

Overall capacity per aircraft the average overall carrying capacity (tons) offered for sale per aircraft in revenue services, derived by dividing the overall available ton-miles by the overall aircraft miles flown in revenue services.

Overall flight stage length the average distance covered per aircraft hop in revenue service, from takeoff to landing, including both passenger/cargo and all-cargo aircraft. Obtained by dividing the overall aircraft miles flown in revenue services by the number of overall aircraft revenue departures performed.

Overbooking the sale of (or the acceptance of reservations for) more space (passenger seats) than is actually available on a flight. A practice that is used sometimes by the air carriers as an allowance for the historical percentage of passengers who fail to utilize the space they have reserved. In those cases in which the actual number of passengers with purchased tickets exceeds the available space, the carrier is liable for denied boarding compensation to those passengers not accommodated on the flight or on comparable air transportation.

Overflight a scheduled flight that does not stop at an intermediate point in its scheduled route because (1) the point is certified as a flag stop, and there is no traffic to be deplaned or enplaned; (2) the carrier has received authority to suspend service to that point temporarily; (3) weather conditions or other safety and technical reasons do not permit landing; or (4) for any other reason. The aircraft need not fly directly over the point.

Passenger enplanements the total number of revenue passengers boarding aircraft, including originating, stopover, and on-line transfer passengers.

Passenger mile one passenger transported one mile. Passenger miles are computed by multiplying the aircraft miles flown on each flight stage by the number of passengers transported on that stage.

Passenger mile, nonrevenue one nonrevenue passenger transported one mile.

Passenger mile, revenue see **Revenue passenger mile**.

Passenger, revenue a person receiving air transportation from the air carrier for which remuneration is received by the air carrier. Air carrier employees or others receiving air transportation against whom token charges are levied are considered nonrevenue passengers. Infants for whom a token fare is charged are not counted as revenue passengers.

Passenger, revenue per aircraft the average number of passengers carried per aircraft in revenue passenger services, derived by dividing the total revenue passenger miles by the total aircraft miles flown in revenue passenger services.

Passenger revenue ton-mile one ton of revenue passenger weight (including all baggage) transported one mile.

Passenger service expenses costs of activities contributing to the comfort, safety, and convenience of passengers while in flight and when flights are interrupted. Includes salaries and expenses of cabin attendants and passenger food service.

Pattern bargaining bargaining that takes place when each airline negotiates its own agreement with a labor union. Each union seeks to better the most recent agreements signed by other airlines, thus establishing a pattern.

Payload the actual or potential revenue-producing portion of an aircraft's takeoff weight in passengers, free baggage, excess baggage, freight, express, and mail.

Payload-range diagram a diagram that shows the relationship between payload (number of passengers and cargo) and the distance the aircraft can fly.

Personal flying any use of an aircraft for personal purposes not associated with a business or profession, and not for hire. This includes maintenance of pilot proficiency.

Physical performance factor used in the fleet-planning process to denote the actual flight performance of an aircraft under consideration. Included are such items as payload-range capability; takeoff, landing, cruise, and approach speeds; runway requirements; noise performance; and flight handling characteristics.

Piston plane an aircraft operated by engines in which pistons moving back and forth work upon a crankshaft or other device to create rotational movement.

Place the element in the marketing mix that includes all institutions and activities that contribute to delivering the product at the times and to the places consumers desire; in other words, a convenient facility or sales outlet where customers can purchase the service.

Planning the function of management that determines what shall be done, how it shall be done, why it shall be done, and who shall do it.

Policy and procedures manual guidelines that employees must follow in making decisions. Each major administration within an airline has policies and procedures regarding the management of its specific operations.

Positioning flights flights designed to *position* or put an aircraft in a location for a heavy bank of flights at a popular time—for example, late-evening flights into a large hub.

Preferred stock a share in the ownership of the company that carries a fixed annual dividend that must be paid before dividends can be declared on common stock.

Price the consideration or level of remuneration established by the seller for a product or service.

Primary-use categories categories developed by the FAA to categorize general aviation aircraft by use as reported by aircraft owners in an annual survey. The primary-use categories include business, commercial, instructional, personal, and other. Business flying has two divisions (executive and business); commercial has three (air taxi/commuter, rental, and aerial application and observation and other work).

Priority mail mail bearing postage for air transportation on a priority basis at air mail service rates.

Priority reserved air freight freight service designed for shippers of heavy or bulky freight who need the advantage of reserved space on a specific flight.

Privately owned airport an airport owned by a private individual or corporation.

Private-use airport an airport that is not open for the use of the general public.

Procurement the process whereby the executive agencies of the federal government acquire goods and services from enterprises other than the federal government.

Product the physical entity or service that is offered to the buyer, plus a whole group of services that accompanies it. For example, the airline product includes not only a seat departure but also frequency of departures, in-flight cabin services, ground services including ticketing and baggage handling, aircraft type, and even the carrier's perceived image. The sale of a general aviation aircraft includes not only the aircraft itself but also its availability, methods of financing, maintenance requirements, and so forth, which marketing people refer to as extensions to the product.

Production certificate a certificate issued by the FAA to an aircraft manufacturer after the type certificate and only when the manufacturer's capability to duplicate the type design has been established. The aircraft is then ready to go into production.

Production-oriented period the period of airline marketing before World War II during which the market demand for air travel was just sufficient to absorb the available capacity provided by the carriers.

Profit in ordinary accounting terms, the excess of sales revenues after all related expenses are deducted.

Profit sharing an incentive system whereby employees can share in the profits of the company.

Progress payments payments that an airline makes to a manufacturer while an aircraft is under production.

Projected industry environment projection used in the fleet-planning process to denote the national, industry, and company's economic outlook over the next one-, five-, and ten-year periods.

Promotion part of the marketing mix; persuasive communication between the carrier and the customer. This communication can be made in various ways, but the two most important forms of promotional communication are *advertising* (sometimes referred to as *mass selling*) and *personal selling*. In a broader sense, everything the company does has a promotional potential: the courtesy of employees and uniform styling can promote sales.

Promotional fares see **Fare, discount**.

Promotion and sales expenses costs incurred in promoting air transportation generally and in creating a public preference for the services of particular air carriers. Includes the functions of selling, advertising and publicity, making space reservations, and developing tariffs and flight schedules for publication.

Publicly owned airport an airport that is owned by a city, state, or county or by the federal government.

Public service revenues (subsidy) payments by the federal government that provide for air service to communities in the United States where traffic levels are such that air service could not otherwise be supported.

Public-use airport an airport that is open for the use of the general public.

RAA (Regional Airline Association) a trade organization of regional and commuter air carriers.

R & D see **Research and development**.

Railway Labor Act a special federal law applicable only to the airlines and the railroads. This act was passed to provide a clear series of steps to the settlement of transport labor disputes.

Rate of return, corporate (return on investment, or ROI) an overall rate of return on investment representing a return on the air carrier's total operations, including nontransport ventures. The corporate rate of return is obtained by dividing the net income after taxes plus interest expenses on debt by the total investment in the carrier.

Regional air carriers a class of certificated air carriers. Airlines are classified as **large regional** air carriers if their annual gross revenues are between $10 million and $75 million and as **medium regional** air carriers if their annual gross revenues are under $10 million.

Regional Airline Association see **RAA**.

Related products and services all nonaircraft, non-space vehicle, and nonmissile products and services produced or performed by those companies and establishments whose principal business is the development or production of aircraft, aircraft engines, missile and spacecraft engines, missiles, and spacecraft.

Research and development (R & D) research is the systematic study directed toward fuller scientific knowledge or understanding of the subject studied. Research is classified as either basic or applied, according to the objectives of the sponsoring agency. **Basic research** has the objective of gaining fuller knowledge or understanding of the fundamental aspects of phenomena and of observable facts without specific applications toward processes or products in mind. **Applied research** has the objective of gaining knowledge or understanding necessary for determining the means by which a recognized and specific need may be met. **Development** is the systematic use of scientific knowledge directed toward the production of useful materials, devices, systems, or methods, including design and development of prototypes and processes.

Reservation the agreement between an airline and a customer that assures that the customer will have a seat on the flight(s) he or she wants. It may be subject to requirements for date or time of ticket purchase.

Reserves for depreciation accruals for depreciation of property and equipment.

Reserves for obsolescence and deterioration, expendable parts accruals for losses in the value of expendable parts.

Reserves for overhaul accruals for overhauls of flight equipment.

Reserves for uncollectible account accruals for estimated losses from uncollectible accounts.

Responsibility the creation of an obligation on the part of subordinates for satisfactory performance.

Restricted-use airport an airport whose use by the general public is prohibited, except in the case of a forced landing or by previous arrangement.

Retained earnings corporate profits that are not paid out in cash dividends but are reinvested in the company to foster its growth.

Retained earnings adjustments charges or credits to unappropriated retained earnings, other than dividends, that reflect transfers to paid-in capital accounts or appropriations.

Retained earnings, appropriated retained earnings segregated for contingencies and other special purposes, including retained earnings segregated in connection with self-insurance plans.

Retained earnings, unappropriated the cumulative net income or loss from operations of the air carrier less dividends declared on capital stock and amounts appropriated for special purposes.

Return on investment see **Rate of return, corporate**.

Revenue compensation or remuneration received by the carrier.

Revenue aircraft departures performed the number of aircraft take-offs actually performed in scheduled passenger/cargo and all-cargo services.

Revenue aircraft miles the total aircraft miles flown in revenue service.

Revenue passenger see **Passenger, revenue**.

Revenue passenger mile (RPM) one revenue passenger transported one mile in revenue service. Revenue passenger miles are computed by summation of the revenue aircraft miles flown on each interairport flight stage multiplied by the number of passengers carried on that flight stage.

Revenue ton-mile one ton of revenue traffic transported one mile. Revenue ton-miles are computed by multiplying tons of revenue traffic by the miles this traffic is flown.

ROI (return on investment) see **Rate of return, corporate**.

Route a system of points to be served by an air carrier, as indicated in its certificate of public convenience and necessity. A route may include all points on a carrier's system or may represent only a systematic portion of all of the points within a carrier's total system.

Route, certificated a listing of points to which an air carrier is authorized to provide air transportation, subject to the terms, conditions, and limitations prescribed in a carrier's certificate of public convenience and necessity.

Routine scheduled maintenance regular scheduled maintenance activities, usually in the form of a letter check—A through D—all performed at regular intervals and involving different levels of maintenance requirements.

RPM see **Revenue passenger mile**.

Safety recommendation the final recommendation made by the NTSB following a major accident. Safety recommendations are made as soon as a problem is identified, not necessarily upon completion of the investigation.

Sales, aerospace sales net of returns, allowances, and discounts; the dollar value of shipments less returns and allowances, including dealer's commission, if any, that have passed through the sales account See also **Aerospace sales**.

Sales-oriented period the airline marketing period following World War II when the air carriers' capacity increased and many companies began to take an active role in convincing consumers to purchase the new services offered. It was referred to as a shotgun approach to marketing: convincing people to fly rather than drive or take the railroad.

Scheduled aircraft miles the sum of the airport-to-airport distances of all flights scheduled, excluding those operated only as extra sections to accommodate traffic overflow.

Scheduled aircraft miles completed the aircraft miles performed on scheduled flights, computed solely between those scheduled points actually served.

Scheduled service transport service operated over an air carrier's certificated routes, based on published flight schedules, including extra sections and related nonrevenue flights.

Schedule, published an official schedule of an air carrier published in the *Official Airline Guide* (OAG) or the *ABC World Airways Guide* showing all flights that will be operated by the air carrier between various points and the time of arrival and departure at each point.

Schedule types four basic schedule types used by the air carriers: (1) skip-stop, (2) local service, (3) cross-connection, and (4) nonstop.

Scheduling the art of designing systemwide flight patterns that provide optimum public service, in both quantity and quality, consistent with the financial health of the carrier.

Scheduling department the department, generally under the marketing administration, charged with the responsibility of developing systemwide schedules. The department works closely with all other departments and field stations in carrying out its responsibilities.

Seasonal trends changes in an economic index that are caused by or related to changes in the seasons of the year.

Seat-mile one passenger seat transported one statute mile. Used to report available passenger-carrying capacity on an aircraft; however, when the seat is occupied by a revenue passenger, the measurement unit is referred to as a **revenue passenger mile (RPM)**.

Seat-miles, available the aircraft miles flown on each flight stage multiplied by the number of seats available for revenue use on that stage. See also **Available seat miles (ASMs)**.

Sensitivity of schedule salability the highly sensitive nature of even minor changes in scheduled departure and arrival times. Schedule convenience ranks high among the competitive elements affecting the passenger's choice of an airline; consequently, even minor changes can affect salability.

Severe Acute Respiratory Syndrome (SARS) is a respiratory disease in humans caused by the SARS coronavirus.

Short-term loan a loan negotiated for seasonal needs or for working capital and paid back within one year.

Show cause order an order soliciting parties to present to the DOT reasons and considerations as to why a particular DOT order relating to the fitness of a carrier should not be put into effect.

Shuttle service a relatively low-fare, no-frills service. The lower fare is based on the cost savings of high-density seating, no reservations, and no meal or beverage service. This service is usually offered only in high-traffic markets and may also require passengers to carry their own baggage to the boarding gate.

Sidewalk check-in a service that enables customers to check baggage outside the terminal entrance. This allows ticketed passengers to proceed directly to the gate.

SOC see **System operations control**.

Sovereignty of airspace the control or authority of each nation over the airspace above its borders. The principle of sovereignty of each nation over the air above its territories and territorial waters was affirmed at the Paris Convention of 1919.

Space available a term applied to passengers who, for lack of reservations or for reduced-rate charges, must await the boarding of other passengers and will not themselves be boarded unless there is additional space available on the aircraft.

Space vehicle an artificial body operating in outer space (beyond the earth's atmosphere).

Span of control the number of subordinates a manager can effectively supervise. Sometimes called *span of management*.

Special air freight services services air carriers provide shippers, such as assembly service (consolidating shipments), distribution service (distribution to different customers), pickup and delivery service, and other specialized services, such as armed guards and shipment of human remains and restricted articles.

Special Flight Permit commonly referred to as a ferry permit. May be issued by the FAA to any U.S. registered aircraft that may not currently meet applicable Airworthiness Requirements but is capable of safe flight.

Special funds funds not of a current nature and restricted as to general availability. Includes items such as sinking funds, pension funds under the control of the air carrier, equipment purchase funds, and funds segregated as part of a plan for self-insurance.

Special income credits and debits, net (special items) extraordinary credits and debits that are of sufficient magnitude that inclusion in the accounts for a single year would materially distort the total operating revenues or total operating expenses.

Special income tax credits and debits, net income taxes applicable to special income credits or debits and other extraordinary income tax items not allocable to income of the current accounting year.

Specific commodity rate special air freight rate established for unusually high-volume shipping of certain products between certain cities.

Speed package service small-package, fast-delivery service, airport-to-airport, with certain carriers on their system. Packages are accepted at the airport passenger terminal, at the baggage check-in position, or at the air freight office.

Spoils Conference a series of meetings held in Washington, D.C., in May 1930 between Postmaster General Walter Folger Brown and the heads of the larger airlines with the purpose of establishing three transcontinental trunk air mail routes. The spoils went to United Air Transport, Transcontinental and Western Air Express, and American Airways.

SSBJ Supersonic Business Jet is a business aircraft capable of travelling above the speed of sound (Mach 1).

SST see **Aircraft, supersonic transport**.

Staff departments departments that assist the line departments in carrying out their responsibilities. They fall under the following administrations: finance and property, information services, personnel, community relations and publicity, economic planning, legal, and medical.

Staffing the positions provided for by the organizational structure.

Staff personnel those whose orders and authority do not flow in a straight line down from the top of the organization. Staff personnel report to a specific person in the organization; however, they may at times perform work for people at levels above or below them. Often referred to as *non-volume-related people* because their numbers are generally not directly related to some volume such as flying hours or departures.

Stage, flight see **Flight stage**.

Stage length, average see **Overall flight stage length**.

Station plotting chart a visual layout of the schedule at a particular station. All flights are plotted, portraying sequence and schedule time of operation and utilizing certain standards and codes. The chart shows the time an aircraft requires to maneuver into a gate position, the scheduled arrival time, the period of time it is at the gate, its scheduled departure time, and the length of time needed to clear the gate.

Stockholder equity the aggregate book value of stock held by all stockholders in the company.

STOL an aircraft capable of taking off and landing in a short distance (short takeoff and landing).

Subsidy see **Public service revenues (subsidy)**.

Supersonic is a speed greater than that of sound.

Supersonic transport (SST) see **Aircraft, supersonic transport (SST)**.

Supplemental air carrier a former class of air carrier holding a certificate of public convenience and necessity issued by the CAB, authorizing it to perform passenger and cargo charter services supplementing the scheduled service of the certificated route air carriers. Supplemental air carriers were often referred to as *nonskeds* (nonscheduled carriers). The remaining former supplemental carriers are now classified as national or as large or medium regional air carriers.

Surplus, capital an increase in an owner's equity not generated through the company's earnings.

Surplus, earned an archaic term for retained earnings.

System constraints the constraining factors that a carrier must take into consideration in the fleet-planning process. **External constraints** might include facility requirements, including runway, gate, and terminal capacity. **Internal constraints** might include lack of funds and maintenance and crew-training facilities.

System operations control (SOC) a central operations department that dispatches and coordinates all aircraft movements systemwide.

Tariff the notice of fares and rates applicable to the transportation of persons or property, and the rules relating to or affecting such fares and rates of transportation. Effective January 1, 1983, the CAB no longer approved tariff filings by the carriers.

Taxable income for federal income tax purposes, the amount of income, less exemptions, on which income tax is determined.

Tax write-off an investment loss that can be offset against gross income when determining adjusted gross income.

Thrust the driving force exerted by an engine, particularly an aircraft or missile engine, in propelling the vehicle to which it is attached.

Ticket a printed document that serves as evidence of payment of the fare for air transportation. Generally, this takes the form of the standard Air Traffic Conference ticket, which is composed of an auditor's coupon, agent's coupon, flight coupons, and passenger's coupon. It authorizes carriage between the points and via the routing indicated and also shows the passenger's name, class of service, carriers, flight numbers, date of travel, and all conditions of the contract of carriage.

Time-series analysis the oldest, and in many cases still the most widely used, method of forecasting air transportation demand. Often referred to as *trend extension,* it consists of interpreting the historical sequence and applying the interpretation to the immediate future. Historical data are plotted on a graph, and a trend line is established. Frequently, a straight line is extended into the future.

Time zone effect an important factor affecting schedule development: the fact that we gain three hours on the clock going westbound coast to coast but lose three hours coming eastbound has a major impact on scheduling a jet fleet.

Ton a short ton (2,000 pounds).

Ton-mile one short ton transported one statute mile. Ton-miles are computed by summing the aircraft miles flown on each interairport flight stage multiplied by the number of tons carried on the flight stage.

Total general services and administration expenses passenger service, aircraft and traffic servicing, promotion and sales, and general and administrative expenses.

Total number of employees the number of full- and part-time employees, both permanent and temporary, during the pay period ending nearest to December 15. Air carriers with more than one operation (domestic or international and territorial) generally do not report a breakdown of total employees corresponding to these operations; thus, employee counts do not provide a reliable basis for measuring average productivity per employee in such separate operations.

Tour, inclusive a round-trip tour that combines air transportation and land services and that meets additional requirements of minimum days of accommodations and other land services to be included in the price of the tour.

Tour package a joint service that gives a traveler a significantly lower price for a combination of services than could be obtained if each were purchased separately. Thus, the total price of a package tour might include a round-trip plane ticket, hotel accommodations, meals, several sight-seeing bus tours, and theater tickets.

Trade balance the difference between the value of U.S. goods exported to other countries and foreign goods imported into this country. The trade balance is generally regarded as favorable when exports exceed imports—a trade surplus—and unfavorable when imports exceed exports—a trade deficit.

Traffic, air the passengers and cargo (freight, express, and mail) transported on any aircraft movement.

Traffic density the total amount or units of traffic traveling or carried between two points, over a route, over a route segment, or on a flight.

Traffic flow passengers making connecting flights at each station that allows for adequate load factors over an entire route structure with intermediate stops.

Transport-related expenses expenses from services related to air transportation, such as in-flight sales of liquor, food, and other items; ground, restaurant, and food services; rental expenses as lessor; interchange sales; general service sales; mutual aid; substitute service; and air cargo service (other than actual air movement).

Transport-related revenues revenues from transportation by air of all classes of traffic in scheduled and nonscheduled service, including charters.

Treasury stock the cost of capital stock issued by the air carrier that has been reacquired by it and not retired or canceled.

Trend a direction of movement, as shown in a trend line.

Trend extension see **Time-series analysis**.

Trip in common usage, the term *trip* includes both the going and returning portions of a journey. In airline usage, it is important to distinguish between trip used in a one-way and a round-trip sense. Published statistics on average length of air trips almost always use one-way distances, because it is virtually impossible to determine from reported data what the round-trip distance is. Fares, on the other hand, are sometimes quoted as one-way prices and at other times as round-trip prices, and the round-trip price is not always equal to twice the one-way price.

Trunk carriers a former class of certificated route air carriers receiving original certification under the so-called grandfather clause of the Civil Aeronautics Act of 1938 and whose primary operations were in domestic scheduled passenger service between medium and large hubs. These carriers are now classified as major air carriers.

Turbine (turbo) a mechanical device or engine that spins in reaction to a fluid flow that passes through or over it.

Turbine-powered aircraft see **Aircraft, turbine**.

Turbofan planes see **Aircraft, turbofan (fan jet)**.

Turbojet planes see **Aircraft, turbojet**.

Turboprop planes see **Aircraft, turbo-propeller (turboprop, prop jet)**.

Twelve-five rule refers to the standard (12,500 pounds) that the CAB set in 1938 to distinguish between large and small aircraft. Those carriers operating small aircraft were deemed air taxis and thus exempted from certification requirements under Section 401 of the Civil Aeronautics Act.

Two Freedoms Agreement the International Air Services Transit Agreement that arose out of the Chicago Conference of 1944 proposing that each contracting state grant to the other contracting states the following freedoms of the air with respect to scheduled international air services: (1) the privilege of flying across its territory without landing, and (2) the privilege of landing for nontraffic purposes.

Two-tier wage structure a wage scale in which newly hired workers are paid considerably less than current workers for similar jobs.

Type certificate a certificate indicating that a new aircraft prototype has passed an extensive series of FAA ground and flight tests and meets FAA standards of construction and performance.

UAM Urban Air Mobility is a safe and efficient aviation transportation system that will use automated aircraft to operate and transport passengers and cargo at lower altitudes within urban and suburban areas.

UAS Unmanned Aircraft Systems are aircraft piloted without a human in the aircraft and are controlled by an operator on the ground in most cases.

Uncontrollable variables certain marketing conditions over which the company exercises little or no control but which they must recognize and respond to. These include: (1) cultural and social differences, (2) the political and regulatory environment, (3) the economic environment, (4) the existing competitive structure, and (5) resources and objectives of the company.

Unfair competition the use of competitive methods that have been declared unfair by statute or by an administrative agency.

Unicom frequencies authorized for aeronautical advisory services to private aircraft. Only one such station is authorized at any landing area. The frequency 123.0 mHz is used at airports served by an airport traffic control tower or a flight service station, and 122.8 mHz is used for other landing areas. Services available are advisory in nature, primarily concerning the airport services and airport utilization.

Uniform system of accounts and reports a standardized system of financial and traffic reports that the certificated air carriers must submit during the year to the DOT.

Unity of objectives the idea that each administration, department, division, section, group, and unit of a company must contribute to the accomplishment of the overall goals of the firm. This is one of the basic principles of organization planning.

Universal Air Travel Plan begun in 1936, one of the world's oldest credit cards. The UATP's Air Travel card today is good for transportation on practically all of the world's scheduled airlines. Participating airlines now number more than 200. The contracting airline bills the subscriber on a monthly basis for all air transportation used, regardless of the number of airlines involved.

Unused (dormant) authority a certificate issued to the first carrier that qualifies when an air carrier that is authorized to provide round-trip service nonstop each way between two points fails to provide at least a minimum of service, as prescribed by the Airline Deregulation Act of 1978. Unused authority may also be issued to an air carrier between points where service is being provided if the service is being provided by no more than one other carrier.

U.S.-flag carrier (American-flag carrier) one of a class of U.S. air carriers holding certificates of public convenience and necessity or other economic authority issued by the former CAB or the DOT and approved by the president authorizing air transportation between the United States and/or its territories and one or more foreign countries.

U.S. mail revenues revenues from the transportation by air of U.S. mail at service mail rates established by the U.S. Postal Service. Includes priority and nonpriority mail revenues.

Utility aircraft an aircraft designed for general-purpose work.

Utility Airplane Council formerly under the AIA; the forerunner to the GAMA.

Utilization the average daily use of aircraft for a period of time, usually monthly or yearly. Obtained by dividing the total hours flown by the number of aircraft and then dividing the result by the number of days for the time period.

Variable costs those costs that increase or decrease with the level of output or available seat-miles that an airline produces.

Venture capital money invested in business enterprises that generally do not have access to conventional sources of capital. Venture capitalists are particularly interested in situations that will ultimately produce sizable capital gains.

Very large aircraft (VLA) term used for the new generation of large wide-body aircraft.

VFR see **Visual flight rules**.

Visual flight rules (VFR) rules specified by a qualified authority establishing minimum flying altitudes and limits of visibility to govern visual flight.

VLA see **Very large aircraft**.

Volume-related personnel see **Line personnel**.

V/STOL an aircraft capable of taking off and landing vertically or in a short distance.

VTOL an aircraft capable of taking off and landing vertically.

Weight, allowable gross the maximum gross weight (of the aircraft and its contents) that an aircraft is licensed to carry into the air on each flight stage.

Weight, maximum certificated takeoff the maximum takeoff weight authorized by the terms of the aircraft airworthiness certificate. This is found in the airplane operating record or in the airplane flight manual, which is incorporated by regulation into the airworthiness certificate.

Weight, maximum gross takeoff the maximum permissible weight of an aircraft and its contents at takeoff. Includes the empty weight of the aircraft, accessories, fuel, crew, and payload.

W.H.O. World Health Organization is a specialized agency of the United Nations responsible for international public health.

Working capital investable funds that are not currently tied up in long-term assets; current assets minus current liabilities. The excess of current assets over current liabilities, or those funds used to finance day-to-day operations.

Work stoppage an incident of labor–management strife arising from disputes over wages, benefits, hours, rules, or conditions of work, as well as from jurisdictional problems of craft representation of airline employees; a strike or lockout. Such incidents may not affect normally scheduled services.

Yield the air transport revenue per unit of traffic carried in air transportation. May be calculated and presented several ways, such as passenger revenue per passenger mile, per aircraft mile, per passenger ton-mile, or per passenger.

INDEX

B

E

F

G

H

I

J

K

L

N

O

S

T

U